Computer-Generated Images

The State of the Art

Proceedings of Graphics Interface '85

Editors: Nadia Magnenat-Thalmann
         Daniel Thalmann

With 278 Figures
121 of them in Color

Springer-Verlag
Tokyo Berlin Heidelberg New York

Prof. Dr. Nadia Magnenat-Thalmann
Hautes Etudes Commerciales
Université de Montréal
Montréal H3T 1V6 Canada

Prof. Dr. Daniel Thalmann
Département d'Informatique
et de Recherche Opérationnelle
Université de Montréal
Montréal H3C 3J7 Canada

ISBN-13:978-4-431-68035-2   e-ISBN-13:978-4-431-68033-8
DOI: 10.1007/978-4-431-68033-8

Library of Congress Cataloging-in-Publication Data

Computer-generated images.
Papers presented to Graphics Interface '85, held May 27–31,1985
in Montreal and presented jointly by the Computer Graphics Society
and the Canadia Man-Computer Communications Society.
Includes bibliographies and index.
1. Computer graphics-Congresses. I. Magnenat–Thalmann, Nadia, 1946–
II. Thalmann, Daniel. III. Graphics Interface '85 (1985: Montreal, Quebec)
IV. Computer Graphics Society. V. Canadian Man-Computer Communications Society.
T385.C5936 1985   006.6   85-27933
ISBN-13:978-4-431-68035-2 (U.S.)

All rights reserved. No part of this publication may be reproduced or transmitted in any
form or by any means, electronic or mechanical, including photocopy, recording, or
any information storage and retrieval system, without permission in writing from the
publisher.

© Springer-Verlag Tokyo 1985
Softcover reprint of the hardcover 1st edition 1985

Preface

Research, development, and applications in computer graphics have dramatically expanded in recent years. Because of decreasing prices, superior hardware is now being used and image quality is better than ever. Many people now require image-synthesis techniques and software for their applicaions. Moreover, the techniques of computer animation have become very popular. In this book, we present a wide range of applications of computer graphics.

This book is a collection of 44 papers in various areas of computer graphics selected from papers presented at Graphics Interface '85. Graphics Interface '85, held from May 27 to 31 in Montreal, was the first truly international computer graphics conference in Canada. This year, for the first time, the conference was presented jointly by the Computer Graphics Society and the Canadian Man-Computer Communications Society. This new arrangement gave the conference international scope. The conference was sponsored by the Department of Communications in Ottawa, the Department of Science and Technology in Quebec, Supply and Services Canada, the Natural Sciences and Engineering Research Council of Canada, Hydro-Quebec, the "Association Canadienne Française pour l'Avancement des Sciences", and the Canadian Broadcasting Corporation. Graphics Interface '85 was organized by "l'Ecole des Hautes Etudes Commerciales" of the University of Montreal.

Over 100 papers were submitted to the conference, but 64 were selected by the international program committee for presentation. This book contains new expanded versions of the papers. Moreover, authors have taken the opportunity of insert many color pictures, thus adding to the quality of their papers.

Computer-Generated Images spans the broad spectrum of computer art and computer graphics technology, including image synthesis, image processing, geometric modelling, computer animation, user interface, CAD/CAM, artificial intelligence, and graphics databases. The applications presented here are very wide—geography, statistics, transportation, simulation of circuits, business, project management, editing, and publishing. This volume offers the reader insight into a broad variety of topics and consolidates the various research areas in computer graphics into a single book.

Nadia Magnenat-Thalmann
Daniel Thalmann

Table of Contents

Chapter 1
Image Synthesis 1

Image Synthesis: Optical Identity or Pictorial Communication
(M.I. Mills) 3

A Theoretical and Empirical Analysis of Coherent Ray-Tracing
(L.R. Speer, T.D. DeRose, B.A. Barsky) 11

High Level Descriptions for 3D Stochastic Models
(B. Wyvill, C. McPheeters, M. Novacek) 26

Frame Buffer Algorithms for Stochastic Models
(A. Fournier, T. Milligan) 35

Animating Lights and Shadows
(M. Fortin, N. Léonard, N. Magnenat-Thalmann, D. Thalmann) 45

An Analysis and Algorithm for Filling Propagation
(K.P. Fishkin, B.A. Barsky) 56

Chapter 2
Image Processing 77

Non-Rigid Body Motion
(A.R. Dill, M.D. Levine) 79

Selection of Segment Similarity Measures for Hierarchical Picture Segmentation
(J.-M. Beaulieu, M. Goldberg) 87

Computer Analysis of Cardiac Wall Motion Asynchrony
(O. Ratib, A. Righetti) 98

Multi-Robot Assembly of IC's
(C. Michaud, A.S. Malowany, M.D. Levine) 106

A Computerized System for Spot Detection and Analysis of Two-Dimensional Electrophoresis Images
(R. Appel, M. Funk, C. Pellegrini, D. Hochstrasser, A.F. Müller) 118

Hologram-like Transmission of Pictures
(P. Prusinkiewicz, M. Christopher) 125

Chapter 3
Geometric Modelling 135

CSG and Ray Tracing Using Functional Primitives
(T.L. Kunii, G. Wyvill) 137

Geometric Continuity with Interpolating Bézier Curves
(A. Fournier, B.A. Barsky) 153

An Intuitive Approach to Geometric Continuity for Parametric Curves and Surfaces
(T.D. DeRose, B.A. Barsky) 159

Octree Data Structures and Creation by Stacking
(W.R. Franklin, V. Akman) 176

Chapter 4
Computer Animation 187

ANIMENGINE: An Engineering Animation System
(T. Noma, T.L. Kunii) 189

Dynamics for Animation of Characters with Deformable Surfaces
(W.W. Armstrong, M.W. Green) 203

Using Dynamic Analysis to Animate Articulated Bodies such as Humans and Robots
(J.P. Wilhelms, B.A. Barsky) 209

Towards an Integrated View of 3-D Computer Animation
(D. Zeltzer) 230

Controlling Evolution and Motion Using the CINEMIRA-2 Animation Sublanguage
(N. Magnenat-Thalmann, D.Thalmann) 249

Computer Animation in Distance Teaching
(J.M. Greenberg) 260

Chapter 5
User Interface 267

The Interactive Planning Work Station: A Graphics-Based UNIX Tool for Application Users and Developers
(R. Bournique, R. Candrea, D. Hartman) 269

The Higgens UIMS and its Efficient Implementation of Undo
(S.E. Hudson, R. King) 278

Graphics Interaction in Databases
(C. Frasson, M. Erradi) 291

Interface Abstractions for an *naplps* Page Creation System
(E. Chang) 302

Colour Coding Scales and Computer Graphics
(A.M. Heath, R.B. Flavell) 307

Chapter 6
CAD/CAM 319

An Innovative User Interface for Microcomputer-Based Computer-Aided Design
(L. Lichten, R. Eaton) 321

A Geometric Modeller for Turbomachinery Applications
(B. Ozell, R. Camarero) 330

Low Cost Geometric Modelling System for CAM
(W.B. Ngai, Y.K. Chan) 342

The CADME Approach to the Interface of Solid Modellers
(C. Bizzozero, U. Cugini) 356

Chapter 7
Artificial Intelligence 365

Generative Design in Architecture Using an Expert System
(E. Gullichsen, E. Chang) 367

Knowledge Engineering Application in Image Processing
(K. Mikame, N. Sueda, A. Hoshi, S. Honiden) 376

Heuristic Rules for Visualization
(L.R. Scholl) 386

Chapter 8
Applications 393

Computer Graphics for Multivariate Data
(R. Cléroux, Y. Lepage, N. Ranger) 395

A Graphics Interface for Interactive Simulation of Packet-Switched Networks
(J.L. Houle, L. Richardson) 411

Design and Implementation of an Interactive Route Editor
(G. Lapalme, M. Cormier) 419

Business Graphics and the Stakeholder Approach: An Exploratory Field Experiment
(A. Lejeune, F. Bolduc, N. Magnenat-Thalmann) 425

An Integrated System for Printing and Publishing Applications
(S. Cavaliere, M. Fantini, A. Turtur) 436

Project Management Using Graphics
(F. Pettinati) 448

Chapter 9
Geographic Information and Databases 455

How Map Designers can Represent their Ideas in Thematic Maps: Effective User Interfaces for Thematic Map Design
(T. Yamahira, Y. Kasahara, T. Tsurutani) 457

Challenges in the Application of Graphics Technology to the Management of Geographic Information
(I.K. Crain, C.L. MacDonald) 469

An Image Management Kernel for the Design of Relational and Pictorial Data Bases
(Ph. Chassignet) 478

The Scientific and Technical Issues in Integrating Remotely Sensed Imagery with Geocoded Data Bases
(W.M. Strome, B. Grush) 485

Author Index 493

Subject Index 495

Chapter 1
Image Synthesis

Image search

Image Synthesis
Optical Identity or Pictorial Communication

Michael I. Mills

The Interactive Telecommunications Program, New York University, 725 Broadway, New York, NY 10003, USA

INTRODUCTION

"Our goal in realistic image synthesis is to generate an image that evokes from the visual perception system a response indistinguishable from that evoked by the actual environment." (Hall and Greenberg, 1983, p. 10) This quote, taken from a recent article in IEEE Computer Graphics and Applications, conveys how many workers in the field of image synthesis interpret their mandate. At first glance, this seems like a sensible research objective. It provides a straightforward criterion for progress. We judge the success of this synthesized image by comparing our perception of it to our direct perception of the identical scene in the real-world.

Now it is true that researchers in image synthesis are constantly finding new ways to mathematically model the physical behaviour of light as it is propagated throughout the environment. And one day these models may enable observers to experience experience in computer "surrogates" many of the important patterns of stimulation available in the visual world--including perhaps those patterns dependent on binocular vision (Schmandt, 1983) and on real-time changes in the observer's station point. But I believe that short of actually building physical replicas, there will always be fundamental differences between looking at images and looking directly at the real thing. (c.f. Gibson's discussion of "Pictures as substitutes for visual realities" in Reed and Jones, 1982).

An important question one can raise then is this: Is there a better--or at least more sophisticated--way of conceiving of the task of depiction in computer graphics than as a contest with reality, a quest to "fool" the perceptual system via imitation of the real world? The communication of visual truths in an image may have less to do with the manufacturing of perfect copies of retinal images than with the skillful manipulation of evocative forms; less to do with transcribing reality than with suggesting it pictorially. And to learn more about the underlying principles of this communicative process--in which the brain imposes interpretations on patterns of light that reach it--we must turn to the domains of art history and perceptual psychology, rather than computer graphics.

CHANGING STANDARDS OF REALISM

If there is one book I would urge computer scientists in the synthetic imaging area to read, it would not be a treatise on technology or the physics of light, but E.H. Gombrich's masterpiece, Art and Illusion (Gombrich, 1960). I think that graphics scientists would find this book particularly valuable because they would see many similarities between artists' "experiments" in using paint to simulate the effects of light and their own quest to simulate the visible world in computer displays. Obviously, I cannot do justice to all the insights in Gombrich's wonderful book. But I would like to highlight several examples of particular relevance to the problem of making realistic images by computer.

In a chapter entitled "From Light to Paint", Gombrich tells of a controversy surrounding "Wivenhoe Park"--a marvelous landscape by the nineteenth-century English artist John Constable in which we can see "...the play of sunlight on green pastures, the gentle ripples on the lake with its swans, and the beautiful landscape that encloses it all." (P. 33) Now we would never mistake this oil painting for a photograph; but we easily accept it as a reasonably faithful record of what Constable might actually have seen when he stood on that spot to paint the picture. It is therefore difficult for us to grasp that this painting was considered by nineteenth-century eyes as an avant-garde, if not revolutionary, "experiment" in depiction.

Constable was widely rebuked for trying out a greater range of tonal contrasts--especially the use of brighter shades of green-- in reconciling the local colour of grass with the tonal gradients needed to suggest depth, than had heretofore been attempted in landscapes of the era. At first, there was great resistance to his use of lighter shades. Legend has it that Constable's patron, Sir George Beaumont, chastised him for not making the grass in the foreground "the requisite mellow brown of an old violin." Constable's retort, so Gombrich tells us, was to "take a real violin and put it on the grass before him to show his friend the difference between fresh green grass and the warm tones demanded by convention." (Gombrich, 1960, p. 44)

Over time, Constable's transgression became the rule, not the exception, and paved the way for brighter and more "realistic" landscapes. But we should not come away from this story thinking that Constable's victory lay in his ability to perform as a kind of human camera--a copying machine capable of matching the "true" colour of grass to the corresponding green on his pallette. In fact, as Gombrich points out, his genius was rather more subtle. The colour of the grass in Constable's painting is still closer to the brown violin than to the green of fresh grass.
Constable's gift was not that he could copy nature better than his predecessors, but rather his intuition that the human visual system could be stretched in its response to the way pigment can suggest relationships in light: that by expanding the contrast between light and dark tones, the artist could force the perception of new "visual truths".

MORE DETAIL, MORE REALISM?

A first lesson from Gombrich, then, is that judgements of realistic portrayal are not so much a process of comparing images with reality, but rather that our criteria for what we accept as visual reality shifts with the discovery of novel techniques for suggesting the effects of light. A second lesson, perhaps even more important to our present purpose, concerns the assumption by many workers in digital imaging that, simply by cramming more and more details (adding more pixels), we automatically achieve more realistic and "useful" images of things and people.

Interestingly, Gombrich tells us that the "more detail, more realism" hypothesis was also shared at first by the old masters, who learned through trial and error that adding more and more detail did not necessarily lead to better paintings.

Rembrandt, for example, in his early portrait work, would struggle to render the "microstructure" of small segments of the visual array corresponding to, say, shiny gold braid on his subject's garment. In his later work, however, he learned that a few well-placed brushstrokes enabled the observer to achieve an even superior experience of gold braid. The secret was that when viewed at the appropriate distance, the small segment representing the gold braid fell on the periphery of the eye and the viewer's mind would "fill in the gaps" so to speak; i.e. the broader brushstrokes could convey the immediacy of the visual system's response to smooth shiny surfaces and glitter better than the more detailed, laborious rendering.

A modern-day counterpart to the old masters' experiments on the relationship between "redundancy removal" and "realism" is the by now well-known computer-generated "block portraits"--for example, a grid of say 14 x 18 squares, each of which can assume any of sixteen grey levels. What is interesting about these reduced-information block portraits, of course, is that viewed close-up, they are merely arrangements of light and dark squares. Seen from a distance of several feet, however, the individual squares seem to fuse magically into a clearly recognizable picture of a human face. Moreover, if the viewer shakes his head or someone jiggles the picture, there seems to be more _apparent_ detail in what is actually quite a coarse-grained image. The intriguing question for students of perception is why stepping back from such images, or blurring them intentionally--actions which are the opposite of what we usually do when we want to get a better look at something--should improve the identification process. No one as yet has a complete answer; but as Rembrandt realized in his rendering of gold braid, the secret must lie not just in the physical qualities of the image, but in accounting for what we will call, after Gombrich, the "beholder's share" in picture perception. (In the case of block portraits, "blurring" through head movement or backward lococmotion serves to "filter out" the high frequency spatial components -- the sharp block edges -- allowing the critical low frequency "portrait" information to get through. C.F. Harmon, 1974).

OPTICAL IDENTITY VERSUS OPTICAL SIMULATION: INSIGHTS FROM HOCHBERG

It would appear then that Rembrandt beat Bell Laboratories by several centuries in exploring methods of redundancy removal in picture making! But surely Rembrandt did not paint this way just to save on bandwidth. Somehow he knew (although we cannot be certain what was going on in his mind) that a few brush strokes could conjure up an impression of smooth, shiny metal better than a more detailed rendering. Can we say more about why he may have been right? Fortunately, we can--thanks to Julian Hochberg, one of the few perceptual theorists who has probed the complex links between art, pictures and the workings of the human visual system: what we have been calling, following Gombrich, the beholder's share.

In an important articile called "Some of the things that paintings are", Hochberg hypothesizes that the techniques used by Rembrandt are breakthroughs in depiction, in the way they exploit fundamental differences between central and peripheral vision. Hochberg reminds us that it is only the center of the retina--the foveal region--that picks up full colour and resolves fine detail. As the distance from the fovea increases, the eye's ability to resolve detail falls off dramatically. Peripheral vision responds mostly to abrupt changes in luminance, indicating edges, large surfaces, and movement. Consider what would occur if, when viewing a Rembrandt portrait, our gaze happens to land on a spot away from the middle region of the painting--i.e., away from the portion of the picture encompassing the face and hands. Even though our foveae can resolve great deatil in these outer regions, there is no fine detail to be had.

Hochberg notes two important consequences of this fact. Firstly, our gaze will drift back to the middle region of the picture--the face and hands--which are the points of interest, where fine detail does exist. According to Hochberg, this "forced focusing" has obvious advantages from a compositional point of view.

A second, more subtle consequence concerns the use of "simultaneous contrast" effects to overcome the limits of paint to represent apparent brightness: highlights, reflections and so on. Simultaneous contrast effects occur when we look at two neighboring areas of a scene, one of which is dark and the other light. Our brains do not merely register the objective difference in brightness between the two adjacent patches, but actually enhance the perceived brightness contrast. This works as follows. The neural receptors in the eye are linked so that the more a particular retinal region responds to light, the more it inhibits the response of adjacent receptors. In a given scene, a light patch surrounded by a dark region will be seen as subjectively brighter than a patch of the same tonality surrounded by a light region. The receptors receiving the central image are being <u>less</u> inhibited by neighboring receptors in the former case, with the net effect of raising the apparent brightness contrast. (Painters discovered early on that by surrounding a grey patch with a black background, they could make the grey patch appear

brighter than it would have looked on a white background.)
Moreover, as Hochberg points out, simultaneous contrast effects
are even stronger in the periphery of the eye than in focal
vision. Although Rembrandt may not have been able to articulate
his awareness of this phenomenon, he seems to have used it to
good effect. Hence, as we mentioned earlier in conjunction with
Rembrandt's attempt to render gold braid, he learned that by
placing large brushstrokes of extreme lights and darks just
outside the area just outside the area of focal interest (outside
of foveal vision), he was able to enhance the apparent brightness
of the highlights and shiny surfaces in the picture.

We can now better understand Gombrich's claim that Rembrandt's
rendering of gold braid in his later portraits have an
"immediacy" and "glitter" not conveyed by its more detailed
counterpart--but with an important corollary. The enhancement of
brightness only works if the braid lies outside the focal area of
the painting. Once we fix our eyes on the gold braid, inspecting
it closely, the global quality--the illusion of glitter--is
destroyed as our eyes resolve the individual brushstrokes.

To Hochberg, these facts are extremely important if we are to
grasp the special, dual character of pictures: i.e., pictures are
themselves perceptibly flat objects, yet they can be seen as
"surrogates" for other objects, usually three-dimensional. In
normal vision, when we search a scene for information, we do
resolve fine detail when we move our gaze onto the periphery.
When we shift from the central to the outer regions of the
Rembrandt painting, however, a mental "switch" occurs: instead of
fine detail which we interpret in terms of the scene--paint
depicting a face--we notice the rough-hewn, individual
brushstrokes, dobs of paint; not an object. This fact, according
to Hochberg, serves to remind us (perhaps unconsciously) that we
are indeed looking at a painting--itself a flat object covered
with pigment--not a real scene or a replica. This is the
artist's way of telling us that he is not engaging in a contest
with reality: not trying to copy, in a one-to-one mapping, the
light emitted from the scene. Rather, he is using paint to
"simulate" certain important effects of light on our visual
system--a process of pictorial communication better thought of as
optical simulation than as optical identity or equivalence.
The difference between the self-conscious use of paint to achieve
optical simulation, as opposed to optical identity, can most
clearly be seen in the experiments of the Impressionists. Their
avowed goal, like that of modern-day workers in image synthesis,
was "...to use optical science to produce paintings that would
provide the same impression to perceptual experience as does the
light in a (usually outdoors) scene." (Hochberg, 1979, p. 33)
No one, however, would ever mistake Monet's impressionist
painting "Rouen Cathedral" for a photograph of the real scene.
Unlike Rembrandt's portraits which contained pockets of fine
detail in focal regions, Monet's painting provides no resting
place for our eyes--no islands of fine detail. The entire canvas
is built out of rough-hewn swatches of colour. How could Monet
do this and still claim to be following the goals of
Impressionism?

Hochberg, again, provides a penetrating analysis which brings us full circle to the computer-generated block portraits mentioned earlier:

> In an impressionist painting, when it is viewed from a normal distance, there are no places at which the fovea can pick up fine detail. To peripheral vision, on the other hand, the Impressionist painting looks veridical, as it does when viewed with deliberately out of focus ("abstracted") gaze and when viewed from a distance that is considerably greater than normal. As Harmon and Julesz (1973) showed, the perceptibility of the object represented by a patchwork picture, like those most characteristic of Impressionist painters, is increased when the perceptibility of the small details or "high spatial frequencies" (provided by the edges of the brushstrokes) is reduced, as in peripheral viewing or viewing from increased distance. At a normal viewing distance, the scene dissolves into patches wherever the fovea leaves them, and they are reclaimed by peripheral or parafoveal vision. (Hochberg, 1979, p. 35)

For Hochberg, then, one might say that Monet's intent was to convey, or more precisely, to simulate the first fleeting impression--the dazzle and freshness of a momentary glance at a sunlit cathedral; an evoking of the events in peripheral vision, undetailed, with gross volumes and colours. Monet's goal was not to fool us into believing that we are looking at a real scene, but to show us how pictures can be used to capture novel "truths" of visual experience.

CONCLUSION

At the outset we saw that the goal of image synthesis research was to use computers to make images of objects and people which would be optically identical to direct perception of the visible world. Most of the effort to date has been spent developing mathematical models of the physics of light, the geometrical modeling of solid objects, and building the hardware to generate scenes based on these formal descriptions. I hope that my brief review of pictorial realism in art, based on the writings of Gombrich and Hochberg, has convinced you that image synthesis and research might profit not only by considering the physics of light and solid geometry, but by learning more about the "beholder's share" in picture perception. Let me summarize the lessons we have gleaned thus far from these authors.

First, we saw that judgements of realism in picture-making are always context-bound; what is considered a realistic image may depend more on comparisons between one picture and another, according to a particular period's criteria for realistic picture-making, than on any fixed or absolute standards of reality based on looking at the visible world. Second, we saw that adding more and more detail, either with paint or pixels, does not necessarily lead to more realistic looking pictures--if one takes into account the limits of the display medium and the functioning of the visual system (i.e., the differences between central, parafoveal, and foveal vision, simultaneous contrast effects, etc.). Finally, we saw that by acknowledging and experimenting with the interactions between the visual system and the limits of the medium of depiction, artists redefined their basic mission. Rather than trying to create objects (paintings) which would be optically identical to the real scene, they strove instead for optical <u>simulation</u> through painting: a self-conscious process of pictorial communication which acknowledges the dual character of pictures (e.g., perceptibly flat objects treated so as to depict a different set of objects. And where the departures from realism--the techniques of optical simulation themselves--become a focus of interest and investigation in their own right.

We should not conclude from these arguments that computer graphics researchers should abandon the quest for realism via sophisticated formal models of light propagation and solid modelling. Nor are we saying that computer imaging should imitate the techniques of Rembrandt and the Impressionists. We are claiming, however, that learning more about the "beholder's share" in pictorial communication, including developing an awareness of how computer imagery fits in with the history and psychology of picture making, could have payoffs in such nitty-gritty matters as developing techniques for redundancy removal in picture encoding, and might tell us more about what styles of pictorial rendering might be acceptable in specific contexts, in different task environments. (C.F. Hearty, 1983).

ACKNOWLEDGEMENTS

Many of the ideas in this paper stem from a larger report entitled "Simulating Reality in Computer Images: Insights from Art History and Cognitive Science" written by the author and funded by the Canadian Department of Communication (contract 36100-3-0057).

I would like to thank Dr. Paul J. Hearty of the Canadian Communications Research Centre for his valuable guidance in helping to formulate these ideas.

REFERENCES

Gibson, J.J. Pictures as substitutes for visual realities. In E.Reed and R.Jones (eds), *Reasons for Realism: Selected essays of James. J. Gibson*. Lawrence Erlbaum, 1982.

Gombrich, E.H. *Art and illusion*. Princeton University Press, 1960.

Hall, R. and Greenberg, D.A. A testbed for realistic image synthesis. *IEEE Computer graphics and its applications*, vol. 3, no. 8, 1983.

Harmon, L. The recognition of faces. *Image, object and illusion: Readings from the Scientific American*, 1974.

Hearty, P.J. Behavioural research on Telidon graphics. Paper presented at the workshop on Telidon and the graphic arts, Science and Technology Centre, Vancouver, British Columbia, 1983.

Hochberg, J. Some of the things that paintings are. In C.Nodine and D.Fisher (Eds.), *Perception and pictorial representation*, Praeger, 1979.

Schmandt, C. Spatial input/output correspondence in a stereoscopic computer graphic workstation. *Computer graphics*, 17(3), 1983, 253-261.

A Theoretical and Empirical Analysis of Coherent Ray-Tracing

L. Richard Speer, Tony D. DeRose and Brian A. Barsky

Berkeley Computer Graphics Laboratory, Computer Science Division, Department of Electrical Engineering and Computer Sciences, University of California, Berkeley, CA 94720, USA

Abstract

The use of *coherence* has been advocated as a means of reducing the large computational cost of the ray-tracing method of image synthesis. This paper examines the theoretical and empirical performance of a typical coherent ray-tracing algorithm, one that exploits the similarity between the intersection trees generated by successive rays. It is shown that despite the large degree of coherence present in a scene, the need to ensure the validity of ray-object intersections prevents any significant computational savings. This indicates that other algorithmic methods must be used in order to substantially reduce the computational cost of ray-traced imagery.

Résumé

L'utilisation de la *cohérence* a été proposée afin de réduire le coût élevé de la méthode de synthèse d'image basée sur le traçage de rayons lumineux. Cet article examine la performance, tant d'un point de vue théorique qu'empirique, d'un algorithme typique qui met de cohérence de rayons, c'est-à-dire un algorithme qui exploit la ressemblance entre les arbres d'intersections générés par des rayons successifs. Nous montrons qu'en dépit du degré élevé de cohérence présent dans une image, l'obligation de maintenir la validité des structure d'intersection fait obstacle à l'obtention de gains importants. Ces résultats donnent à penser que des méthodes algorithmiques plus fondamentales sont nécessaires pour réduire de façon substantielle les coûts de calcul du traçage de rayons lumineux.

KEYWORDS: ray-tracing, coherence, image synthesis.

This work was supported in part by the Defense Advanced Research Projects Agency under contract number N00039-82-C-0235, the National Science Foundation under grant number ECS-8204381, and the State of California under a Microelectronics Innovation and Computer Research Opportunities grant.

1. INTRODUCTION

The technique of tracing rays through a scene ("ray-tracing"), first used to generate shadows[1] and solve the hidden-surface problem for quadrics,[10] has become the centre of a great deal of research activity. Beginning with two papers on realistic image generation,[16,25] the method has been applied to algebraic surface rendering[12,15] and a number of problems in solids modelling.[2,17,19] Probably the most striking application of the method, however, remains its use in generating highly realistic imagery.[11,14,25] The ray-tracing method is unique in its ability to compute inter-object reflections, shadows, and accurate refraction, features that are difficult or impossible to achieve with other techniques.

The price of such effects, however, is not small. Computation times for ray-traced pictures, for example, are often measured in CPU-hours.[11,24,25] The chief reason for this is that a very large number of rays (250,000 - 1,000,000 or more) must be traced for high-quality imagery.

One strategy for reducing ray-tracing computation time relies on hardware. A number of papers have been published in this area, including one on the use of a "supercomputer",[18] two on co-processor designs[3,4] and several on multiprocessor-based systems.[5,6,23]

A second strategy uses algorithms that adaptively subdivide scenes into a number of sub-volumes. The resulting sub-volumes may or may not be disjoint from one another. One study[7] examined a "cellular" subdivision, that is, one in which all sub-volumes were disjoint, though they together contained the whole scene volume. Other papers[9,14,20] have presented algorithms based on hierarchical scene subdivisions. Such scene structures generally permit fast determination of the nearest object intersected by a ray.

Another technique which has been mentioned by several authors[13,15,25] but not tried, centres on the use of *ray coherence*. As Heckbert[13] noted, "...in many scenes, groups of rays follow virtually the same path from the eye..." (see Figure 1). As a result, the tree-like paths that are traced through the scene by successive rays from the viewpoint are often very similar. This similarity can be used to predict the path of any such ray, given the path of its predecessor, as follows. First, the ray currently being traced from the viewpoint is checked against the object intersected by the previous ray from the viewpoint. If the current ray does not intersect that object, it must be checked against all other objects in the scene, as in standard ray-tracing.[25] Otherwise, a check of the other objects need not be done, resulting in a computational savings. In this case, we say that the two rays in question are *coherent*. Also in this case, we can apply the idea recursively: any reflective ray that results is checked against the object hit by the reflective ray of the last ray from the viewpoint; and so on. It should be apparent that the degree of similarity of these paths indicates (roughly) the computational savings that coherence can provide over standard ray-tracing.

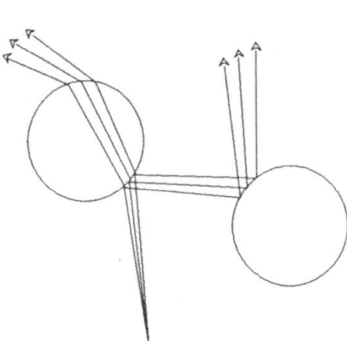

Figure 1 - Groups of Rays Follow Similar Paths

Before proceeding any further, we must add that the detection of coherence is not quite as simple as just described. Even when *corresponding rays* (two rays at the same recursion level, one of which is either the last ray from the viewpoint or one of its children, the other the current ray from the viewpoint, or one of its children) intersect the same object, the current ray might also intersect a nearer, intervening object just missed by its correspondent (Figure 2). These false-coherence cases must be detected, to produce correct results.

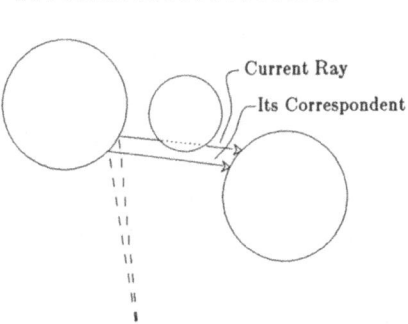

**Figure 2 - Current Ray Intersects Object Hit by
Its Correspondent, and Interceding Object**

In the rest of this paper we describe, analyze and present performance data of an algorithm for coherent ray-tracing. Coherence ("the extent to which the environment or the picture of it is locally constant")[22] has often been used in graphic algorithms.[21,22] It is natural to expect coherent ray-tracing to yield the same kinds of benefits seen in other rendering algorithms. Empirically, however, we have found that this is not the case. The following sections explain why.

We should note that the algorithm we will be discusssing is most naturally used on scenes containing objects enclosed by spherical bounding volumes. The general approach, however, could also be used with other kinds of volumes, such as "box enclosures".[19]

In Section 2, the coherent algorithm is presented and compared with the standard one. Section 3 gives a probabilistic analysis of the new algorithm's performance. Finally, in Section 4 we discuss our implementation and give statistics from test pictures that were made.

2. RAY-TRACING ALGORITHMS

2.1. Terminology

We begin by defining terms that will be used throughout the rest of the paper. A ray is specified by an *anchor* and a *direction vector*. The anchor is the three-dimensional location of the origin of the ray. The direction vector specifies the direction of propagation of the ray.

The *image plane* is a rectangular region positioned (conceptually) in or near the scene. Elemental regions in the plane correspond to pixels of the frame buffer. Along with the plane, a *viewpoint* is specified. To simplify the discussion, we distinguish rays that originate at the viewpoint from all others, labelling them *initial rays*. A *ray-set* is composed of an initial ray and any reflected and refracted rays that it generates, together with their descendants.

As mentioned in Section 1, the scene consists of some number of spherical *bounding volumes*. It will aid the discussion if we assume that relatively few of these volumes intersect, although this is not required. The volumes surround *objects* composed of primitive geometric elements such as triangles or more general polygons. We refer to the latter simply as *primitives*.

Since most rays that are traced are the result of an intersection with an object, we say that a ray has an associated *originating object*. For consistency, we will regard even initial rays as having such objects.

We now define some terms that describe the relations between a given ray and the bounding volumes present in a region or scene. Every ray naturally divides space into two half-spaces, the boundary being a particular plane (Figure 3). This plane, which we call the *bounding plane* for the ray, is defined as the plane passing through ray's anchor, having the direction vector of the ray as its normal. We call the half-space in the direction of ray propagation the *front half-space* of the given ray, and the other the *rear half-space*. A bounding volume that lies entirely in the rear half-space is said to lie "behind" the ray associated with the plane; those that do not are said to lie "in front" of the ray. We refer to the process of classifying all the volumes like this as *partitioning the region*.

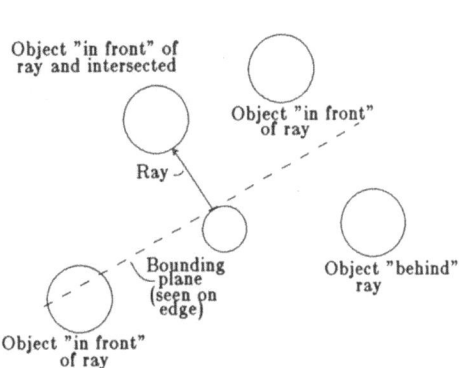

Figure 3 - Partition of Space by a Ray
(Cross-sectional View)

Finding the intersection of a given ray and the primitives in a region requires determining which bounding volumes are intersected by the ray. All the volumes in a region that are in front of a ray divide into two groups, those that are actually intersected by the ray and those that are not. And any volume behind a ray cannot be intersected by it. Therefore, we note that a ray divides all the volumes in a region into three disjoint sets: those behind the ray, those in front but not intersected, and those in front and intersected. We call these sets *B, N* and *I*, respectively.

A few other terms that are more easily defined in context are presented later.

2.2. Standard Algorithm

We now consider the standard ray-tracing algorithm. In its simplest form, a ray-tracing program consists of two nested loops surrounding a call to a ray-tracing routine. The loops serve to scan the rows and columns of the image.

The ray-tracing routine itself is usually written recursively. If the initial ray passed into the routine intersects an object, calls may in turn be made in the directions of reflection and refraction. In the standard algorithm,[25] recursion terminates when a ray either does not intersect anything or intersects an opaque, non-reflective surface. More recent papers[8,11] have noted that recursion can also terminate when a special attenuated-intensity coefficient that is associated with a ray drops below a threshold.

As the recursion proceeds, a record is kept of the objects intersected. Due to the fact that in many implementations, no more than two rays are spawned at an intersection, the record is often kept in the form of a binary tree (the "intersection tree" referred to in Section 1). When recursion has stopped for all members of the ray-set, the pixel's colour is computed by applying an appropriate shading rule[11,25] to the tree. After shading, the tree is discarded and the entire process repeated for the next pixel.

In addition to those traced recursively, rays are also traced from intersection points toward each light source, to test for shadowing. The results of this test are stored in the nodes of the intersection tree and used in the shading calculation.[25]

2.3. Coherent Algorithm

2.3.1. Containers Around Rays

As discussed in Section 1, a coherent ray-tracing algorithm can use the path generated by the last ray-set to predict the path of the current ray-set. Thus, one immediate difference between the new coherent algorithm and the standard one is that after colour computation, the intersection tree is *retained* for one more program iteration. It is used during this iteration as a guide, providing hints as to which objects will be intersected by rays in the current ray-set. When tracing for the current ray-set terminates, the last intersection tree is discarded and the tree that was just generated in turn is retained, to play the role of intersection-guide for the next ray-set.

However, we must be able to detect cases such as those illustrated in Figure 2, as we mentioned; this can be done as follows. A logical "container", a kind of "safety zone", can be constructed around every ray in a ray-set. These containers will be centred around the ray with which they are associated and extend outward *to the nearest object not intersected by that ray* (Figure 4). It can be seen that if a corresponding ray from the next ray-set does not "pierce" (intersect) the side of the relevant container, and intersects the same object intersected by this ray, then that object must be the foremost object intersected by the corresponding ray. Thus, if each ray in the last ray-set has associated container information, the situation shown in Figure 2 can be avoided: rays in the next ray-set that pierce the container of their corresponding ray or fail to intersect the object intersected by that ray, require a region partition, as in standard ray-tracing. Rays that do not pierce the relevant container, on the other hand, and intersect the object intersected by their corresponding ray do not require a region partition.

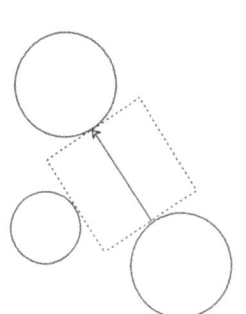

**Figure 4 - "Safety Zone" Around a Ray
(Cross-sectional View)**

Since the savings that can be achieved by this strategy depend on trading the cost of checking every object in the region for the cost of "pierce-checking" the container, it is important that the latter operation be as computationally simple as possible. A radially-symmetric container is a great help in achieving this goal. For this reason, we chose *cylinders* for the containers. Such a cylinder starts at the point of origin of a ray, has its central axis aligned with it, and ends at its point of intersection with an object.

2.3.2. Container/Cylinder Construction

It is not difficult to construct a cylinder like the one just described. Notice that every bounding volume in a region becomes a member of one and only one of the sets B, N and I, defined in Section 2.1, in the course of a region partition for some ray. Let us now consider the set N. If it is not empty, then we can simply check each element in the set to find any that is between the bounding plane of the ray and a parallel plane that passes though the nearest object intersection point. Of these, we take the distance of the volume that is nearest to the ray, radially, as the cylinder radius (Figure 5). The cylinder has its central axis aligned with the ray, which we call the *formative ray* for the cylinder, and is bounded by the two planes mentioned. We store the cylinder information in an intersection tree node simply by storing the radius defined above and the ray direction. The other attributes (the cylinder bounds) are defined implicitly by information stored in the intersection tree by the standard algorithm,[25] namely the point of origin of the ray and its point of intersection with an object in front of it.

2.3.3. Containers/Cylinders for Light Sources

To compute shadows, rays are traced from object intersection points in the direction of each light source, as mentioned in Section 2.2. If one of these rays intersects an object "en route",

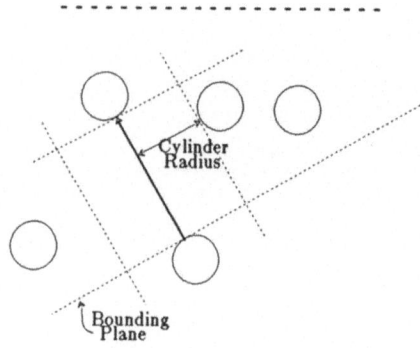

Figure 5 - Safety-Cylinder Construction

the point in question is in shadow with respect to that source. Rays traced for this purpose are somewhat different than those traced for object intersection in that no rays are traced recursively from any object that they intersect.

Coherence cylinders can also be constructed and used for these light-testing rays. If an object is intersected by such a ray, a cylinder is built in the manner discussed earlier (Figure 5).

2.4. Summary

In summary, our algorithm differs from the standard one in two major ways: first, the standard intersection tree is retained across program iterations. Although the discussion above was couched in terms of two distinct intersection trees, the previous being used as a guide for the current one, we can in fact simply update the previous intersection tree as necessary. Tree updates are needed whenever a ray in the current ray-set pierces the corresponding safety cylinder in the retained tree. A tree update involves discarding some or all of the intersection tree (depending on whether the current ray is an initial one or not) and rebuilding as dictated by any new ray intersections.

The second major difference in the new algorithm is that the intersection tree is augmented with "safety cylinder" information. This information is used to indicate when the intersection information of a previous ray is no longer valid and that a region partition will, therefore, be required.

3. PROBABILISTIC ANALYSIS

We now consider two major questions: first, for a scene with a given percentage of coherent rays, what order of computational savings can be achieved using the new algorithm and, second, since it has additional costs beyond standard ray-tracing (due to cylinder construction and pierce-checking), what percentage of rays must be coherent for the new algorithm to outperform standard ray-tracing?

Beginning with the first question, a simple argument can be made to derive an upper bound on the savings that can be achieved using the new algorithm. Suppose that a ray found to be coherent cost *nothing* computationally. Denote the time required to render a given scene using standard ray-tracing as T_{ST}. Then, if a fraction C of the number of rays traced by the algorithm are coherent, an expression for the amount of time saved is $Savings = C * T_{ST}$. This is an upper bound since any implemented algorithm must do some work to process even a coherent ray.

From the above, we note that *the savings that can be achieved by the new algorithm are linear in the amount of coherence present.* For example, if half the rays traced in a scene are found to be coherent ($C = 0.5$), computation time can be reduced by no more than 50%.

We now turn to the second question, concerning the percentage of coherent rays needed before the new algorithm shows a savings. We start by deriving expressions for the amount of time needed to process a ray in the standard algorithm and in the new one.

In standard ray-tracing, there are two costs associated with each ray. First, a scene partition must be performed, at a cost proportional to the number of volumes n in the scene. Second, the volumes that are intersected must be checked to find the one that is nearest to the ray anchor. The time needed to determine this is a weak function of n due to the fact that on average, few volumes will need to be checked. Therefore, we treat this time as a constant, α. We also say that this constant includes the cost of computing the directions of any recursive rays. Altogether then, the amount of time needed for each ray in standard ray-tracing, which we denote t_{ST}, is $t_{ST} = kn + \alpha$.

We now look at the cost of a ray in the new algorithm. There are two cases to consider, corresponding to whether or not a safety cylinder must be constructed. The cost of a ray when a cylinder must be constructed is similar to the cost of a ray in standard ray-tracing: the scene must be partitioned and the nearest intersected object found. An amount of additional work λn must then be done to determine the cylinder radius. Thus, the time needed to process a ray in this case is $t_{cylinder} = kn + \alpha + \lambda n$. Simplifying in terms of t_{ST} yields $t_{cylinder} = t_{ST} + \lambda n$.

The cost of a coherent ray, on the other hand, is simply the cost of computing the intersection point with the object intersected by the formative ray, together with the cost of computing any recursive rays. This cost is less than or equal to α. (The cost of detecting that a cylinder is pierced is negligible compared to the cost of a scene partition, for any scene containing more than a few objects.)

We can now give an expression for the maximum cost of a ray in the new algorithm, t_{CT}. Denoting the probability of a ray being coherent as C, the time needed for its processing is

$$t_{CT} \leq C(\alpha) + (1-C)t_{cylinder}, \text{ for } 0 \leq C \leq 1.$$

Rearranging yields

$$t_{CT} \leq t_{cylinder} - C(t_{cylinder} - \alpha), \text{ for } 0 \leq C \leq 1.$$

Now, by setting t_{ST} equal to t_{CT} and solving for C, we can find the threshold value C_T at which the new algorithm costs less than standard ray-tracing.

$$t_{ST} \leq t_{CT}$$
$$\leq t_{cylinder} - C(t_{cylinder} - \alpha)$$

Solving for C yields

$$C_T \leq \frac{t_{cylinder} - t_{ST}}{t_{cylinder} - \alpha}$$

By substituting in for $t_{cylinder}$ and t_{ST}, this reduces to

$$C_T \leq \frac{1}{1 + \frac{k}{\lambda}}$$

If the coherent fraction of all rays traced is greater than the maximum value of C_T, the new algorithm will outperform standard ray-tracing. To examine this further, we look again at the last equation. It is clear that the larger the ratio of k/λ, the lower the threshold value will be. We will discuss this ratio further in the next section.

Finally, in the worst case, the new algorithm will require more computation time than the standard algorithm. Consider a scene in which rays are *never* coherent, for example. In such a case, partitions are required for every ray, as in the standard algorithm but, in addition, work must be done to construct cylinders and check for piercing. Zero coherence is clearly the limit case as the number of objects in the scene increases. This underscores the point that coherent ray-tracing can only be considered for low- or moderate-density scenes.

4. IMPLEMENTATION RESULTS

We have implemented the new algorithm in Pascal under Berkeley Unix 4.2 BSD. The computers used were Digital Equipment Corporation's VAX-11/750 and VAX-11/780.

We rendered a group of scenes using two versions of the new algorithm. The first version was the new algorithm as presented above. The second version was a modification of the new algorithm to simulate standard ray-tracing. The modification was accomplished by commenting out all code dealing with coherency; the N set was not retained or processed and the intersection tree for a given image point was discarded after the overall colour computation for that point.

Both versions incorporate the same recursion-halting criteria. This includes the standard criteria such as "nothing intersected" or "intersection with an opaque, non-transparent object", as well as the "dynamic recursion termination" condition mentioned in Section 2.2.[8,11]

The programs were tested on four scenes containing an increasing number of randomly-positioned spheres. A typical example is shown in Figure 6. The test results are tabulated below. It can be seen that the coherent technique is no better than the standard algorithm for scenes containing on the order of 8 or 9 spheres.

Perhaps the most important result in this paper is contained in the last row of Table 1. It shows that *despite the fact that nearly two-thirds of the rays behaved coherently, the new algorithm produced no savings over standard ray-tracing*. How can this be the case? There are two likely answers.

First, pierce-checking even as simple a shape as a cylinder is not cheap; the cost is about as much as two ray-sphere intersection tests. Thus, even in the absence of other negative factors, there would have to be a certain number of objects in a scene before a savings over standard ray-tracing could be realized.

\multicolumn{5}{c}{Results}				
Number of spheres	CPU time, std. alg (hrs)	CPU time, coher. alg (hrs)	Percent rays coherent	Ratio, coherent / std.
1	0.283	0.232	76.0	.80
2	0.552	0.48	74.7	.86
4	1.351	1.208	78.0	.875
8	3.396	3.539	66.2	1.02

Table 1.

However, as the number of objects in a scene increases, the average cylinder radius and length *decreases*; more and more time is spent constructing and checking cylinders that will only be pierced. This means that ultimately, for some "crossover" number of objects, coherent ray-tracing will inevitably cost more than the standard method. The only question is whether that crossover value is large enough that the technique is of practical value. Table 1 shows that this is not the case.

Combining the last line of Table 1 with the final equation of Section 3 shows that the ratio k/λ is approximately 0.5. Recall that k is the proportionality constant for a scene partition while λ is a similar constant for cylinder construction. Notice that if λ could be reduced relative to k, C_T could also be reduced; this in turn implies that coherent ray-tracing could be applied to scenes with less coherence than the amount in the 8-sphere scene. However, since cylinder construction is already done by simple comparisons, it is difficult to see how the speed of this operation could be significantly increased.

5. CONCLUSIONS

An algorithm for coherent ray-tracing has been presented. The algorithm uses coherence to reduce the average amount of computation required to construct the intersection tree needed for colour computation. An analysis and empirical study of the algorithm was performed. The results show that the algorithm fails to out-perform standard ray-tracing on scenes of practical size. This indicates that other algorithmic techniques must be considered in order to reduce the large computational cost of ray-tracing.

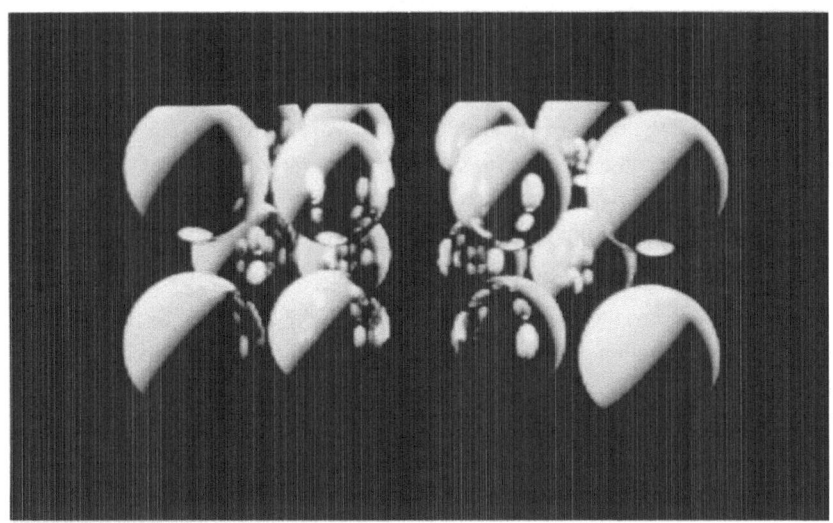

Figure 6 - A Typical Test Figure Used to Generate Table 1 Data

Figure 7 - Another Image Made Using the Technique

References

1. Arthur Appel, "Some Techniques for Shading Machine Renderings of Solids," pp. 37-45 in *Proceedings of the Spring Joint Computer Conference, Vol. 32*, AFIPS, Thompson Books,Washington, D.C.(1968).
2. Peter R. Atherton, "A Scanline Hidden-Surface Removal Procedure for Constructive Solid Geometry," pp. 73-82 in *SIGGRAPH '83 Conference Proceedings*, ACM,(July, 1983).
3. Chris Brown, "Special Purpose Computer Hardware for Mechanical Design Systems," pp. 403-414 in *Proceedings of the 1981 National Computer Graphics Association Conference*, National Computer Graphics Association, Inc.,Washington, DC.
4. Arthur G. Chang, *Parallel Architectural Support for Raytracing Graphics Techniques*, Master's Thesis, Computer Science Division, EECS Department, University of California, Berkeley, Berkeley, California.
5. John G. Cleary, Brian Wyvill, Graham M. Birtwistle, and Reddy Vatti, *Multiprocessor Ray Tracing*, Technical Report No. 83/128/17, Department of Computer Science, The University of Calgary (October, 1983).
6. Hiroshi Deguchi, Hitoshi Nishimura, Hiroshi Yoshimura, Toru Kawata, Isao Shirakawa, and Koichi Omura, "A Parallel Processing Scheme for Three-Dimensional Image Creation," pp. 1285-1288 in *Proceedings of the International Symposium on Circuits and Systems*, IEEE,Montreal(1984).
7. Mark E. Dippé and John A. Swensen, "An Adaptive Subdivision Algorithm and Parallel Architecture for Realistic Image Synthesis," pp. 149-158 in *SIGGRAPH '84 Conference Proceedings*, ACM,Minneapolis(July 23-27, 1984).
8. Patrick A. Fitzhorn, *Realistic Image Synthesis: A Time Complexity Analysis of Ray Tracing*, Master's Thesis, Colorado State University, Fort Collins, Colorado (Spring, 1982).
9. Andrew S. Glassner, "Space Subdivision for Fast Ray Tracing," *IEEE Computer Graphics and Applications*, Vol. 4, No. 10, October, 1984, pp. 15-22.
10. Robert Goldstein and Roger Nagel, "3-D Visual Simulation," *Simulation*, Vol. 16, No. 1, 1971, pp. 25-31.
11. Roy A. Hall and Donald P. Greenberg, "A Testbed for Realistic Image Synthesis," *IEEE Computer Graphics and Applications*, Vol. 3, No. 8, November, 1983, pp. 10-19.
12. Patrick M. Hanrahan, "Raytracing Algebraic Surfaces," pp. 83-90 in *SIGGRAPH '83 Conference Proceedings*, (July, 1983).
13. Paul Heckbert and Pat Hanrahan, "Beam Tracing Polygonal Objects," pp. 119-129 in *SIGGRAPH '84 Conference Proceedings*, ACM,(July, 1984).
14. James T. Kajiya, "New Techniques for Raytracing Procedurally Defined Objects," *ACM Transactions on Graphics*, Vol. 2, No. 3, July, 1983, pp. 161-181.
15. James T. Kajiya, "Ray Tracing Parametric Patches," pp. 245-254 in *SIGGRAPH '82 Conference Proceedings*, (July, 1982).

16. Douglas S. Kay, *Transparency, Refraction, and Ray Tracing for Computer Synthesized Images*, Master's Thesis, Cornell University, Ithaca, N.Y. (January, 1979).

17. Yong Tsui Lee and Aristides A. G. Requicha, "Algorithms for Computing the Volume and Other Integral Properties of Solid Objects, I : Known Methods and Open Issues, and II: A Family of Algorithms Based on Representation Conversion and Cellular Approximation," *Communications of the ACM*, Vol. 25, No. 9, September, 1982, pp. 635-650.

18. Nelson L. Max, "Vectorized Procedural Models for Natural Terrain: Waves and Islands in the Sunset," pp. 317-324 in *SIGGRAPH '81 Conference Proceedings*, (August, 1981).

19. Scott D. Roth, "Ray Casting as a Method for Solid Modelling," *Computer Vision, Graphics and Image Processing*, Vol. 18, No. 2, February, 1982, pp. 109-144.

20. Steven M. Rubin and J. Turner Whitted, "A 3-Dimensional Representation for Fast Rendering of Complex Scenes," pp. 110-116 in *SIGGRAPH '80 Conference Proceedings*, ACM,(July, 1980).

21. Kim L. Shelley and Donald P. Greenberg, "Path Specification and Path Coherence," pp. 157-166 in *SIGGRAPH '82 Conference Proceedings*, (July, 1982).

22. Ivan E. Sutherland, Robert F. Sproull, and Robert A. Schumacker, "A Characterization of Ten Hidden Surface Algorithms," *ACM Computing Surveys*, Vol. 6, No. 1, March, 1974, pp. 1-55.

23. Michael Ullner, *Parallel Machines for Computer Graphics*, Ph.D. Thesis, California Institute of Technology, Pasadena, California (1983).

24. J. Turner Whitted, "Processing Requirements for Hidden Surface Elimination and Realistic Shading," pp. 245-250 in *IEEE Compcon Digest of Papers*, (Spring, 1982).

25. J. Turner Whitted, "An Improved Illumination Model for Shaded Display," *Communications of the ACM*, Vol. 23, No. 6, June, 1980, pp. 343-349.

High Level Descriptions for 3D Stochastic Models

Brian Wyvill, Craig McPheeters and Milan Novacek

Department of Computer Science, University of Calgary, 2500 University Drive N.W., Calgary, Alberta, T2N 1N4, Canada

ABSTRACT

Many graphics systems allow a user to describe three dimensional objects with polygon meshes or surface patches. However to achieve realistic scenes for making animated film some objects are better described with stochastic techniques. Some examples would be clouds, fire and mountains. We describe here a hierarchical graphics system consisting of objects which contain geometrical transformations of other objects or primitives. Each object is treated in a consistent fashion whatever the types of primitives that are ultimately called, for example an object may consist of polygon mesh sub-objects and stochastic objects. The system has been designed so that it may easily be extended to include new primitive types, so far a sub-system for generating particles (fire, volcanos etc.) and a sub-system for generating fractal polygons have been implemented. Examples are given of the results obtained with this technique.

KEYWORDS: Hierarchy, Fractals, Recursion

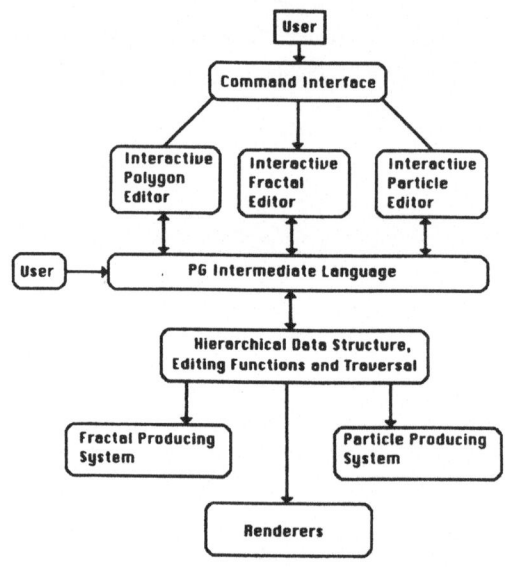

Figure 1 Graphicsland Overview

OVERVIEW

In designing a 3D graphics system one of the problems is to decide what classes of primitives will be used for constructing the objects. The end user may wish to define solid objects of a deterministic nature such as a building and also define a cloud which is perhaps best defined in terms of some stochastic function. Graphicsland is a system which has been designed to include different types of primitives and offers a consistent way of handling them. The system stores 3D objects as a hierarchy of geometric transformations, each object may refer to a number of other objects which in turn refer to objects and so on. At the leaves of this tree hierarchy are the primitives which may be geometrical primitives such as polygons or procedures for generating fractal surfaces or particle systems. We have designed the system in an extensible way so that other primitives such as beta-spline surfaces may be easily added later. Figure 1 shows a diagram of the system. It is layered with the data-structure and associated editing and traversal routines as the central core. A user interacts via a control interface and invokes one of a series of specialised user interface modules.

Each of the user interface modules produces an intermediate command language, called PG, which is interpreted by the system controlling the object hierarchies. Various graphical editors are being designed; so far only the polygon editor has been implemented with a graphical interface. Currently fractal and particle descriptions can be made via the intermediate command language. The design of this language is such that Graphicsland can be extended by writing special purpose interfaces which will interact with the language layer of the system. For example an interactive fractal mountain package is being written which uses contours drawn by the user. Currently landforms such as mountains may be defined in the intermediate language, by entering specifications for a number of parameters such as height of snow line, density of snow, angle of slope to which the snow will stick, and so on.

This approach also has the advantage that new ideas may be tried out very quickly by implementing commands in the intermediate language. Thus Graphicsland is a research oriented system which provides a test bed for new techniques.

It is useful to compare our approach to other methods. Porter & Duff [Porter 84] describe an image compositor which allows pictures to be composed from a series of images. These images are calculated for a particular viewpoint and can be combined as parts of different pictures reducing the overhead of having to render common parts between like frames. Once the view point is moved the component images would have to be re-rendered. We are providing a facility for composing pictures in object space which has the advantage that a view point can be moved and the correct view rendered. Thus image compositing will have an advantage when there are few camera moves. Object composing has the advantage of working in true 3D as compared to a 2½ D approach.

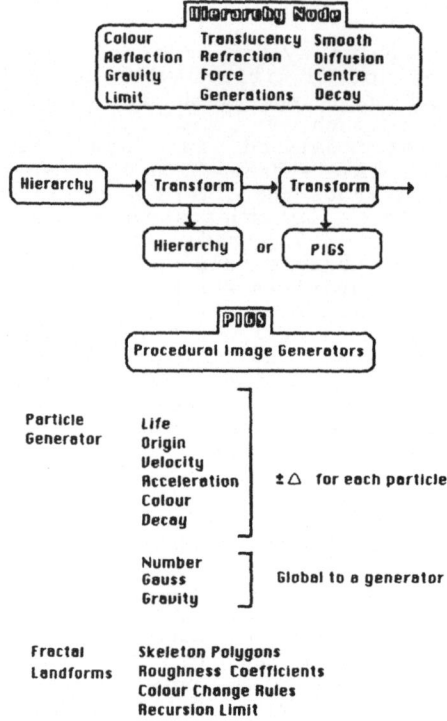

Figure 2 Hierarchical Data Structure

THE HIERARCHICAL DATA STRUCTURE

Figure 2 shows how the object hierarchy is stored as a series of geometric transformations. Each node contains a transformation matrix and a reference to the hierarchy to be transformed. To show a view of the object the structure is traversed as described in [Wyvill 84] in which each new node transforms the current set of coordinates until a primitive is encountered. In the current work the scheme has been generalised in that the polygon primitive has been substituted for a Procedural Image Generator (PIG in the diagram). So far three PIGs have been implemented to generate polygons, particles and fractals. We are currently working on this approach to extend the system to beta-spline surfaces.

THE COMMAND LANGUAGE - PG

The PG (Polygon Groper) command language is fully described in [Wyvill 85], the language provides a simple textual interface between the user and the modelling system. Each object in the system has a unique name and may refer to any other object or primitive. Self referencing objects have been found to be extremely useful and the method used to terminate recursion is to impose a numeric limit stored with each hierarchy node. A simple example is a row of squares. We define the row called <u>row</u> to consist of a square (presumed to be defined previously as a primitive polygon) and a reference to <u>row</u>. A limit of ten has been put on <u>row</u>. This means that when an instance of <u>row</u> is required the data structure is traversed sending ten instances of the primitive square to the renderer. Any combination of the geometrical transformations: translation (origin command) rotation and scaling can be applied. In the following example each instance of row has its origin moved 2 units in the x direction. In PG the definition appears thus:

```
open row
  add square
  add row origin 2 0 0
  limit 10
close
```

One way that randomness has been introduced into the system is to allow the user to specify that a picture instance may be chosen randomly within a certain range. For example the row of squares in Figure 3 has been produced from the following definition:

```
open row1
  add square
  add row1   origin 2[1] 0 0
  limit 10
close
plot row1   #See Figure 3
```

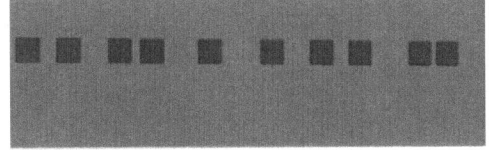

Figure 3 Row

The xorigin specification: 2[1] indicates that the translation in the x direction will be chosen in the range: 2 plus or minus 1. When the data structure is traversed, a matrix representing the translation is evaluated each time round the recursive loop representing the row. This means that the origin of each primitive square will be placed, normally distributed, in the defined range. Figure 4 shows a second example in which squares have been arranged in a random circular pattern. The PG definition is as follows:

```
open circle
   add square origin 5[5] rotate 0[360]
   add circle
   limit 50
close

open pik
   add circle colour red
   add circle colour green
   add circle colour blue
close

plot pik #Figure 4
```

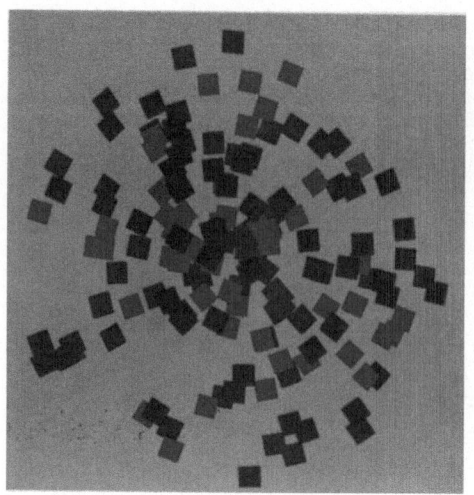 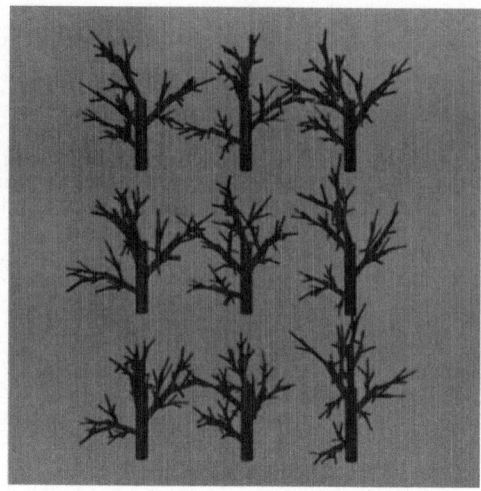

Figure 4 Circle   Figure 5 Trees

Multiply recursive objects, objects that refer to themselves more than once are also useful. Figure 5 shows nine trees. The trees are simply collections of cylinders; the cylinders themselves collections of rectangles. Each tree contains four branches, each branch is a recursive reference to tree. The four branches are scaled, rotated around two axes and translated to different distances along the mother branch. Since each transformation can be specified with a random variation, the nine trees of Figure 5 are all different but produced from the same simple definition.

THE PARTICLE SUB-SYSTEM

A particle system based on the work of Reeves described in [Reeves 83] has been implemented with some extensions. For example, Gauss filtering of particles has been included, this has the effect of defocusing the particles which reduces the number required to represent certain special effects. The user has the option of having particles rendered as simple points, or as fuzzy balls. The former case allows very fast rendering on raster devices. Particles are assumed to be pixel sized, and the colour of the affected pixel is simply increased by the particles' own colour intensity. In the latter case a Gauss function is applied as discussed under rendering.

Figure 2 shows the information stored in the object hierarchy node and the PIG node for a particle generator. These specifications differ from Reeves' in that two parameters which control Gauss filtering are associated with each particle generator along with a third parameter which controls the probability that a given particle will become a generator. It has been found that Gauss filtering particles produces some realistic effects with considerably fewer particles than previously used, this is discussed in the section on rendering.

THE FRACTAL SUB-SYSTEM

The method for generating fractals in the fractal mountain package is largely based on the work of Mandelbrot [Mandelbrot 83] and Fournier et al [Fournier 82]. A recursive algorithm is employed to subdivide a set of intermediate polygons. After each subdivision the coordinates of the vertices are modified by a random value constrained by a roughness factor. The intermediate polygons determine the gross overall shape of the mountain. They may have been generated by hand or by any other suitable method, for example by a preprocessing program that accepts a set of contour polygons and converts these to a set of tiles covering the requisite surface.

Such a scheme need not be excessively restrictive nor need it require a detailed contour specification in order to yield a pleasing result. The mountains in our examples have each been generated from a single input polygon. A mountain range is simply a number of instances of the one mountain with different geometric transformations applied.

The controlling parameters are summarised in Figure 2. Output from this package is a polygon list in the intermediate command language.

RENDERING

The rendering of polygons is well understood, but special attention should be paid to particles. Unlike Reeves system we assume that particles do interact with other surface-based modeling primitives. We have implemented two methods of rendering, z-buffer and Ray Tracing. In both cases the particles are fully integrated into the algorithm as a primitive.

Several options are available for the interaction of particles with other primitives, for example particles may act as luminous entities and be added into the image (as in Reeves' system). A weighted replacement option is also available. Note that particles are not proper light sources in that they do not illuminate other objects.

Particles may also be single points or fuzzy balls, as noted in the particle subsystem description. In the latter case, fuzzy balls are particles with a radius of influence (r) assigned by the user at the definition stage. At the rendering stage a particle is treated as a sphere of radius r, with varying translucency. The edge of the sphere is nearly perfectly translucent, contributing almost nothing to the image, while at the centre the full colour intensity of the particle is added to the pixel value. A negative exponential function is used to provide a smooth transition between the two extremes:

$$f = e^{\frac{d^2}{\sigma^2}}$$

This gives the fraction of the intensity to add to the image at a distance d from the centre of the particle. σ^2 is proportional to the radius of influence, r.

In the z-buffer algorithm we first render all polygons, and then do the particles. Particle intensities are added into the frame buffer according to f. In the case of non-transparent particles a weighted partial replacement is done, with the replacement weight again given by f.

Work on raytracing is still in the experimental stage, but in general particles are treated in a similar manner, as spheres, and the simple point-particles discussed above are simply assigned a small radius.

EXAMPLES

A few examples are shown of combined fractal, particle and polygonal figures. Figures 6 and 7 show some objects built from polygons combined with particle systems. Figure 8 shows some high quality fractal mountains consisting of 128k polygons for each of six mountains. The road and fields are defined by plain polygons. Figure 9 shows two types of particle rendering. The Gauss filter has been used for the super nova and point rendering for the rings of Saturn. The planet is built from polygons. The first two slides represent frames from a short film sequence currently under production to show the application of these techniques to animation.

CONCLUSION

We have presented a way of combining some different primitives in a 3D animation system. These include particles, fractals and polygons. Randomness has been built into the system in a simple and consistent fashion. We are planning to expand the available set of primitives and to implement new user interfaces to allow animators easy access to these facilities.

ACKNOWLEDGEMENTS

The JADE project at the University of Calgary has been particularly supportive of our work in distributed graphics. This work and JADE is supported by the Natural Science and Engineering Research Council of Canada. Special mention is also given to Andrew Pearce, who not only built the castle, but also made it explode.

Figure 6 Martian

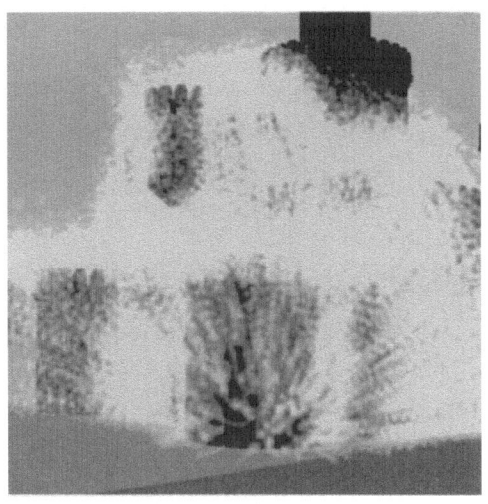

Figure 7 Castle Exploding

Figure 8 Road Fractal

Figure 9 Saturn

REFERENCES

Fournier, A, Fussel, D, and Carpenter, L (June 1982) "Computer Rendering of Stochastic Models" Commun. ACM, 25, 6, 371-384.

Mandelbrot, Benoit. (1983) "The fractal geometry of nature." W.H. Freeman and company.

Porter, T and Duff, T (July 1984) "Compositing Digital Images" Proc. ACM SIGGRAPH '84, 253-259.

Reeves, William. (Apr 1983) "Particle systems- A technique for modeling a class of fuzzy objects" ACM Transactions on Graphics, 2, 91-108.

Wyvill, B.L.M., Liblong, B., and Hutchinson, N. (June 1984) "Using Recursion to Describe Polygonal Surfaces." Proc. Graphics Interface 84, Ottawa.

Wyvill, B.L.M., Liblong, B., Hutchinson, N., and McPheeters, C. (July 1985) "The PG User Manual" Research Report No. 85/205/18 University of Calgary, Dept. of Computer Science..

Frame Buffer Algorithms for Stochastic Models

Alain Fournier and Tom Milligan

Computer Systems Research Institute, Department of Computer Science, University of Toronto, Toronto, Ontario, M5S 1A4, Canada

ABSTRACT

Stochastic modelling is a technique that allows shifting the complexity of the picture away from the modelling database while rendering a class of "natural" looking objects. When implementing this technique within traditional rendering systems, however, one has still to deal with a very large number of geometric and display primitives.

We present here a test system where most of the database expansion is done at the display level. A simple display processor, acting directly on the frame buffer, receives sparse 3-D geometric data, generates dense 2-D stochastic arrays, and determine their colour, shade and visibility to write the final image on the frame buffer.

The system allowed us to explore the issues of reentrant stochastic subdivision, priority and visibility determination, quick shading techniques and filtering at the frame buffer level with a bit-slice display processor. Examples of the images produced and performance statistics are given for the system.

KEYWORDS: stochastic modelling, terrain modelling, frame buffer algorithms, adaptive subdivision.

1. Motivations

The complexity of a picture can be measured by the number of basic elements (or *primitives*) necessary to display it. This complexity can be introduced at the modelling level or delayed until the display level. At the modelling level complexity may manifest itself as a large number of primitives or the use of higher degree surfaces, stochastic models [Four82], or particle systems [Reev83]. Since these are normally broken down into simpler geometric objects such as line segments or polygons, geometric and display operations still have to be performed on a large number of primitives. As an example, the landscape image in Figure 1 is composed of 16 bicubic patches subdivided into about 2000 triangles each. Roughly 30 minutes of a VAX 11/780 processor time were required to model and display the scene.

If we want to postpone the "data base amplification" step as long as possible, algorithms must be developed to perform operations as close to the frame buffer as possible. Processes like clipping, 3-D to 2-D mapping, filtering, visibility and shading computations should be performed with simple, fast, dedicated processors. An example of this strategy is the well known technique of *texture mapping* [Catm75, Blin78, Will83]. Instead of being described by dense data in 3-D, objects are described by sparse data in 3-D and dense data in 2-D in the form of 2-D texture arrays. Then a complex image is obtained from a sparse database, but even more importantly the geometric transformations have only been applied to sparse data. In the case of texture mapping, the 2-D mapping is facilitated by the fact that the position of the surface is not affected by the mapping, and therefore the shading (except in the case of *bump mapping* [Blin78, Haru84]) and visibility are not modified.

In [Four82] we developed the techniques for stochastic modelling as applied to computer graphics, and in particular the reentrant subdivision techniques that allowed to generate approximations to *fractional Brownian motion*. This process, introduced by Mandelbrot [Mand68, Mand82], permits realistic approximation of earth terrain. In [Pipe84] we described the *STINT*, a hardware board designed to generate a stochastic array of values using our subdivision algorithm. We demonstrated that the subdivision algorithm is simple enough to be implemented easily in hardware, and that such an implementation yields a two order of magnitude improvement in the speed of generation of stochastic data over a general purpose processor. The other important point is that the data is next to the display processor (*i. e.* in its address space) and the speed of the generation of the stochastic data has to be matched to the speed at which this processor can use the data.

This paper will describe a group of techniques to generate complex images in a display processor operating directly on the frame buffer. These techniques include the generation of the stochastic data defining implicitly the complex model, using either the STINT board or a firmware simulation, the mapping of that data to create the screen projection of a stochastic surface, the shading computations, the visible surface determination and possible filtering techniques.

This represents a heavy burden for a processor normally dedicated to more mundane tasks, such as line drawing or area filling. This is further complicated by two types of constraints. In most cases in a graphics system, simple primitives are used to describe the objects and must obey constraints at their boundaries. Then the geometric transformations and the rest of the rendering process operate piecewise on these primitives (such as polygons or parametric patches). Clearly then, the dense data generation and display algorithms which operate "close to the frame buffer" must be prepared to deal with and respect the constraints imposed on them. These can be called the *external coherence* constraints. Since most of the data is generated at the frame buffer level, and only as needed, as the objects appear and disappear, move farther and closer, more or less data is actually generated. We have to make sure that in every circumstance the picture appears to be a correct reconstruction of a virtual object. In a traditional system, the details are permanently stored in the data base, and the problem is only of correctly sampling and filtering it. In our system, we have to be careful to respect these *internal coherence* constraints as we generate the dense data "on the fly".

An intelligent division of labour between a general purpose host processor and one or more special purpose display processors greatly improves the speed of the display process. The host processor does the work which requires complex operations such as 3-D floating point calculations. Special purpose processor(s) perform the simple repetitive tasks typical of display processing based on dense 2-D data. The processors are inexpensive and very fast in their limited repertoire. Such a trend is now fairly obvious, and merely one more turn of the *wheel of reincarnation* [Myer68]. It is interesting in this respect to point out that we have seen in the past processors dedicated to raster operation and display tasks (more recently [Levi84]), geometric tasks [Clar82] and modelling tasks [Pipe84]. We are in this paper exploring the issues dealing with the design of a display processor to which some of the modelling and geometric tasks have been transferred.

2. The Experimental System

We have developed an experimental display system which generates terrain scenes from a very sparse 3-D database consisting of a network of square patches. Each patch is "painted" with a terrain texture generated from an array of stochastic data. The software runs on a VAX 11/780 host processor with an Adage 3000 graphics system. Resident on the Adage are two special purpose processors. One (the STINT) is custom built to generate the stochastic data [Pipe84]. The second is a commercial bit-slice processor which is part of the raster system. For added flexibility, we have also implemented a STINT simulation in microcode, which allows quick exploration of alternatives for the algorithms or the architecture of the STINT. All the microcode has been written using a high level compiler, and we have incorporated macros that allow compilation of the same code into C, to be run on the host processor if necessary.

The terrain scene is initially modelled as a single square patch. This patch is recursively subdivided into smaller squares which are of a suitable size for painting. At the same time the totally invisible subpatches are eliminated, using a *extent* based on an estimate of the final height of the fully formed surface. The painter module asks for a dense data array using the stochastic interpolation algorithm and then maps it to the screen space definition of the patch. Colour, height and lighting information are added to the image during the process and clipping and visible surface determination are performed. The entire system runs on the special processors with the exception of the geometric subdivision itself.

3. The Subdivision

The display system passes the single square "world" patch through a perspective projection and determines its size and location in screen coordinates. If it is too large to be processed as an entity it is subdivided into four smaller patches and the process is repeated. The criterion for size is based on the maximum size of the stochastic arrays generated by the system. In the current implementation, it is 129x129. Therefore a patch is subdivided if any of its sides has a "Manhattan" length greater than 129 screen units (pixels). This continues until the subpatches are completely invisible or until they are the appropriate size for painting. Subdivision proceeds in an order which supports the visible surface determination algorithm used by the patch painter, that is the subpatches are generated in a front to back priority ordering, determined from the eye position.

A patch is considered visible if any part of it could appear on the display. This is not a clear cut operation since the planar patches represent only the base area over which the stochastic surface will be drawn (*cf* Figure 2). For this purpose patches are considered to be three dimensional blocks whose vertical dimension is the highest value expected on the stochastic surface. This is similar to the well known technique of "boxing" objects for quick intersection tests, and more specifically to the use of "cheesecake" extents [Kaji83] in ray tracing stochastic surfaces. The height of the extent box is a function of the scaling factor to be used to map the stochastic data, and is deterministically bounded by the size of the entry in the lookup table used for the Gaussian increments and the size of the elements in the STINT array [Pipe84]. Subpatches which are of the right size, but partially outside the window are clipped during the painting process. This means that only a small fraction of the total painting effort will be expended on invisible portions of the patches.

Subdivision performed in this manner guarantees that the work done in data generation and mapping will be closely matched to the size of the final image on the screen. Figure 3 illustrates the subdivision of a patch under a perspective view with a large, but not uncommon, foreshortening. The top of Figure 3 shows the patch boundaries resulting from the subdivision. At the bottom of the figure are the patch boundaries in screen space. Note that the bottom corners have been subdivided less than their neighbours because they have been clipped out.

The modelling and the geometric modules of the graphic system have then to deal only with subpatches. With the sizes used in our implementation (a 512x512 screen and 129x129 stochastic data arrays) this translates into about 20 to 200 geometric primitives (the subpatches) and 1 modelling primitive (the initial "world" patch) instead of about 50,000 geometric primitives (assuming polygons covering about 5 pixels each, which is conservative for an detailed image). As we will see later, the figures would be even larger if stochastic modelling were not used.

4. Dense Data Generation

The stochastic data is generated using the recursive interpolation algorithm described in [Four82], and whose hardware implementation is described in [Pipe84]. The algorithm generates approximations of fractional Brownian motion. It ensures external or boundary coherence by setting the initial seeds of the pseudo-random number generators and it ensures internal coherence by tying the subsequent seeds to the values of the points used in the computation of the new points. It should be noted that in a software implementation, it is better to tie the seeds to the indices of the point being computed. Then changing parameters, such as the dimension, which influence all the values, will not change totally the macroscopic features of the patch. This will make possible animations where only the dimension changes, for instance.

It must be stressed that purely recursive subdivision is not correct, since the process we want to approximate is not Markovian. This means that the knowledge of the boundary of a subpatch is not sufficient to compute its interior. Enough information has to be carried over from the neighbours to insure the required coherence between levels of interpolation. Figure 4 illustrates the reentrant process. Note that the boundary elements of the new array are not usable, since they cannot be computed from all their neighbours. The elements of the array that can safely be used are the ones at a distance from the boundaries equal to or greater than the distance between the points reentered.

This property will automatically limit the level of subdivision that can be safely used, if we insist on computing the subdivision in only one step from the "world" patch. In fact, since we use a 129x129 array, anything past the 12th or 13th level of subdivision (7 for the "world" patch and 5 or 6 for the subpatch) will introduce noticeable discontinuities between subpatches. There are two ways to overcome that limit: one is to use a bigger "world" patch. This means more memory, but is easily obtained. A 1M byte memory would easily accommodate a 513x513 array of 16 bit elements. This would allow about 16 levels, that is an amplification of 9 decimal orders of magnitude from the original square. The other way is to carry the subdivision in steps, carrying from step to step enough array elements to exactly compute the interpolation of the needed points. This is what the original software does. Here the limit (beside the additional time) is in the precision of the array elements. The values of the elements adjacent at some level will tend to be equal, and the standard deviation will eventually go to 0. So in both cases there is a practical limit to the "amplification" effect. But to keep the limit in perspective, in the present case it means that the fully evolved world has more than 100 million data points (13 levels, corresponding to a 2^{13} linear amplification, or 2^{26} data points).

5. The Display Operations

The challenge of implementing the rendering algorithms in a very simple processor can largely be overcome with a few clever programming techniques. A notable example is the calculation of complex arithmetic functions using inverted lookup into precomputed tables. It is even possible in some cases to avoid the search of the inverted index and move incrementally through it.

It is often expedient to resort to approximation. Careful choice of the approximation leads to results which are good in all but the most extreme cases. For example, the strips used to render the surface are actually not vertical in screen space, due to the perspective projection. Fortunately, the direction can be safely approximated as vertical with a large saving in computation. Otherwise the visibility algorithm would be more complex [Ande82].

The quadrilaterals passed to the painter are modelled as bilinear parametric patches. These patches represent the base area over which the surface will be drawn. Each data point is mapped first to a location in the patch and then to the surface by drawing a vertical strip originating from the patch (*cf* Figure 2). The length of the strip is determined from the value of the data point and scaled by a factor provided by the perspective system. Only the visible portion of the strip is drawn. It is clipped to fit the display window and then visible surface determination is performed.

Note that **all** data points are mapped to the base patch. In a conventional texture mapping the data array would be sampled to match the actual size of the patch. In this case that is incorrect; the size and shape of the base patch can be quite different from that of the surface which is constructed over it.

The bilinear mapping of the data array to the patch can be viewed as a linear interpolation of the two screen space coordinates of the patch over the data array. This is useful since there is another parameter which must be interpolated over the patch. The length of the vertical strips drawn to represent the surface must be scaled as in any perspective projection by the inverse of the distance from the eye.

To allow simple visible surface determination, the patch is always filled from front to back (*i.e.* from the bottom of the screen up) and the strips are constrained to fit into vertical columns on the screen. It is then sufficient to record the highest point reached thus far in each column. As the fill process proceeds up the screen, only the portions of strips above the highest already seen are visible. It is crucial that this process execute quickly, even though it places strict ordering requirements on the preceding steps. Both patches and fill line traces must be performed in the correct order. Whenever data is mapped to the screen (a patch or a data point) the lowest item must be done first.

The strips are coloured using a simple height to colour lookup table. The first colour mapping scheme we used was designed to match the traditional colours of a geography atlas. Since the pictures illustrating this paper are grey, there was no need to choose them otherwise. We have, however, experimented with more "realistic" colour schemes.

The shading model used is based on Lambert's law:

$$I = I_i \, k \, (\mathbf{L} . \mathbf{N})$$

The intensity of light (I) reflected from a surface is determined by the angle of incidence of the light rays and the surface normal. The calculation involves the normalized dot product of the incident light vector ($\mathbf{L}$) and the surface normal ($\mathbf{N}$). The surface normal is calculated as the cross product of two tangent vectors. These are approximated using the vertical displacement between adjacent data points and a scale factor related to the interpoint variance. This scaling compensates for the decrease in variance and corresponding lighter shading which accompany increasing depth in the stochastic interpolation.

6. Examples and Performance

The most exhaustive way to test a modelling and display system is to use it to create an animation. We produced a ninety second "flyby and look around" animation, where the "world" was expanded several million fold. The dimension (see [Mand82] for the definition of the dimension) was 2.1.

Figures 5 to 7 give an idea of the images produced. Figure 5 is an orthographic projection of the whole world. The original square (4 data points) now contains 512x512 points, that is to say 16 129x129 arrays. The time to compute it was 36 seconds. Figure 6 is a view of the world from the south. One can recognize the islands in the bay, and the point at the tip of the southern cape. The level of subdivision ranges from 9 to 11. The whole scene has 54 subpatches and took 61 seconds to compute. Figure 7 is a view in roughly the same direction but much closer to the cape. Compare the point now to its size in Figure 5. The time to compute that image was 160 seconds, and the level ranges from 9 to 13.

It should be noted that 30 to 40% of the bit-slice time in the figures given is spent simulating the STINT algorithm. For example, in the last picture, out of the 160 seconds, 60 seconds were spent simulating the STINT interpolation, 50 seconds were spent in the 3-D to 2-D mapping, and about 50 seconds in the display operations. The time spent in the host processor was about 2 seconds, totally overlapped with the bit-slice time.

7. Enhancements

There are of course many improvements that can be made to the display system. We already discussed how to expand further the levels of subdivision. Another straightforward improvement is to use a more sophisticated shading model. In order not to pay too high a price in performance, the best is to use the same lookup table techniques already used in other computations. The use of lookup tables for shading in the frame buffer has already been reported [Evan84] and our situation is similar, since we have a normal and we want to compute quickly the intensity. From the differences in elevation between points and from the precision needed, we can establish that 3 to 4 bits for each normal vector component is enough, giving a 512 to 4K entry lookup table for the intensity. Separate specular and diffuse reflection tables would be used. The same inverted lookup techniques already reported can be used to provide more precision.

Although the current system makes no attempt at anti-aliasing, *supersampling* can be used without too much additional effort. The display operations on the current system operate at pixel resolution. We can compute the location, width and length of the vertical strips used to represent the surface at subpixel resolution and make the columns used for visible surface determination of subpixel width. It is not necessary to generate more data than are already being used. The ratio of data points to patch pixels is currently between one and two. The subpixel strips corresponding to one data point will typically total between one half and one pixel across and may cover portions of more than one pixel both horizontally and vertically. The height of the strips is already computed to the necessary precision.

Figure 8 illustrates a portion of the frame buffer a few pixels across. The display process is using a 4 by 4 subpixel resolution. In this example data points are being mapped to three consecutive strips. The pixel contribution of the strips can be computed 'on the fly' using the information that is already being recorded for visible surface determination. The frame buffer itself can be used for pixel construction. The only additional storage required is that needed to extend visible surface determination to subpixel resolution. The result is equivalent to supersampling to 4x4 subpixels.

8. Conclusions

The system as it stands permits one more step towards the display of some visually complex objects in a reasonable time. It is also a case study of processor specialization within a display system. We have shown with it most of the advantages of the adaptive subdivision technique to generate surfaces, and some of its limitations for data amplification due to the limited sizes of the arrays and the limited precision of the numbers.

The gain in speed from a traditional modelling and rendering system is about two orders of magnitude, but we are still far from real time. The modelling operations and the geometric transformations represent only 20,000 operations (100 subpatches at 200 per subpatch), which can be easily executed in real time by a 1Mips processor. The display operations, on the other hand, represent up to 8×10^8 microinstructions in the bit-slice. Thus it would take the equivalent of about 500 pairs of 50ns processors to accomplish the same task in real time, if the work is fairly distributed among them.

Our experimental system can only model objects which are suited to a dense 2-D data representation. Traditional dense 3-D modelling is appropriate for a large class of (typically man-made) objects. Techniques must be developed to merge these two classes of objects in a single system. Fortunately this is often quite easy. In a flight simulator, for instance, the separation between terrain and cloud cover on one hand and airfields and buildings on the other is quite clear. Among the problems we will investigate next are the mapping of the stochastic data over surfaces more complex than bilinear patches, and the visibility problems introduced by merging them with polyhedral objects.

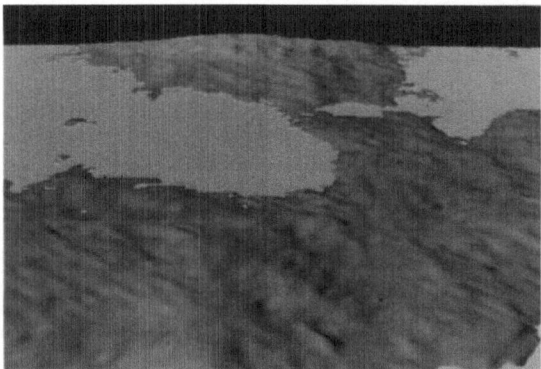

Figure 1. A terrain scene generated by a traditional modelling system. Comprises about 32,000 triangles.

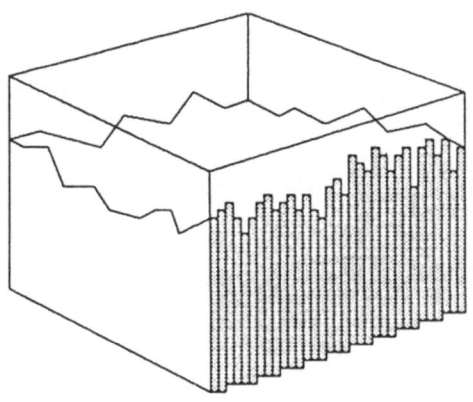

Figure 2. The stochastic surface is drawn over a planar base area using a series of vertical strips. The parallelepiped is the surface extent for the purpose of clipping.

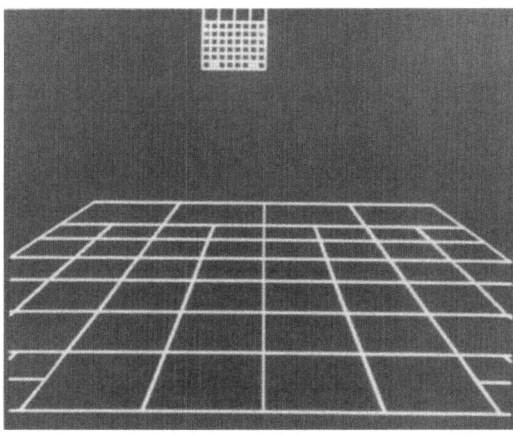

Figure 3. The subdivision step: the patch boundaries resulting from subdivision of the 'world' patch, and the boundaries in screen space.

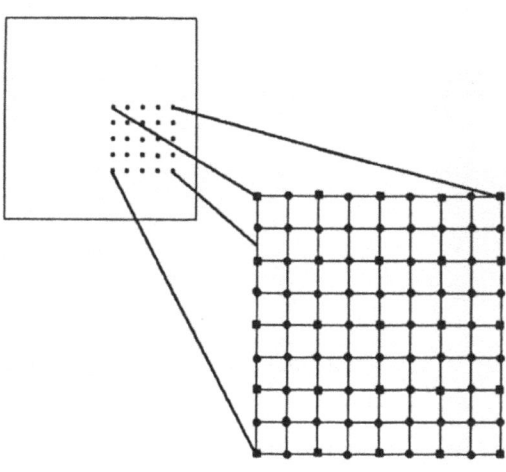

Figure 4. Stochastic interpolator re-entry. All data points available from the initial patch are included as precomputed levels in the new interpolation.

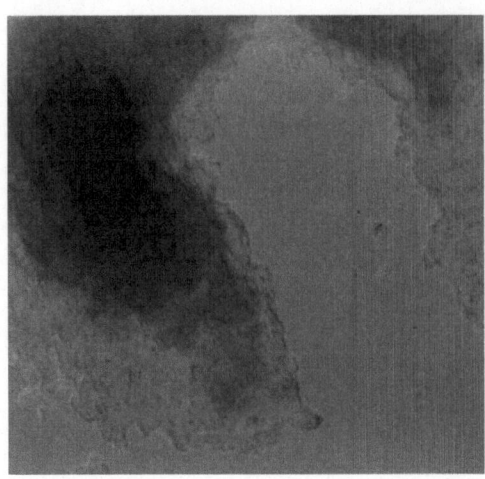

Figure 5. Orthographic projection of the "world" patch. Contains 16 subpatches.

Figure 6. A view from the south. Contains 54 subpatches, and levels from 9 to 11.

Figure 7. A closer view. Note the point in the center of the picture. Contains 120 subpatches, and levels from 9 to 13.

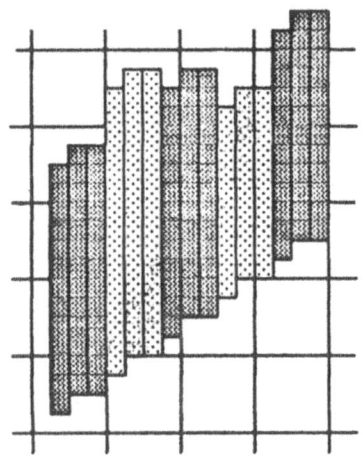

Figure 8. Supersampling: One row of data points mapped to the surface. Subpixel resolution is 4 by 4. Data points mapped to three consecutive strips.

Acknowledgements

We gratefully acknowledge the support of the Natural Sciences and Engineering Research Council of Canada and of the Communication Research Centre of the Department of Communications.

References

[Ande82] Anderson. D. P. "Hidden Line Elimination in Projected Grid Surfaces", ACM Transactions on Graphics, *1*, 4, (October 82), 274-288.

[Blin78] Blinn, J. F. "Simulation of Wrinkled Surfaces", in *Proceedings of SIGGRAPH '78*, also published as Comput. Graphics, *12*, 3, (Aug 1978), 286-292.

[Catm75] Catmull, E., "Computer display of curved surfaces", in *Proc. IEEE Conference on Computer Graphics, Pattern Recognition and Data Structure*. (May 1975).

[Clar82] Clark, J. H. "The Geometry Engine: A VLSI Geometry System for Graphics", in *Proceedings of SIGGRAPH 82*, also published as Comput. Graphics, *16*, 3, (Aug 82), 127-133.

[Evan84] Evans, K. B. "Realtime Lighting Manipulation in Color via Lookup Tables", *Proceedings of Graphics Interface '84*, (May 1984), 173-177.

[Four82] Fournier, A., Fussell, D. and Carpenter, L. "Computer Rendering of Stochastic Models", Communications of the ACM, *25*, 6, (June 1982), 371-384.

[Haru84] Haruyama, S. and Barsky, B. A. "Using Stochastic Modelling for Texture Generation", IEEE Computer Graphics and Applications, *4*, 3, 7-19.

[Kaji83] Kajiya, J. T., "Ray Tracing Procedurally Defined Objects", in *Proceedings of SIGGRAPH 83*, also published as Comput. Graphics, *17*, 3, (July 83), 91-102.

[Levi84] Levinthal A. and Porter, T., "Chap- A SIMD Graphics Processor", in *Proceedings of SIGGRAPH 84*, also published as Comput. Graphics, *18*, 3, 77-82.

[Mand68] Mandelbrot, B. B. and Van Ness, J. W. "Fractional Brownian motions, fractional noises and applications", SIAM Review, *10*, 4, (Oct 1968), 422-437.

[Mand82] Mandelbrot, B. B. *The Fractal Geometry of Nature*. Freeman, (1982).

[Myer68] Myer, T. H. and Sutherland, I. E., "On the Design of Display Processors", Communications of the ACM, *11*, 6, (June 68), 410-414.

[Pipe84] Piper, T. S. and Fournier, A. "A Hardware Stochastic Interpolator for Raster Displays", in *Proceedings of SIGGRAPH 84*, also published as Comput. Graphics, *18*, 3, (July 84), 83-91.

[Reev83] Reeves, W. T., "Particle Systems-A Technique for Modeling a Class of Fuzzy Objects", Transactions on Graphics, *2*, 2, (April 83), 91-108.

[Will83] Williams, L. "Pyramidal Parametrics", in *Proceedings of SIGGRAPH 83*, also published as Comput. Graphics, *17*, 3, (July 83), 1-11.

Animating Lights and Shadows

M. Fortin, N. Léonard, N. Magnenat-Thalmann and D. Thalmann
MIRA Lab., HEC/IRO, Université de Montréal, Montréal, H3C 3J7, Canada

ABSTRACT

The motion of lights and shadows in a computer-generated film gives spectacular effects. In our extensible director-oriented animation system MIRANIM, any motion may be applied to multiple virtual cameras and to various kinds of lights: directional lights, positional lights and spots. Light may be limited by conic and cylindric surfaces and fading lights may be controlled. Moreover objects may be non-convex, may have holes and may be translucent. Such possibilities mean that the restrictions imposed by a shadow algorithm must be avoided. The shadow algorithm, based on the Crow shadow volume algorithm, and its implementation in MIRANIM are described. Various problems and their solutions are discussed.

INTRODUCTION

For any realistic computer-generated film, light sources have to be considered as key elements in the scenes. However, unless the light source is unique and located at an eyepoint, or illumination is very diffuse, as with an overcast sky, images are not complete without shadows. As noted by Crow (1977), algorithms for shadows require considerable computation time and are rarely used in computer-generated films.

In fact, the main problem is that most algorithms are not able to produce shadows for any object, any virtual camera and any light condition, except ray tracing (Whitted, 1980; Kay and Greenberg, 1979; Kajiya, 1983), which is too expensive in terms of CPU time to be used for computer-generated films. In a computer animation scene, where the lights and/or the cameras are moving, an algorithm which gives perfect results for 100 frames, may give a bad result for the 101st, just because of a particular case.

In our extensible director-oriented animation system MIRANIM (Magnenat-Thalmann et al. 1985; Magnenat-Thalmann and Thalmann, 1985), any motion may be applied to multiple virtual cameras (Magnenat-Thalmann and Thalmann, 1985a) and to various kinds of lights: directional lights, positional lights and spots. Light effects may be limited by conic and cylindric surfaces and it is possible to control decrease in the light intensity with distance. Moreover, objects may be non-convex, may have holes in them and may be translucent. Such possibilities mean that restrictions in the production of shadows must be avoided.

This paper emphasizes the light possibilities of the MIRANIM system. It then describes how shadows have been implemented in the system using an extension of the Crow (1977) shadow volume algorithm. Different typical cases and their solutions are explained.

THE EXTENSIBLE DIRECTOR-ORIENTED SYSTEM MIRANIM

MIRANIM is mainly based on three components:
1) an object modelling and image synthesis system BODY-BUILDING
2) the director-oriented animation editor ANIMEDIT
3) the actor-based sublanguage CINEMIRA-2

ANIMEDIT is a scripted system; the director designs a scene with decors, actors, cameras and lights. Each of these entities is driven by animated variables, which are, in fact, state variables following evolution laws. There are 8 modes in ANIMEDIT: MAIN, VARIABLES, OBJECTS, DECOR, CAMERAS, LIGHTS, ACTORS and DIRECTOR. Only the LIGHTS mode and the VARIABLES mode are discussed in this paper. Details on other modes may be found in other publications (Magnenat-Thalmann et al. 1985; Magnenat-Thalmann and Thalmann, 1985).

CINEMIRA-2 (Magnenat-Thalmann, 1985b) allows the director to use programmers to extend the system. An entity programmed in CINEMIRA-2 is directly accessible in ANIMEDIT. This not only extends the system, but also enables specific environments to be created.

LIGHTS AND SPOTS

The LIGHT Mode in ANIMEDIT

Four kinds of lights may be defined in an ANIMEDIT script:
1) ambient light, defined by its intensity
2) directional sources light, defined by their intensity and direction
3) positional source light, defined by their intensity and location
4) spots similar to these introduced by Warn (1983), defined by their intensity, a location, a direction and a concentration factor. Spots are light sources with a direction which may be controlled independently of the source location. A factor may determine the spatial concentration of the directed light source, allowing spotlights and flood lights to be simulated.

Intensity, for each light is defined using the RGB color system.

In ANIMEDIT, each source light is defined in the LIGHT mode and has a name, except for ambient light. Typically the commands used are as follows:
AMBIENT <RGB intensity vector>
SOURCE <source identifier> <RGB intensity vector> D <direction vector>
SOURCE <source identifier> <RGB intensity vector> P <location vector>
SOURCE <source identifier> <RGB intensity vector> S <location vector>
                <direction vector> <concentration factor>

Parameters of each command are constants or variables defined in the VARIABLES mode of ANIMEDIT. When they are variables, any evolution law may be applied to these variables, including procedural laws (Magnenat-Thalmann and Thalmann,1985c).

For example, a positional light source LUX may be defined as
SOURCE LUX INTENSITY P LOCATION
Assume now that the lux intensity linearly varies from red to green and the location changes according to an oscillation movement. We define:
VEC INTENSITY A <1,0,0> <0,1,0>
LAW LINEAR LIN
EVOLUTION INTENSITY LINEAR 0 10
VEC LOCATION A <10,20,30>
LAW ALTERNATE OSCILLATION
EVOLUTION LOCATION ALTERNATE 0 10

Decreasing light intensity factor

A decreasing light intensity factor may be applied to any directional or positional light source. Intensity is calculated by the following formula:
$I = I_0 * e^{-FACT*DIST(P,S)}$

I_0 is the normal intensity without the decreasing factor; FACT is the decreasing factor; P is the lighted point location and S the light source location. DIST(P,S) is the distance between P and S.

Light cones and cylinders

Influence of light may be limited to a conic volume for a positional source light or a cylindric volume for a directional source light. Corresponding commands in MIRANIM are as follows:
LIGHTCONE <source identifier> <axis direction> <cone angle>
LIGHTCYLINDER <source identifier> <point on the axis> <cylinder radius>
Each parameter may be animated, which may have an important influence on shadows.

SHADOW ALGORITHMS

Apart from ray tracing, several shadow algorithms have been proposed in the past. Nishita and Kakamae (1974) have published a method for generating shadows based on a convex polyhedron-clipping algorithm. In 1977, a shadow volume approach was proposed by Crow (1977). Atherton et al. (1978) have introduced a polygon shadow generation algorithm based on an object space polygon-clipping algorithm (Weiler and Atherton, 1977). With depth-buffers, methods have been proposed by Williams (1978) and more recently by Brotman and Badler(1984).

As the rendering algorithm in MIRANIM is a scan-line z-buffer algorithm, we have choosen an algorithm based on the Crow shadow volume technique. The shadow volume is the space region within which an object "intercepts" the light. This volume is theoretically unlimited, however, it is normally restricted to the view volume. Polygons which bounds the shadow volume are added to the list of polygons for display processing, just like the polygons of objects. During display processing, shadow polygons are considered as

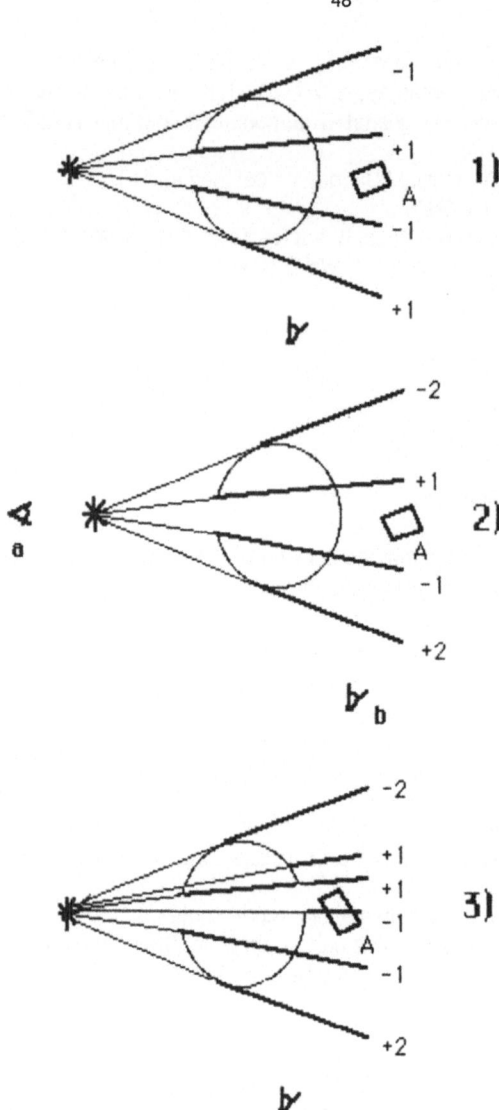

Fig.1 1) For the observer, the object A is lighted
2) For the observer in a, the object is
in shadow;for the observer in b,
if A is transparent, A is lighted
3) is same as 2)

invisible and when they are crossed over, this produces a transition inside or outside the object shadow. Two kinds of shadow polygons have to be considered: frontfacing polygons and backfacing polygons. Any point in front of a backfacing polygon and behind a frontfacing polygon is in the shadow. Consider now a line from the camera eye to a polygon, this polygon is frontfacing if we go into the shadow volume, but backfacing if we go out. A number +1 is associated with frontfacing polygons and a number -1 to the backfacing polygons. The general idea of the algorithm is to consider a line from the eye to the graphical object and to examine the shadow polygons that are crossed by the line. If the sum of their associated numbers is greater than zero, the pixel is in shadow, because we have entered more frontfacing polygons than backfacing polygons.

One way of accelerating the algorithm is to consider the silhouette of the object as viewed from the light source. This silhouette is obtained by considering the edges of the object. There are two kinds of edges:
1) edges in the boundary of the object (category 1)
2) edges shared by two polygons with only one lighted (category 2)

Problems may be found, as shown in Fig.1, where there are edges of both categories in the same object. One way of solving this problem (Bergeron, 1985) is to associate a value of 1 to category 1 edges and a value of 2 to category 2 edges. The method is satisfactory except with translucent objects.

Another problem in animation with shadows occurs when the camera eye comes into shadow; in this case, the count of edges is 0 or -1 which means that there is no region of the view volume in shadow. This is due to the fact that the shadow volume is not closed. One way of solving the problem is to calculate the projection of each polygon on the front plane. After a clipping, a shadow polygon is obtained that closes the shadow volume. In these calculations, other special cases may cause difficulties:

1. The light source is between the extremities of the polygon in the direction z (depth) (Fig.2a)
2. The object overlaps the front plane (Fig.2b)

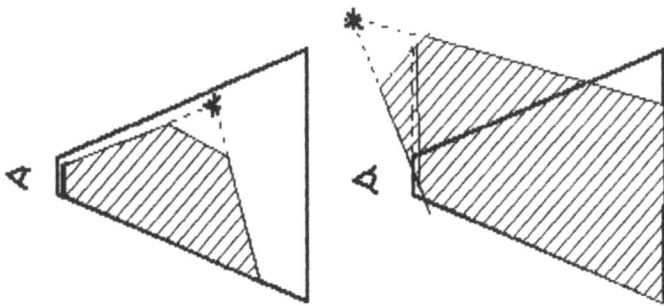

Fig.2 Two special cases

THE MIRANIM IMPLEMENTATION OF SHADOWS

This extended shadow volume algorithm has been incorporated into the MIRA-SHADING language (Magnenat-Thalmann et al., 1985b) which is the implementation language of MIRANIM. To accelerate the calculations of the silhouette, neighbors of the edges of objects are computed. In fact this calculation has already been performed for each standard object in MIRA-SHADING. Moreover, once this calculation of neighbors is performed for an object, it is still valid even if the object, the camera or the light changes.

The data structure for an edge is defined in PASCAL as:

type EDGETYPE =
   record
      NOVERT: 1..NBMAXVERT; (*vertex number in the object*)
      NOEDGE: 0..NBMAXEDGES; (*edge number in the face*)
      NONEIGHB: 0..NBMAXPOLY (*number of neghbor polygon*)
   end;

The silhouette is obtained by inspecting the object polygon by polygon, edge by edge. An edge of a polygon Pi is part of the silhouette if the following condition is true:
    (NONEIGHB=0) **or** ((Pi is lighted) **and** (PNONEIGHB is not lighted))

During the building of a shadow polygon, the value of the increment is negative for a backfacing polygon and positive for a frontfacing polygon. The absolute value of the increment is 1 for an edge of category 1 and 2 for an edge of category 2.

The display algorithm is a scan-line z-buffer algorithm. Fig.3 shows the data structure used in this algorithm. For each pixel, we store the depth, the normal to the corresponding point and the position of this point. Two pointers are also stored for each pixel, POLYPTR and SHADOWPTR. POLYPTR is a pointer to the description of the polygon which gives access to the polygon attributes (shading type, color, transparency, reflectance,...). The SHADOWPTR is a pointer to a list of blocks, each one describing the active light source and a counter.

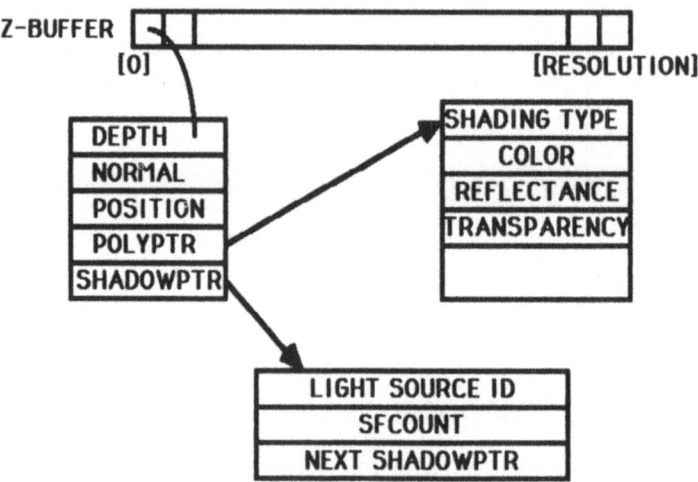

Fig.3 Data structure for the scan-line z-buffer with shadows

The algorithm has 3 steps:

1. All active polygons of an object are scan-converted in the scan-line buffer; information for calculating illumination is stored.
2. All active shadow polygons are also scan-converted; for each shadow polygon in front of a visible point, its increment is added to the counter.
3. The final intensity of each pixel in the scan-line buffer is computed using the counters $SFCOUNT_i$ in the list accessed via the SHADOWPTR pointer. We have:

   if $SFCOUNT_i <= 0$ **then** $I_{total} := I_{total} + I_i$

The ambient light term is then added to I_{total}.

Non-convex objects and holes

This algorithm can process shadows for non-convex objects such as letters in Fig.4. Shadows for objects with holes are also correctly produced as shown in Fig.5

Transparency

This algorithm does not always give good results for transparent objects. In fact, the case of an opaque object with a shadow on a transparent object is well processed as shown in Fig.6. However, the shadow produced by a transparent object is incorrect. Only a ray tracing algorithm would be convenient for this.

Stereoscopic cameras

The camera mode in MIRANIM allows the user to define stereoscopic cameras. In this case, two images are computed, one viewed from the right eye and one viewed from the left eye. Both images are mixed in a unique image during the scan-line processing using complementary color separation. Shadows may also be produced stereoscopically, as shown in Fig. 7.

Texture

Three kinds of textures are possible in MIRANIM: image mapping, three-dimensional bump mapping and fractals. Fig. 8 shows an example of shadows produced in the case of image mapping.

CONCLUSION

This paper illustrates various problems in animating lights; the most important is the impact on shadow animation. Because of changing light and camera conditions, it is essential that shadow calculations be processed quickly but with an algorithm without too many restrictions. Except for shadows of translucent objects, our implementation of the MIRANIM system has no major restrictions. However, we plan in the near future to integrate shadows with particle systems (Reeves, 1983, 1985) which are also available in MIRANIM (Magnenat-Thalmann and Thalmann, 1985c).

Fig.4 Shadows for non-convex objects

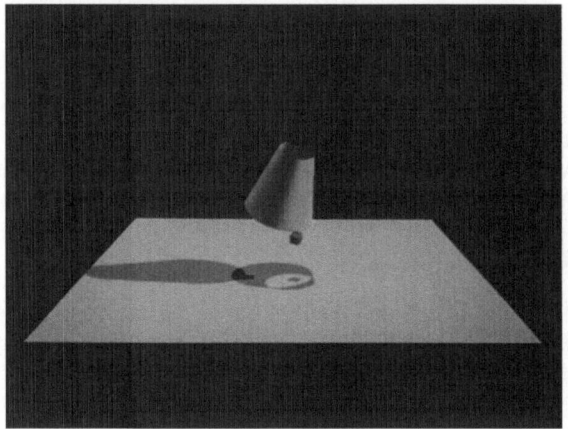

Fig.5 Shadows for objects with holes

Fig.6 Shadows and transparency

Fig.7 Shadows produced stereocopically

Fig.8 Image mapping, spotlight and shadows (antialiased)
designer: Denis Rambaud

ACKNOWLEDGEMENTS

The authors are grateful to Ann Laporte who revised the English text. The research was supported by the Natural Sciences and Engineering Council of Canada and the Government of Quebec. Spots were implemented by D.Rambaud, research assistant at Hautes Etudes Commerciales, Université de Montréal. The idea of introducing two kinds of increments into the Crow algorithm comes from P.Bergeron, graduate student at the Department of Computer Science (IRO), University of Montreal. Stereoscopic cameras were implemented by M.Choquette, also student at the Department of Computer Science.

REFERENCES

Atherton, P.; Weiler, K. and Greenberg, D. (1978) **Polygon Shadow Generation**, Proc. SIGGRAPH '78, pp. 275-281

Bergeron, P. (1985) **Shadow Volumes for Non-planar Polygons**, Proc. Graphics Interface '85, pp.417-418 (abstract only)

Brotman, L. and Badler, N.I. (1984) **Generating Soft Shadows with a Depth Buffer Algorithm**, IEEE Computer Graphics and Applications, Vol. 4, No10 ,pp.5-12.

Crow, F. (1977) **Shadow algorithms for Computer Graphics**, Proc. SIGGRAPH '77, Vol.11, No2, pp. 242-248.

Kajiya J.T. (1983) **New Techniques for Ray-tracing Procedurally Defined Object.**, Proc. SIGGRAPH '83, pp.91-99.

Kay, D.S. and Greenberg, D. (1979), **Transparency for Computer Synthesized Images**, Proc. SIGGRAPH '79, pp.pp.158-164.

Magnenat-Thalmann, N.; Thalmann, D. and Fortin, M. (1985) **MIRANIM: An Extensible Director-Oriented System for the Animation of Realistic Images**, IEEE Computer Graphics and Applications, Vol. 5, No 3, pp. 61-73

Magnenat-Thalmann N. and Thalmann, D. (1985) **Computer Animation: Theory and Practice**, Springer, Tokyo Berlin Heidelberg New York

Magnenat-Thalmann, N. and Thalmann, D. (1985a) **Single and Multiple Virtual Movie Cameras for Special Cinematographic Effects**, Proc. Computer Graphics Tokyo '85.

Magnenat-Thalmann, N. and Thalmann, D. (1985b) **Controlling Evolution and Motion Using the CINEMIRA-2 Animation Sublanguage**, New Electronic Images, Springer, Tokyo Berlin Heidelberg New York.

Magnenat-Thalmann, N. and Thalmann, D. (1985c), **3D Computer Animation: More an Evolution Problem than a Motion Problem**, IEEE Computer Graphics and Applications, Vol. 5, No 10.

Magnenat-Thalmann N.; Thalmann, D.; Fortin, M. and Langlois, L. (1985b) **MIRA-SHADING: a Language for the Synthesis and the Animation of Realistic Images**, Frontiers in Computer Graphics, Springer, Tokyo Berlin Heidelberg New York, pp.101-113.

Nishita, T. and Nakamae, E. (1974) **An algorithm for half-toned representation of three-dimensional objects**, Information Processing Society of Japan, Vol.14

Reeves, W.T. (1983) **Particle Systems - a Technique for Modeling a Class of Fuzzy Objects**, Proc. SIGGRAPH '83, pp.359-376.

Reeves, W.T. (1985) **Approximate and Probabilistic Algorithms for Shading and Rendering of Structured Particle Systems**, Proc. SIGGRAPH '85, pp.359-376.

Warn, D.R. (1983) **Ligthing Controls for Synthetic Images**, Proc. SIGGRAPH '83, pp.13-21.

Weiler, K; Atherton, P. (1977) **Hidden Surface Removal Using Polygon Area Sorting**, Proc.SIGGRAPH '77, pp.214-222

Whitted, T. (1980) **An improved illumination model for shaded display**, Comm.ACM, Vol.23, No6, pp.343-349

Williams, L. (1978) **Casting Curved Shadows on Curved Surfaces**, Proc. SIGGRAPH '78, pp.270-274

An Analysis and Algorithm for Filling Propagation

Kenneth P. Fishkin and Brian A. Barsky
Berkeley Computer Graphics Laboratory, Computer Science Division, Department of Electrical Engineering and Computer Sciences, University of California, Berkeley, CA 94720, USA

Abstract

Fill algorithms are a common graphics utility used to change the colour of regions in the frame buffer. The *propagation algorithm* is a key component of filling algorithms. The problem of propagation within a fill algorithm is presented and defined, and the difficulties of formalization and comparison are discussed. The previous algorithms are presented and analyzed under a new comparison metric whose validity is confirmed by run-time tests. A new algorithm is developed, and is shown to have better average and worst case behaviour than the others.

Résumé

Les *algorithmes de remplissage* sont souvent utiles en infographie. Ils servent à produire des changements chromatiques de certaines régions dans la mémoire d'image. La *propagation du remplissage* est un aspect important de ces algorithmes. Dans cet article, nous commençons par définir le problème de la propagation. Nous discutons ensuite des difficultés inhérentes à la formalisation de cette notion, ainsi qu'à la comparaison d'algorithmes servant à résoudre ce problème. Nous proposons une métrique simple permettant d'effectuer de telles comparaisons. La validité de cette métrique est confirmée par des tests empiriques. Les algorithmes précédemment proposés sont alors présentés et analysés à la lumière de cette métrique. Un nouvel algorithme est finalement développé, et nous montrons que celui-ci se comporte mieux que les précédents en moyenne comme en pire cas.

This work was supported in part by the Semiconductor Research Corporation under grant number 82-11-008, the National Science Foundation under grant number ECS-8204381, and the State of California under a Microelectronics Innovation and Computer Research Opportunities grant.

1. INTRODUCTION AND PROBLEM DEFINITION

A *region* is a group of connected pixels in a frame buffer consisting of a set of connected *spans*. A span is a horizontal row of pixels that are all within the region. Furthermore, a span is the *largest* such row; the pixels horizontally adjacent to the span are assumed to be *outside* the region. The region may be *4-connected* ("Manhattan geometry") in which case spans may only be connected vertically, or *8-connected*, in which case spans may be connected across diagonals. We focus on 4-connected filling, as have others. We show in Section 1.1 that most 4-connected propagation algorithms can be trivially changed into an 8-connected algorithm, if need be.

Every pixel in the region possesses some property P (for example, possessing a certain colour). The region is delimited by a set of *boundary pixels* that do not have P. We assume a Boolean function INSIDE, which returns **true** if and only if the pixel has P. We wish to perform a certain SET operation exactly once upon each pixel in the region (for example, writing a certain colour into the pixel).

Application of the INSIDE function across the frame buffer creates a Boolean matrix. The *propagation algorithm* explores this matrix. Given a seed pixel known to be inside the region, the propagation algorithm finds the region's boundaries. The propagation algorithm calls the SET procedure (exactly once) on each connected INSIDE pixel, where the SET and INSIDE procedures can be varied to achieve different effects (see Fishkin[1] for examples).

The set of pixels that are in the region can be defined inductively:
1) The seed pixel is INSIDE the region.
2) A pixel is in the region if and only if it is INSIDE, and connected to another pixel that is in the region.

Another formalism is to consider each span in the region as a vertex in a graph, and to connect two such vertices with an edge if and only if those two spans are connected. In this case, the propagation algorithm is essentially a graph-traversal algorithm, which finds a connected component from a single vertex. We will show that the propagation algorithms can be easily classified according to which of these two formalisms they use.

The composite process of finding and SETting the pixels in the region is known as *filling*. In this paper, we focus on the propagation method, to the exclusion of the other parts. We assume only that INSIDE and SET exist, and may be called as necessary.

Once a span has been found, the algorithm must explore outwards from it. As per Smith,[7] we define a *shadow* of a span to be some set of pixels connected to the span that are to be explored by the algorithm. A shadow has a key property: any span that lies (wholly or partially) in a shadow is connected to the region. The propagation process consists of pushing shadows from known spans onto a stack, and then later finding the set of spans that contact that shadow, which we term the *spanset*. Figure 1 summarizes our notation, and our representational convention. A span may cast as few as one or as many as three shadows.

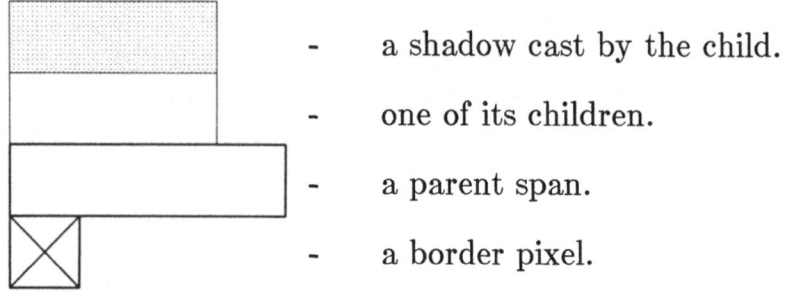

Figure 1.
Basic terms and figures to represent them

When a span is created, it occupies a certain topological relationship to its parent span. There are three possible cases. First, it is possible that the child span does not extend beyond the parent span by more than one pixel on either end (Figure 2). Lieberman[3] terms these *S-turns*.

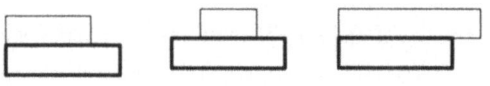

Figure 2.
An S-turn: the child span does not overlap the parent by more than one pixel on either end

Secondly, the child could extend beyond the parent span on one end, but not on the other (Figure 3). Lieberman[3] terms these *U-turns*.

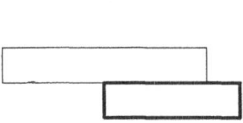

Figure 3.

A U-turn: the child partially overlaps the parent

Finally, the child could extend beyond the parent span on both ends (Figure 4). We term these W-turns.

Figure 4.

A W-turn: the child wholly overlaps the parent

1.1. 8-Connected Propagation

Since a span is added to the region if and only if it contacts a shadow, it is easy to convert 4-connected propagation algorithms into 8-connected algorithms. When a shadow is pushed, it consists precisely of those pixels that could extend the region from the parent span. Therefore, if we simply extend the borders of a shadow by one pixel in each direction when we push it on the stack, the 4-connected algorithm becomes 8-connected.

2. COMPARING ALGORITHMS

There are a number of fast propagation algorithms[2,3,4,6,7,8] extant. Three factors motivate our decision for re-examination:

1) The algorithms are required to solve large problems in real-time.
2) Recently, filling algorithms have been presented[1] that require much more expensive computation on a per-pixel basis.
3) A desire for formalism.

Unfortunately, it is very difficult to compare propagation algorithms, for the following reasons:

1) *Topology.* Algorithm performance depends upon the topology of the region, which is not known in advance.
2) *Seed.* Within a certain topology, performance is also a function of the starting point.
3) *Calls* to the other components. The algorithm makes repeated calls to INSIDE and SET, whose expenses vary with the particular type of filling.[1]
4) *Machine dependence.* The cost and power of the instruction set depend on the particular target machine.

2.1. Comparison Metrics

We will compare algorithms based on two metrics:

1) *Space.* Regions may be cyclic. The propagation algorithm should not "rediscover" pixels that have already been filled, since this could lead to infinite looping. Some algorithms keep one bit per pixel as a "visited" bit. Other algorithms don't need this bit; they avoid infinite looping via internal data structures.
2) *Exploration behaviour.* As mentioned previously, a span may have three different topological relationships to its parent. The main difference between the algorithms lies in their differing behaviour in the different cases; they may push different shadows onto the stack and push them in different orders.

We measure the efficiency of the exploration by ρ, the average number of reads per pixel over the region; that is, the total number of pixel reads performed by the propagation algorithm divided by the number of pixels in the region. In addition to those pixels inside the region, those pixels adjacent to the region ("boundary pixels") are also read at least once. We will not count these pixel reads in our comparison, for three reasons: the ratio of boundary to interior pixels is usually very low, the analysis is greatly simplified if they are neglected, and memory requirements can be reduced if the interior ρ achieves 1.0, regardless of the boundary reads.

Since filling is a linear-time problem, we will be comparing constant-factor reductions in ρ. An extra pixel read represents not only a wasted frame buffer access, but indicates wasted control logic. Our contention is that this single number ρ (within the context of the previous assumptions) measures the efficiency of a propagation algorithm; our run-time tests confirm the strength of this metric.

2.2. Other Criteria

The algorithms were compared on three other criteria, which tests showed to be non-crucial. We list them for the sake of completeness.

1) *Computational cost, for a given p.*
2) *Stack area.*
3) *Instruction set* needed to implement the algorithm. Each of the algorithms can be implemented with only assignments, negations, tests, increments, and decrements.

Table 3 shows that the main algorithms were all approximately the same when evaluated on these criteria; we will not mention them for the rest of the paper.

3. THE ALGORITHMS

There are two schools of propagation algorithms, corresponding to the two formalisms mentioned in Section 1. Considering the region as a connected graph gives rise to algorithms that are *global* and *vertex-based*. These algorithms consider each span as a vertex, and connect two vertices if and only if their corresponding spans are connected.

Second, if the region is considered solely as a Boolean matrix, the algorithms engendered are *local* and *pixel-based*. They pay little or no attention to graph-theoretic properties, considering solely the topology of the current span.

A Taxonomy of Filling Algorithms		
Author	Year	Class
Lieberman	1978	graph
Smith	1979	pixel
Shani	1980	graph
Pavlidis	1981	graph
Smith	1982	pixel
Levoy	1982	pixel
new	1985	pixel

Table 1.

3.1. Graph-Oriented Algorithms

Lieberman: The first published propagation algorithm is that of Lieberman.[3] This graph-oriented algorithm keeps two sorted lists consisting of unexplored edges (shadows) leading up and down, respectively.

This algorithm avoids cycling by referring to the lists of unexplored edges. Intuitively, the unexplored edges represent the border of the current region; if exploration contacts these edges, they represent an "imaginary boundary", and the exploration will retreat. This requires that the list be searched on every pixel (since a vertex (span) may cross more than one edge), that pushes perform insertion into a sorted list, and that edges on the stack be modified *in situ* if spans contact them. Therefore, the algorithm's behaviour depends heavily on the "bushiness" of the region, the density of the region's graph.

Lieberman's algorithm is mainly of historical interest. Shani[6] shows that it is not always correct, and it can be quite slow. However, it does contain five important ideas used by later algorithms:

1) The treatment of the region as a graph, with one vertex per span, and edges between connected spans.
2) Recognition of U-turns.
3) Storage of parental information in a data element.
4) The use of stacked shadows to represent a imaginary boundary enclosing the region.
5) Noting that regions with holes represent the worst case.

Shani: Shani[6] avoids cycling by *explicitly* drawing the imaginary boundaries mentioned above. Boundary lines are drawn temporarily, and then erased.

The algorithm traverses the region's graph, but *only* pursuing edges which go in a certain direction (upwards, say). When no such edges remain, the algorithm reverses direction; only downwards edges are pursued, until *they* are exhausted. This series of back-and-forth waves continues until no unexplored edges remain.

Newly discovered edges are pursued if they lead in the current direction, and *blocked* if they lead in the opposite direction. An edge is blocked by drawing a physical barrier along that edge, on the side of the discovering vertex.

If a vertex is explored, and there is a blocked edge preventing further exploration, then a cycle has been found; the blocked edge is removed from the stack and the current exploring process is terminated. This blocked edge prevented the exploring process from re-entering the blocked vertex, which would have caused an infinite loop.

When all upwards edges have been pursued, the direction is reversed. Any previously blocked edges in the current direction are re-drawn (unblocked) and then pursued. In this manner, all downwards edges are pursued, and all upwards edges are blocked for the next upwards sweep.

Shani uses a *deque*-like structure for his main data structure. Unexplored edges leading in the current direction are pushed on the top of the deque, and blocked edges are pushed on the bottom of the deque. This technique ensures that direction will be changed only when all edges in the current direction have been exhausted. This deque-like structure combines the two sorted lists of Lieberman, by pushing onto the two different ends. This deque-like structure is not a "pure" deque, which would only allow removal from the ends. When a cycle is discovered, the blocking edge is removed from the structure, wherever it may be.

This algorithm is qualitatively different from the pixel-based algorithms, and cannot be compared solely on the basis of ρ. First, the algorithm doesn't need a bit per pixel, a decided advantage. However, the algorithm pays for this by (1) blocking edges, and (2) removing blocked edges that are found to form a cycle. This latter step requires that the deque be searched after each span, to see if that span was claimed by a blocked edge. Depending on the region, this step can be very expensive.

Shani never explicitly describes the behaviour of his algorithm when confronted with U and W turns. However, his paper contains a figure that shows the algorithm performing optimally on a U-turn, and his algorithm requires that non-cycle-causing spans not be revisited. For these two reasons, our implementation of his algorithm uses both U and W turn optimization.

The algorithm visits every non-cycle-causing span once, and every potentially cycle-causing span twice. This leads to a worst-case ρ of 1.5, but this is extremely rare; our test regions had an average-case ρ of 1.09. This is almost identical to (but slightly higher than) the ρ of our algorithm, the only other one that optimizes both U and W turns. This is because Shani's algorithm only revisits pixels that *could* form a cycle, and ours only revisits those that *do* form a cycle.

This algorithm, unfortunately, is not extendible to 8-connected propagation. When a blocked edge is found, the blocking line must be drawn on the side of the blocking vertex, not the blocked vertex. Otherwise, a span could (wholly or partially) traverse any number of blocking edges; the deque would have to be consulted not on every span, but every *pixel*, and shadows have to be modified in-place.

Drawing the line on the side of the blocking vertex is only correct in 4-connected propagation; it is only in this case that we are guaranteed that the blocking edge overlays a set of pixels in the blocking vertex that are all inside the region. For example, consider a to-be-blocked span that lies diagonally and one pixel away from the blocking span. In this case, no pixels in the blocking span will both (1) block the cycle and (2) correctly re-discover the blocked vertex when direction is changed.

Pavlidis: Pavlidis' algorithm[4] notes that the graph formed by the region is implicitly defined by a graph that defines the *border* of the region. Furthermore, this border graph is usually much sparser than the interior graph. His algorithm, then, explores not the interior graph but rather the border graph.

His algorithm uses a stack as the main data structure, containing the address of a border span, and its direction with respect to its parent.

If the interior and border have I and B pixels, respectively, Pavlidis' algorithm makes $I + 3B$ pixel visits, for a ρ of $(I+2B)/I$. In the worst case, the ratio of B to I can be arbitrarily large; the algorithm has worst-case ρ approaching infinity.

We did not implement Pavlidis' algorithm for testing because of two disadvantages:

1) The algorithm assumes that the border of the region has a distinct colour, distinct even from the surrounding background. If this is not the case (e.g. when the picture has only two colors), then the algorithms' behavior is not defined.
2) Pavlidis' algorithm is unique among the graph-oriented algorithms in reserving a bit per pixel.

3.2. Pixel-Based Algorithms

Smith0: Smith has published two propagation algorithms.[7,8] His first,[7] which we will term "Smith0", is the only algorithm that keeps no parental information of any kind on the stack.

The endpoints of the shadow and the values of the parent span are kept as program variables rather than as stack data. This means that when the algorithm switches direction the algorithm has no recourse to parental information.

This algorithm detects S-turns by these program variables (except for immediately after a change of direction), but does not detect U or W-turns. Therefore, the algorithm will always push one shadow continuing in the same direction, and will push one shadow in the opposite direction of the same size as the child in the case of a U or W turn, (see Figure 5).

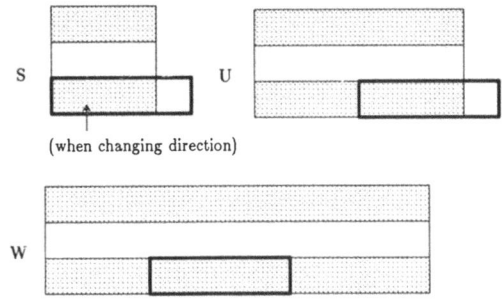

Figure 5.
The Smith0 algorithm acting upon S (left), U (right), and W (bottom) turns

On both U and W turns, the algorithm will read pixels at least twice; those pixels that are in the parent span and also in shadow. This can also happen on S turns, when the algorithm changes direction. Since spans are pushed in both directions, this algorithm can achieve a worst-case ρ of 3, as noted by Pavlidis.[4]

Smith: At the SIGGRAPH '82 2-D Animation tutorial, Smith presented an improvement on his first algorithm.[8] It is this algorithm that we will refer to as "Smith's algorithm" for the rest of the paper.

Smith's algorithm keeps the endpoints and y coordinate of the span explicitly on the stack, and therefore avoids the S-turn anomaly noted above after a switch of direction. However, the algorithm still performs the same in the case of a U or W turn; two shadows are pushed, of the same size of the child, in either direction (see Figure 6).

The worst case is a region that consists exclusively of children that barely exceed their parents on one end, as shown in Figure 7. In this case, we have n rows of m pixels each. Each row is a U-turn with relation to its parent. On the top and bottom rows, pixels will be read only once. On the other rows, $m-2$ pixels will be re-read by each of the adjoining spans. This leads to a worst-case ρ of

$$\rho = \frac{2m + (n-2)[3(m-2)+2]}{mn} = 3 - \frac{4}{n} - \frac{4}{m} + \frac{8}{mn}$$

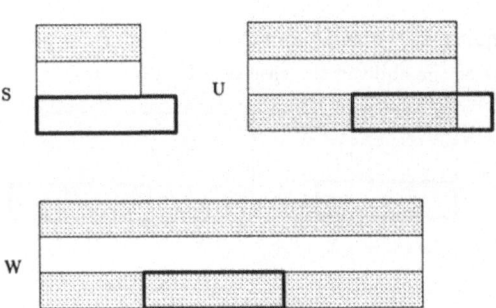

Figure 6.
Smith's algorithm acting upon S, U, and W turns

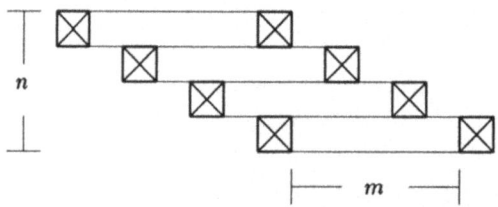

Figure 7.
Worst case for Smith's algorithm

As m and n approach infinity, this approaches a worst-case ρ of 3. In our tests, the algorithm had an average-case ρ of 2.02.

Levoy: At the same tutorial, Levoy presented a propagation algorithm[2] which, though similar to Smith's, makes more use of the parental information.

The endpoints of the shadow, when popped, are compared to the endpoints of the span that pushed it. At this time, S and U turns are detected. If the shadow represents the downward side of an S turn, it is discarded, and if it represents the downward side of a U turn its endpoints are shaved.

Levoy's algorithm delays stack pushes as long as possible; as shown in Table 3, it tends to have the lowest stack heights of any algorithm.

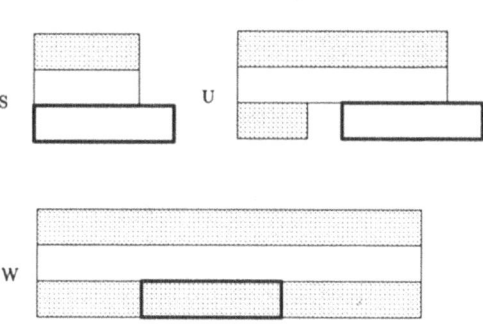

Figure 8.
Levoy's algorithm acting on S, U, and W turns

The behaviour of Levoy's algorithm is summarized in Figure 8. Since it does not detect W turns, the worst case arises when the region consists entirely of W turns, with edges as small as possible (Figure 9). If the seed point is at the apex of the triangle, then the algorithm will read every pixel twice except for those in the top row. If the triangle has n rows, it consists of $2n^2-n$ pixels, $4n-3$ of which are in the top row. Then

$$\rho = \frac{2(2n^2-n)-(4n-3)}{2n^2-n}$$

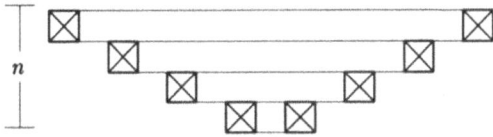

Figure 9.
Worst case for Levoy's algorithm

As n approaches infinity, ρ approaches a worst-case of 2. In our tests, Levoy's algorithm had an average ρ of 1.53. Levoy's algorithm shows substantially better worst and average case behaviour than Smith's, solely due to the detection of U turns.

The new algorithm: This section presents a new algorithm for fill propagation. Like Levoy's and Shani's, it keeps full parental information on the stack. Only the direction that the parent came from is kept, rather than its y value; this simplifies the logic considerably.

The algorithm checks each span against its parent for the S, U, or W configuration. The shadows pushed are the largest set of pixels that could extend the region and *do not* contact the parent span. The algorithm's performance is most easily shown visually by Figure 10.

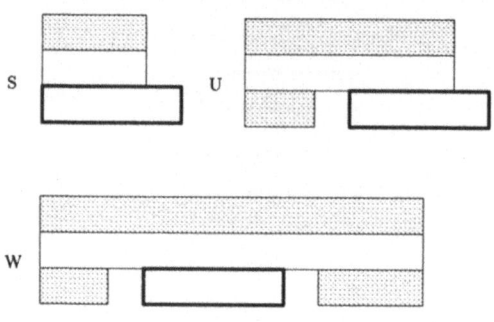

Figure 10.
Our algorithm acting on S, U, and W turns

In any serially-implemented recursive algorithm, recursive calls must be evaluated in some order. In the previous algorithms, the order is arbitrary. Our algorithm uses the well-known heuristic of "do the smallest piece first".[5] In practice, shadows pushed in the opposite direction for U and W turns are almost always very small, corresponding to local bumps in the region; therefore, we always push those spans last.

The new algorithm is the only one with a non-arbitrary stacking order. Otherwise, it is very similar to Levoy's, except that ours detects W-turns. Our tests show that these two minor improvements reduce run-time by roughly 25% on our test data. The new algorithm is also very similar to Shani's, except that ours needs a bit/pixel but does not require a data structure search, reducing run-time by roughly 75% on our test data.

Even though our algorithm pushes as many as three shadows per span, as opposed to the two of most other algorithms, our stack height is virtually identical to theirs, due to this simple heuristic. Of course, there could be narrow spans leading into arbitrarily complex regions, but this rarely happens in practice.

If the region has a hole, the algorithm will re-discover some of those pixels that formed the cycle, as shown in Figure 11.

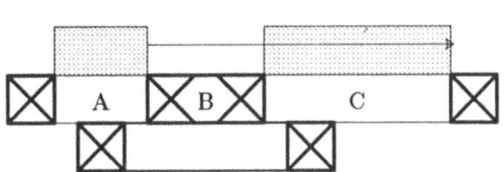

Figure 11.

Our worst case; a hole (region B)

If the widths of the left span, hole, and right span are A, B, and C, respectively, the child of the left span will bleed over on top of the hole and revisit the pixels which are the responsibility of the right span. This results in C pixels being read twice.

The region has A+B+C pixels in the top row, A+C in the middle row, and at least B+2 in the bottom row, giving the region 2A + 2B + 2C + 2 pixels. All pixels are visited once except for the C cycle-forming pixels on the top right, which are visited twice. Therefore, the worst-case ρ is

$$\rho = \frac{2A+2B+3C+2}{2A+2B+2C+2}$$

When C approaches infinity and A and B are minimized, ρ approaches its worst-case value of 1.5.

Behaviour on simply connected regions. In this section, we show that the algorithm achieves ρ of 1.0 on regions without holes (simply connected regions).

We need only consider two shadows whose spansets overlap. Those shadows must lie on the same line, by the definition of spanset. Suppose, then, that we have some overlap of spansets. There are four possible cases, depending on whether or not the shadows overlap and whether or not the parent spans are on the same line. We only prove the result for one case: the others follow similarly.

Case 1: The parent spans lie on different lines, and the shadows don't overlap (Figure 12).

At any point in the algorithm, the set of pixels that have been SET is 4-connected. Furthermore, we defined the shadows for our algorithm such that they don't overlap any

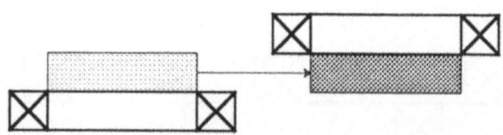

Figure 12.

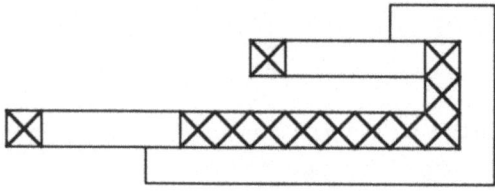

Figure 13.

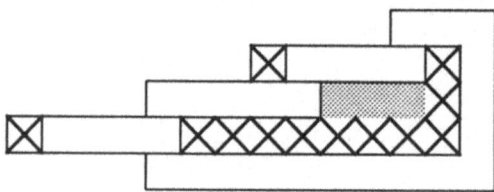

Figure 14.

previous parents. Therefore, the parent spans must be 4-connected by a path that does not touch either of the shadows (Figure 13). Then, we fill in the current spanset, a spanset which, by assumption, contacts both parent spans. This forces a hole either to the right of the upper span, or to the right of the lower span (Figure 14). Again, there are other symmetrical cases.

The algorithm achieves the optimal ρ if the arbitrary region turns out to be simply connected. If we know *in advance* that the region is simply connected, is our algorithm optimal? Unfortunately, no. Consider any region whose border has area proportional to the square root of the area of the entire region (a square, for example). If the border of the region is traversed, and the region is known not to have holes, then the entire interior must be entirely within the region (see Figure 15). Since we only visit the border, this process gives us a ρ of $O(\sqrt{n})$, where n is the area of the region.

Therefore, although our algorithm achieves the lower bound for a subset of the possible regions, it is not necessarily optimal if we know in advance that we are dealing with an element of that subset.

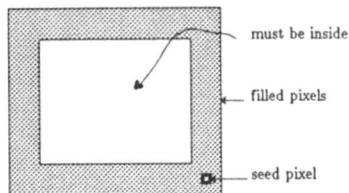

Figure 15.
After $\sqrt{n}$ visits, we can fill n pixels

4. AN ANALOGY

All the algorithms explore (either explicitly or implicitly) the graph defined by the topology of the region.

Both Smith's and Levoy's algorithms proceed in some fixed direction until reaching a dead end, then back up to the last node where a choice was possible, and pursue that. This recalls *depth*-first graph traversal.

Our algorithm always changes direction if possible. Branches are filled before the main trunk, as in *breadth*-first graph traversal.

Shani's algorithm proceeds in one direction as long as there are unexplored arcs anywhere in the region in that direction, repeating the process in the other direction, This exploration by back-and-forth waves recalls network flow or *spanning tree* algorithms.

5. COMPARISON OF THE THREE ALGORITHMS

Four of the algorithms were implemented in C under 4.2 BSD UNIX on a VAX-11/750, using an Adage/Ikonas RDS3000 frame buffer. The **gprof** command provided run-time profiling. The "CPU time" row in Table 3 represents the relative total CPU time to fill each region, using *boundary fills*[7] INSIDE and SET procedures.

One of the 21 regions was a grid. This region represents a maximally dense graph (the greatest possible number of holes), and was created specifically to demonstrate worst-case behaviour. Each of the algorithms fared the worst by far on this region, especially Shani's; the list of blocked spans was so long that his algorithm's behaviour was extremely poor. Without this region, Shani's algorithm performed quite well; it's relative CPU time dropped from 2.17 times Smith's to 0.79 times.

	An Overall Comparison of the Filling Algorithms						
	Lieberman	Smith0	Shani	Pavlidis	Smith	Levoy	new
year	1978	1979	1980	1981	1982	1982	1985
taxonomy	graph	pixel	graph	graph	pixel	pixel	pixel
data structure	sorted list	stack	deque	stack	stack	stack	stack
element width	2 int	2 int	5 int, 3 Bool.	2 int 1 Bool.	3 int	5 int	5 int, 1 Bool.
space requirement?	No	Yes	No	Yes	Yes	Yes	Yes
detects S turns?	Yes	usually	Yes	No	Yes	Yes	Yes
detects U turns?	Yes	No	Yes	No	No	Yes	Yes
detects W turns?	No	No	Yes	No	No	No	Yes
gradient fills?	No	Yes	No	No	Yes	Yes	No
8-connected?	Yes	Yes	No	Yes	Yes	Yes	Yes
pushes/span	1-2	1-2	1-3	NA	1-2	1-2	1-3
ρ, worst case	2	3	1.5	∞	3	2	1.5
av. ρ, test cases	--	--	1.09	--	2.02	1.55	1.05
relative CPU time, test cases	--	--	217.2	--	100.0	83.5	60.2

Table 2.

Average per-region statistics, 4 algorithms, 21 regions				
	Algorithm			
	Shani	Smith	Levoy	new
pushes	821.3	724.9	618.0	780.0
max height, stack/deque	198.1	192.3	98.7	102.7
max area (bytes), stack/deque*	2575.3	1153.8	987.0	1129.7
ρ	1.09	2.02	1.53	1.05
incr	25.18	2.11	1.99	1.20
decr	23.07	0.24	0.30	0.20
negate	0.01	0.00	1.05	0.04
test	94.69	2.20	4.23	3.76
assign	1.22	0.48	0.76	0.27
CPU time	217.2	100.0	83.5	60.2

Table 3.

* assuming 2 bytes/integer, 1 byte/Boolean

6. CONCLUSION

A number of algorithms to fill regions were presented and compared under a new metric. A new algorithm was developed with better average and worst-case behaviour under this metric. The appendix gives code to implement the algorithm.

7. ACKNOWLEDGEMENTS

The authors wish to thank Marc Levoy of the University of North Carolina at Chapel Hill for his many helpful comments and discussions, and the reviewer for suggesting re-examination of the graph-oriented algorithms.

References

1. Kenneth P. Fishkin and Brian A. Barsky, "A Family of New Algorithms for Soft Filling," pp. 235-244 in *SIGGRAPH '84 Conference Proceedings*, ACM,Minneapolis(July 23-27, 1984). Extended abstract in *Proceedings of Graphics Interface '84*, Ottawa (28 May - 1 June 1984), pp. 181-185.
2. Marc S. Levoy, *Area Flooding Algorithms*, Report, Hanna-Barbera Productions (June, 1981). Presented at SIGGRAPH '82 2-D Animation Tutorial.
3. Henry Lieberman, "How To Color in a Coloring Book," pp. 111-116 in *SIGGRAPH '78 Conference Proceedings*, ACM,Atlanta(1978).
4. Theo Pavlidis, "Contour Filling in Raster Graphics," pp. 29-36 in *SIGGRAPH '81 Conference Proceedings*, ACM,Dallas(3-7 August 1981).
5. Robert Sedgewick, *Algorithms*, Addison-Wesley.
6. Uri Shani, "Filling Regions in Binary Raster Images: A Graph-Theoretic Approach," pp. 321-327 in *SIGGRAPH '80 Conference Proceedings*, ACM,Seattle(July, 1980).
7. Alvy Ray Smith, "Tint Fill," pp. 276-283 in *SIGGRAPH '79 Conference Proceedings*, ACM,Chicago(August, 1979). Also Technical Memo No. 6, New York Institute of Technology.
8. Alvy Ray Smith, *Fill Tutorial Notes*, Report No. 40, LucasFilm (April 27, 1982). Presented at SIGGRAPH '82 2-D Animation Tutorial.

APPENDIX

Here we list C source for the key portion of our algorithm, with pseudo-code provided for the other parts.

```
struct {
int    MyLx, MyRx;    /* endpoints of this shadow*/
int    DadLx, DadRx;  /* and parent span    */
int    Myy;           /* my shadows y coord    */
TWO_VAL Mydir;        /* only holds values of +1 or -1 */
} Stack[STACK_HEIGHT];
macro PUSH(a,b,c,dd,e,f)  {
    push a shadow from (a) to (b), inclusive,
    on line (e), going in direction (f)
    from the parent span of of [(c)..(dd)].
}

/* pop top of stack into local variables */
macro POP()   {
```

pop the top shadow into local variables
lx,rx,y,direction, DadLx, DadRx
}

/* stack a shadow on the stack. The current span is
[lx..rx] on line y, the parent is [DadLx..DadRx],
and the current direction is (direction) */
macro STACK(direction,DadLx,DadRx,lx,rx,y)   {
/* store the *shoulders* of the span,
to simplify testing 3,6 lines down */
   pushrx = rx + 1; pushlx = lx - 1;
   PUSH(lx,rx,pushlx,pushrx,y+direction,direction);
   /* U turn to the right */
   if (rx > DadRx)
      PUSH(DadRx + 1,rx,pushlx,pushrx,
         y-direction,-direction);
   /* U turn to the left */
   /* W turn handled implicitly */
   if (lx < DadLx) /* U turn to the left;
      PUSH(lx,DadLx - 1,pushlx,pushrx,
         y-direction,-direction);
}

/* fill a region, with seed at (seedx,seedy) */
Fill(seedx,seedy)
int   seedx,seedy;
   {
   int   x,y;
   int   lx,rx,DadLx,DadRx;
   int   pushlx,pushrx;
   int   direction;
   /* are the pixels from [lx..x) in a run?   */
   BOOLEAN   WasIn;

   (*Start) ();

   find the span containing the seed point.
   suppose it goes from (lx) to (rx), inclusive.

PUSH(lx,rx,lx,rx,seedy+1,1);
PUSH(lx,rx,lx,rx,seedy-1,-1);

```
while (tos >= 0) {
  POP();
  if ((y < TOP) OR (y > Bottom))
    continue;
  x = lx + 1;
  if (WasIn = (*Inside)(lx,y)) {
    (*Set)(lx,y); lx = lx -1;
    while ((*Inside)(lx,y) AND (lx >= Left)) {
      (*Set)(lx,y); lx = lx -1;
    }
    lx = lx + 1;
  }
  /* now looking at pixel (x).
  If (WasIn), then am inside a run of pixels from [lx..x)
  else, lx is meaningless   */
  while (x <= Right) {
    if (WasIn) '
      if ((*Inside)(x,y)) {
        (*Set)(x,y);
      } else {
        /* just found the end of a run */
        STACK(direction,DadLx,DadRx,lx,(x-1),y);
        WasIn = FALSE;
      }
    } else {
      if (x > rx) break;
      if ((*Inside)(x,y)) {
        (*Set)(x,y);
        /* just found the start of a run */
        WasIn = TRUE; lx = x;
      }
    }
    x = x + 1;
  }
  if (WasIn) {
    /* hit an edge while inside a run */
    STACK(direction,DadLx,DadRx,lx,(x-1),y);
  }
 }
}
```

Chapter 2
Image Processing

Non-Rigid Body Motion

A.R. Dill and M.D. Levine

Computer Vision and Robotics Laboratory, Department of Electrical Engineering, McGill University, 805 Sherbrooke Street West, Montréal, Quebec, H3A 2K6, Canada

ABSTRACT

During the last few years motion analysis has developed into a major field of interest in image analysis and understanding. Considerable progress has been made as evidenced by the number of publications. However, most of these have been confined to the study of rigid body motion. Very few have addressed the issue of non-rigid body motion which poses many interesting and difficult problems. We propose a new technique for analyzing non-rigid body motion of closed boundary shapes that is based on the computation of skeletons at multiple resolutions. This technique is used for analyzing the structural changes in the morphology of locomoting lymphocytes and, in particular, of their pseudopods.

KEYWORDS: motion analysis, non-rigid body, skeleton, multiple resolutions, matching, computer vision.

INTRODUCTION

Methods for motion analysis are quite commonly categorized into two main classes: *intensity based schemes* and *token matching schemes* [Hildreth and Ullman 1982]. The former are based on the computation of local changes in light intensity values whereas *token matching schemes* compare certain previously computed features over time. Any identifiable feature can be chosen as a token no matter how complex it is; that is, the token can be composed of several more primitive features. Tokens that suggest themselves are: termination points of lines and edges, edge segments, boundary segments, points of curvature discontinuity, regions, to name only a few. The main difficulty of this scheme is the correspondence problem. In other words a token must be found at time t_j that corresponds to the given token at time t_i $(j > i)$.

Whereas in the case of rigid body motion the tokens between which correspondence must be established are well defined, the choice of these tokens for non-rigid body motion is a very difficult task. For example, to define the tokens in the case of a locomoting white blood cell, its shape must be partitioned into meaningful subparts. In general, this problem can certainly not be solved. Part of the difficulty resides in the fact that the notion of *meaningful* depends on the scene. In other words, not only syntactic knowledge is required for partitioning a planar curve but also, to a great extent, semantic knowledge. Thus, Fischler and Bolles [1983] point out that the partitioning problem is *not* a generic task independent of purpose. They also mention that the segments into which a curve is partitioned change when the purpose of the partitioning is altered.

Pseudopods are temporary protrusions of the protoplasm of a cell. Therefore one is interested in partitioning the cell shape into tokens that represent convex subparts of the cell. A typical cell input image is shown in Fig. 1.

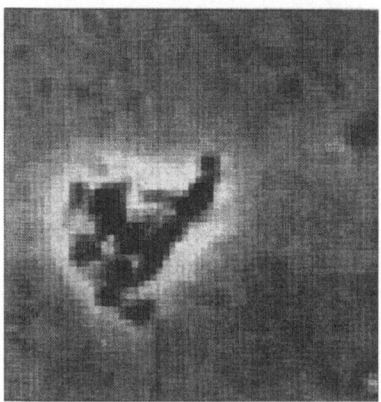

Fig. 1. Typical frame of input image sequence

The symmetric axis transform, introduced by Blum and Nagel [1978], or its discrete version that is usually referred to as skeleton, is a natural way of representing convex subparts of biological shapes. Any locally convex segment of contour, as well as a more globally convex segment of contour that comprises several local convexities, could be a pseudopod. Hence the skeleton would be better computed at different resolutions. Since the local as well as the global context must be maintained over time, smoothing operations as proposed by Dyer and Ho [1984] cannot be applied. In their approach small local convexities cause a new skeleton branch only if they are not incorporated in a large global convexity. This is because their approach is based completely on syntactic knowledge.

By computing skeletons at different resolutions a filtered version can be produced without violating the constraints imposed by the semantic knowledge. The resolution at which the shape is examined is related to the degree of smoothing, in that the lower the resolution, the higher the degree of smoothing. Skeleton branches that persist over several resolutions arise from convexities that are locally as well as globally significant. Their stability is related to their perceptual significance. Witkin [1983] proposes a similar stability criterion that depends on the persistence of events over scale changes. In contrast to the shape centered descriptions of which the skeleton is an example, he uses a boundary-based description.

Having computed the skeleton at different scales, we use those computed at the lower resolutions as a measure of how global the underlying convexity is. Clearly the skeletons computed at higher resolutions represent the exact location and orientation of the underlying convexities. The structural changes of the locomoting cell are then quantified by comparing the filtered skeleton version of the cell at different time instances [Dill 1985].

COMPUTATION OF SKELETONS

The technique used for computing the skeleton is based on an algorithm by Arcelli [1981]. The resulting skeleton can be interpreted as a discrete version of the symmetric axis transform. Given an object as a connected set of pixels O, the skeleton is derived by iteratively tracing its 8-connected contour C. After every iteration, contour pixels that are neither multiple nor lie on a significant convexity are assigned to a set of pixels R, according to some measure of significance that will be explained later. A pixel is multiple if it is traversed more than once during contour tracing, if it has no neighbors in the interior of O (interior: set of pixels $O - C$), or if it has at least one D-neighbor (D-neighbor: horizontally or vertically displaced neighbor of a pixel) which belongs to the contour but is not one of the two direct neighbors along the contour. Before the next iteration, O is assigned to $O = O - R$. The algorithm stops when $R = \emptyset$. The skeleton S then corresponds to the set O. The different sets are illustrated in Fig. 2.

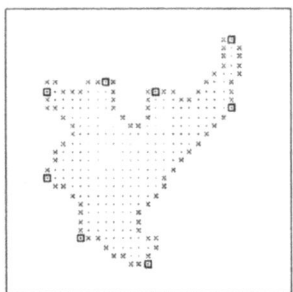

Fig. 2. Iteration 1 of the skeletonization algorithm. The contour (set C) is composed of the symbols ▫ and ×. The set O corresponds to the union of the three different sets of symbols. Contour pixels that lie on a significant convexity are marked with the symbol ▫. Contour pixels marked as × are assigned to the set R.

The significance of a convexity is measured as a function of the discrete curvature computed at a given contour pixel. At every contour pixel that is not already labelled multiple, i.e., pixels that are assigned to the set R, discrete curvature values are computed. Assuming that the chain code is available, a curvature value is readily obtained if only the two direct contour neighbors, i.e., the preceding and succeeding contour pixel, are considered. The resulting curvature is referred to as the 1-code c_i^1 at contour pixel i. A negative 1-code results from anti-clockwise rotation of the contour; -1 corresponds to a rotation of -45deg, -2 to -90deg, and -3 to -135deg. Positive values range from 0 for a straight line to 4 for an inversion. However, the 1-code cannot be used for evaluating the significance of the underlying convexity because it is too noise sensitive.

The discrete curvature function represented by the 1-code must undergo some smoothing operations in order to be useful. Several methods have been proposed to obtain a more reliable measure of discrete curvature and thereby a better estimate of the significance of the underlying convexity. Rosenfeld and Johnston [1973] introduced k-curvature for this purpose whereas Freeman and Davis [1977] used a similar measure called the incremental curvature. We are smoothing the sequence of 1-codes that represent the discrete curvature along the contour by correlating it with a triangular mask $f_{\Delta n}(i)$. Its Fourier transform $F_{\Delta n}(\xi)$ is represented by a quadratic *sinc* function. In other words, the correlation of the 1-code sequence with a triangular mask is equivalent to a low pass filter operation in the frequency domain. Thus,

$$f_{\Delta n}(i) = \begin{cases} (n - |i|)/n^2 & \text{if } |i| \leq n; \\ 0 & \text{elsewhere}. \end{cases} \quad n = 2, 3, \ldots, k \quad (1)$$

$$F_{\Delta n}(\xi) = \frac{\sin^2(\pi \xi n)}{(\pi \xi)^2} \quad (2)$$

The correlation of the 1-code sequence with the triangular mask $f_{\Delta n}(i)$ leads to a new discrete curvature measure that was first used by Gallus and Neurath [1970] and given the name n-code c_i^n, defined as

$$\begin{aligned} c_i^n &= f_{\Delta n}(i) \times c_i^1 \quad \text{(where:} \quad \times \stackrel{\text{def}}{=} \text{correlation)} \\ &= \sum_{k=-n}^{k=n} f_{\Delta n}(k) c_{i+k}^1 \\ &= n c_i^1 + \sum_{k=1}^{n-1} (n-k) \left(c_{i-k}^1 + c_{i+k}^1 \right), \quad n \geq 1. \end{aligned} \quad (3)$$

This n-code can now be used for computing whether a contour pixel lies on a significant convexity. At a given resolution n, contour pixels whose n-codes exceed a certain threshold θ are considered significantly convex. By increasing n, the size of the neighborhood that contributes to the curvature value of a contour pixel grows larger.

This is equivalent to lowering the resolution at which the object is examined. If a continuous string of contour pixels is considered significantly convex only the mid-point of this string is labelled convex. New candidates that are too close to a contour pixel that is either labelled multiple or significantly convex are not included. Pixels are regarded as too close if they lie within n contour pixels on either side of a previously selected skeletal pixel.

The set of pixels S which constitutes the skeleton consists of the following types of pixels: pixels with only one neighbor in S which we will refer to as end-nodes; pixels with two neighbors which are normal skeletal pixels; and pixels with three or more neighbors which we shall call branch-nodes. Skeleton branches that emerge from branch-nodes and lead into end-nodes are called end-branches.

Once the set R is empty some postprocessing techniques are applied. First, lines that are of width 2 are thinned without violating the connectivity constraints and then spurious branches of length 1 are deleted. In Fig. 3 a few iterations of the algorithm are shown.

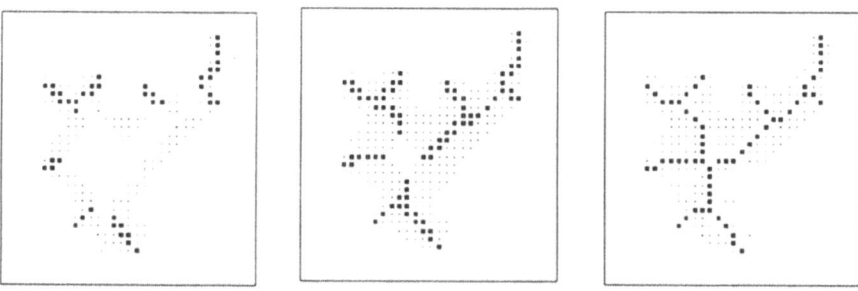

Fig. 3. Some iterations of the skeletonization algorithm. The rightmost diagram shows the final skeleton with all end-branches of length 1 deleted. Skeletal pixels are depicted as ∎.

REPRESENTATION AT MULTIPLE RESOLUTIONS

Before the skeletons computed at different resolutions can be related, another aspect needs some consideration. The question arises whether the numerical values of the n-codes computed at different scales have the same meaning. In other words, will a given contour point on a piece of arc with constant curvature result in the same absolute n-code values for different n's? This should obviously be the case as long as the mask $f_{\Delta_n}(i)$ does not exceed the part of the contour with constant curvature. Quite clearly the definition of the n-code as given in equation (3) violates these constraints. For an arc with constant curvature the resulting n-code values will increase as a function of n. However, it can be shown that this requirement is satisfied by normalizing the triangular mask $f_{\Delta_n}(i)$ so that the area between the mask and the x-axis is always 1, independent of n. As a matter of fact the normalized n-code becomes independent of the resolution n [Dill 1985]. Thus, the employed mask is the normalized n-code $\bar{c}_i^n$, where

$$\bar{c}_i^n = \frac{c_i^n}{n^2} \tag{4}$$

These normalized n-codes are used for computing the skeletons at different resolutions as detailed in section 2.

In other techniques that employ multiple resolutions for representing perceptually prominent points of a planar curve but use a boundary centered description over a shape centered description, the comparison between different resolutions can be quite tedious [Witkin 1983]. This is because prominent points along a planar curve, whether they correspond to concavities, convexities or to zero crossings of the curvature function, will be displaced with respect to their true physical position as the resolution is lowered. The position of the point that reflects a certain feature is only equivalent to the exact position at a very high resolution.

In contrast to the above, the skeletons computed at different resolutions can be compared in a straightforward manner. It is true that the end-nodes of the end-branches also change position as a function of resolution but the corresponding branch-nodes do not alter as long as the accompanying end-branch persists. Because of this, it is sufficient to compare the coordinates of the branch-nodes from which the end-branches emerge in order to verify whether a convexity persists over a certain range of resolutions.

In the following example (Fig. 4), the skeleton is computed at two different resolutions: $n = 5$ and $n = 7$. At both resolutions the threshold is set to $\theta = 0.12$. Convexities that persist over both scales, hence signalling a global convexity, are included in the filtered version. Local convexities that appear only at the smaller scale are filtered. If two end-branches that are considered local share the same branch-node, they are merged creating a new end-node that lies between the old end-nodes; otherwise, they are deleted. The leftmost diagram of the figure corresponds to the unfiltered version of the skeleton computed at the small scale and the diagram in the middle to the unfiltered version at the large scale. The rightmost diagram of the figure shows the filtered version of the skeleton. The branches displayed with the symbol ▪ in the unfiltered skeleton at the small scale refer to branches that are either deleted or merged. In the filtered version they refer to the corresponding new end-branches. Matching branches that are not altered are displayed as ⊡.

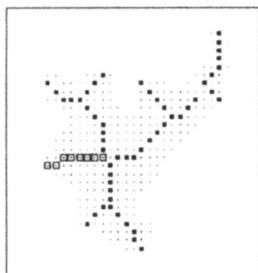 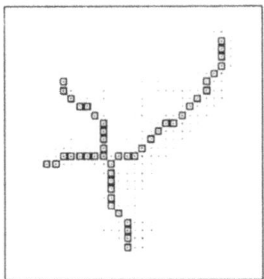 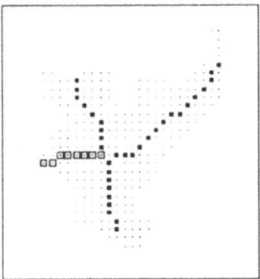

Fig. 4. Skeleton filtering process. The skeleton to the left was computed at $n = 5$ and the skeleton in the middle at $n = 7$. Both were computed with a threshold of $\theta = 0.12$. The skeleton to the right is the filtered version. Branches at the high resolution that match a branch at the low resolution are characterized by the symbol ▫. Non-matching branches that are deleted or merged at the high resolution and thus newly created in the filtered version are depicted as a sequence of ■.

CONCLUSIONS

We have presented a new technique for representing perceptually salient points on a closed planar curve with skeletons computed at different resolutions. One of the merits of this technique is the ease with which descriptions at different scales can be compared. The representation of convexities by branches of a skeleton is particularly well suited for analyzing non-rigid motion. That is because they do not only correspond to locally and globally significant convexities but also preserve the true orientation (as opposed to the orientation of the convexity with respect to the center of the shape) of these subparts.

ACKNOWLEDGEMENTS

This research was supported in part by the Medical Research Council of Canada under Grant No. MA-3236, and the Province of Québec under Grant No. EQ-633. A.R. Dill was in part supported by the Canadian Government Award for foreigners. M.D. Levine would like to thank the Canadian Institute for Advanced Research for its support.

REFERENCES

Arcelli, C., 1981, Pattern Thinning by Contour Tracing, Computer Graphics and Image Processing, Vol. 17 pp. 130-144

Blum, H. and Nagel, R.N., 1978, Shape Decription Using Weighted Symmetric Axis Features, Pattern Recognition, Vol. 10, pp. 167-180

Dill, A.R., 1985, Expert System for the Analysis of Cell Locomotion, M.Eng thesis, Computer Vision and Robotics Lab, McGill University, Montréal, Québec, Canada, in preparation

Dyer, C.R. and Ho S., 1984, Medial-Axis-Based Shape Smoothing, Proceedings of the 7th ICPR, Montréal, Québec, Canada, pp. 333-335

Fischler, M.A. and Bolles, R.C., 1983, Perceptual Organization and the Curve Partitioning Problem, Proceedings of the 8th IJCAI, Karlsruhe, West Germany, pp. 1014-1018

Freeman, H. and Davis, L.S., 1977, A Corner-Finding Algorithm for Chain-Coded Curves, IEEE Trans. on Computers, Vol. C-26, No. 3, pp. 297-303

Gallus, G. and Neurath, P.W., 1970, Improved Computer Chromosome Analysis Incorporating Preprocessing and Boundary Analysis, Phys. Med. Biol., Vol. 15, pp. 435-445

Hildreth, E.C. and Ullman, S., 1982, The Measurement of Visual Motion, A.I. Memo No. 699, MIT Artificial Intelligence Lab, Cambridge, Mass.

Rosenfeld, A. and Johnston, E., 1973, Angle Detection on Digital Curves, IEEE Trans. on Computers, Vol. C-22, pp. 875-878

Witkin, A., 1983, Scale-Space Filtering, Proceedings of the 8th IJCAI, Karlsruhe, West Germany, pp. 1019-1022

Selection of Segment Similarity Measures for Hierarchical Picture Segmentation

J.-M. Beaulieu[1] and M. Goldberg[2]

[1] National Research Council of Canada, NAE, Ottawa, Ontario, K1A 0R6, Canada
[2] Electrical Engineering Dep., University of Ottawa, Ottawa, Ontario, K1N 6N5, Canada

RÉSUMÉ

Différentes mesures de la similarité entre segments sont étudiées pour la segmentation de l'image. Une segmentation agglomérative hiérarchique compare et fusionne deux segments s'ils sont similaires. L'algorithme utilisé fusionne, à chaque itération, les deux segments les plus similaires. Regardant la segmentation de l'image comme un problème d'approximation, la mesure de similarité est reliée à l'erreur totale d'approximation; l'accroissement de l'erreur produit par la fusion de deux segments est utilisé. Une image de télédétection est segmentée par l'approximation de chaque région soit par une constante ou soit par un plan. Une mesure de similarité sensible à la variance locale de l'image est aussi présentée. Les avantages de la combinaison de différentes mesures sont aussi soulignés. Différentes régions d'une image peuvent nécessiter différentes mesures qui doivent donc être combinées pour obtenir, dans l'ensemble, un bon résultat. De plus, dans une segmentation hiérarchique, une mesure simple peut être utilisée lors des premières fusions, tandis que des mesures plus complexes vont être employées par la suite.

ABSTRACT

The problem of defining appropriate segment similarity measures for picture segmentation is examined. In agglomerative hierarchical segmentation, two segments are compared and merged if found similar. The proposed Hierarchical Step-Wise Optimization (HSWO) algorithm finds and then merges the two most similar segments, on a step-by-step basis. By considering picture segmentation as a piece-wise picture approximation problem, the similarity measure (or the step-wise criterion) is related to the overall approximation error. The measure then corresponds to the increase of the approximation error resulting from merging two segments. Similarity measures derived from constant approximations (zeroth order polynomials) and planar approximations (first order polynomials) are applied to a Landsat picture, and the results are presented. An adaptive measurebased upon local variance is also used. The advantages of combining similarity measures (or cirteria) are also stressed. Different picture areas can require different measures which must therefore be combined in order to obtain good overall results. Moreover, in hierarchical segmentation, simple measures can be used for the first merging steps, while, at a higher level of the segment hierarchy, more complex measures can be employed.

KEYWORDS: Hierarchical segmentation, similarity measures, clustering.

I - INTRODUCTION

A hierarchy of segments can be represented by a segment tree in which nodes correspond to segments. Each segment S_i^k is linked to segments of the lower level, S_j^{k-1}, which are disjoint sub-sets of S_i^k, and which are called "sons" of S_i^k. A picture partition thus corresponds to a sub-set of these tree nodes. Starting from the bottom of the tree, an agglomerative hierarchical segmentation algorithm climbs up the tree by merging similar segments. Different similarity measures can be used to decide if two adjacent segments must be merged.

Brice and Fennema (1970) use two heuristics, based upon information from the segment boundaries, to evaluate the similarity of two segments: the phagocyte and the weakness heuristics. The phagocyte heuristic guides the merging of regions in such a way as to smooth or shorten the resulting boundary. Two regions are merged if their common boundary is weak and if the segment boundary length does not increase too quickly. The weakness heuristic merges two regions if a prescribed portion of their common boundary is weak. The phagocyte heuristic is applied first, followed by the weakness one.

Freuder (1976) presents an algorithm where the similarity of two segments is a function of the surrounding segments. For each segment, S_i, the adjacent segment, S_j, which is the most similar to S_i is selected. A directed link is drawn from S_i to S_j. The similarity is related to the difference between segment means values and the segment sizes. Thus, each segment points to one of its neighbours, the one with the closest mean value (weighted to take account of segment sizes). All segments related by a "double link" are then merged. A double link indicates a local minimum of the segment similarity measure, with S_j being minimum among the neighbours of S_i, and S_i among the neighbours of S_j.

Horowitz and Pavlidis (1976) propose a split-and-merge approach using a pyramidal data structure. The data structure defines the way in which segments can be merged or split. A pyramid is a stack of regular picture blocks of decreasing sizes. The picture blocks (or segments) of one level are split into four regular sub-parts to form the next lower level. A pyramid can be regarded as a segment tree where each node corresponds to a block of $2^k \times 2^k$ pixels. A segment is considered as homogeneous if the segment approximation error is smaller than a predefined threshold. The algorithm consists of 1) merging the homogeneous segments, if the resulting segments are also homogeneous, or 2) splitting the segments that are not homogeneous into their four sub-parts.

Chen and Pavlidis (1980) employ a statistical decision process in the preceding split-and-merge approach. The segments of the initial partition are first tested for uniformity, and if not uniform, they are divided into smaller segments. The uniform segments are then subjected to a cluster analysis to identify similar types which are then merged.

The Hierarchical Step-Wise Optimization (HSWO) algorithm is first presented in the next section. Different segment similarity measures derived from a picture approximation model are defined and employed for the segmentation of a remote sensing picture. In section IV, a measure that takes into account the local variance is examined. The advantages of combining similarity measures are studied in section V. The different proposed measures are used to segment a remote sensing picture, and experimental reuslts are presented.

II - THE HIERARCHICAL STEP-WISE OPTIMIZATION ALGORITHM

A hierarchical segmentation algorithm based upon step-wise optimization is used in this paper (Beaulieu and Goldberg 1982, 1983). A segment similarity measure, $C_{i,j}$, is defined as the step-wise criterion to optimize. At each iteration, the algorithm employs an optimization process to find the two most similar segments, which are then merged.

The Hierarchical Step-Wise Optimization (HSWO) algorithm can be defined as follows:

  i) Define an initial picture partition.

  ii) For each adjacent segment pair, (S_i, S_j), calculate the step-wise criterion, $C_{i,j}$; then find and merge the segments with the minimum criterion value.

  iii) Stop, if no more merges are needed; otherwise, go to ii).

Different segment similarity measures (step-wise criteria) can be employed, each one corresponding to different definitions of the picture segmentation task. Different measures are examined in the following sections.

III - PICTURE APPROXIMATION

Let $f_i(x,y)$ designate the pixel values for the segment S_i, ($f_i(x,y)=f(x,y)$ for $(x,y) \in S_i$). Piece-wise picture approximation, therefore, consists in approximating each segment by a polynomial function, $r_i(x,y)$. The approximation error for each segment is defined as the sum of the squared deviations:

$$H(S_i) = \sum_{(x,y) \in S_i} [f_i(x,y) - r_i(x,y)]^2 \qquad (1)$$

The goal of picture approximation is then to find the partition, $\{S_i\}$, that minimizes the overall approximation error, $H(S_i)$.

The segment similarity measure, thus, can be related to the increase of the approximation error produced by the merging of two segments, S_i and S_j:

$$C_{i,j} = H(S_i \cup S_j) - H(S_i) - H(S_j) \qquad (2)$$

The utilization of $C_{i,j}$ in the HSWO algorithm ensures that each iteration does it best to minimize the overall approximation error. Segmentation results produced by constant value and planar approximation are now examined.

Constant Value Approximation

A portion of a Landsat picture (64x64 pixels) is presented in Fig. 1, together with an enlargement of the lower left area. The first model assumes that constant value regions constitues a representation of this picture. The segment approximation function is therefore

$$r_i(x,y) = u_i \qquad (3)$$

where u_i is the segment mean value. This approximation function is employed for the calculation of $C_{i,j}$. The segmentation results for the constant approximation are shown in Fig. 2. The picture is divided into 100 segments, and an approximation picture is produced by replacing each segment by its mean value.

Planar Approximation

The constant value approximation is seen to be generally appropriate but its limitations are clear. For example, in Fig. 3, a 1-dimensional case is shown where a constant value region is appropriate for regions 1 and 3, while it is inappropriate for region 2. A planar approximation is more suitable:

$$r_i(x,y) = a_i + b_i(x) + c_i(y) \qquad (4)$$

This approximation function is now used in the calculation of $C_{i,j}$ for the segmention of the Landsat picture of Fig. 1 and the results are shown in Fig. 4. Region 4 is an example where a planar approximation is needed.

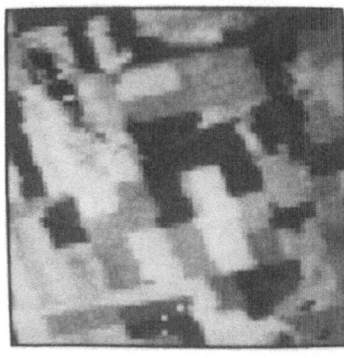
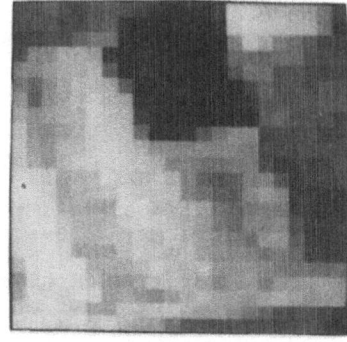

a) the entire picture   b) sub-area

Fig. 1 : Landsat picture.

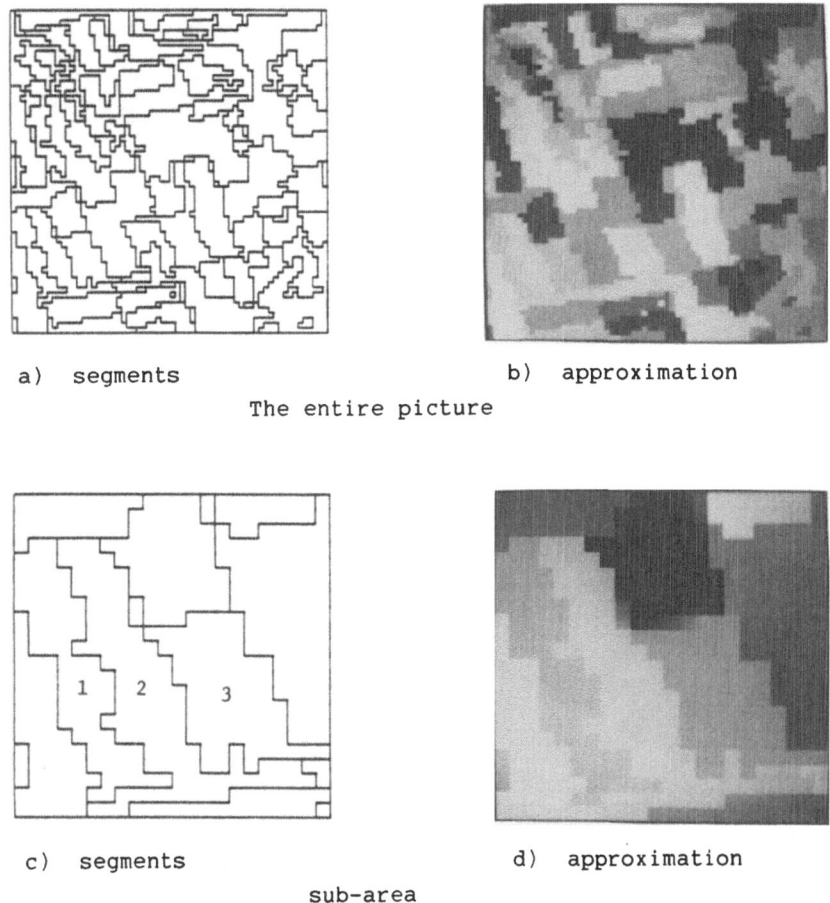

Fig. 2 : Segmentation results for constant approximation.

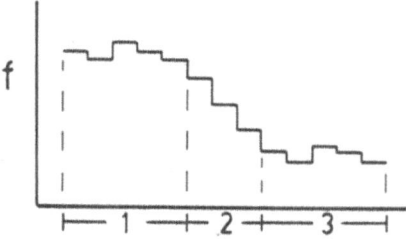

Fig. 3 : An example with constant value and inclined line regions.

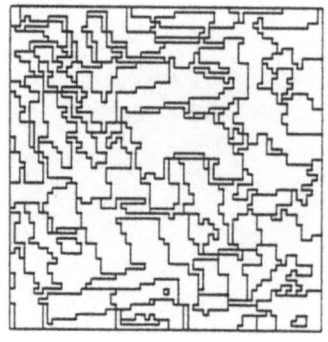
a) segments

b) approximation

The entire picture

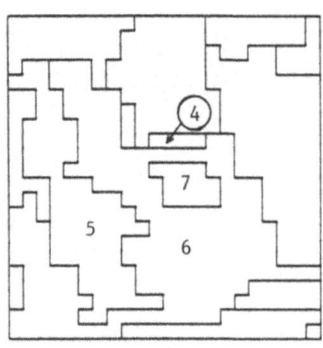
c) segments

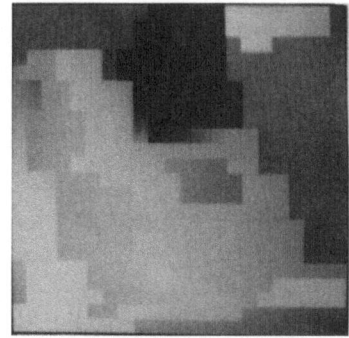
d) approximation

sub-area

Fig. 4 : Segmentation results for planar approximation.

The utilization of a higher degree polynomial however can cause spurious results to arise, as illustrated in Fig. 5. The original signal (a) is composed of two constant value regions which are then corrupted by noise (b). In this case, the true regions would be correctly detected by a constant approximation, (c), while, a first order approximation leads to misleading results, (d). Higher degree polynomials, having more degrees of freedom, attempt to match more closely the noise deformation, thus yielding spurious results. A similar situation is observed by comparing regions 1, 2 and 3 of Fig. 2-c, and regions 5, 6 and 7 of Fig. 4-c. Region 2 resulting from a constant approximation, is divided between regions 5 and 6 in the case of planar approximation. The inclined plane of region 6 represents both the light values of region 2 and the darker values of region 3. The pixels of region 7 do not fit this plane and therefore form a distinct region. The constant approximation results are, therefore, more appropriate for these regions.

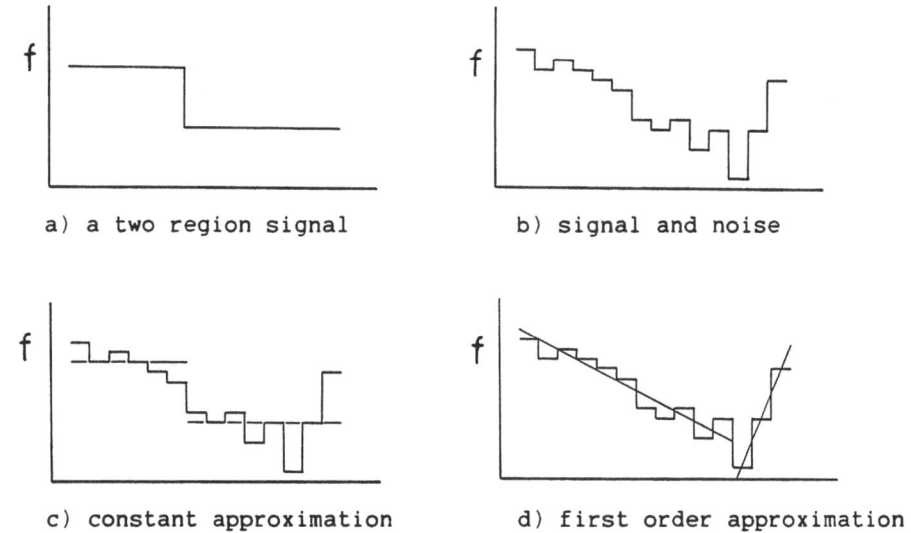

Fig. 5 : A 1-D function composed of two regions (a), with added noise (b), and approximated by constant values (c) and inclined lines (d).

IV - LOCAL VARIANCE

The HSWO algorithms based upon constant or planar approximation attempts to minimize the approximation error. The evaluation of the error for a given pixel does not consider the importance of the gray level variance in the surrounding area. Thus, in Fig. 6, both examples, a and b, have the same criterion value with respect to the regions 1 and 2. It can be advantageous to make the criterion value depend upon the segment variance, and define a new criterion such as:

$$C^*_{i,j} = C_{i,j} / (1 + \sigma_{i,j}) \qquad (5)$$

where $\sigma^2_{i,j}$ is the mean value of the squared approximation error :

$$\sigma^2_{i,j} = (H(S_i) + H(S_j)) / (N_i + N_j) \qquad (6)$$

Here, $H(S_i)$ is, as previously defined, the sum of the squared approximation error for segment S_i, and N_i is its size. For constant approximation, $\sigma^2_{i,j}$ corresponds to the combined variance of both segments. Thus, the criterion $C^*_{i,j}$ is equal to $C_{i,j}$ when $\sigma_{i,j}$ is zero, and decreases for large values of the variance.

The results given by this new criterion are shown in Fig. 7. The regions marked by "X" correspond to a zone of large gray level variation, and thus the utilization of $C^*_{i,j}$ produces smaller criterion values and forces more segment merging in this area. This new criterion seems preferable, as it adjusts itself to local picture variations.

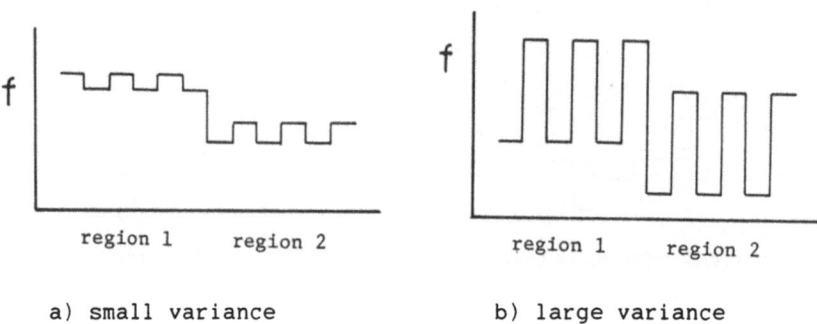

a) small variance   b) large variance

Fig. 6 : Examples of regions with the same criterion values but different variances.

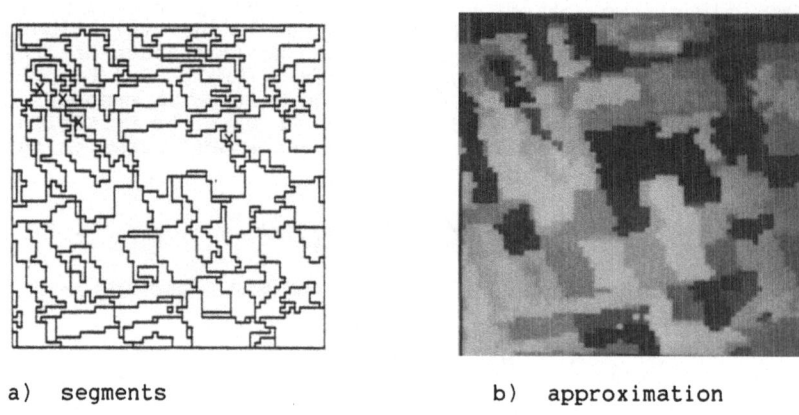

a) segments   b) approximation

The entire picture

Fig. 7 : Segmentation results for the local variance adaptable approximation.

V - SIMILARITY MEASURE COMBINATION

The step-wise optimization algorithm can employ different similarity measures, which correspond to different segment description models. Those previously introduced involve very simple models. However, more complex models can be required for segmentation tasks. Complex measures can be obtained from combinations of simpler ones.

Zobrist and Thompson (1975) point out that human vision employs many cues such as brightness, contour, color, texture and stereopsis to perform perceptual grouping. They stress the limitations of using only one cue at a time for computer grouping, and show the importance of studying mechanisms that combine many cues. For computer simulation of human perception, they derive from each cue a distance function that measures the similarity of two scene parts. Then, they perform a weighted sum of these distances to obtain a global perceptual distance.

Applying this approach to picture segmentation, it can be noted that different picture areas can require different segment models (cues) and that these models must be combined in order to obtain good overall results. Hence, the constant approximation can be appropriate for some parts of a picture while the planar approximation can be preferable for some other parts. Thus, it can be advantageous to combine the similarity measures associated with both models. For example, a composite measure can be obtained as follows:

$$C_{(composite)} = C^*_{(constant)} * C^*_{(planar)} \quad (7)$$

This corresponds to using the geometric mean of the two measures to form the composite one. $C^*_{(.)}$ indicates a local variance adaptive measure as defined in the preceding section.

In picture segmentation, an ordering of segment descriptions can also be considered (Pavlidis 1979). For example, the pixel gray level can be employed to form small homogeneous regions, then more complex descriptors, such as segment contour shape, can be considered for forming larger regions. Many segment descriptors, such as contour shape, or higher order approximation coefficients, are meaningless for small regions and only become useful at a latter stage. In the hierarchical segmentation scheme, this corresponds to using a simple measure for the first merging steps, then, as we get to a higher level in the segment hierarchy, more complex measures, involving more complex segment descriptors, are introduced.

The ordering of segment descriptions and composite measures are now employed to segment the Landsat picture. The constant approximation measure, $C_{i,j}$, is first used to obtain a partition with 1000 segments. Then the previously defined composite measure is employed to continue the segment merging. The results which combine the characteristics of the preceding measures are shown in Fig. 8. For example, in Fig. 8-c, region 8 is represented by an inclined plane as is shown in Fig. 4-c for the planar approximation. While regions 9, 10 and 11 correspond to those obtained by constant value approximation in Fig. 2. Thus, the advantages of planar approximation are exploited, while the previously noted artifacts are avoided. The constant value approximation is still predominant for large constant areas.

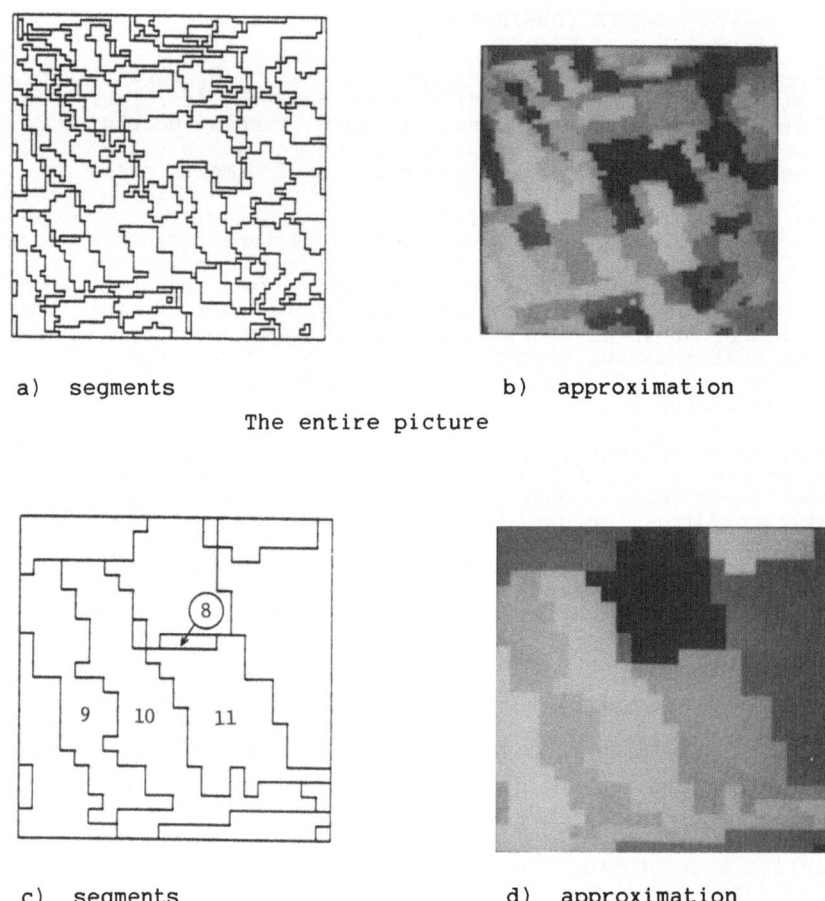

a) segments b) approximation

The entire picture

c) segments d) approximation

sub-area

Fig. 8 : Segmentation results from criterion combination.

REFERENCES

Beaulieu JM, Goldberg M (1982) Hierarchical Picture Segmentation by Approximation. *Canadian Communications and Energy Conference*, Montreal (Canada): 393-396.

Beaulieu JM, Goldberg M (1983) Step-Wise Optimization for Hierarchical Picture Segmentation. *Conf. on Computer Vision and Pattern Recognition*, Washington, D.C.: 59-64.

Brice C, Fennema C (1970) Scene Analysis Using Regions. *Artif. Intell.* 1: 205-226.

Chen PC, Pavlidis T (1980) Image Segmentation as an Estimation Problem. *Comput. Graphics & Image Process.* 12: 153-172.

Freuder EC (1976) Affinity: A Relative Approach to Region Finding. *Comput. Graphics & Image Process.* 5: 254-264.

Horowitz SL, Pavlidis T (1976) Picture Segmentation by a Tree Traversal Algorithm. JACM 23: 368-388.

Pavlidis T (1979) Hierarchies in Structural Pattern Recognition. *Proc.* IEEE 67: 737-744.

Zobrist AL, Thompson WB (1975) Building a Distance Function for Gestalt Grouping. *IEEE Trans. Comput.* C-4: 718-728.

Computer Analysis
of Cardiac Wall Motion Asynchrony

Osman Ratib and Alberto Righetti

Cardiology Center, University Hospital of Geneva, 1211 Geneve 4, Switzerland

ABSTRACT

Digital image processing is emerging as an increasingly important modality in the evolution of different types of image acquisition and analysis in cardiology. It has become an integral element in the technologies that are being developed and explored. New mathematical concepts in the assessement of cardiac function have been applied to digital images of the heart. Among them, the measurement of temporal changes in regional wall motion of the heart using Fourier analysis led to a significant improvement in the detection of regional alterations in ventricular function. Several imaging modalities can benefit from this approach for the assessement of the temporal sequence of cardiac wall motion.

INTRODUCTION

With the recent developpement of digital imaging techniques, dynamic images of the heart motion have become accessible to computer processing and analysis. Several cardiac imaging modalities benefit nowdays from digital recording, particularly the radionuclide angiograms, the contrast cine-angiograms and the echocardiograms. All these images can be converted in digital form and processed by computer analysis programs. Such programs not only allow the extraction of morphological information about the heart structures but also permit a quantitative evaluation of the motion of the different regions of the heart. Digital image processing hardware components are largely similar among different systems. Software can also be broken down into separate algorithms that are image independent. The same methods can be applied to images irrespective of their source (isotope, ultrasoud, radiographic). Before the developpment of computer analysis techniques, the evaluation of dynamic images of the heart could only be done visually by a higly trained cardiologist. A significant improvement in diagnostic accuracy when using dynamic analysis techniques for the evaluation of the heart motion has been well demonstrated. Recent analysis techniques relying on a temporal evaluation of the heart wall motion are significantly more sensitive in detecting cardiac abnormalities than conventional global morphological parameters. Computer techniques offer a more objective and reproducible evaluation. The heart wall motion being a complexe mechanism, conceptual models and mathematical algorithms are needed to adequately analyze the temporal sequence of changes occuring during the heart cycle. We have particularely studied the application of Fourier transformation methods for the evaluation of segmental cardiac motion. The Fourier transform concept is based on the hypothesis that any periodic function can be represented as the sum of cosine and sine waves of different frequencies, each frequency characterized by a specific amplitude and phase. Expressed alternatively, Fourier analysis describes a signal in terms of its frequency content. Because cardiac contraction is generally a regular, reccurent event, it has periodicity and is well suited for the use of temporal Fourier analysis. The displacement of a point within the ventricle through the heart cycle can roughly be approximated with one cosine wave at the fundamental frequency, the heart rate. This cosine wave at the fundamental frequency is referred as the first Fourier harmonic. The first harmonic amplitude is an estimate of the total extent of motion. The phase shift of the first harmonic is a reasonably good approximation of the timing of the oscillation and can be used as a parameter to measure delays in wall motion between different regions of the heart. The changes in the first harmonic phase however does not differentiate between delays in the filling and in the emptying phase of the heart cycle. Higher order harmonics provide more information about the motion profile in the different parts of the cycle but they are more sensitive to artefacts and noise interferences related to each imaging technique (Cramer et al. 1981). The assessement of regional abnormalities in the temporal sequence of wall motion is of great interest for the clinical evaluation of heart diseases. It allows the detection of subtle changes of cardiac function in several types of cardiac disease before any changes in the global cardiac performance could be identified. Computer processing of digitized images not only allows functional parameters to be extracted from a sequence of images but also offers the possibility of displaying the resulting distribution on parametric or functional images representing a topographic map of the changes of the measured parameter in each point of the image. In fact, the advantage of parametric imaging is to enable the eye to easely dectect regional changes in dynamics that are otherwise not readily apparent on visual inspection of the original data.

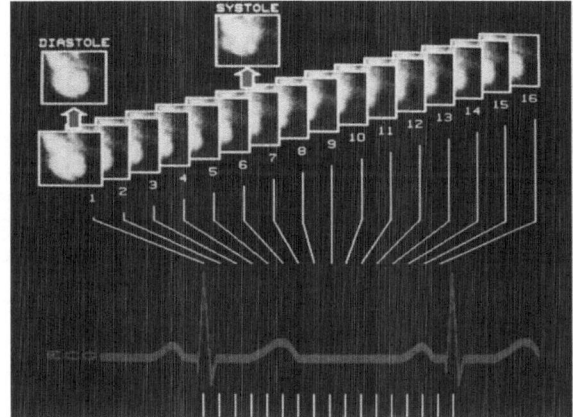

Fig 1 : Recording of a sequence of ECG gated radionuclide angiographic images. The average heart cycle period is divided into 16 intervals and acquisition starts at the begining of each cycle. Successive cycles are added during 3 to 5 minutes in order to obtain an average cycle with satisfactory target to background count ratio.

Temporal Fourier analysis of cardiac motion applied to different imaging modalities:

(1) Radionuclide angiogram was the first imaging modality to benefit from computer processing due to the fact that the dynamic recording of sequential isotopic images of the moving heart could only be performed by computer recording triggered by the electrocardiographic (ECG) signal. Images of the heart cavities obtained after labeling the red blood cells with radioactive Tc-99m are obtained by a gamma scintillation camera connected to a computer. The average time interval of the cardiac cycle obtained fron the ECG is divided by the computer into a fixed number of subintervals. The information acquired from each subinterval of the cardiac cycle is then stored into separate frame in the computer memory. The process is then repeated usually for several hundred cardiac cycles, until sufficiently high count densities per image frame are obtained. The data are then formulated in a multiple frame mode and displayed in a closed loop movie form providing a visual assessment of the chamber dimensions and wall motion.

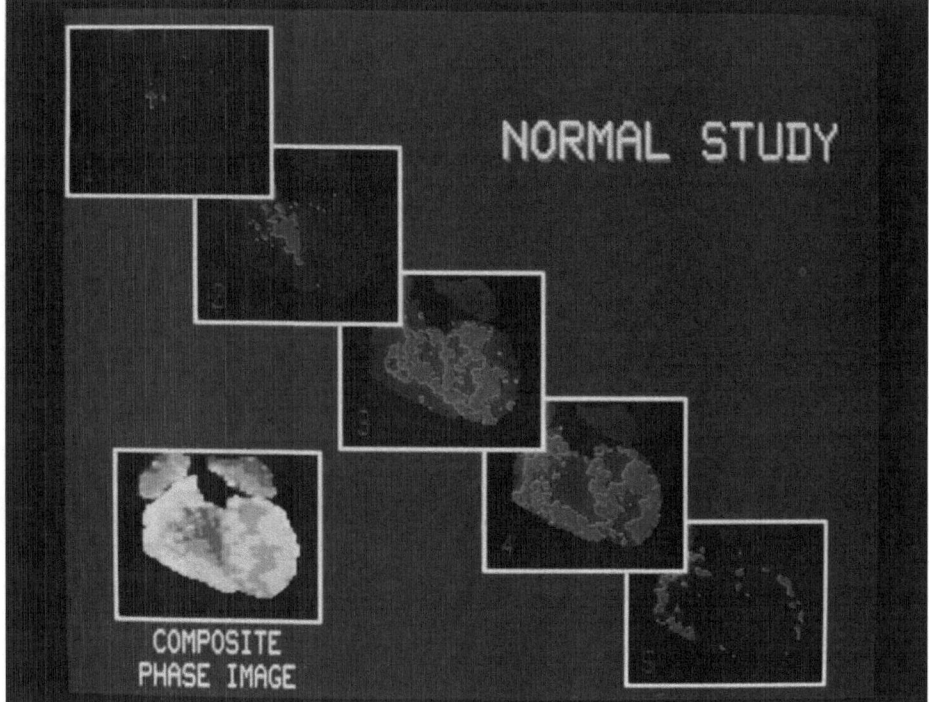

Fig 2 : Successive parametric images showing the temporal sequence of normal regional ventricular wall motion recorded by radionuclide angiography. Motion starts close to the septal area between right and left vetricle and spreads symetrically towards the two ventricles. A composit phase image in the lower left corner shows in shades of gray the same temporal sequence of wall motion; yellow regions being regions wich move later during the cardiac cycle than the dark red regions.

The counts present in any point of a given frame, after background substraction are proportional to the volume contained in that ponctual region of the heart chambers. For each pixel in the images a time activity curve can be extracted and Fourier analysis is applied to calculate the phase and amplitude of the first harmonic. These two parameters being calculated in each point are then displayed in color coded parametric images showing the topographic distribution of the temporal sequence (phase) and amplitude of wall motion of the different parts of the heart (Adam et al. 1979).

Many clinical studies performed in our institution and in many other centers have well demonstrated the usefulness of this new quantitative approach for the evaluation of cardiac wall motion abnor- malities. This technique depicts not only delays due to electrical conduction abnormalities but also regional asynchrony due to mechanical distur- bances. In coronary artery disease for example this method was found to be more sensitive than conventional criteria for the detection of ischemia induced abnormalities during exercise (Ratib et al. 1982).

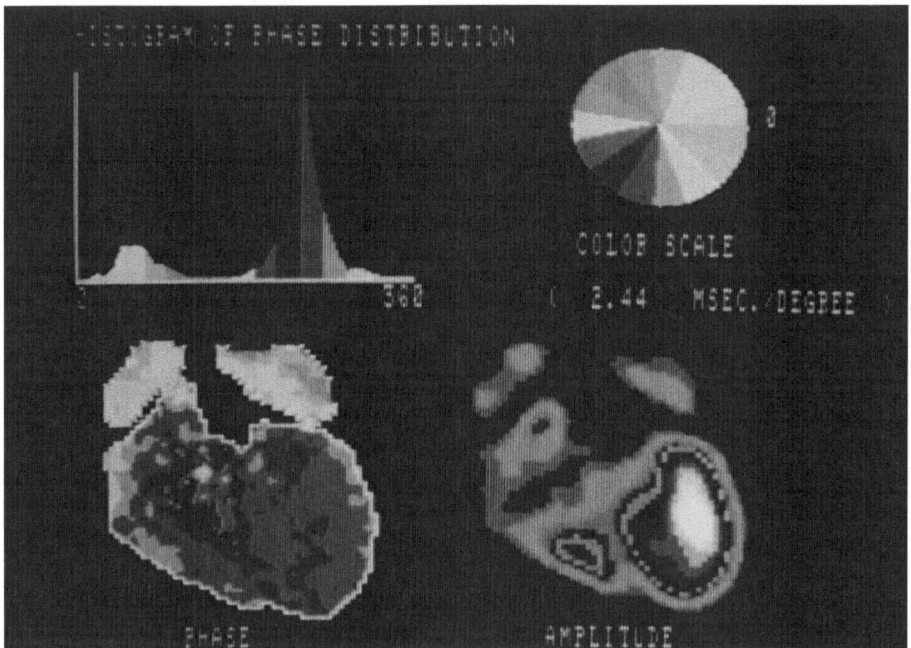

Fig 3 : Phase analysis results from a normal patient. The phase image shows the topographic distribution of temporal sequence of wall motion in each picture element. Areas with early phase are in purple and red and areas moving last are in yellow. The histogram of phase distribution shows two peaks, an initial small peak corresponding to the atrial phases (blue) and a second sharp peak corresponding to the ventricular phases (red and yellow). The histogram is colored using the same color scale as for the phase image. The narrow ventricular peak in this example indicates a normal synchronous ventricular wall motion. The amplitude image depicts the amplitude of count changes in each picture element.

(2) **X ray cineangiograms** consist of radiological images recorded on film after injection of radioopaque contrast medium into the blood ciculation to visualize the different chambers of the heart. The recent developpement of digital imaging techniques offers an alternative to film as the primary recording medium for radiography, and digital image processing methods can be applied. This type of images has a much better spatial resolution than radionuclide angiograms but due to inhomogeneity of dilution of the contrast medium with the blood, changes in image density in each point of the cardiac cavities is not always directly proportional to changes in blood volume. Such inhomogeneity is particularly evident in images obtained by conventional injection of contrast medium directly into the heart cavities.

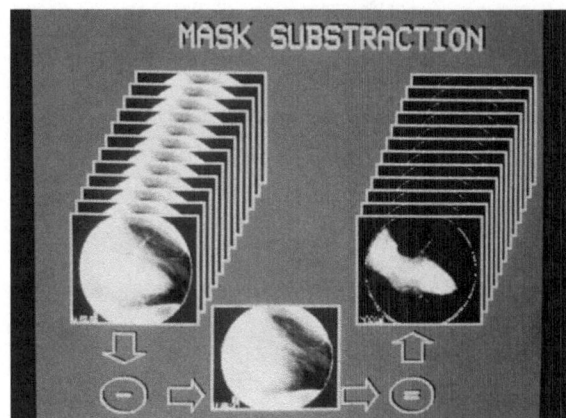

Fig 4 : Mask substraction technique applied to digitized cineangiographic images obtained by intravenous injection of contrast medium: A single mask image obtained prior to the injection of the contrast medium is substracted from successive images representative of a single heart cycle.

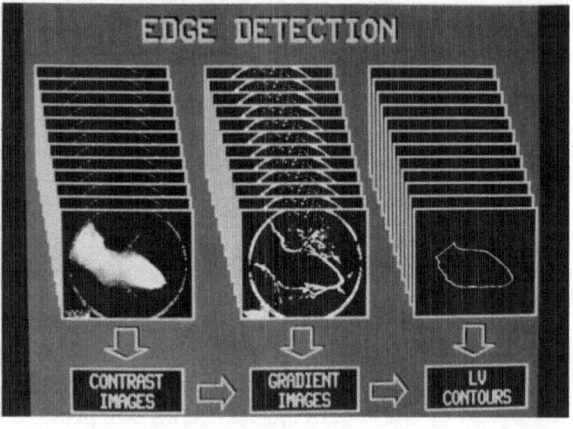

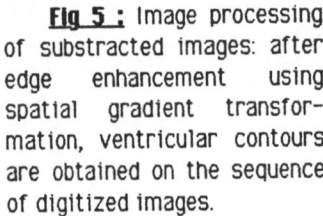

Fig 5 : Image processing of substracted images: after edge enhancement using spatial gradient transformation, ventricular contours are obtained on the sequence of digitized images.

With digital image enhancement methods it is however possible to obtain satisfactory images of the heart cavities by intravenous injection of contrast medium.

In this case the contrast material is more homogenousely mixed to the blood when it reaches the heart and changes in image density is directly related to changes in blood volume (Widmann et al. 1983). To avoid the artefacts due to inhomogeneity of contrast medium dilution we have developped and applied a Fourier analysis technique of ventricular wall motion based on a radial evaluation of the ventricular wall displacement along 180 radii drawn from the center of mass of the ventricle over 360 degrees (Ratib et al. 1982). This technique can therefore be applied to images obtained either by conventional intraventricular injection or by intravenous injection of contrast medium. Quantitative information about the timing of motion of the different segments of the ventricle are computed and displayed on parametric color coded images. Functional parameters can be extracted from the parametric images in order to assess quantitatively heart function and dynamics. Furthermore, the promise of functional or parametric imaging is to enable the eye to dectect subtle changes in dynamics that are otherwise not readily apparent on inspection of the original data.

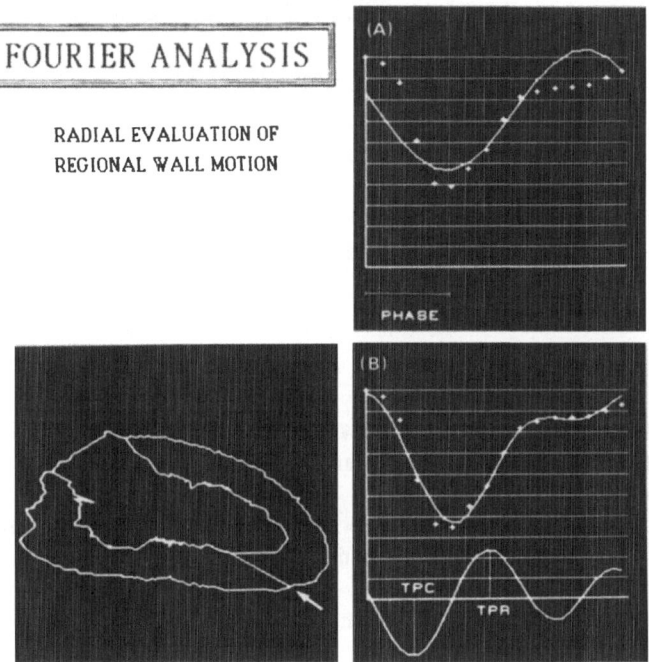

Fig 6: Fourier analysis of ventricular wall motion along one single radius (arrow).
A)- First harmonic of the Fourier transform (solid curve) of a selected radial motion curve (dotted curve). This sinusoidal curve gives a simple approximation of the timing of motion but does not differentiate between contraction and relaxation.

B)- The solid curve is obtained from the two first harmonics the Fourier transformation of the same segmental motion curve (dots). The first derivative of this curve is also plotted and represents the rate of changes in length. The maximum rate of emptying and maximum rate of filling are depicted and referred to as TPC and TPR standing for time of peak contraction and time of peak relaxation.

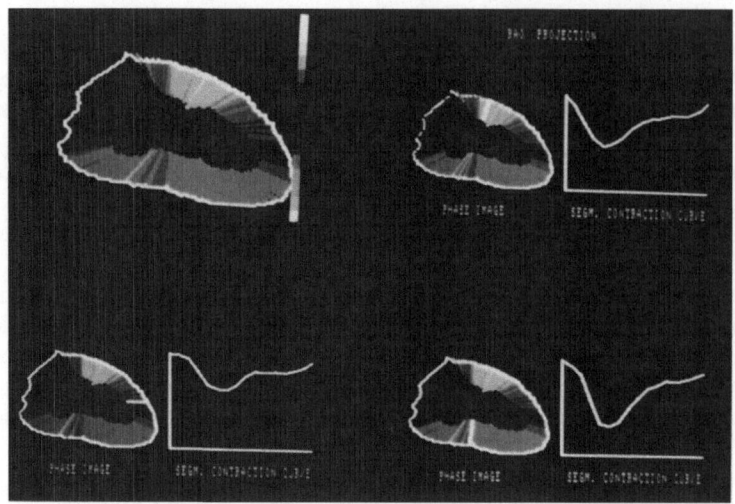

Fig 7:

Parametric phase image obtained by Fourier analysis of digitized cineangiogram in a subject with normal ventricular wall motion. The temporal sequence of wall motion is displayed in a predefined color scale. Bright areas are segments which move first while darker regions move later during the cardiac cycle. Radial motion curves of three selected segments are displayed.

(3) **Ultrasound two dimensional echocardiogram** with its comprehensive display of left ventricular cavity, size, shape, and wall motion was a logical candidate for the application of computer techniques. Some difficulties and limitations surrounding computer interpretation of ultrasound data must however be considered. The mechanism underlying image degradation must be clearly understood before algorithms can be developped to reverse them. Grayscale manipulation, smoothing, and integration of information from several heart beats are methods which have been borrowed from other imaging systems and applied to echocardiographic images. Two distinct problems exist with this technique: the location of a pictorial boundary on the image, and the determination of the relation of this pictorial boundary to an anatomic one. Early techniques required the manual outlining by an operator of cardiac chamber surfaces for subsequent computer measurement, but more recent method employ automated methods of boundary recognition which are more or less reliable depending on the underlying image quality and image acquisition performance.

However when cardiac chambers are easely outlined, a Fourier analysis technique of ventricular wall motion can be applied offering the same advantages described for angiographic images.

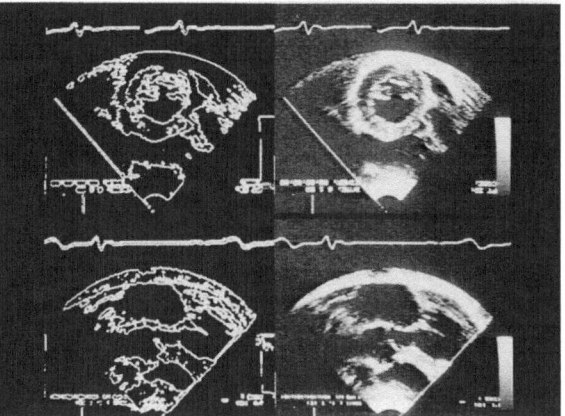

Fig 8 : Ultrasound echographic images of the heart before (left) and after (right) edge enhancement using a gradient transformation.

REFERENCES

Adam WE, Tarkowska A, Bitter F, Strauch M, Geffers H (1979): Equilibrium gated radionuclide ventriculography. Cardiovasc. Radiol 2:161-173.

Cramer JA, Ehrhardt JC, Collins SM (1981): Second Harmonic analysis in the assessement of ventricular contraction patterns from radionuclide images. IEEE Engineering in Med. and Biol. Society, Houston, pp.97-101.

Ratib O, Henze E, Schon H, Schelbert HR (1982): Phase analysis of radionuclide angiograms for detection of coronary artery disease. Am. Heart. J. 104:1-9.

Ratib O, Righetti A, Brandon G (1982): A new method for the temporal evaluation of ventricular wall motion from digitized ventriculography. Comp. in Card. Seattle:409-413.

Widmann T, Tubau J, Ashburn W, Bhargava C, Higgins C, Peterson K (1983): Evaluation of regional wall motion by phase analysis of intravenous contrast fluorangiography. Int. Symp. on Ventricular Wall Motion, ed. Thieme Verlag: 24-33.

Multi-Robot Assembly of IC's

C. Michaud, A.S. Malowany and M.D. Levine

Computer Vision and Robotics Laboratory, Department of Electrical Engineering, McGill University, 805 Sherbrooke Street West, Montréal, Quebec, H3A 2K6, Canada

ABSTRACT

This paper presents a multi-robot system which assembles integrated circuits. The problems addressed are the calibration of the robotic station, the control of several robots working concurrently, and pattern recognition. These problems are discussed in the context of a distributed system.

The use of image processing is omnipresent. For instance, vision feedback is used to acknowledge almost every move of the robots and also to calibrate the camera itself. Pattern recognition techniques are employed to detect the exact orientation of an IC die.

Several robots are used in order to give more flexibility to the system and allow us to acquire experience which could lead toward a multirobot multitasking system.

KEYWORDS: Multirobot, Flexible Manufacturing Systems, Integrated Circuit assembly, Pattern Recognition, Vision Feedback, Error Recovery

INTRODUCTION

Until recently, few attempts have been made to create multirobot cooperative systems which have practical application in industry. The designers of such systems have to take into account factors such as ease of programming, task parallelism, error recovery, collision avoidance and so on. F.Ruoff (1980) has proposed such a system but every robot must be programmable with the same programming language. Unfortunately, industrial robots usually come with their own programming language and generally, robot vendors offer little support to those who want to implement their own language. As a result, few customers implement their own language because it is expensive, takes a lot of time, and incurres risk of damaging the robot. Here, we will discuss the implementation of a flexible IC assembly station, which deals with some of these problems. The proposed station does not require any special robot programming language. Paler et al. (Paler 1983) have already implemented a system that assembles IC's. However, they used one robot, which involved a single task. Therefore, they were not concerned about synchronization between robots. Here, the assembly of IC's is used as a means to work in a multi-robot environment. This paper is divided in five sections. First, a description of the robotic environment is given, which is followed by a functional description of the tasks to be done. Thereafter, the important features of the system are discussed. This includes the start-up procedure, task synchronization and vision feedback.We conclude with some ways to improve the system.

The start-up procedure discusses efficient ways to model the environment and to calibrate the cameras. The modeling is based on *basic guiding* (Lozano-Perez 1983) and the camera calibration is done by inferring the position of the camera and correcting its position by evaluating a proper correction offset. This technique has been described by Mansouri (Mansouri 1985).

Task synchronization is done by means of message passing (1976)(1978) (Gauthier 1985). Processes are synchronized with each other by means of a ''*rendez-vous*'' scheme. The vision feedback will mostly be used for locating the position and the orientation of objects. It requires the use of template matching and the local features method(1982). Finally, the implementation of forward recovery techniques(1981) and a simple scheme for collision avoidance based on the method of Freund and Hoyer(1984) are intended.

DESCRIPTION OF THE ROBOTIC ENVIRONMENT

The McGill University Computer Vision and Robotics Laboratory is based on three VAX minicomputers and a wide variety of peripheral equipment for research. A VAX 11/780 running VAX/VMS and Eunice, a Unix emulator, is linked with two VAX 11/750 minicomputers running UNIX 4.2BSD, by the Ethernet local area network. The VAX 11/780 is used for the AI oriented programs which control the overall station. The two VAX 11/750s are used for the robots, the control of peripheral equipment and the vision processing. A Matrox frame grabber system which can handle up to 4 different video inputs, is linked to the vision VAX 11/750. The system is configured as a distributed system shown in Fig.1.

There are two robots available in the laboratory: A PUMA 260 from Unimation and a ECUREUIL from Microbo. Each robot has its own command language, VAL for the PUMA 260 and IRL for the ECUREUIL. Fortunately, software packages have been written in the C programming

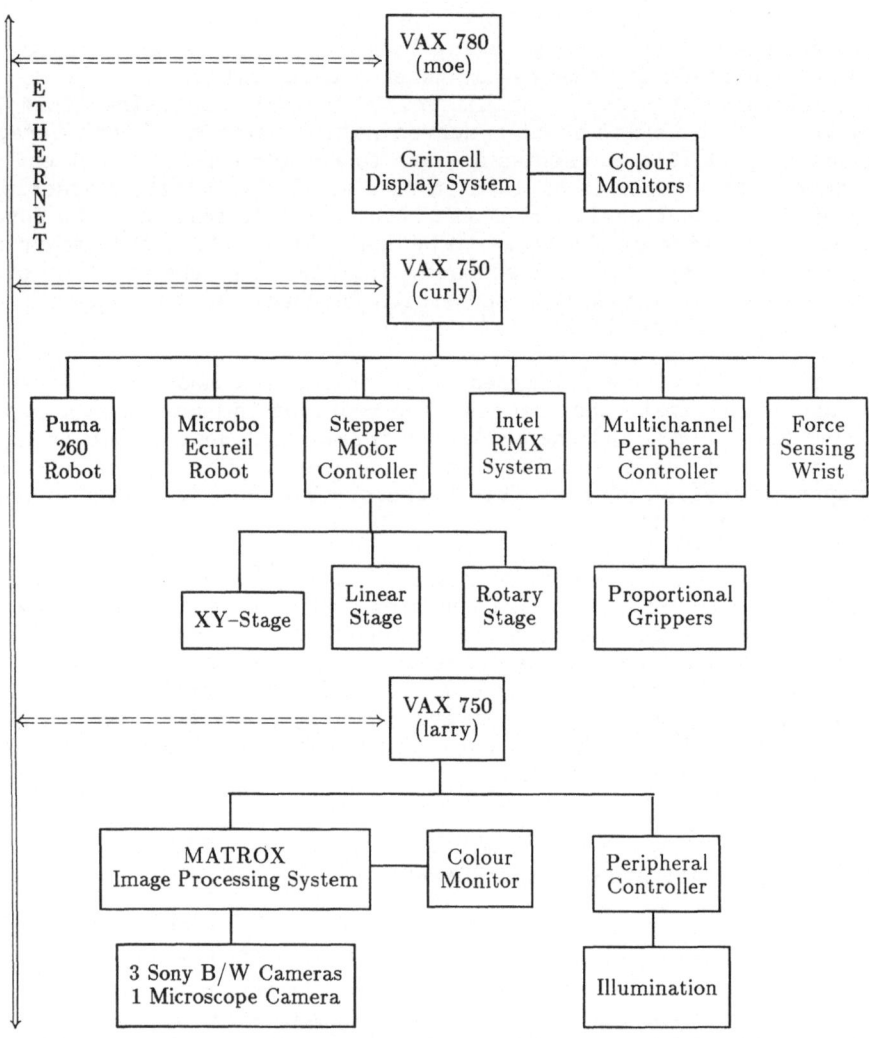

Figure 1: The CVaRL research environment

language to emulate these two robot languages. Basically, these programs convey commands as remote terminals to the robots by way of RS-232 links. This greatly simplifies the control of the robots by allowing them to be accessed by a single program. The main advantage is that no special language is required to use both robots at their full capabilities. This saves a great deal of time at the implementation level and seems to be one of the easiest ways to use several robots efficiently. However, the user is limited by the power of the emulation package available as well as the vendor's programming language. For instance, the ECUREUIL's controller offers an easy way to do concurrent processing because every time a command is received, the ECUREUIL's controller returns an acknowledgement immediately, which is not the case for the PUMA's controller, as shown in Fig.2.

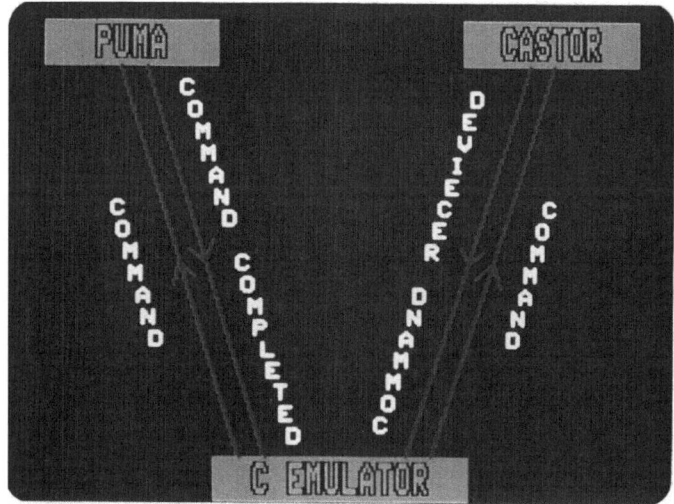

Figure 2:   Difference of behavior between the two robot controllers.

It is also possible to change the robot trajectory while it is moving by sending a new trajectory command before the previous one is completed. On the other hand, the IRL command language does not have any facilities for making the robot move along a straight line. The only available motion is joint interpolated.

A variety of automatically interchangeable end effectors have been built to work with the PUMA 260 robot. They will soon be available for the ECUREUIL robot as well. Meanwhile, a specialized multitool has been built for the Microbo. These exchangeable tooling facilities provide great flexibility to the present robotic station. The robots can perform a wide range of complex tasks without any human intervention. The special gripper and some of the tools are shown in Fig.3 and Fig.4.

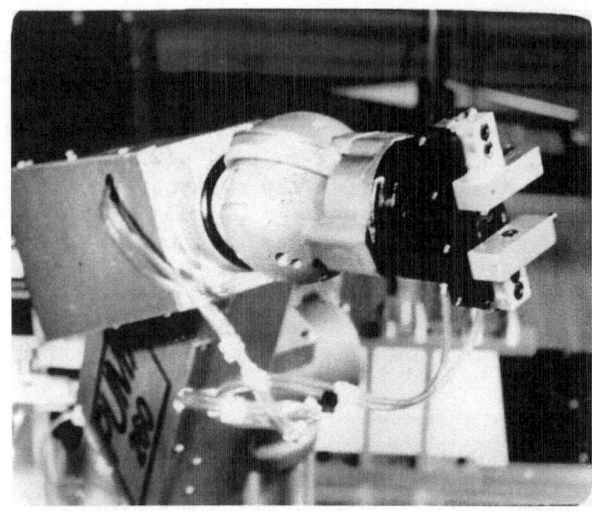

Figure 3: A Puma 260 robot equipped with a special gripper to allow it to perform with a wide variety of tools

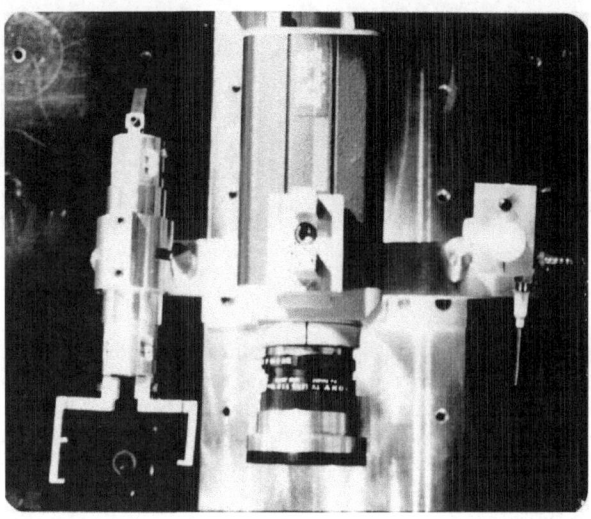

Figure 4: Some interchangeable end effectors available in the laboratory. From left to right; a hybrid circuit gripper, a camera and the special tool required for the microbo, which is not interchangeable.

In addition, a set of high resolution CCD cameras and a 50x microscope, with remote focus and zoom, are available for the vision task. Also, an XY stage can achieve extremely fine positioning under the microscope. Finally, several kinds of feeders have been built to fulfill the different needs of the laboratory.

The minimum set-up requirements for the present project includes:

- Two robots to perform the assembly task.
- IC feeder.
- Dice array carrier to hold the dice array for assembly.
- Fixture for holding the dice array during the operation.
- Vacuum end effector to pick up the 40 pin IC dice carrier.
- Vacuum end effector to pick up a 3mm x 3mm die.
- Syringe to dispense the soldering paste on the IC dice carrier.
- End effector to pick up the dice array.
- Set of CCD cameras and a microscope with a frame grabber system.
- XY stage.

The Matrox frame grabber generates images of 512 x 512 pixels with 128 grey levels. However, only 256 x 256 pixels of resolution and 64 grey levels are used. This has been chosen for two reasons. First, it greatly reduces the amount of processing required per image which speeds up the processing time by several orders of magnitude. Second, knowing that the welding pads are $\approx$ 10 pixels square when full magnification is used, this 256 x 256 image resolution allows locating their centers with a possible precision of 10 percent, which is acceptable. Because of its higher repeatability, the ECUREUIL robot is used to handle the dice. Its repeatability is about +/- 10 microns. The repeatability of the PUMA 260 is only 40 microns, so it is used for the less demanding tasks. The XY stage used for positioning under the microscope has an accuracy of 5 microns.

The multi-tool used by the ECUREUIL robot consists of a small vacuum tube that can accurately take a die and a syringe that is used to put the solder paste on the IC dice carrier. Presently, this microbo tool is not yet automatically interchangeable, which constrains the use of the ECUREUIL to these two tasks only. On the other hand, the PUMA 260 uses two interchangeable tools. The first one is a vacuum tube built to pick up 40 pin IC dice carrier. The second tool consists of two fingers for picking up a dice array by holding it by the border.

FUNCTIONAL DESCRIPTION

The overall process consists of putting dice on a IC dice carrier on which solder paste has been applied. This will be done in several steps involving many concurrent operations. Consequently, the functional description stresses on this.

The operation begins with the calibration of the station. Then, the PUMA 260 robot takes a dice carrier and puts it on the XY stage. Meanwhile, the ECUREUIL robot has moved close to the microscope and is ready to put on the paste. As soon as the PUMA 260 has finished its move, it goes to get the dice array and puts it in the fixture close to the ECUREUIL robot while the latter is putting on the paste. Then, the ECUREUIL goes to take a die and puts it on the XY stage. Thereafter, the XY stage moves the die under the microscope. When it is in position, a picture of the die is taken and the XY stage moves immediately back to where it was and the vision VAX 11/750 computes the exact position of the center of the die. When the result is known and the XY stage is in position, the ECUREUIL picks up the die at the center and moves it over the dice carrier. By that time, the orientation of the die is known, which enables the ECUREUIL to put it in place. Meanwhile, the PUMA 260 has replaced the dice array by the next required kind of dice. This interleaved sequence is shown in Fig.5.

The reader may have noticed that sometimes during the process one robot is idle, doing nothing! Our goal would be to make the robotic station work with an efficiency close to 100%. This problem has not been fully resolved. A great deal of research and experimentation are in progress involving image processing algorithms, networking and operating systems.

START-UP

We feel that the station start-up procedure is very important. In order to do this nicely, special routines have been written to ease the world modeling and the calibration of the camera. The world modeling of the station is done by basic guiding, which means that one can teach the desired position using the robot teach pendant. Both robots can be used for the modeling of the environment. The routines written allow the user to modify part or all of the environment in the database. When a modification is done or a new element is introduced, the database is immediately updated. Furthermore, a graphic routines package will be added to help the user during the modeling. It will guide the user by displaying the suggested séquence of points for teaching any particular object in the robotic station. For instance, if someone wants to teach the position and orientation of an object X, the routines will display the particular robot to be used for the teaching of this particular object and the object itself.

The camera calibration is done automatically. The only requirement is that the robot program must know the approximate location of the

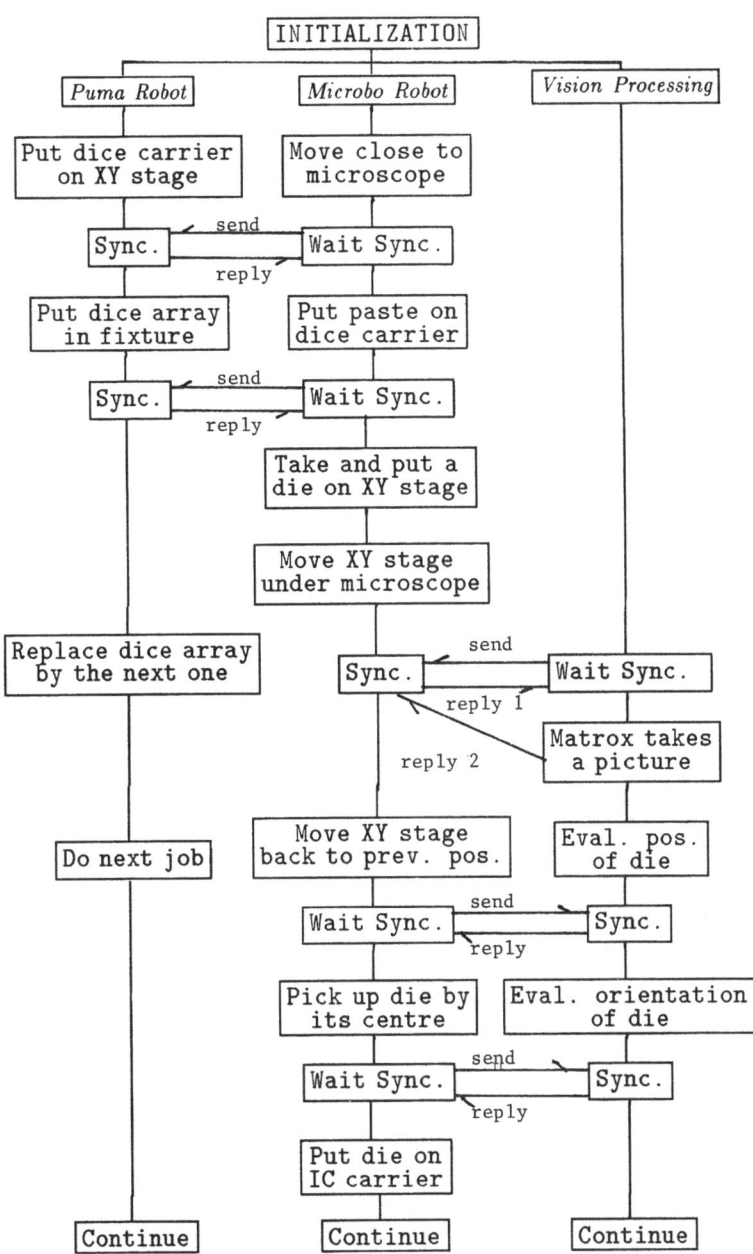

Figure 5: Process flow chart

camera. This can be provided during the basic guiding. During the
camera calibration process, the robot is brought under the camera and
the equations relating the camera and the robot coordinate systems
are evaluated.

The calibration of the XY stage is also done automatically with the
use of the camera. It is done by precisely locating the position of a
marker on the XY stage.

TASK SYNCHRONIZATION

Anyone working in a distributed environment must deal with the synchronization of tasks running in parallel on different computers.
This is being done by way of message passing. Every time a process has
to be synchronized with another, one of the processes acts as message
sender and the other one as message receiver. When the sender process
has
reached its synchronization point, it sends a message to the other
process. It will not go further until a proper acknowledgement message is sent back. In the case of the receiver process, it will run
until it reaches the ''rendez-vous'' point where it expects a message, see Fig.6. If there is no message, it waits for the message unless a watchdog procedure stops it. In this latter case, a recovery
procedure is fired. Otherwise, it reads the message and sends an acknowledgement.

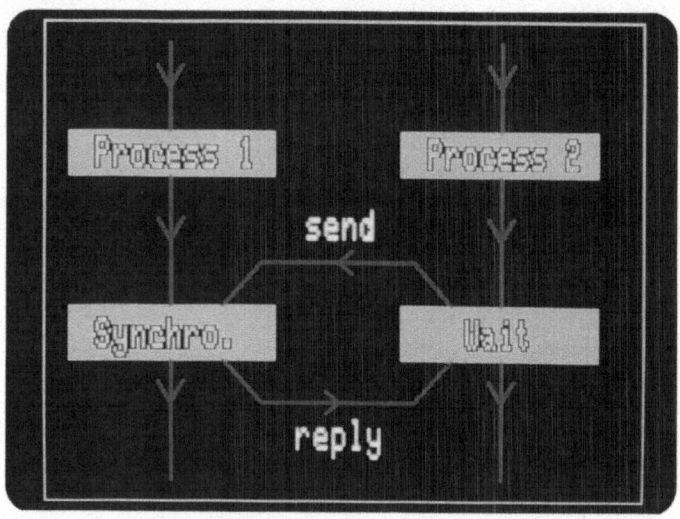

Figure 6: Process synchronization

Every process involving direct object movement runs on the same VAX 11/750. This was done because if a sensor detects a possible collision, it can stop the robots immediately with a minimum of delay.

Figure 7: Result of a contour follower on a thresholded picture of a die magnification 50x.

VISION FEEDBACK

Extensive use of vision feedback is made starting with the calibration of the station until the termination of a working session. Every time the robots move objects, vision feedback is used to detect any malfunctioning. However, most of the vision processing will be used for the detection of the position and orientation of the IC dice.

It is very important to detect the position of the die accurately. We propose to do it in two steps. First, an approximative evaluation of the position of the die is done. Then, using this knowledge, the program tries to match known local features from a database to the present object. When this is done, the knowledge of the exact position of these features can be used to obtain the precise position of the die.

The finding of the approximate position is done as follows. First, a predefined grey level threshold is applied to the picture of the dice. Then, thinned edges are obtained by running a contour tracing program which stores the contours in chain codes, see Fig.7. The chain codes are noise filtered by applying a filter that retains only the relatively long straight edges. Thereafter, the shape of the desired dice is fitted to the exterior of the residual edges. The quality of the fitting is critical.

The detection of the orientation is done using local feature extraction. In order to do so, the program uses the database containing available features of the dice and their relative positions. Since these features can be matched within a few passes and involve only small part of the picture, the process can be very fast. Having accurately located the IC die, other operations would be possible. For example, getting the position of the welding pad.

SYSTEM RELIABILITY

In order to improve the reliability of the system, forward recovery will be extensively applied. Forward recovery implies that every time an error is detected, the program tries to recover without having to restart from a predetermined previous position. It also does not require knowledge of the state of the program before it failed.

In addition, the implementation of a collision avoidance program is being attempted. However, since the topic of collision avoidance is still under active research, we have decided to apply Freund and Hoyer's approach(1984). He considered the problem in the XY plane where all the robots are described an translational and rotational joints. It turns out that most robots can be described that way. This approach, based on decision rules and tables, leads toward a relatively simple algorithm to plan the robot's trajectory. This method is much more efficient than freezing one robot when another is in the common working area, and will significantly increase the performance of the system by eliminating most of the robot's waiting.

CONCLUSION

This system will provide us with some first hand experience with multiple robots. It will be used as a basis for implementing a multi-robot multitasking system for repairing IC and hybrid circuits. In the future, other repair and assembly tasks with concurrency will be added. This will ensure a better percentage of robot use and will provide much flexibility to the user.

The required tooling and programming development for the assembly of hybrid circuits and IC dies are presently in progress.

ACKNOWLEDGEMENTS

The financial support of NSERC and FCAC are gratefully acknowledged. Martin Levine would like to acknowledge the support of the Canadian Institute for Advanced Research.

REFERENCES

Anderson T. & Lee D.A., *Fault Tolerant Principle and Practice*, Prentice Hall International

Bolles C.Robert and Cain A.Ronald (1982) Recognizing and Locating Partially Visible Objects:The Local-Features-Focus Method. Int. Journal of Robotics Research, Vol 1,(3)

Freund E. and Hoyer H. (1984) Collision Avoidance for Industrial Robots with Arbitrary Motion. Journal of Robotics System, Vol. 1(4)

Gauthier D., Carayannis G., Freedman P., Malowany A.S. (1985) A Session Layer Design for the CVaRL Local Area Network. Technical Report Tr-85-7R, Computer Vision And Robotic Lab., Dept. of Elec. Eng. McGill University

Hoare C.A.R. (1978) Communicating Sequential Processes, CACM, Vol 21

Lozano-Perez T. (1983) Robot Programming. Proceeding of IEEE, Vol 71(7)

Manning and Peebles (1976) A Homogeneous Network for Data-Sharing Communications. Computer Networks, Vol 1, (2)

Mansouri A.R. and Malowany A.S. (1985) Using Vision Feedback in Printed Circuit Board Assembly. Proc. of IEEE Microprocessors Forum Atlantic City,NJ

Paler K. et al. (1983) Automatic Packaging of Integrated Circuits, Proc. of RoViSec 3. SPIE Vol 449, Cambridge Massachusetts

Ruoff F. (1980) Multitasking Robot System, Industrial Robot

A Computerized System for Spot Detection and Analysis of Two-Dimensional Electrophoresis Images

R. Appel[1], M. Funk[1], C. Pellegrini[1], D. Hochstrasser[2] and A.F. Müller[2]

[1] Centre Universitaire d'informatique, 24, rue du Général-Dufour, 1211 Geneva 4, Switzerland
[2] Hôpital Cantonal Universitaire, 1211 Geneva 4, Switzerland

INTRODUCTION

Objectives

The 2-dimensional electrophoresis technique is very powerful to separate complex mixtures of proteins. It is estimated that it is possible to separate 19,000 proteins on a single gel (O'Farrel 1975; Anderson 1977). Because of this large number, the only practical solution for using 2-dimensional electrophoresis is through a computerized system. The main tasks of the system are :

- image digitization,
- noise reduction or elimination,
- spot detection or separation,
- normalization and standardization.

Programs have been developed at the University of Geneva which constitute the first part of a large project called MELANIE (Medical ELectrophoresis ANalysis Interactive Expert-system). These programs are intended for image processing and medical diagnosis and are based on Artificial Intelligence methods. This research project is multidisciplinary and involves groups of researchers in medicine and in computer science (at the University of Geneva), in biochemistry (at the Federal Polytechnic Institute in Zürich) and in computer science (at NIH-Bethesda, Maryland, USA). The wide range of activities in this domain, in particular the work of Harrington et al. (1984) and of Wiederkehr and Vonderschmitt (1985), confirms the present interest in adapting the 2-dimensional electrophoresis technique to a clinical environment and of developing a new diagnostic tool.

This paper describes only the image-processing section of MELANIE.

Main Difficulties in the Processing of Two-dimensional Electrophoresis Images

The aim of processing 2-dimensional electrophoresis images is the detection of spots and their characterization by their coordinates and the density of protein they contain.

The biochemical technique of electrophoresis produces images that are not of high quality and which contain a lot of noise. This noise is of three types :

- background noise,
- horizontal and vertical streaks,
- "noise" superimposed on spots.

On the one hand, the image-processing program must compensate for these noises and, on the other hand, must have the following qualities in order to be used in an operational environment :

(a) display of all the significant spots,
(b) fast processing,
(c) portability.

TWO EXISTING SYSTEMS

In the field of computerized spot detection in electrophoresis images, one can cite two important works : TYCHO (Coultec 1981) and ELSIE (Miller 1982).

TYCHO

The TYCHO system runs on a PDP-11/60 using an AP-120B array processor. The purpose of the system is :

- background subtraction,
- spot detection,
- Gaussian spot modelling, pattern matching and comparison.

TYCHO is based on a Gaussian model of the spots. This method has many good qualities, but it is not adapted to our needs; also the execution time is too long and the qualitative aspect of the original image is not preserved.

The general approach adapted for eliminating the background noise and the streaks is to find the minimum element in some selected region surrounding each image pixel. The regions are vertical and horizontal line segments, which are used to scan the image in x and y directions. This method allows background noise and streaks to be removed. Unfortunately, despite the use of an array processor, the CPU time necessary to process an image is much too long to be used for an interactive system such as MELANIE. For this reason, only the general method of background and streaks subtraction was retained, but this is implemented in MELANIE in another form.

ELSIE

The ELSIE system, developed by M. Miller on a VAX-11/750, is a sophisticated and complex set of programs, which perform a large number of operations on 2-dimensional electrophoresis images. Among them we can mention :

- spot detection,
- density measurements,
- image comparison.

The algorithm used to detect the spots is based on the principle that a point p belongs to a spot if the following condition is satisfied :

$$J(P) = \sum_{P} F(x,y) * G(x,y) < S$$

where : F is a second degree function of two variables;
G is the discrete function describing the image;
P is a square region centered on the point p;
S < 0 is a predefined limit.

ELSIE offers the user a very powerful tool for detection and comparison of spots. However, it has some inconvenient properties :

- the total number of operations is too large,
- small spots are not always detected,
- the use of a third-degree function to approximate the background noise introduces some imperfections (bad limit conditions, lack of precision to approximate small differences, etc.).

MELANIX - THE IMAGE PROCESSING PART OF MELANIE

Introduction

Collaborating with Dr. Miller's group allowed us to benefit from previous work done in the processing of 2-dimensional electrophoresis images. We have based our developments on the existing ELSIE system, but we have implemented new algorithms for noise subtraction and for spot detection. Moreover, we have augmented the range of image display options by adding to the common 2D pictures in grey levels or in false colors, a pseudo-3D representation, for which the user can interactively define or modify the parameters (see Fig. 3 and following figures).

MELANIX

MELANIX is the image-processing subsystem of MELANIE, and it executes the following sequence of operations :

- background and streak subtraction,
- elimination of the high frequency noise,
- detection and separation of the spots,
- computation of the surface of spots and of protein density.

In addition to this basic set of operations, MELANIX offers the user various display options : grey levels, pseudo-colors, 2D representations and pseudo-3D representations (see illustrations). To produce the pseudo-3D representation, and in order to emphasize the details without loosing the global view of the image, we consider the 2-dimensional gel as a projection of a three-dimensional picture with the values of the pixels representing the third dimension.

An algorithm to remove the hidden lines gives the picture a better quality and makes the small spots easier to visualize and to detect.

Below are the detailed descriptions of the four phases of image-processing.

Background and Streak Subtraction

The basic idea used in the TYCHO system for background and streak subtraction is improved in MELANIX to give better results and run faster.

The method consists of the following steps:

1) Determining a horizontal segment of n pixels length centered on a given pixel $p(i,j)$.

2) The minimum value over the segment is placed in a matrix at the position (i,j).

3) Steps 1 and 2 are repeated for every pixel of the gel.

At the end of the process we have a matrix of the same resolution as the image. In order to avoid fuzziness at the edges of the streaks, we determine the maximum values over the matrix using the same method as explained above. Finally, the matrix represents the value of the background noise and the horizontal streaks. We subtract this matrix from the image.

The same process is performed vertically. Figures 3 to 5 illustrate the different steps of this process.

In order to reduce the CPU time necessary to execute the algorithms of background and streak subtraction, the points of the overlapping segment are organized in a binary-tree. This structure allows a very fast determination of the minimum (or maximum) value. When the segment is shifted to the adjacent pixel (vertically or horizontally), the extraction of the outgoing pixel and the insertion of the incoming one is easily achieved. A great amount of time can be saved using this method.

An option in the system allows the user to eliminate the background noise without suppressing the streaks. This is done by considering a segment which is diagonal to the picture. This is an interesting possibility, because the streaks are produced by proteins which may be significant in certain cases and we want to keep them visible.

Elimination of the High Frequency Noise

This step consists mainly in the elimination or the noise local to a spot. This is done by the following smoothing algorithm.

Given a function $F(X,Y)$, this function is "smooth" if its Laplacian equals zero or :

$$\nabla F = - \frac{\partial^2 F(X,Y)}{\partial X^2} + \frac{\partial^2 F(X,Y)}{\partial Y^2} = 0$$

Thus we compute the Laplacian of the discrete function $G(X,Y)$, describing the gel, at each point (X_i, Y_j) and by using the Gauss-Seidel method we compute its solutions.

$$\nabla G(X_i, Y_j) = 2G(X_i, Y_j) - G(X_{i+1}, Y_j) - G(X_{i-1}, Y_j)$$
$$+ 2G(X_i, Y_j) - G(X_i, Y_{j+1}) - G(X_i, Y_{j-1})$$

$$\nabla G(X_i, Y_j) = 4G(X_i, Y_j) - G(X_{i+1}, Y_j) - G(X_{i-1}, Y_j)$$
$$- G(X_i, Y_{j+1}) - G(X_i, Y_{j-1}) = 0$$

By factorisation

$$G(X_i, Y_j) = (G(X_{i+1}, Y_j) - G(X_{i-1}, Y_j)$$
$$- G(X_i, Y_{j+1}) - G(X_i, Y_{j+1}))/4$$

$G(X_i, Y_j)$ is then taken as the new value of the point (X_i, Y_j). This is in fact the mean of the four neighboring points of the point (X_i, Y_j). This is done for all the points of the original image and it produces the smoothed image.

Detection and Separation of the Spots

Once the image is processed for noise subtraction, one has to detect and separate the spots in order to give the user a synthetic view of the gel and to be able to perform the computation of the protein density for each spot.

The algorithms implemented in MELANIX for spot detection and separation are completely different from those used in TYCHO or ELSIE. They are based on the following concepts :

(1) the Laplacian of that function is positive at it's peak;

(2) the minimum value of the second derivative with respect to x and y is negative on the boundary of the edges of a spot or in the region separating two very close spots.

A point p belongs to a spot if the following condition is satisfied :

$$\min \left\{ -\nabla G(p) - L, \frac{\partial^2 G(p)}{\partial x^2} - R, \frac{\partial^2 G(p)}{\partial y^2} - C \right\} > 0$$

where L, R and C are positive constants.

Computation of the Surface of the Spots and of the Density of Protein

The method used in ELSIE was implemented for MELANIX. This method consists of computing the integral for every spot. The density of protein is then determined in relation to certain reference spots whose concentration is precisely known.

At its present stage of development, MELANIX performs the complete processing of an image of medium complexity (512 x 512 pixels and approximatively 500 spots) in around 10 minutes of VAX-11/780 CPU time (running UNIX BSD 4.2).

REFERENCES

Anderson NL et NG (1977) High resolution two-dimensional separation of human plasma proteins. Proc. Natl. Acad. Sci. USA, 5421-5425.

Coultec BP, Anderson NG (1981) The TYCHO system for computer analysis of two-dimensional gel electrophoresis patterns. In Clin. Chem., vol. 27,11, p. 1807-1820.

Harrington MG, Merril CR, Goldman G, Xu XH, McFartin DE (1984) Two-dimensional electrophoresis of cerebrospinal fluid proteins in multiple sclerosis and various neurological deseases. In electrophoresis, vol.5, p. 236-245.

Miller MJ et al. (1982) Computer analysis of two-dimensional gels : semi-automatic matching. Clin. Chem., vol.28,4, p. 867.

O'Farrel PH (1975) High resolution two-dimensional electrophoresis of proteins. J. Biol. Chem. 250, 4007-4021.

Wiederkehr F, Vonderschmitt DJ (submitted 1985) Zweidimensionale Elektrophorese des liquor cerebrosbinalis verschiedener neurologischer Patienten.

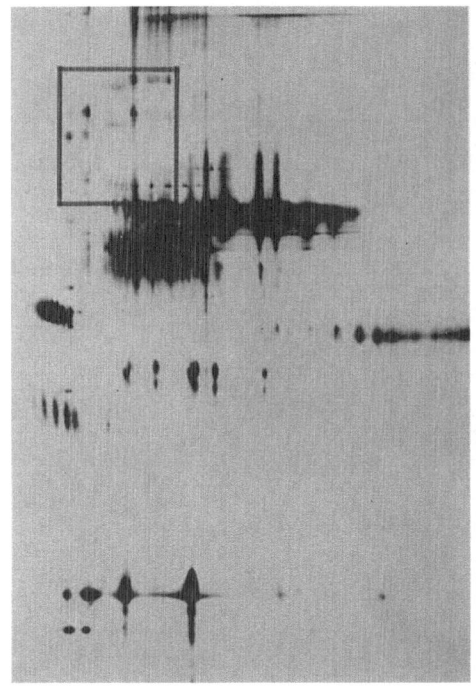 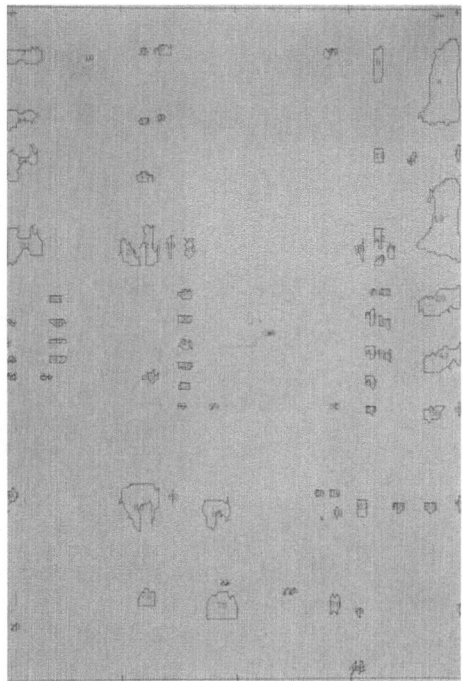

Fig. 1 An electrophoresis image.

Fig. 2 Part of fig. 1 after processing.

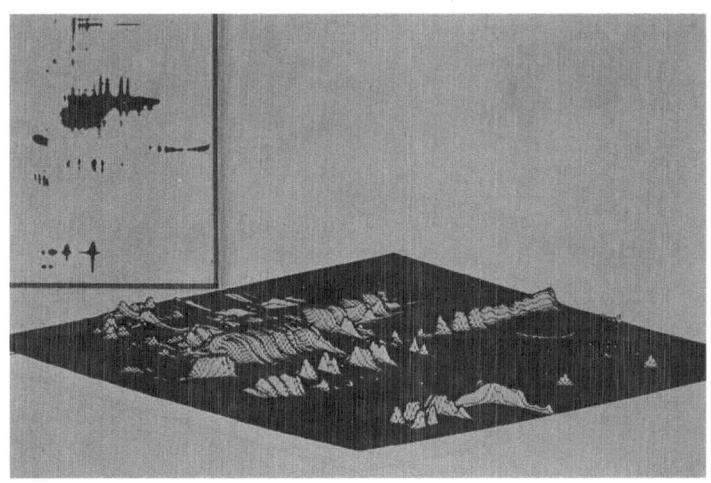

Fig. 3 A pseudo-3D representation of the digitized original image.

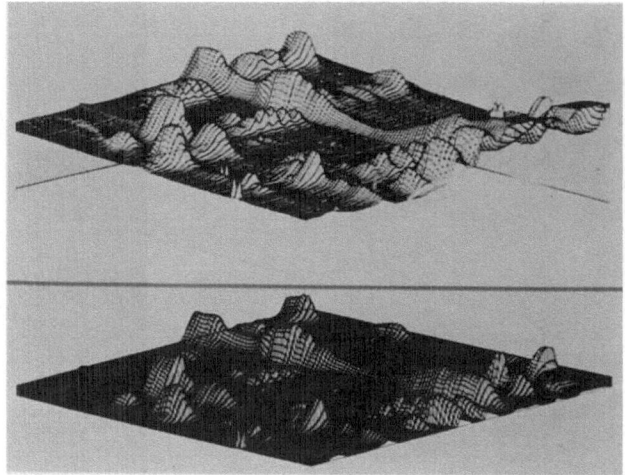

Fig. 4 The values of the background noise and of the x-streaks (in the lower part) extracted from the original image (in the upper part).

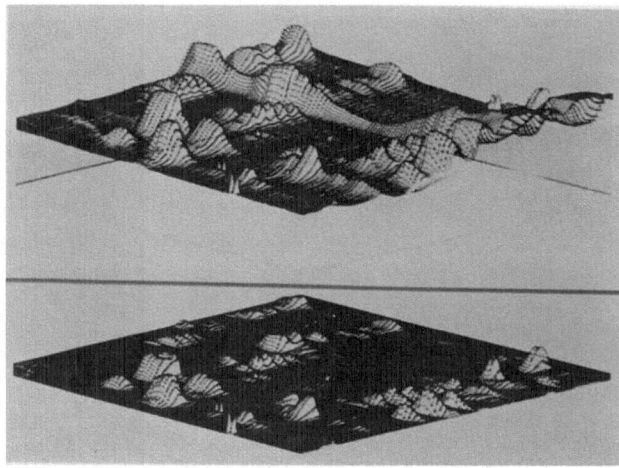

Fig. 5 Result of the subtraction of the background noise and x-streaks (in the lower part) from the original image (in the upper part).

Hologram-Like Transmission of Pictures

Przemyslaw Prusinkiewicz and Mark Christopher

Department of Computer Science, University of Regina, Regina, Saskatchewan, S4S 0A2, Canada

ABSTRACT

A new digital representation of pictures is proposed. The main feature of this representation is: Given a string of data Z representing a picture with full resolution, various substrings of Z represent the same picture with appropriately lower resolution. This is analogous to a well-known property of holograms. The new representation is based on a particular picture traversal algorithm and uses overlapping sampling areas. The paper presents the principle of this representation, analyzes its overhead, and provides examples of picture reconstruction. An application of the hologram-like representation to the transmission of pictures with progressive resolution is indicated.

KEYWORDS: progressive transmission, sampling and reconstruction, picture traversal.

INTRODUCTION

Numerous methods for the transmission of pictures have been studied in the past. In the simplest case, a picture is represented as an array of samples. Its transmission and display proceed along rows or columns, referred to as scan lines. If t_c is the time necessary to display the whole picture, in $\frac{1}{k} \cdot T_c$ time only one kth of the picture will be displayed. This part will be presented at full resolution. In some applications, for example slow transmission of visual information (videotex), or browsing through a database of stored images (Hill and Walker 1983), it may be desirable for the resolution of a picture, rather then its visible area, to increase while the transmission proceeds. To this end, methods of progressive transmission of pictures were developed (Pavlidis 1982). They use quad trees (Sloan and Tanimoto 1979) or binary trees (Knowlton 1980) as underlying data structures. Consequently, various initial substrings of the string of data representing the entire picture can be used for its reconstruction, with the resolution proportional to the length of the substring. However, non-initial substrings are meaningless.

This paper describes a new representation of pictures suitable for their transmission with progressive resolution. The main feature of this representation is: Given a string of data Z representing a picture with full resolution, various (not necessarily initial) substrings of Z represent the same picture with an appropriately lower resolution. This is analogous to the well-known feature of holograms: Any portion of a hologram represents the same picture as the whole hologram, but with a lower resolution. The new representation is based on a traversal algorithm (i.e. the selection and ordering of sampling points) with the following key property: Given a string of sampling points, $P = \langle p_0, p_1, p_2, ... \rangle$, various substrings of P consist of points uniformly distributed in the sampling region Q. Hence the longer a substring of sampled values is, the better the resolution of the reconstruction of the original picture can be achieved. An earlier version of this traversal algorithm was described in (Prusinkiewicz 1984).

This paper is organized as follows. First, the traversal algorithm is formally defined, and its essential properties are stated. A suitable sampling technique and the corresponding reconstruction method are described next. The subsequent section provides an analysis of the overhead of the hologram-like representation. Finally, a possible application of the method is indicated. The appendix contains proofs of the theorems.

PICTURE TRAVERSAL ALGORITHM

Intuitively, the traversal algorithm is based on two observations (Fig. 1):
- A translation of a set of sampling points uniformly distributed in a region of a plane is a set of uniformly distributed points;
- The union of appropriately translated sets of uniformly distributed points is also a set of uniformly distributed points, with a reduced distance between the adjacent points.

The string (sequence) of sampling points is defined recursively, by translating and concatenating previous strings. Consequently, various substrings consist of points uniformly distributed in the plane.

A formalization follows.

Let $P = \langle p_0, p_1, p_2, ... \rangle$ be a string of points in a plane. By $P(n,h)$ we denote the following substring of P:

$$P(n,h) = \langle p_{h \cdot 4^n}, p_{h \cdot 4^n + 1}, ..., p_{(h+1) \cdot 4^n - 1} \rangle$$

Furthermore, by $S(\langle p_0, p_1, ..., p_m \rangle, \vec{c})$ we denote translation of the substring $\langle p_0, p_1, ..., p_m \rangle$ by the vector $\vec{c}$:

$$S(\langle p_0, p_1, ..., p_m \rangle, \vec{c}) = \langle p_0 + \vec{c}, p_1 + \vec{c}, ..., p_m + \vec{c} \rangle$$

We will represent the translation vector $\vec{c}$ as $c_x \vec{1}_x + c_y \vec{1}_y$, where $\vec{1}_x$ and $\vec{1}_y$ are the unit vectors in the directions of axes x and y, respectively.

Definition 1. Let $T>0$ denote the edge size of the square sampling region $Q(T)$ (its vertices are: $(0,0)$, $(0,T)$, (T,T), and $(T,0)$). The string of sampling points is then defined as follows:

$P(0,0) = \langle p_0 \rangle = \langle T,T \rangle$

$P(n,1) = S(P(n,0), -T \cdot 2^{-n-1} \vec{1}_x)$

$P(n,2) = S(P(n,0), -T \cdot 2^{-n-1} \vec{1}_y)$

$P(n,3) = S(P(n,0), -T \cdot 2^{-n-1} (\vec{1}_x + \vec{1}_y))$

$P(n+1,0) = P(n,0) \circ P(n,1) \circ P(n,2) \circ P(n,3)$

where o denotes concatenation of strings, and $n = 0,1,2,...$.

Theorem 1. Let the binary word $r_{2n-1} r_{2n-2} ... r_1 r_0$ represent index k of a sample point $p_k = (x_k, y_k)$ in the pure binary number system:

$$k = \sum_{i=0}^{2n-1} r_i 2^i$$

The coordinates of point p_k are then defined as:

$$x_k = T(1 - \sum_{i=0}^{n-1} r_{2i} 2^{-(i+1)})$$

$$y_k = T(1 - \sum_{i=0}^{n-1} r_{2i+1} 2^{-(i+1)})$$

Proof in the Appendix.

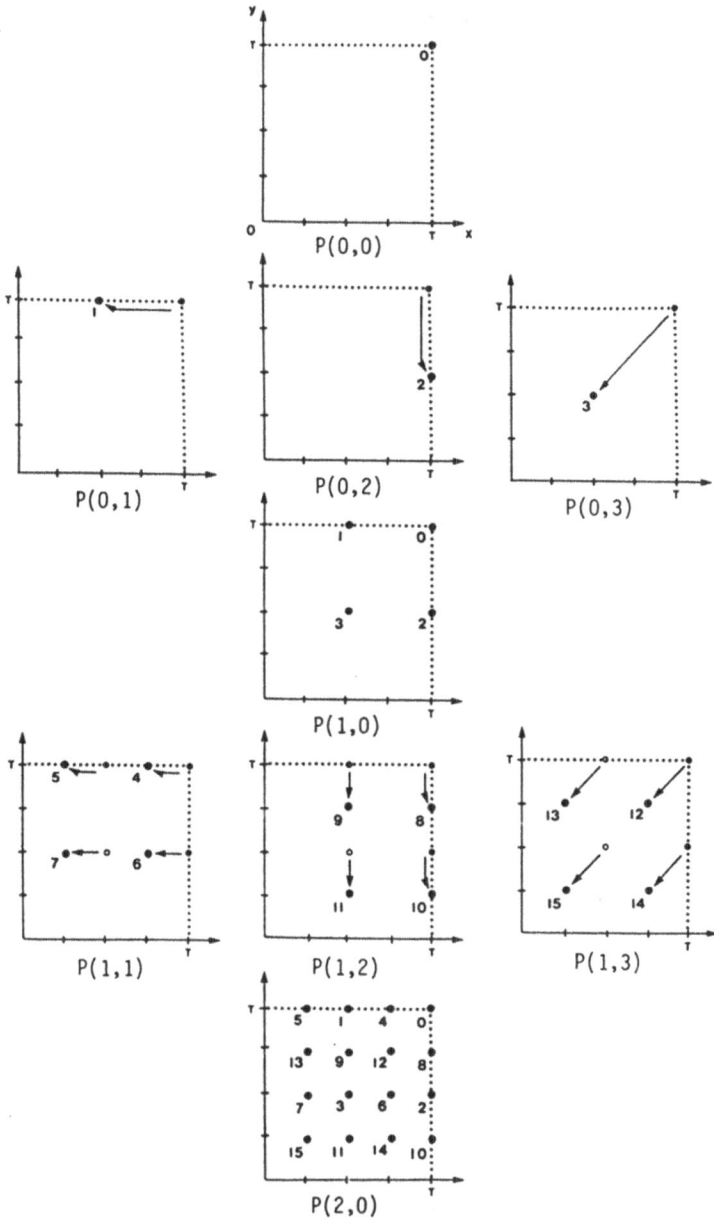

Fig. 1. Definition of the sequence of sampling points P.

Theorem 1 provides an explicit (non-recurrent) relationship between the index of a sampling point and its coordinates. This relation can also be used as a definition of sequence P (Prusinkiewicz 1984). It lacks, however, the intuitive flavor of definition 1.

The central property of the string of sampling points P is given by Theorem 2. It refers to definition 2 (Rosenfeld and Kak 1982), formalizing the notion of $m \times m$ points uniformly distributed in the square $Q(T)$.

Definition 2. Given a sampling region $Q(T)$, the sampling lattice of $m \times m$ elements, with the origin in point (c_x, c_y), is the set:

$$M_{m \times m}(c_x, c_y) = \{(c_x + (i-1)\frac{T}{m}, c_y + (j-1)\frac{T}{m}): i, j = 1, 2, ..., m\}$$

Theorem 2. Let $\hat{P}(n,h)$ denote the (unordered) set of elements of the substring $P(n,h)$:

$$\hat{P}(n,h) = \{p_{h \cdot 4^n}, p_{h \cdot 4^n + 1}, ..., p_{(h+1) \cdot 4^n - 1}\}$$

For any $n, h = 0, 1, 2, ...$, the set $\hat{P}(n,h)$ is a sampling lattice in the region $Q(T)$:

$$(\forall n, h = 0, 1, 2, ...)\ (\exists c_x, c_y \in [0, \frac{T}{2^n}))\ \hat{P}(n,h) = M_{2^n \times 2^n}(c_x, c_y)$$

Proof in the Appendix.

SAMPLING AND RECONSTRUCTION

The sampling method used for the hologram-like transmission of pictures should make it possible to reconstruct a picture f from any number of uniformly distributed samples, with the resolution proportional to the number of samples considered.

The simplest sampling method – Shannon's sampling – does not meet this requirement. Since the number of samples which will actually be used to reconstruct picture f is not known when sampling, it is not possible to adequately filter out high frequency components of f. Consequently, a reconstruction of f from a small number of samples may be totally misleading, due to aliasing (Rosenfeld and Kak 1982).

Let us define the area sample z_k in point $p_k = (x_k, y_k)$ as the total amount of light which falls in the rectangle $(0,0)$, $(x_k, 0)$, (x_k, y_k), $(0, y_k)$:

$$z_k = \int_0^{x_k} \int_0^{y_k} f(x,y)\ dxdy \quad\quad (*)$$

A reconstruction of f can be performed, given area samples corresponding to any set of sampling points $\hat{P}(n,h)$. Following Theorem 1, the set $\hat{P}(n,h)$ forms the sampling matrix $M_{m \times m}(c_x, c_y)$ for some m, c_x, c_y. Consequently, each sampling point p_k can be expressed as

$$(c_x + (i-1)\frac{T}{m},\ c_y + (j-1)\frac{T}{m})$$

where $i, j \in \{1, 2, ..., m\}$. We will use i and j as indices, and write $p_{i,j}$ instead of p_k. Similarly, if $p_{i,j} = p_k$, we will write $z_{i,j}$ instead of z_k. By referring to the definition of the area sample, we then obtain:

$$\frac{m^2}{T^2} \int_{x_i}^{x_i+\frac{T}{m}} \int_{y_i}^{y_i+\frac{T}{m}} f(x,y)\, dx\, dy = \frac{m^2}{T^2} (z_{i+1,j+1} - z_{i+1,j} - z_{i,j+1} + z_{i,j})$$

where $i, j = 1,2,...,m-1$ (an extension to $i = 0$ and $j = 0$ is straightforward). The above equation is the basis of picture reconstruction. The left side represents the average value of function f (average gray level) in the square $Q_{i,j}$ with vertices:

$$(x_i, y_j),\ (x_{i+\frac{T}{m}}, y_j),\ (x_{i+\frac{T}{m}}, y_{j+\frac{T}{m}}),\ (x_i, y_{j+\frac{T}{m}})$$

This value (known as standard sample) can be directly used as an approximation of f in $Q_{i,j}$. Due to averaging, the reconstruction of f based on standard samples will be automatically antialiased.

Examples of the reconstruction of pictures from their hologram-like representations are shown in Fig. 2 and Fig. 3. These figures were obtained on a laser printer, with an 8×8 dither matrix (Foley and van Dam 1982) used to simulate 64 gray levels.

ANALYSIS OF OVERHEAD

Suppose that the original picture is sampled using a lattice of $2^n \times 2^n$ points. Furthermore, suppose that the gray level function f takes values from the set $\{0,1,...,2^d-1\}$ (after quantization). From the formula (*) it follows that the area sample $z_{i,j}$ in point $p_{i,j}$ can take any value from 0 to $i \cdot j \cdot (2^d-1)$. The number of bits necessary to represent this sample is equal to:

$$\lceil \log_2(i \cdot j \cdot (2^d-1)) \rceil \approx d + \lceil \log_2(i) + \log_2(j) \rceil$$

where $\lceil x \rceil$ denotes the ceiling function. Consequently, the total length of the hologram-like representation of f (in bits) is equal to:

$$N_1 = 4^n d + \sum_{i=1}^{2^n} \sum_{j=1}^{2^n} \lceil \log_2(i) + \log_2(j) \rceil$$

Since the number of bits required to send 4^n d-bit samples is equal to $4^n \cdot d$, the overhead related to the hologram-like representation can be expressed as:

$$O_1 = \frac{N_1 - 4^n \cdot d}{4^n \cdot d}$$

Value N_1 is calculated under the assumption that representations of area samples $z_{i,j}$ may have variable lengths. Decoding of the picture can actually be simplified if all samples are represented by words of equal length: $d+2n$. The length of the hologram-like representation is then equal to $N_2 = 4^n \cdot (d+2n)$. The corresponding overhead is equal to:

$$O_2 = \frac{N_2 - 4^n \cdot d}{4^n \cdot d} = 2\frac{n}{d}$$

The overheads O_1 and O_2 calculated for various values of n and d are shown in Fig. 4. The overheads are approximately proportional to the logarithm of the number of samples n, and inversely proportional to the number of bits per standard sample d. The variable-length representation of samples does not significantly reduce the overhead.

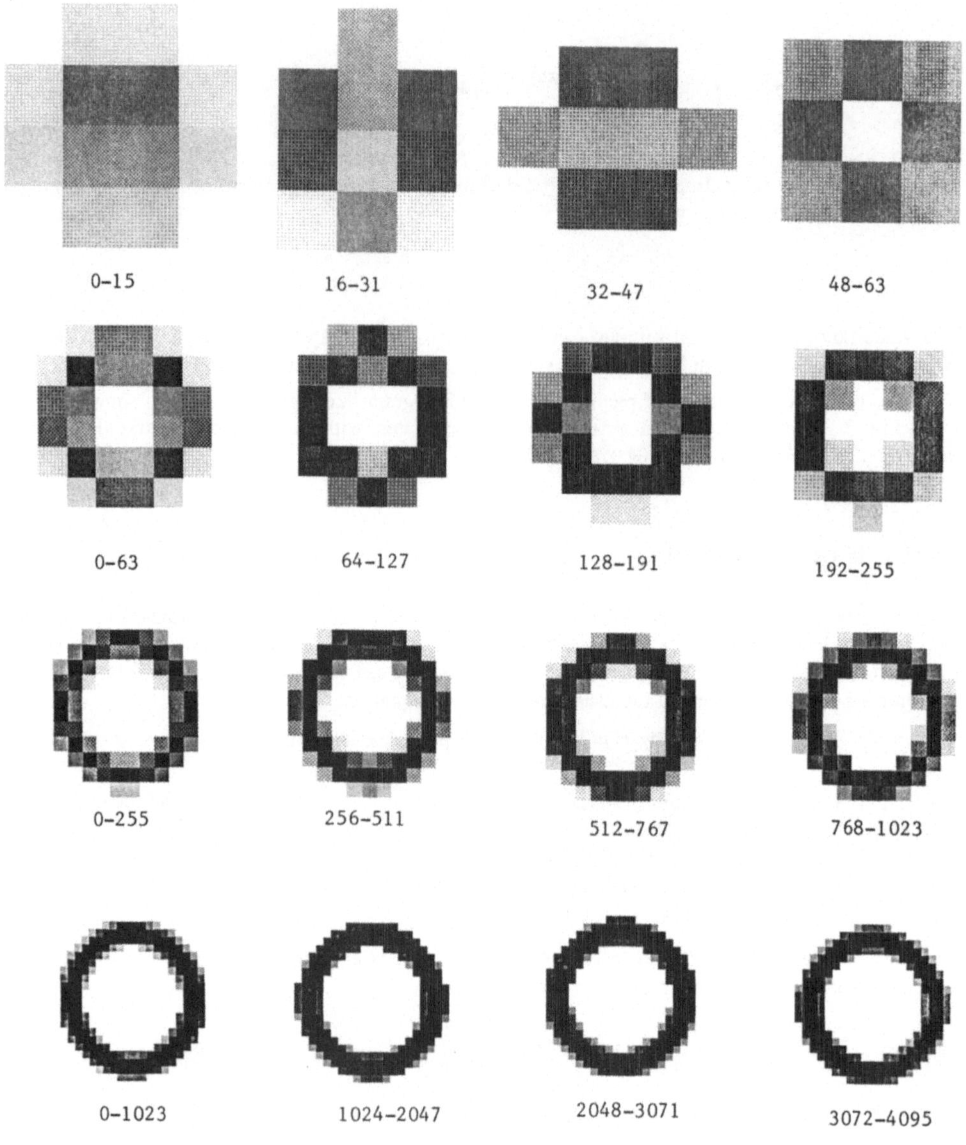

Fig. 2. Example of the hologram-like transmission of a picture.

0-4095

Numbers indicate indices of area samples z_k used for reconstruction.

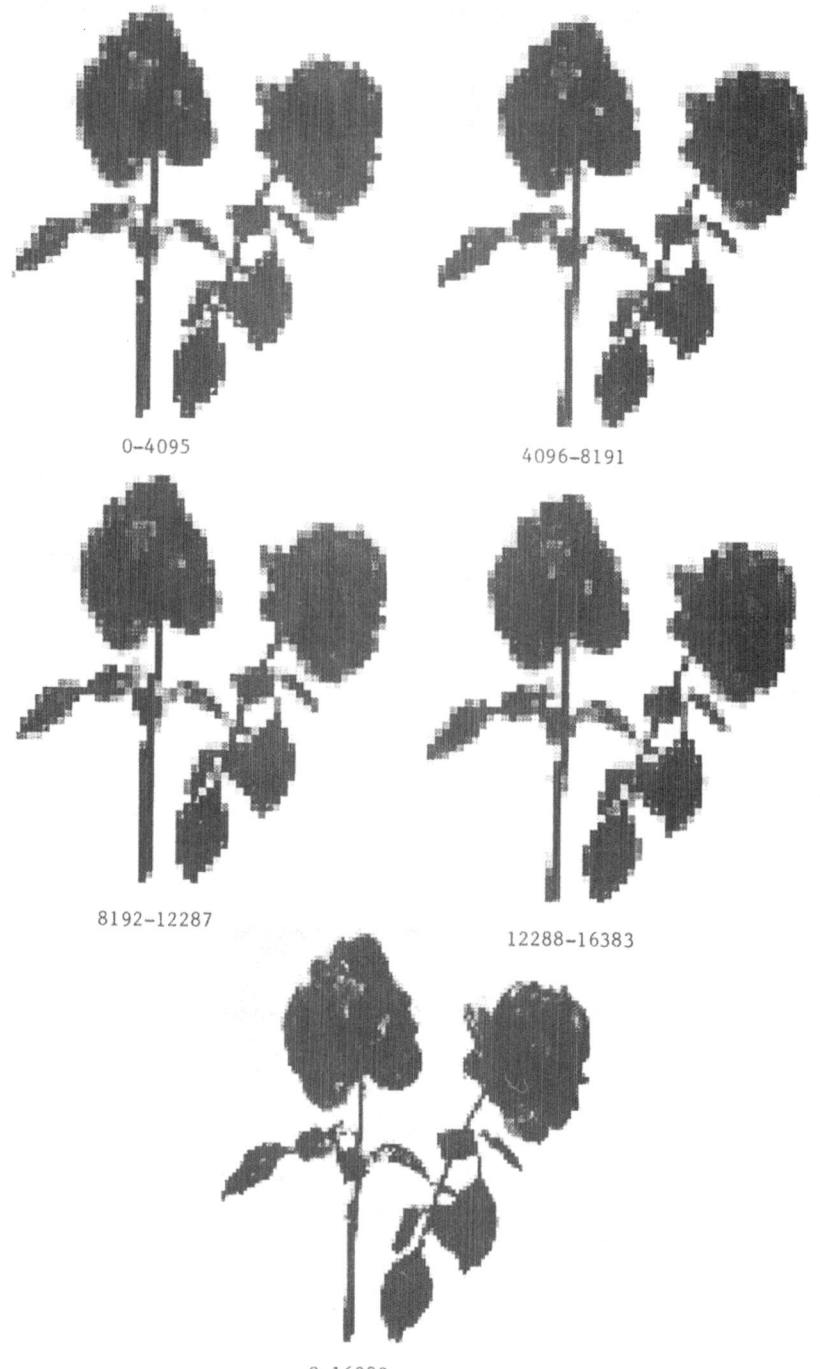

Fig. 3. Example of the hologram-like transmission of a picture. Numbers indicate indices of area samples z_k used for reconstruction.

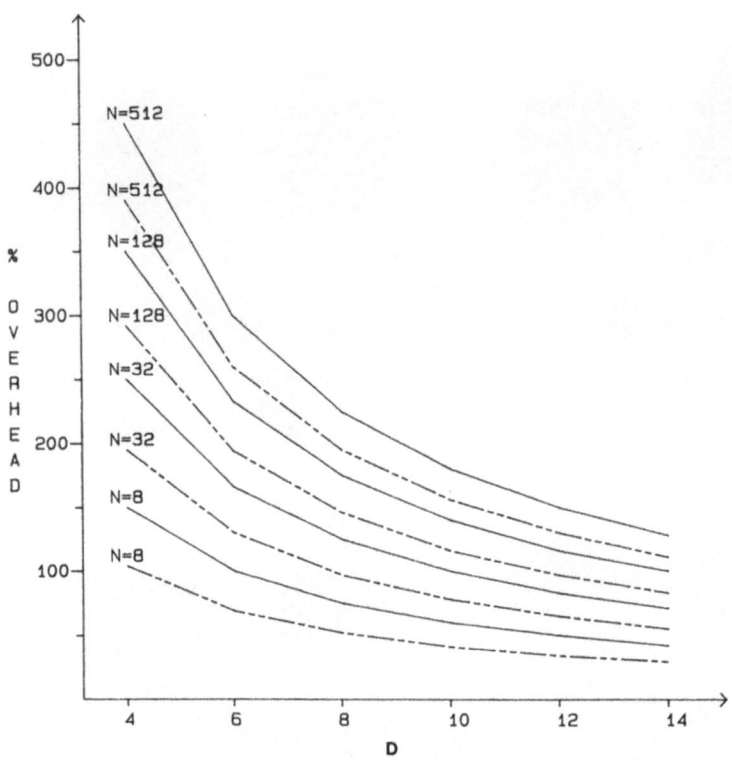

Fig. 4. Overhead of the hologram-like representation of pictures. N indicates the total number of area samples taken (N^2). D is the number of bits per area sample (pixel). Dashed lines correspond to the variable-length representation of samples (overhead O_1). Continuous lines correspond to the fixed-length representation (overhead O_2).

CONCLUDING REMARKS

A new method for the transmission of pictures has been proposed. The main property of this method is: given a data string Z representing a picture f with full resolution, various substrings of Z represent f with a resolution proportional to the length of the substring. Analysis of the overhead of the method is given. Examples of the reconstruction of pictures from the hologram-like representation are presented.

The method is applicable, for example, to browsing through a set of pictures sent round robin over a communications channel (in a videotex system). Pictures can be quickly reconstructed from a small number of samples, allowing for previewing before the full resolution reconstruction of the selected picture proceeds.

ACKNOWLEDGMENT

This research was supported by Grant No. A0324 from the Natural Sciences and Engineering Research Council of Canada.

REFERENCES

Foley JD, van Dam A (1982) *Fundamentals of interactive computer graphics.* Addison-Wesley, Reading

Hill FS, Walker S (1983) Interactive image query system using progressive transmission. *Computer Graphics,* 17 (3) : 323-330

Knowlton K (1980) Progressive transmission of gray-scale and B/W pictures by simple, efficient and lossless encoding schemes. *IEEE Proceedings,* 68: 885-896

Pavlidis T (1982) *Algorithms for graphics and image processing.* Computer Science Press, Rockville

Prusinkiewicz P (1984) A hologram-like digital representation of pictures. *Proceedings of the 22nd Allerton Conference on Communications, Control, and Computing,* Monticello : 796-797

Rosenfeld A, Kak AC (1982) *Digital picture processing.* Academic Press, New York

Sloan KR, Tanimoto SL (1979) Progressive refinement of raster images. *IEEE Trans. Comput.,* C-28: 871-874

APPENDIX: PROOFS OF THE THEOREMS

Proof of Theorem 1. Let $L(R)$ denote the number represented by the binary word R in the pure binary number system. Specifically, the numerical value of the empty word λ is zero: $L(\lambda)=0$. As usual, point (.) can be used to separate the fractional part of R from its integer part. Using this notation, Theorem 1 can be restated as follows:

Let the word $b_{n-1}a_{n-1}...b_0a_0$ represent index k in the pure binary number system: $k = L(b_{n-1}a_{n-1}...b_0a_0)$. The point q_k with coordinates

$$x_k = T(1-L(.a_0...a_{n-1})) \qquad y_k = T(1-L(.b_0...b_{n-1}))$$

coincides with point p_k specified by Definition 1.

Proof by induction on n.

- For $n = 0$ the word $b_{n-1}a_{n-1}...b_0a_0$ is empty. Consequently, $k = L(\lambda) = 0$, $x_0 = T(1-L(\lambda)) = T$, and $y_0 = T(1-L(\lambda)) = T$. Thus, $q_0 = (T, T)$ is equal to p_0.

- Suppose the theorem true for $n \geq 0$. Thus, $q_k = p_k$ for any k represented as $b_{n-1}a_{n-1} ... b_0a_0$. For $n+1$ four cases can be distinguished: $b_na_n = 00, 01, 10$ and 11. The case $b_na_n = 00$ is trivial because it leads to a previously considered value of k. (The coordinates x_k and y_k are not affected by trailing zeroes in their binary representations.) In the next case ($b_na_n = 01$) index $k' = L(01b_{n-1}a_{n-1}...b_0a_0)$ can be represented as $k' = 4^n + k$, where $k = L(b_{n-1}a_{n-1}...b_0a_0)$. Point $q_{k'}$ has coordinates:

$$x_{k'} = T(1-L(.a_0...a_{n-1}1)) = x_k - T \cdot 2^{-n-1}$$

$$y_{k'} = T(1-L(.b_0...b_{n-1}0)) = y_k$$

Or, $q_{k'} = q_k - T \cdot 2^{-n-1}\vec{1}_x$. On the other hand, from the definition 1 it follows that $p_{k'} = p_k - T \cdot 2^{-n-1}\vec{1}_x$. Since $q_k = p_k$ (by the inductive hypothesis), $q_{k'} = p_{k'}$ as well. In the remaining cases ($b_{n+1}a_{n+1} = 10$ and 11) the equality $q_{k'} = p_{k'}$ can be proved the analogous way. Thus, the theorem is true for all $n = 0, 1, 2,....$ □

Proof of Theorem 2.

- Let us first consider the case $h = 0$. Following Theorem 1, the set $\hat{P}(n, 0)$ consists of all points p_k with coordinates

$$x_k = T(1-L(.a_0...a_{n-1})) \qquad y_k = T(1-L(.b_0...b_{n-1}))$$

It is known that the 2^n numbers represented by the words $.a_0...a_{n-1}$ form the arithmetic sequence with the first element 0 and the difference 2^{-n}. Naturally, the 2^n numbers represented by the words $.b_0...b_{n-1}$ form the same sequence. Hence,

$$\hat{P}(n,0) = \{(T(1 - i \cdot 2^{-n}), T(1 - j \cdot 2^{-n})) : i, j = 0,1,...,2^n-1\} = M_{2^n \times 2^n}(2^{-n}, 2^{-n})$$

- For $h > 0$ index k' of any element of the set $\hat{P}(n, h)$ can be expressed as $k' = h \cdot 4^n + k$, where $k \in \{0,1,...,4^n-1\}$. Consequently, the binary representation of k' can be written as

$$b_{s-1}a_{s-1}...b_n a_n b_{n-1}a_{n-1}...b_0 a_0$$

where $h = L(b_{s-1}a_{s-1}...b_n a_n)$ and $k = L(b_{n-1}a_{n-1}...b_0 a_0)$. As a result, the coordinates of point $p_{k'}$ can be expressed as:

$$x_{k'} = T(1-L(.a_0...a_{n-1})) - T \cdot 2^{-n}L(.a_n...a_{s-1})$$

$$y_{k'} = T(1-L(.b_0...b_{n-1})) - T \cdot 2^{-n}L(.b_n...b_{s-1})$$

Thus, $p_{k'} = p_k - c_x \vec{1}_x - c_y \vec{1}_y$, where c_x and c_y are constants dependent only of h. Consequently, $\hat{P}(n,h)$ is a translation of the sampling lattice $\hat{P}(n,0)$, or $\hat{P}(n,h)$ is also a sampling lattice. □

Chapter 3
Geometric Modelling

CSG and Ray Tracing Using Functional Primitives

Tosiyasu L. Kunii[1] and Geoff Wyvill[2]

[1] Department of Information Science, Faculty of Science, The University of Tokyo, 3-1, Hongo 7-chome, Bunkyo-ku, Tokyo, 113 Japan
[2] Department of Information Science, University of Otago, Box 56, Dunedin, New Zealand

ABSTRACT

A simple system is described for computer aided design by constructive solid geometry (CSG). The system allows the design of engineering components by combining 'basic components' which represent shapes produced by standard machining operations.

The system has four significant original features:

1. The primitive components are described in an object oriented fashion, data plus procedures.

2. A new kind of octree structure is used to render various displays from descriptions.

3. Certain objects can be directly associated with components of tool paths. For example, a cylindrical object might represent a drill moving along its length or a prism might represent the shape of material cut by a milling tool sweeping horizontally. An object built from these basic objects can, in principle, be cut using combinations of their associated tool paths.

4. The system consists of four conceptual modules with well-defined interfaces. One module, for example, is the set of primitive objects and their associated procedures. Another is the octree generator. Because of this design technique, it is easy to modify or even replace modules. This meta-structure provides us with a general, if informal method of describing CSG systems.

KEYWORDS: CAD/CAM, Geometric modelling, CSG, Octree, Ray tracing.

INTRODUCTION

In the last few years the method of constructive solid geometry (CSG) has become increasingly popular as an alternative to surface-based models for Computer Aided Design [1, 2, 3, 11, 13, 14, 20, 22]. In a CSG system, objects are represented as collections of 'primitive objects' connected by set operations on the space they occupy. This leads, naturally, to the representation of objects as a tree structure where the leaves represent primitive objects. The nodes, other than leaves, represent set operations between sub-objects. Since the sub-objects can be different copies of the same object description, we prefer to represent this as a directed acyclic graph (DAG) or node-sharing tree. The edges of this graph carry geometrical transformation information. (Diagram 1.)

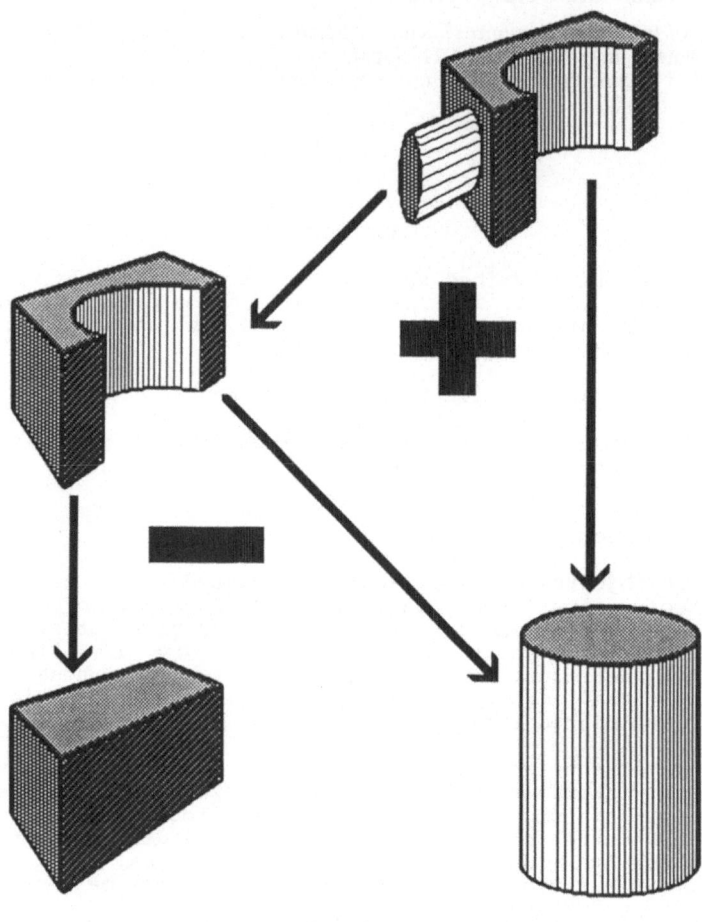

Diagram 1

A compound object is represented by a DAG. The same cylinder is subtracted and subsequently added with a different size and orientation.

This structure is also a natural extension of the recursive picture languages PG, Pictures 68 and PDL-2 [9, 23, 24, 25]. The structure can be built from text descriptions, algebraic descriptions or, in principle, interactively with a graphics console. The user interface is a substantial separate problem which we intended to address in a subsequent paper.

In order to extract useful information from the DAG, a rendering process is needed. Usually, this implies building a secondary structure which can be processed by conventional display algorithms. For this structure, surface models have been used [2, 3, 13 and others] and more recently octree and other solid grid representations [8, 10, 26]. We use a modified octree structure. It provides a spatial ordering to reduce the complexity of a scene (e.g. for ray tracing) while retaining almost all of the information from the primitive CSG objects.

Each primitive object is represented as a collection of procedures which describe its properties. Some of these procedures are called by the rendering algorithm as it processes the intermediate (octree) structure. Others are called as the octree is being built. This means that new primitives can be added in a systematic way, by writing procedures which describe them.

Similarly, new rendering algorithms can be added, for example to generate n.c. machine tool paths. Depending on its purpose, an algorithm can extract information from the DAG, the intermediate structure or both.

The system consists of four parts.

1. The primitives and their procedures.

2. The CSG structure and user interface.

3. The intermediate structure and its creation algorithm.

4. The renderers

These communicate through well-defined interfaces. In principle, any part can be replaced by a functional equivalent, although in the pilot version, the renderers include some knowledge of the intermediate structure and a radical change in the CSG structure would require changes in the 'creation procedure'.

THE DAG STRUCTURE

The language PDL-2 [25] is for describing pictures. The line:

DEFINE stool leg leg AT 1,0 top AT 0,1 TURNED 90

defines a (2-D) object called "stool" which consists of two copies of the object called "leg" and a copy of the object "top". The phrases "AT 1,0" and "AT 0,1 TURNED 90" convey information about the position and orientation of the copies of "leg" and "top". The representation of this in DAG form is shown in diagram 2.

A definition is a list of "instances" of sub-pictures and each instance includes a pointer to a definition.

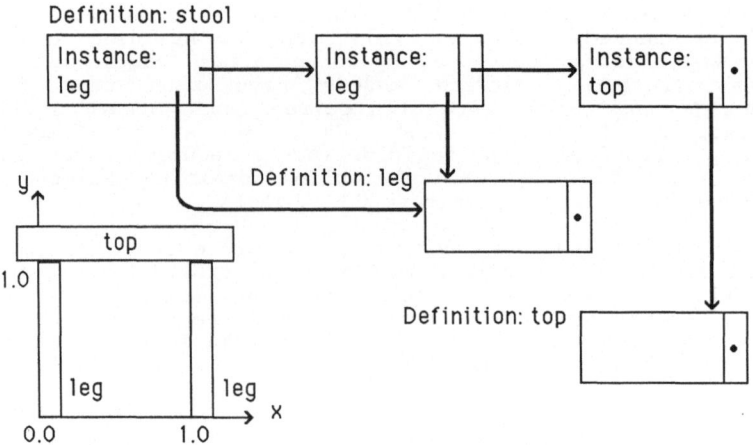

Diagram 2: Definitions and Instances

Similarly in our DAG structure a list of elements constitutes an object's definition and each element contains a pointer to a definition. Our DAG elements have five fields:

Mode: PLUS or MINUS

Trans: A pair of matrices which describe the position of this instance in the current definition.

This: A pointer to another object's definition.   (This instance.)

Next: A pointer to the next element of this definition.

Props: A pointer to another structure containing properties of this instance.

The mode PLUS indicates that this object is to be added in the current definition. Mode MINUS indicates that the object represents a volume cut away.

The matrices are simple matrices of linear transformation. For example:

$$\begin{pmatrix} a & b & c & d \\ e & f & g & h \\ i & j & k & l \\ 0 & 0 & 0 & 1 \end{pmatrix} * \begin{pmatrix} x \\ y \\ z \\ 1 \end{pmatrix} = \begin{pmatrix} ax+by+cz+d \\ ex+fy+gx+h \\ ix+jy+kz+1 \\ 1 \end{pmatrix}$$

This matrix transforms the point <x,y,z> into some other coordinate system. The elements d,h,l describe a translation of <x,y,z> and the other elements describe rotation and magnification. Because matrix multiplication is associative, we can accumulate a number of matrices, M1*M2* ... Mn and observe that for a position p=<x,y,z>:

M1*M2*... Mn*p = M1*(M2*(M3... (Mn*p)))

We use this in traversing the DAG to find the final position of each primitive element in the world space. (See [24, 25]).

The properties are other information that can be associated with an object. In our pilot system, the only properties are surface colour and reflectivity, but other information such as density, elasticity or material cost could be represented according to the needs of applications. The pointer "This" can also point to a 'primitive object' which is a collection of procedures. In this case, we say the DAG element is 'primitive'.

THE INTERMEDIATE STRUCTURE

An octree model [8, 10, 26 and others] divides a cubic region of space recursively into eight sub-cubes at each level of a tree structure. Each leaf of the tree represents an undivided cube which is either 'full' or 'empty'. 'Full' elements can have other associated information e.g: colour. A modified structure has also been described, in which the leaves of the tree contain a strictly limited set of surface elements [4, 26]. This has the advantage of compactness. Also less information is lost in transforming to this model.

Our intermediate structure is a modified octree in which space is divided until each leaf:

1. is Full,

2. is Empty,

3. contains boundaries between empty space and one primitive object,

4. contains boundaries between full space and one primitive object (In this case the object is being subtracted from full space),

or

5. represents a volume of space less than the limit of system resolution.

Nodes of the tree, other than leaves, represent cubes which are further divided into eight sub-cubes recursively until a leaf node is reached. Such cubes and nodes are called 'partial'. Note that the leaf nodes in (5) above, would also be partial and have 'children' but for the limit on resolution. We refer to these cells as "nasty" as there is no easy way to extract information from them. Because they occupy only a small proportion of the total space, this is acceptable.

See also, that this structure differs from [4, 26] in that the leaf nodes refer to a primitive solid object and not to part of a plane, edge or vertex.

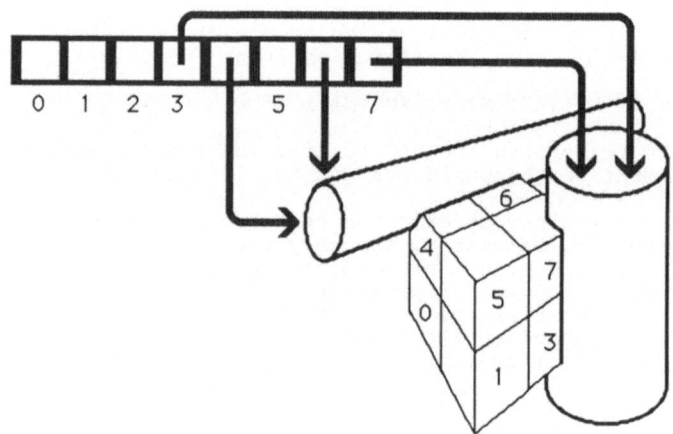

Diagram 3: Modified Octree Structure

Each leaf node points to a representation of an instance of a primitive. Where the primitive extends over more than one voxel, several leaf nodes point to the same data record.

THE CREATION ALGORITHM

Creation of the octree is accomplished in two phases. First the DAG structure is traversed top-down using a current transformation matrix, 'forward' which describes the position and orientation of the current object in the world space. There is also a 'return' matrix which is the inverse of the 'forward' one.

As each DAG element is encountered, this current matrix is pre-multiplied by the element's own matrix to obtain the transformation for the sub-components of the DAG. At the same time a new 'return' matrix is computed by pre-multiplying the 'return' matrix of the DAG element and the current 'return' matrix. This procedure is repeated, recursively on the DAG until a primitive element is encountered. At the primitive element, therefore, we have a matrix which describes the position of the primitive object in world space, and also a matrix for the inverse transformation.

When a primitive element is encountered, we create an elementary octree structure consisting of a single leaf. The matrices are copied into the octree leaf node and the mode is set to PLUS. These elementary structures are merged into a single tree in phase two.

The traversal algorithm can be summarised thus:

1. If DAG is empty, return the empty octree.

2. Traverse DAG.next recursively to obtain an octree for the background to which this element will be added or subtracted.

3. Calculate new matrices for DAG.

4. If DAG is primitive create an octree leaf element called foreground.

5. If DAG is not primitive, traverse DAG.this recursively using the new matrices to return an octree called foreground.

6. If the mode of DAG is PLUS, add the foreground to the background and return the result.

7. If the mode of DAG is MINUS, subtract the foreground from the background and return the result.

The addition and subtraction phase is thus separate from the traversal only in a conceptual sense. Add and subtract are called as sub-procedures of the traversal algorithm.

To add two octrees a,b we proceed as follows:

1. If a is empty, result is b, otherwise:

2. If b is empty, result is a, otherwise:

3. If a is full, then the objects interfere. This is not allowed.

4. If b is full, the objects interfere, otherwise:

5. If we have reached the limit of resolution, create a nasty (type 5) cell, otherwise:

6. Subdivide a and b. If a or b is a partial node, this just means we access its child nodes. If a or b is a leaf node, we create child nodes for it.

7. Add the eight sub-elements of a,b recursively.

Notice that we do not permit conventional set union. It is a feature of the system design that we imitate nature. We do not permit two objects to occupy the same space. This check for interference also is the basis for our approach to tool path generation.

To subtract two octrees a,b we proceed as follows:

1. If a is empty, result is empty, otherwise:

2. If b is empty, result is a, otherwise:

3. If b is full, result is empty, otherwise:

4. If a is full and b is a leaf node, return the inverse of b, otherwise:

5. If we have reached the limit of resolution, create a nasty (type 5) cell, otherwise:

6. Subdivide a and b as for addition.

7. Subtract the eight sub-elements of a,b recursively.

When we subdivide a primitive octree, we construct the co-ordinates of the boundaries of the eight sub-cubes. Now using the 'return' matrix of the leaf element, we transform the co-ordinates of the voxel boundary back into the space belonging to the primitive. These transformed points are passed to the appropriate primitive routine which returns one of three values:

IN   indicates that the voxel boundary is completely contained. This means that the voxel is full. (Empty in subtractive mode.)

OUT   indicates that the voxel boundary is completely outside the space occupied by the primitive; the reverse of IN.

BORDER means that the child voxel still contains part of the primitive boundary.

Thus some of the child nodes will be full or empty and this enables the recursive calls of add and subtract to do their job. Others will require further subdivision.

The only information required of the primitives to build the intermediate structure, is defined through one uniform procedure interface. This is an example of the value of our meta-structure.

THE RAY TRACER

To illustrate the octree algorithms, we have written a simple ray tracer which operates on an octree structure. Since each leaf voxel refers to only one primitive, the ray tracer does no searching among objects. Instead, each ray is followed through the structure until it encounters a non-empty voxel. At this point, a primitive function is called to deal with the intersection.

The rest of the ray tracer's function requires knowledge of surface properties which are described in the DAG and octree structure and are independent of the primitives. This information comes fom the octree leaf.

To achieve a reasonable speed, it is important that we skip over empty voxels fast. Our 'next voxel' algorithm is a refinement of Glassner's [7].

THE NEXT VOXEL ALGORITHM

Like Glassner [7], we find a point which is guaranteed to be in the next voxel. But we avoid most of the computation of solving plane intersections as follows. (Uppercase is used for vectors so P[z] is the z component of P.)

Consider a ray from P to Q within a voxel v. Let D=Q-P and note that D does not change during the traversal of many voxels.

Now find R such that R[i] (i=x,y,z) is the distance from P to the exit point of v in direction i. R[i] will have the same sign as D[i].

Now find t such that t is the minimum value of:

abs(R[x]/D[x]), abs(R[y]/D[y]) and abs(R[z]/D[z])

The point P[x]+tD[x], P[y]+tD[y], P[z]+tD[z] is guaranteed to lie on the voxel boundary. This, of course, assumes that we can perform the divisions in an exact mathematical way with no rounding error.

To avoid floating point calculation and its attendant uncertainties we have to rearrange the calculation slightly. For a voxel bounded by L,H (bottom southwest and top northeast corners) we consider P to be inside v if L[i]<=P[i]<H[i], (i=x,y,z). If D[i] is positive, then:

   R[i]=H[i]-P[i]   but if D[i] is negative, let:

   R[i]=L[i]-P[i]-1

so R[i] is the minimum movement on axis i which takes us into the next voxel.

The divisions (above) don't work with integers. D[i] is usually greater than R[i]. So instead we find the direction of movement by cross multiplication. For example: if R[x]D[y] < R[y]D[x] it indicates that the ray will intersect the voxel on the x co-ordinate before the y co-ordinate. The new P is thus found from the old as follows:

```
for i:=x to z do
    if D[i]>=0 then R[i]:=H[i]-P0[i]
    else R[i]:=L[i]-P0[i]-1;
k:=x;
for i:=y to z do
    if abs(R[k]*D[i])>abs(R[i]*D[k]) then k:=i;
for i:=x to z do
    if i=k then P[i]:=P0[i]+R[i]
        else P[i]:=P0[i]+(D[i]*R[k])/D[k];
```

This works even when the smallest voxel is only one unit wide. The truncation error in the division is always a fraction of a unit. And in the awkward case where the ray reaches two or three boundaries simultaneously, there is no error.

Since we consider only the exit surfaces of the voxel for the ray, we repeat this calculation for each voxel always using the original value of P, P0. Thus the truncation errors from the divisions do not accumulate and each P is guaranteed to be in the correct voxel. Notice that R[i] can never be zero, so that D[k] can only be zero in the trivial case where D[x], D[y], D[z] are all zero.

This algorithm uses only eight integer multiplications and two divisions per voxel.

Once we have a point guaranteed to be in the correct voxel, finding the voxel is straightforward (see Glassner[7]).

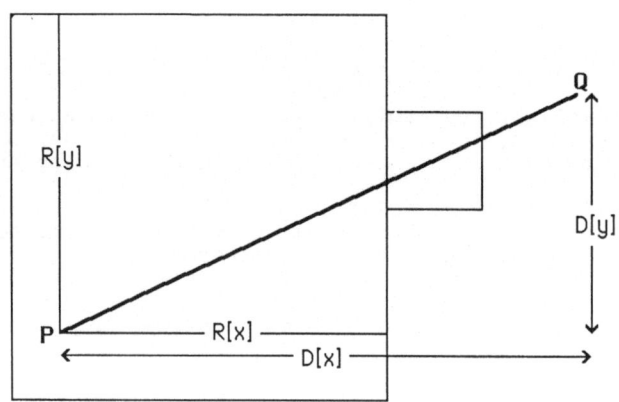

Diagram 4: 2-D Example of Next Voxel Algorithm

Since R[x]*D[y] < R[y]*D[x] the intersection is at:

P[x]+D[x], P[y]+(D[y]*R[x])/D[x]

D[x] cannot be zero so the division is safe.

THE RAY TRACING PRIMITIVE ROUTINES

Having found a non-empty voxel, the ray tracer must analyse the ray impact. This is done by a procedure from the appropriate primitive. First the intersection points of the ray with the voxel boundary are found. These points are then transformed back into the primitive's space using the inverse matrix associated with the octree leaf. The primitive procedure, therefore, is presented with the end points of a short ray. It returns TRUE or FALSE depending on whether the ray intersects the ideal object between its end points. When intersection occurs, it also returns the intersection point, and two others from which the ray tracer finds the surface normal. We don't allow the primitive routine to find the surface normal, because that would limit us to transformations which preserve angles. Our DAG building routines include stretching operations so that we can make ellipsoids from spheres and cylinders.

THE SYSTEM PRIMITIVES

An important feature of our system is the logical separation of procedures which describe primitives from the rest. These procedures provide us with a very flexible way to describe the nature of the primitive objects.

To date, we have implemented only a plane half-space and a cylinder as primitives. Because the only functions of our system are octree building and ray tracing, each of these primitives has only two associated procedures: "in" and "intersect".

"In" takes as arguments, eight points which are the transformed corners of a voxel. It tells us whether the voxel is completely inside the primitive, completely outside or neither. "Intersect" takes two points as arguments and finds intersections as described above.

Other routines which could be associated with primitives would perform functions appropriate to the needs of a system's applications. For example:

1. A volume procedure returning the proportion of a voxel's volume occupied.

2. A sketch procedure which generates line segments for sketching that part of a primitive lying inside a voxel.

3. A tooling procedure which creates elements for tool path generation.

TOOL PATH GENERATION

One of the objectives in our design is to facilitate the generation of tool paths for the automatic machining of objects described by the system. Yamaguchi, Kunii et al. [26] have described the generation of a simple tool path from an octree. Our system is designed to generate tool paths from the description in the DAG. The octree is used only as a check for interference.

Consider the operation of a drill. The volume cut out is described by a (subtracted) cylinder. The volume swept out by the chuck holding the drill can similarly be described by a cylinder, possibly with a shaped front end. We can describe the drilling action as the subtraction followed by adding the cylinder representing the chuck. If the chuck movement interferes with any part of the work piece, this will be detected during the octree construction.

Similarly a milling operation can be described by combining the shapes of diagram 5.

The use of a tool is described thus:

1. Subtract tool volume.

2. Add 'head' volume.

3. Subtract 'head' volume.

This should produce the same object as step 1 alone. For tool path generation, we start by describing the work piece. We then describe the finished shape by subtracting from the work piece, a sequence of objects each having an associated tool path component. Then we generate an octree and if no interference is detected, we have described an object which can be created by using the specified cutting operations in sequence. Finally, we can use the ray tracer to display the object. If it appears correct, then we have a sequence of machine operations to produce it.

In complicated cases, we can combine objects which represent a sequence of cutting operations. The tool path sequence is then determined by a top down traversal of the DAG.

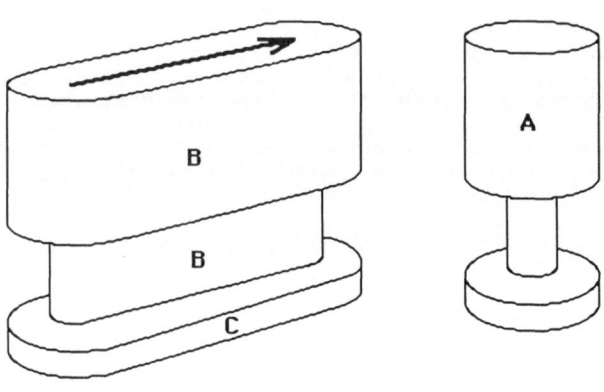

Diagram 5

An idealised milling tool, A, is shown together with its associated object. The volume C is subtracted and B is added to check for interference. The arrow shows the tool path.

DISCUSSION

The simple octrees of Tanimoto[8] and Meagher[10] have a number of leaves approximately proportional to the surface area of the objects represented. Our octrees have a number of leaves approximately proportional to the sum of the lengths of all the edges of the objects. An edge is, by definition, a line along which two primitive objects meet. It would be interesting to experiment with a system which permitted up to two primitive objects per voxel instead of one. Long edges would then be contained in large voxels and the 'nasty' cells would be confined to places where three or more primitives intersect.

Our algorithms are not particularly fast or space saving. For example, in the ray tracer, we transform each ray into a different space for processing by the primitive. Perhaps it is possible to create a package of data at octree creation which the primitive can use to operate on the ray in its original coordinates. This might take longer, but it need be done only once for each leaf in the octree, rather than many times in the ray tracer.

Although our ray tracer is not fast (50-100 rays per second on a VAX 750), it must be remembered that each intersection is calculated with respect to an ideal primitive object. We do not get the faceted look of cylinders aproximated by swept polygons.

We do not handle colours very well. When we make a hole, for example, by subtracting a blue cylinder from a red cube, the inside of the hole is blue! This is because we have only one kind of 'full' voxel. Arranging proper inheritance of colour or other properties is a substantial problem demanding attention.

The need for sets of points in space to be regular has been pointed out by Tilove [17, 18] and Voelcker and Requicha [14]. In essence a regular set of points is one from which dangling points, lines and planes of no thickness have been removed. Since our system allows for arbitrary set subtraction, it is capable of generating such dangling points and they are represented by unnecessary 'nasty cells' at the limit of resolution. These cells can be eliminated and we call this process regularisation. At the time of writing, we have designed a regularisation algorithm, but it has not been tested. Regularisation of an octree with superfluous cells reduces the storage needed. It may prove desirable to regularise the octrees during creation. We hope to report on this later.

ACKNOWLEDGEMENT

We are grateful to The Software Research Centre of Ricoh Co., Ltd. for financial support in this project.

CONCLUSION

A very simple pilot system for CAD by CSG has been produced to test some new principles and algorithms. Preliminary results suggest that this is a promising approach but more experimentation is needed to assess its performance. A new octree related structure has been designed and algorithms appropriate to its exploitation have been written. This new structure retains in its leaf elements, references to descriptions of the system primitive objects. This avoids the loss of information usually associated with this kind of structure.

REFERENCES

1. Atherton Peter R.
   A Scan-line Hidden Surface Removal Procedure for Constructive Solid Geometry
   Computer Graphics Vol. 17 No. 3 July 1984 pp 73-82

2. Boyse, J.W. and Gilchrist, J.E.
   GMSolid: Interactive Modelling for Design and Analysis of Solids
   IEEE Computer Graphics and Applications
   Vol. 2 No. 2 March 1982 pp 86-97

3. Brown, C.M.
   PADL-2: A Technical Summary
   IEEE Computer Graphics and Applications
   Vol. 2 No. 2 March 1982 pp 69-84

4. Carlbom, Ingrid; Chakravarty, Indranil; Vanderschel David
   A Hierarchical Data Structure for Representing the Spatial Decomposition of 3D Objects
   Frontiers in Computer Graphics: Proceedings
   of Computer Graphics Tokyo '84 Springer-Verlag 1985

5. Dippe, Mark; Swenson, John
   An Adaptive Subdivision Algorithm and Parallel Architecture for Realistic Image Synthesis
   Computer Graphics
   Vol. 18 No. 3 July 1984 pp 149-158

6. Frieder, Gideon; Gordon, Dan; Reynolds, Anthony R.
    Back-to-front Display of Voxel-Based Objects
    IEEE Computer Graphics and Applications
    Vol. 5 No. 1 January 1985 pp 52-60

7. Glassner, Andrew S.
    Space Subdivision for Fast Ray Tracing
    IEEE Computer Graphics and Applications
    Vol. 4 No. 10 October 1984 pp 15-22

8. Jackins C.L.; Tanimoto S.L.
    Oct-trees and Their Use in Representing Three Dimensional Objects
    Computer Graphics and Image Processing
    Vol. 14 No. 3 November 1980 pp 249-270

9. Liblong B; Hutchison N
    PG A Graphical Editor
    University of Calgary, CPSC project 1982

10. Meagher D.
    Geometric Modeling Using Octree Encoding
    Computer Graphics and Image processing
    Vol. 19 1982 pp 129-147

11. Myers, W.
    An Industrial Perspective on Solid Modeling
    IEEE Computer Graphics and Applications
    Vol. 2 No. 2 March 1982 pp 86-97

12. Norio Okino, Yukinori Kakazu, Masamichi Morimoto
    Extended Depth-Buffer Algorithms for Hidden Surface Visualization
    IEEE Computer Graphics and Applications
    Vol. 4 No. 5 May 1984 pp 79-88

13. Requicha, A.A.G. and Voelcker, H.B.
    Geometric Modelling of Mechanical Parts and Processes.
    IEEE Computer December 1977 pp 48-57

14. Requicha, A.A.G. and Voelcker, H.B.
    Solid Modeling: A Historical Summary and Contemporary Assessment
    IEEE Computer Graphics and Applications
    Vol. 2 No. 2 March 1982 pp 9-24

15. Roth, S.D.
    Ray Casting for Modelling Solids
    Computer Graphics and Image Processing
    Vol. 18 1982 pp 109-144

16. Sequin C.H.; Strauss P.S.
    Unigrafix (three dimensional graphics modelling)
    ACM IEEE 20th Design Automation Proceedings
    1983 pp 374-381

17. Tilove, R.B.
    Set Membership Classification: A Unified Approach to Geometric Intersection Problems
    IEEE Trans. Computers
    Vol. C-29 No. 10 October 1980 pp 874-833

18. Tilove, R.B.; Requicha, A.A.G.
    Closure of Boolean Operations on Geometric Entities
    Computer Aided Design
    Vol. 12 No. 5 September 1980 pp 219-220

19. Tuy, Heang, K.; Tuy, Lee Tan
    Direct 2-D Display of 3-D Objects
    IEEE Computer Graphics and Applications
    Vol. 4 No. 10 October 1984 pp 29-33

20. Voelcker, H.B.
    Algorithms and Applications
    Tutorial on Solid Modelling
    SIGGRAPH '82 (ACM)

21. Whitted, J. Turner
    An Improved Illumination Model for Shaded Display
    CACM
    Vol. 23 No. 6 June 1980 pp 343-349

22. Wolfe, R., Fitzgerald, W. and Gracer F.
    Interactive Graphics for Volume Modeling
    Proceedings of the IEEE Eighteenth Design Automation Conference
    pp 463-470

23. Wyvill, B.L.M., Liblong B. and Hutchison N.
    Using Recursion to Describe Polygonal Surfaces
    Proceedings of Graphics Interface '84
    Ottawa 1984, pp 167-171

24. Wyvill, B.L.M.
    Pictures-68 MK1
    Software: Practice and Experience Vol. 7 No. 2 1977 pp 251-261

25. Wyvill, G
    Pictorial Description Language 2
    Interactive Systems:
    Proceedings of The European Computing Conference
    Brunel University 1975

26. Yamaguchi, K.; Kunii, T.L.; Fujimura, K.; Toriya, H.
    Octree Related Data Structures and Algorithms
    IEEE Computer Graphics and Applications
    Vol. 4 No. 1 January 1984 pp 53-59

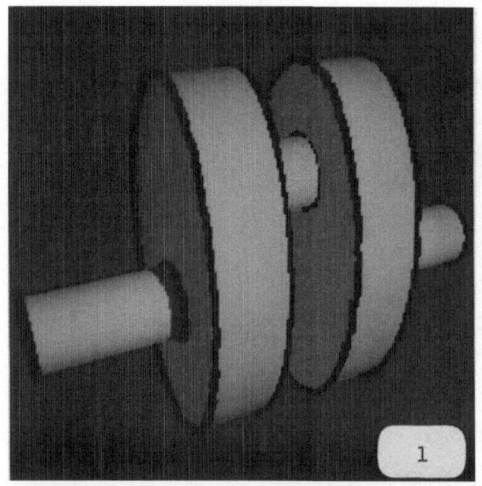
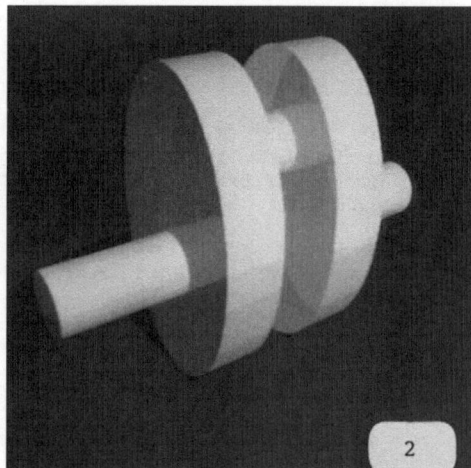
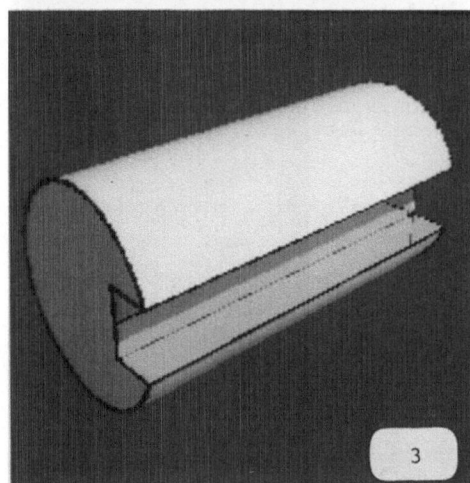
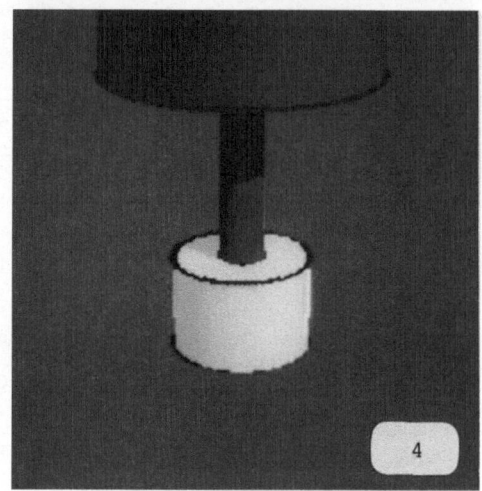
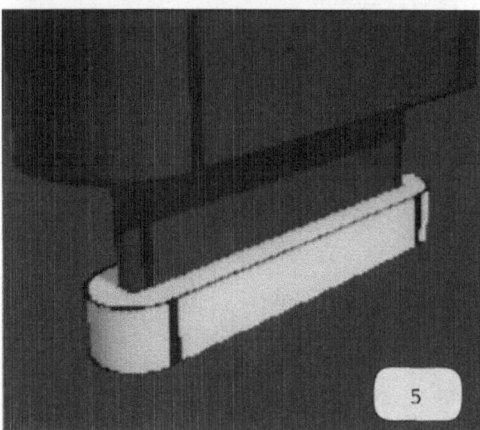

1. A crankshaft shown at low resolution (Octree depth 8). The 'nasty' cells appear black. Note that the webs are elliptical and not circular.
2. The same crankshaft at higher resolution (Octree depth 10).
3. A short shaft in which a keyway has been cut.
4. The idealised Milling tool used to cut the keyway.
5. The toolpath object which represents the cutting of the keyway. The yellow part represents the path of the tool to be subtracted from the shaft. The red part is the shape which is added to test for interference.

Geometric Continuity
with Interpolating Bézier Curves
Preliminary Report

Alain Fournier[1] and Brian A. Barsky[2]

[1] Computer Systems Research Institute, Department of Computer Science, University of Toronto, Toronto, Ontario, M5S 1A4, Canada
[2] Department of Electrical Engineering and Computer Sciences, University of California, Berkeley, CA 94720, USA

ABSTRACT

The Bézier formulation for parametric curves has many qualities, among them the intuitive relationship between the shape of the *control polygon* and the shape of the curve, and the ease of computation and subdivision. Other formulations, however, have become more popular because they offer local control, or because they are interpolating, or even more recently because they provide the added flexibility of *shape parameters*.

We present here techniques to use the Bézier formulation to interpolate the two-dimensional points given by a user with cubic piecewise Bézier curves, while maintaining up to $G^{[2]}$ continuity, and to interactively manipulate the *bias* and *tension* of each span, with geometric entities clearly related to the curve, while preserving the degree of geometric continuity prescribed by the user.

RESUME

La méthode de Bézier pour définir des courbes paramétriques a de nombreuses qualités, parmi lesquelles la relation intuitive entre la forme de la courbe et la forme du *polygone de contrôle*, et la facilité avec laquelle les courbes sont calculées et subdivisées. D'autres méthodes, cependant, sont devenus plus populaires parce qu'elles permettent le contrôle local, parce qu'elles interpolent, ou bien plus récemment parce qu'elles permettent de plus la possibilité de *paramètres de formes*.

Nous présentons ici des techniques pour utiliser la méthode de Bézier pour interpoler les points en deux dimensions donnés par l'utilisateur avec des arcs de courbes de Bézier, tout en maintenant la continuité géométrique jusqu'à $G^{[2]}$. Le système permet aussi à l'utilisateur de manipuler de façon interactive par l'intermédaire d'objects géometriques intuitivement reliés aux propriétés dsirées le *biais* et la *tension* de la courbe obtenue.

KEYWORDS: geometric modelling, Bézier curves, geometric continuity, font design systems.

1. Bézier Curves

The use of piecewise *spans* of parametric polynomial curves joined together under some continuity constraints to design curves (and surfaces) goes back to Coons and Bézier. Later, Riesenfeld used B-splines for the same purpose. Each of the various formulations used have qualities and drawbacks, but behind all is the desire to provide the user (the designer) with a more direct and more intuitive control of the shape of the curves.

Bézier curves use a simple and efficient formulation where the curve is defined solely in terms of a set of points called *control vertices* connected in a sequence to form a *control polygon* (Figure 1). The curve mimics the overall shape of the control polygon, but interpolates only the first and last vertices of the control polygon. The curve is defined by a polynomial whose degree is equal to the number of edges in the control polygon (that is the number of control vertices minus one). It follows immediately from this definition that the formulation has *global* not *local* control; that is the motion of a control vertex affects the shape of the entire curve. Likewise the curve is infinitely differentiable by virtue of being a polynomial. A Bézier curve $Q(u)$ defined by a set of control vertices $\{V_i\}$ is given by:

$$Q(u) = \sum_{i=0}^{d} V_i B_i(u)$$

where d is the degree of the curve and B_i are the binomial coefficients:

$$B_i(u) = \binom{n}{i} u^i (1-u)^{n-i} \quad , i=0,...,d$$

The Bézier formulation has numerous advantages: the shape is better related to the control points than in others, there is an easy geometric construction for the curves, and splitting a curve into two spans is also geometrically easy.

It is frequently desirable to decouple the number of control vertices from the degree of the curve, and to have local control as well. In the Bézier formulation it is easy to raise the degree of the curve, by creating a new set of vertices that generate the exact same curve with a (degenerate) polynomial of higher order (Figure 2). If we have the set $\{V_i\}$ with $i = 0,......,d$, the following formula gives the set $\{W_i\}$ of control vertices with $i = 0,......,d+1$:

$$W_i = (\frac{i}{d+1}) V_{i-1} + (1 - \frac{i}{d+1}) V_i \quad i = 0,......,d+1$$

To obtain local control, we use a piecewise representation of the curve. The entire curve is composed of *curve segments*, each of which is a Bézier polynomial. The common point between them is called a *joint*. The problem we face now is to maintain some amount of *continuity* at the joints.

2. Parametric and Geometric Continuity

The smoothness of a piecewise curve has traditionally been measured by maintaining *parametric continuity* at the joints; that is, a continuity in the parametric derivatives on both sides of the joint. Parametric continuity is usually noted $C^{[n]}$ where n is the order of the parametric derivative which is equal on both sides of the joint. Recent work has shown that parametric continuity is overly restrictive; more relaxed constraints of *geometric continuity* have recently been proposed [Fari82, Bars81, Bars83, DeRo85]. The key insight is that the traditional measure of continuity is affected by reparametrization. Geometric continuity provides a metric which is independant of the parametrization. The use of geometric continuity entails the use of *shape parameters* which provide further control of shape above and beyond that of control vertices. β_1 is known as *bias* and measures the relative influence of the tangent direction at a joint on each span. β_2 is called *tension* and controls the sharpness or flatness of the curve. These parameters appear in the equations of geometric continuity which are hence referred to as *beta constraints*. When two shape parameters are used, the continuity is denoted $G^{[2]}$ continuity. The reader is referred to [DeRo85] for a generalization of geometric continuity to any order $G^{[n]}$ and for the principle to construct the beta constraints of any order based on the chain rule of calculus. There are domains of application where parametric continuity is important, since the parametrization is directly related to the speed along the curve. But in other applications, only the shape is important, and this is where geometric continuity is the relevant concept.

For geometric continuity up to $G^{[3]}$, the necessary relationships are, given that the span $R(t)$ has a common joint with the span $Q(u)$ for the values of the parameters t_1 and u_0:

$$R^{(0)}(t_1) = Q^{(0)}(u_0)$$

$$\beta_1 R^{(1)}(t_1) = Q^{(1)}(u_0)$$

$$R^{(2)}(t_1) = \beta_1^2 Q^{(2)}(u_0) + \beta_2 Q^{(1)}(u_0)$$

$$R^{(3)}(t_1) = \beta_1^3 Q^{(3)}(u_0) + 3\beta_1 \beta_2 Q^{(2)}(u_0) + \beta_3 Q^{(1)}(u_0)$$

The formulations to which geometric continuity has been applied so far, besides being somewhat expensive to compute, suffer from another problem: the extra freedom given by the new parameters β_1 and β_2 is not intuitively related to some geometric entity to be manipulated by the user, but is controlled by setting some *dials* provided by the program [Koch84]. This is counter to the general philosophy of parametric curves. We propose here to remedy this by the use of the geometric characteristics of the Bézier formulation.

3. Parametric and Geometric Continuity in Bézier Curves

The relationships between the parametric derivatives curves and the control vertices are simple and well known [Faux79]. For example, for cubic curves, and the first two derivatives, assuming the spans defined above have the control vertices $\{W_i\}$ and $\{V_i\}$ (Figure 3):

$$R^{(1)}(t_1) = 3(W_3 - W_2)$$
$$Q^{(1)}(u_0) = 3(V_1 - V_0)$$
$$R^{(2)}(t_1) = 6(W_1 - 2W_2 + W_3)$$
$$Q^{(2)}(u_0) = 6(V_0 - 2V_1 + V_2)$$

To ensure geometric continuity ($G^{[2]}$) the preceding relationships together with the beta constraints given above give the following relationships for the vertices of span Q as a function of the vertices of span R:

$$V_0 = W_3$$
$$V_1 = (1 + \beta_1)W_3 - \beta_1 W_2$$
$$V_2 = \beta_1^2 W_1 - (2\beta_1^2 + 2\beta_1 + \frac{\beta_2}{2})W_2 + (\beta_1^2 + 2\beta_1 + 1 + \frac{\beta_2}{2})W_3$$

In other words, only V_3 can be freely chosen if we insist on $G^{[2]}$ geometric continuity once β^1 and β^2 are chosen. The crucial point is that the relaxation of the continuity constraints gives us two more degrees of freedom. In particular, we can adjust β_1 and β_2 to be able to ensure $G^{[2]}$ on both sides of the span. The usefulness of the Bézier formulation is in the fact that the control vertices and the shape parameters are directly and simply related. [Rams85] discusses the issues of parametrizations, geometric continuity and geometric constructions in Bézier formulations.

4. The Interactive System

The user first interactively inputs a set of two-dimensional points. These are the points that will be interpolated by the system, and the points the user will see most of the time and use to modify the basic shape of the curve. The system then draws a smooth interpolating curve through the points. The default method is to fit the cubic interpolating version of Catmull-Rom splines [Catm74]. In order to accomplish this while interpolating the end points, more information (two values per end point) has to be provided. One solution is to ask the user for "phantom" vertices. But it is better to have the system provide "reasonable" extra vertices on its own. A good solution when the intended curves have definite symmetries is to take the mirror image of the third point through the perpendicular bisector to the first segment (and similarly at the end; see Figure 4).

The curve obtained is only $C^{[1]}$ continuous at the joints. More continuity could be provided (actually the curve could be made $G^{[2]}$ continuous everywhere) but that would be, in general, at the price of undesirable variations between the joints. Note also that $C^{[1]}$ continuous means $G^{[1]}$ continuous with $\beta_1 = 1.0$.

The next step is to create the extra control vertices that define Bézier spans identical with the spans already computed. It is a straighforward change of basis. To simplify the terminology, we will call *points* the points originally defined by the user. Note that they are also joints between the spans. We will call *control vertices* the added vertices of the Bézier control polygons. Of course the joints are also control vertices. We will mention them explicitly if need be (Figure 5).

Now the user has available two kinds of control: shape and shape parameters. Shape is controlled through the points (joints) and shape parameters through the control vertices. The system maintains the continuity required by default or as specified by the user. We will illustrate some possibilities.

The original points given can be manipulated to change the overall shape of the curve. These changes can be made while respecting the local continuity that the user wants respected. Note that these changes are only local, since they affect only a small number of spans. Four spans are affected for $C^{[2]}$ continuity, two for $C^{[1]}$ or $G^{[2]}$ continuity. Of course the user can choose to split the curve at this joint. While acting on the original points, in general the control vertices are not even displayed. They are automatically updated by the system to maintain the required constraints.

The other group of options is to manipulate the control vertices to influence the shape parameters of the curve at a joint. In this case, the vertices are visible, but move only according to the continuity constraints required. For instance, to manipulate the bias at a joint, while respecting $G^{[1]}$ continuity, the user only has to slide the control vertex along the line defined by the tangent. The program automatically maintains the vertex on this line (Figure 6). To adjust the tension, while for example keeping tangent continuity at each end of the span, the user grabs the segment defined by the two middle control vertices, and moves it closer to or farther from the segment defined by the two original points (Figure 7).

The fact that the shape and the shape parameters are locally controlled, and that they are controlled through geometric entities visibly related to their effects is a great help in the interaction. The problem with local control of shape parameters is the often undesirable behaviour of the curves between the joints. By having a "visible" control of shape, the user is better able to avoid these problems, and to understand them if they occur.

5. Conclusions

Bézier curves are easier to compute and to subdivide than most formulations. They also allow easy control over geometric continuity by the manipulation of the control vertices. The scheme we presented here exploits these properties to give the user explicit and intuitive control over bias and tension with interpolating curves.

The scheme is currently limited to planar curves. There are many areas of applications where good shape control in the plane is useful. One of the most important ones is font design. Some systems have already been implemented using parametric curves [Plas83, Knut79, Pavl84]. It is our intention to implement a prototypical system to apply the techniques described in this paper to that particular task.

Acknowledgements

We gratefully acknowledge the support of the Natural Sciences and Engineering Research Council. Mark Corbould has implemented the prototype system, and contributed many ideas, and Avi Naiman provided some of software for the interface and wise advice.

References

[Bars81]
Barsky, B. A., *The Beta-Spline: A Local Representation Based on Shape Parameters and Fundamental Geometric Measures*, Ph. D. Thesis, Department of Computer Science, University of Utah, Salt Lake City, Utah, December 1981.

[Bars83]
Barsky, B. A. and J. C. Beatty, "Local Control of Bias and Tension in Beta-Splines", ACM Transactions on Graphics, Volume 2, Number 2, April 1983.

[Catm74]
Catmull, E. E. and Rom, R. J., "A Class of Local Interpolating Splines", *Computer Aided Geometric Design*, Barnhill, R. E. and Riesenfeld, R. F., Eds, Academic Press, (1974), 317-326.

[DeRo84]
DeRose, T. D. and B. A. Barsky, "Geometric Continuity and Shape Parameters for Catmull-Rom Splines", in *Proceedings of Graphics Interface '84*, Ottawa, Ontario, May 1984, 57-62.

[DeRo85]
DeRose, T. D. and Barsky, B. A., "An Intuitive Approach to Geometric Continuity for Parametric Curves and Surfaces", in *Proceedings of Graphics Interface '85*, Montréal, May 1985, 343-351.

[Fari82]
Farin, G., "Visually C^2 Cubic Splines", Computer-Aided Design, Volume 14, Number 3, May 1982, 137-139.

[Faux79]
Faux, I. D. and M. J. Pratt, *Computational Geometry for Design and Manufacture*, John Wiley and Sons, 1979.

[Knut79]
Knuth, D. E., *Metafont: A System for Alphabet Design*, Technical Report STAN-CS-79-762, Department of Computer Science, Stanford University, Stanford, California, September 1979.

[Koch84]
Kochanek, D. H. and R. H. Bartels, "Interpolating Splines with Local Tension, Continuity, and Bias Control", *SIGGRAPH 1984 Proceedings*, published as Computer Graphics, Volume 18, Number 3, July 1984, 33-41.

[Pavl83]
Pavlidis, T., "Curve Fitting with Conic Splines", ACM Transactions on Graphics, Volume 2, Number 1, January 1983, 1-31.

[Plas83]
Plass, M. and Stone, M., "Curve-Fitting with Piecewise Parametric Cubics", *SIGGRAPH 1983 Proceedings*, also published as Computer Graphics, Volume 17, Number 3, July 1983, 229-239.

[Rams85]
Ramshaw, L., "A Euclidean View of Joints between Bézier Curves", to appear in ACM Transactions on Graphics.

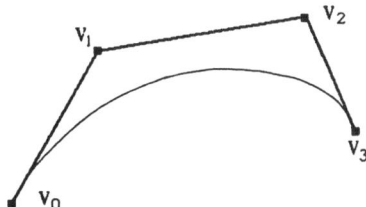

Figure 1. Bézier curve and its control polygon.

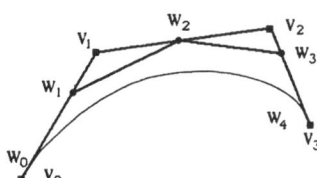

Figure 2. Raising the degree of a Bézier curve from cubic to quartic.

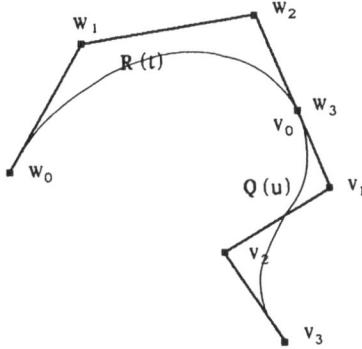

Figure 3. Continuity constraints at the joints.

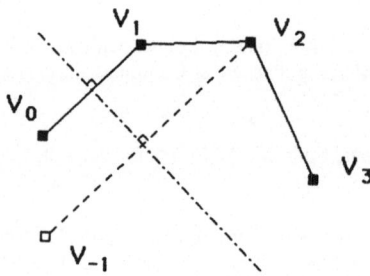

Figure 4. Creating the phantom vertex by symmetry.

Figure 5. Interpolated points and control vertices.

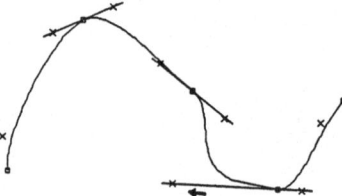

Figure 6. Controlling the bias at a joint.

Figure 7. Controlling the tension.

An Intuitive Approach to Geometric Continuity for Parametric Curves and Surfaces

Tony D. DeRose and Brian A. Barsky

Berkeley Computer Graphics Laboratory, Computer Science Division, Department of Electrical Engineering and Computer Sciences, University of California, Berkeley, CA 94720, USA

Abstract

Parametric spline curves and surfaces are typically constructed so that some number of derivatives match where the curve segments or surface patches abut. If derivatives up to order n are continuous, the segments or patches are said to meet with C^n, or n^{th} order *parametric continuity*. It has been shown previously that parametric continuity is sufficient, but not necessary, for geometric smoothness.

The geometric measures of *unit tangent* and *curvature* vectors for curves, and *tangent plane* and *Dupin indicatrix* for surfaces, have been used to define first and second order *geometric continuity*. In this paper, we extend the notion of geometric continuity to arbitrary order n (G^n) for curves and surfaces, and present an intuitive development of constraint equations that are necessary and sufficient for it. The constraints (known as the *Beta constraints*) result from a direct application of the univariate chain rule for curves and the bivariate chain rule for surfaces. For first and second order continuity, the Beta constraints are equivalent to requiring continuity of the geometric measures described above.

The Beta constraints provide for the introduction of quantities known as *shape parameters*. If two curve segments are to meet with G^n continuity, n shape parameters may be introduced. For surfaces, the use of the constraints for G^n continuity provides for the introduction of $n(n + 3)$ shape functions, defined along the boundary between two surface patches. For polynomial splines, the use of the Beta constraints allows greater flexibility through the shape parameters without raising the polynomial degree.

The approach we take is important for several reasons. First, it generalizes geometric continuity to arbitrary order for both curves and surfaces. Second, it shows the fundamental connection

---

This work was supported in part by the Defense Advanced Research Projects Agency under contract number N00039-82-C-0235, the National Science Foundation under grant number ECS-8204381, the State of California under a Microelectronics Innovation and Computer Research Opportunities grant, and a Shell Doctoral Fellowship.

between geometric continuity of curves and that of surfaces. Finally, due to the chain rule derivation, constraints of any order can be determined more easily than using derivations based exclusively on geometric measures.

Résumé

Les courbes et surfaces paramétriques à base de splines sont généralement construites de façon à ce qu'un certain nombre de dérivées coïncident aux raccordements entre les arcs de courbe ou les carreaux de surface. Lorsqu'additionnellement les n premières dérivées sont continues, les arcs ou les carreaux se rencontrent avec *continuité paramétrique C^n*, ou d'ordre n. Il a déjà été établi que la continuité paramétrique est suffisante à l'obtention d'un lissage géométrique, mais qu'elle n'est pas nécessaire.

Les premier et deuxième ordres de continuité géométrique sont généralement définis à l'aide de mesures géométriques tels le *vecteur tangent unitaire* et le *vecteur de courbure* dans le cas des courbes, ainsi que le *plan tangent* et l'*indicatrix de Dupin* dans le cas des surfaces. Dans cet article, nous généralisons la notion de continuité géométrique à n'importe quel ordre n (G^n) aussi bien pour les courbes que pour les surfaces. Nous présentons également un développement intuitif des équations de contrainte nécessaires et suffisantes. Ces contraintes, que nous appelons les *contraintes-beta*, découlent directement des règles de chaîne à une variable pour les courbes et à deux variables pour les surfaces. Pour les premier et second ordres de continuité, les contraintes-beta sont équivalentes à la continuité des mesures géométriques décrites ci-dessus.

Les contraintes-beta offrent l'occasion d'introduire certaines quantités connues sous le nom de *paramètres de formes*. Si deux arcs de courbe doivent se raccorder avec continuité G^n, n paramètres de formes peuvent être introduits. Pour les surfaces, l'utilisation des contraintes de continuité G^n permet d'introduire $n(n+3)$ *fonctions de formes*, lesquelles sont définies le long des limites communes entre les surfaces de deux carreaux mitoyens. Dans le cas des splines polynomiaux, l'utilisation des contraintes-beta permet une flexibilité accrue grâce aux paramètres de formes, sans pour autant augmenter le degré du polynôme.

Cette approche est importante pour maintes raisons. Premièrement, elle généralise la notion de continuité géométriques aux ordres quelconques, autant pour les courbes que pour les surfaces. Deuxièmement, elle met en évidence la similarité fondamentale entre la continuité géométrique des courbes et celle des surfaces. Finalement, les règles de chaîne facilitent la détermination de contraintes d'ordre quelconque, comparativement à ce qu'auraient permis des dérivations basées uniquement sur des mesures géométriques.

KEYWORDS: geometric modelling, continuity, parametric curves, parametric surfaces, shape parameters.

1. INTRODUCTION

Curves are defined or *generated* by *parametrizations* (surfaces will be addressed in Section 3). A *univariate* (one variable) parametrization is a function such as $\mathbf{q}(u) = (X(u), Y(u))$, where the *domain parameter* u is allowed to range over some interval $[u_0, u_1]$. For a given value of u, the function $\mathbf{q}(u)$ can be thought of as locating a particle in Euclidean two-space. As u is increased over the interval, the particle traverses a path defined by $\mathbf{q}$, tracing out a curve in the process (see Figure 1). If $[u_0, u_1]$ is thought of as an oriented line segment, then $\mathbf{q}$ can be thought of as a deformation producing an *oriented curve*. One advantage of the parametric representation is that a curve in Euclidean space of arbitrary dimension m can be described by a parametrization such as $\mathbf{q}(u) = (x_1(u), x_2(u), ..., x_m(u))$.

For a curve generated by $\mathbf{q}(u)$, the first derivative vector $\mathbf{q}^{(1)}$ represents the *velocity* of the particle[†]. The velocity is a vector quantity and, as such, contains information about orientation and *rate*, or speed. The second derivative vector $\mathbf{q}^{(2)}$ represents the *acceleration* of the particle, so it too contains information about the rate (specifically, the change of rate). Thus, a parametrization contains information about the *geometry* (the shape or image of the curve), the orientation, and the rate.

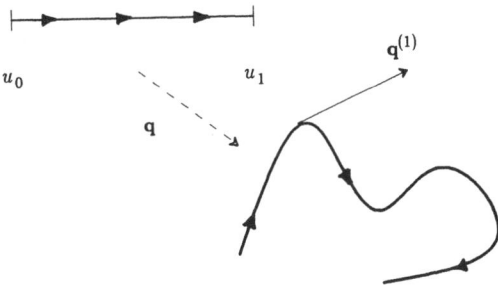

Figure 1. *The univariate parametrization* $\mathbf{q}$ *generates an oriented curve by deformation of the oriented line segment* $[u_0, u_1]$.

Figure 2 show the curves generated by three different parametrizations. The shape of the curves is identical; they differ only in orientation and rate. Curves (a) and (b) have the same orientation at each point, but the rates differ. The curve labelled (c) differs from (a) and (b) in orientation and rate. If a curve is defined to be simply the geometry of a parametrization, one would conclude that figures (a), (b), and (c) represent *equivalent* curves. We will refer to this as the *G model* of a curve. Another possibility is to consider the geometry and orientation, which we call the *GO*

[†] In general, we denote the ith derivative of a univariate function by superscript (i).

model. Using the GO model, one would say that (a) and (b) are equivalent, but (c) is different. The last possibility we will consider is the *GOR model*, where geometry, orientation, and rate are all relevant to the definition of a curve. Using this model, no pair of the curves is equivalent.

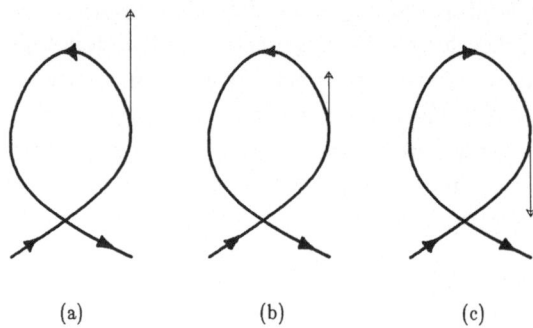

Figure 2. *Each of the curves above has the same image; they differ only in orientation and rate. Orientation is indicated by arrowheads and rate is indicated by vectors tangent to the curves.*

In recent years, heavy use has been made of piecewise parametric functions known as *parametric splines*. Parametric spline curves are typically constructed by stitching together univariate parametric functions, requiring that some number of derivatives match at each *joint* (the points where the curve segments meet). If n derivatives agree at a given joint, the parametrizations there are said to meet with n^{th} *order parametric continuity* (C^n continuity for short).

We maintain that the choice of a particular model for a curve, and hence the choice of how the curve segments are stitched together, should be application dependent. For instance, if a spline is being used to define the motion of an object in an animation system, the GOR model is most appropriate since the orientation and rate are of importance. In this type of application, parametric continuity is required to maintain smoothness of rate. In other words, parametric continuity will ensure that the object will *move* smoothly.

However, in CAGD the rate aspect of a parametrization is often unimportant. Consider for example the use of splines to describe numerically-controlled cutters. It may be necessary to specify uniquely the direction of the cutter at each point on the path, but the speed of the cutter may depend upon the hardness of the material being cut. For this type of application, the GO model is most suitable, but parametric continuity is overly restrictive since it places emphasis on irrelevant rate information. Many other applications in CAGD require only the G model, but it seems difficult to develop a useful formalism without the structure provided by orientation. We therefore adopt the GO model, and develop an appropriate measure of continuity — one based only on the geometry and orientation; we refer to this as *geometric continuity*, a term first introduced by Barsky & Beatty[3].

It has recently come to our attention that many authors have independently defined this kind of continuity of first and second order (which we denote by G^1 and G^2, respectively) for curves and/or surfaces using geometric means. For curves, Fowler & Wilson[12], Sabin[19], Manning[15], Faux & Pratt[10], and Barsky[1] each (independently) defined first order continuity by requiring that the *unit tangent vectors* agree at the joints. To achieve second order continuity, both the unit tangent and *curvature* vectors were required to match. Nielson's ν-spline[16] possesses a similar kind of continuity. These geometric measures essentially ignore the rate information by "normalizing" the parametrization before determining smoothness.

For surfaces, it is common to require matching of *tangent planes* for first order geometric continuity (cf. Sabin[20] and Veron et al[22]). For surfaces of second order geometric continuity, Veron et al and Kahmann[14] require continuity of *normal curvature* in every direction, at every point on the boundary shared by the constituent surface patches. As Veron et al and Kahmann each show, this is equivalent to requiring that the *Dupin indicatrix* (cf. DoCarmo[8]) of each patch agree at the boundary curve. The Dupin indicatrix is a measure of curvature, but the curvature properties of surfaces are sufficiently complex that they cannot be characterized by something as simple as a scalar or a vector.

Although the geometric approaches described above are convenient and intuitive for first and second order continuity, a more algebraic development is better suited for the extension to continuity of higher order. The approach we take is based on *reparametrization* — the process of obtaining a new parametrization given an old one. Under the GO model, reparametrization may change rate, but not geometry or orientation. By allowing reparametrization before making a determination of continuity, the rate aspects of parametrizations may be ignored. Alternately stated, our approach is based on the following simple idea:

P1: *Don't base continuity on the parametrizations at hand; reparametrize, if necessary, to obtain parametrizations that meet with parametric continuity. If this can be done, the original parametrizations must also meet smoothly, at least in a geometric sense.*

The above concept is not a new one; similar principles have been discussed by Farin[9] and Veron et al[22]. What is new is the use of the principle to construct constraint equations (known as the *Beta constraints*) that are necessary and sufficient for geometric continuity of arbitrary order for both curves and surfaces.*

The Beta constraints generalize the parametric continuity constraints through the introduction of freely variable quantities called *shape parameters*. Once the Beta constraints are determined for a given order of continuity, they may be used in place of the parametric continuity constraints when building splines, thereby obtaining increased flexibility. For instance, if the C^2 constraints are

---

* Goodman[13] and Ramshaw[17] have independently derived the univariate Beta constraints from the univariate chain rule.

replaced with the G^2 constraints in the uniform cubic B-spline[18], the cubic Beta-spline results[1,2]. The cubic Beta-spline is an *approximating* spline technique that possesses two shape parameters; an *interpolating* technique is described in DeRose & Barsky[7]. Faux & Pratt[10], Farin[9], and Fournier & Barsky[11] use the extra freedom allowed by geometric continuity to place *Bézier control vertices*.

An important aspect of these techniques is that the additional flexibility of geometric continuity is added without increasing the degree of the polynomials. This is particularly important for algorithms that manipulate the spline. For instance, the complexity of Sederberg's algorithm[21] to intersect two polynomial curves of degree d grows at least as fast as d^3. Substantial savings can therefore be realized by minimizing the degree of the polynomials involved.

In the remainder of this paper, we extend the notion of geometric continuity to arbitrary order n (G^n) and show (in a nonrigorous way) that the derivation of the Beta constraints results from a straightforward use of the univariate chain rule for curves and the bivariate (two variable) chain rule for surfaces. For a more complete treatment, the reader is referred to Barsky & DeRose[4] and DeRose[6].

2. GEOMETRIC CONTINUITY FOR CURVES

We begin the study of geometric continuity for curves by examining the reparametrization process. Two parametrizations are said to be *GO-equivalent* if they have the same geometry and orientation in the neighborhood of each point. Given a parametrization $\mathbf{q}$, all GO-equivalent parametrizations may be obtained by *functional composition*. More specifically, if $\mathbf{q}(u)$ and $\tilde{\mathbf{q}}(\tilde{u})$ are GO-equivalent, then they are related by $\tilde{\mathbf{q}}(\tilde{u}) = \mathbf{q}(u(\tilde{u}))$, for some appropriately chosen *change of parameter* $u(\tilde{u})$ (see Figure 3). Since $\mathbf{q}$ and $\tilde{\mathbf{q}}$ must have the same orientation, u must be an increasing function of $\tilde{u}$, implying that u must satisfy the *orientation preserving condition* $u^{(1)} > 0$. Intuitively, $u(\tilde{u})$ deforms the interval $[\tilde{u}_0, \tilde{u}_1]$ into the interval $[u_0, u_1]$ without reversing the orientation of the segment $[\tilde{u}_0, \tilde{u}_1]$. This in turn implies that $\mathbf{q}$ and $\tilde{\mathbf{q}}$ will have the same geometry and orientation, but they may differ in rate.

A univariate parametrization is *regular* if the first derivative vector does not vanish. It is well known from differential geometry[8] that regularity is, in general, essential for the smoothness of the resulting curve. We will therefore restrict the discussion to regular parametrizations. We now give a more precise definition of G^n continuity:

Definition 2.1: Let $\mathbf{q}(u), u \in [u_0, u_1]$ and $\mathbf{r}(t), t \in [t_0, t_1]$ be two parametrizations such that $\mathbf{q}(u_1) = \mathbf{r}(t_0) = \mathbf{J}$ *(see Figure 4)*. These parametrizations meet with G^n continuity at $\mathbf{J}$ if and only if there exist GO-equivalent parametrizations $\tilde{\mathbf{q}}(\tilde{u})$ and $\tilde{\mathbf{r}}(\tilde{t})$ that meet with C^n continuity at joint.

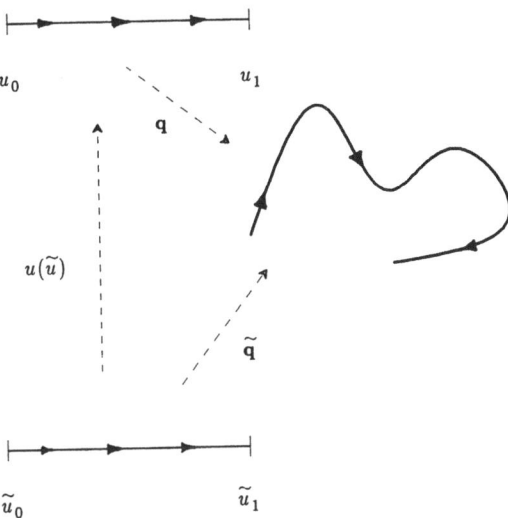

Figure 3. *The equivalent parametrizations* q *and* q̃ *are related by the change of parameter* $u(\tilde{u})$.

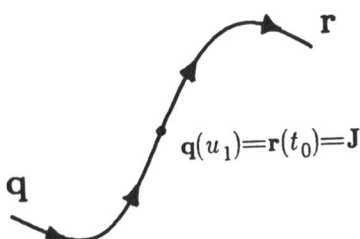

Figure 4. *The parametrizations* q(u) *and* r(t) *meet at the common point* J.

Definition 2.1 is simply a restatement of principle P1, but in practice one cannot examine all GO-equivalent parametrizations in an effort to find two that meet with parametric continuity. However, it is possible to find conditions on **q** and **r** that are necessary and sufficient for the *existence* of GO-equivalent parametrizations that meet with parametric continuity.

Although Definition 2.1 suggests that both **q** and **r** need to be reparametrized, it is possible to show that Definition 2.1 holds if and only if there exists a **q̃** that meets **r** with parametric continuity. In other words, only one of the parametrizations needs to be reparametrized to determine smoothness.

We will ultimately be interested in the derivative properties of **q̃**. The *univariate chain rule* allows derivatives of **q̃** to be expressed in terms of the derivatives of **q** and u. For example, the first derivative is given by

$$\tilde{\mathbf{q}}^{(1)} = \frac{d\tilde{\mathbf{q}}}{d\tilde{u}} = \frac{d\mathbf{q}(u(\tilde{u}))}{d\tilde{u}}$$
$$= \frac{du}{d\tilde{u}}\frac{d\mathbf{q}}{du} \qquad (2.1)$$
$$= u^{(1)}\,\mathbf{q}^{(1)}.$$

In general, the ith derivative of $\tilde{\mathbf{q}}$ can be written as some function, call it $\mathcal{CR}_i$, of the first i derivatives of u and $\mathbf{q}$. That is,

$$\tilde{\mathbf{q}}^{(i)} = \mathcal{CR}_i(\mathbf{q}^{(1)},\cdots,\mathbf{q}^{(i)},u^{(1)},\cdots,u^{(i)}). \qquad (2.2)$$

We are actually interested in $\tilde{\mathbf{q}}^{(i)}$ evaluated at its *right parametric endpoint* $\tilde{u}_1$. Thus, derivatives of $\mathbf{q}$ and u must also be evaluated at their right parametric endpoints:

$$\tilde{\mathbf{q}}^{(i)}(\tilde{u}_1) = \mathcal{CR}_i(\mathbf{q}^{(1)}(u_1),\cdots,\mathbf{q}^{(i)}(u_1),u^{(1)}(\tilde{u}_1),\cdots,u^{(i)}(\tilde{u}_1)). \qquad (2.3)$$

Since u is a scalar function, evaluating one of its derivatives results in a real number. In particular, let $u^{(j)}(\tilde{u}_1) = \beta_j$, $j = 1, ..., i$. Equation (2.3) then becomes

$$\tilde{\mathbf{q}}^{(i)}(\tilde{u}_1) = \mathcal{CR}_i(\mathbf{q}^{(1)}(u_1),\cdots,\mathbf{q}^{(i)}(u_1),\beta_1,\cdots,\beta_i). \qquad (2.4)$$

The orientation preserving quality of u implies that $\beta_1 > 0$.

We are now in a position to state the primary result of geometric continuity for curves. Recall that $\mathbf{q}$ and $\mathbf{r}$ meet with G^n continuity if $\mathbf{q}$ can be reparametrized to $\tilde{\mathbf{q}}$ so that derivatives of $\mathbf{r}$ and $\tilde{\mathbf{q}}$ agree. That is, we require that

$$\mathbf{r}^{(i)}(t_0) = \tilde{\mathbf{q}}^{(i)}(\tilde{u}_1), \qquad i = 1, ..., n. \qquad (2.5)$$

Positional continuity is implicitly assumed (see Figure 4). Substituting equation (2.4) into (2.5) yields

$$\mathbf{r}^{(i)}(t_0) = \mathcal{CR}_i(\mathbf{q}^{(1)}(u_1),\cdots,\mathbf{q}^{(i)}(u_1),\beta_1,\cdots,\beta_i) \qquad i = 1, ..., n. \qquad (2.6)$$

The constraints resulting from equation (2.6) are the *univariate Beta constraints* and the numbers $\beta_1, ..., \beta_n$ are the *shape parameters*. The above discussion is not a proof that the Beta constraints are necessary and sufficient conditions for geometric continuity, but such a proof can be constructed[4,6]. Thus, if equations (2.6) are satisfied for any choice of the β_i's, subject to $\beta_1 > 0$, then the coincident curve segments will meet with G^n continuity. For instance, the Beta constraints for G^4 continuity between $\mathbf{q}$ and $\mathbf{r}$ are

$$\begin{aligned}
\mathbf{r}^{(1)}(t_0) &= \beta_1\,\mathbf{q}^{(1)}(u_1) \\
\mathbf{r}^{(2)}(t_0) &= \beta_1^2\,\mathbf{q}^{(2)}(u_1) + \beta_2\,\mathbf{q}^{(1)}(u_1) \\
\mathbf{r}^{(3)}(t_0) &= \beta_1^3\,\mathbf{q}^{(3)}(u_1) + 3\beta_1\beta_2\,\mathbf{q}^{(2)}(u_1) + \beta_3\,\mathbf{q}^{(1)}(u_1) \\
\mathbf{r}^{(4)}(t_0) &= \beta_1^4\,\mathbf{q}^{(4)}(u_1) + 6\beta_1^2\beta_2\,\mathbf{q}^{(3)}(u_1) + (4\beta_1\beta_3 + 3\beta_2^2)\,\mathbf{q}^{(2)}(u_1) + \beta_4\,\mathbf{q}^{(1)}(u_1).
\end{aligned} \qquad (2.7)$$

The discussion leading from equation (2.3) to equation (2.4) suggests that the ith Beta constraint is determined by repeated application of the chain rule, followed by evaluation at the right parametric endpoint. There is, however, an easier way to derive the Beta constraints. The method is based on the observation that CR_i is obtained by differentiation of CR_{i-1}, suggesting that the ith Beta constraint can be obtained by "differentiating" the $i-1^{st}$ order constraint. Differentiating in the normal way makes little sense because the Beta constraints are not functions. However, recall that β_i results from the evaluation of $u^{(i)}$, and that $u^{(i+1)}$ results from differentiating of $u^{(i)}$, so in some sense, β_{i+1} results from differentiation of β_i. More specifically, consider the derivative of $(u^{(i)})^k$:

$$\frac{d(u^{(i)})^k}{d\tilde{u}} = k(u^{(i)})^{k-1} u^{(i+1)} \qquad (2.8)$$

which can be interpreted at the right parametric endpoint as

$$\frac{d\beta_i^k}{d\tilde{u}} = k\beta_i^{k-1}\beta_{i+1}. \qquad (2.9)$$

Similarly, using the chain rule, the derivative of $\mathbf{q}^{(i)}$ with respect to $\tilde{u}$ is

$$\frac{d\mathbf{q}^{(i)}}{d\tilde{u}} = u^{(1)}\mathbf{q}^{(i+1)} \qquad (2.10)$$

which can be interpreted at the right parametric endpoint as

$$\frac{d\mathbf{q}^{(i)}(u_1)}{d\tilde{u}} = \beta_1 \mathbf{q}^{(i+1)}(u_1). \qquad (2.11)$$

Using the heuristic rules (2.9) and (2.11) together with the heuristic

$$\frac{d\mathbf{r}^{(i)}(t_0)}{d\tilde{u}} = \mathbf{r}^{(i+1)}(t_0) \qquad (2.12)$$

and the product rule for differentiation, the ith order constraint can be obtained by differentiating the $i-1^{st}$ order constraint with respect to $\tilde{u}$. One can easily verify that equations (2.7) result from these rules.

It is important to check that we have indeed generalized geometric continuity by showing that our definitions reduce to the previous geometry-based definitions of unit tangent and curvature vector continuity. This is easily done by noting that the first two equations of (2.7) are identical to the constraints resulting from a geometric derivation using unit tangent and curvature vector continuity[2,15]. Thus, our approach reduces to previous definitions of G^1 and G^2 continuity for curves. It can also be shown that Beta constraints for n^{th} order continuity are equivalent to requiring continuity of the first n derivatives with respect to *arc length* [4,6].

When constructing a spline technique, if the Beta constraints are used in place of the parametric continuity constraints, new freedom is introduced through the shape parameters. These parameters may be made available to a designer in a CAGD environment to change the shape of the target curve, as the following example shows.

Example 2.1: *To demonstrate the use of the Beta constraints, we will sketch the construction of the geometric continuous analogue of the uniform quartic B-spline called (naturally enough) the quartic Beta-spline.*

The jth segment of the quartic B-spline is generated by

$$\mathbf{q}_j(u) = \sum_{k=-2}^{2} \mathbf{V}_{j+k} B_k(u), \qquad u \in [0,1] \qquad (2.13)$$

where the basis functions $B_k(u)$ are quartic polynomials that satisfy

$$B_{k+1}^{(i)}(1) = B_k^{(i)}(0),$$
$$i = 0, 1, 2, 3, \qquad (2.14)$$
$$k = -2, ..., 1.$$

The sequence of control vertices $\mathbf{V}_{j+k}$ comprise a control polygon.

Since the derivative properties of the basis functions are inherited by $\mathbf{q}_j$, equation (2.14) implies that the curve segments meet with C^3 continuity. The quartic Beta-spline is constructed by building quartic polynomials $b_k(u)$ that satisfy the G^3 constraints instead of the C^3 constraints of equation (2.14). That is,

$$b_{k+1}^{(i)}(1) = C\mathcal{R}_i(b_k^{(1)}(0), \cdots, b_k^{(i)}(0), \beta_1, \cdots, \beta_i) \qquad i = 0, 1, 2, 3. \qquad (2.15)$$

Equation (2.15) implies that the basis functions are dependent upon the shape parameter values. Changing a shape parameter therefore changes the shape of the resulting curve (see Figure 5).

3. GEOMETRIC CONTINUITY FOR SURFACES

In this section, we extend the notions of geometric continuity to surfaces. Since care was taken in Section 2 not to base the development of geometric continuity on concepts (such as arc length) that don't apply to surfaces, the machinery developed for univariate parametrizations can be readily extended to bivariate parametrizations.

A *surface patch* is defined by a bivariate function such as $\mathbf{G}(u,v) = (X(u,v), Y(u,v), Z(u,v))$, where u and v are allowed to range over some region D of the uv plane (see Figure 6). Loosely speaking, a *surface* is a collection of surface patches. We use the notation $\mathbf{G}^{(i,j)}(u,v)$ to denote the ith partial derivative with respect to u, and the jth partial with respect to v. In general, a superscript (i,j) denotes the ith partial with respect to the first variable, and the jth partial with respect to the second variable. A bivariate parametrization such as $\mathbf{G}$ is *regular* if the first order partials ($\mathbf{G}^{(1,0)}$ and $\mathbf{G}^{(0,1)}$) are linearly independent; we will deal exclusively with regular parametrizations.

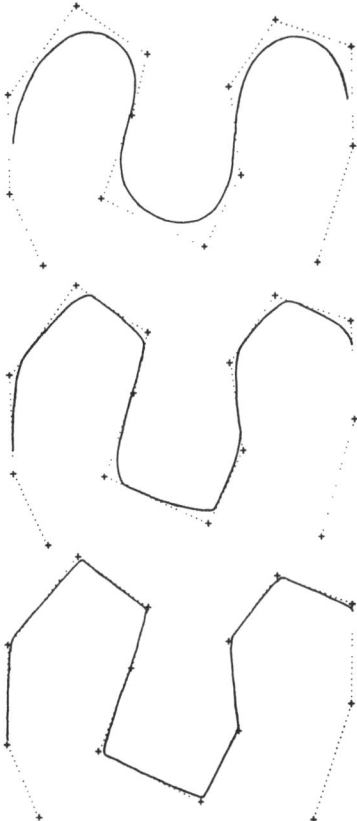

Figure 5. *The curves above share the same control polygon, and all have $\beta_1 = 1$ and $\beta_3 = 0$; they differ only in the value of β_2. The top curve has $\beta_2 = 0$, the middle curve has $\beta_2 = 20$, and the bottom curve has $\beta_2 = 100$.*

In Section 1, we saw that univariate parametrizations contain information about geometry, orientation, and rate. The same is true of bivariate parametrizations. Orientation can be defined by treating D as an *oriented plane* having a "top side" and a "bottom side." $\mathbf{G}$ can then be thought of as deforming the oriented plane to produce an oriented, or two-sided, surface patch. The rate information enters through the magnitudes of the partial derivatives of the parametrization. We can therefore speak of the G, GO, and GOR models of surfaces. Just as for curves, the use of a particular model should be application dependent. We will adopt the GO model for two reasons: first, orientation is necessary in applications, such as rendering, where the two-sidedness of surfaces is important; second, it seems difficult to develop a useful formalism without the structure provided by orientation.

We now examine the reparametrization process for surface patches. Two bivariate parametrizations are GO-equivalent if they have the same geometry and orientation in the neighborhood of

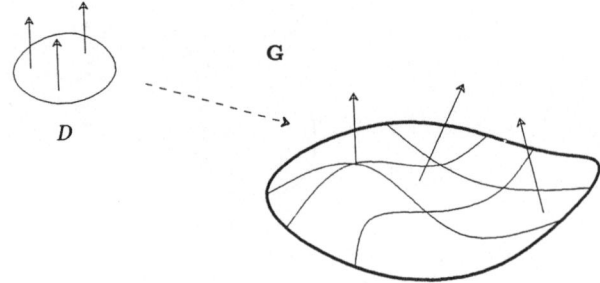

Figure 6. *The bivariate parametrization G deforms the oriented domain D to generate an oriented surface patch.*

---

each point on the surface patch. If $\mathbf{G}(u,v)$ and $\tilde{\mathbf{G}}(\tilde{u},\tilde{v})$ are GO-equivalent, then they are related by

$$\tilde{\mathbf{G}}(\tilde{u},\tilde{v}) = \mathbf{G}(u(\tilde{u},\tilde{v}), v(\tilde{u},\tilde{v})) \tag{3.1}$$

where the functions u and v satisfy the orientation preserving condition**

$$u^{(1,0)}v^{(0,1)} - u^{(0,1)}v^{(1,0)} > 0. \tag{3.2}$$

We now examine how surface patches are stitched together with parametric continuity. Referring to Figure 7, $\mathbf{F}(s,t)$ and $\mathbf{G}(u,v)$ meet with n^{th} order parametric continuity if and only if all like partial derivatives of order up to n agree for each point of the boundary curve. That is,

$$\mathbf{F}^{(i,j)}(\gamma) = \mathbf{G}^{(i,j)}(\gamma), \qquad i+j = 1, ..., n, \tag{3.3}$$

where evaluation at γ is to be interpreted as evaluation at all points $\mathbf{P}$ of γ.

Just as for curves, parametric continuity is appropriate for the GOR model of a surface, but it is not suitable for use with the GO model since it places emphasis on irrelevant rate information. The determination of continuity can be made insensitive to rate by allowing reparametrization. Thus, we say that $\mathbf{F}$ and $\mathbf{G}$ meet with G^n continuity if and only if there exist GO-equivalent parametrizations $\tilde{\mathbf{F}}$ and $\tilde{\mathbf{G}}$ that meet with C^n continuity.

In complete analogy with curves, only one of the parametrizations actually needs to be reparametrized, implying that $\mathbf{F}$ and $\mathbf{G}$ meet with G^n continuity if and only if there exists a $\tilde{\mathbf{G}}$ such that

$$\mathbf{F}^{(i,j)}(\gamma) = \tilde{\mathbf{G}}^{(i,j)}(\gamma), \qquad i+j = 1, ..., n. \tag{3.4}$$

** Readers familiar with multivariate calculus may recognize equation (3.2) as the Jacobian of the change of parametrization (cf. DoCarmo[8]).

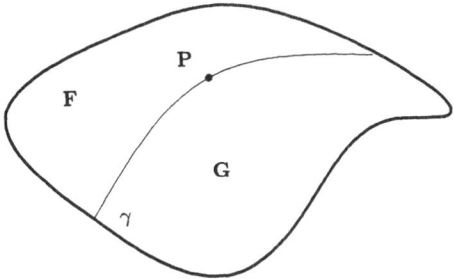

Figure 7. *The surface patches generated by the parametrizations* **F** *and* **G** *meet at the boundary curve* γ.

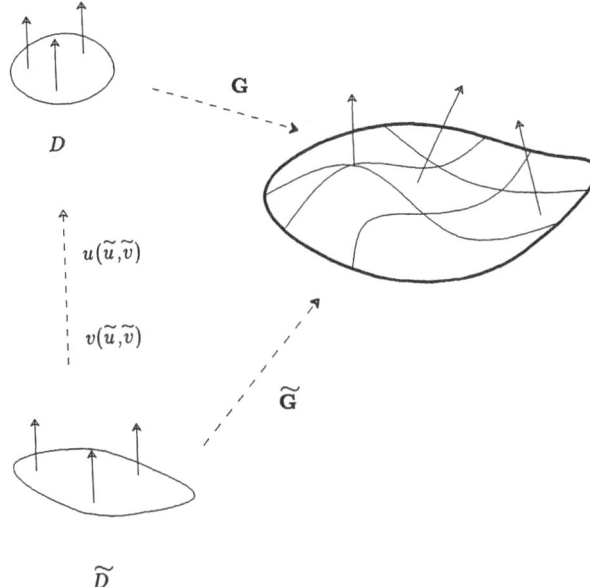

Figure 8. **G** *and* $\widetilde{\mathbf{G}}$ *are GO-equivalent parametrizations related by the change of parametrization determined by* $u(\widetilde{u},\widetilde{v})$ *and* $v(\widetilde{u},\widetilde{v})$.

Once again, in complete analogy with curves, the bivariate chain rule can be used to express derivatives of $\widetilde{\mathbf{G}}$ in terms of **G**. In general, the i,j^{th} partial of $\widetilde{\mathbf{G}}$ can be expressed as some function, call it $\mathcal{CR}_{i,j}$, of the partials of **G**, u, and v, up to order $i+j$. Stated mathematically,

$$\widetilde{\mathbf{G}}^{(i,j)} = \mathcal{CR}_{i,j}(\mathbf{G}^{(k,l)}, u^{(k,l)}, v^{(k,l)}), \qquad (3.5)$$

where the indices (k,l) are to take on all positive values such that $k+l = i+j$.

We may now obtain the *bivariate Beta constraints* by evaluating (3.5) along the boundary curve, followed by substitution into equation (3.4) to get

$$\mathbf{F}^{(i,j)}(\gamma) = \mathcal{CR}_{i,j}(\mathbf{G}^{(k,l)}(\gamma), u^{(k,l)}(\gamma), v^{(k,l)}(\gamma)) \tag{3.6}$$

for $k + l = i + j$ and $i + j = 1, ..., n$.

The equations resulting from (3.6) are the bivariate Beta constraints, and the scalar functions $u^{(k,l)}(\gamma)$ and $v^{(k,l)}(\gamma)$ are the shape functions. To simplify the determination of the bivariate Beta constraints, a set of heuristics similar to those derived in Section 2 can be derived. A simple counting argument can then be used to show that it is possible to introduce $n(n + 3)$ shape functions when two patches are stitched together with G^n continuity.

Just as the univariate Beta constraints can supplant the parametric continuity constraints when building spline curves, the bivariate Beta constraints can replace the parametric constraints when building spline surfaces. It can be shown that the Beta constraints for first and second order are equivalent to requiring continuity of tangent planes and Dupin indicatrices of the patches match along the boundary curve[6]. Thus, the chain rule derivation agrees with geometric intuition for both G^1 and G^2 continuity. Moreover, the chain rule derivation yields the second order constraints with less effort than the geometric approach. For higher order continuity, geometric intuition becomes more feeble, but the chain rule still applies.

4. CONCLUSION

We have defined n^{th} order geometric continuity for parametric curves and surfaces, and derived the Beta constraints that are necessary and sufficient for it. The derivation of the Beta constraints is based on a simple principle of reparametrization in conjunction with the univariate chain rule for curves, and the bivariate chain rule for surfaces. This approach therefore uncovers the connection between geometric continuity for curves and geometric continuity for surfaces, provides new insight into the nature of geometric continuity in general, and allows the determination of the Beta constraints with less effort than previously required.

The use of the Beta constraints for G^n continuity allows the introduction of n shape parameters for curves, and $n(n + 3)$ shape functions for surfaces. The shape parameters and shape functions may be used to modify the shape of a geometrically continuous curve or surface, respectively. However, geometric continuity is only appropriate for applications where rate aspects of the parametrizations are unimportant since discontinuities in rate are allowed.

As a final comment, the approach we have taken is not based on measures that are inherent to curves and surfaces, so the generalization to k-variate objects (volumes, hyper-volumes, etc.) can be made very simply: two k-variate parametrizations are GO-equivalent if they are related by a change of parametrization with positive Jacobian; the corresponding Beta constraints may be derived in complete analogy to the development of Section 3, using the k-variate chain rule[5] in place of the bivariate chain rule.

ACKNOWLEDGMENTS

The authors gratefully acknowledge Ron Goldman of Control Data Corporation whose contributions to this work are too numerous to list. We would also like to thank the students of CS 284 and the members of the Berkeley Computer Graphics Laboratory for enduring early (and erroneous) reports of this research.

REFERENCES

1. Brian A. Barsky, *The Beta-spline: A Local Representation Based on Shape Parameters and Fundamental Geometric Measures*, Ph.D. Thesis, University of Utah, Salt Lake City, Utah (December, 1981).

2. Brian A. Barsky, *Computer Graphics and Computer Aided Geometric Design Using Beta-splines*, Springer-Verlag, Tokyo. To appear.

3. Brian A. Barsky and John C. Beatty, "Local Control of Bias and Tension in Beta-splines," *ACM Transactions on Graphics*, Vol. 2, No. 2, April 1983, pp. 109-134. Also published in *SIGGRAPH '83 Conference Proceedings* (Vol. 17, No. 3), ACM, Detroit, 25-29 July, 1983, pp. 193-218.

4. Brian A. Barsky and Tony D. DeRose, *Geometric Continuity for Parametric Curves*, Technical Report No. UCB/CSD 84/205, University of California, Berkeley (October, 1984).

5. R. C. Buck, *Advanced Calculus*, McGraw-Hill Book Company, Inc., New York (1956).

6. Tony D. DeRose, *Geometric Continuity: A Parametrization Independent Measure of Continuity for Computer Aided Geometric Design*, Ph.D. Thesis, University of California, Berkeley. In preparation.

7. Tony D. DeRose and Brian A. Barsky, "Geometric Continuity and Shape Parameters for Catmull-Rom Splines (Extended Abstract)," pp. 57-62 in *Proceedings of Graphics Interface '84*, Ottawa (27 May - 1 June, 1984).

8. Manfred P. DoCarmo, *Differential Geometry of Curves and Surfaces*, Prentice-Hall, Inc., Englewood Cliffs, New Jersey (1976).

9. Gerald Farin, "Visually C^2 Cubic Splines," *Computer-Aided Design*, Vol. 14, No. 3, May, 1982, pp. 137-139.

10. Ivor D. Faux and Michael J. Pratt, *Computational Geometry for Design and Manufacture*, Ellis Horwood Ltd. (1979).

11. Alain Fournier and Brian A. Barsky, "Geometric Continuity with Interpolating Bézier Curves (Extended Summary)," pp. 337-341 in *Proceedings of Graphics Interface '85*, Montreal (27-31 May, 1985).

12. A. H. Fowler and C. W. Wilson, "Cubic Spline, A Curve Fitting Routine," Union Carbide Corporation Report, Y-1400 (Rev. I.) (1966).

13. T. N. T. Goodman, "Properties of β-Splines." Submitted for publication.

14. Juergen Kahmann, "Continuity of Curvature Between Adjacent Bézier Patches," pp. 65-75 in *Surfaces in Computer Aided Geometric Design*, ed. Robert E. Barnhill and Wolfgang Boehm, North-Holland Publishing Company (1983).

15. J. R. Manning, "Continuity Conditions for Spline Curves," *The Computer Journal*, Vol. 17, No. 2, May, 1974, pp. 181-186.

16. Gregory M. Nielson, "Some Piecewise Polynomial Alternatives to Splines under Tension," pp. 209-235, in *Computer Aided Geometric Design*, ed. Robert E. Barnhill and Richard F. Riesenfeld, Academic Press, New York (1974).

17. Lyle Ramshaw, "A Euclidean View of Joints between Bézier curves." Submitted for publication.

18. Richard F. Riesenfeld, *Applications of B-spline Approximation to Geometric Problems of Computer-Aided Design*, Ph.D. Thesis, Syracuse University (May, 1973). Available as Tech. Report No. UTEC-CSc-73-126, Department of Computer Science, University of Utah.

19. Malcolm A. Sabin, *Parametric Splines in Tension*, Technical Report No. VTO/MS/160, British Aircraft Corporation, Weybridge, Surrey, England (July 23, 1970).

20. Malcolm A. Sabin, *The Use of Piecewise Forms for the Numerical Representation of Shape*, Ph.D. Thesis, Budapest (1976).

21. Thomas W. Sederberg, *Implicit and Parametric Curves and Surfaces for Computer Aided Geometric Design,* Ph.D. Thesis, Purdue University (1983).

22. M. Veron, G. Ris, and J.-P. Musse, "Continuity of Biparametric Surface Patches," *Computer-Aided Design,* Vol. 8, No. 4, October, 1976, pp. 267-273.

Octree Data Structures and Creation by Stacking[†]

Wm. Randolph Franklin[*] and Varol Akman[**]

Electrical, Computer, and Systems Engineering Dept., Rensselaer Polytechnic Institute, Troy, NY 12180, USA

INTRODUCTION

Efficient, compact data structures are necessary for the representation of octrees. First, several concrete data structures for the octree abstract data type will be compared in terms of storage space required and execution time needed to perform operations such as to find a certain node or obel. We compare information theoretic minimal representations, digital search trees sometimes storing some information in an immediate mode without pointers, and storing the set of rays, which is often the most compact.

It is also necessary to convert from other formats into octrees. Therefore, a fast method to convert a quadric surface into rays is described next. Finally, a new algorithm to stack these rays into an octree is given. It is very fast, has no intermediate swell in the storage, and does not thrash virtual memory. These algorithms have been implemented and tested on large examples. For example, the stacking program, implemented in Fortran on a Prime 750, converted an object with 12,985 rays into an octree with 106,833 obels in 3 minutes.

HISTORY

The *Octree* data structure is a space partitioning method of representing 3-D objects with the following properties:

- It is suited for representing irregular objects to a medium precision, such as one part in 256.

- Operations such as boolean combinations, transformations, and display can be implemented much more easily than with a boundary representation.

- Since the storage tends to rise with the square of the resolution, octrees are not suitable very precise objects such as machine parts.

- An octree approximates the volume of an object; the surface is not stored. Thus realistic display usually requires also storing surface normals, which can multiply the storage needed several times.

- Octrees use *spatial coherence* to reduce space and time. They are more suitable for medical objects such as human organs than for long thin objects such as geological strata.

The octree is a form of the quadtree of Bentley (1975) and Finkel, Bentley, and Stanat (1974). For some examples of quadtree algorithms, see Hunter and Steiglitz (1979) , and Samet (1980). Tanimoto (1977) applied the concept to images. The extension to representing irregular three dimensional graphic objects and implementation was by Meagher (1980, 1982a, 1982b, 1984). He formulated the basic algorithms and implemented them in a massive effort involving about 20,000 lines of code that resulted in an interactive system that allows the user to create quadtrees interactively on a graphic terminal, extend them to octrees, and then transform and combine them. Some other valuable references are Doctor and Torborg (1981) , Jackins and Tanimoto (1980) , and Yamaguchi,

---

[†] This material is based upon work supported by the National Science Foundation under grant number ECS-8351942, and by the Schlumberger-Doll Research Labs, Ridgefield, CT. The second author was also supported in part by a Fulbright award.

[*] Until June 1986 visiting at: Computer Science Division, Electrical Engineering and Computer Science Dept., 543 Evans Hall, University of California, Berkeley CA 94720 USA.

[**] Current address: Dept. of Computer Science, University of Utrecht, Budapestlaan 6, P.O.Box 80.012, 3508 TA Utrecht, the Netherlands

Kunii, Fujimura, and Toriya. (1984) Samet (1984) has an exhaustive survey of quadtrees and similar data structures.

The octree is one of several methods for representing three dimensional objects. For a survey of the methods used in some Computer Aided Design systems, see Baer, Eastman, and Henrion (1979) and Requicha (1980). Tamminen (1981, 1982) studied the related EXCELL (extendible cell method). Franklin (1980, 1981, 1983) has devised and implemented the efficient adaptive grid data structure. Hoskins (1979) describes box geometries as applied to architecture. F. Yao (1983) has presented the octant tree, which uses three planes which do not necessarily pass through its middle to divide the universe.

DEFINITIONS

An octree is logically the abstract data type called the *Digital Search Tree*. The object is contained in a universe which is a cube of size 1x1x1 with coordinates ranging from 0 to 1. The primitive component of the octree is an *Obel* of level L is a cube of linear size 2^{-L} whose lower left front corner has each coordinate of the form

$$k \cdot 2^{-L}, \quad 0 \leq k < 2^L$$

Every obel in the system is either *Empty*, *Full*, or *Partial*. When we wish to emphasize the data structure instead of the geometry, we will use *Node* for obel, and *Tree* for octree.

The universe is considered to be a level zero obel. If the object is not empty but also does not fill the universe, then the universe obel is marked as partially full. The object is now defined by the following recursive process. If L is less than the maximum level allowable, then a partial obel of level L, is divided evenly into 8 obels of level $L+1$. Each one of these obels is marked full, empty, or partial, and the process repeats on the partial ones. Partial obels at the highest level are arbitrarily declared to be full.

Each full obel is either a *Surface* obel of the object, that is it is adjacent in an orthogonal direction (not diagonally) to either an empty obel or the exterior of the universe, or else is an *Interior* obel of the object. This is not to be confused with an internal node (i.e. not a leaf) of a tree. A graphical representation of the subclassifications is shown in figure 1.

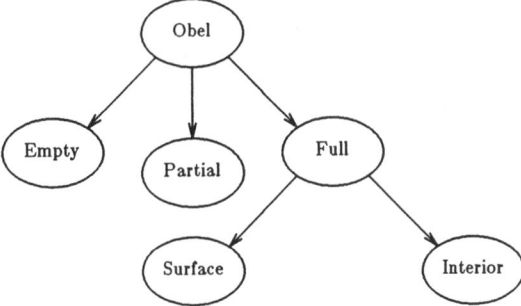

Figure 1: Types of Octree Obels

Surface obels contain associated information that is used to display the object realistically so that the user can determine its shape, especially if it is irregular. The associated information can include the local surface normal and color, which are necessary to create an understandable image.

TYPICAL NUMBERS

Some idea of the typical sizes of various components of an octree is necessary when designing an optimal implementation. Although this is dependent on the object's exact position and orientation, we can still determine some rough figures. We will let our sample object be a cube which is aligned as badly as possible: if we intend to approximate it down to level $L \geq 2$, then the cube will be the whole universe except for a single layer of level L obels removed from just inside the perimeter of the universe. Thus its side length will be $1-2^{1-L}$. This will give the number of empty obels, all at level L, as

$$N_e = (2^L)^3 - (2^L-2)^3 = 2 \cdot 4^L - 4 \cdot 2^L + 8$$

The number of full obels at level l, $2 \leq l \leq L$, is $N_{fl} = (2^l-2)^3 - (2^l-4)^3$

The total number of full obels is $N_f = \sum_{l=2}^{L} N_{fl} = 8 \cdot 4^L - 72 \cdot 2^L + 56L + 56$

The number of partial obels in the tree can be determined by working backward from L to 1. There are no level L partial obels since all the obels at the finest level are either full or empty. The level $l=L-1$ partial obels occur where the level L full and empty obels are adjacent. This occurs in a layer around the outside of the universe, and thus the level $L-1$ partial obels are precisely those obels which would be empty if the bottom level of the tree were $L-1$ instead of L. This process continues until $l=1$. Finally, at $l=0$, the whole universe is a partial obel. Thus the total number of partial obels is:

$$N_p = 1 + \sum_{l=1}^{L-1} (2^l)^3 - (2^l-2)^3$$

$$= 2 \cdot 4^L - 12 \cdot 2^L + 8L + 9, \quad \text{for } L>0$$

The total number of obels will be

$$N = N_e + N_f + N_p$$
$$= 12 \cdot 4^L - 56 \cdot 2^L + 64L + 73, \quad L>1 \qquad (1)$$

SPACE REQUIRED

In this section, we will analyze the minimal space required to store an octree, that is the information content. Let N be the number of nodes in a given octree. Since every internal node of the octree has exactly eight sons, and every exterior node (leaf), has exactly zero sons, regardless of how well balanced the tree is, then I, the number of internal nodes, is exactly $(N-1)/8$. This may be proved inductively. Therefore most of the octree is composed of leaves (that is, full or empty obels) so it is important to store them compactly.

Now the minimal storage required for a tree (apart from the nodes' attributes) is to note whether each node is full, partial, or empty, which can be done in two bits per node. If we measure storage in bytes, and assume eight bits per byte, then the simple storage required is $S_1 = 1/4 N$.

Given that P_p, the probability of a partial obel (interior node) is about 1/8, the worst case for the full and empty obels is to have equal probabilities: $P_f = P_e = 7/16$. Now, using a Huffman coding, Abramson (1963), the minimum storage per node reduces to $S_2 = 0.177 N$. However, this improvement would be at the cost of a complicated coding algorithm that would be harder to implement, and the resulting octree would be harder to modify.

The associated information, such as surface normals, required for each surface node also makes this compact encoding irrelevant. A convenient representation for one normal is one byte per component, for a total of three bytes. We could precalculate the intensity at each node from some given light source and store that instead. However, storing red, green, and blue components would still require three bytes. This would also prevent us from changing the light source after the octree had been created. Therefore, S_3, the extra storage required per full surface node is 3.

Now using the P_f, P_p, and P_e given before, and assuming that almost all of the full obels are surface obels, we get

S_4 = extra storage required for surface obel attributes
= (extra storage per surface obel)
· (number of surface obels per full obel)
· (number of full obels per leaf node)
· (number of leaf nodes per general node)
· (number of nodes)
= $3 \cdot 1 \cdot 1/2 \cdot 7/8 \cdot N$
= $21/16$ N

Since this totally dominates both S_1 and S_2, the simple encoding of S_1 suffices. Thus

S_5 = storage required to represent an octree with attributes
= $S_1 + S_4$
= $25/16 N$

We have not added a bit to tell whether a full node is a surface or interior node, since it can be fitted in easily.

We will now consider some possible realizations of the abstract octree.

STORING A MINIMAL OCTREE

It is possible to store an octree using only S_5 bytes by traversing the tree in a breadth first manner and packing the nodes together. The root is listed first, followed by the eight level 2 nodes, then by all the level 3 nodes in order, and so on. Unless the level 2 nodes are all partial, there will be less than 64 level 3 nodes. Thus finding a particular level 3 node requires examining all the level 2 nodes, and so on. Thus, in general, accessing a given leaf whose coordinates we know requires reading the whole tree up to that point. Thus an $\theta(logN)$ time process degenerates to a much worse $\theta(N)$ process. It is also impossible to modify the tree, for example to change a full node to a partial node with eight sons without rewriting the whole tree after that point.

While this method may be suitable for archival storage where space is critical, it is totally unsuited for computation. Thus we need another data structure for manipulation.

STORING A GENERAL DIGITAL SEARCH TREE

Instead of storing the octree as compactly as given above, we might store it as a general digital search tree, Knuth (1973). In this format, the nodes are separately allocated from a storage heap and are referenced by their address. A two byte address will be too small (there may be over 64K nodes) so we will allocate four bytes. Each partial node will contain an array of the addresses of its eight sons. All the empty nodes can be represented by one node at a distinguished address (such as 00000), as can all the interior full nodes by address 00001. Thus each partial node will require 32 bytes. Each surface full node requires at least three bytes for the normals. If we allocate four bytes, then it will be the same size as the partial nodes.

We need to distinguish between a full node and a partial node; there are two methods. First, we might allocate the two types of nodes from separate address spaces. Second, we might reserve a tag bit to identify them. The latter method is more flexible, but requires that extra bit. Since we are not using the full range of our node address space (32 bits), we can reserve the most significant bit as a tag, so these two methods are equivalent in this case.

This method requires the following storage. Since a partial node requires 32 bytes, an empty node zero bytes, an interior full node zero bytes, and a surface full node 4 bytes, then using the aforementioned probabilities with the additional worst case assumption that essentially all of the full nodes are surface, then we get:

S_6 = storage to represent the octree as a general digital search tree with attributes

$$= (\tfrac{1}{8}\cdot 32 + \tfrac{7}{16}\cdot 0 + 0\cdot 0 + \tfrac{7}{16}\cdot 4)\, N$$

$$= \tfrac{23}{4}\, N$$

that is, about 6 bytes per node.

STORING A MODIFIED DIGITAL SEARCH TREE

We observe that in the general digital search tree method given above, since there may be so many nodes, and each node is rather small, the pointer to a surface full leaf is as big as the leaf itself (4 bytes in either case). This suggests that we store leaves in *Immediate* mode, as an immediate operand is stored in an instruction in assembly language. In this format, a partial node is an array of eight 4 byte fields, one per son. For a partial son, the field is the son's address. For a full surface son, the field is the 4 byte description of the surface of the octree at that point, i.e. the surface normal. As before, empty nodes and full interior nodes are represented by distinguished values.

The storage required by this method is the same as before, except that a surface full node requires no storage since its associated information (i.e. the surface normal) is encoded in place of its address. Therefore,

S_7 = storage for modified digital search tree format with attributes

$\quad = 4N$

that is, about 30% less than before. With this method, we must reserve one bit of each field to indicate whether it is an address or an immediate field. It is convenient to represent the amount of storage in terms of the maximum level number in addition to the number of nodes. Using equation (1) with the number of nodes down to level L in a generally aligned cube, we get

$$S_7 = 48\cdot 4^L - 224\cdot 2^L + 256 L + 292$$

STORING A HYBRID TREE

In a general tree such as described above, most of the storage is consumed by nodes that are near the leaves, while most of the search time is spent reading nodes nearer the root. This allows us to graft the compact format onto the general digital search tree format. The process consists of using the general format, where each node has a four byte pointer to each of its sons, for the first several levels of the tree. Every leaf of this tree then becomes a separate compact subtree where all the nodes are packed together with only two flag bits per node. Although the general part of the tree will have most of the depth, it will have only a few of the nodes, and so will occupy little space. In contrast, since most of the nodes are stored in compact subtrees, they will require only 2 bits of flags instead of a 4 byte pointer. In addition, since each compact subtree is small, adding or deleting a node, which requires copying the whole compact subtree that the node occurs in, will take little time. This method is part of the database folklore, Willard (1984), but not is easily available in a reference. We can choose the time/space tradeoff as desired by choosing the proportion of the tree to be in each format. Thus,

S_8 = storage for hybrid format, w/o attributes

$\quad = 1/4N$

Adding in the storage for the attributes, we get

S_9 = storage for hybrid format with attributes

$\quad = S_8 + S_4$

$\quad = \tfrac{25}{16}\, N$

$\quad = \tfrac{75}{4}\cdot 4^L - \tfrac{175}{2}\cdot 2^L + 100 L + \tfrac{1825}{16}$

However, this method is much more complicated.

STORING THE OCTREE AS A SET OF RAYS

The usual method of generating an octree from an irregular object, such as a conic section is by intersecting a regular grid of rays with the object. This set of rays can then be transformed to an octree; however the set is a useful and efficient data structure in its own right. Each element has the following format:

$$(X, Y, Z_1, Z_2, N_1, N_2)$$

This represents a ray with fixed (X,Y) that enters the object at $Z=Z_1$ and leaves at $Z=Z_2$. The surface normals at the two points are N_1 and N_2, respectively. If we wish to construct an octree whose highest level is L, then

$$X, Y = k \cdot 2^{-L}, \quad k = 0, 1, \cdots 2^L - 1$$

Z_1 and Z_2 are also rounded to the nearest multiple of 2^{-L}. Each ray requires 10 bytes composed of three bytes per normal and one byte per coordinate (assuming that $L \leq 8$). There will be about 4^L rays running through the object. This is affected by some rays not intersecting the object at all and some intersecting more than twice. Thus approximately

S_{10} = storage for set of rays format with attributes

$\quad = 10 \cdot 4^L$

For large L, S_{10} is half as large as S_9, the best method using the explicit octree data structure. In addition, all of the usual octree operations except rotation can be performed efficiently on the ray format. A Boolean operation on two octrees reduces to Boolean operations on pairs of rays which is trivial since the rays are one dimensional. Translation of a ray is also easy. Finally, to display an octree composed of rays, we can paint the rays into the frame buffer back to front. This works for any display angle. Another advantage of this data format is that the smaller number of data objects may allow shorter addresses, two byte instead of four byte, to be used to refer to them.

Finally, since the rays do form a somewhat regular grid, we might omit the (X,Y), and just store the (Z_1, Z_2, N_1, N_2). This reduces the total storage for the octree to about

$$S_{11} = 8 \cdot 4^L$$

The special cases of objects folding back on themselves and objects that don't intersect all the rays, might be handled with exception tables if their number is limited. This is reasonably only for fairly regular objects.

RAY TRACING QUADRIC SOLIDS

An efficient algorithm for converting a quadric solid, such as an ellipsoid, was designed and implemented in Fortran-77 on a Prime 750 midicomputer by the authors. A quadric is defined by a matrix M, such that

$$(x \ y \ z \ 1) M \begin{bmatrix} x \\ y \\ z \\ 1 \end{bmatrix} = 0, \quad M = \begin{bmatrix} a & b & c & d \\ b & e & f & g \\ c & f & h & i \\ d & g & i & j \end{bmatrix}$$

After the solid is clipped to a $[0,1]^3$ universe, the output is a set of rays and surface normals as described in the last section. We assumed that each ray goes through the lower left corner of the obel; the alternative assumption would have been that the rays go through the center.

The algorithm is as follows:

a) Iterate up the quadric solid in Y. For each Y, find the 2-D conic in X and Z.

b) For each conic in the (X,Z) plane, find the range of X for which Z is real. This range contains 0, 1, or 2 segments that may be finite or infinite.

c) Iterate in X and solve the quadratic equation for Z_1 and Z_2. Clip them to $[0,1]$.

d) Calculate the normals the usual way. If Z_i was clipped, the the associated normal is $(0,0,\pm 1)$.

The above method is fast because it does not work with rays that do not intersect the solid. These are typically the majority of all the rays. To determine the range of X for which the 2-D conic $f(X,Z)$ is real, six cases must be considered depending on the discriminant, Q, of the formal solution for Z in terms of X. That is, if

$$f(X,Z) = a\,z^2 + (b_0+b_1x)z + (c_0+c_1x+c_2x^2) = 0,$$

then

$$Q(X) = (b_0+b_1x)^2 - 4a(c_0+c_1x+c_2x^2)$$

The six cases and an example of each are:

a) $Q(X)$ is always positive (X^2+1).

b) $Q(X)$ is positive outside a finite interval (X^2-1).

c) $Q(X)$ is positive inside a finite interval $(-X^2+1)$.

d) $Q(X)$ is never positive $(-X^2-1)$.

e) $Q(X)$ is positive above a certain value (X).

f) $Q(X)$ is positive below a certain value $(-X)$.

For ray tracing higher order solids, such as bicubic patches, we propose to use the following observation. The functions $Z(X,Y)$ and $N(X,Y)$, for intersections and normals, although complicated, are smooth. Therefore efficient simple approximations using splines can be found. It appears that 17 evaluations of either function along a scan line, followed by linear interpolation, would allow the determination of the function at every pixel to 8 bit accuracy (instead of say 512 evaluations).

STACKING

We invented and implemented a new algorithm called *Stack* for converting the set of rays into an octree. The algorithm has the following advantages over previous algorithms:

- It is simple to program and easy to understand.

- It does not lead to intermediate storage swell.

- It accesses memory in an orderly fashion that does not thrash virtual memory when processing large objects.

- It produces a minimal octree.

Only a brief description is presented here; for more formal details and the complete code in a high level language see Franklin and Akman (1985). Another similar symmetric recursive indexing method is given in Srihari (1981). Yau and Srihari (1983) give an algorithm for constructing a tree of a d-dimensional image from trees of its (d-1) dimensional cross sections.

In this section we will consider the universe to be of size $[0,2^L]^3$ instead of $[0,1]^3$. The algorithm proceeds by iterating in dimensions as follows.

a) Each ray is partitioned into a set of *rows* which comprise a 1-D octree. That is, each row has a length which is a power of two, and a starting Z which is a multiple of its length. Rows are to obels as 1-D is to 3-D.

b) The rows are sorted by their starting point (X,Y,Z).

c) Adjacent rows are combined into squares whenever possible. A square has a side of 2^l for some $0\leq l\leq L$ and starting X and Z multiples of 2^l. 2^l rows with positions

$$(i\cdot 2^l+m,\ j\cdot 2^l,\ k\cdot 2^l),\quad m = 0,\cdots,2^l$$

can be combined into one square. The process starts at $l=L$ and interates down to $l=0$. At any l, after all the rows that can be are combined into squares, the remaining rows are each split into two rows of length 2^{l-1}. These smaller rows may be later combined into smaller squares. At the end, the remaining rows are of size one and can be considered to be obels of size one.

d) Next the squares are either combined into obels or split into squares of size one that are obels of size one.

e) Finally, the obels are formed into the new octree.

Note that the combination requires inspecting only adjacent items in memory and when a new object is created, it is appended sequentially to a list in memory. Since efficient external sorts are known, the whole process will execute efficiently in a virtual memory environment.

We implemented Stack in Ratfor. Building a 1/8 sphere with $L=6$ read 833 rays and created an octree with 6569 obels. The execution time was 9.2 seconds on a Prime 750. A higher resolution sphere consisting of 12,985 rays was transformed into an octree with 106,833 obels in 3 minutes. This octree has $N_f=67,570$, $N_p=13,354$, and $N_e=25,909$ and is larger than many of the examples cited in Tamminen (1984) and Yau (1983).

THE SYSTEM

These features have been integrated into a system with the following data flow as shown in figure 2.

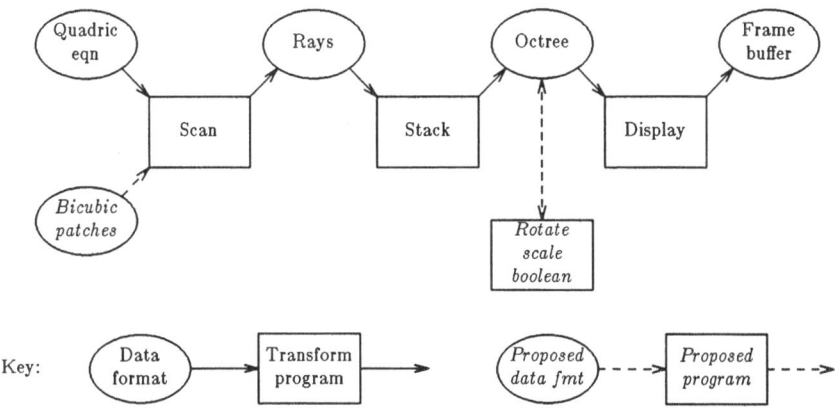

Figure 2: Dataflow in the System

The display algorithm is a back to front paint into a frame buffer. Depending on the octant in which the viewer is situated, there is a certain permutation of the numbers from 1 to 8 that is easy to determine. If the octree is traversed recursively with the eight sons of each internal node being visited in this order, then the leaves will be visited in back to front order. Note that traversing the tree is this order is no harder than traversing the tree in the usual lexicographic order.

The alternative display algorithm is to paint the image front to back and never paint any pixel twice, Meagher (1982). A quadtree in the frame buffer records which pixels have been painted once. Our method paints some pixels twice but has one less complicated (and slow to manage) data structure.

SUMMARY

Of the various data structures considered with which to implement the abstract octree, we see that the most efficient are 1) the digital search tree with surface full nodes stored as immediate data, and 2) a set of the rays. We have also presented a very fast stacking algorithm for converting a set of rays into an octree.

REFERENCES

Abramson, N. (1963) *Information Theory and Coding*, McGraw-Hill Electronic Sciences Series.

Baer, A., Eastman, C., and Henrion, M. (Sept. 1979) "Geometric Modelling: A Survey," *Computer Aided Design*, vol. 11, no. 5.

Bentley, J.L. and Stanat, D.F. (July 1975) "Analysis of Range Searches in Quad Trees," *Information Processing Letters*, vol. 3, no. 6, pp. 170-173.

Doctor, L. J. and Torborg, J. G. (1981) "Display Techniques for Octree Encoded Objects," *IEEE Computer Graphics and Applications*, vol. 1, no. 3, pp. 29-38.

Finkel, R.A. and Bentley, J.L. (1974) "Quad Trees: A Data Structure For Retrieval On Composite Key," *Acta Informatica*, vol. 4, pp. 1-9.

Franklin, Wm. Randolph (July 1980) "A Linear Time Exact Hidden Surface Algorithm," *ACM Computer Graphics*, vol. 14, no. 3, pp. 117-123.

Franklin, Wm. Randolph (April 1981) "An Exact Hidden Sphere Algorithm That Operates In Linear Time," *Computer Graphics and Image Processing*, vol. 15, no. 4, pp. 364-379.

Franklin, Wm. Randolph and Akman, Varol (October 1985) "Building an Octree from a Set of Parallelepipeds," *IEEE Computer Graphics and Applications*.

Franklin, Wm. Randolph (16-21 October 1983) "Adaptive Grids For Geometric Operations," *Proc. Sixth International Symposium on Automated Cartography (Auto-Carto Six)*, vol. 2, pp. 230-239, Ottawa, Canada.

Hoskins, E.M. (November 1979) "Design Development and Description Using 3D Box Geometries," *Computer Aided Design*, vol. 11, no. 6, pp. 329-336.

Hunter, G.M. (April 1979) "Operations on Images Using Quad Trees," *IEEE Trans. Pattern Analysis and Machine Intelligence*, vol. PAMI-1, no. 2, pp. 145-153.

Jackins, C. L. and Tanimoto, S. L. (1980) "Quadtree, octree, and K-trees: A Generalized Approach to Recursive Decomposition of Euclidean Space," *IEEE Trans. Pattern Analysis and Machine Intelligence*, vol. 5, no. 5, pp. 533-539.

Knuth, D.E. (1973) *The Art of Computer Programming, Volume 3: Sorting and Searching*, Addison-Wesley.

Meagher, Donald J. (October 1980) *Octree Encoding: A New Technique for the Representation, Manipulation and Display of Arbitrary 3-D Objects by Computer*, IPL-TR-80-111, Rensselaer Polytechnic Institute, Image Processing Lab.

Meagher, Donald J. (April 1982) *The Octree Encoding Method for Efficient Solid Modelling*, Rensselaer Polytechnic Institute, Electrical, Computer, and Systems Engineering Dept., Ph.D. thesis.

Meagher, Donald J. (1982b) "Geometric Modelling Using Octree Encoding," *Computer Graphics and Image Processing*, vol. 19, pp. 129-147.

Meagher, Donald J. (November 1984) "The Solids Engine: A Processor for Interactive Solid Modelling," *Proc. Nicograph*.

Requicha, Aristides A. G. (December 1980) "Representations for Rigid Solids: Theory, Methods, and Systems," *ACM Computing Surveys*, vol. 12, no. 4, pp. 437-464.

Samet, H. (December 1980) "Deletion in Two-Dimensional Quad Trees," *Comm. ACM*, vol. 23, no. 12, pp. 703-710.

Srihari, S. N. (1981) "Representation of Three-Dimensional Digital Images," *ACM Computing Surveys*, vol. 13, no. 4, pp. 400-424.

Tamminen, M. (1981) *Expected Performance of Some Cell Based File Organization Schemes*, REPORT-HTKK-TKO-B28, Helsinki University of Technology, Laboratory of Information Processing Science, SF-02150 Espool 5, Finland.

Tamminen, M. (June 1982) "The Excell Method for Efficient Geometric Access to Data," *ACM IEEE Nineteenth Design Automation Conference Proceedings*, pp. 345-351.

Tamminen, M. and Samet, H. (1984) "Efficient Octree Conversion by Connectivity Labelling," *ACM Computer Graphics*, vol. 18, no. 3, pp. 43-51. (SIGGRAPH'84 Proceedings)

Tanimoto, S.L. (June 1977) "A Pyramid Model for Binary Picture Complexity," *Proc. IEEE Computer Society Conference on Pattern Recognition and Image Processing*, Rensselaer Polytechnic Institute.

Willard, Dan E. (1984) *personal communication*, State University of New York at Albany.

Yamaguchi, K., Kunii, T. L., Fujimura, K., and Toriya, H. (1984) "Octree-related Data Structures and Algorithms," *IEEE Computer Graphics and Applications*, vol. 4, no. 1, pp. 53-59.

Yao, F. F. (April 1983) "A 3-Space Partition and Its Applications (extended abstract)," *ACM 15th Symposium on the Theory of Computing*, pp. 258-263, Boston.

Yau, M. and Srihari, S. N. (1983) "A Hierarchical Data Structure for Multidimensional Images," *Comm. ACM*, vol. 26, no. 7, pp. 504-515.

Chapter 4
Computer Animation

ANIMENGINE
An Engineering Animation System

Tsukasa Noma and Tosiyasu L. Kunii

Department of Information Science, Faculty of Science, The University of Tokyo, 3-1, Hongo 7-chome, Tokyo, 113 Japan

ABSTRACT

Animation for engineering is very different from traditional animation for entertainment. We do not require realistic images and we cannot afford the cost, or the time, for their production. At the same time, there are other requirements which must be met. Firstly, it must be possible, in an engineering animation, to identify, unambiguously, each separate, mechanical part in a scene. Secondly, the animation must be produced quickly: ideally, in real-time.

As an attempt to satisfy these requirements, a new engineering animation system called ANIMENGINE has been implemented. To achieve clear visual identification of objects, we mark each of them with a unique, characteristic color or texture. For fast production and almost real-time display, we use a combination of on-line video display and recording. Algorithms have been developed for hidden surface removal with moving objects and a special, geometric model, the "template model" has been used to facilitate the production of scenes using many similar, common parts.

KEYWORDS: engineering animation, animation system design, interactive video, simulation, hidden surface removal

INTRODUCTION

Animation is one of the best ways to visualize the movement of an object. It suits not only entertainment but also flight simulation (Schachter 1981) or crash simulation (Badler 1979). Moreover, in the area of computer integrated manufacturing(CIM), an animation is very useful for engineering design, especially, as a means of communicating the results of assembly simulation.

ANIMENGINE is an animation system for engineering, and it aims to help designers to find and solve, the problems encountered in the design process with a superior man/machine interface, that is, an engineering animation. In contrast with costly and realistic image-oriented entertainment animation, an engineering animation system needs to meet the following requirements:

1. Exact and Unambiguous Display of Objects:
   Objects in engineering animation are parts, modules, and units of production and assembly machines such as robots. It must be possible to distinguish the different objects in a picture unambiguously. So the style of display must make this possible. This is more important than making the pictures realistic. Also, the parts must

look solid. Line drawings do not convey the impression of solid working parts. For an engineer to gain an understanding of the three dimensional motion of the animation, it is much easier if the pictures have a solid appearance.

2. High-speed and automatic production of engineering animations:
An engineering animation is also a way of communicating between designers, engineers, and workers. It needs to be produced as fast as possible so as to encourage their communication.

In addition, engineering animations are usually produced by designers who are not professional animators. For this reason, an engineering animation system should work automatically.

3. Lower Host Dependency and Cost Saving:
An engineering animation system must be constantly available during the design process. There is little point in having a fast system if you have to wait to use it. Typically, several work stations will share a central host computer and these must not put too large a load on the host. The work stations should be inexpensive too.

THE DESIGN OF ANIMENGINE

Based on the three requirements of the previous section, we made the following design decisions for ANIMENGINE.

1. Since a vector display works faster than a raster display, it is better for animation. In spite of this, we selected a raster display because we needed to display solid areas of color and patterns to make the components of our pictures identifiable, requirement 1 (above).

2. High-speed production of animation needs a high-speed display. A real-time animation system is ideal, but hardware for a real-time raster graphics animation system is too expensive, requirement 3. Instead, we decided to use an interactive video display combined with a video recorder. The designer can see his animation a frame at a time and record each frame for later display as a smooth animation. This system configuration produces frames fairly quickly, several frames per minute, and the designer can get a good impression of what the animation will look like as it is produced. Through smooth animation produced with ANIMENGINE, workers are also able to understand how the automated work cells move. We call this "pseudo real-time animation". We prefer video tapes to film because we can see the animation playback immediately and we do not need the film quality fine resolution of pictures. Another advantage of using video signal is that we can easily store and transfer engineering animations through digital and analogue crossover network systems (Kunii 1985).

3. In order to achieve the lower host dependency, we need to utilize an intelligent graphic device. If the device has a segment buffer and enables us to shift, rotate, and scale the figures up and down with simple commands, we can construct an engineering animation system which is practicable even if the connection with the host and the graphic device is only a low-speed serial interface, for example: a local area network.

Two-Dimensional Display

For the internal data of the intelligent graphic device, three dimensional data are preferable, but two-dimensional, intelligent graphic devices are useful, too. This comes from the fact that much of the motion we wish to display is parallel motion combined with simple rotation and this can be done with a two-dimensional display.

If the movements of the displayed objects are parallel and the projection is a parallel projection or oblique projection, then we can treat shifting (translation) of an object in the three-dimensional object space as shifting in the two-dimensional projected plane. The case of parallel projection is shown in Fig. 1. The projection of an object M which is shifted by (x,y,z) in the object space is the same as the projection of M shifted $xP_x+yP_y+zP_z$ in the projected plane, where P_x, P_y, P_z are projections of unit vectors in the object space. Accordingly, we decided to employ a two-dimensional graphic device and to adopt parallel projection, especially, axonometric projection. This means that for parallel motion we need only transmit a projection of an object's shape to the work station once, and the animation can be produced locally. Of course, in the case of rotating objects we have to transmit a different projection for each frame. As a matter of fact, most of the rotations can be treated easily by "template models" described later.

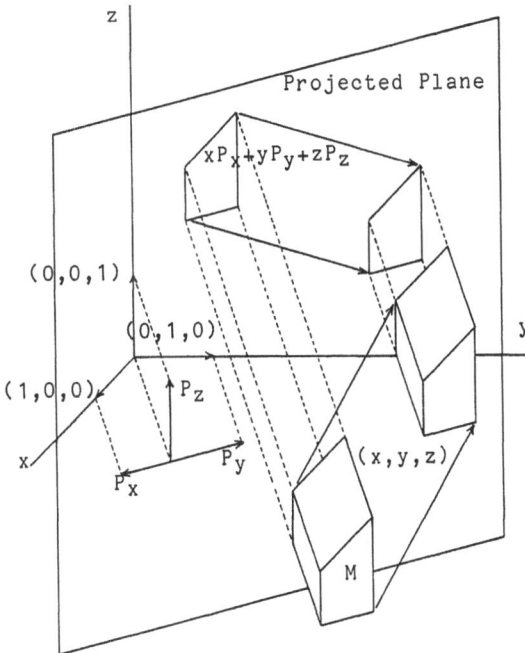

Fig. 1. Parallel motion in the object space and parallel motion in the projected plane

Hardware

The hardware of ANIMENGINE is shown in Fig. 2. The host computer is VAX 750 running UNIX. The graphic device is YAMAHA GC-100 with 752x480 pixels. It can put out RGB signals whose timing matches NTSC(RS-170A) signals, and with a PHOTRON ENCODER/DECODER ED-1000, we can get NTSC video signals directly from the GC-100.

We are using a Japan Victor U-matic video tape recorder. Ideally, the video tape recorder should be controlled by the host. For the moment, we are using a MSX personal computer with a Japan Victor time lapse unit as a video device controller and recording each picture at regular intervals frame by frame.

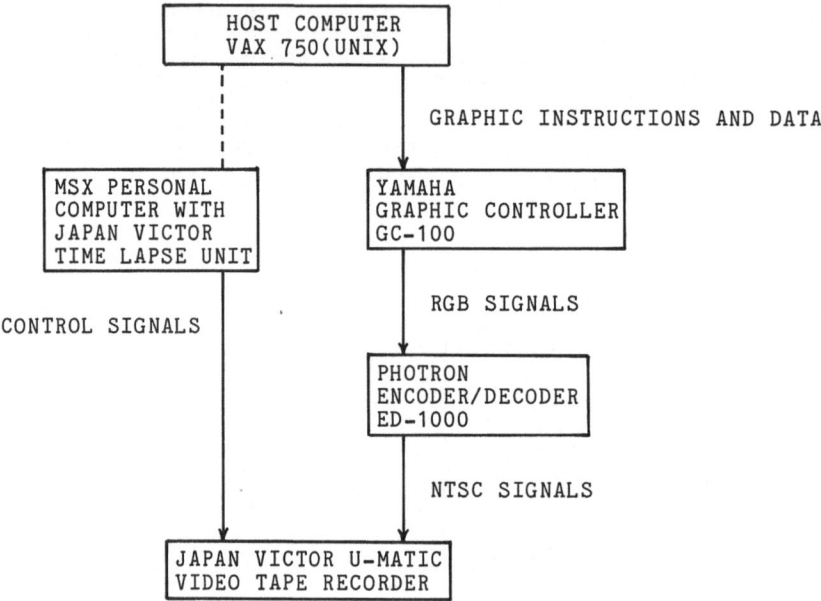

Fig. 2. ANIMENGINE hardware configuration

Software

The software of ANIMENGINE consists of three units, called Global Controller, Display Manager, and Recording Manager (Fig. 3). Global Controller manages the whole system and it has interfaces with other systems and users. Display Manager is computer graphics display software and it has interfaces with Object Database, Movement Database, and Template Database. Object Database contains the shape data of displayed objects and Movement Database contains data which describes their positions and motion. In a working application these databases would also be shared by other systems, for example, a computer aided design system and a dynamical simulation system. There is another database called Template Database, described later.

Recording Manager controls recording and reports at the end of each frame, but because of the restrictions of existing hardware, described above, Recording Manager is only a time keeper.

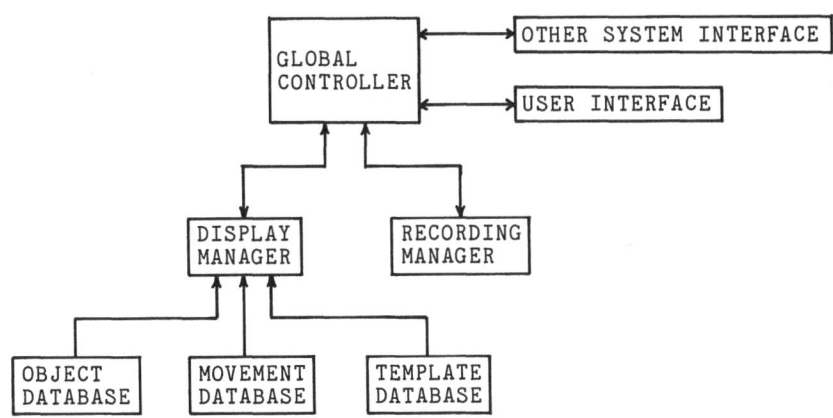

Fig. 3. ANIMENGINE system architecture

DISPLAY PRINCIPLES

As described in the first section, an engineering animation must have a solid appearance in order to help designers to recognize the shape, position, and direction of displayed objects. Methods of giving computer generated pictures a solid appearance are, for example, ray-tracing, shading, making distant objects darker and/or more obscure (Badler 1979; Yokokawa 1980), and the use of texture.

Now, in our case, ray-tracing is unsuitable because of the amount of computation required. Since distant objects are often important in an engineering animation, we cannot make distant objects darker and/or more obscure. ANIMENGINE uses shading and texture to produce a solid appearance.

Shading

For shading, we use a diffuse reflection model with parallel illumination (Harrington 1983) owing to its simplicity. Consequently we need not change the colors of objects while they are moving in parallel in the object space.

Cartographic Display Technics

As is the case with cartographic displays, colors of each object need not be realistic, but just need to be unique to each object. Of course, the color of each face varies within a certain limit depending on the shading effect. This makes identification of each object easier. Characteristic textures are also used for the same purpose.

ANIMENGINE can display symbolic marks and/or additional lines. Exactness and unambiguity often contradict. For example, small holes, drawn exactly, are hard to notice. It is much more convenient to display a kind of symbols than to draw the holes exactly. Symbolic marks are used to express the positions of such small holes or unseen points. Additional lines can represent the directions of movements or the center lines of shafts. We name these "cartographic" display technics.

Anti-Aliasing

ANIMENGINE does not support anti-aliasing. This is because pictures of NTSC signals are less clear than RGB signals and anti-aliasing is unnecessary.

DRAWING EDGES

In engineering animation, it is important to recognize the edges of displayed objects. Although edges of shaded objects are generally identifiable by sharp changes in color, it is sometimes the case that two surfaces, painted almost with the same color, cannot be distinguished.

Figure 4 presents such an example. The face ABCD and the face EFGH have the identical normal vector and they are painted with the same color (and shading property). Consequently the edge CD is not identifiable. Considering this and similar cases, the designers very often wish to draw the edges as distinct lines.

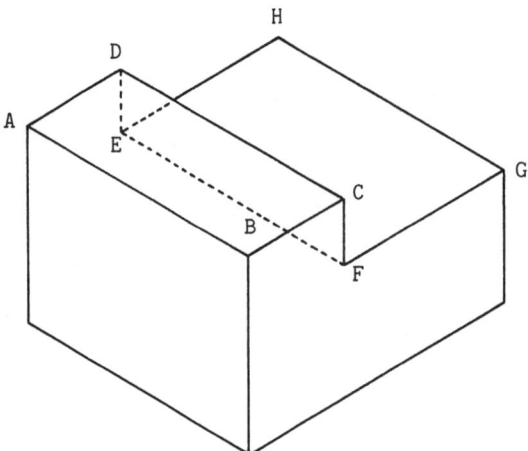

Fig. 4. A solid with an unidentifiable edge CD

Transparency Effect

As described above, edges of visible surfaces make the shape of an object clear. The geometry model of ANIMENGINE is based on polyhedra (Baumgart 1975), and all the surfaces are flat. In such cases, the set of edges contains all the profile lines of an object, which is indispensable for clear identification of objects. In addition, drawing edges has another advantage, called "transparency" effect.

Generally speaking, drawing solid areas is better than wire frame drawing. However, wire frame has a merit in making the hidden surfaces recognizable. So displaying edges of hidden surfaces together with visible surfaces and edges makes the picture transparent and enables us to recognize the whole shape of a given object.

Visibility of Edges

It is interesting to note that it is difficult to distinguish boundary edges worthy of being displayed from useless ones. In other words, edges of visible surfaces are not necessarily visible edges.

An example is given in Fig. 5. It is clear that a number of rectangles represent the curved surface. We don't have to draw edges between such rectangles. (In case of wire frame drawing, such edges are useful. In our case, however, it is important to recognize "sharp" edges.)

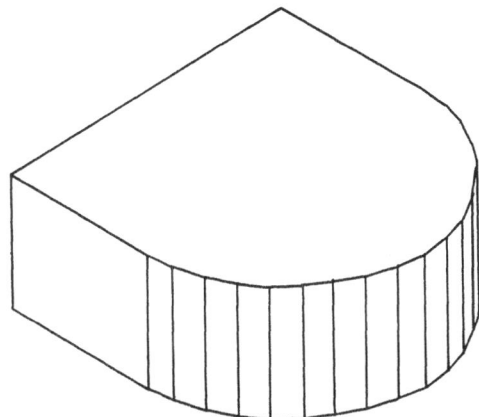

Fig. 5. A solid with an approximated curved surface

We decided that the visibility of the boundary edge should depend on the angle between two surfaces which share the edge, and we adopt the following algorithm.

```
ALGORITHM EDGE_VISIBILITY_DECISION(E)
begin
   (* Symbols PFACE and NFACE are used as defined by Baumgart (1975) *)
   vp <- normal vector of PFACE(E);
   vn <- normal vector of NFACE(E);
   vp <- vp/ |vp| ;
   vn <- vn/ |vn| ;
   if(vp·vn<1-ε) then
      set E visible;
   else
      set E invisible;
end
```

This can decide the visibility of each edge. This is not enough. We need another algorithm to avoid losing profile lines.

```
ALGORITHM MAKE_PROFILE_LINE_VISIBLE
(* E_1,...,E_n are all the invisible edges. *)
begin
   for i=1 to n
```

```
   begin
      vp <- normal vector of PFACE(E_i);
      vn <- normal vector of NFACE(E_i);
      vv <- normal vector of projected plane;
      if((vp·vv)*(vn·vv)<=0) then
         set E visible;
   end
end
```

HIDDEN SURFACE PROBLEM IN A DYNAMIC ENVIRONMENT

Hidden surface removal (Sutherland 1974) is usually done with a static environment and a static view-point. If we apply it to an animation, it takes a lot of time because it is necessary to repeat the calculation for each picture.

A method of decreasing the amount of computation for each picture with appropriate preprocessing has been reported (Fuchs 1980). It is only for a static environment and a dynamic view-point for such applications as flight simulation. Conversely, we want to remove hidden surfaces in a dynamic environment and the view-point may be static. Therefore we thought that global hidden surface removal should be done. "Global" means that hidden surface removal of several frames is done at the same time.

Our algorithm is based on the painter's algorithm (Harrington 1983), to make the most of the intelligent functions of graphic devices. We paint each scene from back to front so that hidden surface removal becomes a matter of deciding in which order to draw each face. The most important point of this algorithm is to determine whether or not the projections of two faces intersect each other in the projected plane within a given period. Our algorithm deals with two cases: first, one face is stationary and the other face is in parallel motion; second, the faces are in parallel and uniform motion. The latter case applies to the following.

Determining whether or not the projections of two faces intersect each other in the projected plane within a given time period is equivalent to interference detection between two oblique prisms in the three-dimensional space composed of two axes in the projected plane and a time axis. In Fig. 6, two oblique prisms represent the motion of the projections of two faces over a time ΔT. If the two oblique prisms intersect each other then the projections of the two faces intersect each other within the time ΔT. If we compute in the three-dimensional space, we can decide whether they intersect each other or not. This is the most general method but inefficient for an engineering animation.

Accordingly, we want to compute in the projected plane. One of the alternative ways is to examine the loci of the projections of the two faces (Fig. 7). If the loci do not intersect each other, the projections do not intersect within the given period. The converse is not true. The loci can intersect although the projections of the objects do not interfere. Thus, this test is necessary but not sufficient to decide whether the projected faces intersect.

Now, objects of engineering animation are mainly rigid ones. In parallel motion, faces of rigid objects do not change the shape of their projections. If we take a new origin of coordinates from a fixed point in one of the object's projections, the motion of the other object's projection in the new coordinates will be a difference of the original two motions. The projection of the first object intersects the locus of the projection of the second object in the new coordinates if and only if the original two projections intersect (Fig. 8). The algorithm follows.

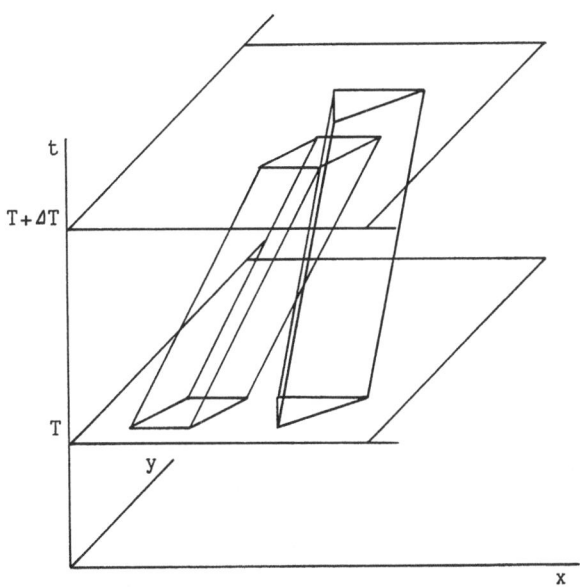

Fig. 6. Interference detection over time ΔT

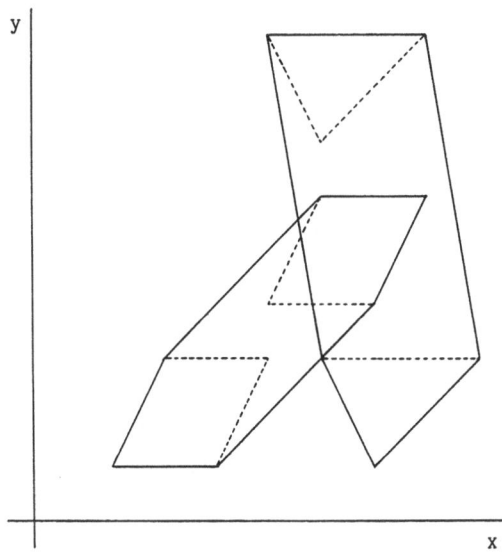

Fig. 7. Interference detection by loci of two projections

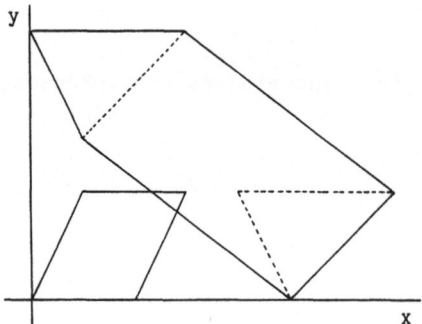

Fig. 8. Interference detection by loci of two projections in the relative coordinates

```
ALGORITHM GLOBAL_DEPTH_BUFFER_OF_TWO_SURFACES(A,B)
begin
   ta <- end of the current parallel and uniform motion of A;
   tb <- end of the current parallel and uniform motion of B;
   tmin <- min(ta,tb);
   split A into convex polygons A_1, A_2, ..., A_k;
   split B into convex polygons B_1, B_2, ..., B_l;
   for i=1 to k
     for j=1 to l
        GLOBAL_DEPTH_BUFFER_OF_TWO_CONVEX_POLYGONS(A_i, B_j);
end

ALGORITHM GLOBAL_DEPTH_BUFFER_OF_TWO_CONVEX_POLYGONS(P,Q)
begin
   LQ <- locus of Q in the relative coordinate;
   split LQ into triangles LQ_1, ..., LQ_m;
   for i=1 to m
     if(P and LQ_i intersect) then
       begin
         set priority between P and Q until tmin;
         break;
       end
end
```

In case that one face is stationary and the other in parallel motion, we take a new origin of coordinate from a static object, that is, the static surface becomes A. Consequently it is equivalent to taking an absolute coordinate except for a constant displacement.

The above-mentioned algorithm cannot deal with penetrating faces and cyclic overlap (Harrington 1983). ANIMENGINE is designed as one of the tools of the CIM system which includes an interference detection mechanism as a separate tool. Since that mechanism checks interference among solids, it is unnecessary to treat penetrating faces.

Solving the problem of the interference/collision detection of moving rigid objects in a three-dimensional space (Comba 1968; Boyse 1979; Esterling 1983), it seems promising to consider rigidity of objects combined with a relative coordinate system. Further research is under way.

TEMPLATE MODEL

ANIMENGINE adopts boundary representation as its figure model. It is a general and advantageous model for animation. It is not always appropriate to have boundary representation data for all objects. For example, shafts, rings, bolts, nuts, and screws appear quite frequently in an engineering animation. They have the same shape within a particular type of part and only the sizes differ from one to another.

Just as a template is used, when drafting, to draw figures which often appear but are hard to draw, so ANIMENGINE enables us to specify regular parts as "template models".

A template model consists of the the part name and a list of numbers to specify its size, and when the template model is drawn, drawing information in Template Database is used. Generally, drawing information in Template Database does not include solid models or full specifications of the shape in three-dimensional space. It only provides rules for drawing. Therefore invisible 'back' surfaces can be omitted.

Two examples of template rules for drawing a cylinder are shown in Fig. 9. Figure 9 (a) is with shading effects on the curved surface and Fig. 9 (b) is without shading. Note that the back faces are not considered. Whether Fig. 9 (a) or (b) is adopted is determined by the entry in Template Database.

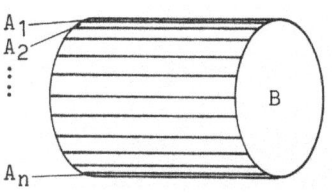

```
begin
   for i=1 to n
      draw A_i;
   draw B;
end
```

(a) With shading effect

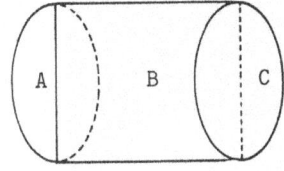

```
begin
   draw A;
   draw B;
   (* A and B have the same color *)
   draw C;
end
```

(b) Without shading effect

Fig. 9. Template rules for drawing a cylinder

Rotations

Template models have another advantage, for handling object rotation. For example, when a shaft, specified as a "template model", rotates around its center line, it need neither be redrawn nor does it require its shape data transferred from the host computer. This is because its rotation does not change the way it is drawn. Note that the way in which the template is designed is important here. Suppose a shaft is defined by an inappropriate boundary representation, say a polygonal approximation, the view of its boundary differs after rotation

(Fig. 10). So it becomes necessary to redraw its shape repeatedly during its rotation. What is even worse, is that in this case, the shape data would be transmitted from the host, repeatedly.

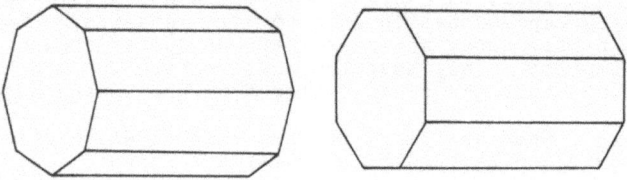

(a) Before rotation   (b) After rotation

Fig. 10. Rotation of a shaft specified by the polygonal boundary representation

EXAMPLES

Figure 11 is a simulation of assembling a copier. Each module is identified with its characteristic colors and a robot hand and its arm, gripping a drum module are identified with a texture. Two sets of three red triangles are symbolic marks. The right-hand set represents the positions of screws on a drum module and the left-hand set is the corresponding positions on a base module. Edges of hidden surfaces help to represent the whole shape of each module.

Figure 12 is a simulation of setting rings onto a shaft. The shaft and the rings are defined as a template model. Additional lines indicate the center line of the shaft.

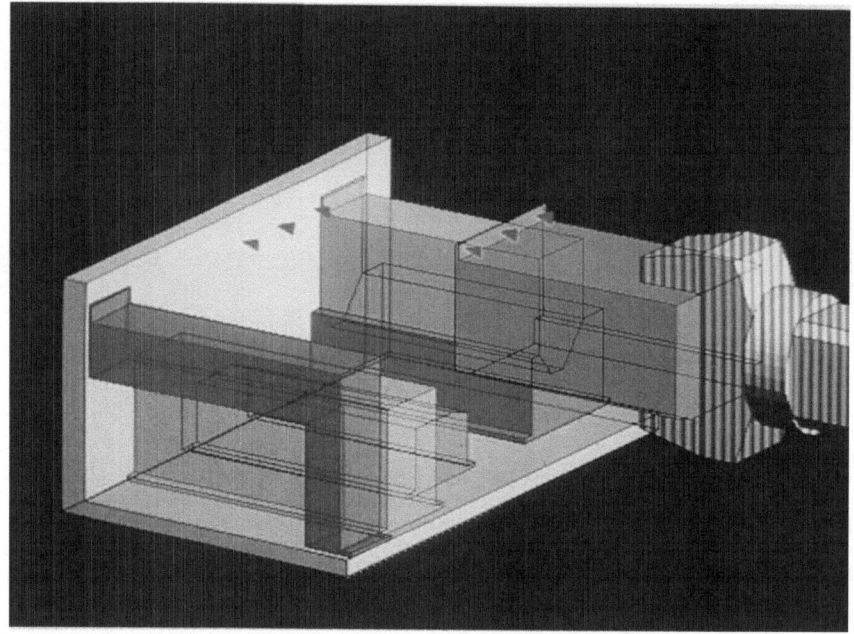

Fig. 11. A simulation of assembling a copier

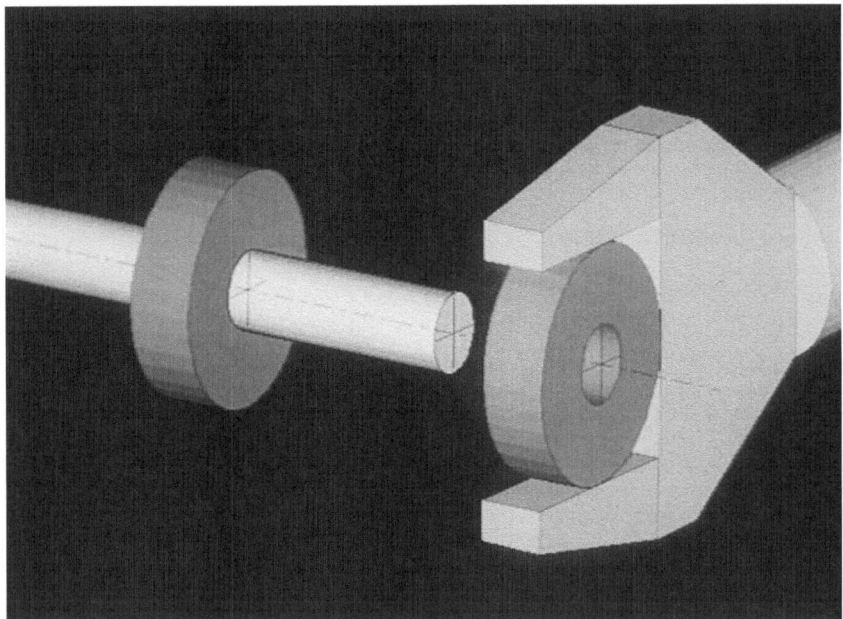

Fig. 12. A simulation of setting rings onto a shaft

CONCLUSION AND FUTURE WORK

ANIMENGINE satisfies our requirements for engineering animations, that is, exact and unambiguous display of objects, high-speed and automatic production of engineering animation, low host dependency and modest cost.

The presentation of colored and shaded areas needed for easy identification of picture components is a requirement which conflicts with the need for fast display. We have used a novel method for hidden surface removal which enables us to produce displays of sufficient quality, fast enough to be of practical use.

There is room for improvement in the following points.

1. Engineering animation needs exact display. When the displayed objects are too complicated, it should be possible for the system to simplify them automatically when the detail is not required.

2. There are some characteristics of engineering which make the job of animation simpler than in a more general context. We have tried to take advantage of this by means of our "Template model". There may be other such characteristics which can be exploited.

3. Computer graphics and video technology need to be combined and unified. In the near future, we will use a video disk recorder rather than a frame-by-frame video tape recorder. A random-access video disk recorder can substitute for a frame buffer and it excels in cost and the number of frames to be recorded.

ANIMENGINE is a growing system and the developed system will be described in a succeeding paper.

ACKNOWLEDGEMENTS

This work was partially supported by Nippon Gakki Co., Ltd., Ricoh Co., Ltd., and Japan Victor Co., Ltd. We are grateful to Prof. Geoff Wyvill, Prof. Brian Wyvill, Prof. Alain Fournier and Mr. Yasuto Shirai for their thoughtful comments.

UNIX is a trademark of AT&T.

MSX is a trademark of MICROSOFT.

REFERENCES

Badler NI, O'Rourke J, Toltzis H (1979) A Spherical Representation of a Human Body for Visualizing Movement. Proc. IEEE 67: 1397-1403

Baumgart BG (1975) A Polyhedron Representation for Computer Vision. AFIPS Conf. Proc. 44: 589-596

Boyse JW (1979) Interference Detection Among Solids and Surfaces. CACM 22: 3-9

Comba PG (1968) A Procedure for Detecting Intersections of Three-Dimensional Objects. JACM 15: 354-366

Esterling DM, Van Rosendale J (1983) An Intersection Algorithm for Moving Parts. Computer-Aided Geometry Modeling (NASA Conf. Publication 2272) 129-133

Fuchs H, Kedem ZM, Naylor BF (1980) On Visible Surface Generation by a Priori Tree Structures. Computer Graphics 14(3): 124-133

Harrington S (1983) Computer Graphics --- A Programming Approach. McGraw-Hill, New York

Kunii TL, Shirota Y (1985) CrossoverNet: A Computer Graphics/Video Crossover LAN System. Proc. Computer Graphics Tokyo '85

Schachter BJ (1981) Computer Image Generation for Flight Simulation. IEEE CG&A 1(4): 29-68

Sutherland IE, Sproull RF, Schumacker RA (1974) A Characterization of Ten Hidden-Surface Algorithms. Comput. Surveys 6: 1-55

Yokokawa K, Kunii TL (1980) A Definition of Neighborhood of a Region for Picture Processing. Computer Graphics and Image Processing 14: 112-144

Dynamics for Animation of Characters with Deformable Surfaces

William W. Armstrong and Mark W. Green

Department of Computing Science, University of Alberta, Edmonton, Alberta, T6G 2H1, Canada

INTRODUCTION

The animation of human and human-like characters is one of the major problems in computer animation (Badler 1982). The key aspect of this problem is achieving realistic motion with a minimal amount of effort on the part of the animator. The control of a dynamic animation by means of joint torque and force functions has been described by Wilhelms and Barsky (1985). Their solution to the dynamics problem uses a Gibbs-Appell formulation, according to which the time to set up the equations grows at least as the cube of the number of links. After that, the solution time is at least quadratic, due to the fact that a square matrix having several rows for each link is employed. Formulating the problem using such a matrix is not essential for animating tree-like figures, however. The fact that the only dynamic interactions which occur between links are those between parents and their children means that the solution can be carried out more efficiently.

The approach to human figure animation presented here is based on incorporating dynamics into the model of the figure, as well as some information on surface deformations due to the changes in joint angles of the character. Once the model has been constructed, a wide range of motions can be achieved by applying forces or torques to joints in the model at key points in the animation. The fast solution method of the dynamic equations of motion makes real-time control by the animator a possibility.

In our view of human figure animation a human figure model must have the following characteristics:

1) The model should produce realistic motion sequences when given realistic input data.

2) The amount of information the animator must provide should be minimal and proportional to the complexity of the motion. If the character is standing still, for example, the animator should not need to specify any motion data.

3) The model should be able to react to and act upon its environment. If someone pushes the character, or if it runs into an obstacle, it should react to that force without animator intervention.

This suggests using a model that accounts for such physical properties as mass, force, inertia, torque, and acceleration.

THE EQUATIONS OF MOTION AND THEIR SOLUTION

A treatment of manipulator dynamics based on Lagrangian mechanics is given in a book by R. P. Paul (1981). Hollerbach has given a recursive Lagrangian formulation of manipulator dynamics (1980). Details of our formulation and solution of the equations of motion are to be found in our paper (1985). In this section, only a sketch will be given.

For dynamic modeling of linkages, it is convenient to choose frames which move along with the links to represent some vectors. In addition to frames which move with the links, we also use an inertial frame, considered fixed and non-rotating. The transformation from one frame to another is done by multiplying a column vector on the left by a 3-by-3 orthogonal matrix. The cross product is denoted by $\times$.

We shall use the following quantities:

Scalar:
  m_r the mass of link r;

Representations in the inertial frame:
  a_G the acceleration of gravity;

  p^r position vector of the hinge of link r proximal to root;
  v^r the velocity of the proximal hinge of link r;
  f_E^r external force acting on link r at p_E^r;
  g_E^r external torque acting on link r;

Representations in the frame of link r:
  a^r the acceleration of the proximal hinge of link r;
  ω^r the angular velocity of link r;
  $\dot{\omega}^r$ its rate of change;
  c^r vector from proximal hinge to center of mass of link r;
  f^r force link r exerts on its parent at the proximal hinge;
  g^r torque link r exerts on its parent at the proximal hinge;

Representation in the frame of the parent of link r:
  l^r vector from proximal hinge of parent to that of link r;

Rotation matrices:
  R^r converts vector representations in the frame of link r to the representations in the frame of the parent link;
  R_I^r converts from representations in frame r to the inertial frame;

Matrix representation in frame r:
  J^r the moment of inertia matrix of link r about its proximal hinge;

The first equation of motion expresses the fact that the rate of change of angular momentum of link r is equal to the applied torques from various sources.

$$J^r \dot{\omega}^r = g_\Sigma^r - m_r c^r \times a^r + \sum_{s \in S_r} l^s \times R^s f^s \qquad (1)$$

where

$$g_\Sigma^r = -\omega^r \times (J^r \omega^r) - g^r + \sum_{s \in S_r} R^s g^s + R_I^{r\,T} g_E^r \qquad (2)$$
$$+ m_r c^r \times R_I^{r\,T} a_G + p_E^r \times R_I^{r\,T} f_E^r$$

The next equation of motion gives the force f^r acting on the parent of link r at the proximal hinge of link r.

$$f^r = f_\Sigma^r - m_r a^r + m_r c^r \times \dot{\omega}^r + \sum_{s \in S_r} R^s f^s \qquad (3)$$

where

$$f_\Sigma^r = - m_r \omega^r \times (\omega^r \times c^r) + R_I^{r\ T} (f_E^r + m_r a_G) \qquad (4)$$

The last equation describing the motion relates the acceleration at the proximal hinge of a son link s of link r to the linear and angular accelerations at the proximal hinge of r:

$$R^s a^s = a_c^s + a^r - l^s \times \dot{\omega}^r \qquad (5)$$

where

$$a_c^s = \omega^r \times (\omega^r \times l^s) \qquad (6)$$

In order to get the motion, we must solve these equations to get the motion (accelerations, velocities, positions and orientations of the links through time) given the torques at the hinges and the external forces and torques. This will let the animator control the motion interactively using hand and perhaps other controllers. The solution method used (Armstrong and Green 1985) grows linearly with the number of links, and is appropriate, we feel, for animation purposes, where the number of links may be large.

DEVELOPING FIGURE MODELS

Our approach to human figure modeling consists of three steps. The first step is developing a skeleton for the figure. This skeleton consists of a set of links representing the figure's limbs and a set of joints representing the places where the limbs are connected. The set of links representing the figure form a tree with each link having at most one parent. The skeleton represents the topology and some physical properties of the figure. The skeleton itself can be viewed as a stick figure. The graphical display of the figure used in an animated sequence is generated from the skeleton. Techniques for converting skeletons to graphical displays were treated by Burtnyk and Wein (1976), and Zeltzer (1982). Associated with each link in the model is its mass, center of mass, and moment of inertia matrix. These quantities must be calculated or estimated from the figure being modeled, but some values may have to be modified to keep the integration stepsize from being too small.

In order to have realistic motion the skeleton data must be augmented by information pertaining to the elastic behavior of joints, determined in the second step in this modeling process. The third step is determining the joint torques and the external forces and torques required for specific motions such as walking, throwing, or diving.

The following example is based on a human body model consisting of twelve links. Figure 1 shows a sequence of images generated by the program "DynaTree" simulating the first 0.5 second of a diving motion very simply defined by applying external forces downward and forward on the head and arms, forward on the lower body, and upward and backward on the feet. The hinge torques generated by stiffness and friction were sufficient to maintain reasonable behavior without any intervention by joint motor programs. The moments of inertia of the links were increased by about an order of magnitude from the correct values for the large links, and by three orders of magnitude for the small links (like the neck). Further experiments are required to determine the allowable modification of the moments of inertia still giving reasonable behavior. With this falsification of the true dynamics, the integration step size could be taken to be 1/30 second. It was possible to generate one second of motion on the VAX † 11/780 in 9.5 seconds of CPU time. Doing some computations less frequently than every cycle cut this time in half. The shaded color display in Fig. 1 was prepared using software developed by Robert Lake.

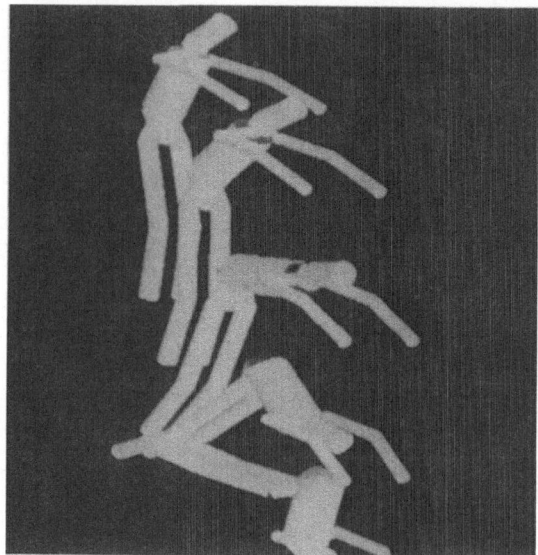

Figure 1

Clearly, we have a long way to go before having near-real-time simulation and display of shaded images, but stick-figure simulation in real time is very close to being a reality. Use of distributed processing and perhaps dropping some of the non-essential terms in the equations of motion would be enough to attain it. We are thus already facing the difficult question of how the animator can control the motion interactively.

DEALING WITH DEFORMABLE PARTS

In this section we briefly describe two approaches that can be used to model the motion of nonrigid body parts. The two approaches differ in the types of body parts they model.

Some body parts under normal circumstances closely follow the motion of the underlying skeleton. Examples of these body parts include fingers, hands, arms, face, and legs. When the skeleton moves the skin covering these body parts follows the general motion of the corresponding bone. However, when the limb bends the skin deforms somewhat and tends to bunch

---

† VAX is a trademark of Digital Equipment Corporation.

around the joints. This type of behavior can be modeled in the following way. First, a radius is associated with each limb in the skeleton. This radius could be constant or vary along the length of the limb. At fixed intervals along the limb, lines perpendicular to the limb are constructed. The lengths of these lines is nominally the radius of the limb at that point. The ends of these lines are used as control points for either spline curves or surface patches representing the skin. In order to model deformations of the skin, the length of the perpendicular lines is modulated by the rotation angle of nearby joints. If the limb is straight the limb radius is used as the line length. As the limb bends, the line length is increased near the center of the limb. This causes the curve or surface representing the skin to bulge out.

The other approach to modeling nonrigid body parts and attachment deals with more flexible parts. As an example consider a fat person landing on the ground after a jump. The body will undergo visible deformations which are not computed by the equations of motion. A related problem is simulating the movement of clothing and hair in a manner which is consistent with our expectations of their dynamic behavior, such as the long dress and long hair of a woman dancing the waltz. For this type of object, dynamic properties can have as much (or more) influence on the motion as the underlying skeleton. A more elaborate modeling scheme is called for. Extra "sensor" links in the tree structure are introduced whose dynamics reflect the forces and torques acting on the parts in question. For example, one can think of an extra (invisible) link attached to the spine and pointing forward to sense the forces acting on a fat abdomen. Springs and viscous damping can cause the link to behave somewhat like the actual abdomen. Then the positions of the neighboring structural links, i. e. the torso and the hips, and the position of the sensor link together can be used to determine a set of control points, which in turn define the shape of the deformed surface.

Of course, the introduction of extra links adds to the computational burden of solving the equations of motion, however this is mitigated by the use of the present technique which grows linearly with the number of links. An even better approach is to use the inherent parallelism possible in the technique, as we shall now explain.

A DISTRIBUTED SOLUTION TO THE EQUATIONS OF MOTION

The solution of the equations proceeds in cycles which treat the links in the tree linkage in succession either on an inbound pass towards the root or in an outbound pass towards the leaves. Since the dependencies among the quantities are limited to connected links, the computations along separate branches from the root can be done concurrently. This suggests using several processors to solve the equations. One processor could handle computations for the root and for all the links along one simple path to a leaf. Another processor could handle a disjoint path from a child of the root to another leaf, and so on. The time required for a complete cycle in the solution of the dynamic equations should be roughly proportional to the length of the longest path from the root to a leaf if enough processors are available. This approach is currently being investigated on a virtual tree machine distributed over several computers at the University of Alberta (Armstrong, Marsland, Olafsson, Schaeffer 1985).

CONCLUSIONS

In this paper we have discussed the dynamics of articulated rigid bodies, and a method for solving their equations of motion in time which grows linearly with the number of links, or as the depth of the tree linkage if a multiprocessor system is used. We have described a technique for developing figure models including surfaces which deform under the effects of kinematics and dynamics. Real-time interactive control of figures appears to be within the realm of possibility if this approach is taken.

REFERENCES

Armstrong WW, and Green MW (1985) The Dynamics of Articulated Rigid Bodies for Purposes of Animation, Proc. Graphics Interface '85, Montreal, pp. 407-415.

Armstrong WW, Marsland TA, Olafsson M, Schaeffer J (1985) Solution of the Equations of Motion of Tree-Linkages on a Virtual Tree Machine, Technical Report, Dept. of Computing Science, University of Alberta.

Badler N ed. (1982) Special Issued IEEE Computer Graphics and Applications on Human Body Models and Animation, vol. 2, no.9.

Burtnyk N, Wein M (1976) Interactive Skeleton Techniques for Enhancing Motion Dynamics in Key Frame Animation, Comm. ACM vol.19, no.10, p.564-569.

Hollerbach JM (1980) A Recursive Lagrangian Formulation of Manipulator Dynamics and a Comparative Study of Dynamics Formulation, IEEE Trans. on Systems, Man and Cybernetics, SMC-10, 11, pp. 730-736.

Paul P (1981) *Robot Manipulators: Mathematics, Programming, and Control*, MIT Press, Cambridge, Mass.

Wilhelms J, and Barsky B (1985) Using Dynamic Analysis to Animate Articulated Bodies such as Humans and Robots, Proc. Graphics Interface '85 , Montreal, pp. 97-104.

Zeltzer D (1982) Motor Control Techniques for Figure Animation, IEEE Computer Graphics and Applications, vol. 2, no. 9, p.53.

Using Dynamic Analysis to Animate Articulated Bodies such as Humans and Robots

Jane P. Wilhelms and Brian A. Barsky

Berkeley Computer Graphics Laboratory, Computer Science Division, Department of Electrical Engineering and Computer Sciences, University of California, Berkeley, CA 94720, USA

Abstract

A method of animating articulated (linked) bodies such as humans, animals and robots using *dynamic analysis* is presented. Dynamic analysis predicts motion by analyzing the effect of forces and torques on mass; this is different than the usual *kinematic* method of specifying motion, where positions, velocities, and accelerations are given without considering the forces and torques producing motion. It is difficult to kinematically specify realistic motion, particularly in cases where the body is moving fast, in complex patterns, or with great freedom. In such cases, animation based on dynamic analysis, though more expensive, may be preferable. Animation using dynamic analysis is also useful in the design and control of robots and other mechanical manipulators, and for analyzing the movement of humans and animals in biomechanics and sports.

Résumé

Nous présentons une méthode pour l'animation d'objets articulés, tels que les humains, les animaux et les robots. Cette méthode est basée sur *l'analyse dynamique*, ce qui permet de prédire les mouvements grâce à une analyse des effets des forces et des moments sur les masses. Ceci diffère de l'approche *kinématique* plus habituelle consistant à spécifier les mouvements en précisant uniquement les position, vittesse et accélération des objets sans accorder aucune attention aux forces et moments à l'origine de ces mouvements. Il est ardu de spécifier kinématiquement un mouvement réaliste, surtout lorsque l'objet se déplace rapidement, de façon complexe, ou avec beaucoup de liberté. Dans de tels cas, une animation basée sur l'analyse dynamique peut être préférable malgré son coût plus élevé. Cette approche à l'animation peut également être pratique pour la conception et le contrôle des robots et autres manipulateurs mécaniques, ainsi que pour l'analyse des mouvements humains et animaux aussi bien en biomécanique qu'en sports.

KEYWORDS: animation, human modeling, dynamics, simulation

This work was supported in part by the Defense Advanced Research Projects Agency under contract number N00039-82-C-0235, the National Science Foundation under grant number ECS-8204381, and the State of California under a Microelectronics Innovation and Computer Research Opportunities grant.

1. OVERVIEW

Considering the physical properties of the natural world when modeling imaginary worlds in computer graphics has consistently led to more realistic and aesthetically pleasing images. A natural next step in this process is to consider the physical principles governing moving objects in producing animations; these principles form the study of that part of physics known as *dynamics*. The motion of an object is determined by its own nature and its interaction with the environment, and is described dynamically as a relation between forces and torques and the behavior of masses under their influence. A simpler means of describing motion is *kinematics*, which differs from dynamics in that kinematics describes motion only in terms of positions, velocities and accelerations, neglecting the forces and torques responsible.[12] An effective means of motion specification is particularly important in animating articulated (linked) bodies, such as humans, other animals, and robots, since these bodies are capable of extremely complex movement.

Present systems for animating articulated bodies tend to do so kinematically.[3,6,7,16] A major problem with kinematic motion specification is determining a sequence of positions that produces a realistic animation. The two major alternatives for finding such a sequence are: (1) recording the actual movement occurring in the real world (e.g. filming animals) or (2) using trial-and-error, testing motion sequences until an acceptable solution is found. Neither of these methods is completely satisfactory; measurements may not be easily available, and trial-and-error depends on the ability and patience of the user.

The use of dynamic analysis to avoid the limitations of kinematic motion specification has been suggested before,[6] but the cost and complexity involved have kept it from being implemented. An advantage of dynamic analysis is that the motion predicted is accurate for the specified conditions and it would occur under these conditions in the real world. Dynamic analysis coupled with computer animation has applications outside the field of computer graphics proper -- for example, in the design and control of robots and mechanical manipulators, biomechanical exploration of the engineering principles underlying animal motion,[14] and in the evaluation of the safety and efficiency of motion in sports.[10]

Previous use of dynamics to simulate articulated bodies in motion has largely been limited to crash studies,[15] where dynamics is used to predict the uncontrolled motion of bodies under the influence of large external forces, such as those occurring in auto and plane crashes. Graphical output tends to be simple and motion is often limited to two dimensions. The method described here differs from crash simulations in that dynamics is used to *control* the motion, by using internal forces and torques simulating muscles and motors. Recently, Armstrong and Greene[1] have presented an alternative method for controlling animation using dynamics.

This paper introduces a method of specifying three-dimensional motion dynamically. Although the principles involved are particularly oriented towards animating articulated bodies, they are equally applicable to simpler structures. The use of dynamic analysis is explained first, followed by a brief description of the system (*Deva*) that has been implemented to investigate dynamic and kinematic motion specification, and concluding with some discussion of future research directions.

2. DYNAMIC ANALYSIS USING THE GIBBS-APPELL FORMULATION

For dynamic analysis, it is necessary to develop the dynamic equations of motion (one for each degree of freedom) that describe the relationship between masses and the forces and torques affecting them. In the case of articulated bodies, each body segment (e.g., the leg) can be modeled as a rigid body. An unconstrained rigid body is capable of six degrees of freedom of motion; however, in articulated bodies motion is restricted by attachments to neighboring segments. Because the motion of each segment of the articulated body is affected by the motion of others, the dynamics equations are complex and coupled.

A variety of formulations of the dynamics equations are available, all of which produce the same result in slightly different terms. The most familiar formulation is that of Newton, exemplified in simple form in his *Second Law* ($\mathbf{F} = m\mathbf{a}$); that is, the sum of all forces ($\mathbf{F}$) acting on a particle is equal to the particle's mass (m) times its acceleration ($\mathbf{a}$). Another formulation, the Gibbs-Appell, more easily describes the complex dynamics of articulated bodies and was chosen for use here.[2,9]

The dynamics equations can be solved in either of two directions: the *direct solution* involves providing the accelerations of the bodies involved and solving the equations for the forces and torques that produced these accelerations; the *indirect solution* involves providing the forces and torques, and solving for accelerations. The indirect problem is of relevance here, where the desired output is a prediction of realistic motion. Besides the controlling input (forces and torques), solution of the dynamics equations also requires knowledge of the present state of the body including, for each segment, its mass, the location of its center of mass and the distribution of the mass around the center, and its present position and velocity. Once the equations are formulated, they can be integrated using numerical methods.[8] The cost of dynamic analysis is bounded by the cost of solving the set of equations, and is $O(n^3)$ for n degrees of freedom.

2.1. The Gibbs Formula: The Basis for the Gibbs-Appell Formulation

The Gibbs-Appell dynamics formulation is based on the Gibbs Formula, which describes the *energy of acceleration*.[9] For rigid bodies consisting of n segments, this formula is

$$G = \sum_{k=1}^{n} (\frac{1}{2} m_k \mathbf{a}_k^T \mathbf{a}_k + \frac{1}{2} \alpha_k^T \mathbf{I}_k \alpha_k + \alpha_k^T (\omega_k \times \mathbf{I}_k \omega_k) + f(\omega_k))$$

where, for segment k,

$m_k =$ *mass*
$\mathbf{a}_k =$ *acceleration vector of center of mass*
$\alpha_k =$ *angular acceleration vector*
$\omega_k =$ *angular velocity vector*
$f(\omega_k) =$ *scalar disappears with differentiation*

$$\mathbf{I}_k = \begin{bmatrix} I_{xx} & I_{xy} & I_{xz} \\ I_{xy} & I_{yy} & I_{yz} \\ I_{xz} & I_{yz} & I_{zz} \end{bmatrix} = \text{ inertial tensor}$$

$I_{xx} = \int (y^2 + z^2) dm;$ *etc., moments of inertia*
$I_{xy} = \int xy\, dm;$ *etc., products of inertia*

The actual dynamics equations are found by partially differentiating the Gibbs formula with respect to the local acceleration relative to each degree of freedom. For n degrees of freedom, this results in n equations, which relate local accelerations at the degrees of freedom to the *generalized forces* acting on the body. A generalized force can be thought of as the net force (for sliding degrees of freedom) or torque (for revolute degrees of freedom) active at this degree of freedom, and is the result of all forces and torques acting within the system.

2.2. Dynamic Analysis Using the Gibbs-Appell Formulation

The dynamics equations can be stated in a succinct form as

$$\mathbf{M}\ddot{\mathbf{c}} + \mathbf{V} = \mathbf{q} \quad or \quad \mathbf{M}^{-1}(\mathbf{q} - \mathbf{V}) = \ddot{\mathbf{c}}$$

For a body with n degrees of freedom, $\ddot{\mathbf{c}}$ is an n-length vector of the local acceleration occurring at each degree of freedom (e.g. a rotation about the X-axis or a translation along the Z-axis) and $\mathbf{q}$ is an n-length vector specifying the generalized force active at each degree of freedom. **M** is an $n \times n$ inertial matrix dependent upon the configuration of the system masses. **V** is an n-length vector dependent upon the position of the masses and their motion relative to each other. Thus, if the generalized force vector **q** is available, the equations can be solved for accelerations $\ddot{\mathbf{c}}$ which can then be used to update the positions of the body segments.[9]

The elements of both the matrix **M** and the vectors $\ddot{\mathbf{c}}$, **V**, and **q** are arranged so that those referring to revolute degrees of freedom precede those referring to sliding degrees of freedom. A coordinate frame is associated with each degree of freedom such that its Z-axis is the axis of sliding or revolution. Indexing is such that degree of freedom k lies between segments $k-1$ and k.

For dynamic analysis, multiple-degree-of-freedom joints can be depicted as a sequence of single-degree-of-freedom joints connected by massless and dimensionless segments. Thus each degree of freedom has its own *joint* and *segment*, and in the following dynamics discussion "joint" and "segment" refer to these generalized forms.

The formulation of the dynamics equations described below does not exploit the recursive nature of the terms, and the cost of setting up the equations is $O(n^4)$. A recursive Gibbs-Appell formulation has been suggested by Athan and Horowitz[2] which is $O(n^3)$. Armstrong and Green[1] have presented a slightly less general, recursive dynamics formulation that is linear ($O(n)$) in the number of joints.

Explanation of Terms: The partial differentiation of the Gibbs formula leaves motion described in inertial world space terms; however, these equations can be restated in terms of local joint configuration because of the known relation between local and world frames. The following kinematic configuration information is necessary for dynamic analysis ($k = 1, \ldots, n$ for n degrees of freedom).

$\mathbf{r}_k =$ *3-D position vector of joint connecting segments $k-1$ and k*

$\mathbf{g}_k =$ *3-D position vector of center of mass of segment k*

$\mathbf{u}_k =$ *3-D unit vector of rotation or sliding axis of joint k*

$s_k, \dot{s}_k, \ddot{s}_k =$ *sliding along axis $\mathbf{u}_k$, its velocity, and acceleration*

$\theta_k, \dot{\theta}_k, \ddot{\theta}_k =$ *rotation angle about axis $\mathbf{u}_k$, its angular velocity, and acceleration*

$\mathbf{R}_k =$ *3×3 matrix describing rotation about axis $\mathbf{u}_k$*

Finding the Inertial Matrix (M-Matrix): $\mathbf{M}$ is an $n \times n$ matrix which takes into account the present distribution of body mass. $\mathbf{M}$ consists of four submatrices.

$$\mathbf{M} = \begin{bmatrix} \mathbf{M}^\theta & \mathbf{M}^{\theta s} \\ [\mathbf{M}^{\theta s}]^T & \mathbf{M}^s \end{bmatrix}$$

The upper left submatrix $\mathbf{M}^\theta$ is an $r \times r$ matrix describing the relation between revolute degrees of freedom. Its elements are defined by the following equation

$$m_{ij}^\theta = m_{ji}^\theta = \sum_{k=distal(i,j)}^{Todistal} (m_k [\mathbf{u}_i \times (\mathbf{g}_k - \mathbf{r}_i)]^T [\mathbf{u}_j \times (\mathbf{g}_k - \mathbf{r}_j)] + \mathbf{u}_i^T \mathbf{I}_k \mathbf{u}_j)$$

(for $i = 1, \ldots, r$ and $j = 1, \ldots, r$).

(Note that $distal(i,j)$ refers to whichever of i or j lies further from the initial world segment, and if i and j lie on separate branches the calculation does not take place. $Todistal$ refers to the furthest segments continuing out this branch.)

The upper right submatrix $\mathbf{M}^{\theta s}$ (whose transpose is the lower left submatrix) is an $r \times t$ matrix describing the relation between revolute and sliding degrees of freedom. Its elements are

$$m_{ij}^{\theta s} = \sum_{k=distal(i,j)}^{Todistal} m_k \mathbf{u}_j^T [\mathbf{u}_i \times (\mathbf{g}_k - \mathbf{r}_i)]$$

(for $i = 1,\ldots,r$ and $j = 1,\ldots,t$).

The lower right submatrix $\mathbf{M}^s$ is a $t \times t$ matrix describing the relation between sliding degrees of freedom. Its elements are

$$m_{ij}^s = m_{ji}^s = \sum_{k=(i,j)}^{Todistal} m_k \mathbf{u}_i^T \mathbf{u}_j$$

(for $i = 1, \ldots, t$ and $j = 1, \ldots, t$).

Velocity-Dependent V-Vector: The **V**-vector takes into account such velocity-dependent contributions as the Coriolis and centrifugal forces. The **V**-vector contains two sub-vectors: $\mathbf{V}_\theta$ is an r-length vector representing revolute degrees of freedom, and $\mathbf{V}_s$ is a t-length vector representing sliding degrees of freedom.

$$\mathbf{V} = \begin{bmatrix} \mathbf{V}_\theta \\ \mathbf{V}_s \end{bmatrix} \quad \mathbf{V}_\theta = \begin{bmatrix} V_{\theta 1} \\ \cdots \\ V_{\theta r} \end{bmatrix} \quad \mathbf{V}_s = \begin{bmatrix} V_{s 1} \\ \cdots \\ V_{s t} \end{bmatrix}$$

The elements of the $\mathbf{V}_\theta$ vector for revolute degrees of freedom ($V_{\theta k}$ for $k = 1, \ldots, r$) are found using the following equation.

$$V_{\theta k} = [\dot\theta_1, \ldots, \dot\theta_r, \dot s_1, \ldots, \dot s_t] \begin{bmatrix} \mathbf{N}_\theta^{k\theta} & \mathbf{N}_\theta^{ks} \\ [\mathbf{N}_\theta^{ks}]^T & 0 \end{bmatrix} [\dot\theta_1, \ldots, \dot\theta_r, \dot s_1, \ldots, \dot s_t]^T$$

where the components of the $\mathbf{N}_\theta$ matrix are found by

$$n_{\theta ij}^{k\theta} = n_{\theta ji}^{k\theta} = \sum_{l=distal(k,j)}^{distal} (m_l [\mathbf{u}_k \times (\mathbf{g}_l - \mathbf{r}_k)]^T [\mathbf{u}_i \times (\mathbf{u}_j \times (\mathbf{g}_l - \mathbf{r}_j))]$$
$$+ \mathbf{u}_k^T [\frac{1}{2} trace(\mathbf{I}_l) \mathbf{u}_i \times \mathbf{u}_j + \mathbf{u}_j \times \mathbf{I}_l \mathbf{u}_i])$$

where $trace(\mathbf{I}_l) = I_{l11} + I_{l22} + I_{l33}$
(for $i = 1, \ldots, r$ and $j = 1, \ldots, r$)

and

$$n_{\theta ij}^{ks} = \begin{bmatrix} \sum_{l=distal(k,j)}^{distal} m_l [\mathbf{u}_k \times (\mathbf{g}_l - \mathbf{r}_k)]^T [\mathbf{u}_i \times \mathbf{u}_j] \\ \quad\quad\text{for } i \text{ proximal to } j \\ 0 \quad\quad\text{for } i \text{ distal to } j \end{bmatrix}$$

(for $i = 1, \ldots, r$ and $j = 1, \ldots, t$)

The elements of $\mathbf{V}_s$ vector for sliding degrees of freedom (V_{sk} for $k = 1, \ldots, t$) are found using the following equation.

$$V_{sk} = [\dot\theta_1, \ldots, \dot\theta_r, \dot s_1, \ldots, \dot s_t] \begin{bmatrix} \mathbf{N}_s^{k\theta} & \mathbf{N}_s^{ks} \\ [\mathbf{N}_s^{ks}]^T & 0 \end{bmatrix} [\dot\theta_1, \ldots, \dot\theta_r, \dot s_1, \ldots, \dot s_t]^T$$

where the components of the $\mathbf{N}_\theta$ matrix are found by

$$n_{\theta ij}^{k\theta} = n_{\theta ji}^{k\theta} = \sum_{l=distal(k,j)}^{distal} m_l \mathbf{u}_k^T[\mathbf{u}_i \times (\mathbf{u}_j \times (\mathbf{g}_l - \mathbf{r}_j))]$$

(for $i = 1, \ldots, r$ and $j = i, \ldots, r$)

and

$$n_{\theta ij}^{k\theta} = \begin{bmatrix} \sum_{l=distal(k,j)}^{distal} m_l \mathbf{u}_k^T[\mathbf{u}_i \times \mathbf{u}_j] & i \text{ proximal to } j \\ 0 & i \text{ distal to } j \end{bmatrix}$$

(for $i = 1, \ldots, r$ and $j = 1, \ldots, t$)

2.3. Forces and Torques Contributing to Motion

A variety of forces and torques contribute to motion, some of which can be calculated automatically, others of which can be input by the user to control the movement. The forces and torques that can be computed automatically include those due to gravity, to collisions between parts of the body, to joint limits, and to contact with external objects such as the ground or objects in the environment whose position and behavior is known to the system. Those forces and torques that should be input include internal forces applied across joints and external applied forces unknown to the system; these forces and torques will be called *controlling forces* and *torques*. All forces and torques are calculated for each degree of freedom; by summing their contributions to each degree of freedom, the generalized force for that degree of freedom is found. A more detailed description of the calculation of these forces is forthcoming.[13]

Gravitational Forces and Torques: The gravitational component of each generalized force can be determined simply by considering the effect of the mass of distal segments at a particular degree of freedom. In the case of each revolute degree of freedom, this involves finding the torque around its axis of rotation, which depends upon the gravitational force acting on each distal segment and the perpendicular distance of the point of force's application from the axis of rotation. The equation for torque due to gravity at degree of freedom k is

$$\tau_{gk} = -g_c \sum_{i=k}^{distal} m_i \mathbf{z}_{0T}[\mathbf{u}_k \times (\mathbf{g}_i - \mathbf{r}_k)]$$

where $z_0 = (0,0,1)$ is a vertical direction vector, $g_c = 9.81$ m/sec^2 is the acceleration due to gravity, and the other terms are as explained previously.

In the case of each sliding degree of freedom, the gravitational component (f_{gk}) contributing to the generalized force there is dependent upon the component of the gravitational force acting on each distal segment that lies along the axis of sliding; that is,

$$f_{gk} = -g_c \sum_{i=k}^{distal} m_i z_0^T u_k$$

Figure 1 shows a body falling freely under the influence of gravity. By altering the gravitational constant, motion on other planets or in space can be simulated.

External Applied Forces: Where the magnitude and direction of an external applied force (such as a pull from a rope or a shove) is known, the contribution of this force to the generalized force at each degree of freedom can be calculated using a method very similar to that used for gravity. Assume that a force represented by vector $\mathbf{F}_a$ is applied to segment a at a location designated by the world-space vector $\mathbf{a}$. Each revolute degree of freedom i which lies proximal to segment a feels the effect of this applied force as the torque τ_{app_i} defined by the equation

$$\tau_{app\_i} = \mathbf{F}_a [\mathbf{u}_i \times (\mathbf{a} - \mathbf{r}_i)]$$

Each sliding degree of freedom j which lies proximal to segment a feels the effect of the applied force as the force F_{app_j} defined by the equation

$$F_{app\_j} = \mathbf{F}_a \mathbf{u}_j$$

At present, arbitrary external applied forces cannot be specified by the system *Deva*, though this would be a relatively simple extension.

Joint Limit Forces and Torques and Damping:. Although the specification of the dynamics equations automatically restricts motion to the designated degrees of freedom, it does not restrict motion within a particular degree of freedom; thus, segments are quite capable of moving through each other. To restrict motion to more realistic patterns, limiting positions for joints must be established and appropriate counteracting forces and torques applied when the motion threatens to pass beyond these limits. Simulating exact joint limit forces and torques, particularly for multiple-degree-of-freedom joints, would be extremely difficult. However, they can be adequately represented by spring and damper pairs that become active as joint limits are approached. The natural damping of friction can also be simulated by applying a damping force or torque during all joint movements.[11] Linear springs are simply specified as the product of a *spring constant* times the distance that the spring is compressed. Damping force or torque is the product of a *damping constant* times the local speed at that degree of freedom. However, the use of such a simple spring and damper is undesirable because the user must determine appropriate constants for each degree of freedom (the opposing force needed being dependent upon the nature of the joint). The method implemented is somewhat more complex, but automatically calculates joint limit forces and torques. The spring and damper used are linear; however, the stiff spring necessary to quickly stop motion might be better simulated with an exponential function.

The end limit forces (for sliding joints) or torques (for revolute joints) each have three components. The first component counteracts other forces and torques pushing the joint beyond its limit and is simply equal in magnitude and opposite in direction to all other forces (for sliding joints) or torques (for revolute joints) contributing to the generalized force at that degree of freedom (such as gravity or actuator forces). The second component is a spring whose strength is a function of the amount the joint limit has been exceeded, the local velocity, and the mass (for sliding joints) or moment of inertia (for revolute ones) distal to this degree of freedom. The third component is a damper which is a function of the local velocity and the mass or moment of inertia due to distal segments.

A damping action is normally active throughout the range of joint motion. This damper is calculated in the same manner as the end limit damper but is weaker (usually 60% of end damping).

Ground Reaction Forces: Bodies must be prevented from moving through the ground by counteracting reaction forces. Ideally, reaction forces can be calculated by considering the present state of the entire body. However, they are not automatically calculated in the course of dynamic analysis as done here, because the Gibbs-Appell formulation avoids the calculation of all reaction forces in the interest of speed. Reaction forces can be included, but this would involve considerable increase in the number of degrees of freedom that must be analyzed. An alternative is to set up and solve another set of dynamics equations that will predict reaction forces when a portion of the body is in contact with the ground. In order to avoid this considerable cost, a method of simulating ground reaction forces with an approximated force plus springs and dampers has been found satisfactory.

Simulating ground reaction forces proved an interesting problem, because the necessary normal force can vary from one to several times the body weight, because it can be distributed over several support points, and because a suitable tangential frictional force must be found to provide the desired amount of horizontal slipping on the ground. The normal force must be sufficient to stop vertical motion before the body descends noticeably into the ground, and yet not be so much as to cause unrealistic bouncing. A further problem involves the sampling rate at which dynamic analysis is done. If the body is moving rapidly it may descend significantly below the floor between sample times. A combination of an estimated counteracting force plus a spring and damper has proved an acceptable solution. Reaction forces consist of a normal force perpendicular to the ground and two orthogonal tangential forces.

Calculating Normal Forces: Normal forces are calculated as a combination of an estimated reaction force plus, possibly, a contribution from a spring and damper. The estimated force is based upon the body's total mass and momentum. This force is distributed among all contact points in proportion to their depth below the ground surface. Floor contact points are recognized by checking the height of each of the eight corners of the max/min boxes of each of the body segments against the height of a planar horizontal ground.

Because this force is only approximate, additional force is added as the contact point continues to descend. This force is due to a spring whose strength is a function of estimated normal force described above and the amount of descent beyond the original contact depth. A damper is also introduced to slow motion.

Calculating Tangential Frictional Forces: Frictional forces act to oppose tangential motion along the surface and are dependent upon both the normal force pressing into the ground and the characteristics of the surfaces. To simulate frictional forces, a combination of an estimated force plus a spring and damper are again used.

The estimated tangential force for a particular contact point is merely the product of a coefficient of friction and the normal force calculated as indicated above and applied in a direction to oppose sliding. If the contact continues to be displaced tangentially, a tangential spring is applied to contribute further opposition. (A maximum tangential force can be indicated so that sliding will occur where desired.) A damping force is also added to subdue motion.

The reaction force is then treated as an applied force acting on the contact point, as described in Section 2.3. The effect of reaction forces can be altered by varying the constants described above to simulate more or less springiness, damping, and friction; e.g. bodies sliding on ice or bouncing on trampolines. Figure 2 shows a body falling onto the ground with no frictional force; Figure 3 shows the same body falling forward on a surface with friction.

Actuator and Muscular Forces: Actuators in mechanisms such as robots and muscles in animals serve the same function: applying a force or torque across the joint that joins segments for the purpose of movement. Actuators are far simpler than muscles, since they can (ideally) be designed to apply the force or torque relative to only one degree of freedom, and as such can map directly into a component of a single generalized force. Muscles are more complex for several reasons. In particular, they apply a force between two or more fixed points so the resultant torque varies with the joint angle. The joint is usually capable of more than one degree of freedom. Typically several muscles cross one joint and some muscles cross more than one joint. The effect of all the muscles controlling a joint can, however, be simplified to a single net force or torque, and components of these net forces and torques can be found relative to the axis of motion of each of the joint's degrees of freedom. These components are then equivalent to ideal actuator forces or torques and can be mapped directly onto the generalized forces for each degree of freedom. Because of the great complexity of modeling individual muscles, the present implementation of *Deva* starts with a controlling input of actuator forces and torques, rather than muscles.

Controlling forces are input by the user, usually as control functions which describe the force or torque versus time for each degree of freedom. Figure 4 shows a more complex body bringing its knees up from a prone position. Although this method is suitable for experimentation, the number of iterations necessary to develop a desired movement makes it unsuitable for a practical animation system.

Various low-level control schemes are being investigated to give the user more general control over the motion. A simple example of this is the *freeze* function which allows clamping of specified degrees of freedom to their present position by applying a spring and damper combination on either side of this position. A similar method is being explored to automatically adjust for balance, a major problem in unstable two-legged animals.

3. DEVA: A SYSTEM FOR ANIMATING ARTICULATED BODIES

Deva is an experimental graphical system for simulating the motion of articulated bodies. More detailed descriptions of the system are available elsewhere.[13] *Deva* consists of a central *body model* describing the present characteristics (dimensions, mass properties, display properties, connectivity, etc.) and configuration (positions of segments) of the body, and a set of subroutines for modifying, displaying, and animating the body. The body can be displayed either as a vector figure on a calligraphic display (see Figure 5) or as a solid figure on a raster display (see Figure 6).

The body model consists of a number of segments (e.g., a human body is typically simplified to 15 segments) connected by joints capable of from one to six degrees of freedom of motion (three translational, three rotational). Each segment has its own local coordinate frame whose position and orientation are defined relative to its more proximal segment. It is possible to associate limits with joints to constrain their range of motion.

The body can be moved either kinematically or dynamically. For kinematically-specified motion, the user describes a sequence of local positions taken by each degree of freedom. For dynamically-specified motion, the user describes the controlling forces and torques acting on and in the body. Dynamic analysis routines evaluate the effect of these forces and torques and output an updated configuration of the body. As the body configuration is altered, the calligraphically-displayed image of the body is repositioned.

The use of *control functions* provides a convenient means of specifying motion control information for either kinematic or dynamic animation. A control function is a curve of either position versus time (for kinematic control) or force/torque versus time (for dynamic control). A unique control function is associated with each degree of freedom, and evaluating the control functions provides positions or forces (for sliding joints) and torques (for revolute joints) that specify the motion at that degree of freedom. An interactive graphical editor, *Virya*,[13] has been developed to define control functions for each degree of freedom (see Figure 7). Control functions are *cubic interpolatory spline curves*[5,4] which are defined by user-specified *defining points*. This method allows the user to specify quite complex and smooth curves by designating relatively few defining points.

4. CONCLUSIONS

The use of dynamic analysis for the animation of articulated bodies has been briefly presented, and a system (*Deva*) using this method described. In computer graphics, dynamic analysis provides an alternative means of motion specification that avoids some of the problems involved in pure kinematic animation. Graphical simulation of dynamically-predicted motion is also a tool useful in such fields as robotics and bioengineering. Kinematic motion specification is much less expensive and far easier to implement than dynamic specification and is preferable in cases where an acceptable kinematic description is available. When this is not the case, particularly when motion is complex, fast, or involves contact with powerful external forces and torques, dynamic analysis may be preferable. A combination of kinematic and dynamic motion specification which provides the best of both techniques could provide the best of both worlds.

Research is now concentrating upon the practicality and usefulness of dynamic specification for producing realistic animation. This involves a number of problems and complexities. For example, how does one choose the appropriate applied forces and torques that produce realistic motion? How can one best model motion such as walking, where the body is sometimes restricted by the ground, and at other times not? How can one best provide a balancing mechanism, a particularly complex problem for two-legged bodies? What kind of high-level control will make the system practical to use? These issues provide fertile ground for future research and are currently being investigated.

References

1. William W. Armstrong and Mark W. Green, "The Dynamics of Articulated Rigid Bodies for Purposes of Animation," pp. 407-415 in *Proceedings Graphics Interface '85*, Computer Graphics Society,(May, 1985).

2. Tim Athan, *An Analysis of Complex Multi-Link Chains*, Master's Thesis, Dept. of Mechanical Engineering, University of California, Berkeley (June, 1984).

3. Norman I. Badler, Joseph O'Rourke, Stephen Platt, and Mary Ann Morris, "Human Movement Understanding: A Variety of Perspectives," pp. 53-55 in *Proceedings 1st Annual National Conference of Artificial Intelligence*, (1980).

4. Brian A. Barsky and Spencer W. Thomas, "TRANSPLINE -- A System for Representing Curves Using Transformations among Four Spline Formulations," *The Computer Journal*, Vol. 24, No. 3, August, 1981, pp. 271-277.

5. Richard H. Bartels, John C. Beatty, and Brian A. Barsky, *An Introduction to the Use of Splines in Computer Graphics*, Technical Report No. UCB/CSD 83/136, Computer Science Division, Electrical Engineering and Computer Sciences Department, University of California, Berkeley, California, USA (August, 1983). Also Tech. Report No. CS-83-9, Department of Computer Science, University of Waterloo, Waterloo, Ontario, Canada.

6. T. W. Calvert, J. Chapman, and A. Patla, "The Integration of Subjective and Objective Data in the Animation of Human Movement," pp. 198-203 in *SIGGRAPH '80 Conference Proceedings*, ACM,(July, 1980).

7. Don Herbison-Evans, "NUDES 2: A Numeric Utility Displaying Ellipsoid Solids, Version 2," pp. 354-356 in *SIGGRAPH '78 Conference Proceedings*, ACM,(August, 1978).

8. Robert W. Hornbeck, *Numerical Methods*, Quantum Publishers, Inc., New York, New York (1975).

9. Roberto Horowitz, *Model Reference Adaptive Control of Mechanical Manipulators*, Ph.D. Thesis, Mechanical Engineering, University of California, Berkeley, CA (May, 1983).

10. D. I. Miller, "Computer Simulation of Human Motion," in *Techniques for the Analysis of Human Motion*, ed. D. W. Grieve, et. al.,Lepus Books,London(1975).

11. Al Pisano, Department of Mechanical Engineering, University of California, Berkeley, CA (1984). Personal communication.

12. Robert Resnick and David Halliday, *Physics Part I*, John Wiley and Sons, Inc., New York (1966).

13. Jane Wilhelms, *Computer Graphics Simulation of the Motion of Articulated Bodies such as Humans and Robots, with Emphasis on the Use of Dynamic Analysis (Tentative Title)*, Ph.D. Thesis, Computer Science Division, Department of Electrical Engineering and Computer Sciences, University of California, Berkeley. Forthcoming.

14. R. J. Williams and Ali A. Seireg, "Interactive Computer Modeling of the Musculoskeletal System," *IEEE Transactions on Biomedical Engineering*, Vol. BME-24, No. 3, May, 1977, pp. 213-219.

15. K. D. Willmert, "Visualizing Human Body Motion Simulations," *IEEE Computer Graphics and Applications*, Vol. 2, No. 9, November, 1982, pp. 35-43.

16. David Zeltzer, "Motor Control Techniques for Figure Animation," *IEEE Computer Graphics and Applications*, Vol. 2, No. 9, November, 1982, pp. 53-60.

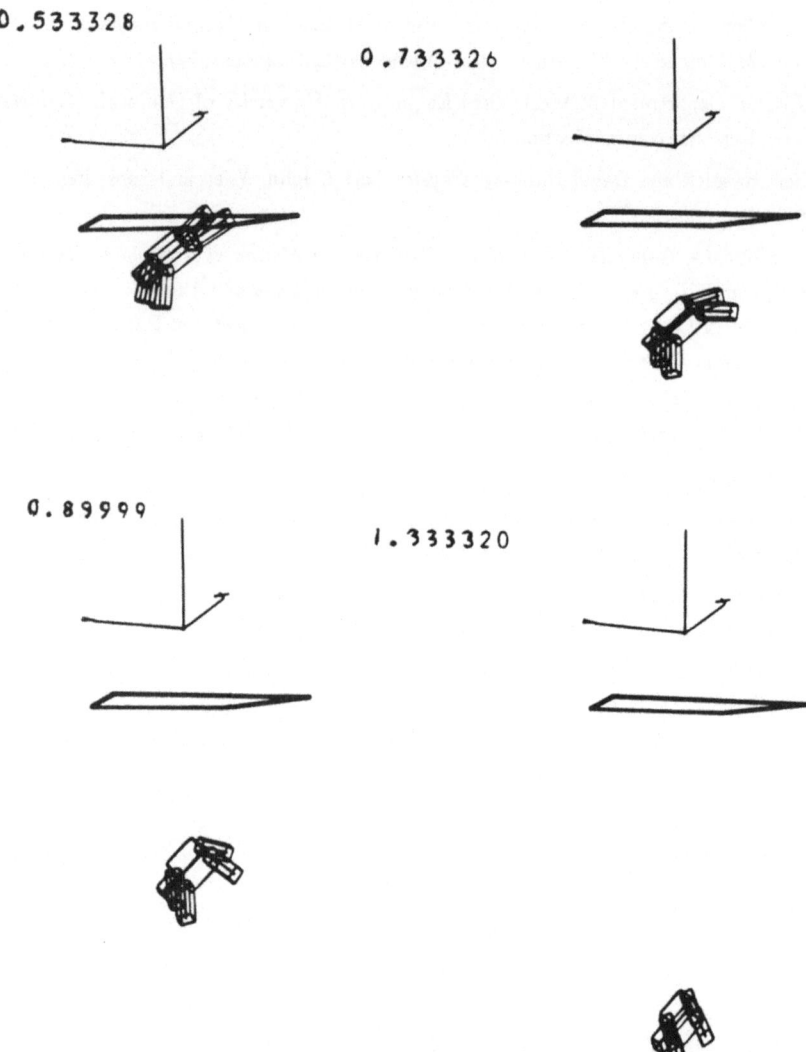

Figure 1. *Figure Falling Freely*

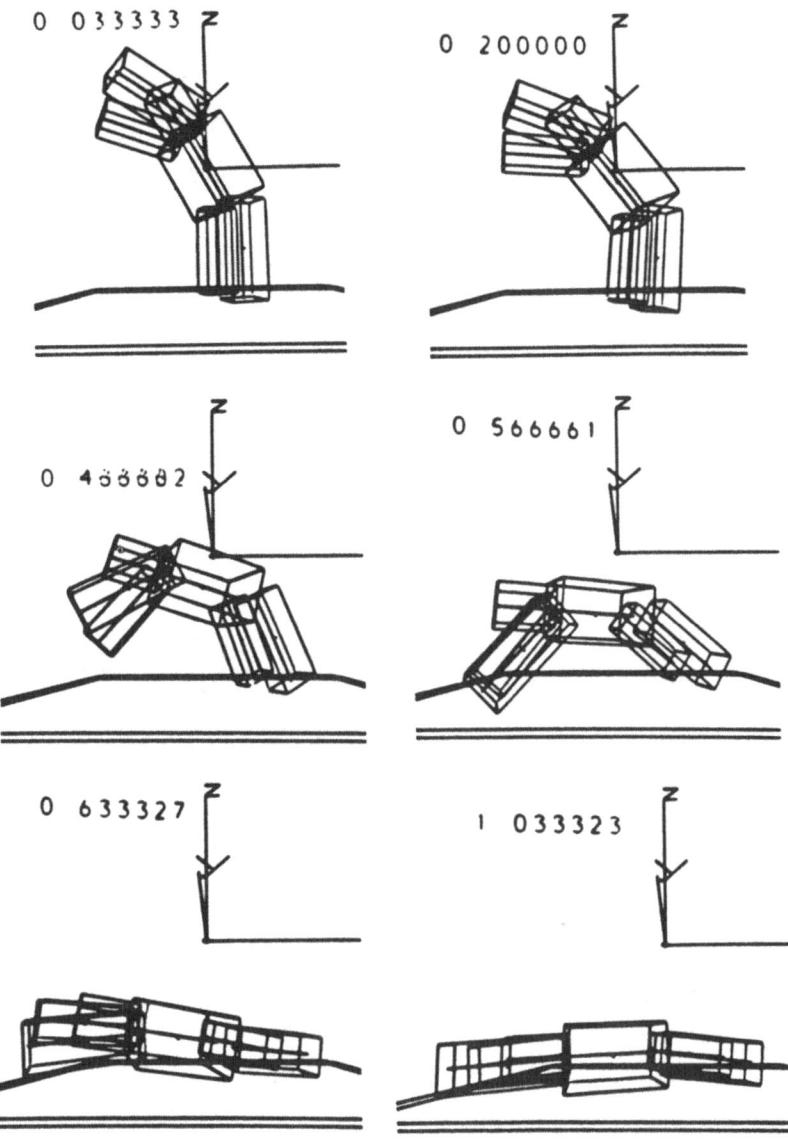

Figure 2. *Figure Falling on a Frictionless Surface*

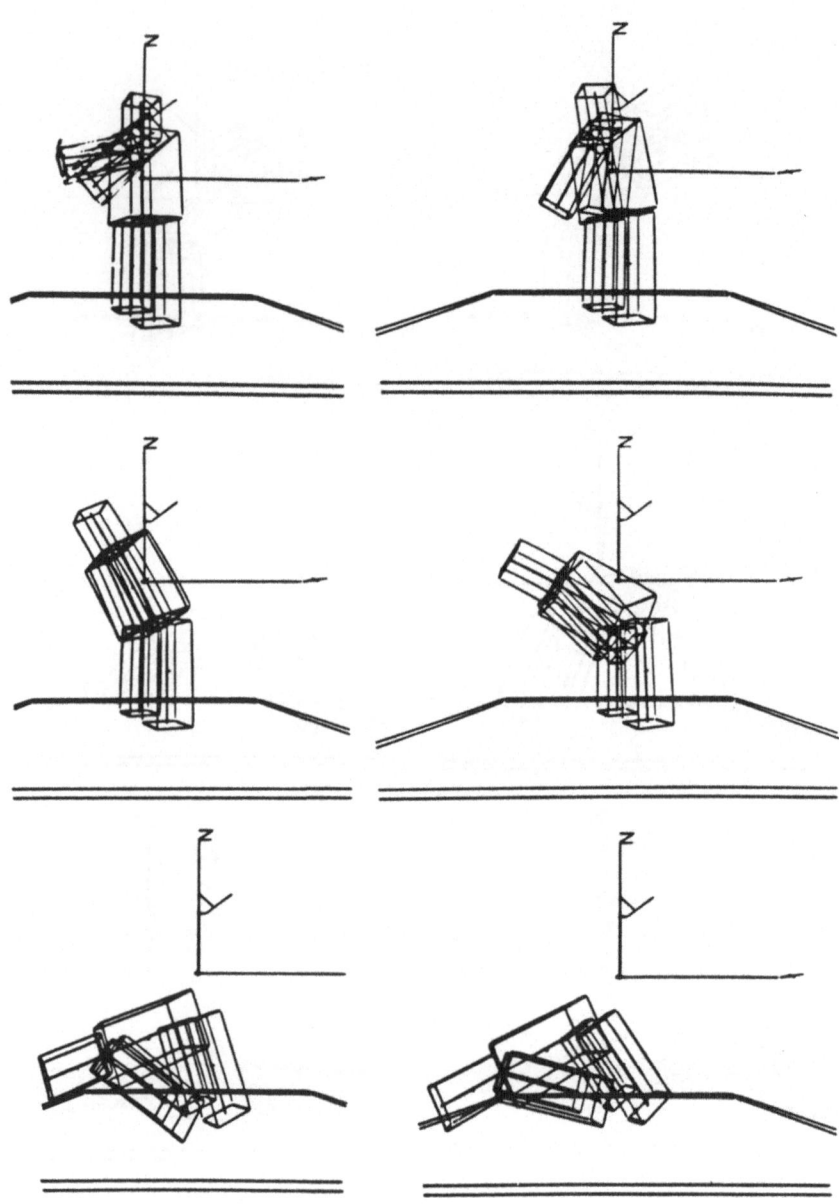

Figure 3. *Body Falling on a Surface with Friction*

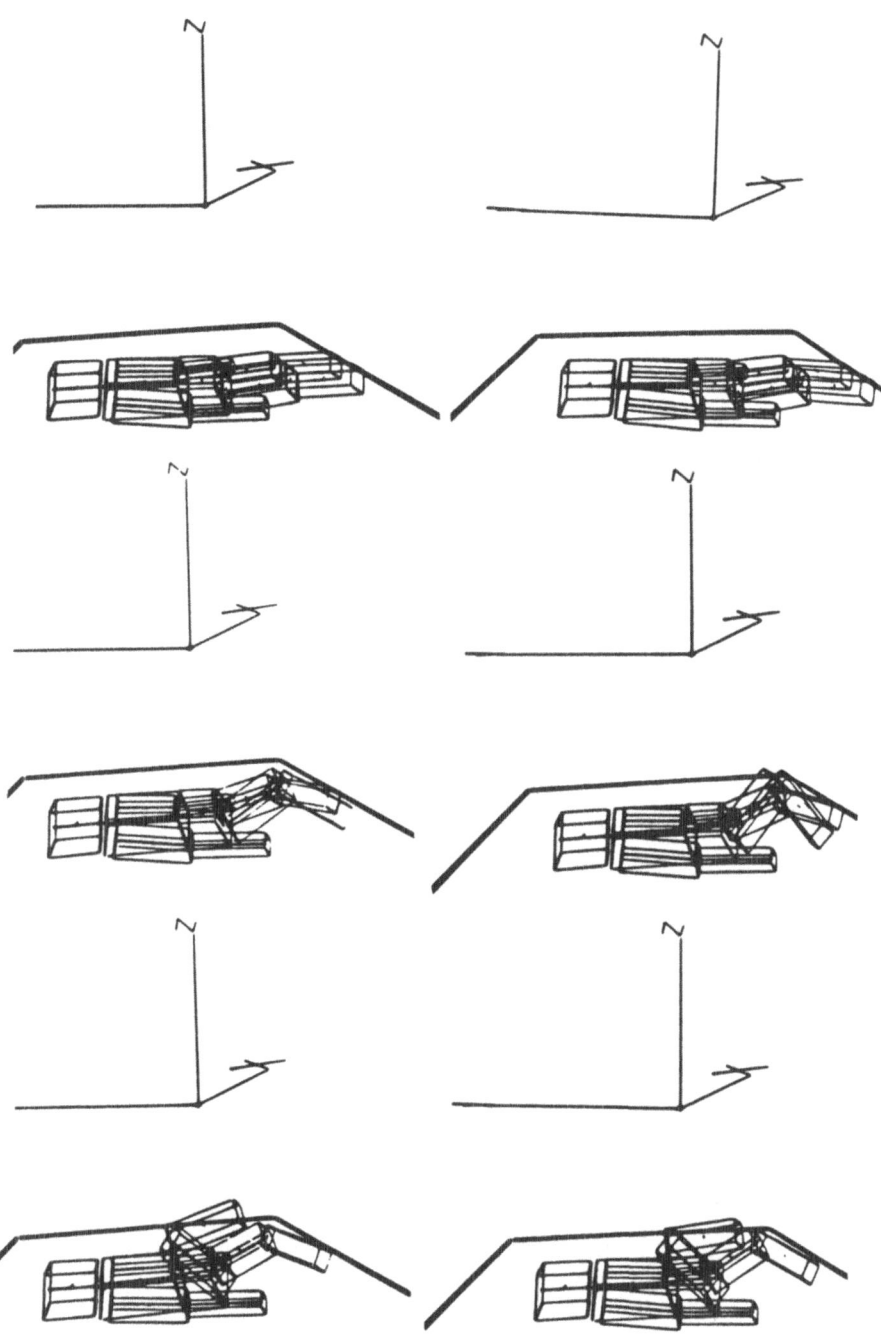

Figure 4. *Man Exercising Legs*

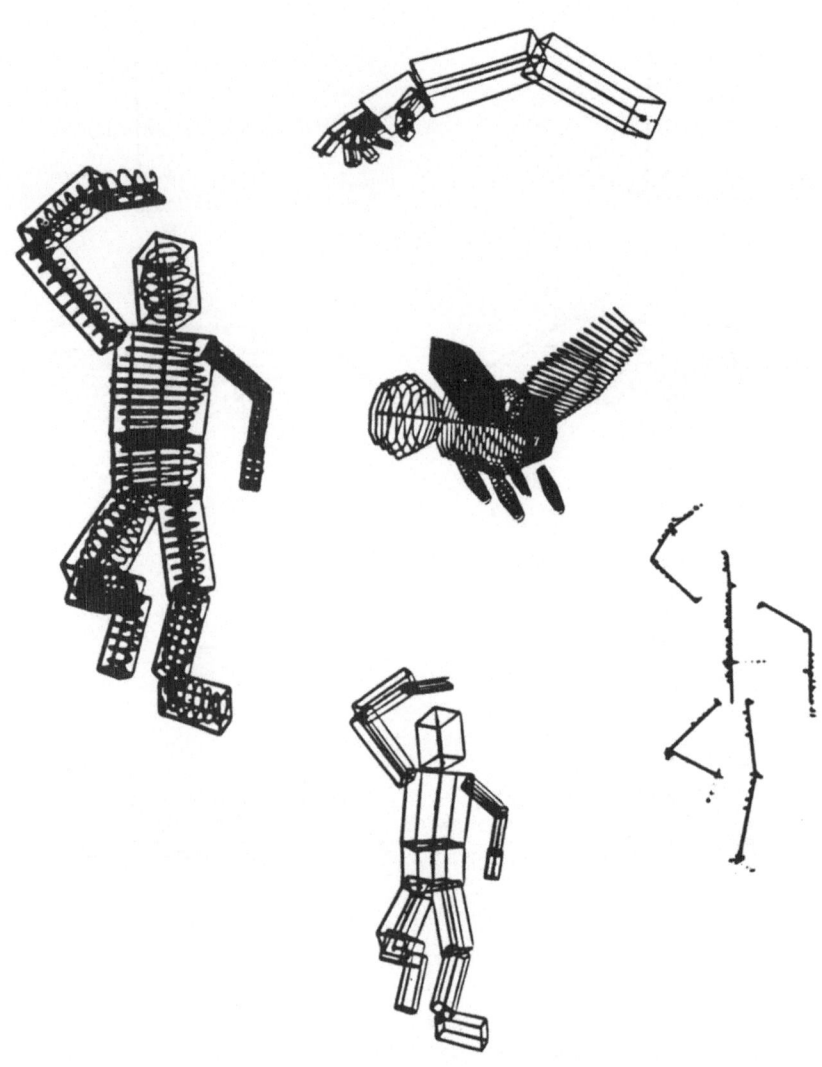

Figure 5. *Calligraphic Display Figures*

Figure 6. *Raster Display Figure*

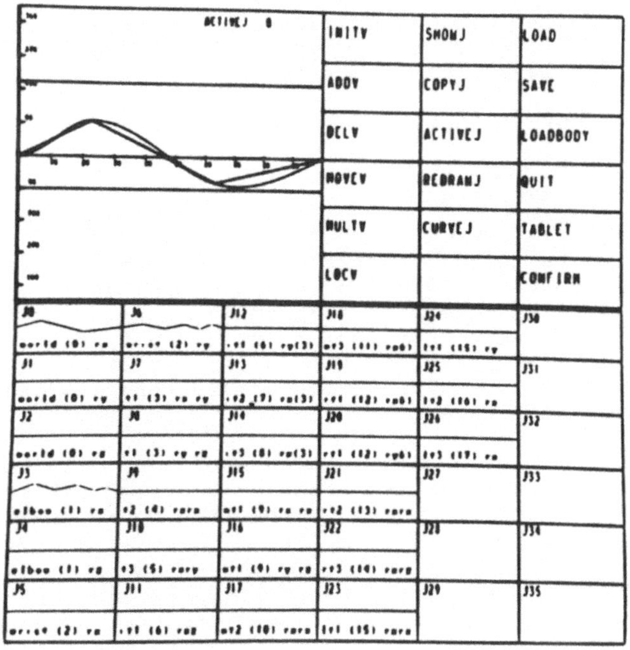

Figure 7. *Virya Graphical Editor Display*

Towards an Integrated View of 3-D Computer Animation

David Zeltzer

Computer Graphics and Animation Group, The Media Laboratory, Massachusetts Institute of Technology, Cambridge, MA 02139, USA

ABSTRACT

To automate character animation and extend it to 3-D we need to create and manipulate three-dimensional models of articulated figures as well as the worlds they will "inhabit". <u>Abstraction</u> and <u>adaptive motion</u> are key mechanisms for dealing with the <u>degrees of freedom</u> problem, which refers to the sheer volume of control information necessary for coordinating the motion of an articulated figure when the number of links is large. A three level hierarchy of control modes for animation is proposed: <u>guiding</u>, <u>animator-level</u>, and <u>task-level</u> systems. Guiding is best suited for specifying fine details but unsuited for controlling complex motion. Animator-level programming is powerful but difficult. Task-level systems give us facile control over complex motions and tasks by trading off explicit control over the details of motion. The integration of the three control levels is discussed.

KEYWORDS: computer animation, simulation, human-machine interface.

ANIMATION AS SIMULATION

Currently there is much controversy about the nature of 3-D computer animation. Should such systems be based on simulation, keyframing, or an animation programming language? Should the interface be through graphical input devices, or through the keyboard? It is my purpose here to provide a conceptual framework for 3-D computer animation in general, and character animation in particular.

Automatic inbetweening has been the focus of attention in moving from conventional to computer-assisted 2-D animation (Burtnyk 1976; Catmull 1978). From this point of view, it seems a natural extension to apply automatic inbetweening to 3-D animation, and in fact, a number of such systems have been developed (Chuang 1983; Gomez 1984; Magnenat-Thalman 1983). Here I will argue that 3-D keyframing belongs to the first level of a three level hierarchy of control regimes for animating articulated figures.

In order to produce convincing character animation, conventional 2-D animators refer constantly to living models, or study motion pictures of living models, or draw directly from still frames of such motion pictures (rotoscoping). That is, character animation is not a process of transforming lines and shapes a on 2-D surface, nor is it simply the art of squashing, stretching, or otherwise exaggerating and caricaturing motion. Thomas and Johnston (1981) make quite clear that the great success of the Disney animators was due in large part to the long hours they devoted to studying and observing the movements of humans and animals in preparing for a particular sequence. A character was successful precisely in proportion to how well the animator understood the kinematics of the figure, the structure and timing of a movement, and the effects of a movement on soft tissue and clothing. Once these elements were mastered, only then could the animator develop a character's personality by the judicious exaggeration or de-emphasis of particular attributes.

As long as animation requires the generation of many drawings by hand, simplicity and economy will be essential elements. 3-D computer animation, however, is an entirely different medium. The animator's energy is no longer invested in drawing and the tedium of inbetweening. Instead, the focus is on creating an environment -- designing microworlds and populating them with interesting characters. Since frames are no longer generated by hand, rather than expecting simplified and stylized imagery, we assess computer animation in large part by noting how convincing is the simulation of three-dimensionality, lighting, background scenery, and surface texture. Animated images can take on added complexity and detail; they can be made to look more realistic, if that is desired, or more convincing in their other-worldliness. This applies equally to the behavior of figures and objects as well as their physical appearance.

3-D computer animation is thus a process of simulation in its most general sense: the specification of objects and transformations on objects. The notion of the computer as a simulation medium is not new; Turing showed after all, that a computer could simulate itself or any other -- a theme echoed often by Alan Kay (1977, 1985). The work of early graphics researchers was aimed at apprehending the visual complexity of the world by learning to simulate the effect of light, shade, texture and so on. Current synthetic imagery has achieved near photographic realism for certain classes of geometric and stochastically tractable objects and environments. Now the task is to try and apprehend the procedural complexity of the world, which, as we shall see, requires computational models of many highly complex or only partly understood processes, including the dynamics and inverse kinematics of articulated motion, and commonsense planning and problem solving.

How can we specify and coordinate the behavior of the objects we wish to animate? There are three basic approaches.

1. We can explicitly describe the behaviors we are interested in. This is the _guiding_ mode.

2. We can describe behaviors algorithmically, in some programming notation. This is the _animator level_.

3. Lastly, we can describe behavior implicitly, in terms of events and relationships. This is the _task level_.

For our purposes we can consider the domain of 3-D computer character animation to be the control and coordination of the motion of articulated structures made up of rigid links. Differential scaling and other shape transformations are important but secondary to the motor control problem. In the next section I examine the fundamental problem we face in trying to coordinate the motion of articulated figures, and we will look at mechanisms for dealing with the complexities of figure animation. Later we will see that the graded implementation of these mechanisms gives the above three-tiered hierarchy of control modes.

THE DEGREES OF FREEDOM PROBLEM

The essential problem of coordinating the motion of an articulated figure is to generate appropriate values of the joint variables that control the position and orientation of each link. Joints may be modeled as _lower pairs_ (Denavit 1955) such as rotary or sliding joints, or they may be more complex, as in a detailed model of the human knee. For a figure with n joints, we can think of an n-dimensional _pose space_, where we assign a coordinate axis to each of n degrees of freedom; and an n-component _pose vector_, which completely specifies a particular configuration. To animate the motion of a jointed figure, a pose vector must be specified for each frame of the sequence. To animate a minute of complex motion for a reasonably detailed figure, say, with 30 links, tens of thousands of values will need to be specified for the joint variables to display a new configuration each frame. Even if the sequence is keyframed, with a keyframe every two seconds, 30 pose vectors -- nearly a thousand values -- need to be specified. This is an example of the _degrees of freedom_ (DOF) problem (Turvey 1982) which refers to the sheer volume of control information necessary for coordinating the motion of an articulated figure when the number of links is large, as in a human figure. It is the reason why animators find 3-D character animation so tedious.

Of course we are not interested in random motion; the movements of a figure must be "correct" in some sense to be of any use -- the robot programmer may wish to optimize energy expenditure, for example, and the animator will want the figure to move in some expressive manner. Viewed in this way, character animation is a problem of _search_. Not only do we have to generate pose vectors, we need to find a _particular_ set of variables out of an immense pose space -- if each of 30 joints has only 2 possible positions, there are over a billion potential configurations!

To complicate the problem, many figures of interest are
kinematically _redundant_, possessing "extra" degrees of freedom
that allow multiple solutions -- perhaps an infinity of pose
vectors -- all of which satisfy a particular movement problem.
The human arm, for example is redundant -- you can reach for
an object with the elbow held high, low, or in between. That
is, there are many arm configurations that will position the
hand at some fixed location in space. This redundancy gives
us the extra flexibility we need to reach around and over
objects, and in general, to maneuver in a cluttered environment. And it is why individuals can develop characteristic
and expressive "styles" of movement.

For animation, of course, we are not interested in a single
configuration, but a sequence of pose vectors -- a "hyper-path"
through a many-dimensional pose space. So it is not surprising
that even when the main features of a motion are known, it may
take an animator many iterations to get the movement "just
right".

In the next sections we look at two important techniques for
dealing with the degrees of freedom problem.

ADAPTIVE MOTION

By adaptive motion I mean the ability of a figure controller
to use information about the environment and the figure itself
in the control process. That is, feedback can be used to guide
the search through the huge space of potential configurations.
To do this, at least the location and orientation of objects
and their surfaces must be available to the animation software,
and not just to the the rendering programs, as is usually the
case. Physical interactions between figures and objects are
so ubiquitous in the real world -- touching, grasping, pushing,
not to mention locomotion over a wide variety of surfaces --
that automatic collision detection, long of interest in CAD/CAM
and robotics, should become an integral part of the animation
environment.

Adaptive motion makes possible goal-directed and constrained
behavior, since it allows the animator to describe movement in
terms of relations among objects and figures. It lends generality to animation sequences, since animation software can
adjust motion sequences for different scenes. This helps to
hide unnecessary detail from the animator, since the burden of
generating much of the control information can be left to the
animation software. See Fig. 1.

Reynolds (1982) has suggested that it would be desirable if an
animator could establish "rules of behavior" for objects and
characters in some imagined microworld. After establishing
the initial conditions of this simulated universe, the animator
would sit back and let the animation system generate the
sequence. This amounts to a 3-D, computerized extension of the
straight ahead style of 2-D animation (Thomas 1981). Adaptive
motion makes possible the extension of this technique to 3-D
computer animation.

ABSTRACTION

The importance of abstraction in dealing with the intellectual
complexity of computer programming is well-known (Shaw 1980)
and it is a basic tool for dealing with the kinematic and
behavioral complexities of articulated motion as well.

There are five kinds of abstraction useful for controlling
character animation: structural, procedural, functional,
character and world modeling.

Structural Abstraction

A structural abstraction describes the kinematic properties of
a figure, i.e., the transformation hierarchy, the nature of
the allowable joint motions, and whether links are rigid or
non-rigid (although we will deal only with rigid motion here).
The notion of a transformation hierarchy is a generalization
to 3-D of the familiar 2-D instancing systems described in
graphics texts. Most 3-D animation systems provide some means
of representing transformation hierarchies, e.g., Crow's scn
assmblr (Crow 1982), Blinn's artic (Blinn 1982), and Reynolds'
ASAS (Reynolds 1982). In these systems, joint transformations
are represented as simple rotations and translations, sometimes
including scaling, although more general representations for
articulated motion, e.g., Denavit-Hartenburg (D-H) notation
(Denavit 1955; Lee 1982) have long been used in the field of
mechanism design, and more recently, robotics (Paul 1981).
sdl, the skeleton description language, is the tool for specifying structural abstractions for use in sa, an articulated
motion system described in (Zeltzer 1984). A similar tool,
mat, is in use at the New York Institute of Technology (Williams
1982).

At the Media Laboratory we are developing a set of graphical
tools, implemented on a Symbolics 3600 Lisp machine, for
designing and editing standardized kinematic descriptions of
jointed figures. See Fig. 2. These descriptions have been
expanded to include D-H representation for prismatic and
rotary joints; the representation is extensible such that
other joint types may easily be added. Such a standardized
representation is essential in a distributed computing environment in which many programmers and animators, working on a
variety of machines, wish to share graphical data and software.
In addition, we can readily integrate robotics control algorithms
into the animation software, since D-H notation provides a
convenient and powerful representation for such motor control
techniques.

Procedural Abstraction

A procedural abstraction (Tennent 1981) is the representation
of a movement algorithm independent of the structure of the
figure it controls.

For example, the DOF problem is not so severe in the case of a robot manipulator with six or seven joints. Even so, humans are not good at calculating the necessary joint angles for controlling even a simple manipulator, and <u>resolved motion</u> (Klein 1983; Whitney 1972) is generally used. That is, the position and orientation of a target location are input, and the manipulator controller automatically computes the pose vector necessary to reach it.

Resolved motion control is an important example of the use of procedural abstraction in the solution of the DOF problem: a computation is specified that will transform the input parameters, i.e., the position and orientation of the target, into the output object, here the set of joint angles that will position and orient the end effector at the desired location in the workspace, if possible. Resolved motion control is independent of a particular kinematic structure, and can be applied to figures of 6, 8 or more links, and for a human figure, can be applied equally well to control either arms or legs (Girard 1985; Ribble 1982). Other examples of procedural abstraction are the computation of trajectories for falling objects, the computation of the paths of colliding objects, or the use of spline curves for generating smooth motion. Such facilities are often provided for the animator ready-made, but may be constructed by the animator in animation systems embedded in high-level programming
languages.

<u>Functional Abstraction</u>

For the robot arm the number of links is small and the arm is treated as a single kinematic entity. But for a figure with many links, we want to be able to group together both the structural elements and the procedures that are necessary to effect a particular class of motions. Alternatively, we can impose constraints on the movements of a set of joints. We call such a grouping a <u>functional</u> abstraction. Functional abstractions are important because they allow the animator to <u>factor</u> the pose space into motor skills. If we already know the general "shape" of a motion, we need only consider a subregion of the total pose space. Say we want a figure's hand to grasp an object -- we already know which joints need to move, roughly how they should move, and moreover, we know this is a useful motion that we want to repeat often. We can cluster this group of joint movements around the task "to grasp", and attach one or more procedures to implement it (perhaps resolved motion). Once this motor skill has been defined, the details of its execution can be suppressed. That is, we need only supply the appropriate parameters, e.g., target location, fast or slow, hard or soft, to the motor program for the grasping skill. By specifying functional abstractions for grasping and other tasks, the animator is spared the burden of generating pose vectors and can instead think of the figure motion at a higher level -- in terms of the tasks and events that are to be performed.

Functional abstractions allow us to attach implicit _goals_ to figure motion. By decomposing a figure's potential movements into a repertoire of skills we can associate the events and relationships the animator specifies with the skills (implemented as functional abstractions) that the figure controller "knows" about. Moreover, if we allow functional abstractions to refer to other functional abstractions, it is possible to construct _behaviors_ as compositions of simpler movements.

Character Abstraction and World Modeling

In the physical world objects and figures interact in complex ways at many levels of detail. Adaptive motion requires at least efficient geometric representations for collision testing and path planning; goal-directed animation control requires in addition sophisticated mechanisms for knowledge representation.

Part of the problem involves structuring high-density graphical data bases to avoid exhaustive searches through long lists of surface elements to do, say, collision testing. Rather, we want to consider only those objects in the scene that are "near" to the figure. This means that the data base must be carefully organized spatially so that searches always proceed at the appropriate level of detail. Various hierarchical methods of structuring data to speed up occlusion testing have been reported (Clark 1976; Fuchs 1980; Rubin 1980). Franklin (1981) describes a set of algorithms which are useful for intersection testing as well.

But the larger problem is to represent attributes, functionality, and relationships of objects in a scene so that we can simulate the mechanical behaviors and interactions of objects in general. We want this representation to be uniform such that there is no distinction between agents and objects. That is, while humans are in some sense active agents they also obey the laws of Newtonian mechanics; a person falls just like a rock when pushed off a cliff. On the other hand, an animator may want the chairs and tables to dance around the room when the villain leaves. It should be easy to ascribe such behaviors to otherwise inanimate objects.

In order to do this, we need to specify three things about any object: what it is, how it's put together, and how it behaves. The problem of representing physical objects is an active area of research in artificial intelligence (Wasserman 1985). Briefly, objects can be described in terms of a generalization hierarchy, such that instances of particular things appear as specializations of more general classes of objects. 'Inheritance' is a key notion which means that object instances may make use of attributes and procedures associated with the class of which they are members. These serve as default values which may be overridden by specifying particular values for these 'slots' in the instances themselves. Often _multiple-inheritance_ is supported such that an object may inherit attributes from more than one superior class. For this reason, the generalization "hierarchy" is often a lattice, rather than a tree. A number of programming systems support this view of object representation, which is well-described in the literature (Stefik 1983; Tesler 1981).

An object's location in such a generalization lattice tells us what it is, and what it looks like (i.e., how to render it). We can describe the structure of an object by associating with each node in the generalization lattice a transformation hierarchy as described above. The node for a human figure, for example, would have an associated tree structure describing the joints and links that make up the figure. Each of the links, in turn, would be an instance of a monolithic object located elsewhere in the generalization lattice. Instances of the class of human figures can inherit this structural description with local variables that specify the dimensions and movement constraints of a particular human being.

Like structural descriptions, each object must have an associated behavioral description. For simple objects, the behaviors would be correspondingly simple. The prototypical physical object, for example, might obey some subset of the laws of Newtonian mechanics. Articulated figures would have a repertory of skills, such as walking and grasping. But since behaviors too can be inherited, human figures, being instances of the class of physical objects, can inherit all those simple Newtonain behaviors we'd expect.

In addition, it is necessary to represent the mechanical interaction of objects in terms of a small, well-defined set of relationships. Since we want to represent a world changing over time, these relationships must be dynamic, and include links between objects that signify support, contact, containment, epsilon-proximity, and whether one object is a part-of, or a movable-part-of another. The part-of relationship may well apply to objects that are themselves complicated assemblies, each with their own structural description, e.g., an engine is part-of a car.

Lastly, in order to do simple motor problem solving, we want to embed commonsense knowledge in object descriptions. That is, we want to be able to encode such knowledge as "One usually leaves a room by finding and opening the door".[1] Such knowledge represents cultural information learned by individuals early on; it is "common knowledge" we all know about doors. It is appropriate to associate such information with the objects themselves. That is, in addition to modeling the physical and geometric properties of a microworld, the world knowledge base must contain cultural information attached to objects as well. We are currently investigating techniques for encoding such information in terms of uniform behavioral descriptions for all the objects contained in the generalization lattice.

---

[1] This is not always the case in animation, of course! Therefore such representations must be easily modifiable.

Text-Mediated and Device-Mediated Interaction

The power of an animation system derives ultimately from its available abstraction mechanisms and the implementation of adaptive movement, not simply by providing the animator with joysticks, knobs and dials. Much has been made of device-mediated interaction in computer graphics, especially in early work (Baecker 1969; Sutherland 1963), begun at a time when Fortran or assembly code may have been the only alternative means of human-machine communication. However, language will probably remain the medium of choice for describing algorithms and complicated spatial, temporal, and behavioral relationships. Much of the objection to text-mediated interaction really is an objection to typing.

Progress in improving the ergonomics of the typewriter keyboard and ultimately, developments in speech recognition will go a long way towards ameliorating this aspect of the human-machine interface.

At the same time, there are many functions, e.g., picking, locating, and sketching, for which the the graphical gesture clearly is the preferred mode of interaction. Perhaps the ultimate example of graphical interaction is that of flying a simulated airplane, or steering the six-legged walk of a science fiction robot ant with a joystick. But these are large simulation programs built on a complex set of procedures. The user interacts with the top level of a hierarchy of abstractions, and it is this organization that allows small movements of the operator's hand on a joystick to be amplified into a complex of meaningful control signals with such a powerful result.

In the following sections, we will see how three levels of control result from the graded implementation of adaptive motion and abstraction mechanisms.

A THREE LEVEL HIERARCHY FOR CHARACTER ANIMATION

We can classify animation systems as being either guiding, animator level, or task level systems. (For a similar classification of robot programming systems, see (Lozano-Perez 1982)).

Guiding

Guiding systems are those with no mechanisms for user-defined abstraction or adaptive motion. There are a wide range of guiding systems, including motion recording (Calvert 1980; Ginsberg 1983), shape interpolation (Gomez 1984), key-transformation systems (Chuang 1983; Gomez 1984; Williams 1982), and notation-based systems (Calvert 1982; Weber 1978).

In motion recording, various devices are used to acquire kinematic data from a moving figure. The kinematic data is then used to control an animated figure. Such systems are usually limited to measurements of a restricted range of human movement in a laboratory setting, but offer a potentially rich source of data on human motion. Shape-interpolation (also known as "metamorphosis") is the 3-D analog of 2-D keyframing. Where there is a one-to-one correspondence between the points and faces of separate objects, inbetween frames can be computed by interpolating between the data points of the two objects. In key-transformation systems, whole objects are manipulated by affine transformations. Inbetween frames are generated by interpolating the transformation parameters and transforming the objects. Such systems usually allow the specification of transformation hierarchies, making articulated motion possible. In such key pose systems, e.g., BBOP, a p-curve facility (Baecker 1969) is provided so that the user can graphically specify velocities. Notation-based systems are an example of text-mediated guiding in which the user describes a movement in a choreographic notation or an alphanumeric equivalent (i.e. (Calvert 1982)).

Limitations of Guiding Systems: In guiding systems, the animator must specify in advance the details of motion. This is reasonable only in a relatively featureless environment. Suppose a human character is to walk over rough terrain. Walk cycles are not difficult to generate using keyframing or shape interpolation, but in this case, the walk cycle changes with each step, requiring a large number of intermediate configurations to ensure that the motion looks right. This is because the inbetween frames are computed without regard for other objects in the scene. If a foot goes through the floor, or the figure walks right through a wall, so be it. What is worse, if the character is to walk in another direction over different terrain, none of the earlier key configurations can be used.

In guiding, the animator has nearly complete control over the motion of a figure. Because of the nature of the DOF problem, this is both a blessing and a curse. The animator is free to design an expressive motion sequence in toto, but for complicated figures or intricate mechanisms this is a demanding or perhaps an impossible task, even with a well-designed device-mediated interface (Lundin 1982).

Most guiding systems include predefined procedural abstractions for smoothing motion based on one or several spline techniques Rogers 1976). Often these tools allow the animator to interactively adjust the spline parameters until some desired trajectory is achieved. Splining allows the animator to more closely simulate the dynamics of rigid bodies, e.g., acceleration and deceleration due to inertia, friction, or gravity, since motion that is linear and jerky doesn't look right and is often unpleasant to view. (In conventional animation acceleration and deceleration are referred to as ease in and ease out respectively, and must be calculated by hand and from tables).

In general, splining provides convenient control over the
velocity of many kinds of transformations, including changes
in size, shape and color, in addition to changes in position
and orientation. The value of using parameterized curves to
control animation was recognized early on and the refinement
of these techniques remains an active area of interest (see
e.g. (Kochanek 1984)). While the use of spline curves is a
powerful simulation mechanism, spline techniques alone are not
a general solution to the DOF problem, since the control of
many transformations requires the generation and refinement of
many splines.

To date, a number of interesting animation sequences have been
produced using guiding systems at various commercial production
houses and university laboratories. However, since powerful
abstraction mechanisms are not provided, and because adaptive
motion is not possible at all, guiding systems do not scale up
well for use with complicated figures, and their utility for
controlling animation in complicated environments
is limited.

Animator-Level Systems

A number of animator level systems have been designed to allow
the animator to specify motion algorithmically. A few of
these systems, while not specifically designed as character
animation systems, do provide some measure of one or both
adaptive motion and abstraction.

GRAMPS, ASAS, and MIRA: GRAMPS (O'Donnel 1981) has no facility
for adaptive motion, but does allow the construction of motion
macros based on functional abstraction. Joints can be grouped
together and their input derived from dials, and the motion at
the joints can be explicitly constrained to lie within some
range of values. This is a good example of the interaction of
a guiding mechanism (dials) and a functional abstraction
(motion macros). While not designed as a character animation
system, GRAMPS has been used to generate interesting animation
of a human figure.

Craig Reynolds' ASAS (1982) provides a set of low-level mechanisms for both abstraction and adaptive motion. The actor
paradigm explicitly provides a general abstraction mechanism
allowing the definition of transformation hierarchies (structural abstraction) and behaviors (procedural and functional
abstractions). The message passing mechanism makes it possible
to implement adaptive motion, since animated entities can
report aspects of their physical attributes or their internal
states.

Another recently reported animation system, MIRA (Magnenat-
Thalman 1983) is based on a programming paradigm closely
related to actor-based systems, namely, the data abstraction
(Shaw 1980). MIRA provides a set of important abstraction
facilities nearly identical to those of ASAS. While MIRA is

not a message-passing system, the animator can set and examine the values of variables (of various data types), so that attributes of figures and objects can be used to influence the generation of movement.

TEMPUS: The group led by Norman Badler at the University of Pennsylvania has long been involved in research on representing and portraying human movement. They have developed TEMPUS (Badler 1982; Korein 1983) a system for analyzing and displaying the movements of realistic human figures in a workspace. While not a general-purpose animation system, TEMPUS has sophisticated features for defining and modifying human figures, and for resolved motion control.

Because the domain of TEMPUS is restricted, unlike MIRA and ASAS, to positioning and orienting human figures, TEMPUS can be largely device-mediated. Users pick actions from a graphically displayed menu, and control motions using displays of simulated potentiometers. Available movements are rotation and translation of the whole figure, rotations at selected joints, and resolved motion of the limbs.

TEMPUS has no facilities for adaptive motion, and abstraction mechanisms available to the animator are limited to a parameterless macro facility which allows the user to group movement commands. The implementation of a flexible resolved motion algorithm for positioning the limbs of a human figure is an important step towards task-level animation.

Discussion: Because it is possible to implement adaptive motion, and to define structural, functional and procedural abstractions, animator level systems provide significant improvements over guiding in terms of the DOF problem. But as usual, there is a trade-off. Guiding systems are relatively easy to learn and use, but lack the power to control complicated animation. Animator level systems, on the other hand, provide the computational power of a general programming language but at the same time saddle the user with all the problems so closely associated with software development. Thalman et al note that "it took 14 months to produce [a] 13-minute film," certainly highlighting the problem (Magnenat-Thalman 1983). That is, while it is possible to develop complex motion in either ASAS or MIRA, it is not necessarily easy, since neither language provides explicit, high level support for developing functional abstractions or adaptive motion. Interestingly, Thalman et al. note that they found it necessary to integrate a guiding system, MUTAN (Fortin 1983) into their production scheme. I will have more to say about integrating control modes later on.

Task Level Animation

At the task level, the animation system must schedule the execution of motor programs to control characters, and the motor programs themselves must generate the necessary pose vectors. To do this, as we have seen, a knowledge base of objects and figures in the environment is necessary, containing information about their position, physical attributes, and functionality.

In (1983) I outline one approach to task level animation in which motor behavior is generated by traversing a hierarchy of skills (represented as frames (Minsky 1975) or actors (Hewitt 1979) in an object-oriented system) selected by rules which map the current action and context onto the next desired action. Albus of the Bureau of Standards has designed a robot control system based on a hierarchy of table-driven computing elements (Albus 1981). Powers (1973) has outlined a behavioral control hierarchy based entirely on servomechanism theory. Both of these latter approaches seem to work well at the lower levels of motor control and what we might call instinct-driven behavior, but seem rather vague when it comes to behavior requiring symbolic interaction with the environment.

Task level motor control is a difficult problem under study by cognitive scientists, roboticists, and of course those interested in high level animation systems. In the near term we can expect the development of prototype systems capable of generating rather simple behaviors. How well such systems scale up depends on our understanding of the motor control problem itself.

With task level control, the animator can only specify the broad outlines of a particular movement and the animation system fills in the details. See Fig. 3. Whether this approach is appropriate depends on the particular application. A non-expert user may be satisfied with the 'default' movements and figures the system provides if he or she can produce, in a reasonable amount of time and at a reasonable cost, an animation that gets the point across. A user in the entertainment industry may want nearly total control over every nuance of a character's movement to make a sequence as expressive as possible. However, control over the expressive qualities of movement does not mean that the animator needs or wants a pure guiding system to generate pose vectors. The animator does need access to different levels of the control hierarchy in order to generate new motor skills and to 'tweak' the existing skills.

INTEGRATION OF CONTROL MODES

Guiding is the prevalent mode in most current interactive animation systems. The necessity for integrating all three modes of control stems from the inability of any one mode to provide complete yet economical control. Guiding is best suited for specifying fine details but unsuited for controlling complex motion. Animator level programming is powerful but difficult. Task level systems give us facile control over complex motions by trading off explicit control over the details of motion.

Part of the solution lies in applying guiding techniques at appropriate points in the motion control hierarchy. The key is the ability to decompose the movement repertoire into a manageable set of hierarchically organized skills. The notion of <u>browsers</u>, as implemented in Smalltalk (Tesler 1981) or Loops (Stefik 1983) suggests a powerful method for attaching guiding controls to motor skills. Suppose I have on my monitor a shaded display of a human character. On my terminal screen is a representation of the structure of the character and its skills. Now suppose I trace a curve on the graphics tablet. If I specify that that curve represents a particular joint rotation, -- i.e., I point to the node for the little finger on my terminal, I should immediately see on the display the little finger of my character wiggling. Suppose now I point to the node for "grasping with the left hand" -- I should see the figure's left hand open and close with the velocity I have specified. Lastly, if I pick the node labeled "walk", the figure should begin to walk across the screen, and this time, the curve I have drawn could determine, say, the speed of the gait. This modular, hierarchical organization allows the user to identify the motion qualities that need to be adjusted, and at the same time it helps to localize the effect of such changes. This calls for a uniform representation of motor skills that incorporates, for each skill, a specification of the kinds of adjustments that are possible and in addition, a uniform set of mechanisms, e.g., p-curves, for interacting with skills.

CONCLUSION

I have presented a conceptual analysis of the domain of three dimensional computer animation, which is viewed as the process of simulating objects and their behaviors in a microworld specified by the animator. The degrees of freedom problem is the central issue in the coordination of articulated figures. Computer animation systems must be based on the appropriate set of domain concepts, namely adaptive motion and the five abstraction mechanisms, to enable the animator to define and manipulate interesting characters and environments in an expressive way.

The discussion of the three control modes suggest criteria for good guiding and animator level systems. Guiding systems have received the greatest attention to date -- the notion of an interactive, device-mediated interface has come to be viewed almost as a standard way of communicating with computers, as evidenced by the popularity of the "mouse-and-window" style of computing. In general, however, guiding should be seen as a mechanism for developing and controlling the behavior of complex systems, rather than just picking points, drawing lines, or generating scalar values for various transformation parameters. As suggested above, we want to be able to attach the output of a physical input device at arbitrary levels of a behavioral hierarchy. While the meaning of a gesture depends, of course, on the process that is viewing it, the hard question is to find an appropriate set of parameters for controlling a complex process, for example, facial expressions (cf. (Parke 1982) and (Platt 1981)). Once a natural control set has been determined, it is not hard to use input devices to generate parameter values interactively. There are two complementary design themes: How can we "plug in" guiding mechanisms to drive a given complex behavior? How can input device modules serve as standard "gesture amplifiers" that can be easily redirected to various functions of the figure control hierarchy?

An animator level language should incorporate the design features and principles we expect in a powerful programming language. Concealing the programming task from the user or sugar-coating the syntax is not nearly as important as providing the expressive power needed for animation. This is not the place for a discussion of the future of automatic programming, nor of the merits of the latest programming paradigm. The point is that the algorithmic description of behavior -- "Do this, then do that" -- is an essential and fundamental way to communicate about movement. More often than not the so-called "naive user" will quickly learn the syntax of an animation language only to become frustrated because the language is not powerful enough. Animation level languages and systems should therefore combine what we know about software technology with the mechanisms appropriate to motion control e.g., functional abstraction and adaptive motion.

Finally, adaptive motion in the form of collision testing, and resolved motion should be implemented, at least in part, as basic elements of any 3-D computer animation system.

The art and science of 3-D computer animation continues to evolve towards the simulation of hypothetical worlds complete with physical laws and figures possessing behavioral repertoires. It is by learning to construct and control these simulations that we give computer animation its expressive power.

ACKNOWLEDGEMENTS

This work was supported in part by NHK (Japan Broadcasting Company).

REFERENCES

Albus, JS (1981) Brains, Behavior and Robotics. Byte Books, New Hampshire
Badler NI (1982) Design of a Human Movement Representation Incorporating Dynamics. In: Course Notes, Seminar on Three-Dimensional Computer Animation, July 27,1985, ACM SIGGRAPH 82
Baecker RM (1969) Picture-driven Animation. In: Proc. AFIPS Spring Joint Computer Conf., vol. 34, p 273-288
Blinn JF (1982) Systems Aspects of Computer Image Synthesis. In: Course Notes, Seminar on Three Dimensional Computer Animation, July 1982, ACM SIGGRAPH 82
Burtnyk N, Wein M (1976) Interactive Skeleton Techniques for Enhancing Motion Dynamics in Key Frame Animation. Communications of the ACM 19: 564-569

Calvert TW, Chapman J, Patla A (1980) The Integration of Subjective and Objective Data in the Animation of Human Movement. In: Proc. ACM SIGGRAPH 80, vol. 14, p 198-203

Calvert TW, Chapman J, Patla A (1982) Aspects of The Kinematic Simulation of Human Movement. In: IEEE Computer Graphics and Applications, vol. 2, p 41-50

Catmull E (1978) The Problems of Computer-Assisted Animation. In: Computer Graphics, vol. 12, Proc. ACM SIGGRAPH 78, p 348-353

Chuang R, Entis G. (1983) 3-D Shaded Computer Animation -- Step-by-Step. IEEE Computer Graphics and Applications 3: 18-25

Clark JH (1976) Hierarchical Geometric Models for Visible Surface Algorithms. Communications of the ACM 19: 547-554

Crow FC (1982) A More Flexible Image Generation Environment. In: Proc. ACM SIGGRAPH 82, vol. 16, p 9-18

Denavit J, Hartenberg RB (1955) A Kinematic Notation for Lower-Pair Mechanisms Based on Matrices. J of Applied Mechanics 23: 215-221

Fortin D, Lamy J, Thalman D (1983) A Multiple Track Animator System for Motion Synchronizaion. In: April 1983, Proc. ACM SIGGRAPH/SIGART Workshop on Motion, p 180-186

Franklin WR (1981) 3-D Geometric Databases Using Hierarchies of Inscribing Boxes. In: June 1981, Proc. Conf. Canadian Society for Man-Machine Interaction, p 173-180

Fuchs H, Kedem Z, Naylor B (1980) On Visible Surface Generation by A Priori Tree Structures. In: July 1980, Proc. ACM SIGGRAPH 80, p 124-133

Ginsberg C, Maxwell D (1983) Graphical Marionette. In: April 1983, Proc. ACM SIGGRAPH/SIGART Workshop on Motion, p 172-179

Girard M, Maciejewski AA (1985) Computational Modeling for the Animation of Legged Figures. In: Proc. ACM SIGGRAPH 85, To appear

Gomez JE (1984) Twixt: A 3-D Animation System. In: September 1984, Proc. Eurographics '84, North-Holland

Hewitt C (1979) Control Structure as Patterns of Message Passing. Artificial Intelligence: an MIT Perspective, MIT Press, MA, p 433-465

Kay A, Goldberg A (1977) Personal Dynamic Media. Computer, March 1977, p 31-41

Kay A (1985) Computer Software. Scientific American 251: 52-59

Klein C, Huang C (1983) Review of Pseudoinverse Control for Use with Kinematically Redundant Manipulators. IEEE Transactions on Systems Man and Cybernetics 13: 245-250

Kochanek DHU, Bartels RH (1984) Interpolating Splines with Local Tension, Continuity, and Bias Control. In: Proc. ACM SIGGRAPH 84, p 33-41

Korein J, Radack G, Badler N (1983) TEMPUS User Manual. Unpublished, Dept. of Computer and Information Science, University of Pennsylvania, PA

Lee CSG (1982) Robot Arm Kinematics, Dynamics, and Control. Computer 15: 62-80

Lozano-Perez T (1982) Robot Programming. In: AI Memo 698, December 1982, MIT, MA

Lundin D (1982) 3-D Modeling, A Personal Orthodoxy. In: Course Notes, Seminar on Three-Dimensional Computer Animation, July 27, 1982, ACM SIGGRAPH 82

Magnenat-Thalman N, Thalman D (1983) The Use of High-Level 3-D Graphical Types in the Mira Animation System. IEEE Computer Graphics and Applications 3: 9-16

Minsky M (1975) A Framework for Representing Knowledge. In: Winston P (ed) The Psychology of Computer Vision, McGraw-Hill, New York,

O'Donnel TJ, Olson AJ (1981) GRAMPS -- A Graphics Language Interpreter for Real-Time, Interactive Dimensional Picture Editing and Animation. In: Proc. ACM SIGGRAPH 81, p 133-142

Parke FI (1982) Parameterized Models for Facial Animation. IEEE Computer Graphics and Applications 2: 61-68

Paul R (1981) Robot Manipulators: Mathematics, Programming, and Control. MIT Press

Platt SM, Badler NI (1981) Animating Facial Expressions. In: Proc. ACM SIGGRAPH, p 245-252

Powers WT (1973) Behavior: The Control of Perception. Aldine Publishing Co., Chicago

Reynolds CW (1982) Computer Animation with Scripts and Actors. Proc. ACM SIGGRAPH 81, p 289-296

Ribble EA (1982) Synthesis of Human Skeletal Motion and the Design of a Special-Purpose Processor for Real-Time Animation of Human and Animal Figure Motion. MS Thesis, The Ohio State University, Ohio

Rogers D, Adams J (1976) Mathematical Elements for Computer Graphics, McGraw-Hill, New York

Rubin S, Whitted T (1980) A 3-Dimensional Representation for Fast Rendering of Complex Scenes. Proc. ACM SIGGRAPH 80

Shaw M (1980) The Impact of Abstraction Concerns on Modern Programming Languages. Proc. of the IEEE 68: 1119-1130

Stefik M, Bobrow D, Mittal S, Conway L (1983) Knowledge Programming in Loops: Report on an Experimental Course. AI Magazine 4: 3-13

Sutherland IE (1963) Sketchpad: A Man-Machine Graphical Communication System. In: Proc. AFIPS Spring Joint Computer Conf., vol. 23, p 329-346

Tennent RD (1981) Principles of Programming Languages. Prentice Hall, New Jersey

Tesler L (1981) The Smalltalk Environment. Byte 8: 90-147

Thomas F, Johnston O (1981) Disney Animation: The Illusion of Life, Abbeville Press, New York

Turvey MT, Fitch HL, Tuller B (1982) The Problems of Degrees of Freedom and Context-Conditioned Variability. In: Kelso J.A.S. (ed), Human Motor Behavoir, Lawrence Erlbaum Associates, New Jersey, p 239-252

Wasserman K (1985) Physical Object Representation and Generalization. AI Magazine 5: 28-42

Weber L, Smoliar SW, Badler NI (1978) An Architecture for the Simulation of Human Movement. In: Proc. ACM Ann. Conf., p 737-745

Whitney DE (1972) The Mathematics of Coordinated Control of Prosthetic Arms and Manipulatotors. Transactions of the ASME, Journal of Dynamic Systems, Measurement, and Control 122: 303-309

Williams L (1982) BBOP. In: Course Notes, Seminar on Three Dimensional Computer Animation, July 27, 1982, ACM SIGGRAPH 82

Zeltzer D (1983) Knowledge-based Animation. In: April 1983, Proc. ACM SIGGRAPH/SIGART Workshop on Motion, Toronto, Canada, p 187-192

Zeltzer D (1984) Representation and Control of Three Dimensional Computer Animated Figure. Ph.D. Thesis, The Ohio State University, Ohio

Fig. 1. An adaptive walk program allows a simulated human figure to walk over changing terrain with no animator intervention.

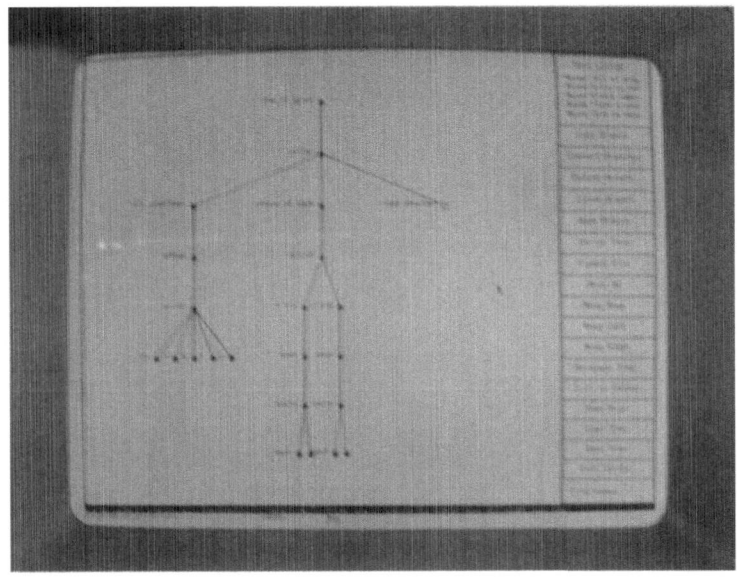

Fig. 2. The "tree editor" allows the animator to graphically design the transformation hierarchy for an articulated figure.

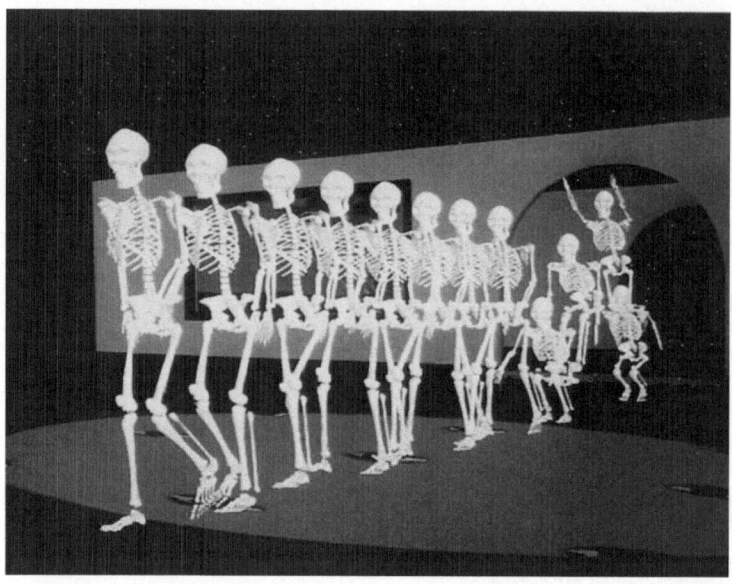

Fig. 3. Three motor programs have been invoked to generate this sequence. The first controls a standing broad jump and recovery to a standing position. The second controls the transition from a rest position to a full stride. The third is an adaptive walk control program.

Controlling Evolution and Motion
Using the CINEMIRA-2 Animation Sublanguage

Nadia Magnenat-Thalmann and Daniel Thalmann
MIRA Lab., HEC/IRO, Université de Montréal, Montréal, H3C 3J7, Canada

ABSTRACT

Interactive systems have the great advantage of being dedicated to artists; however, computer animation programming language does not impose fewer limits on creativity. CINEMIRA-2 is one way of conciliating the two approaches. This is a computer animation sublanguage only designed for extending the MIRANIM animation system. Five kinds of entities may be programmed in CINEMIRA-2: procedural objects, procedural evolution laws, procedural actor transformations, procedural subactor types and animation blocks. These entities are then controlled in a user-friendly way by non-programmer animators. This paper presents an informal description of the CINEMIRA-2 sublanguage with examples.

1. INTRODUCTION

Computer animation (Magnenat-Thalmann and Thalmann, 1985,1985a) was first developed in the mid-sixties (Knowlton, 1964). Early films were produced using programming languages (Sinden, 1967; Alexander and Huggins, 1967) or interactive systems accessible only to computer scientists. User-friendly interactive systems (Baecker, 1969) were then developed and artists could make films without too much intervention by computer scientists. These interactive systems had the great advantage of being dedicated to artists, but they imposed limits on the creativity of artists who would like to exploit all the possibilities of a computer. Two arguments can be used against a programming language for computer animation:

1. The production of computer-animated films using a graphical programming language is time-consuming
2. This approach implies that animators also have to be programmers

Four arguments can be put forward for the development and use of a programming language for computer animation:

1. A computer animation programming language imposes fewer limits on creativity.
2. A computer animation programming language permits the easy development of interactive computer animation systems, especially in terms of graphical data structures and temporal concepts.
3. Recent developments in the design of programming languages have led to new concepts that are fundamental to the control of motion and temporal events: data abstraction, synchronisation, message passing and actor systems.

4. Computer programming knowledge is not yet universal, but it is no longer restricted to computer scientists.

2. THE MIRANIM SYSTEM

MIRANIM is an advanced system which allows the creation, manipulation and animation of realistic images. The most important features of MIRANIM are as follows:

- basic geometric primitives
- ruled and free-form surfaces
- multiple cameras and stereoscopy
- actor motions
- multiple lights and spots, highlights and shadows
    (Magnenat-Thalmann and Thalmann, 1985)
- transparency, texture, fractals, particle systems

The system is mainly based on three components:
1) the object modelling and image synthesis system BODY-BUILDING
2) the director-oriented animation editor ANIMEDIT
3) the actor-based sublanguage CINEMIRA-2

ANIMEDIT is a scripted system; the director designs a scene with decors, actors, cameras and lights. Each of these entities is driven by animated variables, which are, in fact, state variables following evolution laws. These laws are predefined and may be chosen from among a linear law, cosinusoidal acceleration and deceleration, circular motion, gravity etc...There are eight modes in ANIMEDIT: MAIN , OBJECT , DECOR , ACTOR, CAMERA, LIGHT, VARIABLES and DIRECTOR. A complete description may be found in (Magnenat-Thalmann et al., 1985).

Although we have introduced less common laws such as fuzzy laws, this is still limitative for the creator. CINEMIRA-2 allows the director to use programmers to extend the system. The great advantage of this is that the system is extended in a user-friendly way. This means that the director may immediately use the new possibilities. An entity programmed in CINEMIRA-2 is directly accessible in ANIMEDIT. This not only extends the system, but also enables specific environments to be created.

3.THE CINEMIRA-2 SUBLANGUAGE

CINEMIRA-2 is derived from the computer animation language CINEMIRA. CINEMIRA was a complete language based on animated types, actor types and camera types (Thalmann and Magnenat-Thalmann, 1983). CINEMIRA had several characteristics in common with ASAS (Reynolds, 1982), but in a PASCAL environment with a strongly type-oriented definition. The major drawback of CINEMIRA was that it could not be used by artists. For this reason, the implementation was only partial and we have preferred to design and implement a director-oriented system which is extensible by using a sublanguage. CINEMIRA-2 is a sublanguage, which cannot be used without ANIMEDIT. The CINEMIRA-2 sublanguage contains all features defined in the MIRA-SHADING language: vector arithmetic, high-level graphical types (Magnenat-Thalmann,1983), graphical statements, geometric primitives, image transformations, virtual camera facilities and image rendering primitives. For animation, CINEMIRA-2 allows the programming of five kinds of entities:

- procedural objects
- procedural laws of evolution
- procedural actor transformations
- procedural subactors
- animation blocks.

Moreover, three CINEMIRA-2 global variables are accessible at any time:

- GTIME is the global time, in seconds, since the beginning of the scene
- LTIME is the local time, in seconds, since the activation of the procedural entity within which it is invoked
- NIPS is the shooting speed in number of images (frames) per second

In the next sections, we examine in details the different kinds of CINEMIRA-2 entities.

4. PROCEDURAL OBJECTS

Procedural objects are defined in the form of high-level types:

type \<type identifier\> = **object** [(\<list of parameters\>)];
    \<declarations\>
    spec
        \<list of statements\>
    name \<string\>, **shading** \<type of shading\>,
    figure of \<integer expression\> **vertices,**
        \<integer expression\> **faces,**
    transparency \<transmission coefficients\>
    begin
        \<list of statements\>
    end;

A procedural object is a variable of **object** type. It may be created at any time in an ANIMEDIT session using the PROCEDURAL command in the object mode:

PROCEDURAL \<object identifier\> \<type identifier\>
\<parameters\>

However, it cannot have dynamic properties, except if an actor is based on it. A procedural object is generally graphical, but it may also be non-graphical and its purpose in this case is the initialization or modification of states in the animation system.

5. PROCEDURAL EVOLUTION LAWS

A procedural law is similar to a function in a Pascal-like language; however the result is always a VECTOR or a REAL value and there is an implicit parameter: **time**. This means that a procedural law is defined, for exemple, as follows:

law CHANGE(P1,P2:T): VECTOR;
begin
  CHANGE:=f(P1,P2,CLOCK)
end;

In ANIMEDIT, the animator uses a law with the command LAW in the VARIABLES mode; this law is then applied to any animated variable using the EVOLUTION command. For example:

VECTOR MID,A,0,0,0   --defines an animated variable MID
LAW MYLAW, CHANGE   --defines an instance (MYLAW) of the
                                      law CHANGE
EVOLUTION MID,MYLAW,0,1   --applies the law MYLAW to the variable
                                      MID for 10 seconds

The problem in the design of evolution laws is to find a way of expressing them analytically:
    e.g. CHANGE:=f(P1,P2,CLOCK)

Our strategy in CINEMIRA-2 is based on the following principle: if laws may be expressed analytically, we program a simple law. If the evolution law is only expressed as a function of a previous state, we merely store values as global variables and the evolution law then gives a value computed from the global variables. The more general case occurs when evolution laws are modified during the animation process. This is generally not possible in current animation systems. We implement this as follows:

1. We initialize the extended animation system in the main CINEMIRA-2 program
2. We define procedural objects, to initialize global state variables
3. We define animation blocks (subprograms called at each frame) responsible for calculating the values of state variables at the current time
4. We define evolution laws which depend on the global state variables. They compute values that depend on the value of the state variables. which are accessed by the blocks during the animation process.

With this strategy, an evolution law may be completely changed at any time (and consequently at any frame).

We now give an example for texture. Blinn (1977) has developed a method which uses a texturing function to slightly alter the direction of the surface normal before using it in the intensity calculations. In the MIRANIM system, three-dimensional texturing laws may be defined in CINEMIRA-2 in the ACTOR mode and applied to any actor. For example:

In CINEMIRA-2:

```
law BUMP(X,Y,Z:REAL):REAL;
begin
  BUMP:=Fact*SIN(2*PI*CLOCK*(Perx*X+0.1*Ampl*
              (Ampl2*RANDOM(Ran)+SQR(COS(2*PI*CLOCK*Y*Pery)))))
end;
```

In ANIMEDIT:

VARIABLES	-- enters in the VARIABLES mode
LAW WRINKLE,BUMP	-- defines an instance (WRINKLE) of the
	-- BUMP law
0,0,0	-- dummy parameters
*	-- mode exit
ACTOR	-- enters in the actor mode
ACTOR MYACT,MYOBJ	-- defines an actor MYACT
TEXTURE MYACT,WRINKLE	-- applies a texture transformation to
	-- the actor MYACT using the texture
	-- law WRINKLE

Fig.1 and Fig.2 show examples of three-dimensional textures produced with MIRANIM.

6. PROCEDURAL ACTOR TRANSFORMATIONS

A procedural actor transformation has a syntax similar to a Pascal procedure:

actransform <identifier> [(list of parameters)];
   <declarations>
begin
   <list of statements>
end;

However, parameters may only have the types REAL and VECTOR. Moreover, the body of a procedural actor transformation must define a relation between two objects; the original object and the transformed object. These objects are designed by the two predefined identifiers OLDFIG and NEWFIG of type FIG.

Typically, an actor transformation calls an image transformation using the parameters OLDFIG and NEWFIG. For example:

```
actransform EXPLOSION(F:REAL);
   transform EXPLOSE(a,b,c...);
   begin
      ...
   end;
begin
   EXPLOSE(OLDFIG,A1,B1,C1,...,NEWFIG)
end;
```

Fig.1 An example of texture in MIRANIM (created by Alain Brossard)

Fig.2 An example of texture in MIRANIM (created by Alain Brossard)

In ANIMEDIT, procedural actor transformations are invoked by the command PROTRANSFORM:

PROTRANSFORM <actor identifier> <type transformation identifier>
<parameters>

e.g. PROTRANSFORM CAR EXPLOSION
 INTENSITY

INTENSITY is a variable that must be defined in the VARIABLES mode.

7. PROCEDURAL SUBACTOR DATA TYPES

An actor as defined by Reynolds (1982) is a graphical entity with a given role to play. A subactor (Magnenat-Thalmann and Thalmann, 1985b) is an entity which is dependent on an actor. This means that all motions applied to an actor are also applied to all its subactors. The reverse is not true. There are also two other advantages to the subactor approach:

1. Any new subactor may be inserted as dependent on an existing actor
2. Motions of different subactors may be coordinated and synchronized within an actor.

The syntax of a subactor is as follows:

type <type identifier> = **subactor** [(<list of parameters>)];
 <declarations>
 begin
 <list of statements>
 end;

In ANIMEDIT, a subactor is defined using the command SUBACTOR:

SUBACTOR <subactor identifier> <subactor type identifier>
<parameters>

The subactor is then made dependent on an actor using the command HIERARCHY:

HIERARCHY <actor identifier> <subactor identifier>

Subactors are currently used to model human and robot motions. For example, the model in Fig.3 was built using a subactor PERSON. Procedural laws to make this subactor walk have been also programmed.

8. ANIMATION BLOCKS

An animation block is a subprogram executed at each frame; it is similar to the animate block in ASAS (Reynolds, 1982); however, parameters of a block defined in CINEMIRA-2, may be actors and cameras. The syntax of an animate block is as follows:

block <identifier> [(list of parameters)];
  <declarations>
begin
  <list of statements>
end;

In ANIMEDIT a block is activated in the DIRECTOR mode, using the BLOCK command:
BLOCK <block identifier> <activation time> <duration>
    AFTER/BEFORE [<camera identifier>]

As a block may contain instructions manipulating virtual cameras, it may be activated after or before the first image displayed.

Typically, blocks are used to update state variables. For exemple, we have used blocks in our implementation of particle systems (Reeves, 1983)and in designing evolution laws based on simultaneous differential equations (Magnenat-Thalmann and Thalmann, 1986). They may be also used for interfacing other systems with ANIMEDIT. For example, data for each frame may be read into an animation block.

Normally, actors and cameras in ANIMEDIT are activated in the DIRECTOR mode. For example
ACTOR GIRAFFE 0 12 3
means that the actor named GIRAFFE is activated at time 0 for 12 seconds and transformations applied to GIRAFFE only start at time 3.

With CINEMIRA-2 actors and cameras, defined in ANIMEDIT, may be dynamically activated or stopped using the commands **start** and **stop**. In this case, actors and cameras must be formal parameters of the block using the type identifiers ACT and CAM.

1) **start** [<actor>/<camera>] (<activation time> <duration>
                    <start time for transformations>)
    - the actor or the camera will be activated at the time given and for a certain duration; transformations may start later on.

2) **stop** [<actor>/<camera>] (< time>)
    - the actor or the camera will be stopped a certain time after this call

The dynamic activation of ANIMEDIT actors and cameras is very important when activation times cannot be forecasted. For example, we shall assume that when a cable car (Fig.4) is at a certain altitude, a camera is started with the eye in the cable car. The block has the following structure:

block CABLECAR (CAM1,CAM2:CAM);
begin ...
  if ALTITUDE=2000 **then**
  begin
    stop CAM1(0);
    start CAM2(0,10,0)
  end
end;

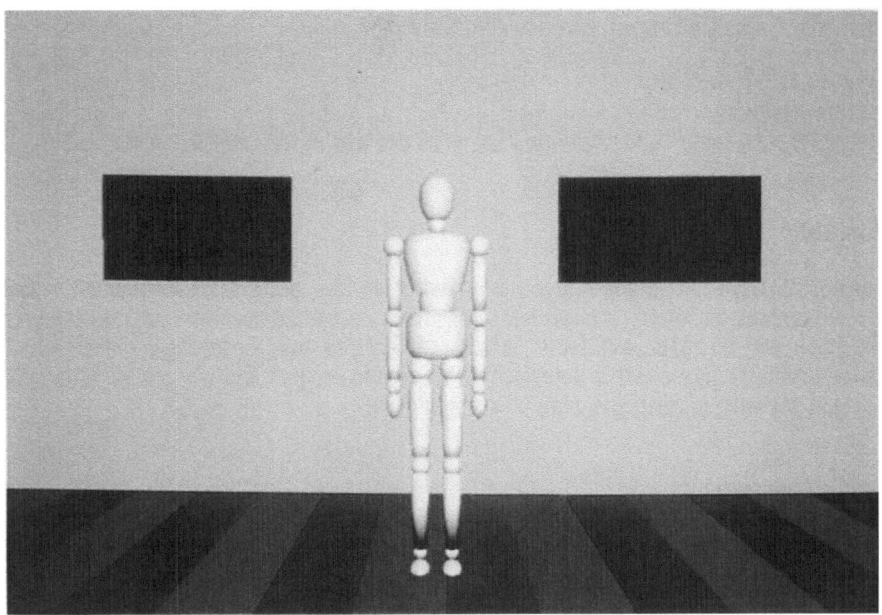

Fig.3 The PERSON the subactor (created by Denis Rambaud)

Fig.4 A cable car (created by Luc Forest)

The block CABLECAR is activated in ANIMEDIT by:

BLOCK CABLECAR,0,20,A
MYCAM1 MYCAM2
where MYCAM1 and MYCAM2 are two cameras defined in the CAMERA mode.

CONCLUSION

The possibility of programming any new evolution law, actor transformation, subactor, object or animation block provides unlimited possibilities for motion. And these possibilities can be made available to artists. Artists may order new commands from computer scientists. This is the approach taken in this project and we are sure it can help fill the gap between artists and computer scientists.

ACKNOWLEDGEMENTS

The authors are grateful to Ann Laporte who has revised the English text. They are also indebted to the students who have worked on this project. Mario Fortin implemented the CINEMIRA-2 sublanguage; Denis Rambaud implemented the PERSON subactor; Alain Brossard implemented the texturing functions. The research was supported by the Natural Sciences and Engineering Council of Canada, the Art Council of Canada and the Government of Quebec.

REFERENCES

Alexander, S. and Huggins, WH (1967) **User's manual on PMACRO**, John Hopkins University.

Baecker, R.M. **Picture-driven Animation**, Proc. Spring Joint Computer Conference, AFIPS Press, Vol.34, pp.273-288.

Blinn, J. (1977) **Simulation of Wrinkled Surfaces**, Proc.SIGGRAPH'77, Computer Graphics, Vol.12, No 3, pp.286-292

Fortin, M.; Léonard, N.; Magnenat-Thalmann, N. and Thalmann, D. (1985) **Animation of Lights and Shadows** in New Electronic Images, Springer, Tokyo Berlin Heidelberg New York (This book)

Knowlton KC (1964) **A Computer-technique for Producing Animated Movies**, Proc. SJCC AFIPS Conference, 25:67-87.

Magnenat-Thalmann, N. and Thalmann, D. (1983) **The Use of High Level Graphical Types in the MIRA Animation System**, IEEE Computer Graphics and Applications, Vol. 3, No 9, pp. 9-16

Magnenat-Thalmann N. and Thalmann, D. (1985) **Computer Animation: Theory and Practice**, Springer-Verlag, Tokyo

Magnenat-Thalmann, N. and Thalmann, D. (1985a) **An Indexed Bibliography on Computer Animation**, IEEE Computer Graphics and Applications, Vol. 5, No7, pp.76-86.

Magnenat-Thalmann, N. and Thalmann, D. (1985b) **Subactor Data Types as Hierarchical Procedural Models for Computer Animation**, Proc. EUROGRAPHICS '85, Nice, France, North Holland, pp.121-128

Magnenat-Thalmann, N. and Thalmann, D. (1985b) **Three-Dimensional Computer Animation Based on Simultaneous Differential Equations**, Proc. Conference on Continuous Simulation, Society for Computer Simulation, San Diego.

Magnenat-Thalmann, N.; Thalmann, D. and Fortin, M. (1985) **MIRANIM: An Extensible Director-Oriented System for the Animation of Realistic Images**, IEEE Computer Graphics and Applications, Vol. 5, No 3, pp. 61-73

Reeves, W.T. (1983) **Particle Systems - a Technique for Modeling a Class of Fuzzy Objects**, ACM Transactions on Graphics, Vol.2, 1983, pp.91-108.

Reynolds, C.W. (1982) **Computer Animation with Scripts and Actors**, Proc. SIGGRAPH'82, pp.289-296

Sinden, FW (1967) **Synthetic Cinematography** (1967), Perspective, Vol.7, No4, pp.279-289.

Thalmann, D. and Magnenat-Thalmann (1983) **Actor and Camera Data Types in Computer Animation**, Proc. Graphics Interface '83, pp.203-210.

Computer Animation in Distance Teaching

Joel M. Greenberg
Academic Computing Service, The Open University, Walton Hall, Milton Keynes, MK7 6AA, UK

ABSTRACT

Television plays an important role in the distance teaching methods of the Open University. The use of computer animation has greatly enhanced the teaching process. Computer images are created using a graphics package based on the SIGGRAPH "Core" system and viewed on a range of colour raster terminals. Previewing animation sequences has been simplified by developing an interactive animation system. Completed sequences are recorded direct to videotape using a system developed jointly by the BBC and the Open University. They are subsequently edited into television programmes for transmission by the BBC.

INTRODUCTION

The Open University is an independent self-governing distance-teaching institution which awards its own degrees and certificates. Students do not attend a campus, but learn at home and in their own time from specially written booklets, recommended textbooks, radio and television broadcasts and other audio-visual material. There are about 65,000 undergraduates at various stages of their degree studies and another 23,000 people taking single courses. At present, there are 131 undergraduate courses covering a wide range of disciplines.

Television programmes are made in partnership with a special unit of the BBC. Some 35 hours of television are broadcast each week over the BBC network. The BBC OU Production Centre is probably the largest and best-equipped educational audio-visual centre anywhere in the world.

Computer animation has proved to be particularly effective in the television programmes produced for the Mathematics and Science faculties of the University. Some forty minutes of computer generated animation has been used in nine half-hour programmes produced for the second-level course "Probability and Statistics". The sequences range from animating simple histograms to 3-D representations of bivariate normal distributions. It has been found that the teaching of many facets of statistics is made simpler by the use of computer animation to illustrate specific points. Other effective applications have been found in physical chemistry, physics and molecular biology.

A particularly interesting sequence in molecular biology resulted in the first solid modelling animation of a Lysozyme enzyme. Co-ordinates of the molecules were generated on a Cray 1 and converted by the IBM UK Scientific Center to solid graphic images. These were then previewed and recorded using the animation system described in this paper.

THE CAVITY ANIMATION SYSTEM

The Cavity system is based on four design objectives:

1. A previewing environment is available which allows the user to view any frame in the sequence easily;
2. Computer images can be modified without having to resort to time-consuming compilations and loading of source code;
3. Single and multiple fairings are available to allow changes to position, angles, colours and other parameters in a visually smooth fashion.
4. Sequences can be recorded direct to video-tape and meet the requirements of BBC videotape standards. The computer controls and operation of the videotape machine (VTR) and the whole recording process once begun, requires no manual intervention.

It should be noted that as many of the animation sequences are illustrating scientific topics, the primary means of control is by numerical model. A fully interactive graphics editor has been developed and integrated into the Cavity system for work requiring manual input.

ANIMATION SOFTWARE

The animation system is made up of the following software components:

1. A Graphics Package

   The graphics package is a full implementation of the SIGGRAPH "Core" system written in FORTRAN 77. The package includes additional routines to allow such facilities as anti-aliasing, hidden line removal, RGB and HLS colour models.

2. Animation Control File (ACF)

   The ACF is a text file which controls which routines will be called to form the images associated with each frame of the animation sequence. The file contains commands which initialise and change entries in a database. Parameters associated with graphics images may be linearly changed to specified values over a specified number of frames. These changes may also be done using several fairing techniques. The system can also cope with large numbers of overlapping changes. Commands are also available to define and enable or disable boolean variables.

3. User Routine

   The user routines are written by the programmer/animator. They produce images by calling routines in the graphics package or obtaining picture segments from metafiles. The routines are generally controlled by boolean variables defined in the ACF and enabled for the relevant frames.

4. The Database

   The database is held in memory and is modified either by commands in the ACF or as a result of actions in the user routines. It holds key variables which change during the animation sequence as well as those modified during development of the sequence. Variables can be boolean, integer, real and arrays of these types and may have names of up to 30 characters.

5. Videotape Control Routines

These routines control the recording process. Appropriate commands are sent from the computer to the VTR to control normal VTR functions such as pre-roll and cue actions. The commands pass through the Cavity convertor box, described later. The VTR also sends data back to the computer through the convertor box, reporting on its status.

6. Animation Package (ANIMAT)

The animation package consists of a set of routines which allow the user to preview individual frames of an animation. The user keys in commands at the terminal and ANIMAT uses the specifications in the ACF together with routines in the graphics package to produce the images.

The user can step forward or backward through the sequence or jump to any specified frame. Images can be altered by using a second terminal to edit the ACF file. The UPDATE command will make the necessary changes to the database and redisplay the relevant frame.

When an animation is completed, ANIMAT is used to initiate the recording process and control the VTR with the videotape control routines.

7. Graphics Environment

The programmer/animator can set up an environment which adds a range of graphics commands to the operating system of the computer. The only source code which need be altered when developing a sequence is in the user routines. The user then specifies which output devices are to be used and invokes the ANIMATE command followed by the file containing the user routines. All relevant graphics routines, output device specific routines and VTR control routines will automatically be loaded together.

ANIMATION HARDWARE

Animation sequences are currently being developed on a DEC 2060. All communications are over serial RS232 lines at 9600 BAUD. The following input/output devices are available for development work:

1. AED 767
2. SIGMA 5000 GOC
3. TEKTRONIX 4012
4. DEC GIGI VK100
5. DEC VT241
6. Pericom 7800
7. BBC Micro
8. CALCOMP81 Plotter
9. Altek Datatab Digitizer
10. GTCO Digi-Pad 5 Digitizer

The recording process uses:

1. AMPEX 1" VPR2
2. Newbury 7000 VDU
3. Cavity convertor box
4. Michael Cox Coder
5. Sony 5860 P U-matic recorder.

Final development work is done on the AED 767, which has a resolution of 767 x 585, compatible with British television requirements. The eight memory planes of the device offer a suitable colour table, easily modified by the programmer/animator.

THE CAVITY CONVERTOR BOX

This device was designed and built by John Franklin and Alan Francis of the BBC Open University Production Centre. Data from the DEC 2060 is sent to a frame store in the BBC Production Centre. Control codes are separated from the graphical data which is assembled into RGB signals. The RGB signals are locked to station sync pulses and fed to the Michael Cox coder to produce a PAL encoded video signal. This signal is then routed to the video input of the VTR.

Some of the control codes command the internal functions of the frame store, while others control the motion of the VTR. The latter are gated to a downstream output of the frame store and fed to the Cavity Convertor. The Convertor is built around a Z80 microprocessor and updates timecodes and cues and records as appropriate. It also keeps the VTR and computer in step by telling the computer when each video recording operation is complete.

PRODUCTION OF A SEQUENCE

The decision to use a computer animation sequence in a programme is generally taken by the BBC producer. Discussions are then held with the Course Team of academics writing the course to assess the teaching potential of the sequence. Once approved by the academics, a storyboard of the sequence is developed in conjunction with a graphic designer from the BBC.

At this stage the programmer/animator becomes involved and decisions are taken with regard to the type of images required and how best to animate them. After the sequence is approved by BBC resources and planning, a detailed storyboard is produced.

The programmer/animator then writes the user routines necessary to generate the images and the associated ACF file to set and control variables used in specific frames. One command in the graphics environment loads all the required modules together and the sequence is edited and previewed on a colour raster terminal. In some sequences, the graphics editor might be used to draw certain images. These are stored in metafiles and accessed from the user routines. Alternatively, a frame generated by the user routines may be stored in a metafile, accessed by the graphics editor and modified as required. Parts of the sequence may be recorded directly onto the Sony U-matic recorder to give some picture of the movement involved in the sequence. When all the images for the sequence are being generated correctly, frame numbers in the ACF are adjusted to synchronise the sequence with its accompanying commentary.

Recording of sequences takes place on two nights each week, although additional sessions are made available as required. The recording process is initiated by a VT editor, operation is entirely automatic and takes place overnight.

The time taken to record a sequence is generally dependent on the complexity of the images being drawn. Inevitably, the VTR has to wait for the computer to complete the frame before recording it. Recording sessions typically last for twelve or thirteen hours if no hardware malfunctions occur.

EXAMPLES OF AN ANIMATION SEQUENCE

Three animation sequences were commissioned for a programme in the course "Probability and Statistics". The sequences were used to illustrate concepts which would have been difficult with traditional graphics techniques. The programme deals with the bivariate normal distribution. Bivariate distributions are probability distributions for two random variables. The distributions of each variable alone when obtained from the joint distribution of the variable is called the marginal distribution.

As an example, consider the heights of fathers and their adult sons in a large population. These are continuous random variables, both of which can be regarded as being normally distributed. They are not independant, since tall fathers tend to have tall sons, so to describe their joint distribution to look at say, the average heights of sons of six-feet tall fathers, requires a continuous bivariate distribution whose marginals are normal.

The bivariate normal distribution has an explicit mathematical representation which, when plotted, results in a 3-D contour. Once the image is drawn, it is easily manipulated using the animation package. The image is rotated, split into independant segments which can move freely. By changing parameters in the mathematical description of the distribution, the whole surface can be animated. Hidden line removal is used where appropriate and limited shading enhances the final image.

Figure 1 shows studio models used in the television programme to represent heights of 1078 father-son pairs. The probability density function (p.d.f.) of a bivariate normal distribution is shown in Fig.2. The animation sequence had to realistically represent the studio model. Manipulation of the RGB colour model allowed the appropriate colours to be generated. The image was further enhanced with text labels which were orientated in 3-D space. Fig.3 shows the p.d.f. as drawn by the computer. In the animation sequence the p.d.f. is split into vertical cross-sections. This reveals that each section has the shape of a normal curve.

FUTURE DEVELOPMENTS

At present, the Cavity system uses the AED 767 as a frame store during the recording process. We are intending to install a PLUTO 11 graphics controller for future work. This is an 8088 based graphics processor with 1 Mbyte of frame buffer memory and complete compatability with the AED 767 with regards to colour table, resolution and performance. Another PLUTO 11 will be available for development work.

Recent applications have demanded more sophisticated images requiring hidden surface removal and shading algorithums. These have been implemented at the user routine level.

The acquisition of a VAX 11/785 has raised the possibility of moving the animation system to a machine with much faster transmission rates. The complexity of images now being produced requires an improvement on the current data transmission rate of 9600 BAUD.

CONCLUSIONS

The Cavity animation system allows BBC producers and graphic designers to work alongside programmer/analysts of the Open University in producing computer animation sequences. In the first two years of operation, the system has resulted in some two hours of computer animation. The system allows completed sequences to be recorded overnight, direct to videotape. No manual intervention is required in the recording process.

Animation sequences are intended as a teaching aid and not simply visual entertainment. To this end, care must be taken not to obscure the teaching point by creating images which are visually distracting to the student.

Fig. 1

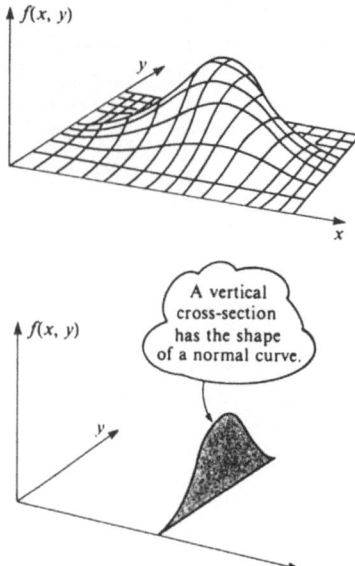

Fig. 2

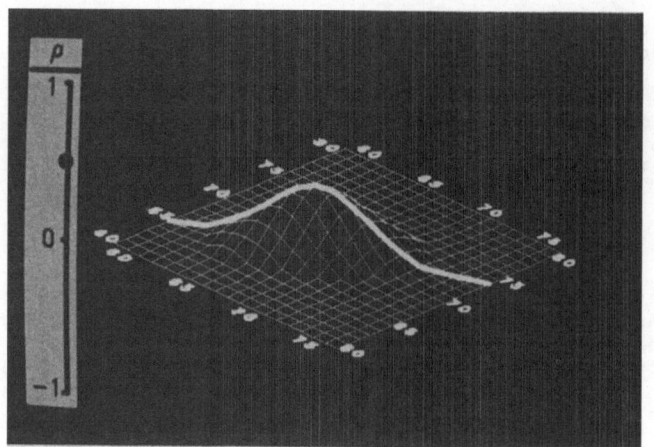

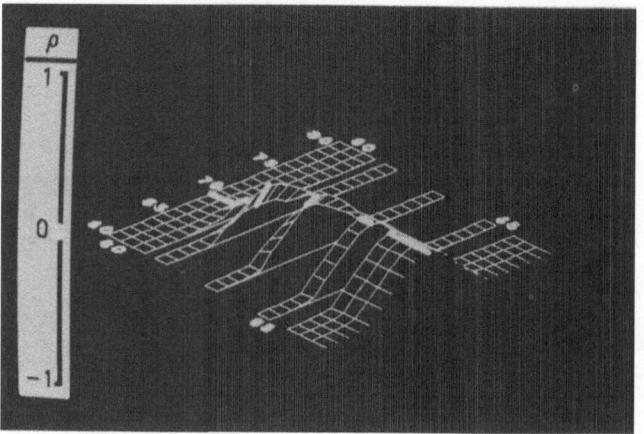

Fig. 3

Chapter 5
User Interface

The Interactive Planning Work Station
A Graphics-Based UNIX™ Tool for Application Users and Developers

R. Bournique[1], R. Candrea[1] and D. Hartman[2]

[1] AT&T Bell Laboratories, Crawford Corners Road, Holmdel, NJ 07733, USA
[2] MLC Inc., 150 E. Riverside Drive, #400, Austin, TX 78704, USA

INTRODUCTION

The Interactive Planning Work Station (IPWS) is a *UNIX™*-based system intended to support planning and other complex decision-making tasks. Network planning at AT&T has always been supported by a wide variety of edp systems. A typical planning system includes a collection of algorithms that produce large amounts of data to produce a network plan. The primary user interface was, for many years, a set of voluminous printouts. If the system contained an interactive component it was usually in the form of a single package for editing data files or submitting batch runs.

As part of AT&T's Bell Laboratories responsibility to design planning methods and tools to support facility planning within AT&T Communications (formerly Long Lines), a study was undertaken in 1978 to review the software architecture of the existing generation of AT&T facility planning systems and propose an architecture for next generation systems. One of the principal conclusions of the study was that next generation systems require a much better user interface than the current ones, and the only reasonable way to provide the required interface is to build a separate system that can be adapted to meet the needs of a variety of applications. It was out of this study that work on IPWS grew. IPWS design began in early 1979; at that time the intent was to demonstrate the feasibility of the concept and provide a testbed for further development.

As IPWS has evolved, more users and applications have been identified and the need for a complete set of underlying tools, reaching beyond those needed simply for network planning, has become even greater. A next generation low-cost work station has since evolved in both hardware and software with potential applications extending into other areas including marketing, operations research studies, and statistical analysis.

WHAT IS IPWS? WHO USES IT?

IPWS can best be viewed as a collection of software capabilities along with a control structure that ties these capabilities together. The IPWS philosophy is distinguished from other work station philosophies in its emphasis upon software. That is, IPWS should not be viewed as a specific hardware device but, rather, as a software architecture that can be implemented on a variety of hardware devices. A typical work station "terminal" consists of an alphanumeric terminal for displaying menus and entering text, a color raster graphics monitor for displaying pictures, and a pointing device such as a tablet or mouse for direct interaction with the graphics screen. One configuration is an AT&T 6300 PC with a high resolution color board and monitor and an AT&T mouse (Fig. 1).

IPWS addresses the needs of at least two classes of users (Hartman 1984a): *end users of an application* (both basic and sophisticated) and *application developers*. Both classes of users have different but overlapping requirements.

End Users of an Application

The basic users of an application are typically non-programmers who have little interest in learning about software or an underlying database structure. Normally they work in a highly structured and tightly controlled environment. To assist these users, IPWS provides the ability to display information graphically and add, delete, or modify the display by pointing at various items on the screen. Typically, these users want to interact through a set of menus which define alternatives available at each step of the application process.

Fig. 1. The Interactive Planning Work Station.

More sophisticated users are those who use the system on a regular basis to manipulate data to, for example, perform special studies and ask one-time "what-if" questions. The tasks to be performed change frequently and the exact functions required are often not known prior to performing the task. These users typically have some programming experience and are frequently motivated to understand an underlying database. The tools needed by sophisticated users are those that generate graphics displays to aid in understanding the data (and to help locate data errors) as well as tools that help users edit, synthesize, and manipulate the data.

Application Developers

Application developers design algorithms and software packages for other users. They require the same capabilities as sophisticated users plus tools to assist in building application packages. Software provided by IPWS here includes a language for building application menus, a database management system, an interactive graphics package, and some general purpose software development packages.

IPWS Features

Both end users and application developers see IPWS as a system with three major features:

(i) A menu-oriented user interface
(ii) Interactive database management capabilities
(iii) Graphical input and output.

These three features are expanded upon in the sections below.

THE MENU-ORIENTED USER INTERFACE

The question of whether it is better to provide users with a command-oriented or menu-oriented user interface to their applications is a difficult one. That issue is resolved in the IPWS environment by essentially providing both.

IPWS Menus

Figure 2 is an example of a work station menu. The menu is displayed at the top of the alphanumeric screen in an application programmer-defined format. The remaining bottom portion of the screen is used as a scrolling region.

```
IPWS - GRAPHICS MENU FEATURING GRADIAL - plots

I Input file    = linkdata
f filter        = bars  (options: bars curve steps stats yours)
x x-axis field = ?
y y-axis field = ?

a auto-axes: on                  U user command file:
A axes-setting menu              u user params: none

K clear whole screen             w window: (d) 0 1 0 1
k clear just viewport            v viewport: (d) 0 1 0 1
s select (using cursor)          c color: 1

l list-dir       d display-fmt   p print-fi    R Runfi:
r run            e exit          G Globals     t tutorial


> I linkdata
> f bars
> r
>
```

Fig. 2. **Plots** is one of the basic menus on the Interactive Planning Work Station. Users type the desired option in the scrolling region below the menu. Online help information and tutorials are available for all the basic work station menus.

Whenever the prompt character, ">", is displayed, the user may select either an option from the current menu (a one-character entry) or any built-in or *UNIX* command (a multiple-character entry). To *UNIX* system users, this appears in practice to be a menu-oriented shell. Menu options may spawn application programs, update entries in the current menu, or invoke other menu pages.

IPWS provides a tree structure of basic work station menus (Witting 1984). These menus include basic capabilities many users want, including database manipulation and graphical display. The basic menus may be run stand alone or may be linked with application-specific menus.

The Menu Language

To facilitate application developers in the creation of menu interfaces for their applications, a menu language (Hartman 1984b) was developed for IPWS. In many ways the Menu Language looks like a subset of C along with some additional functions. Figure 3 is an example of a menu language program.

The most noticeable addition to the Menu Language is the *display* statement which lets users create their own menus. To define a menu entry, the programmer provides in the *display* statement:

      (i) The pick character, i.e., the character typed to choose this menu option
      (ii) The location of the entry using a row- column format (the top of the screen
           is row zero; the left-hand side of the screen is column zero)
      (iii) The explanatory text to be displayed beside the menu entry
      (iv) The action(s) to be performed when the menu option is chosen.

In addition to *display*, other built-in functions, like *getfld* and *update* in Fig. 3, are provided as part of the language for entering data and updating the menu information on the screen.

```
page sortmenu()
{
        static char inf, outf;

        display(0, "Sorting Menu")
                {
                        /* "I" menu option at row 1, col 1 */
                        :I, 1, 1; "Input file = ", inf;
                                {
                                        inf = getfld();
                                        update;
                                }

                        /* "O" menu option at row 2, col 1 */
                        :O, 2, 1; "Output file = ", outf;
                                {
                                        outf = getfld();
                                        update;
                                }

                        /* "R" menu option at row 3, col 1 */
                        :R, 3, 1; "Run sort";
                                {
                                        if ((inf != "") && (outf != ""))
                                                exec(BIN, "sort", inf, outf);
                                        else
                                                print("Missing file name(s)");
                                }
                }
}
```

Fig. 3. A Menu Language program.

INTERACTIVE DATABASE MANAGEMENT

The interactive database management capabilities on IPWS is a relational database management system (DBMS) (Hartman 1984c). Much of the design of the DBMS borrows from other database systems, notably IBM's System R.

IPWS database software has been designed in two levels (Fig. 4). On the bottom lie the low-level database access routines and the C language interface. This level includes record and page managers and an indexed access (B-tree) manager. On top are numerous higher-level tools. They include database menus, some basic database management utilities, a database editor, and a graphical database language. An interactive query interpreter is also in the works.

Low-Level Database Management

IPWS supports both logical *UNIX* databases and physical *UNIX* databases. Logical *UNIX* databases, in which relations are stored as plain *UNIX* files, are intended primarily for personal use where concurrent access and crash recovery are not required. Physical *UNIX* databases, in which relations are stored in a *UNIX* physical file system, are intended for applications that require large shared databases.

Users may process databases sequentially or through indexed access provided through the use of B-trees. Indices may be on a single field or on the concatenation of several fields. Users can also create databases made up of a collection of interdependent relations.

The C language interface consists of a set of low-level C subroutines that are used for processing the database on a record-at-a-time basis. Record-at-a-time access is useful for operations that are inherently procedural. In addition to accessing the database, subroutines have also been provided that support transaction control.

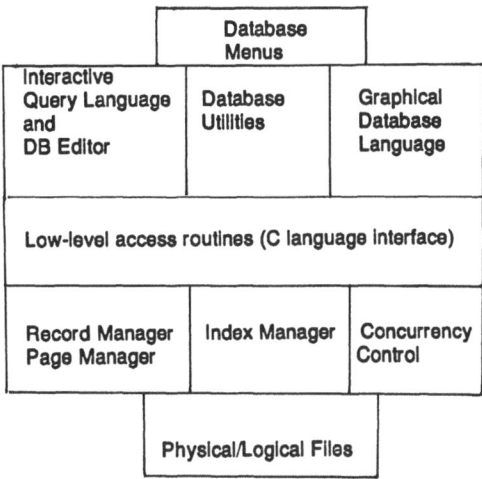

Fig. 4. Levels of IPWS database software.

Higher-Level Database Tools

Database Utilities: Many database functions are so frequently needed that a set of database utilities has been provided for quick and easy access. These utilities include the ability to:

(i) Convert an ASCII file to a database file
(ii) Select and/or join database files
(iii) Print a database file
(iv) Concatenate, sort, and/or summarize database files

Most of these utilities are accessible either through an IPWS command or through one of the basic work station menus.

Interactive Query Language and Editor: A database query language is in the works. The fourth generation interactive query language will allow users to query a database and browse through the results using the database editor.

The database editor, qde (query, display, and edit) is a screen-oriented interactive program that allows a user to browse through a relation in a database (Kashdan 1984). The editor appears much like the *vi* text editor in that a user can easily move around in a relation and add, delete, or modify records. Format files can optionally be provided that define the screen layout for records being displayed. The format file can also make certain fields invisible or protected.

Graphical Database Language: GRADIAL (Graphics and Database Interpreter and Language) is a high-level procedural language that marries database access and graphical display. It has been mentioned here for completeness, since it is both a database as well as graphics language. More is said about GRADIAL below after a more complete discussion of graphical input and output is presented.

GRAPHICAL INPUT AND OUTPUT

Like the database management software, there are distinct levels of graphical functionality (Bournique 1983) to consider (Fig. 5). At the lowest level are the hardware device drivers and a virtual device interface (VDI) that controls and invokes those low-level functions. The next level of software is a set of device-independent routines that permits programmers to develop their own graphical applications in C. Higher-level software, built on top of the device-independent routines, resides at the topmost level. A basic set of graphics utilities are available as well as a graphical database language and an interactive picture editor.

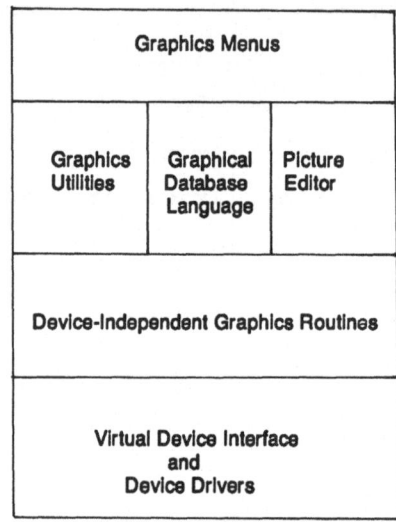

Fig. 5-Layers of IPWS graphics software.

Device Drivers and the VDI

From the beginning, the intent was to allow users to configure their IPWS work stations with the hardware that their particular application dictated. Consequently, many different graphics drivers running under IPWS were anticipated. In the authors' work environment alone, output drivers have been written for the AT&T Teletype 5620 bit-mapped terminal, the Ramtek 9351, the Ramtek 6211, the Printacolor ink jet color printer, the Hewlett-Packard 7221S plotter, the Bausch and Lomb DMP HIPLOT-29 and DMP-9 plotters, the Epson FX-80 black and white printer, and the Scion, Matrox, NEC, and Heurikon graphics boards; input drivers exist for the Summagraphics bitpad, the GTCO and CalComp Wedge tablets, and the AT&T, Microsoft, and Logitech mice.

The highly repetitive and generally well understood task of writing a device driver led to the definition and implementation of a standard set of routines and data structures that must be provided to drive the device. The result is a device-independent/device-dependent (DI/DD) interface (Bournique 1984a) or VDI. The concept of a DI/DD interface is nothing new; but without the prospect of an industry standard soon, it was thought necessary to go ahead and define a standard IPWS interface.

The DI/DD interface allows the inclusion of not only *hardware* devices but so called *pseudo* devices as well. In particular, a device driver was written that stores the graphics calls in an application-independent metafile, thus allowing for the saving and retrieving of images in a picture library.

The Device-Independent Graphics Routines

The device-independent graphics routines comprise the mid-level graphics software of IPWS. In actuality there are two packages. One package is a C implementation of Core, the ACM SIGGRAPH Graphics Standards Planning Committee's industry standard for graphics functions (Status Report 1979). The second package is a C implementation of the newer, internationally popular Graphical Kernel System (GKS) standard (Graphical Kernel System 1982). Newer applications tend to use the more complete GKS package.

Both packages consist of hundreds of user-callable functions (Bournique 1984b) and have, presently, the ability to:

     (i) Draw two-dimensional line, marker, text, or polygon primitives
    (ii) Perform clipping, viewing, and image transformations
   (iii) Group the primitives into higher-level nested segments
   (iv) Set and inquire about various graphical attributes
    (v) Read input from different virtual input devices.

Higher-Level Graphics Software

Graphics Utilities: Many graphics functions are rather basic and are regularly used in an interactive session, regardless of the particular application. Some of these basic functions include:

     (i) Automatic scaling and drawing of axes for charts and graphs
    (ii) Definition of colors to be used in drawing the picture elements
   (iii) Definition of the special markers (icons) to be used as picture symbols
   (iv) Interactive windowing and viewporting
    (v) Production of panels (iconic menus) for the graphics screen.

A set of about a dozen graphics utilities have been provided on IPWS for easy access to these frequently used operations. From the user's viewpoint, these utilities appear to be *UNIX*-like commands that can be invoked directly or through basic menu options.

Graphical Database Language: The IPWS graphical database language, GRADIAL (Graphics and Database Interpreter and Language) (Kretsch 1984) is a high-level language for describing a picture to be drawn, using the information in the records of a database file. The GRADIAL interpreter translates these higher-level constructs into the appropriate lower-level graphics function calls.

Figure 6 is a simple GRADIAL program that displays LATAs (Local Access and Transport Areas).

```
strtpick              " save LATAs for picking
ue                    " continue Until End of file
   read               " read the next database record
   if lata lt 800     " AT&T LATAs are < 800
      color Icolor    " set LATA color
      marker x y 14   " place marker #14 on point
   endif              " end of if
endue                 " end of loop
```

Fig. 6. A GRADIAL program.

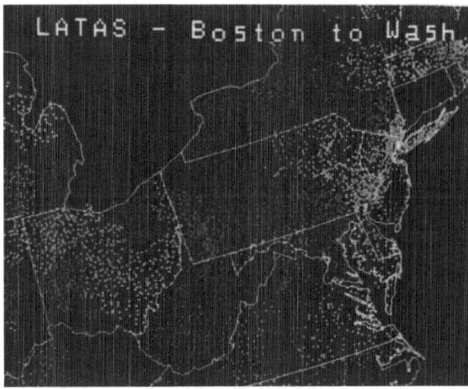

Fig. 7. The GRADIAL program display.

The database file from which the picture was constructed includes the fields *lata* (LATA number), *lcolor* (LATA color), and (*x*, *y*) (location of LATA). With the appropriate database file and GRADIAL program, the interpreter will generate the graphics that, equivalently, would require a C program about fifty lines long. Figure 7 is the color display generated by this program.

In addition to producing the picture, the interpreter can also store the indices to the database records from which the items in the picture were generated. A later application process can let a user point to an item on the screen causing the database record on that item to be displayed on the alphanumeric screen. The *strtpick* statement in Fig. 6 tells the interpreter to store the database records for later picking.

Interactive Picture Editor: In the same way that GRADIAL allows post-inquiry of the picture elements, it was also thought important to provide users with the ability to post-edit a picture, independent of the particular application that produced it. An interactive picture editor (Bournique 1984c) has been provided within the work station for that purpose.

Most of the interaction takes place on the graphics screen, using a tablet and cursor (or mouse). The windows of control information, superimposed on top of the picture, can be shuffled around like sheets of paper on a desk (Fig. 8).

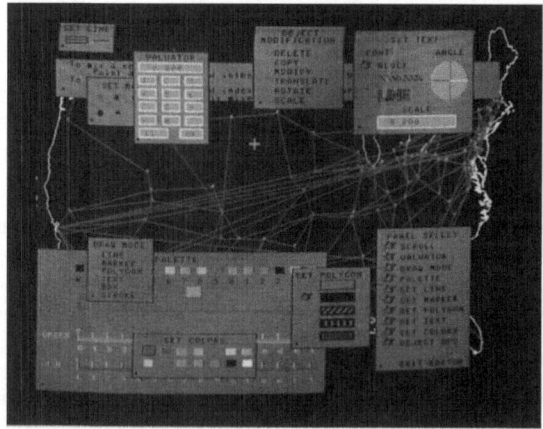

Fig. 8. Picture editor panels are superimposed on top of the picture to be edited. Users can move the panels and make them visible or invisible as needed.

The picture editor allows a user to perform a wide variety of tasks interactively that normally would require some kind of programming effort. Users can, for example, mix new colors, create new marker symbols, stylize networks, and design flowcharts, all interactively.

SUMMARY

The Interactive Planning Work Station is a *UNIX*-based software architecture addressing the needs many different users. Both end users and application developers see IPWS as a system with a menu-oriented user interface, interactive database management capabilities, and graphical input and output. The numerous applications developed and running on IPWS have demonstrated its potential for becoming a valuable decision-maker's assistant in the workplace.

Future IPWS plans include the evolution of the next generation of hardware, movement toward a single-screen multiple-window environment, and the development of other higher-level software tools such as a graphical database editor. Work on IPWS should continue to be challenging and exciting for some time to come.

REFERENCES

Bournique R (1983) Graphics Software Tools on the Interactive Planning Work Station. In: Proceedings of the Application Development Systems Symposium, AT&T Bell Laboratories, Murray Hill p. 89

Bournique R, Mowatt N (1984a) IPWS General Driver Interface. In: Interactive Planning Work Station User's Manual- Volume 3. AT&T Technologies, Winston-Salem, pp 5.1-5.21

Bournique R (1984b) The Definitive Guide to the IPWS Graphics Package. In: Interactive Planning Work Station User's Manual- Volume 2. AT&T Technologies, Winston-Salem, pp 9.1-9.47

Bournique R (1984c) Picture Editing Made Easier: A Guide to the IPWS Picture Editor. In: Interactive Planning Work Station User's Manual- Volume 2. AT&T Technologies, Winston-Salem, pp 4.1-4.28

Graphical Kernel System (1982) - Functional Description. ISO Draft Proposal ISO/TC 97/SC 5 N 728

Hartman D, Russo SJ, and Udovic S (1984a) The Interactive Planning Work Station- an Introduction. In: Interactive Planning Work Station User's Manual- Volume 2. AT&T Technologies, Winston-Salem, pp 1.1-1.13

Hartman D (1984b) Menu Language for the Interactive Planning Work Station. In: Interactive Planning Work Station User's Manual- Volume 2. AT&T Technologies, Winston-Salem, pp 6.1-6.24

Hartman D, Kashdan S (1984c) The IPWS Database Management System. In: Interactive Planning Work Station User's Manual- Volume 2. AT&T Technologies, Winston-Salem, pp 8.1-8.25

Kashdan S (1984) The Database Editor, qde. In: Interactive Planning Work Station User's Manual- Volume 2. AT&T Technologies, Winston-Salem, pp 9.1-9.24

Kretsch K (1984) GRADIAL Language Specification. In: Interactive Planning Work Station User's Manual- Volume 2. AT&T Technologies, Winston-Salem, pp 5.1-5.25

Status Report of the Graphics Standards Planning Committee (1979) Computer Graphics. 13: 1-150

Witting H (1984) A Design Tutorial Using Basic IPWS Menus. In: Interactive Planning Work Station User's Manual- Volume 2. AT&T Technologies, Winston-Salem, pp 7.1-7.56

The Higgens UIMS
and its Efficient Implementation of Undo

Scott E. Hudson and Roger King

Department of Computer Science, University of Colorado at Boulder, Boulder, CO 80309, USA

ABSTRACT

The Higgens user interface management system being developed at the University of Colorado allows an interface designer to rapidly construct graphical user interfaces based on a primarily non-procedural interface specification. This paper discusses how user recovery and reversal, or Undo, is performed within a Higgens generated interface. A special data model is developed which has unique properties which combine to provide an efficient environment for implementing an undo mechanism. New algorithms based on recent work in incremental attribute evaluation are used to efficiently implement both the generated interfaces as a whole, and the undo mechanism in particular. In addition, a formal model of undo is used in an attempt to evaluate the power of the mechanism in order to compare it with other undo implementations.

INTRODUCTION

User reversal and recovery systems, sometimes called *Undo* systems, have recently been recognized as an important feature in user interfaces. Adding an Undo system to a user interface can have a profound effect on the useability and learnability of the interface. It allows the user to freely explore new or unfamiliar features of the interface without the normal fears of catastrophic mistakes. This greatly enhances the user's confidence, and allows more rapid learning. In addition, the capability to Undo actions allows the user to act in a more exploratory way. The user is able to try tentative actions which answer *what if* type questions without committing to those actions. This capability provides an entirely new level of functionality to a system, without changing any of its overt functionality.

Unfortunately, many previous Undo systems (Archer et.al. 1984; Vitter 1984) have been quite expensive. It has been necessary to produce a series of checkpoints which preserved part or all of some previous state of the system, along with a list of commands which are executed to move from one checkpoint's state to the next. Recovery was accomplished by restoring the state saved in some checkpoint, and reexecuting some saved commands, in order to return to the state requested by the user. Unfortunately, the process of creating a checkpoint is normally slow and often requires large amounts of space.

This paper discusses a technique for constructing efficient user recovery and reversal systems. This technique is employed by user interfaces constructed by the Higgens user interface generator. Higgens generated interfaces use a special data model to describe and implement the semantics of the interface, as well as the application itself. Interfaces constructed using this data model are described in a primarily non-procedural (rule-based) manner. Because of some special properties of this rule-based system, it is possible to construct simple inverses for all actions. This makes construction of a general undo system very easy and efficient.

In addition to being able to provide a powerful and general undo mechanism, the Higgens system has many other advantages for constructing graphical user interfaces. By using the algorithms described later (in section 3), it is able to automatically and efficiently construct graphical interfaces from a primarily non-procedural specification. In this way, the interface designer is free to concentrate on describing the behavior of the system without specifying precisely how or when the system will perform the computations necessary to update the graphical display. The system is able to use the rule-based interface specification to determine how to construct and update both the graphical images and the underlying application data, based on user actions.

This work was supported in part by NSF under grant DMC-8505164 and in part by Hewlett Packard under an American Electronics Association Faculty Development Program fellowship.

In the next section we will talk about the Higgens interface generator and the goals behind it. Section 3 will discuss the powerful data model that underlies Higgens, and how it can be used to easily describe and implement powerful interfaces. Section 4 will discuss how undo can be implemented in a general yet very efficient manner within this data model. Section 5 will discuss the power and limitations of the undo mechanism provided, and finally, section 6 will discuss the current state of the implementation and provide conclusions.

HIGGENS

Higgens, the Human Interface Graphical Generation System, is a tool for automatically generating graphics based user interfaces. Higgens accepts a specification which is primarily non-procedural, and generates a user interface from it. Like some previous work done in generating human interfaces (Kasik 1982; Olsen and Dempsey 1983) it borrows techniques from translator writing systems. Higgens, unlike most previous work in this area does not draw a sharp line between the application and the interface. It works with and has knowledge of the semantics of an application, as well of the interface itself.

One of the major goals of Higgens is to be able to support rapid and incremental development. At the present state of the art even if we use the best available design techniques, it is unlikely that we will be able to fully predict in advance all aspects of how real users will actually use a graphical interface. Consequently, it is not usually possible to create interfaces which have good human factors the first time. In order to produce high quality interfaces we are forced to test them with real users and change them to take the problems found into account. This means that we must often revise not only implementations, but also designs. This problem is particularly severe in the case of user recovery and reversal systems. This aspect of the implementation is traditionally a difficult one. If we are forced to reimplement the undo system each time the interface is modified, it will likely be too expensive to build.

Higgens overcomes this problem by allowing incremental development and by automatically providing an undo facility for all actions. Since interfaces are constructed as a set of semi-independent active entities, a partial working interface can be constructed and tested before the entire interface is finished. Only part of the semantics of each entity need be fully defined to construct a prototype interface which tests that part. In addition, since Higgens generated interfaces are described in a high level manner, changes are much easier to perform than they would be if conventional implementation techniques were used. As a result the designer is able to rapidly construct and test an interface in an incremental fashion, without having to discard all of the work that would have been put into one or more prototype systems. In addition, since Higgens provides a powerful undo facility as a primitive, the semantics of undo can be designed and implemented along with the items it affects, and does not need to be added later once the system is stable.

THE ACTIVE SEMANTICS DATA MODEL

In order to understand how the Undo system works within a Higgens generated interface, it is necessary to understand the *active semantics data model* used to implement much of the functionality of the interface. In a Higgens generated interface, the semantics of both the application and the interface are described by this uniform data model. This data model encapsulates both the data of the application and its semantics.

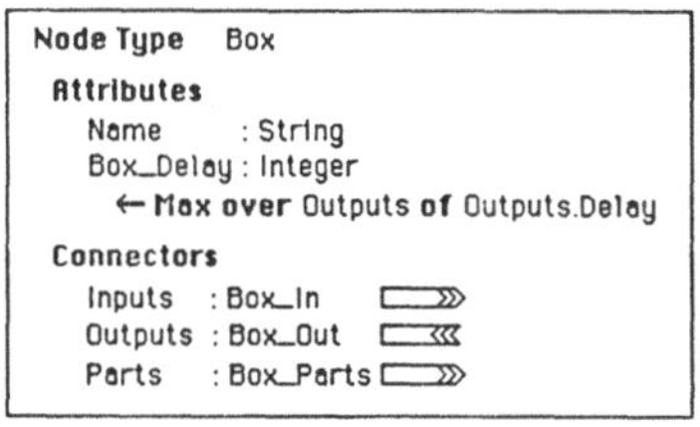

```
Node Type   Box
Attributes
   Name       : String
   Box_Delay  : Integer
      ← Max over Outputs of Outputs.Delay
Connectors
   Inputs  : Box_In    ⟹
   Outputs : Box_Out   ⟸
   Parts   : Box_Parts ⟹
```

Figure 1.

The model employs new algorithms adapted from techniques related to Knuth's attribute grammars (Knuth 1968, 1971) as well as from more recent work on incremental attribute evaluation (Demers et.al 1981; Reps et.al. 1983) used in syntax directed editors. The state of the application and the interface are described in an *attributed graph*. Like the attributed trees often used in compiling, each node of an attributed graph has associated with it a number of *attributes* which describe the internal state of the semantic entity described by that node. In addition, *attribute evaluation rules* are given for computing certain attribute values as a function of other attributes within a given node, and from the values contained in related nodes. This allows the model to actively respond to its environment in a way which reflects its semantics. Finally, the interface designer may attach constraint predicates to attributes to perform error checking, and insure the integrity of the model. These constraints are automatically tested by the system and must always hold.

As an example of how we might use an attributed graph to model an application, we will examine a very simple gate level logic design system. In this system we will design a series of functional units called **Boxes**. As shown in fig. 1, a **Box** consists of (is related to) a set of inputs, a set of output, and a set of parts (gates) which implement its function. For this example, we will be interested in finding the maximum delay time required for each box. Consequently, as shown in fig. 1, we compute an attribute **Box_Delay**, which is defined as the maximum of the **Delay** values transmitted from the outputs.

```
Node Type    Box_Input
Attributes
   Name : String
Connectors
   Owner  : Box_In     ⊏
   Output : Wire       ⊏⟫
   Transmits 0  as Delay
```

```
Node Type    Box_Output
Attributes
   Name : String
Connectors
   Input  : Wire       ⊏
   Owner  : Box_Out    ⊏
   Transmits Input.Delay  as Delay
```

Figure 2.

As shown in fig. 2, these values are in turn derived from the values transmitted along the **Input Wire** relationship. These values come either from a **Box_Input** node (which always supplies 0), or from a **Gate** node. **Gate** nodes calculate a delay as a function of their operation, and logic family type, as shown in fig. 3.

```
Node Type    Gate
Attributes
   Op        : Gate_Operation
   Type      : Logic_Family
   My_Delay  : Integer
      ← Max( In_1.Delay , In_2.Delay ) +
                        Gate_Delay(Op,Type)
Connectors
   Owner     : Box_Parts  ⊏
   In_1, In_2 : Wire      ⊏
   Output    : Wire       ⊏⟫
   Transmits  My_Delay  as Delay
```

Figure 3.

Because of the definition of the attributes in this graph, the model is able to respond automatically to changes. For example, if the user were to change the logic family type of a gate, the system would automatically determine which delay values were no longer correct, and recompute them. This will all happen without the implementor being forced to explicitly describe how or when the computations are to take place. Instead, the system can determine from the attribute evaluation rules exactly what attributes need to be recomputed when a change is made.

Levels of Interface

A Higgens generated interface is divided into 3 levels: application data, views, and abstract devices. The application data level encapsulates the data of the application and implements its semantics. The second level creates one or more *views* of the applications data. A view normally involves selection, filtration, and abstraction of information in order to specificly highlight or emphasize one aspect of the data. In addition, overall decisions about how data will be presented to the user, along with how the user may interact with the data, are done within views. Finally, the third level of abstract devices provides a very abstract and high level interface to the actual graphical I/O devices used.

Each of these levels is implemented using an attributed graph. This means that each level is able to respond to changes in other parts of the system in ways which are meaningful at that level. Entities at the abstract device level can translate the actions of physical devices and affect entities at the level of views. Actions on views can affect the way views are presented, and can be translated into actions on application data. Application data can then respond in ways that are meaningful to the semantics of the application they support. These responses can in turn affect views, abstract devices, and eventually the graphical images presented to the user. This process allows very powerful feedback to occur. This feedback can be not only on the normal lexical and syntactic levels, but can also be on a deeper level which reflects the semantics of the underlying problem domain. It is this powerful semantic feedback which guides the user into forming the helpful mental models needed for good interfaces. In addition, since the specification of the attribute evaluation rules which control this feedback is primarily non-procedural, the designer is free to concentrate on what the feedback will be, and may leave many of the details of how and when it is carried out to the system.

Translating Data Into Views and Images

In order to construct graphical images from data graphs, the conventional approach would be to use programs which traversed the graph extracting information, making decisions, and producing partial images as the traversal proceeds. Such a traversal can in general be very powerful and flexible, since the nature of the traversal can be determined in arbitrarily complex ways based on the actual data encountered in the graph. Higgens uses a traversal process similar to this conventional approach in order to translate its attributed data graphs into views.

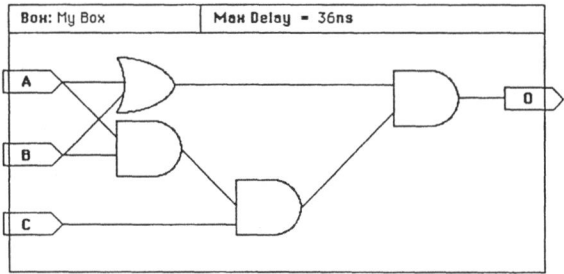

Figure 4.

A Higgens interface specification contains a series of *traversal plans*. These plans determine how traversals proceed based on predicates over the attributes of nodes they visit. However, unlike conventional traversals which exist only as a dynamic series of procedure invocations, Higgens traversals are explicitly represented as data objects. Each visit of a data node is represented by a *viewing* node (thus forming a tree of viewing nodes). These nodes are normal data objects. They are given attributes and attribute evaluation rules. They are persistent, and have access to the attributes of the data node they visit. In this way, they are able to implement the view dependent semantics needed to provide selection, filtering, and abstraction of the underlying data. In addition, each node may render images and accept input from the abstract devices used to implement the graphics of the interface.

For example, in our simple logic design system, the user might want one of several different views of a box. These views could range from a simple summary view showing just a rectangle with the box's name in it, to a complete view like the one in fig. 4, showing all inputs, output, and gates which implement the box. Each of these views can be constructed by a different traversal.

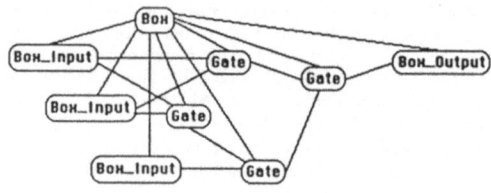

Figure 5a.

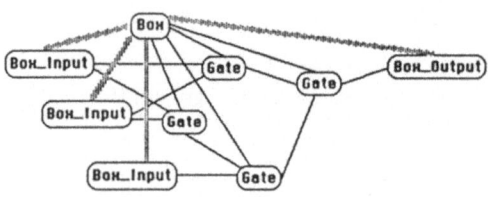

Figure 5b.

As an intermediate example, we will consider a view which shows just the name, maximum delay, inputs, and outputs of a box without showing the gates used to implement it. Figure 5a shows an example data graph corresponding to the view given in fig. 4. Figure 5b shows the path that a traversal would take in order to implement our sample view. This path visits the **box** node itself, then each of the inputs, then finally the single output node. Each of these node visits is represented by a viewing node. Figure 6 shows several of these viewing nodes as they would be created by a traversal.

In order to deal with actual graphical I/O devices, a viewing node communicates with a series of abstract devices. These abstract devices are constructed using the *Planit* picture planning language which is a part of Higgens. Planit allows the interface designer to construct *picture plans*. A picture plan consists of a specification of how (hierarchical) images are to be drawn, and how logical input devices are to be constructed. These specifications describe images and devices based on a set of formal parameters. A viewing node gives a picture plan and provides a set of actual parameters in order to instantiate an abstract device. A viewing node may then at any time change these actual parameters. The images and devices controlled by the picture plan will then be updated to reflect these new actual parameter values. The parameters provided by a viewing node may be intrinsic or derived attributes of the node. In this way, when they are changed, or recomputed, they will directly affect the picture presented to the user. Since picture plans may contain conditionals based on arbitrary expressions of parameters, as well as calls to other picture plans, they can be given arbitrarily complex behavior. Figure 7 illustrates how picture plans would be attached to the viewing nodes of our example.

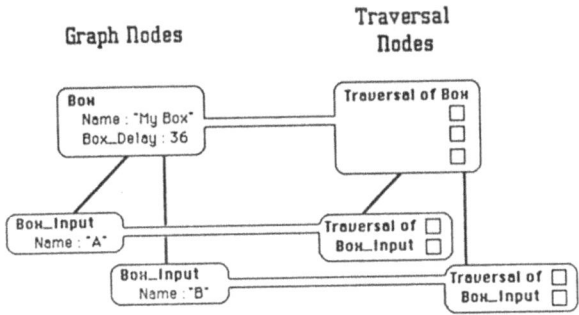

Figure 6.

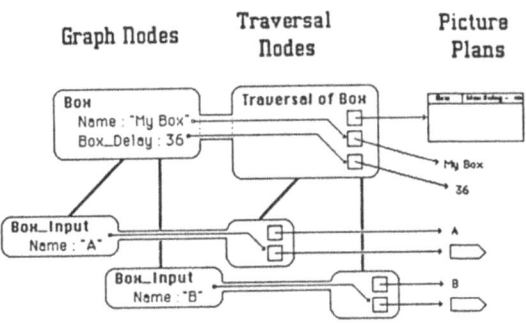

Figure 7.

In addition to presenting output images to the user, abstract devices can respond to user inputs by means of messages sent to viewing nodes. Viewing nodes respond to these messages by invoking editing commands. These editing commands can modify attributes, create and delete data nodes, as well as establish and break relationships within the data graph. In this way, views may translate the actions of devices into actions appropriate to the semantics of the underlying data.

In a Higgens generated interface, feedback can occur at all levels. The user can use actual graphical I/O devices to manipulate the abstract devices presented. The abstract devices send messages to views, which in turn may modify their own attributes, and those of applications nodes in order to carry out user requested actions. These modifications in turn invoke whatever computations are needed in order to satisfy the attribute evaluation rules of the system. These computations propagate their effects throughout the system, and may result in changes to views, or to the traversals that construct views. This in turn may change the parameters of the abstract devices they control. This can finally change the images and logical devices presented to the user. Thus, it is possible for feedback to occur locally at each level, as well as across several levels. In this way, feedback can go beyond the properties of the graphical entities used to present the data, and is able to convey the semantics of the underlying data.

The Attribute Evaluation Algorithm

Whenever changes are made to some part of the attributed graph, the system must ensure that all attributes retain a value which is consistent with the attribute rules given by the interface designer. This requires some sort of an attribute evaluation algorithm. One approach would be to recompute all attribute values every time a change is made to any part of the system. This is clearly too expensive. What is needed is an algorithm for incremental attribute evaluation, which computes only those attributes whose values change as a result of a given modification. This problem also arises in the area of syntax directed editing systems, so it is not surprising that algorithms exist to solve this problem for the attribute grammars used in that application. The most successful of these algorithms is due to Reps (1984). Reps' algorithm is optimal in the sense that only attributes whose values actually change are recomputed, and that the total overhead of the algorithm is $O(|Changed|)$, where Changed is the set of attributes whose values actually change.

Unfortunately, Reps' algorithm, while optimal for attributed trees, does not seem to extend directly to the arbitrary graphs used by a Higgens generated interface. Instead, a new incremental attribute evaluation algorithm has been designed for use with Higgens. This new algorithm is simpler, and exhibits similar behavior to Reps' algorithm. In particular, for any given change it will never recompute an attribute that would not have been recomputed by Reps' optimal algorithm. However, it does have a slightly inferior worst case upper bound on the amount of overhead incurred.

The algorithm works by using a strategy which first determines what work has to be done, then performs the actual computations. The algorithm uses the dependencies between attributes. An attribute is dependent on another attribute if that attribute is mentioned in its attribute evaluation rule (i.e. is needed to compute the derived value of that attribute). When the value of an intrinsic attribute is changed, it may cause the attributes which depend on it to become *out of date* with respect to their defining attribute evaluation rules. Instead of immediately recomputing these values, we simply mark them as out of date. We then find all attributes which are dependent on these newly out of date attributes, and mark them out of date as well.

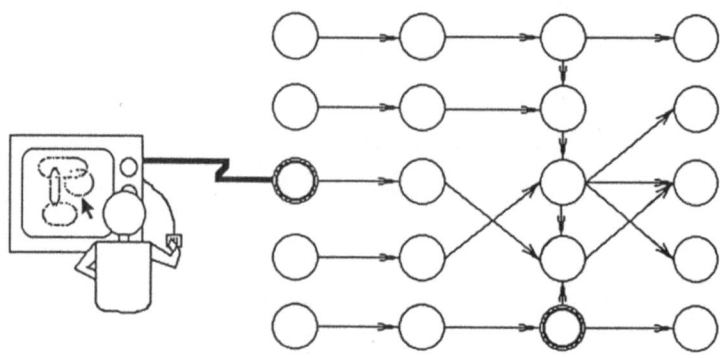

Figure 8.

This process continues until we have marked all affected attributes. During this process of marking, we determine if each marked attribute is *important*. Attributes are said to be important if they have a constraint predicate attached to them, or if part of the current graphical display depends on them. When we have completed marking attributes during the first phase of the algorithm, we will have obtained a list of attributes which are both out of date and important. We can then use a demand driven algorithm to evaluate these attributes in a simple recursive manner. The calculation of attribute values which are not important may be deferred, as they have no immediate effect on the interface or the application. If user actions cause abstract devices or views to be changed, new attributes may become important, and new computations of out of data attributes may be invoked in order to obtain the values needed to construct new displays. In fig. 8, we have presented a set of attributes in order to illustrate how the attribute evaluation algorithm works. The circles represent individual attributes. How these attributes are distributed among nodes is not important to the evaluation algorithm, only the dependencies between attributes are important. In this case, two attributes have been designated important. One provides a parameter to a picture plan which controls part of the current display. The other has a constraint predicate attached. For this example, we will presume that the attribute marked with an X in fig. 9 has been changed by some user action. The first phase of the algorithm responds to this change by marking a series of attributes as out of date. These attributes have been marked in gray in fig. 9.

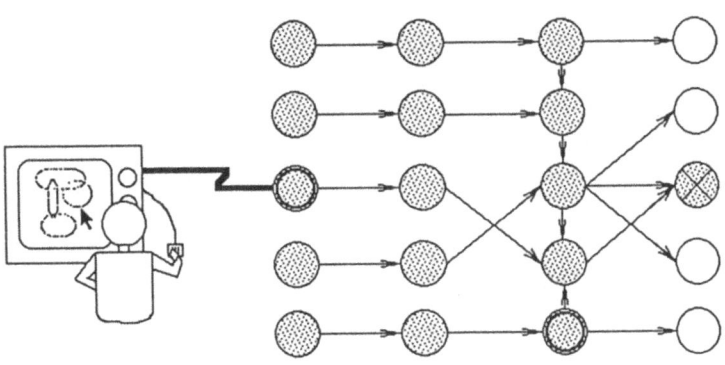

Figure 9.

Notice that along with a number of other nodes, the two important nodes have been marked out of date. These nodes will be remembered for use in the second phase of the algorithm. During the second phase, the system will attempt to obtain correct values for all important attributes using a simple recursive evaluation strategy. The evaluation starts with each important attribute which is also marked out of date, and recursively evaluates only those attributes need to obtain the original important attribute value. The attributes that are reevaluated in the second phase for our example are marked in fig. 10. Once the second phase of the algorithm is complete, the graph will be left in the state shown in fig. 11. Notice that a number of attributes are left with out of date values. The values of these attributes cannot affect the observable state of the system, therefore, we can safely defer their computation. If the same change made here is done several times, the system will not be forced to recompute these values several times despite the fact that none of them will actually be used. Instead, the attributes will retain their old out of date values until the correct values are actually needed.

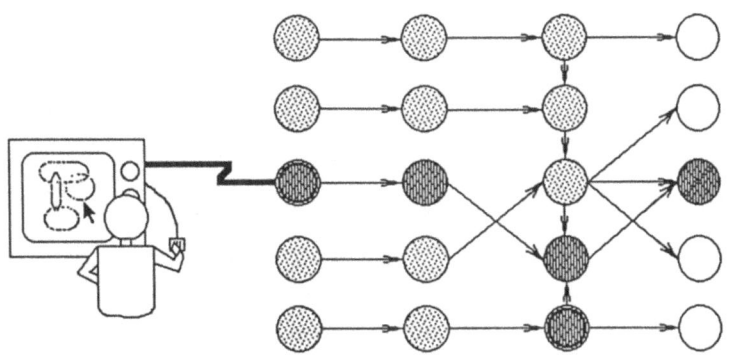

Figure 10.

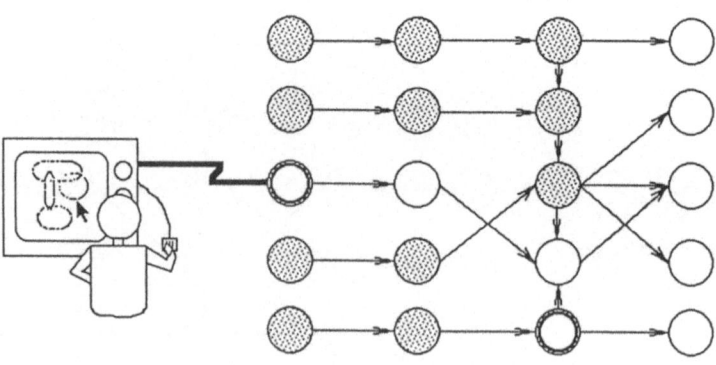

Figure 11.

In order to support actions which change not only the attributes of the application data but also, its structure (i.e. the relationships between entities) a process similar to that used for intrinsic attribute changes is used. When a relationship is broken, the system determines which derived attributes depend on values that are passed across the relationship. These attributes are marked out of date just as if an intrinsic attribute had changed. When a relationship is established, the second half of the attribute evaluation algorithm is invoked to evaluate attributes which are out of date and important. In order to insure that derived attributes can always be given a valid value, and hence a display generated, the system insures that relationships are not left dangling across attribute evaluations. This is either done explicitly by application supplied actions, or where necessary the system will provide special dummy nodes to tie off any dangling relationships.

During the evaluation of attributes, certain attributes will have constraint predicates attached to them. By attaching a constraint predicate to an attribute, the interface designer is able check for error conditions, and insure the semantic integrity of all entities. After an attribute is evaluated, any attached constraint predicates are tested. If any of these evaluates false, a constraint violation exists. By default, this causes the user command invoking the evaluation to fail and be undone. Optionally, a special recovery action associated with the constraint can be invoked to attempt to recover from the violation. In either case, the constraint must be satisfied or the user command invoking the evaluation will fail and be undone. The next section will discuss how user recovery and reversal is actually performed, and how the boundaries between user commands are established.

EXECUTION AND REVERSAL

It would seem that the large amounts of derived data, along with the fact that the order of computations is not defined, and that some computations are deferred, would make creating a general user reversal and recovery system a difficult task. However, as it turns out, the properties of the active semantics data model combine to provide an excellent environment for efficient implementation of a user recovery and reversal system. Note that the set of attribute evaluation rules can be used at any time to obtain the values of derived attributes from the set of intrinsic attribute values. This means that in order to Undo commands which simply change attributes, the only action needed is to restore the old values of those attributes changed, and invoke the normal attribute evaluation mechanism used to respond to these changes. The system will restore itself to its old state automatically. Similarly, commands which change the structure of the attributed graph, need only remember the old structure in order to allow for their complete reversal. It is this simplicity which makes user reversal and recovery efficient in a Higgens generated interface.

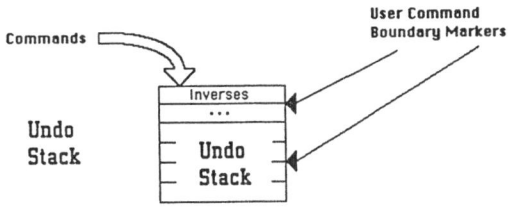

Figure 12.

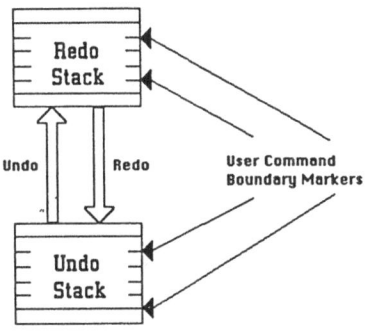

Figure 13.

Primitive Commands

We can now examine the kinds of primitive commands needed to effectively deal with the attributed graphs used to implement the interface, and how the effects of each of these primitives can be reversed. Clearly we need a command to replace the value of an intrinsic attribute. We also need a command to create a new node of a given type, to delete a node, to break a connection between nodes, and finally to establish a new connection between nodes. We will call these primitive commands **assignment, create, delete, cut,** and **connect.** Notice that each of these primitive commands has a simple inverse as shown below.

Operation	Inverse
Assignment	an **assignment** which restores the old value of the attribute
Create	a **delete** of the **created** node
Delete	replacement of the deleted node
Cut	a **connect** between the affected nodes
Connect	a **cut** of the affected relationship

Because each primitive command has a simple inverse, we are not forced to determine or remember the full effects of each command to be able to reverse its action. Instead, we need only remember its inverse. The system is able to derive the reversal of its full effects in the same way it derived the effects to begin with.

In addition, we can use this same capability to provide a Redo mechanism. The user may wish to undo an undo; that is they may wish to redo the original operation. Since all primitive operations have an inverse which is also a primitive command, the system can reconstruct original commands from their inverses in much the same way that the inverses were constructed to begin with. In this way, the system has the ability to redo commands after they have been undone. Unfortunately, whenever new commands are executed after an undo, the system will be unable to redo old commands, since the new commands may have destroyed something which the old commands depend upon. As we will see in section 5, this places a limit on the power of the undo mechanism provided.

In order to make effective use of primitive commands to act upon attributed graphs, we need to embed them in control structures. We need the conditionals, loops, and procedural abstraction mechanisms found in more traditional programming languages. However, in order to reverse commands, we need only record the sequence of inverses for the primitive commands actually executed, without regard for the control structures which arranged for their original execution. Using these inverse commands, it is possible to fully reverse the effect of commands without explicitly reexecuting their control structures.

User Level Commands

Although the primitive commands described above provide a good mechanism for the designer to describe the implementation of the interface, they are not suitable for use directly as user commands. Instead, user commands are normally built as a series of primitive commands embedded in control structures. From the user's point of view, however, this internal structure is invisible, and commands appear as atomic units. Because of this, it would be highly inappropriate to undo and redo individual primitive commands. Instead commands should be undone and redone in groups which correspond to what the user considers atomic operations. In order to accomplish this, Higgens provides a means for declaring the boundaries of user commands. As shown in fig. 12, as operations are performed, their inverses are automatically saved on an undo stack for possible later reversal. In order to allow the manipulation of whole user commands instead of primitives, Higgens allows the interface implementor to use a special command which marks the boundaries of user commands on the undo stack. Later when an undo action is invoked, Higgens will undo all primitive commands up to the last mark and construct a corresponding redo stack for those commands. As shown in fig. 13, an undo operation performs the saved inverse operations, and pushes the recreated original commands onto the redo stack. Similarly, if a later redo action is performed, Higgens redoes all primitive commands up to the last command mark, and places their inverses on the undo stack. In this way, the interface designer is able to implement user commands using whatever primitives and control structures are needed, while still allowing the system to undo actions in chunks which are meaningful to the user.

POWER OF THE HIGGENS UNDO MECHANISM

In (Gordon et.al. 1984) an elegant formal model of undo systems is constructed which allows us to compare and characterize the power of various undo strategies. Their model makes use of the following formal entities:

S	a set of extended states (including history information)
$c(s)$	the contents of an extended state s (excluding history information)
O	a set of operations mapping extended states to extended states [denote applying operation k to state s as ks]
u in O	an Undo operation
K	a subset of O not including u

Notice that a state s in S includes whatever history of previous commands is needed in order to be able to perform undo operations. In a Higgens generated system this includes the attributed graph as well as the undo and redo stacks (which we will refer to as the *history*). The expression $c(s)$ is used to denote the state s without its associated history. In a Higgens generated system this includes just the attributed graph.

Based on these entities, we can define a formal property which captures our intuitive notion of undo. This property is the Basic Undo Property.

Basic Undo Property:
    $c(uks) = c(s)$ for all s in S and all k in K

In addition to this basic property, Gordon et.al. define two other important properties that we would like undo systems to have.

Thoroughness:
$$c(o_n...o_1 uks) = c(o_n...o_1 s)$$
for all s in **S** and o_i in **O** (possibly including u)

Invertibility:
$$c(rus) = c(s) \quad \text{for all s in \textbf{S} and some r in \textbf{O}}$$

Intuitively, the thoroughness property insures that an undo is complete, that the state returned to by using an undo can in no way be distinguished from the original state (even when we consider the behavior of the undo or redo operators). Invertibility insures that a redo operation (r) exists, so that undo operations are not themselves irreversible. Both these properties are highly desirable, unfortunately, it is can be show that no non-trivial system can be both thorough and invertible. As a consequence Gordon et.al. explore a somewhat weaker form of thoroughness called unstacking.

Unstacking:
$$c(u^n f_n...f_1 s) = c(s) \quad \text{for } f_i \text{ in \textbf{K} and any positive n}$$

It can be shown that systems with separate undo and redo operations can be both unstacking and invertible. In fact, these are precisely the properties that a Higgens generated interface has. The user can undo arbitrary sequences of operations by repeated applications of the undo operation, and can redo operations so long as new operations are not performed. More formally, the Basic Undo Property holds since

$$c(upg) = c(g) \quad \text{for any primitive operation p and any}$$
attributed graph (and history) g

The Invertibility property holds since Higgens supports a redo operator r such that

$$c(rug) = c(g) \quad \text{for any attributed graph and history g}$$

The Unstacking property holds since

$$c(u^n p_n...p_1 g) = c(g) \quad \text{for any primitive operations } p_i$$

but, the Thoroughness property fails since

$$c(rrupupg) <> c(ppg)$$

It is not clear at this point if unstacking is the most powerful property that might be achieved in conjunction with invertibility (while still retaining the basic undo property). However, it does seem clear that it is at least near what we can hope to achieve given the theoretical limits that exist, and it compares favorably with existing undo systems.

CONCLUSION

The Higgens system is currently being implemented at the University of Colorado at Boulder. A prototype of the abstract device description language Planit which makes up part of Higgens, has been completed. The current implementation runs on a Silicon Graphics IRIS display device connected to a VAX, and on a SUN workstation. The remainder of the system is under development and is scheduled for completion in middle to late 1985.

In this paper we have discussed the user recovery and reversal mechanism used in the Higgens interface generation system. Despite the very powerful data model used to implement Higgens generated interfaces, they provide an efficient undo mechanism in a way which is fully integrated with the rest of the system. This technique greatly improves the useability of human interfaces, and makes learning to use these interfaces much easier.

Acknowledgements

The authors would like to thank Dan Olsen of BYU. The original form of the incremental attribute evaluation algorithm we use in the Higgens system emerged from a long discussion between Dan and one of the authors. The authors would also like to thank Clayton Lewis for introducing us to the formal notion of undo that he and his colleagues have developed.

REFERENCES

Archer J, Conway R, Schneider FB (1984) User Recovery and Reversal in Interactive Systems. TOPLAS 6: 1-19

Demers A, Reps T, Teitelbaum T (1981) Incremental Evaluation for Attribute Grammars with Application to Syntax Directed Editors. Proceedings 8th Principles of Programming Languages Conference 105-116

Gordon RF, Leeman GB, Lewis CH (1984) Concepts and Implications of Interactive Recovery. IBM Tech Report RC 10562 (#47293), IBM Thomas J. Watson Research Center, Yorktown Heights, NY

Kasik DJ (1984) A User Interface Management System. Computer Graphics 16: 99-106

Knuth DE (1968) Semantics of Context-Free Languages. Math. Systems Theory J. 2: 127-145

Knuth DE (1971) Semantics of Context-Free Languages: Correction. Math. Systems Theory J. 5: 95-96

Olsen DR, Dempsey EP (1983) SYNGRAPH: A Graphical User Interface Generator. SIGGRAPH '83 Conference Proceedings 43-50

Reps T, Teitelbaum T, Demers A (1983) Incremental Context-Dependent Analysis for Language-Based Editors. TOPLAS 5: 449-477

Reps T, (1984) Generating Language-Based Environments. MIT Press, Cambridge, Mass.

Vitter J (1984) US&R: A New Framework for Redoing. SIGPLAN Notices 19: 168-176

Graphics Interaction in Databases

Claude Frasson and Mohammed Erradi

Départment d'informatique et de recherche opérationnelle, Université de Montréal, C.P. 6128, Succ, A., Montréal, Québec, H3C 3J7, Canada

ABSTRACT

This paper is intended to highlight the evolution of interaction techniques between users and database systems. We examine the evolution of database query languages and emphasize the importance of the graphical interface taking in account the availability of new functionalities and the users demand. Then, using examples in a medical environment, we present the characteristics of an interactive graphical language based on icons.

KEYWORDS

Database query languages, interaction techniques, icons, graphics and pictures.

INTRODUCTION

The evolution of database systems was characterized by an increase of the power of data manipulation languages. At the beginning, programming languages were the only means available for interacting with the data. In fact, the method used was complex, long and intended for programmers or specialists. At that time the end user was not given much consideration. Progressively, the need for a more powerful interaction became necessary. The interface particularly evolved with the relational model allowing non procedural languages (Astrahan & Ap 1976; Chamberlin 1980; Relational Software Inc. 1984).

Availability of relational database systems, word processing and others software on micro-computers permitted to reach a new class of users. They are mostly non specialized users who generally wish a ready-to-use and simple system which does not require technical knowledge.

However, professionals requirements also contributed to a more sophisticated interface which might lead to better productivity. In addition, new types of data such as graphics or images, which convey a great quantity of information, are more and more used in various domains.

Finally, recent techniques like the mouse, bit-mapped displays and multiple-window screen management enable users to directly and easily perform their tasks.

In that context, a graphics interface now appears useful. Going further, an icon is sufficiently expressive to be understood by large group of users and used for communicating with databases.

In this paper we highlight the evolution of interaction techniques and justify the present importance of a graphics interface in databases. Then we present the main characteristics of a language which uses icons as a support to easily manipulate various types of data: structured data (numeric or alphanumeric) and unstructured data (text, image, voice) which will be more and more required in an end-user environment. Examples are given in a medical context.

THE EVOLUTION OF QUERY LANGUAGES

Programming languages progressively evolved to be independent of the type of the computer, of the external memories and of the access methods. The concept of physical and logical independence, introduced by Date (Date and Hopewell 1971), and the need for a centralized data management were at the origin of the databases systems.

The development of architectures and languages has successively gone through hierarchical, network and relational models.

a. Hierarchical (IMS/VS 1979) and network (Data Base Task Group of CODASYL 1971) languages are intended for programmers and even for programmers who are familiar with the process of navigating through the database.

Before formulating a query it is necessary to define a set of procedures in order to "communicate" with the portion of the database choosen by the user: for instance, a program communication block (PCB), in IMS, or a schema and a subschema, in a network type language. In addition, procedures to find the data obey a "top-down-left-right" process (for hierarchies) or a list processing approach (network). Generally they have to be included in a host language (COBOL, PL/1, FORTRAN,...).

b. Several high-level data manipulation languages have been designed for the relational model. Four different strategies can be distinguished:

- Languages based on relational algebra which manipulate relations using a set of operators (union, difference, intersection, product, join, projection, selection) and which are procedural because we must know how to get what we want. However the underlying concepts are important.

- Relational calculus is non-procedural and represents a desirable property but it is hard to understand and use.

- Transform-oriented languages are non-procedural languages which provide easy-to-use structures for expressing what is desired in terms of what is known. This approach is represented by SEQUEL (Chamberlin 1980) and other similar languages which served as a basis for industrial products (SQL/DATA 1981; Relational Software Inc. 1984).

The fourth class of relational languages is graphic. They provide users with a picture of the relations to manipulate. The user fills in tables on the screen, entering an example of what he wants in the appropriate place. Query-by-Example (QBE) (Zloof 1975) and CUPID (McDonald and Stonebraker 1975) are the most representative of those languages. We give some examples of QBE in the next section.

Except for the two languages mentionned above, the needs of the non-specialist have been neglected before the eighties. Even SEQUEL required to be included in a host programming language. After 1980, the availability of microcomputers (Frasson 1984) increased the need for a more sophisticated user interface and new languages were developed with this goal: Dbase III (Dbase III 1984), knowledge-Manager (Knowledge Man 1983), Microrim (Rbase 4000, 6000, 1984), for instance. They first provide a very simple way and powerful functions for interacting with the data. Then, additional primitive operations make the languages more powerful, self-contained, providing for better productivity of programmers. Correspondingly, a new layer has been added to SQL in order to be directly used by end-users.

THE IMPORTANCE OF THE GRAPHICAL INTERFACE

The advantage of a graphical query language was first noted by Zloof with QBE (Zloof 1975). A query may be built up in any order the user likes which is important because the perception of a problem and the solution are generally different for different users. When an end-user understands his own needs, he wishes a direct and visual interaction with the computer. He wants to query without having to worry about procedural details. CUPID (McDonald and Stonebraker 1975), implemented on top of a predicate calculus language, is another graphical language in which the user builts queries by light-pen manipulation of a set of symbols.

However, the interest in a graphical interface was not really emphasized before the beginning of the eighties when two forces converged: new developments of researches in graphics and image processing, and the availability of new interactive facilities.

- The Pictorial approach.
    There exists two major types of pictorial processing

First, the pattern recognition and image processing community (PRIP) uses pictorial information for specific applications such as various LANDSAT processing (geography, cartography, earth resources analyses...), medical imaging, shape and fingerprint recognition, ... An original image is transformed into another image (more distinct), a simplified form (sketch) or a symbolic description.

Second, the computer graphics applications lead to an interactive design of pictures from descriptions.

Both approaches aim at utilization of database systems, and particularly relational systems, for supporting the descriptions.

Figure 1 shows the different categories of that the user can interact with.

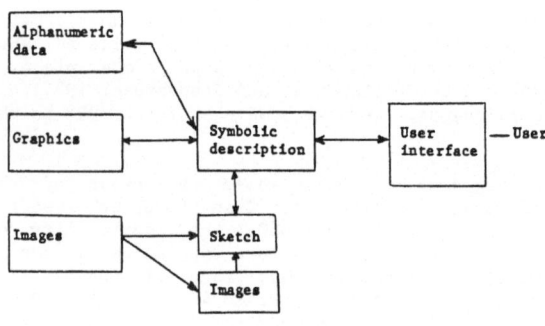

Fig. 1

The need for integrating various types of data in a database system resulted in a vast effort of the different communities.

An interesting survey of the subject is given in (Tamura and Yokoya 1984; Erradi and Frasson 1984). (Kunii and Harada 1980) emphasize the need for graphical interaction in CAD. (Chang and Kunii 1981) present and discuss different approaches to pictorial database design. A fundamental step for enhancement of the man-machine communication is presented by (Chang and Fu 1980, 1981) as an extension of QBE: Query by Pictorial-Example. The user can manipulate images or introduce pictorial examples in order to formulate pictorial queries. To illustrate the following discussion, we will consider a simple relational model concerning patients and teeth:

   Patient (Pat-id, name, address, phone, age)

   Pat-tooth (Frame, Pat-id, tooth-id, tooth-name)

   Jaw (Frame, Tooth-id, Jaw-id)

   Disease-desc (Tooth-id, Disease, tooth, date)

Pictures of teeth (for instance X-Ray) are taken separately, and a jaw presents a general view of all the teeth of a patient. They are identified by a frame number.

Q1: Give the name and age of corresponding patients having a cavity on the molar-37.

In QPE (as in QBE) the user enters Patient, Pat-tooth and Disease-desc as the table-names and fills in the columns.

Patient	Pat-id	Name	Address	Phone	Age
	X̲	P.			P.

Pat-tooth	Frame	Pat-id	Tooth-id	Tooth-name
		X̲.	Y̲	

Disease-desc	Tooth-id	Disease	Tooth	Date
	Y̲	cavity	Molar -37	

Q2: Find the patient whose tooth is pointed on the screen. This request can only be formulated in QPE.

Pat-tooth	Frame	Pat-id	Tooth-id	Tooth-name
		X̲	@	

Patient	Pat-id	Name	Address	Phone	Age
	X̲	P. Y̲			

This illustrates a capability of QPE. For more details about the syntax see (Chang and Fu 1980).

Q3: Show the complete description of the jaw of patient John. Also, this query can be formulated in QPE only, using the DISPLAY (DIS) function.

Patient	Pat-id	Name	Address	Phone	Age
	X̲	John			

Pat-tooth	Frame	Pat-id	Tooth-id	Tooth-name
		X̲	Y̲	

Jaw	Frame	Tooth-id	Jaw-id
Dis.		Y̲	

- New-interactive facilities.

    Graphical aids evidently enhance the interaction. However, there is an increasing need for more sophisticated user interfaces (Herot 1982), (Schneiderman 1982). A user-interface based on interactive techniques, like the mouse and the bit-mapped display (Ellis and Bernal 1982), (Smith et al. 1982) enables users to perform their tasks more directly and easily (Williams 1983).

An important aspect of human behaviour is that it can understand the meaning of a symbolic picture (an icon) at a glance unlike the meaning of a page of alphanumeric data (even in a structured form). In various domains (medicine, scientific applications, mechanic, traffic control, ...) icons are used for an easy communication with group of users. Taking in account this capability of the human brain to process picture more efficiently than text we designed (Frasson and Erradi 1985) an interactive system based on icons.

AN ICON-BASED INTERFACE

Our approach uses an iconic interface for directly handling both alphanumeric data and images. This interface is made up of a set of objects familiar to the user and of a set of operations which can be performed on these objects. We distinguish three areas on the screen (Fig. 2).

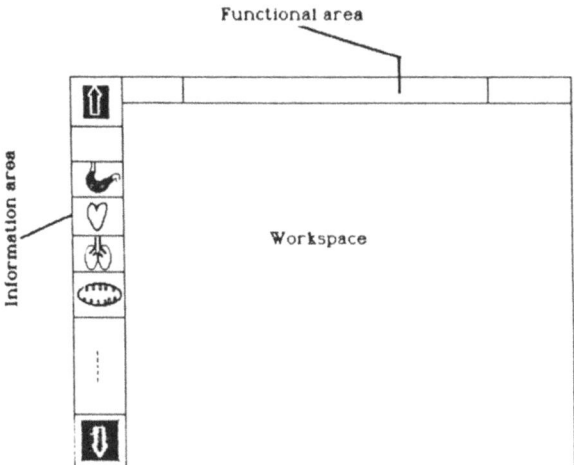

Fig. 2   The areas of interface

The information area can contain the different kind of objects to be manipulated and also the properties associated with an object. Objects represented on Fig. 2 concern a stomach, a heart, lungs and a jaw. The properties appear in the information area by cliking on the selected object while this one appears in the workspace. For instance, diseases such as cancer, pleuristy, pneumonia (which can affect lungs), or cavity, crawn, bridge,... (which can affect the teeth of a jaw). Notice that properties can also be represented by icons.

The functional area contains the types of operations associated with the objects. We distinguish icons commands (creating or modifying icons), retrieval and functions.

The workspace area is a window where an object (selected by clicking on the corresponding icon) can be manipulated using commands in the functional area.

Figure 3 shows a jaw of a patient with a list of properties associated in the information area. They represent diseases of teeth and the icons represented here are actually used by the dentists. For instance, the meaning of those icons is the following:

- • : cavity
- N : open contact
- ⊗ : crown
- / : absent tooth
- ⌒ : present filling

- o—o : fixed bridge
- Ω : chronicle periapical periodontis
- ∥ : present root canal
- ∿ : radicular resorption
- ↻ : rotation

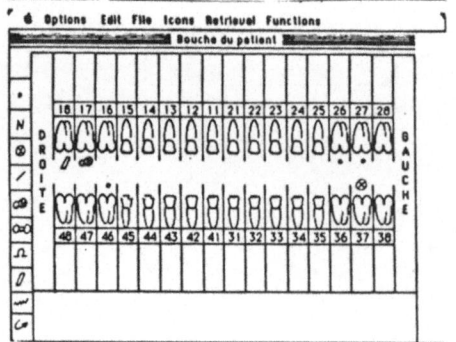

Fig. 3

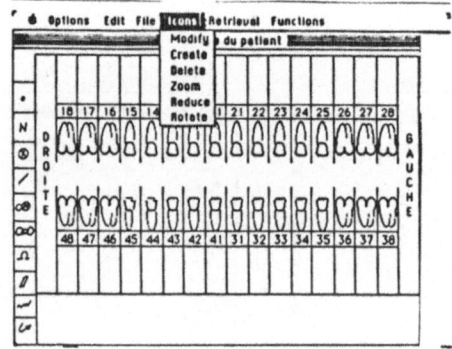

Fig. 4

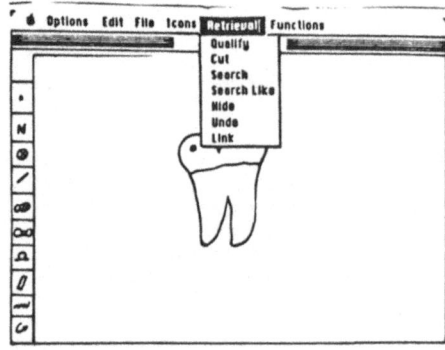

Fig. 5

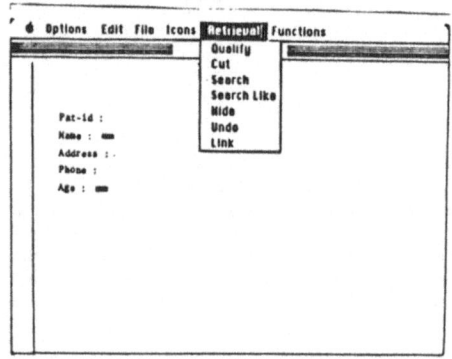

Fig. 6

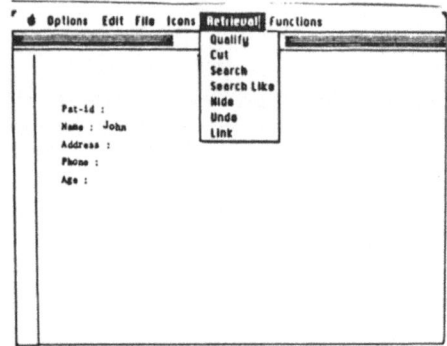

Fig. 7

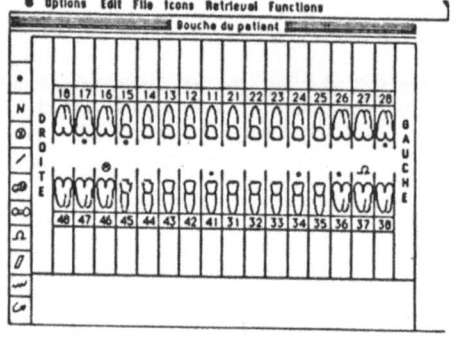

Fig. 8

The user can select properties and assign them to teeth using only the mouse. The resulting object is modified or can serve as a model for a retrieval as we will see in the next examples.

Teeth can also be choosen independently from the information area as indicated on Fig. 5 which represents molar-37.

Figures 4 and 5 exhibit some commands available in the functional area.

Let us see how the queries mentionned above can be formulated in such a system.

Q1: We select the molar-37 in the information area and assign a cavity by clicking successively on the corresponding icon (information area) and on the tooth (Fig. 5). Then, we select the SEARCH LIKE and LINK options in the retrieval commands in order to bind the tooth with other objects. Clicking on the patient icon - this icon is not shown here and looks like:

will bring the attributes of a patient into the workspace. The results will be obtained after a quick selection (by clicking) on Name, Age and on the SEARCH command (Fig. 6).

Notice that all these operations are performed very quickly with the mouse. As in QBE a condition box is available for relational comparisons.

Q2: This query is similar to the previous manipulation, starting with a tooth of a patient.

Q3: Here, we first select "John" by clicking on the patient icon and filling in the attribute name-with the value "John" (Fig. 7. We select the SEARCH option and we bind this occurence using LINK.

Selecting the jaw icon, we obtain the result shown in Fig. 8 which represents John's jaw.

The SEARCH LIKE command retrieves similar pictures. As we can see on Fig. 3 the properties assigned to each tooth mean: "exists somewhere on the tooth". However, the precise location can be obtained by retrieving the corresponding tooth alone.

Other examples in a medical context are given in (Frasson and Erradi 1985). Icons are used as a simplified support for image and textual manipulation. An important fact is that it is not always necessary to consider a precise and complete image of the object to understand the meaning of the underlying information (objects are generally familiar to the user). However a simplified and direct manipulation is more important.

Some aspects of the present system have been implemented on a Macintosh, in Mac-Forth, using file access techniques. Extension to a relational system is under way together with other types of objects.

CONCLUSION

The system we have designed is intended for users interested by the principle of "what you get is what you see". It uses an object oriented interface and a direct manipulation. The interaction is controlled by the system so that only sequences of authorized operations are allowed.

Preliminary tests have shown an easy and rapid manipulation. We are now examining its extension to other domains of application.

ACKNOWLEDGMENTS

We would like to thank Jan Gecsei for his comments and the different students who have participated to the preliminary tests. This research was supported by the NSERC under grant A0196.

REFERENCES

Astrahan M & Ap (1976) System R: A Relational Approach to Database Management. ACM TODS 1,2.

Bachman CW (1973) The Programmer as Navigator. CACM 16, 11.

Chang SK, Kunii T (1981) Pictorial Database systems. Computer 14, 11.

Chang NS, FU KS (1980) Query by Pictorial Example. IEEE. Trans. Soft. Eng. SE6.

Chang NS, Fu KS (1981) Picture Query Languages for Pictorial Database Systems. Computer 14, 23-33.

Chamberlin D (1980) A Summary of User Experience with SQL Data Sublanguage. Proc. International Conference on Data Bases. Aberdeen, Scotland.

Date CJ, Hopewell P. (1971) File Definition and Logical Data Independence. Proc. ACM SIGFIDET Workshop on data description access and control.

Dbase III [TM] (1984) Dbase III Reference Guide. Ashton Tate.

Data Base Task Group of CODASYL (1971) Programming Language Committee Report. Available from BCS, ACM.

Ellis C, Bernal M (1982) Officetalk-d, an Experimental Office Information System. Proc. ACM, SIGOA conf.

Erradi M, Frasson C (1984) Image Database Systems. Département d'informatique et de recherche opérationnelle, Université de Montréal. Internal report no 155.

Frasson C (1984) Bases de données sur micro-ordinateurs. Département d'informatique et de recherche opérationnelle, Université de Montréal. Publication no 498.

Frasson C, Erradi M (1985) An Icon-Based Language for Applications in Medicine. Département d'informatique et de recherche opérationnelle, Université de Montréal. Internal report no 158.

Herot C (1982) Graphical User Interfaces. Proc. of the NYU symposium on user interfaces.

IMS/VS (1979) Information Management System / Virtual Storage. General Information Manual GH20-1260, IBM, White Plains N.Y.

Knowledge Man (1983) Reference Guide. Micro Data Base Systems. Lafayette.

Kunii T, Harada M (1980) SID: A System for Interactive Design. AFIPS Conf. Proc.

Mapper 5 and 6 (1983) Reference Guide. Sperry Inc. Mississauga, Ontario.

McDonald N, Stonebraker M (1975) CUPID, The Friendly Query Language. Proc. ACM Pacific Conference. San Francisco.

Rbase 4000, 6000 (1984) Reference Guide. Microrim Inc. Bellevue.

Relational Software Inc. (1984) ORACLE Introduction Version 1.3. Available from RSI, 3000 Sond Hill Road, Menlo Park, California 94025.

Schneiderman B (1982) The Future of Interactive Systems and the Emergence of Direct Manipulation. Proc. of the NYU Symposium on User Interfaces.

Smith D, Irby C, Kimball R, Verplank B, Harshem E (1982) Designing the Star User Interface. Byte vol 7 no 4.

SQL/Data System General Information (1981). IBM Document GH24-5012-0.

Tamura H, Yokoya N (1984) Image Database Systems: A Survey. Pattern Recognition vol 17 no 1.

Williams G (1983) The Lisa Computer System. Byte vol 8 2.

Zloof, MM (1975) Query by example. Proc. National Computer Conference, vol 44. AFIPS Press.

Interface Abstractions for an *naplps* Page Creation System

Ernest Chang

Department of Computer Science, University of Victoria, Box 1700, Victoria, B.C. V8W 2Y2, Canada

ABSTRACT

Computer programs that allow humans to create pictures are called *paint* systems. Those that use geometrical shapes as building blocks, rather than brushes, are *element-based*, rather than *canvas-based*. The *naplps* graphics encoding standard, used primarily for videotex, lends itself to the creation of element-based paint systems. The user interface for such a system can be rather complex, because of the need to choose shapes, colours, textures, and the need for editing functions. This paper presents some interface techniques that present the user with a number of easily understood abstractions such as a colour bar, function buttons, and element *groups* that facilitate the creation of *naplps* graphics.

1. INTRODUCTION

A paint system [Plebon, Booth 1982; Smith 1978; Tanner 1983] is a computer program that facilitates the interactive creation of graphic images, using techniques analogous to those found in traditional artistic media. Some paint systems treat the screen as a simple canvas, which is successively covered with colours and textures. The software, and user interface, is correspondingly simple since there is only one major function to support, that of adding more colour. The performance of this class of *canvas-based* paint systems is very fast when implemented on a frame buffer.

More flexible paint systems can define graphic elements, that are remembered as unique entities in display lists, even if they are covered on the screen by other elements. These entities, and subsets of them, can be selected, deleted, copied, moved, or modified. These *element-based* paint systems typically require more complex software, and a user-interface that is no longer analogous to traditional techniques in art. This problem is compounded by the addition of facilities for entering text in different sizes, colours, orientations and fonts. This paper deals with the demands that an element-based paint system makes of the user interface, in the context of the naplps [DSA 1983] videotex environment, and the use of abstractions in its implementation.

2. NAPLPS and VIDEOTEX

The North American Presentation Level Protocol Syntax [DSA 1983], known commonly as *naplps*, is a communications standard using 7-bit or 8-bit codes to represent graphical and text images. The idea is to use the same bit combinations to define multiple code sets, with a mechanism for invoking a particular set as the **active** code set. Graphic elements, and their attributes, are represented by one code set, alphanumeric text by another, and so on.

An underlying assumption in naplps is that a function or attribute, once invoked, remains active until specifically reset. There is always a current graphical element, a current colour, etc. Another fundamental premise is that graphical images are constructed from dots, lines, arcs, rectangles and polygons. These are the building blocks for the image creator. The naplps approach to colour is also important: it assumes that a colour map is used, which permits a small number of colour *entries* to take on values from a larger range of colours.

Some implications of these characteristics are that the encoding is **sequential**, that the user **selects** the current active attributes, and that **colours** can be modified. To understand how these affect the user-interface, we must refer to the physical context in which naplps is used.

To date, naplps has been used mainly in videotex [Miller, 1983], which transmits combined text and graphics as *pages* over low-speed communications lines to large numbers of subscribers. The cost-performance characteristics of the videotex market has produced hardware naplps decoders costing about $1000 that typically give 256 X 200 resolution, support 16 displayable from 4096 colours, communicate at 300 to 9600 baud, and use 8-bit microprocessors. This relatively slow graphics system yields figures that take a long time to fill, especially if texture patterns are used. Pictures are therefore built up sequentially over long periods of time, possibly several minutes. To get the actual effect of a page, the page making system must use a decoder similar to the end-user's. Thus, slowness and sequentiality is an inherent property of such systems, which cannot make use of the speed of frame buffers, nor the kinds of icon-based menu interfaces that they can support [Miller 1983; Smith 1978]. Note that software decoders, based on IBM-PC's in the majority, represent no significant advantage of speed.

3. USER INTERFACE REQUIREMENTS for PAGE-MAKING SYSTEMS

Although it is possible to simply establish a one-to-one correspondence between naplps codes and page-creation commands, such a system would be so cumbersome as to be unusable. A more appropriate interface should reflect both the characteristics of the structures being used, as well as the forms of human motion and perception. Functionally, it must support three classes of operations: creating a new element, modifying the current picture, and changing the active environment.

The major user-interface design problems lie in the implementation of this informal set of specifications. They are: methods for accepting input, displaying and changing the current active environment, dealing with colours, and editing the current picture. The user interface must integrate the solutions in as clear and simple a manner as possible.

4. PCS-UVIC and INTERFACE ABSTRACTIONS

The Page Creation System developed by the author at the University of Victoria is based on an IBM Personal Computer, using an external decoder with a graphics monitor and optional input devices. The graphics monitor is treated as the drawing and page display screen, and the IBM monitor as the menu screen. The user-interface is based on a small number of *abstractions*, which present the user with easily understandable objects that are simple to manipulate. The most important of these are: the *cursor*, *virtual buttons*, the *colour bar* and element *groups*.

4.1. The Cursor Abstraction

The user interacts with the system either through the cursor or by entering text with the keyboard. The cursor is active and displayed on only one of the drawing or menu screens. The functions for moving the cursor, "accepting" its present position, and switching it between screens are mapped onto either the keyboard or the optional pointing device, which is a mouse or digitizer tablet. Accepting the cursor while in the drawing screen includes the point into the current graphical element, and in the menu area activates its corresponding function.

4.2. The Virtual Button Abstraction

The menu screen [Fig. 1] is an object used to display and change the current active environment, to invoke functions for editing the page, and to support the colour map. It is divided into a number of contiguous *virtual buttons*, each of which has a display mode. A button is "pressed" by moving the menu cursor there and "accepting" it. As the cursor moves, the current button is outlined in high intensity.

There are four flavours of buttons: *select* buttons, *toggle* switches, *action* buttons, and *function* buttons. Select buttons allow the user to pick one of a group to set an attribute. For example, the user selects one of the buttons DOT, LINE, ARC, RECTANGLE, to set the current drawing element. The selected button is displayed in reverse video.

A toggle button is shown on the menu screen as a box with <a>/<b> on it, where <a> and <b> are its possible values. Only one of these is active, with its descriptor in high intensity. Pressing the button causes the other attribute to become active.

An action button is similar to a firing trigger, whose action is invoked each time it is selected. Every time an action button is pressed, it flashes in reverse video. A colour can be modified by changing its HSV values using action buttons.

Some functions in PCS-UVIC may cover several steps. For example, to modify the current colour, it can be continuously varied until the user is satisfied. When a function button is pressed, it flashes continuously in high intensity, and the function remains in effect until the button is pressed again.

4.3. The Colour Bar Abstraction

The set of displayable colours are presented as a series of contiguous rectangles on the drawing screen, with the current colour outlined. The user can select a different colour by invoking the "New Colour" function, moving the cursor to the desired color on the color bar, and accepting it. The colour bar can be scaled in size, oriented horizontally or vertically, and repositioned, or removed. The system covers its previous position with the background colour, which may render the picture temporarily incorrect, until redrawn. Actions which require the colour bar to be present, such as selecting a new colour, will redraw it on the screen if necessary.

To support the use of only 16 displayed colours out of 4096, the current colour value is displayed on the menu screen in its RGB and HSV coordinates, and can be modified either by entering the exact RGB or HSV values, or step by step using rate buttons. The step size can itself by changed with the menu. What the colour bar represents is a *colour map* from display space (16 possibilities) into value space (4096).

The current colour map can be included in the naplps encoded picture, to support colour map animation[Shoup 1979]. Each colour map that is saved creates a new colour environment during the display of the naplps stream that corresponds to a picture, and by changing the value of a displayed colour, elements can be "hidden" in their backgrounds, or made visible. The slow speed of most decoders permit colour maps to create special effects, such as gradual fade-in or fade-out. Being able to store colour maps also provides a mechanism for the page creator to save and recall previous *palettes*.

5. ELEMENT GROUPS

PCS permits the user to define a sequence of elements as a *group*, which can be given a name, saved as a file, and included in new pictures. By using the **find** command, the user places a *pick* square over the vertex of the first element to be included in the group. If there is more than one element within the pick region, the system will outline and blink them successively, giving the user the ability to select the desired starting element of the group.

Successive elements are displayed in outline and blink form, until the user indicates that the current element is the last one in the group. The group can now be deleted, moved, saved in memory by name, or saved as a file.

Of course, it is possible to select, using the **find** command, a single-element group, by specifying an element as the first and last element of a group. The user has the additional options, in this case, of modifying the attributes of the element, and of appending new elements.

Whenever a new element can be created, the user can invoke the **insert** command, and place a group of elements previously defined, with the starting vertex shown as a blinking dot. The user can now move the group to a new location by specifying the place that the starting vertex is to be placed.

This technique of handling groups of elements has been shown to be versatile and easy to understand. The primary approach taken has been to treat the group as a single abstract entity, consisting of a first element with an initial vertex, and subsequent elements.

5.1. Other Interface Abstractions

Other techniques in the user-interface include the provision of a keyboard to menu mapping, so that buttons can be selected using keys assigned by a user-definable configuration file. Sequences of such keystrokes can be remembered as keyboard *macros*. Since the cursor movement in keyboard is based on current step size in pixels, these macros, used properly, permit a crude method of scaling to be implemented for groups of elements.

The system also used the concept of a background of up to ten previously created pictures, which can be used for inheriting colour maps, texture maps, text fonts (user-defined), as well as a mechanism for displaying commonly used visual backdrops, which would otherwise have to be created redundantly.

6. DISCUSSION

The naplps environment is by no means a simple one, and many page creation systems require a significant period of time to learn. PCS-UVIC has been used by novices after only 15 minutes of instruction to create non-trivial pictures. An interesting aspect of designing user interfaces is to allow entry level skills to be acquired quickly, while providing mechanisms for the professional user to build short cuts. This is the reason why tree-structured menus were rejected in favour of buttons and configurable keyboards with macros.

fig.	DS/CNT	dot	line	horz	vert	arc	circ	rect	poly	text
map.	new	screen	adjust	blink	draw	erase	MOD\MP	select	rgb	hsv
ctrl.	solid	....	----	dotdsh	pel	mask	clrmap	ctlpdi	d:tr	drcs
fill.	FL/OUT	HILGHT	solid	vert	horz	hatch	maskA	maskB	maskC	maskD
edit.	redraw	reset		backgd	find	dele	INS\RT	MOD\FY	move	copy
resp.	yes		no		end					

FCS-UVIC 1984
naplps v1.0

Keyboard

begin	end	curr	rgb
x:			hsv
y:			[+]

	h		+
	s	- R	+
	v		-

Figure 1.

REFERENCES

Canadian Standards Association. Videotex/Teletext Presentation Level Protocol Syntax. Toronto. 1983.

Miller D. Videotex: Science Fiction or Reality? BYTE:42-56. July 1983.

Plebon DA, Booth KS. Interactive Picture Creation Systems. Department of Computer Science Technical Report CS-82-46. University of Waterloo. 1982.

Smith AR. Paint. NYIT Technical Memo. July 1978.

Shoup RG. Color Table Animation. Computer Graphics 13(2):-13. Aug. 1979.

Tanner P et al. Colour Selection, Swath Brushes and Memory Architectures for Paint Systems. Proc. Graphics Interface 83. Edmonton. 1983.

Colour Coding Scales and Computer Graphics

A.M. Heath and R.B. Flavell

Department of Management Science, Imperial College of Science & Technology, London, SW7 2BX, UK

ABSTRACT

Colour is a powerful tool when used to code information on a graphics display, and the growth in the number of colour displays increases the importance of understanding the potential of colour coding.

This paper describes the ways in which colour can be used to code information, and reviews previous guidelines. An experiment examining the quantitative, rather than qualitative, use of colour in ten different ordinal scales is described. The results generate new guidelines that demonstrate the importance of displaying a reference scale, and show that when applied out of context the previous guidelines can significantly underestimate the power of colour coding. The results are interpreted using two examples of quantitative colour coding, and recommendations are proposed.

KEYWORDS: Human factors, Colour coding scales, Colour models.

INTRODUCTION

When displaying information graphically, colour is both extremely effective and efficient in terms of the speed and amount of data absorbed, and the level of recall. Colour coding does not, however, improve accuracy; if accuracy is important then numbers should be used. There are two principal methods of employing colour:

1. Nominal coding, in which colours are used qualitatively and are not ordered in any fashion but one colour represents one aspect of the information, e.g. a complex wiring diagram where each wire is represented by its own colour;

2. Ordinal coding, in which a (discrete or continuous) ordered scale of colour is used quantitatively to represent the ordered values of a set of data, e.g. a temperature scale where the coding is typically from blue (cold) to red (hot), or a contour map where heights above sea level are colour coded.

The research that has been carried out in the use of colour in visual displays has been into the application of nominal coding, especially in the area of enhancing visual search and identification performance under the auspices of US military contracts. In the 1950's the central question was "how many colours can be used for error-free recognition?" and the answers ranged from 6 to 10 depending upon the precise experimental conditions. This work was given impetus by the emergence of information theory as an analysis technique. In later years more complex experiments were constructed to examine the contribution of colour as merely one dimension out of several available, for example shape and size. For a survey of this work, see either Jones (1962) or the later paper of Christ (1975). Most of this work however was concerned with the visual studies with photographs, spectral lights or in one instance, with colour film. Therefore, the applicability of these early studies to colours displayed on a cathode ray tube (CRT) is dubious; the colour of physical objects is dependent on reflected light, whereas a CRT emits light and complicates the way in which colours are perceived.

Previously the cost of graphics equipment offering accurate colour reproduction restricted the use of colour to nominal codes, and the results generated for physical static displays remained satisfactory. However, with colour raster graphics devices, the cost argument is no longer valid, and ordinal scales flowing smoothly from one colour to another may be easily generated. The results for nominal scales do not hold when applied out of context to the use of ordinal scales, therefore research examining the quantitative use of colour needs to be conducted.

The importance of such work grows when one considers dynamic displays; for example, moving a window around a map, displaying the on-line calculations of a computer model, or reporting on the current position of a number of devices. The experiments described here have been performed to identify some guidelines for constructing ordinal scales. The results from the first of a series of experiments will be discussed. The direction of future work is also outlined.

THE DEFINITION OF COLOUR

There are a variety of terms used to described the different aspects of colour. For consistency, the three terms 'lightness', 'hue' and 'saturation' will be used. For a fuller discussion of colour on CRT's see Murch (1983/4) or Foley and van Dam (1982, Chapter 17).

'Hue': determines the name associated with a "colour", for example it distinguishes between red, green, purple, blue etc.

'Lightness': is measured independent of hue, on an achromatic scale going from black through grey to black.

'Saturation': measures the purity of a colour. For fixed hue and lightness, saturation varies from a pure fully saturated colour to a totally desaturated grey.

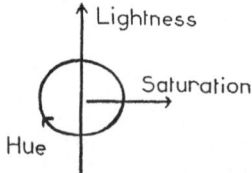

Fig.1: The Perceptual Colour Dimensions

There are a number of systems for specifying the relationships between colours and they fall naturally into three classes.

i. Perceptual

The earliest and probably best known is the Munsell system (1967). It consists of a set of standard colours organised in three-dimensions corresponding to hue, lightness and saturation (HLS); the colours are perceived as being equidistant from their neighbours. The entire system is described in cylindrical co-ordinates, see Fig 1. A second perceptual system has been created by the Optical Society of America (Nickerson, 1981). The use of these systems with graphics systems is considered by Meyer (1980).

ii. <u>Physical</u>

The perceptual systems are purely subjective and in 1931 an objective system based on wavelengths was set up by the Commission Internationale l'Eclairage (CIE). This uses three primary imaginary colours to define all feasible colours.

iii. <u>Graphics</u>

Colour monitors create colours by combining primary colours. A CRT cannot produce all possible colours, and the limit or 'gamut' of colours it can produce is defined within the red-green-blue (RGB) colour model. Because the dimensions do not correspond to perceived colour dimensions this model is difficult to manipulate and consequently user-orientated models, such as the HLS model, have been developed to map the RGB cube into more intuitive space. These mappings are one-to-one but not linear and can be done by a computer; see Foley and van Dam (1982) for more details.

EXPERIMENTS

It is an implicit assumption with the use of ordinal scales that people can look at individual colours from within a scale and be able to locate their relative positions in the scale. It is also implied that if the scale represents some physical property, e.g. height on a contour map, then people are capable of subjectively translating the various colours into appropriate values of the property.

It was decided to start by looking at these fundamental assumptions under very simple environmental conditions. A high resolution colour graphics device (PLUTO, 1982) capable of generating more than 16 million colours was used, controlled by a low-level version of GKS implemented on a SAGE IV microcomputer. The experiments were restricted to static displays of colour placed on a mid-grey background.

The initial experiments were designed to investigate the errors people made when trying to place isolated colours into their correct place in an ordinal scale. Four different types of scale were constructed, corresponding to Fig.2a to d respectively. Colour coded contour maps illustrating the scales are shown in Fig 3.

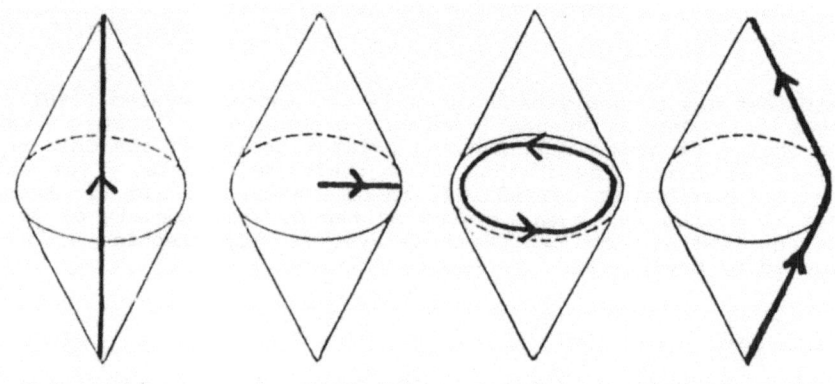

Figure 2: The Four Types of Colour Scales.

i.   achromatic or grey scale; starting with black, then passing through grey to white (Fig.3b)

ii. saturation; ranging from grey to a pure colour (Figs.3c-f)

iii. hue or rainbow; starting with white then running through the pure colours, in a rainbow sequence, ending with red (Fig.3a)

iv. coloured; ranging from black through a pure colour to white (Figs.3h-k)

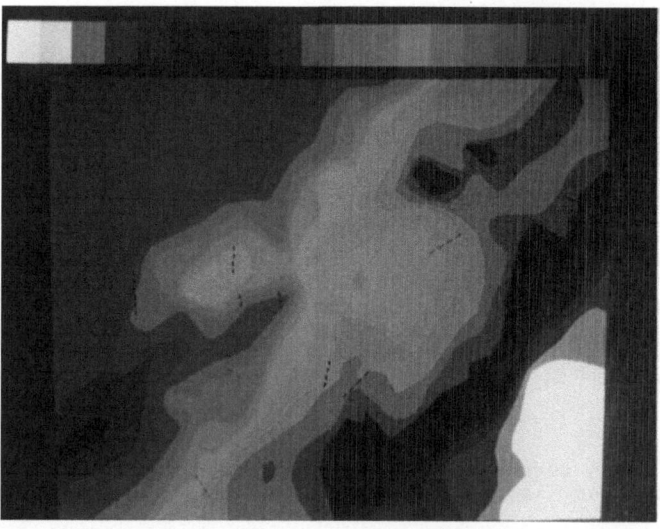

Figure 3: Colour coded geometric contour maps

3a: Rainbow Scale

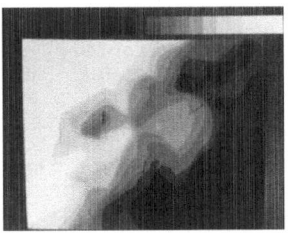

Note : Photographic Processing has significantly distorted the colour reproduction.

3b: Achromatic

3c: Red Saturation

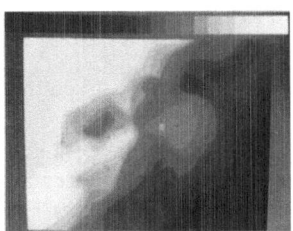

3h: Red Coloured

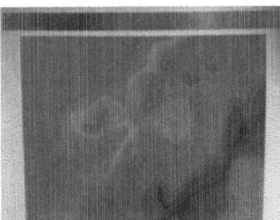

3d: Blue Saturation

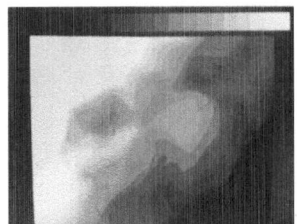

3i: Blue Coloured

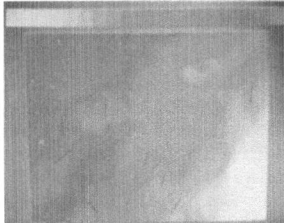

3e: Green Saturation

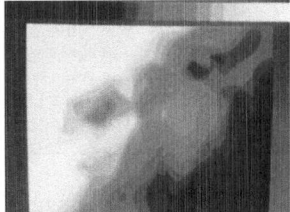

3j: Green Coloured

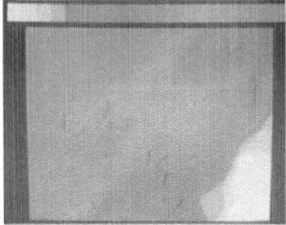

3f: Yellow Saturation

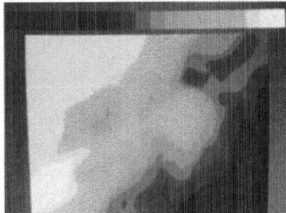

3k: Yellow Coloured

The rainbow scale has no intuitive beginning or end, and yet is probably most widely used in computer graphics; the sequence suggested by Poulton (1975) was implemented. There were four different variations of scales ii and iv, based on pure colours of red, blue, green and yellow.

Each scale consisted of twenty colours, the individual colours were generated by initial matching under controlled lighting conditions with the Munsell colours. The advantage of using Munsell colours is that they ensure equal perceptual spacing although in practice the spacing was modified slightly to overcome induced effects from the background. The length of the scales was selected to be longer than that required for error-free performance (on the basis of the previous work and a few initial trials) and was held constant at 20 colours in this series of experiments.

The experimental procedure was as follows for each subject:

1. The Ishihara colour blindness test was performed

2. A scale was displayed on the graphics screen whilst instructions were given on a neighbouring green monochrome screen; apart from a shaded light for the keyboard, there was no other light in the windowless room. The subject controlled the rate of instructions with a numeric keypad. The scale was 20 uniform rectangles, each 12mm x 15mm in size and arranged horizontally at the top of the screen separated by a grey border. The colours were numbered underneath from 1 to 20 measuring 16mm x 20mm in the centre of the screen. Five examples were given, in which this lower rectangle was filled with a colour from the scale and the correct number was shown underneath. Then another five practice colours were generated and the subject typed in the (subjectively) appropriate number and the computer then responded with the correct one. This was all the training that was received.

3. A sequence of 60 random colours from the scale were now displayed in the centre of the graphics screen. There was a gap of 77mm between the bottom of the reference scale and the top of each of these colours. The colours were shown alone or in groups of either 5 or 20. For each colour the subject had to type the appropriate number. No time limit was placed on the subject to respond, although unbeknown the response time was recorded by the computer, and there were facilities for the correction of errors. The computer did not respond with the correct number. Fig.4 shows the display when the rainbow scale was being tested.

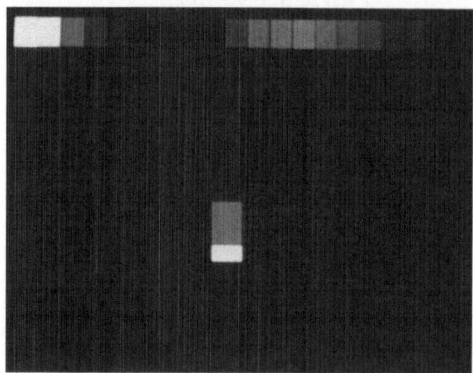
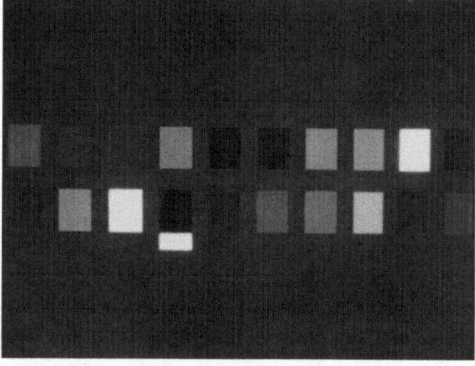

Figure 4   Figure 5

4. The horizontal reference scale was removed, as shown in Fig.5, and the subject repeated stage 3 with a different random sequence of 60 colours.

5. Stages 2 through 4 were then repeated for each of the four types of scales. Each subject only did a single variation of the saturation and coloured scales with an equal number of people doing each variation.

Thus each subject made a total of 480 responses. The total response times ranged from 30 minutes to an extreme of 140 minutes. No subjects were retested, and motivation was generated by offering prizes for lowest error performance.

RESULTS

The experiments were designed to see if people could respond correctly to a colour and place it accurately in an ordinal scale. The criterion is therefore the degree of error involved in this response. The errors made by subjects can be considered to be of three types. Firstly, procedural errors caused by bad typing or confusing the ends of the scale and responding 1 to 20, or 20 to 1. Secondly, perceptual errors due to induced effects of neighbouring colours either in the scale or in the main display area, perceptual errors may also be caused by the difference in size between the stimulus and the colours in the reference scale. The final group of errors are judgemental i.e. comparison errors when the reference scale was shown, combined with errors of memory when the scale was removed. The following analysis includes all types of errors; there were only 13 procedural errors in over 16,000 responses.

A simple measure would be to take the percentage of correct responses but this conceals a lot of information such as the size of error, and the uniformity of error on the scale. The responses were converted into percentage error terms - on a 20 colour scale, an error of 1 is $100/(20-1) = 5.3\%$ - and the results for a total of 33 adult subjects are shown in Fig.6.

The variations of the coloured and the saturated scales are all clumped together; there was no significant difference between the coloured scales, however, the saturation scales were significantly different at the 5% level using a rank-sum test. The yellow saturation scale was the best, followed by the green, blue and then worst of all the red saturation scale. It is unclear whether this result holds for all saturation scales, or if it is simply caused by the specific combination of colours used in this experiment.

As is clear from Fig.6, the penalty for not displaying a reference scale is extremely high, on average doubling the size of error. This is most marked in the rainbow scale, which lacks an intuitive internal structure, making it difficult to associate magnitude with the scale. However, when a reference scale is shown the coloured scales are all significantly better than the achromatic scale at the 5% level using a rank-sum test. However, after the reference scale was removed, the achromatic and coloured scales performed equally well. This is interesting as of course the achromatic scale may be produced on a black-and-white system.

Displaying different numbers of colours clearly showed that they were being used for internal reference purposes; the performance with 20 was better than with 5 which in turn was slightly better than with 1.

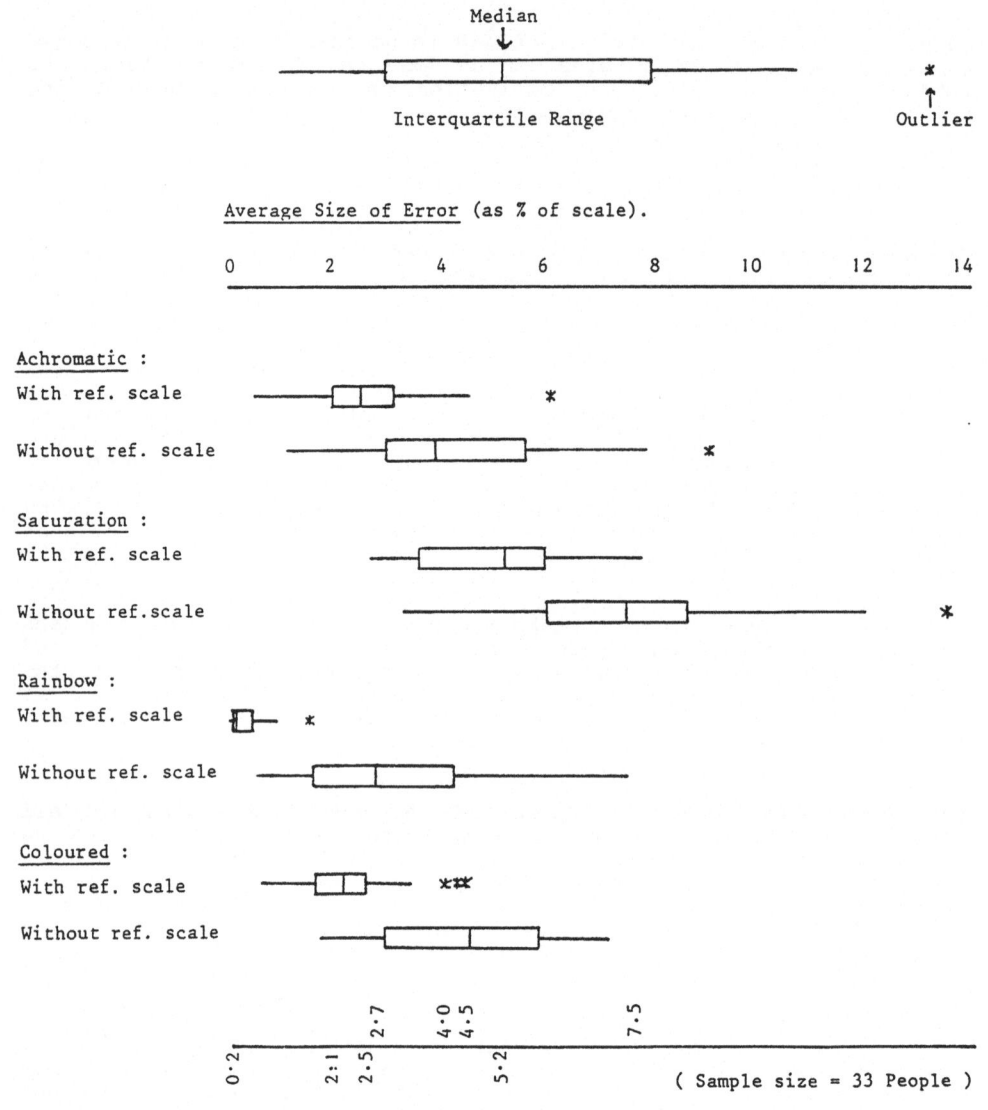

Size of Error = |stimulus-response| / (20-1) * 100%

Figure 6: Box Plots to show Distribution of Average Size of Error

No significant difference was found between males and females but there is a significant difference between those with normal colour vision and those who made mistakes in the colour blindness test. This is despite the fact that four or less mistakes is not considered as evidence of colour blindness. One might consider the mistakes and the poor performance both result from sheer carelessness but if this were the case, these people should have completed the tests more rapidly, which they did not. This suggests a physical rather than psychological reason.

A red-green colour blind person has subsequently taken the tests (but too late to be included in the analysis) and scored in the top third! This may indicate the subject made a conscious effort to compensate, or that the difficulty of the task dominated any errors due to colour matching, the reason is unknown as sample size is obviously too small.

Although two subjects spent considerable time memorising the colours and performed very well, there was no significant correlation between the total response time and the error rate. When the responses within each scale are examined, it is found that the variance of errors increases towards the middle of the scale. This was despite the fact that each colour was selected as being equidistant (as defined by Munsell) from its neighbours. The result is not entirely surprising, especially for scales with natural beginnings and/or endings, which provide subjects with reference or anchoring points.

Finally, Shannon-Wiener information theory was used to measure the real number of separate colours people were using in the scales. The method of analysis is described in Sheridan (1981), and Edwards (1984); the results are shown below in Table 2. The use of the rainbow scale without a reference scale is equivalent to the early experiments on nominal scales, and as expected this result, seven, agrees with previous work, cf. Miller (1956).

Table 2: Number of individual colours used in each scale

Scale	Number of colours used (rounded)	
	With ref.scale	Without ref.scale
Achromatic	8	6
Saturation		
-Red	5	3
-Blue	5	4
-Green	5	4
-Yellow	7	4
Rainbow	17	7
Coloured*		
-Red	11	6
-Blue	9	5
-Green	9	6
-Yellow	10	6

*There was no significant difference between the coloured variations.

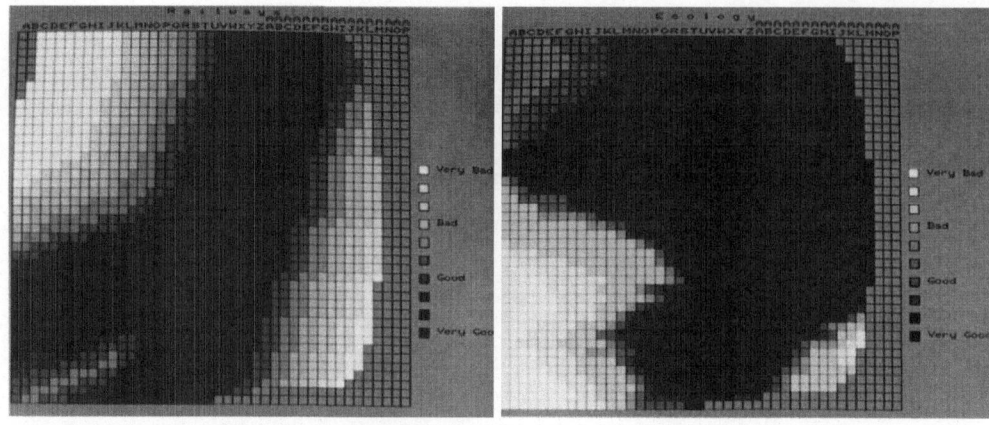

7a: Access to Rail Network   7b: Ecological Factors

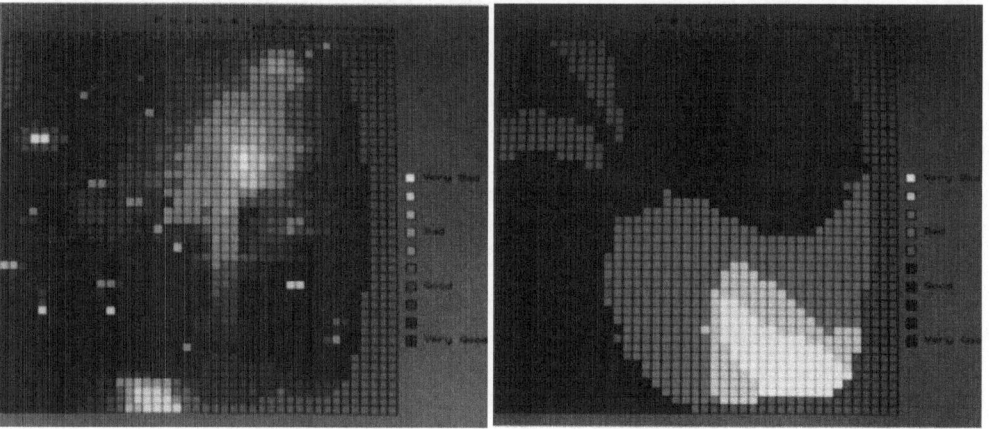

7c: Population Density   7d: Agricultural Factors

Figure 7: Environmental Factors effecting Site Location

DISCUSSION AND RECOMMENDATIONS

These results for ordinal scales differ from the previous experimental results for nominal codes. This highlights the need to ensure experimental results are not applied beyond the context in which the experiment is performed. Of course, this statement also holds for the experimental results presented here. Consider for example, the colour coded contour maps in Fig.3. Phillips (1982) has shown that the performance of scales depends on the task being performed; a rainbow scale is best when a spot height is needed, whereas a 'coloured' scale is better when the direction of the slope is of interest. This task analysis highlights the great failing of the rainbow or hue scale - it uses a perceptually angular dimension and is inappropriate if used to interpret the differences between linear variables. However, because hue is an angular dimension it is therefore ideal for coding qualitative information. An efficient use of the perceptual dimensions of colour is illustrated by the graphical output from an environmental assessment model developed by the Operational Research Executive of the National Coal Board, U.K. The four maps, Figs.7a-d, cover the same geographical area and are coded using 'coloured' scales to show conflicting factors influencing the selection of a new mine site. Lightness is used to indicate the quantitative information in each map, and hue classifies the maps qualitatively:

Black   - Favourable -----> White - Unfavourable

Red   - proximity to rail network
Green   - ecological factors
Blue   - proximity to population
Yellow - agricultural factors

FUTURE WORK

The experiments described here are only preliminary and other experiments are currently continuing. The length of the scale was held constant at 20 for all of these experiments; it is hypothesised that if the length were reduced a maximum number of usable colours would be found and this is being investigated.

Whilst the colours were equidistant in perceptual space the errors were not uniform. It may be desirable in practice to have for each stimulus an approximately equal variance, and new scales of equal discriminability are being constructed based on the methodology of Garner and Hake (1951).

Another hypothesis under investigation is that scales of very uneven discriminability might increase the number of usable colours and that in fact, there is a trade-off between uniformity of error and maximum transmission of information. No time limits were placed on the response time; it is hypothesised that the rainbow scale would be less useful if there was a limit. This has obvious implications for dynamic displays.

The objective of this work is to establish guidelines for the use of ordinal colour scales for display purposes, especially computer graphics. The first results measure the performance of different colour scales both with and without a reference scale, recommendations are made, and further hypotheses are suggested. More work is needed to examine the quantitative rather than qualitative use of colour coding, especially when used in dynamic situations.

REFERENCES

Christ RE (1975) Review and analysis of colour coding research for visual displays. Human Factors, 17(6):542-570
Edwards E (1964) Information Transmission, Chapman & Hall, London,
Foley JD, Van Dam A (1982) Fundamentals of Interactive Computer Graphics, Addison-Wesley
Garner WR, Hake HW (1951) The amount of information in absolute judgements. Psychological Review, 58:446-459
Jones MR (1962) Color Coding. Human Factors 4(6):355-365
Ishihara's Tests for Colour-Blindness, Kanehara & Co.Ltd., Tokyo
Meyer GW, Greenberg DP (1980) Perceptual colour spaces for computer graphics. Computer Graphics 14(3):254-261
Miller GA (1956) The magical number seven, plus or minus two: Some limits on our capacity for processing information. Psychological Review 63(2):81-97
Murch GM (1983/4) The effective use of color, TEKniques 7(4):13-16, 8(1):4-9, 8(2):25-31
Munsell AH (1967) Munsell Book of Color, Baltimore, Munsell Colour Company Inc.
Nickerson D (1981) OSA uniform color scale samples: A unique set. Color Research and Application, 6(1):7-33
Phillips RJ (1982) An experimental investigation of layer tints for relief maps in school atlases. Ergonomics 25(12):1143-1154
Pluto Power! (December 1982) Personal Computer World, p 126
Poulton EC (1975) Colours for Sizes, Applied Ergonomics, 6(4):231-235
Sheriden TB, Ferrell WR (1981) Man-Machine Systems, MIT Press, London

Chapter 6
CAD/CAM

An Innovative User Interface for Microcomputer-Based Computer-Aided Design

Larry Lichten[*] and Ronald Eaton

Manufacturing Engineering Program, University of California, Los Angeles, CA 90024, USA

ABSTRACT

This paper describes an innovative user interface for a general purpose computer-aided design system. It is being developed as part of an investigation into distributed processing in manufacturing environments. The system supports three-dimensional design capabilities for execution locally and incorporates model compatibility for communication with mainframe CAD systems.

INTRODUCTION

A general purpose computer-aided design system is being developed as part of an investigation into distribution of function between microcomputer-based workstations and mainframes in manufacturing environments. Visually-oriented user interaction, good resolution display graphics, powerful interactive three-dimensional manipulations, and model compatibility with mainframe CAD systems are major objectives. The system, herein called MicroDesign, is intended to run on inexpensive hardware; it incorporates new approaches to interfacing with designers and to creating and displaying models. The MicroDesign system models objects in a hierarchical boundary representation while providing a "natural" user interface with standard wireframe operations. Volumes are defined by hierarchical groupings of bounded surfaces or by sweeping planar faces linearly or rotationally.

HARDWARE AND SOFTWARE ENVIRONMENT

MicroDesign is intended for a stand-alone or networked engineering workstation in an integrated manufacturing environment in which both training and production design occur. In evaluating potential engineering workstations, our criteria included
- sufficient power for numerical computation and medium resolution color graphics,
- rich software development and support environments,
- likely upward compatibility to avoid obsolescence, and
- cost.

Furthermore, we evaluated graphics hardware with respect to their networking potential in a distributed computing system. We concluded that the IBM PC/ES series of personal computers with fixed disk and IBM medium resolution graphics best met our requirements. Microcomputers of comparable or greater cost-performance were considered; however, non-obsolescence, quality technical support, and

---

[*] Author's present address: Department of Computer Science
California State University, Northridge
Northridge, California 91330

compatibility with the large installed base of IBM mainframes in manufacturing environments were overriding. The PC AT (or AT/370 if graphics interfaces become available), in particular, with either IBM Enhanced or Professional Graphics provides strong local functionality and networking facilities. Of other IBM PC models available, we considered the 3270 PC and XT/370--the 3270 PC for its multiprocessing windows and multiple host sessions and the XT/370 for its ability to execute mainframe software directly and to network with a remote host. We believe that as applications software and "hardened" PCs for manufacturing environments become available, these systems will predominate as "standard" engineering workstations in factories.

Although MicroDesign software is intended to be usable stand-alone, we feel that workstation-based systems can be significantly enhanced by the addition of networking facilities. In particular, we are addressing some of the problems of communication between existing mainframe packages through host communication, terminal emulation, and the ability to copy information between windows. A critical consideration in such a distributed system is the trade-off between local power and bandwidth; insufficient bandwidth limits the level of interactivity for some applications that necessitate transferring models to a host. From our initial experiences, we anticipate minimal need for remote mainframe execution; for example, only analysis, realistic display, and file and plot serving may be relegated to a host.

Software requirements included
    -high level language programming except where assembler language could exploit special hardware characteristics,
    -support for windows,
    -device independence only within the limits of our initial hardware configurations, and
    -ability to exchange information with existing mainframe CAD systems.

CURRENT DEVELOPMENT STATUS

When we began work on microcomputer-based CAD more than two-and-a-half years ago, we surveyed available hardware and software as well as turn-key systems. At that time, microcomputer CAD was in its infancy; recently, however, several vendors have begun to offer functionally-rich systems. UCLA's Manufacturing Engineering Program has also designed and implemented a special purpose microcomputer-based CAD system, which is described in [Lichten 1984]. Menus, prompts, color queues, and other graphical techniques were investigated during the course of our work. Initial implementation of MicroDesign began more than a year-and-a-half ago; since that time, our target hardware and some significant parts of the software have changed greatly. For example, third-party graphics enhancements to the IBM PC were originally necessary to provide the required resolution and color. Development is currently under way using both PC-DOS and VM/PC. We feel that the lack of multi-processing support in these operating systems may present serious limitations, and implementation in a Unix^{TM} environment is being considered. In order to best utilize our existing equipment and to provide an efficient development environment, we are also implementing low level graphics support for other IBM workstations such as the 5080.

SYSTEM OVERVIEW

Although much current Computer Science research focuses on human-computer interfaces, there seems to be insufficient understanding of engineering design processes and human interaction with computer-aided design and drawing systems. We feel that "user friendliness" is exemplified by some microcomputer software, particularly for the Apple MacIntosh (which, in turn, borrows from Xerox Star office automation technology) and for many computer video games. Mainframe CAD systems' interfaces (notably those with tablet-menu-oriented or keyboard entry) unfortunately approach "user hostility". Our approach to user interface design is supported by several studies of man-machine interaction [Card 1978; IEEE 1984; Ingalls 1981; Irby 1977; Newman and Sproull 1979; Xerox 1982], while choices of modeling and display functions were based primarily on our experience with mainframe CAD systems.

In MicroDesign, users display models in stackable dynamic windows during design sessions; interaction with system functions is through "pop-up" and "pull-down" menus that temporarily overlay model display. Windows may be added, deleted, or changed in size at any time. Windows, as generalizations of engineering drawings, can contain arbitrarily-oriented views of a single model or of separate models. Separate models also may be "assembled" in a window. Geometric operations in a particular window affect model display in all windows containing that model.

Geometric entities are "drafted" in working planes and grouped or "swept" into three-dimensional models. This type of wireframe interaction is supported by geometric definition and manipulation functions and by inclusion of pre-defined volumes that can be scaled and placed within a model. Standard tools used in design and conventional drafting such as temporary grids, construction lines and planes, and dimensional information are supported. For example, a construction grid can overlay a plane without modifying the model being created.

Primary user interaction can be entirely with a mouse or other pointing device. Some of the reasons we believe this to be advantageous are
 -It leaves a user's hand free to browse drawings, documents, or other materials.
 -It frees desk space.
 -We believe new users are intimidated by a number of input devices. A mouse is convenient since one just points and "clicks".
 -Fewer hand movements and keystrokes are required so experienced users should be able to work faster. Function keys and keyboard entries are also supported. Some functions can be invoked immediately at any time during a design session; they include obtaining "help" information, and display pan, zoom, and rotate. Most functions define or operate on geometry in a construction plane, and two-dimensional operations default to this plane. Any visible planar entity can define a new construction plane, which is then displayed normal to a user's line of sight. Closed profiles may be translationally or rotationally swept; alternatively, topologically adjacent "trimmed" surfaces may be grouped into volumetric models.

Hierarchical groupings of such bounded surfaces are all user-directed as in Dassault's CATIA^R system [Dassault 1983]; no algorithmic support of Constructive Solid Geometry (CSG) Boolean operations is anticipated or, we believe, desirable since

-CSG implementation requires considerable computing power,
-set union and intersection have no counterparts in piecepart manufacturing (other than assembly),
-CSG operations may be less "natural" than wireframe "drafting" for many classes of objects, and
-objects' bounding surfaces provide useful information for most manufacturing operations (especially NC cutter paths), and CSG systems often contain no surface information explicitly.

INTERNAL DATA STRUCTURING

For mathematical tractability and host solid modeling compatibility, volumes are modeled as approximating polyhedra. Curves are linearly approximated and surfaces are faceted; techniques used are described by Lichten and Samek [1985]. The underlying polyhedral structure is that of GDP, an experimental solid modeling system [Fitzgerald, et al 1981], which uses a boundary representation containing faces, loops, edges, and vertices. It is similar to the proposed topology of the IGES Experimental Solids Proposal [NBS 1984].

DISPLAY FORMAT

Three classes of entities can be displayed:
(1) geometry and annotation of models,
(2) windows, and
(3) command "icons" containing menu items and prompts.

Specific functions supported are listed in a subsequent section of this paper. Only two command icons--HELP and EXIT--are always selectable and immediately executable. In order to provide consistency, the command language structure is, in a sense, recursive; major functions may be used as sub-functions of other major functions. For example, definition of a horizontal line requires a point through which the line will pass. Within major function LINE, sub-function HORIZONTAL, all options of major function POINT are available with identical icons and actions.

One window is "active" for resizing or re-orienting view of a model. It is possible to copy entities from one window to another or from one place to another within a window. Selecting VIEW provides capabilities to zoom, pan, or change orientation without leaving the current function. An L/R icon allows panning a window left or right by using the left or right mouse button. The UP/DOWN icon provides up and down pan.

When a user presses one of the mouse buttons while the cursor is over an icon and holds it for about a second, a menu will be displayed (or "pulled-down") only as long as the button is depressed. A user may then move the cursor under his next choice in the menu and select with a single key stroke. Icons may react differently depending upon whether the left or right button is pressed. A short information message may also appear as a prompt.

An icon displayed in the upper left corner of the screen represents the current primary function, as shown in figures on the following pages. Selecting this icon "pops-up" a list of primary functions. When one of these is selected from the icons, the chosen primary command appears in the upper left corner. If the function has secondary functions, those appear to the right of the primary function name also as icons. Selecting a secondary or tertiary function icon also "pops-up" a multiple choice menu listing options from which to choose and appropriate prompts.

FEATURES SUPPORTED

In our experiences with mainframe CAD systems, designers generally use only a small subset of a system's functions, which is often based on their initial training with the system. We therefore chose to support a minimum set of geometric, display, and system management functions. Functions to be supported for local execution are listed below:

Geometry Creation

    Points
    Lines
       construction and model lines
       segment and unlimited lengths
    Curves
       circle
       interpolating piecewise cubic spline
       rational B-spline
    Surfaces
       construction and model planes
       tabulated cylinder
       singly-ruled
       bicubic network
       rational B-spline
    Volumes
       enclosed by bounded surfaces
       from basic elements library
       planar entity swept linearly or
          rotationally

Geometric Manipulation

    Intersection and tangency
    Bounding
       line and curve segmenting
       line and curve extrapolating
       cornering
       trimming surfaces
       circular-section filleting
    Projection
       entities onto planar entity
       offset entities
    Assembling (multiple layers)
    Editing
       rescaling
       translation
       rotation
       delete geometric entity

Viewing

    Zoom, pan, rotate object in active window
    Create, delete, resize window
    Display viewing parameters

System Management
    Model
        get, save, merge, delete, and list
        basic elements library
    Plot
        model
        print text from associated file
        screen dump
    Miscellaneous
        dimensioning and annotation
        physical properties calculation
        on-line documentation and tutorial
        "undo"

In addition to saving models on mainframe peripheral storage and communication with other manufacturing functions, host invocation seems desirable for
    -realistic display of complex models
    -CSG operations
    -IGES pre- and post-processing
    -NC code generation
    -interfaces to engineering analysis systems

SAMPLE SESSION

Figures one through five provide an example of MicroDesign's user interface. Figure one displays three models, in which the "top" model is an assembly of the models "below". Major function icons are "popped up", and SURFACE has been selected. Immediate function icons HELP and EXIT are displayed in the upper right corner. Within SURFACE, secondary function CONSTRUCTION PLANE has been selected in Figure two. Figure three displays several views of the model, including the newly-created construction plane in a background window. Other windows were created by VIEW. Figures four and five show definition of concentric circles within the construction plane.

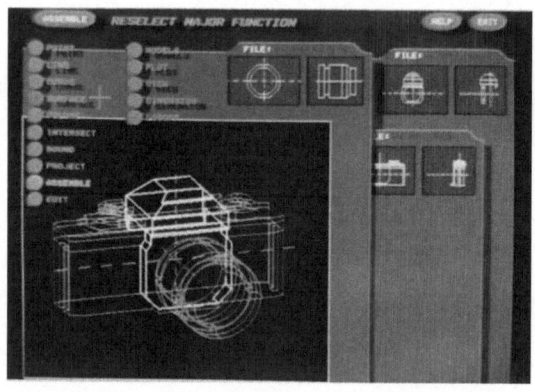

Fig. 1. Stacked windows and pop-up menus

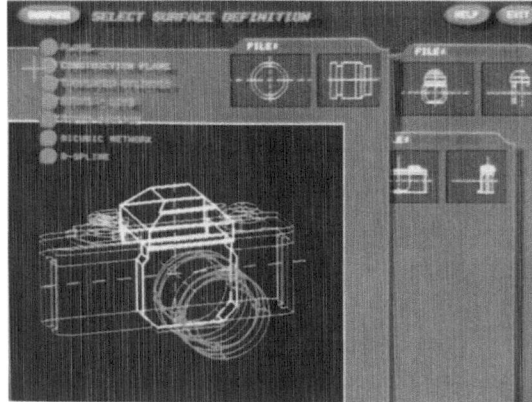

Fig. 2. Surface definition

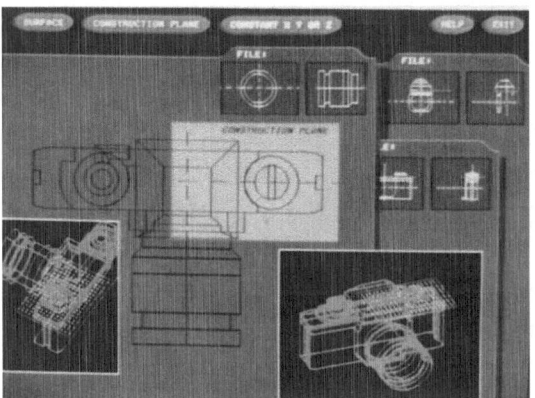

Fig. 3. A construction plane

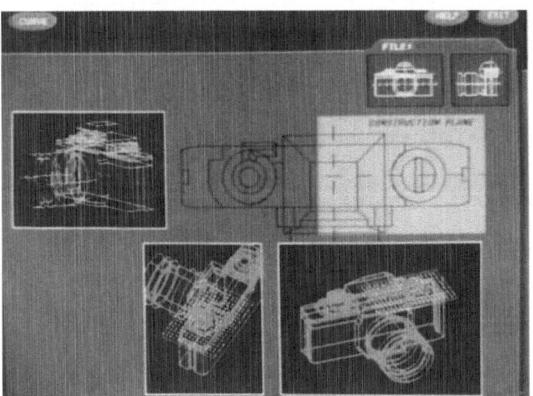

Fig. 4. Curve definition in a plane

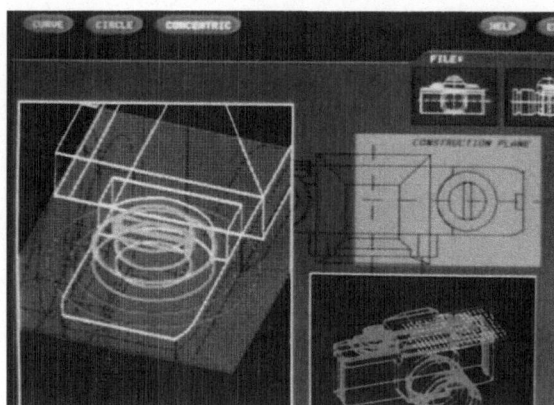

Fig. 5. Zooming in a window

CONCLUSIONS

This paper summarizes the progress of our investigations into distributed computer-aided design and techniques for interaction. We have thus far concluded
- Both standalone and distributed CAD are significant components of integrated CAD/CAM.
- Wireframing with additional surface and grouping information provides an appropriate geometric model for microcomputer-based systems.
- The PC AT with graphics enhancement provides the best workstation based on cost/performance and upward compatibility.
- User interaction through dynamic windows and menus provides flexibility and ease-of-use generally not found in current systems.

System functions have been specified and partitioned into local and remote based on their anticipated computing requirements and the communication speeds in a distributed system. We are currently proceeding with prototype implementation; we feel that MicroDesign's functions and operations provide
- a natural interface to three-dimensional modeling,
- a generalization of multiple-view engineering drawings,
- capabilities for retaining volumetric information in the system's data structures, and
- potential compatibility with mainframe solid modeling systems.

As implementation progresses, we will be testing the system by using it in teaching CAD and in developing a prototype distributed manufacturing system. We will then be able to better evaluate both the system's interface and its functionality in its intended environment.

ACKNOWLEDGEMENT

The authors gratefully acknowledge the assistance of Wade Hokoda in design and implementation of MicroDesign's user interface and in producing the illustrations in this paper.

REFERENCES

Card S, et al (1978) Evaluation of mouse, roto-controlled isometric joystick, step keys, and text keys for text selection on a CRT. Ergonomics 12(8): pp 601-613

Computer-graphics aided three dimensional interactive application (CATIA^R) user manual (1983). IBM Corp SH20-2629-3

Fitzgerald W, et al (1981) GRIN: interactive graphics for modeling solids. IBM J Res Dev 25(4): pp 281:294

IEEE Comp Graph Appl (Nov, Dec 1984). 4(11,12): entire issues

NBS IGES experimental solids proposal (draft 1984). Nat Bureau Stds

Ingalls DA (1981) The smalltalk graphics kernel. Byte 6: pp 168-194

Irby C, et al (1977) A methodology for user interface design. Systm Dev Div Xerox Corp

Lichten L (1984) Computer-aided design applications on microcomputers. IEEE Comp Graph Appl 4(10): pp 25-28

Lichten L, Samek M (1985) An approach to sculptured surface representation in a polyhedral solid modeling system. SIAM Conf Geom Modelling & Robotics

Newman WM, Sproull RF (1979) Principles of interactive computer graphics. McGraw-Hill, pp 443-478

Office Systems Technology (1982) Xerox Corp OSD-R8203

A Geometric Modeller for Turbomachinery Applications

B. Ozell and R. Camarero

CAD Center, Ecole Polytechnique, C.P. 6079, Succursale A, Montréal, H3C 3A7, Canada

ABSTRACT

This paper describes a software package tailored for the geometric modelling of turbines, as well as for the automatic generation of a body-fitted coordinate grid. The package consists of four programs used respectively for:

1. The creation and the modification of a model; the designer can "edit" the model by means of commands whose basic entities are points, profiles, blades, the hub and the shroud.

2. The refinement of the model by the distribution of points over each profile defining the blade, and then by the interpolation of new intermediate profiles between the hub and the shroud.

3. The construction of surfaces delimiting the blade-to-blade channel boundaries (the computational domain).

4. The calculation of a body-fitted coordinate system, inside the channel, by the solution of a system of differential equations.

A set of modeled turbines is shown to illustrate the results of each step.

INTRODUCTION

The design of highly efficient hydraulic turbines necessitates modern and efficient tools to assist the designer in his work. He must indeed reconcile contradictory requirements regarding performance and cost, the size and the machine's reliability.

We distinguish three steps in the design approach:

1. the creation of a model for the turbine.

2. the solution, on this model, of the differential equations that describe the behavior of the fluid flow (Navier-Stokes equations).

3. the analysis of these results in light of the previous designs.

This work presents the first of the above three steps. It consists in part of the development of a software package used for the geometric modelling, and for the automatic grid generation used in subsequent steps as a mesh for the numerical simulation of the flow phenomena.

The actual production of the modeled turbines will hence be possible using a minimum of testing and consequently, will reduce financial risks as well as others, given an indepth study with the aid of the computer.

DEFINITION OF MODELED OBJECTS

A turbine is composed of three main elements: the blades, the hub and the shroud. Since the blades are all identical, the definition of one suffices.

The main objective of the modelling process is to create a geometrical representation of these objects in such a manner as to render them accessible to users for purposes of analysis and visualization or for modification (geometric modelling).

A second main objective, once the shape has been created, is to prepare the physical flow domain for purposes of fluid dynamics calculations (computational modelling).

This, when using numerical methods for the solution of differential equations, requires the usage of a mesh. In the present software package, this step is carried out automatically and the resulting mesh is a curvilinear coordinate system which fits the domain boundaries.

This domain is a closed volume, referred to as the "blade-to-blade channel", reaching from one blade to the next, from hub to shroub and, by extending the blade length, from the the inlet plane of the turbine to the outlet plane. These extensions result in two "ruled surfaces", going from each side of the blade towards the inlet and outlet planes. For convenience, we shall refer to the set of the surfaces bounding the channel as the "shell".

CHARACTERISATION OF ELEMENTS AND DATA STRUCTURE

The blade can easily be represented by a surface folded upon itself in a three dimensional space; the blade being bounded by the hub and the shroud. This surface can be characterized by two sets of lines: the first, traversing from the hub to the shroud, and the second set going around the blade. These two families of curves form a grid where the intersection of one line of a family with that of another results in a node (Fig. 1(a)). These points serve as a base for defining the blade by means of interpolation. Other representations of the blade such as solid hexahedrons or bi-dimensional "patches" are also possible, but would be less suitable for the modelling methods employed here.

This characterisation of the blade permits the use of a well known concept in this domain, that of a profile. A profile is a cross-section along a given surface that is located between the hub and the shroud. These profiles consequently form one of the families of curves characterising the blade, and are defined by interpolation of the coordinates of known points, by means of cubic splines parametrised with respect to the arc length.

The hub and shroud are described by surfaces of revolution (Fig. 1(b)); it is therefore sufficient to define, for each, a curve in a given plane and an axis of revolution.

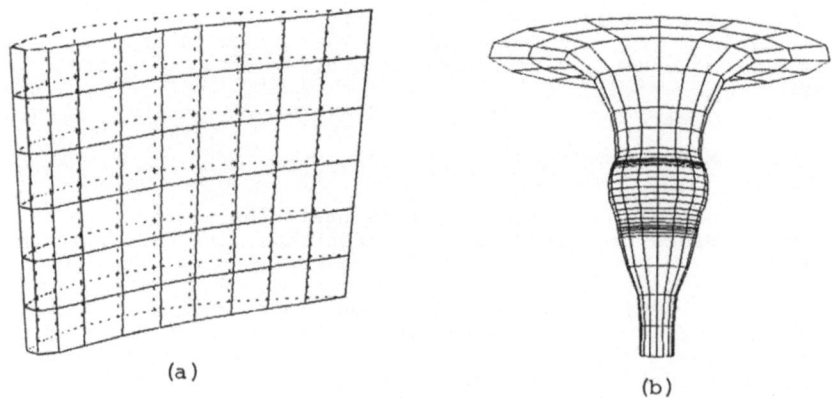

Fig. 1. Characterisation of a blade, and of a surface of revolution

Finally, we should mention that no profile is explicitly defined at the surface of the hub or at that of the shroud; it is by extrapolation that an extension of the blade is computed up to the intersection with the hub in one direction, and with the shroud in the other. This allows the modification of the hub and shroud indepentendly of the profiles at the extremeties of the blade. It is with the addition of the above mentioned profiles to the previously defined profiles that we find, by interpolation of their points, the second set of curves running from hub to shroud.

The database stores the necessary elements for the geometric description of four categories of "objects":

1. the non-refined version of the turbine: the profiles, the hub and the shroud.

2. the refined version of the turbine: the profiles (the "natural" points), the hub and the shroud.

3. the shell (computational domain boundaries).

4. the body-fitted curvilinear grid.

These files form the sole links (input/output) whereby information is transferred between the functional modules.

THE COORDINATE SYSTEMS

The design process can be carried out in one of three different referentials: cartesian (x,y,z), cylindrical (r,θ,z) and toroidal (R,θ,ϕ), as shown in Fig. 2. A certain similarity in their use is established if we agree, for all systems, that their coordinates indicate respectively the distance from the hub to the shroud, from one blade to the next and from the inlet plane to the outlet plane. The programs take advantage of this convention and perform all of their operations, in a general manner, on coordinates one, two and three, without ever really considering the actual referential. Rather it is the user who interprets the results appropriately, according to the coordinate system that he choses to use; a displacement in the direction of one of the coordinates can hence be considered as a rotation or as a translation (depending on whether the coordinate is an angle or not). The application of certain functions may at times seem disconcerting in certain referentials, but do however appear natural enough once their mechanics are understood.

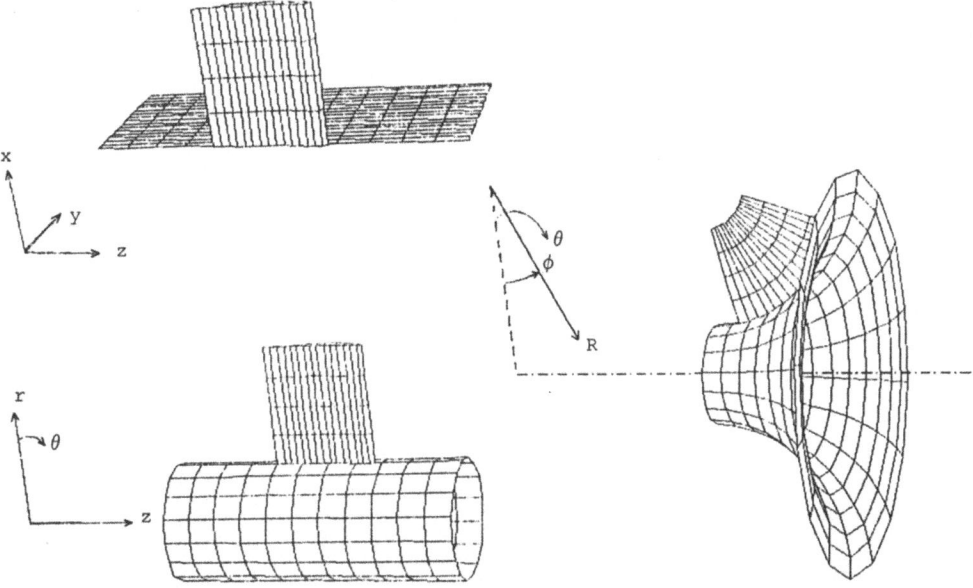

Fig. 2. Cartesian, cylindrical, and toroidal coordinate systems

SCREEN DISPLAY

The display and modification of three-dimensional objects, on a graphic terminal having only two dimensions undoubtedly causes problems. The visualization of 3-D objects by means of various projections is thus necessary and succeeds in rendering rather completely the true geometric characteristics of these objects. The inverse communication that is from the designer to the program is more difficult because the dialogue is restricted by the physical devices such as the flat screen, cursor, pen, mouse, etc. These do not allow for the passage of all the geometrical data that we would desire: only two dimensions can be input to the program at one time, due to the absence of true depth at the screen. Thus, to develop an acceptable method of communication, one must judiciously combine their use with that of a particular projection.

We can easily project the blade profiles on three different surfaces, each corresponding to a constant value of each coordinate (orthogonal projection). This type of projection, because of the speed and ease with which it can be implemented, was retained. This stems from the fact that one of the coordinates is simply dropped while displaying the other two. The creation and modification of profiles is easily made because the screen's surface corresponds to two of the profile's dimensions.

THE PROGRAMS

The Design of a Model

This first program deals with the geometric modelling and modification aspects of the turbine. A menu, displayed on the screen, lists the available editor commands, Fig. 3 gives such an example.

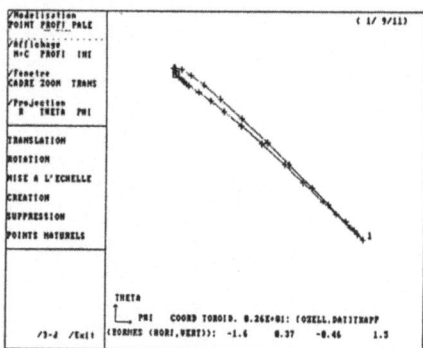

Fig. 3. Typical menu for the geometric modelling

These commands fall into four categories:

1. Those whose basic entity is a point (they are performed with the aid of the graphic cursor):

    - the creation and insertion between other levels of a new profile. Points are entered on the screen on a constant coordinate surface.

    - the modification of either profiles or curves representing the hub and the shroud, by adding, deleting, displacing, duplicating, permuting, or renumbering the points that define them.

2. Those whose basic entity is a profile:

    - scaling.

    - translation.

    - rotation.

    - the addition of profiles by duplicating them.

    - the rearrangement of profiles by moving their order around.

    - deletion.

3. Those who deal with reading or writing the model's geometry in a given file (file and data management) and whose basic entity is the entire model.

4. Those dealing with visualization of the model:

   - the choice of a projection to display a profile.

   - the choice of the displayed element (pointer to a profile, the hub or the shroud) as well as the interval of profiles to display along with the chosen element, and the presence or not of the hub and the shroud.

   - the display of all profiles at one time in a three-dimensional cartesian frame of reference for a better grasp of the turbine's actual shape (with possibilities of rotating the model with respect to the three axes).

   - the modification of the display window by translations, by specifying two new corner points, or by allowing the program to automatically calculate one.

   - the choice of the symbol's size (i.e. the point identifier).

   - the choice of the number of line segments joining two consecutive points for the curve's approximation.

   - the possibility of refreshing the display when too much obsolete data appears on the screen, or simply to visualize the result of a modification to an element.

Certain pertinent information is always listed within the screen's frame:

   - the profile's number currently displayed (upper right-hand corner).

   - a coordinate dyad indicating the coordinates used for the projection (lower left-hand corner).

   - the referential used.

   - the edited file's name.

   - the physical values corresponding to the screen's frame boundaries.

The Refinement of the Model

This second program allows the refinement of the geometrical definition of the turbine. This process permits a description with a greater number of points, and/or mainly with a new distribution as a function of the local curvature. Afterwards, we refine the blade by creating supplementary intermediate profiles by means of interpolation between the hub and the shroud.

The same functions mentioned above are available, in addition to those relevant to the refinement of the model which are in three steps:

1. Firstly, an equal number of points are "naturally" distributed on each profile in proportion to its local curvature. The curvature is calculated, by the program, in two dimensions with respect only to the two last coordinates in order to avoid consideration of the first coordinate's influence (oriented hub to shroud). Concentration is controlled by one parameter specified by the user.

2. Secondly, these new points are then used to automatically create, by means of extrapolation, two profiles at the intersection of the blade with the hub and shroud.

3. Lastly, new intermediate profiles are generated by means of interpolation between the hub and the shroud.

The original profiles, the refined profiles, or the intermediate refined profiles can be displayed in a three-dimensional cartesian system using the functions of the previous program.

The Construction of a Shell

The shell is made up of the pressure side and the suction side of two consecutive blades, four ruled surfaces, the inlet and outlet planes, the hub and the shroud, as shown in Fig. 4.

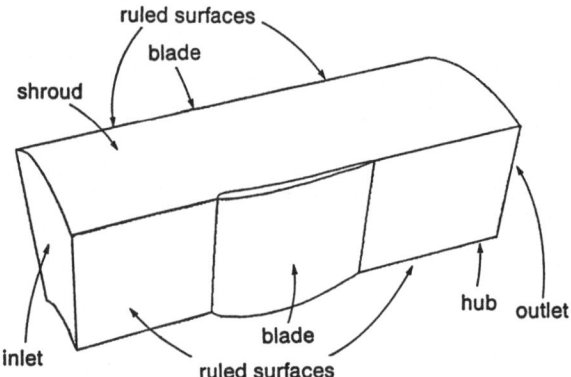

Fig. 4. Definition of the shell bounding the computational domain

It is constructed in two steps:

1. The limits of the ruled surfaces are defined by extending lines from the leading (trailing) edge of the hub and shroud profiles. These lines lie on the surface of the hub and the shroud, going from the blade to the inlet (outlet) plane. The angles and lengths of these lines are specified by the user. Points are then distributed along the lines according to a concentration parameter, also given by the user.

2. By providing the number of blades of the turbine, the user indirectly supplies the blade-to-blade channel distance i.e. the width of the shell. The concentration and the number of points in the blade-to-blade direction are given by the user.

The program automatically performs all the functions related to the display (window calculations, for example), and its execution is sequential.

The Generation of a Body-fitted Curvilinear Coordinate Grid

The approach proposed by certain authors (Thompson 1978; Camarero 1981) for creating a three-dimensional body-fitted coordinate system consists of solving a system of three coupled non-linear elliptic equations. These equations describe the transformation undergone by a cartesian regular mesh in a parallelepiped prism which would be stretched and deformed until it is adapted to the channel. We hence define a relation that enables us to introduce the curvilinear coordinate system.

This transformation of the domain of computation simplifies subsequent calculations by the use of simple finite differences. It also allows a proper application of boundary conditions of fluid mechanics while rendering possible the control of the concentration of nodes.

RESULTS

The described software was written in FORTRAN-77 and the TCS graphic language was used for the display within the package. For more elaborate displays (hidden lines and color), a translation routine is available which writes the data structure in the MOVIE.BYU format.

These programs were tested and applied for the modelling of practical applications to illustrate the package's applicability and range of use. They have been used with a variety of models ranging from FRANCIS and KAPLAN to bulb turbines. Figure 5(a) shows the hub and the shroud of a FRANCIS turbine, in a toroidal system, while Fig. 5(b) shows a bulb turbine, in a cylindrical system.

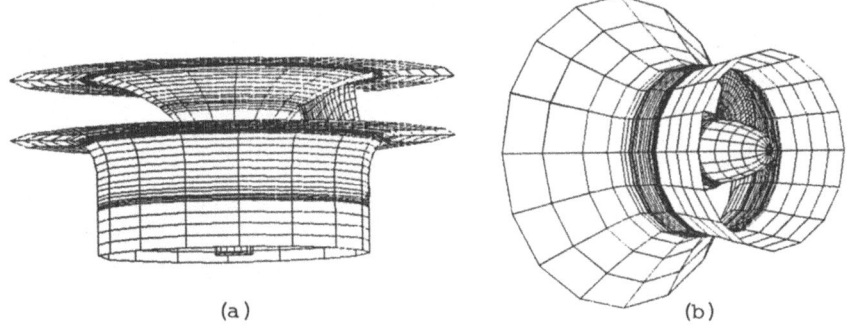

(a)　　　　　　　　　　　　　　　(b)

Fig. 5. Modelled FRANCIS and bulb turbines

The next step is to construct a shell bounding the computational domain. The one corresponding to the FRANCIS turbine is shown in Fig. 6. The inlet plane and a part of the hub are visible in Fig. 6(a), while Fig. 6(b) depicts another view of the same channel after a 160 degree rotation around the central axis. Figure 7 shows the shell constructed for the KAPLAN turbine. Figure 8(b) depicts the same object as Fig. 7(a), after a 180 degree rotation, and allows us to see the inlet and outlet planes.

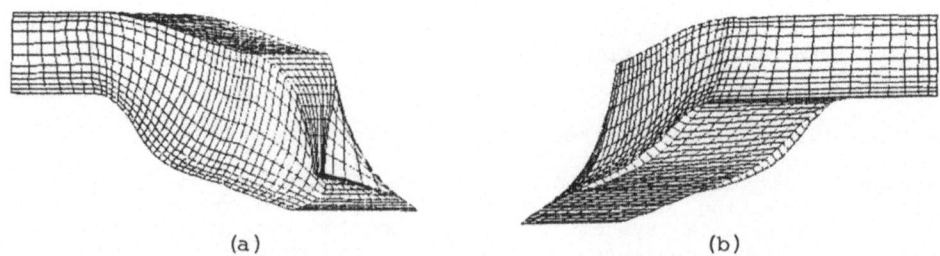

Fig. 6. Three-dimensional projections of the shell for the FRANCIS turbine

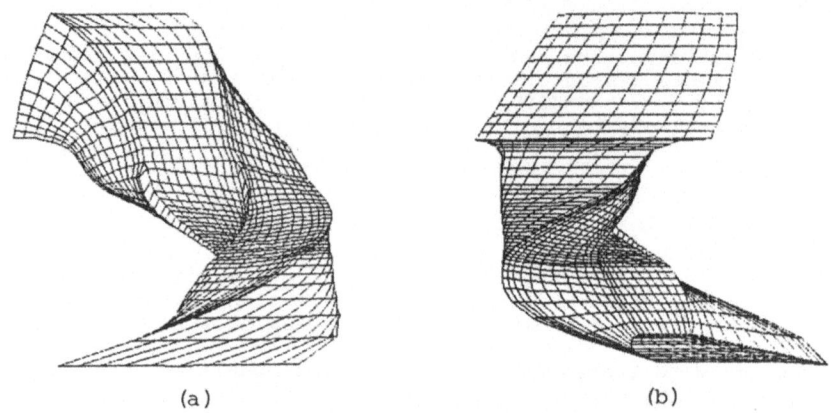

Fig. 7. Three-dimensional projections of the shell for the KAPLAN turbine

Figures 8 and 9 show the body-fitted coordinate system generated automatically within the shells. The coordinate surfaces lying between the hub and the shroud, and the ones that are between the inlet and outlet planes are displayed. Figure 8 gives the same view angle as in Fig. 6(a), while Fig. 9 corresponds to the one in Fig. 7(a).

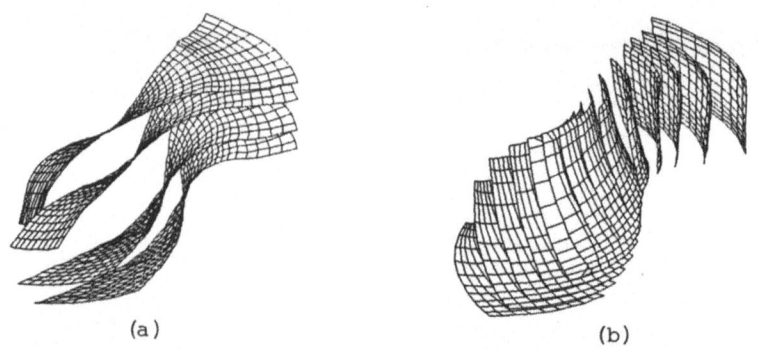

Fig. 8. Hub-to-shroud and inlet-to-outlet curvilinear coordinate surfaces (FRANCIS)

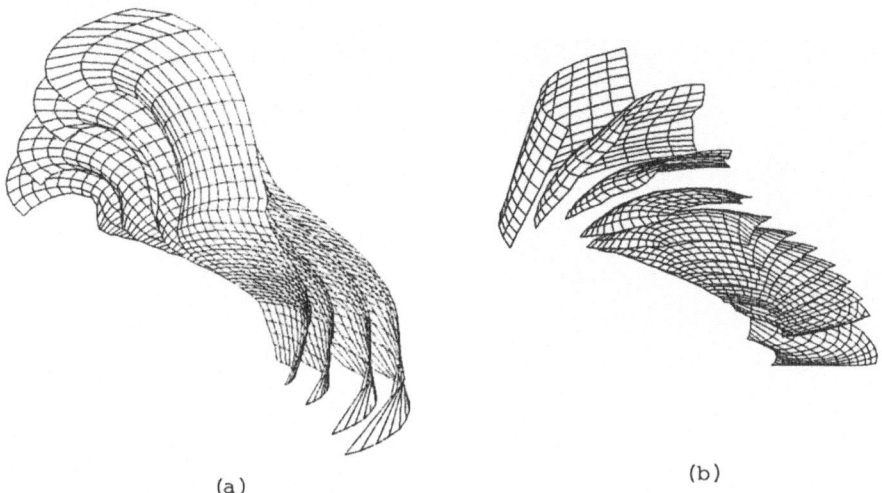

Fig. 9. Hub-to-shroud and inlet-to-outlet curvilinear coordinate surfaces (KAPLAN)

The color and transparency capabilities of the software package MOVIE.BYU have been used to produce the following pictures. Figures 10(a) and 10(b) show respectively the modelled FRANCIS and bulb turbines, with a full set of blades in order to render a more realistic view of the actual turbines. Figure 11 shows the shell constructed for the KAPLAN turbine, along with an almost transparent hub.

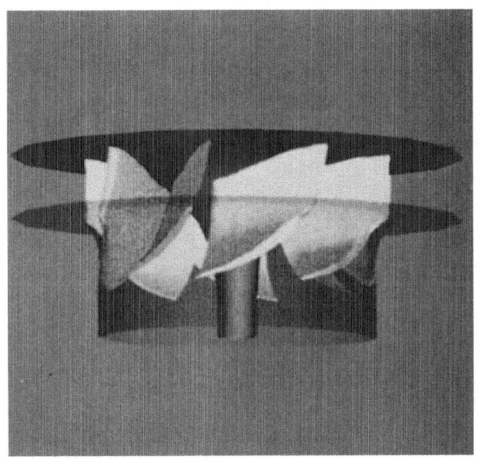
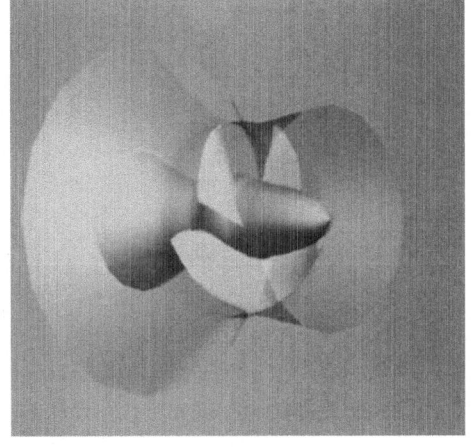

Fig. 10. Modelled FRANCIS (8 blades) and bulb (4 blades) turbines.

Fig. 11. View of the shell constructed for the KAPLAN turbine.

After extensive use, it has been concluded that these programs work well, are reliable, and user-friendly. Furthermore, they require relatively few resources, and give a very good level of interactivity. Besides being well suited to turbomachines, one can envisage applications to other fields such as pumps, and ship hulls (Fig. 12 shows such an example where a keel has been modelled by the present programs).

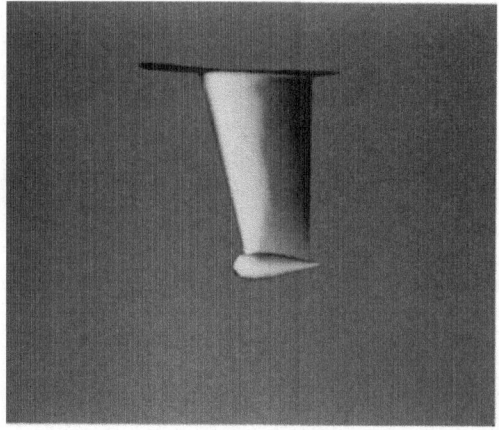

Fig. 12. Modelled ship hull.

REFERENCES

Camarero R, Reggio M (1981) Three-dimensional Body-fitted Coordinates for Turbomachine Applications. In: Ghia KN, Muller TJ, Patel BR (eds) Computers in Flow Predictions and Fluids Dynamics Experiments. ASME, New York, p 51

Thompson JF (1978) Numerical Solutions of Flow Problems using Body-fitted Coordinate Systems. In: Lecture Series 1978-4, Computational Fluid Dynamics. VKI, Brussels.

Low Cost Geometric Modelling System for CAM

W.B. Ngai and Y.K. Chan

Department of Computer Science, The Chinese University of Hong Kong, Shatin, N.T., Hong Kong

ABSTRACT

A geometric modelling system is implemented on a low cost, medium resolution colour graphics workstation. When compared with other CAD/CAM systems for the design and manufacture of engineering components, the proposed system is more oriented towards the manufacturing of 3-dimensional geometric model using Numerical Control machine. The colour graphics capability allows a designer to interactively create simple 3-dimensional geometric shapes as the building blocks for complex 3-dimensional engineering component. By "shape operation" on the building blocks interactively with feed back from the graphical screen, the final design as appeared on the graphical screen can then be manufactured by Numerical Control machine subject to designer specified manufacturing parameters such as Numerical Control machine cutter size and the degree of surface finishing.

KEYWORDS : building blocks, CAD, CAM, cutter path, geometric modelling, Numerical Control machining, shape operation

INTRODUCTION

Currently, there are various CAD/CAM systems available commercially. The application areas covered by these systems range from Computer Aided drafting in building architecture (Kalay 1981) to design and manufacture of sculpture surfaces (Flutter and Rolph 1976). Another application area is the CAD/CAM of engineering components for the production and mechanical engineering industry. Some better known research and commerically available systems addressing the needs of the engineering industry are PADL (Brown 1982) and ROMULUS (Carter 1979). Although these two systems are usually referred to as CAD/CAM systems, the geometric models produced by these systems in research publications and advertising brochures in fact tend to demonstrate visual realism rather than physical realism in the form of physical models manufactured by Numerical Control machine. The system proposed in here is a CAD/CAM system with emphasis on CAM and yet offer design capability to a designer. In as far as using the proposed system is concerned, there can be two approaches. One approach is the traditional practice in which a specification drawing is already available and the user simply interprets the drawing and discretise the complex engineering drawing specification into many "building blocks". The building blocks are then "shape operated" to reproduce the engineering component visually on the graphical screen as well as physically by Numerical Control machine. To put it simply, the user can be considered as a "part programmer" responsible for producing a physical model based on a specification drawing. When compared with part programming language such as APT (Hori 1967) to produce a physical model, the power and the ease-of-use of the proposed system can be easily seen. Furthermore, the turnaround time will only be a matter of hours even for a complex engineering component compared with a matter of days or weeks when using APT or its equivalent. The other way in which the system can be used is that the designer would directly input his design idea into the system in the form of "building blocks". By placing the "building blocks" appropriately and "shape operating" them interactively on the graphical screen, a design can then be obtained. A design as displayed on the graphical screen can then be made available in digital format for engineering analysis. The final approved design can the be produced physically by Numerical Control machine.

The hardware configuration on which the system is implemented is a Seiko-9500 which consists of three processors/co-processor. These are Intel 8086, 8087 running at 5 MHz and an 8088 running at 8 MHz. The 8086 and 8087 are used for executing load module obtained by linking various object modules compiled from a number of Pascal source programs. The 8 MHz 8088 is dedicated to I/O and is used as a "graphics processor" for an eight colour raster display of 512 by 480 resolution. The system has 512 Kbytes of memory and two 5.25-inch floppy disk drives giving 1.2 Mbytes of storage. The operating system is a customised version of Intel iRMX86. In developing the software, an external winchester is used.

AN OVERVIEW OF THE PROPOSED SYSTEM

The proposed system allows a designer/part-programmer to interact with it in order to produce a design and subsequently produce a physical model of the design by the use of a Numerical Control milling machine.

In as far as a typical user of the proposed system is concerned, a session on the system is typically divided into three distinct phases. The first phase can be best described as the initialization phase which basically prepares the ground work for performing the second and the third phase. The second phase of a session allows the user to interactively create "building blocks" from PRIMITIVES avaliable in the system. The third and final phase is the "placement and shape operation" of previously created building blocks incrementally on the graphical screen of the Seiko-9500 until a final design is obtained for Numerical Control machine milling to produce a physical 3-dimensional engineering component.

THE INITIALIZATION PHASE

The proposed system is oriented towards CAM of engineering components by Numerical Control milling. The two most important ingradients which enable the proposed system to be a genuine CAM system are the "creation of building blocks from primitives in the system" and the subsequent "placement and shape operation of the building blocks". However, it is necessary to make preparations before the creation of building blocks and shape operation can take place.

When a user enters the proposed system, he must first define

(1) an area defined by length and width in millimeters on the x-y plane onto which a Numerical Control machine would perform the NC milling,
(2) the cutter size to be used on the Numerical Control machine in millimeters,
(3) the degree of surface finishing specified in millimeters,
(4) the number of building blocks to be created from each of the primitives available in the system.

THE PHASE OF CREATING BUILDING BLOCKS

One of the features of the system is that "building blocks" can be created which are subsequently "shape operated" upon to form a complex engineering component. When using the system, building blocks can be created by assigning physical dimensions to "PRIMITIVES" available from the system. Currently, there are six primitives in the system from which building blocks can be created. These are

(i)   CONE
(ii)   ARC-BLOCK
(iii)   ELLIPSOID
(iv)   PRISM
(v)   TOROID
(vi)   HORIZONTAL CONE

Although there are only six primitives available in the system for creating building blocks, the variety of building blocks that can be generated from these six primitives are tremendous. Figure 1 gives a tree structure representation of the primitives and the variations that can be obtained from these six primitives.

When using the system to create a building block from any one of the above primitives, the user is required to input various parameters. These parameters include:

(a) the Numerical Control machine cutter size for NC milling the building block currently being created,
(b) the degree of surface finishing for the building block currently being created,
(c) the physical characteristics of the building block which are usually length, width, vertical height, etc..

A typical building block created from the system is in fact a series of cutter path positions. When these cutter path positons are traversed by a Numerical Control milling machine with the appropriate cutter as specified in (a) then a physical building block of physical characteristics as specified in (c) is obtained. The smoothness/roughness of this building block is in turn related to the degree of surface finishing as specified in (b). In general, small cutter size should be used for machining small building blocks while as larger cutter size should be used for machining bigger building blocks. In order to produce building block with a high degree of surface finishing a large number of cutter path movements are necessary which might require a long time during Numerical Control machining.

It should be noted that all numerical values are in millimeters and if (a) and (b) are not specified then the values specified in the initialization phase would be used. Building blocks created from various primitives can be retrieved in the shape operation phase by their unique identifier. For example, the first building block created by invoking the CONE primitive will be uniquely referred to as CONE1 and the subsequent building block by invoking the CONE primitive will be uniquely referred to as CONE2.

INCREMENTAL PLACEMENT AND SHAPE OPERATION PHASE

Once the building blocks have been created in the form of cutter path positions, they can be referred to by their respective unique identifiers that were assigned to them when they were created. In other words, after the creation of building block phase, a library of symbols are created and can be instanced and shape operated upon to form the cutter path positions for machining a complex engineering component.

In as far as the placement and shape operation phase is concerned, the user would instance one building block at a time by an unique identifier that is associated with it and then place it in the appropriate orientation on the x-y plane as appear on the graphical screen. When the user is satisfied that it is in the correct position, the user would then instance a second building block and position it relative to the first one. When the user is satisfied that the second building block is also in the correct position, the user would then shape operate on these two building blocks to eliminate overlapping cutter path contours. By incrementally invoking and shape operating one building block at a time the user would finally produce the cutter path contours for Numerical Control machining a complex engineering component.

AN EXAMPLE TO PRODUCE A LEVER FORGING

The manner in which a user would interact with the proposed system is illustrated by means of an example. The aim of this example is to interactively reproduce a design as laydown in a specification drawing. This specification drawing refers to a LEVER FORGING which is illustrated in Fig. 2.

In reproducing the LEVER FORGING specified in Fig. 2 on the graphical screen of the Seiko-9500 and subsequently Numerical Control machining of the LEVER FORGING physical model, it is decided that 4 building blocks are to be used. This 4 building blocks are to be created from the CONE and a variation of the ELLIPSOID primitives.

In fact a hemi-sphere building block is to be created from the CONE primitive and three cylinders with ellipsoid ends are to be created from a variation of the ELLIPSOID primitive.

INITIALIZATION

Photo 3 illustrates that

(a) a block of material upon which the Numerical Control machining will take place and this is an area on the x-y plane equal to 222 millimeters times 111 millimeters,
(b) the physical characteristics of the cutter size in terms of T1 and

T2 as illustrated in Fig. 4 are chosen to be quarter and eighth of an inch (6.35 mm, 3.175mm) respectively,
(c) definition for the degree of surface finishing as illustrated in Fig. 5 which shows the relationship between the CONE primitive, a typical cutter and the two parameters for defining surface finishing in which EPS is equal to 0.3 mm and EPSEDG is equal to 0.3 mm in this example.

Photo 6 illustrates that one building block is to be created from the CONE primitive and three building blocks are to be created from a variation of the ELLIPSOID primitive which is a CYLInder with Ellipsoid ends (CYLIE).

CREATING BUILDING BLOCKS

Photo 7 is a display of the plan view, the two side views and the isometric view of the CONE primitive. A building block can be created by simply assigning dimensions on the right hand side of the graphical screen. The resultant building block in terms of cutter path positions will then be displayed as illustrated in Photo 8 with actual dimensions as specified in Photo 7. This building block will be referred to as CONE1. Notice that the created building block is in fact a hemi-sphere.

Photo 9 is a display of the plan view, the two side views and the isometric view of the cutter path of a building block created from the CYLIE primitive. This building block is then referred to as CYLIE1. The most important point to note in Photo 9 is that the building block CYLIE1 is rotated by 90 degreees. It can be easily seen that CYLIE2 and CYLIE3 can be created in the same way as CYLIE1.

INCREMENTAL PLACEMENT AND SHAPE OPERATION

Photo 10 illustrates the placement of CONE1 within a rectangular area as defined in the initialization phase. Photo 11 illustrates the placement of CYLIE1 with respect to CONE1 and Photo 12 illustrates the shape operation between CONE1 and CYLIE1 in which the elimination of overlapping cutter path can be easily seen. The placements of CYLIE2 and CYLIE3 are shown in Photo 13 and Photo 14 respectively. Photo 15 illustrates the final product as a result of incremental shape operation between CONE1 and CYLIE1 and then total shape operation between CONE1, CYLIE1 and CYLIE2 and CYLIE3.

NUMERICAL CONTROL MACHINING OF THE LEVER FORGING

Photo 16 is a physical model produced by Numerical Control machining. The data that is input to the Numerical Control machine is in fact the cutter path positions illustrated in Photo 15.

RESPONSE TIME AND ELAPSE TIME

The response time for initialization, creating each building block and each placement is in terms of a few seconds. The response time for each incremental shape operation in this case is approximately 20 seconds.

In general terms, the response time for shape operating ELLIPSOID type building block is longer than building blocks created from other types of primitives. This is because the number of cutter path positions for ELLIPSOID is approximately three to four times more than other types of primitives.

The actual elapse time from initialization stage to producing Photo 15 on the graphical screen takes approximately 30 minutes.

CONCLUSION

The proposed system is a low cost geometric modelling system with special emphasis on the manufacturing of engineering components using Numerical Control machine. The applicability of the system is clearly demonstrated by the LEVER FORGING example. The proposed system is a low cost system and this is clearly indicated by the hardware configuration on which the system is implemented. In as far as the user response time and throughput is concerned, current results obtained indicate that for initialization, creating building blocks and incremental placement the typical response time is a matter of seconds. Furthermore, the incremental shape operation is also in the region of seconds except for ELLIPSOID type building blocks. Therefore, it can be concluded that the proposed system is a genuine interactive design and manufacturing system. In as far as throughput is concerned, the system is quite capable of being used to complete one or two designs per day even for complex engineering components.

REFERENCES

Brown CM (1982) PADL-2 : A Technical Summary. IEEE Computer Graphics & Applications:69-97
Carter WA (1979) ROMULUS : The Design of a Geometric Modeller. Pub P-80 CM 01 by CAM-I Inc
Flutter AG, Rolph PN (1976) Polysurf : An Interactive System for the Computer-Aided Design and Manufacturing of Components. CAD 76 Conference London:150-158
Hori S (1967) APT Part Programming. ITT Research Inst McGraw Hill
Kalay YE (1981) Interactive Shape Generation and Spatial Conflict Testing. 18 Design Automation Conference Nashville Tennessee:75-89

6 PRIMITIVES	variations of primitives
CONE	-- hemi-sphere vertical sharp cone vertical cylinder triangular pyramid rectangular pyramid others
ARC-BLOCK	-- typical arc-block horizontal cylinder with sloping end vertical semi-disc
ELLIPSOID	-- typical ellipsoid horizontal cylinder with ellipsoid ends
PRISM	-- typical prism rectangular pyramid lying on one of its sides other variations
TOROID	
HORIZONTAL CONE	

Fig. 1. 6 primitives and their variations

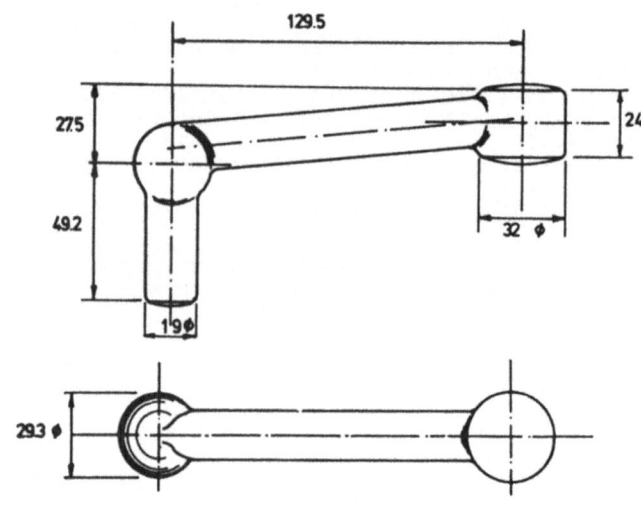

Fig. 2. Specification of a LEVER FORGING

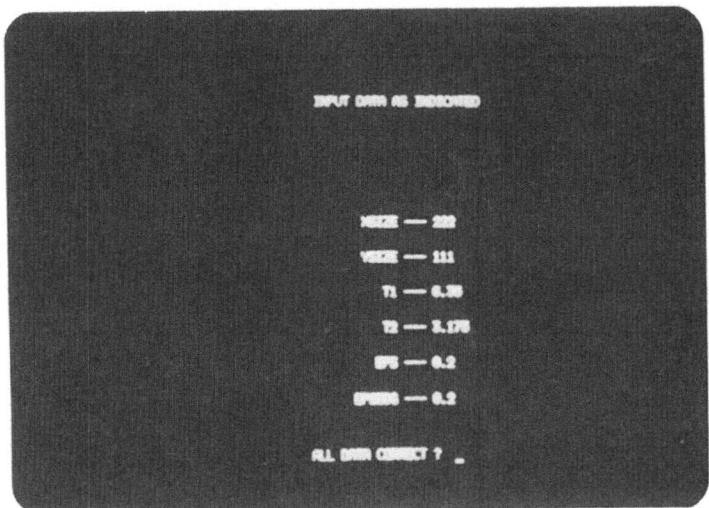

Photo 3. Initialization of machining parameters

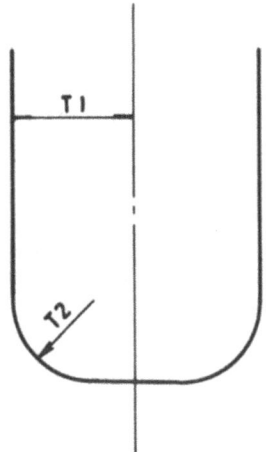

Fig. 4. Cutter characteristics

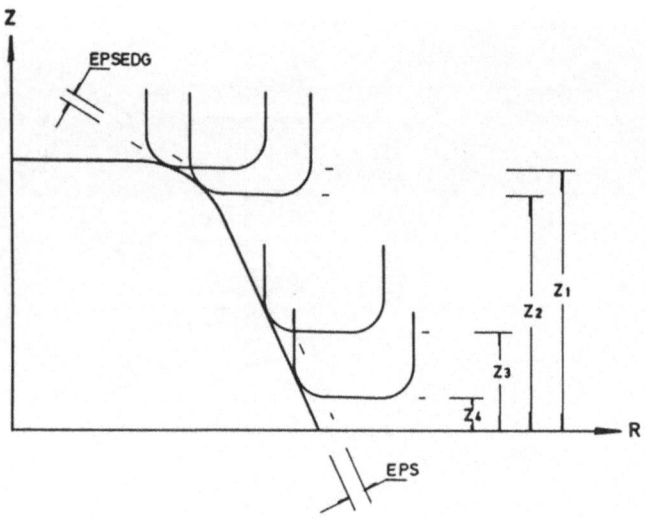

Fig. 5. Surface finishing defined by EPS and EPSEDG

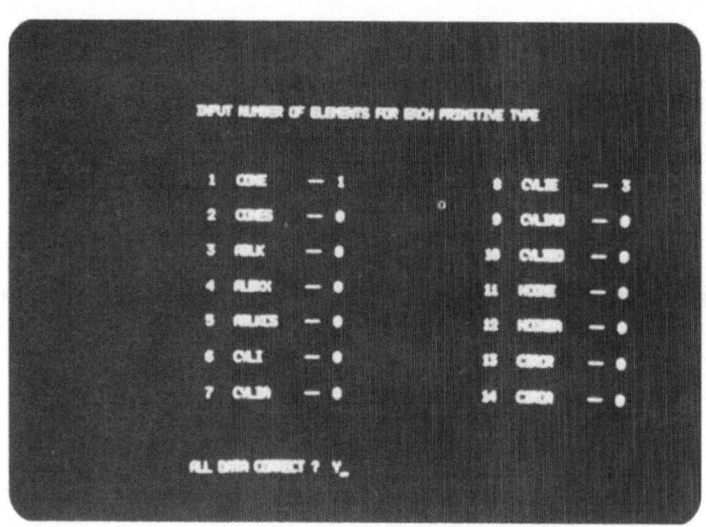

Photo 6. Creating building blocks from CONE and CYLIE

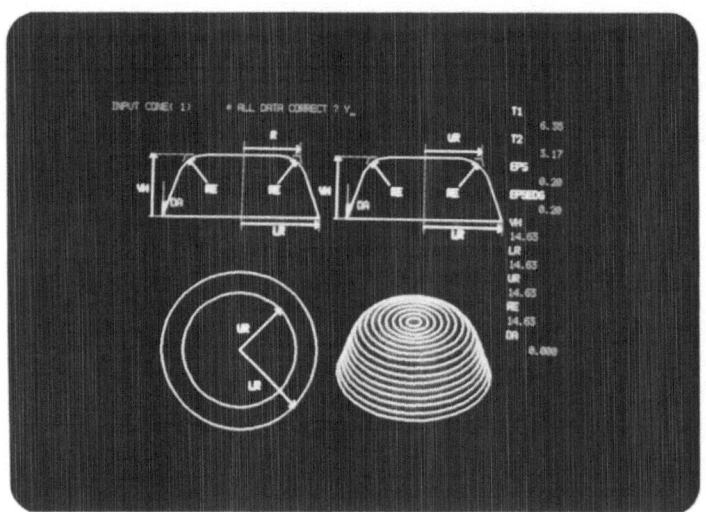

Photo 7. Entering data to create a hemi-sphere

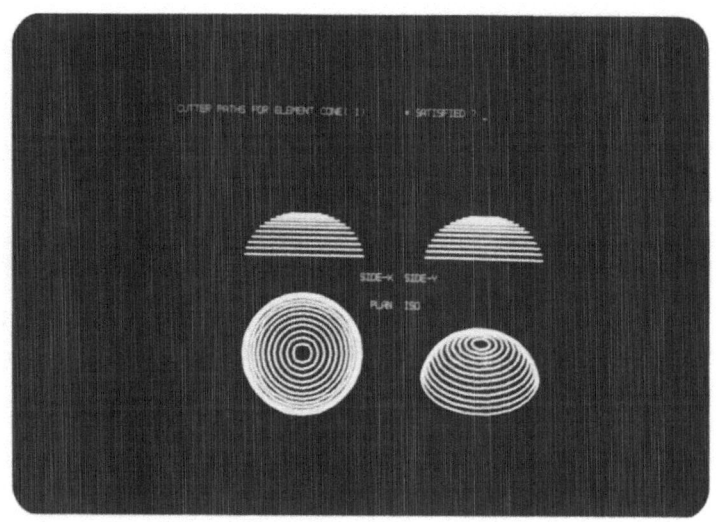

Photo 8. Cutter path of a hemi-sphere

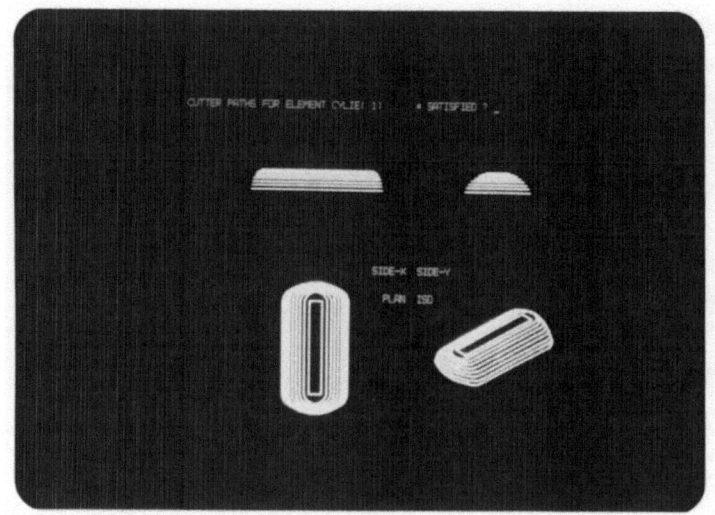

Photo 9.   Cutter path of a cylinder

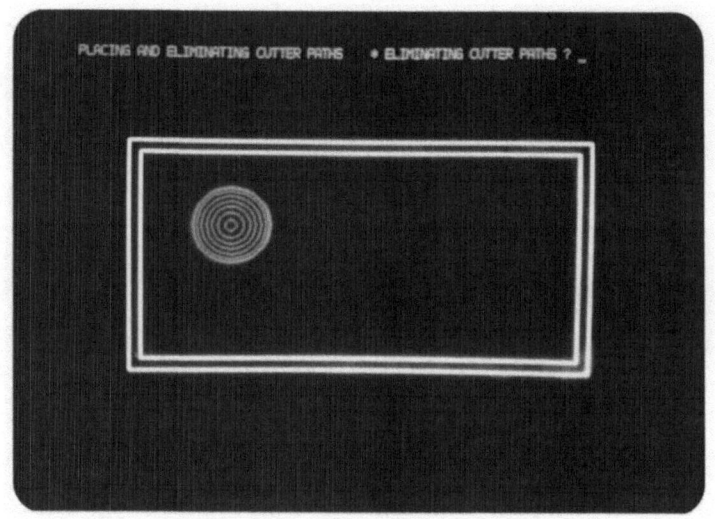

Photo 10.   Placement of CONE1

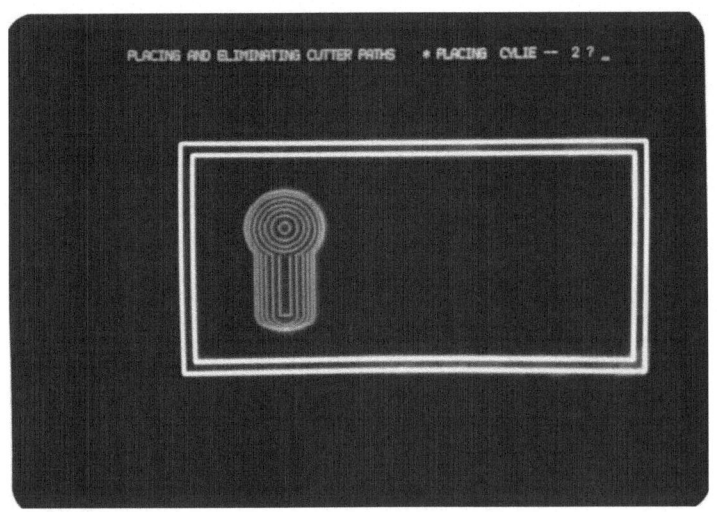

Photo 11. Relative positioning between CONE1 and CYLIE1

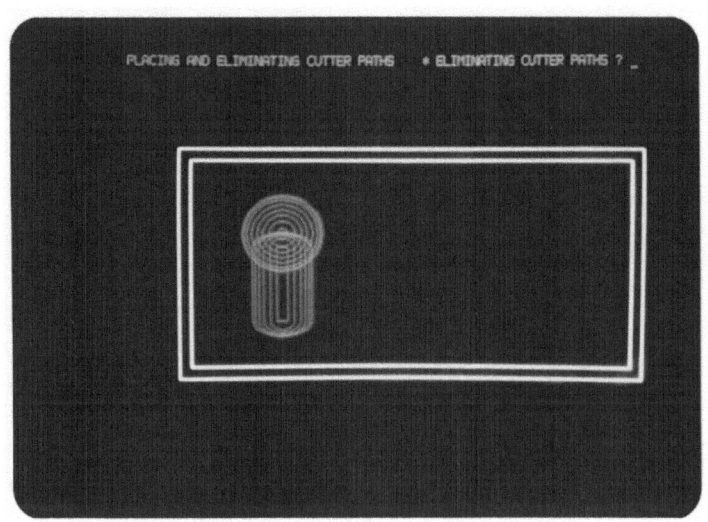

Photo 12. Cutter path elimination between CONE1 and CYLIE1

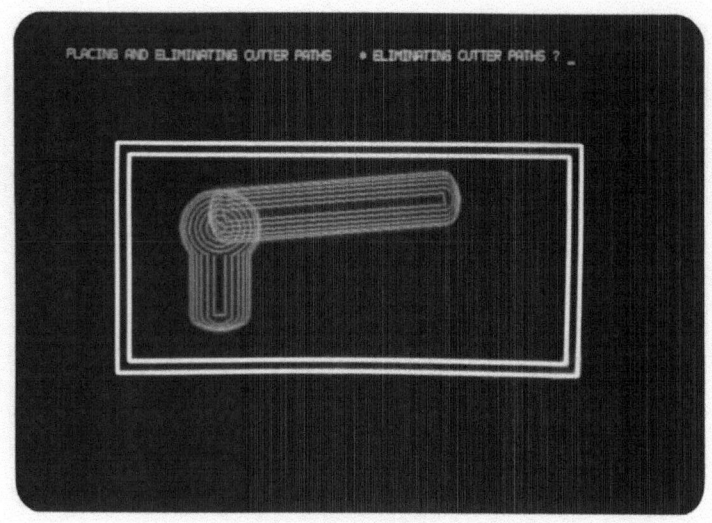

Photo 13. Placement of CYLIE2

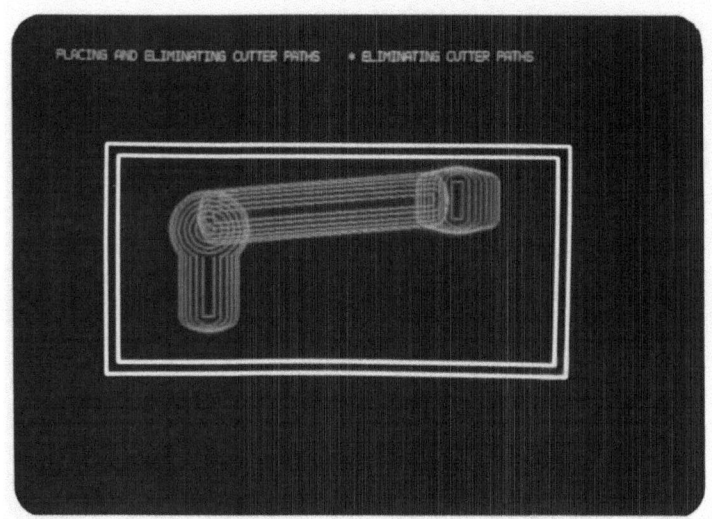

Photo 14. Placement of CYLIE3

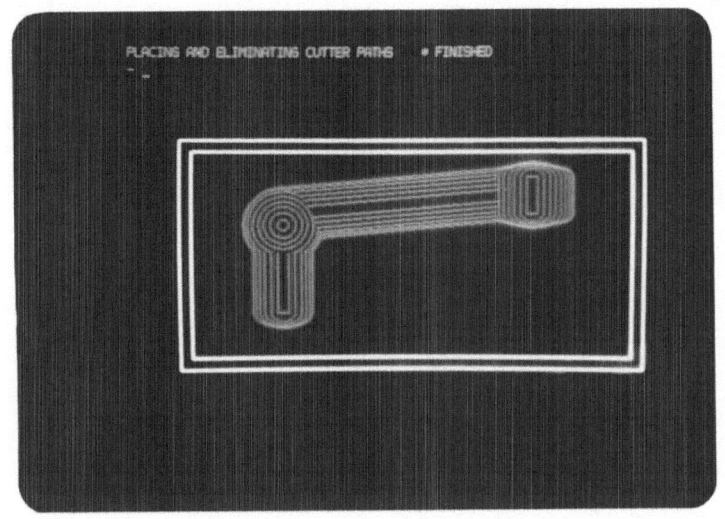

Photo 15. Final cutter path elimination

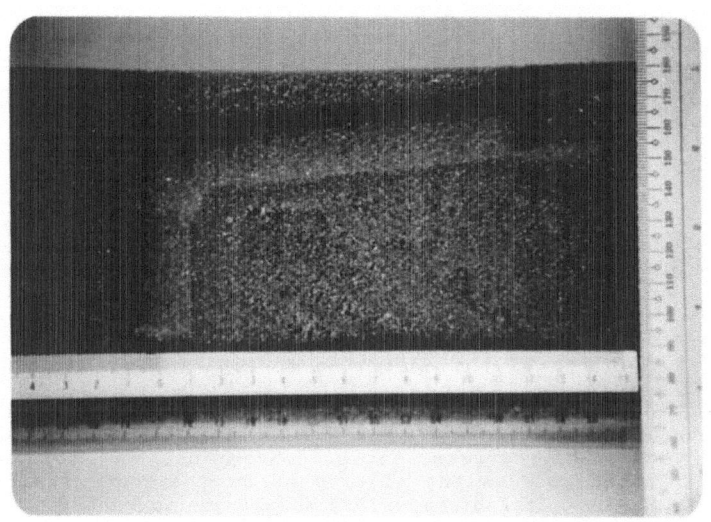

Photo 16. A physical LEVER FORGING

The CADME Approach to the Interface of Solid Modellers

C. Bizzozero and U. Cugini
Politecnico di Milano, dip. di Meccanica, P.za L.da Vinci 32, Milano, Italy

INTRODUCTION

This work stands as a contribution in the area of the man-machine communications. In the field of Computer Aided Design the solution of such a problem has led us to the definition and realization of an indipendent interface placed in front of solid modellers accepting C.S.G. definitions. This system is able to simulate the orthographic projections of the specified part without activating the solid modeller. The illustrated interface is a part of an integrated system called CADME.
To understand the logical process followed in the illustrated system and the software proposed tools we have to clarify the meaning we give, following Stafford Beer (1975), to the words "capacity" and "ability". <u>Capacity</u> stands for a systemic concept: it gives a value of the theoretical performances of a system, without any consideration about the constraints imposed by the environment. On the other hand, <u>ability</u> represents what we can really get from the system, noticing that an informatic system becomes more and more only a component in more complex and integrated ones (Winograd 1979).
If a system is not able to express all its potential features there have to be some phenomena which are restricting its capacity; such bottlenecks may depend, and this is our case, on the big problem of man-machine interaction. Generally the use of a computer imposes new mechanisms of formal communication which are alien to the way of thinking of experts in other disciplines.

THE PROBLEM

A typical example of systems which join high capacity and a usually low ability is that of the Solid Modellers (Requicha, Voelker 1980,1982). These systems have the main characteristic of being able to merge in an unique mathematical model all the informations which are necessary in the industrial process of manufacturing solid objects (typically mechanical parts). Solid modellers are able to maintain all the geometrical and topological features of the described object, logically connected and structured. Traditionally all these informations have to be deduced from a non connected set of geometrical and topological data represented in engineering drawings. Those data must be interpreted by an expert able to correlate them using representations, conventions and standards.
What dramatically reduces the ability of such systems resides in the interaction process: in fact modellers mainly use command languages which lead to the use of complex sentences and describing operations in a three dimensional space: an unfamiliar job to almost all the designers (Cardani, Cugini 1982).

TOWARDS A SOLUTION

This work suggests a step towards the solution of such problems, describing an interface system between Geometric Modellers and designers implemented into CADME system (Cugini, Valle 1983): the interface system is able to

simulate the work of a modeller, being at the same time a more natural tool for the usual user: a draftman.
This system has been designed in such a way to represent an interactive graphic generalized front-end to solid modellers.
The adopted point of view was that of the "designer" who, in a design process, uses the modeller mainly with the aim to create a unique representation of a complex solid. Thus the preliminary study has been devoted to an analysis of the designer's usual ways of working and of the problems arising because of the introduction of modelling systems.

We found that the existing modellers have some disadvantages:
- there is a low level of interaction, which is mainly based on the use of sentences in a specific command language
- the system is oriented towards the modellers' problems rather than those of the users'
- the designer is forced to produce preliminary sketches in order to obtain the geometrical and topological informations needed for the model definition
- it is necessary to evaluate the model to obtain the visual feed-back assuring the user of the correctness of the specified operations

As a matter of fact a mechanical designer does want to use the modeller in a correct and simple way, preserving methods which he is accustomed to, avoiding, as much as possible, other difficulties connected with the introduction of the computer in his work. In other words the use of a modelling system needs more interaction based on of procedures (as much as possible graphical ones) allowing the use of traditional drafting methods (bidimensional representations of solid objects by means of orthographic projections, sections etc.). It also needs an immediate visualization of the results of each action, operating on the graphical bidimensional representations.
The design of a system able to join capacity of the modellers with ability started from the identification of such needs. The resulting system, indipendent from a specific modeller, can be roughly divided in two main parts: the first one allows the user to describe the object via drafting procedures and performs the simulation of the resulting orthographic projections; the second one is really an interpreter, used as a code generator to arrange commands in the language of the modeller, starting from the generalized data structure defined during the designer work and stored by the first module.

This solution also permits to avoid the problems arising when a user, who has learned the command language of a specific modeller, tries to fit the shape of the part he is going to design on the features of the well known modeller; it should be better to use, among different modellers, the one which best performs the particular shape. Thus, the unification of the input modalities adds freedom to the use of different modelling systems.

A 2-D DRAFTING SYSTEM AS AN EMULATOR OF THE SOLID MODELLER

The tipical task of a system which models rigid solids is combining simple primitives in different ways to obtain complex shapes. On the other hand, it is possible to operate solid objects by means of a planar description, more simple and natural for a designer. In order to obtain these planar representations of complex solid objects it is possible to resort to a system which produces the orthographic projections by superimposing several planar figures. These ones, which represent sections of the solid, perpendicular to the point of view, can be obtained applying logical multivalued functions of union, intersection, difference, and finally superimposition, to planar operands which represent co-planar sections of the solids to be combined.

The problem is now that of being able to univocally represent complex shapes by means of a sequence of characteristic sections which are parallel one another. In simple cases (see fig. 1) it is easy to identify such sections; in these situations it's enough to apply the logical function (the set union, intersection, difference) to the co-planar sections of the objects, superimposing the results in a second time applying a procedure for hidden line removal.

By means of the "constructive" approach (Requicha, Voelker 1977), followed by the simulation process, it is easy to translate the graphic commands for the definition and operation of solids in the 3D space into an equivalent set of instructions for the definition of the 2D figures and their combinations.

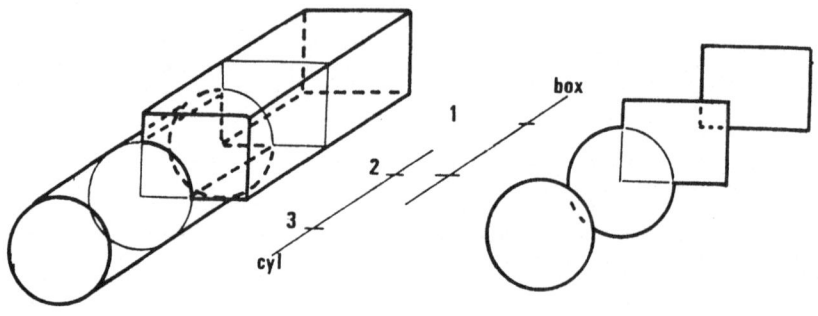

figure 1

CONNECTIONS OF THE SIMULATION SYSTEM

The simulation system's dialog towards its environment is mainly kept by means of two modules (see fig. 2)
    a) a user-interface system
    b) an interface towards the modelling system

The first module is designed to acquire the geometric and topologic data for the definition of the solid primitives in terms of dimentions, absolute and relative positions, and the operations between them; it handles in an interactive way the dialog with the user. Using graphical input software tools which simulate the tipical tools of designers (a ruler, a protractor, a drawing board) and hardware allowing real time 2-D and 3-D transformations for high interaction, a flexible and dynamic user-interface has been implemented.

The interactive part of a design process coincides, in modellers, with a phase of definition of simple solid shapes (primitives). This is performed in our system describing primitives via their three orthogonal projections.

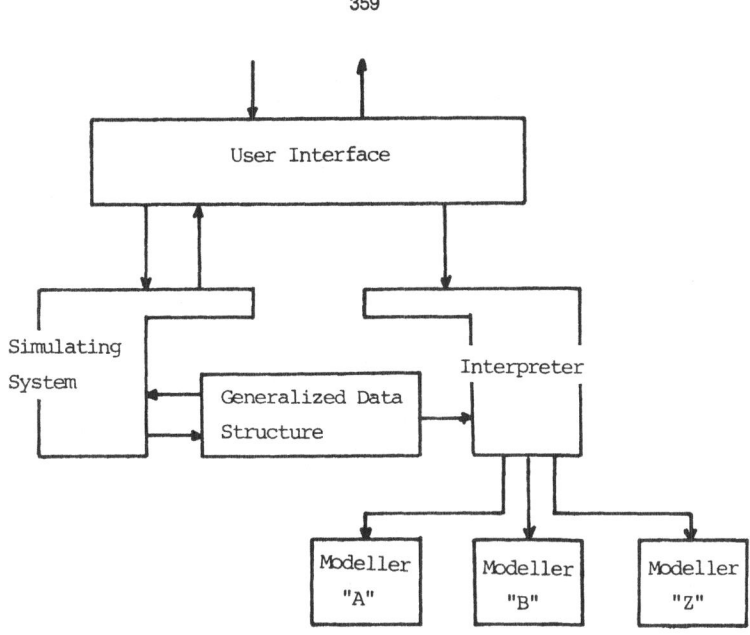

figure 2

These projections are defined by users with interactive procedures (graphic and alphanumeric); permits the use of graphical tools and modalities of interaction which can be chosen and activated via dynamic menus displayed on the screen.
It is possible to select a "direct", exclusively graphic, interaction (without any of the software tools mentioned: ruler, protractor and drawing-board) which is based on the use of a graphical device (a joystick) or an alphanumeric input (pairs of coordinates typed on a keyboard) or a pick device.
On the other hand, it is possible to select one of the three software tools which can be used in one of the three modalities: graphic, alphanumeric, pick.
The use of these tools make it possible to join the ease of use of the graphic interaction instruments with the precision, which is necessary in the definition of shapes via their coordinate values.

The second system, the interface between the simulation system and the modeller, called "interpreter", automatically translates the designer actions into a set of instructions, intelligible for a modeller (Cosmai, Rosoni 1982); this has been done in order to obtain the mathematical model of the defined object. In order to have a generalized channel between the system and the modeller we maintain a common basis for the different modellers: this basic element resides in the "constructive" approach for the input modalities of the different modelling systems.
The interface between the simulator and the modeller is a processor which, starting from a generalized data structure created during the phase of definition of complex solids, is able to generate the shape (geometry and topology) of the designed object.
This modularity lets a possibility of using the user interface and the simulating system combined with different modellers.

Our applications deal with three different "translators", each of which related to a particular modeller. The first two modellers used are: PADL1, developed by the University of Rochester, N.Y. (Requicha et al. 1977,78,79,80), TIPS1, developed in Japan by a research group of the Hokkaido University (Okino et al. 1978). As a note we underline the substantial difference between the languages of this two modellers.
We have built up a third "translator", which is necessary for the system to support a modeller, based on a C.S.G. approach and a Ray Casting technique (Scardaccione 1984), developed in the CADME research group, Politecnico di Milano.

AN EXAMPLE

In the design of a simple mechanical part are defined the geometrical and topological features of the part itself. In figures 3 and 4 are shown two moments of this phase. In the pictures it is possible to note the four graphic windows: in one of the three bidimensional ones the user is interacting with the system via the simulation of a drawing board. The three-dimensional window maintains a wire frame echo of the object already created. The other parts of the screen are devoted to the menus (commands, instruments, swithes, figure's names) and to the alphanumeric interaction.
At the end of the interactive phase, which gives as a result the object representation via its orthogonal projections, the user may instance the chosen modelling system; this one creates the mathematical model of the solid object.

Figures 5, 6 and 7 show three results obtained submitting to three different modellers the results of the implemented interpreters; the pictures refer respectively to PADL1, TIPS1 and CADME.

CONCLUSIONS

The present implementation is able to deal with objects in "two and half" dimensions defined using two primitives: box and cylinder. The extension for fully three dimensional objects is under development and testing.

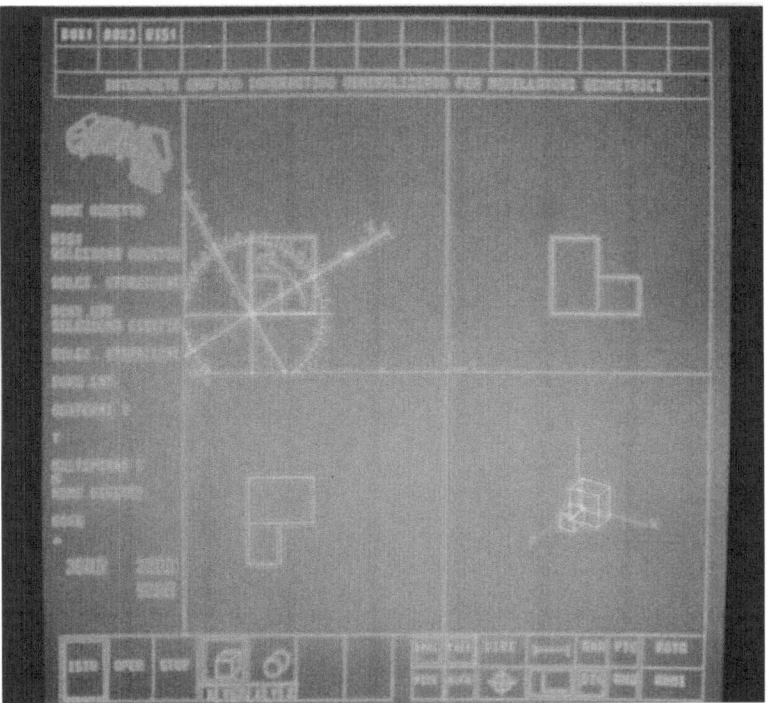

figure 3

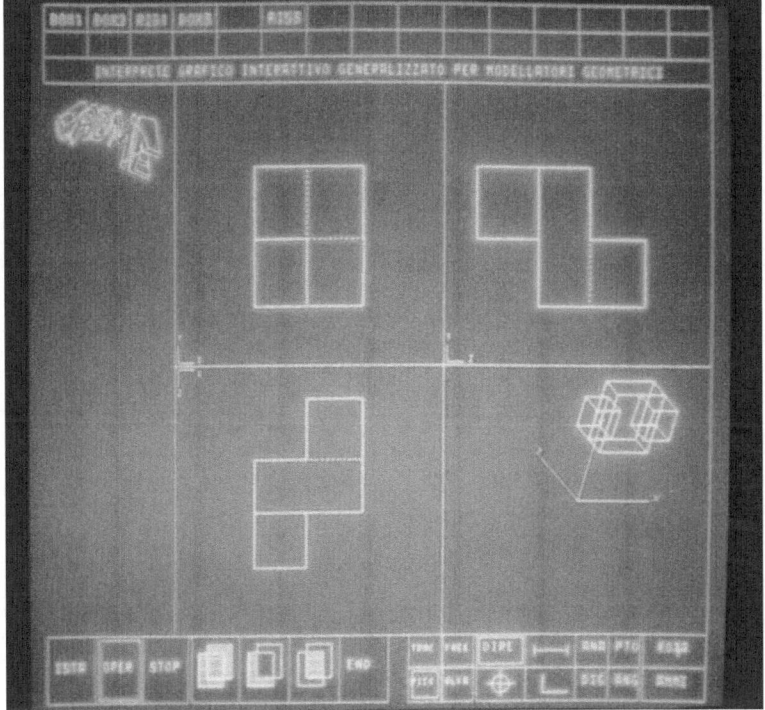

figure 4

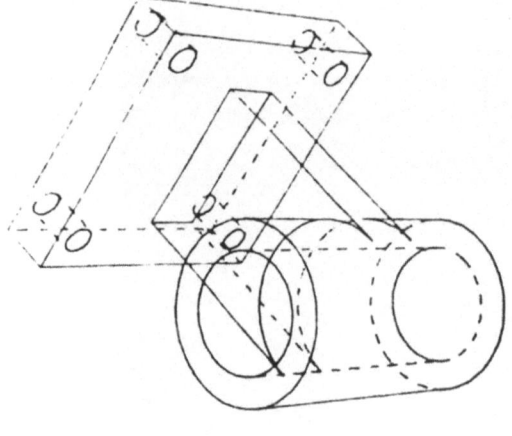
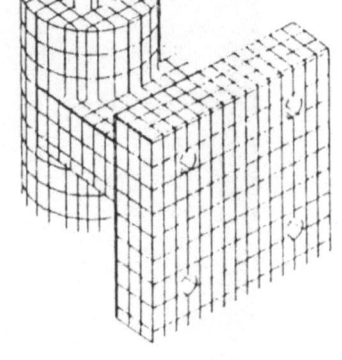

figure 5 figure 6

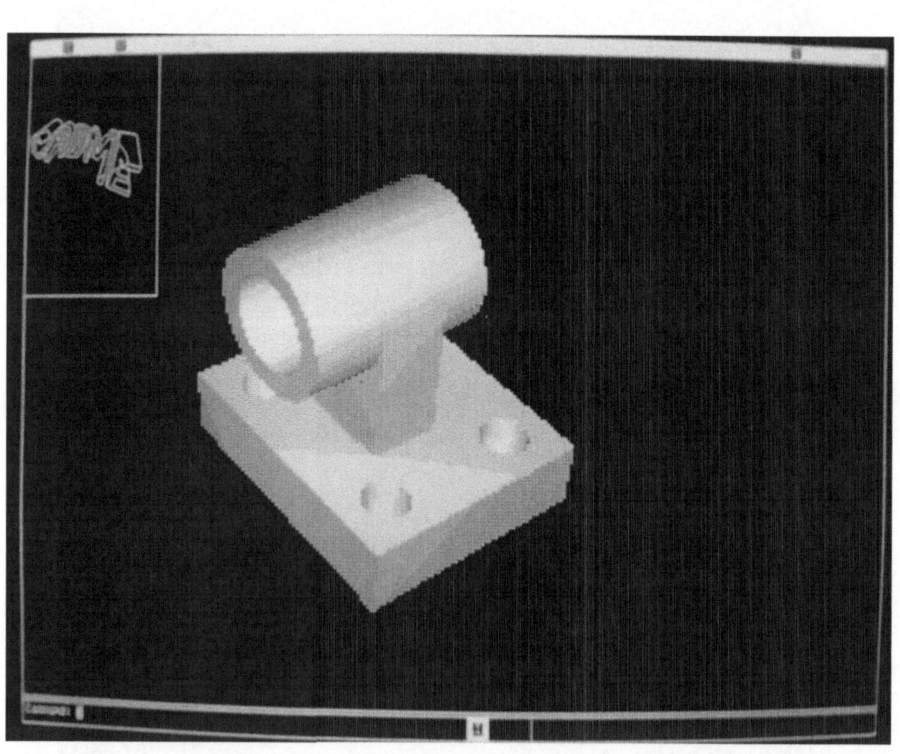

figure 7

ACKNOWLEDGMENTS

This research was supplied by "Consiglio Nazionale delle Ricerche" under contracts number 83.03025.97 and 83.03007.97 in "Progetto Finalizzato Informatica".

REFERENCES

Beer S. (1975)
 'Fanfare for effective freedom: cybernetic praxis in government'
 from: Beer S. 'Platform for Change' Wiley and Sons
Cardani A., Cugini U. (May 1982)
 'Analisi critica dell'impiego dei modellatori PADL1 e TIPS1'
 P.F.I. Obbiettivo CADME, technical report
Cosmai G., Rosoni R. (October 1982)
 'Studio ed implementazione di un interprete grafico interattivo generalizzato per modelli geometrici 3-D' P.F.I. Obbiettivo CADME, technical report.
Cugini U., Valle G. (February 1983)
 'L'obbiettivo CADME del Progetto Finalizzato Informatica del C.N.R.'
 in: "Il CAD, la progettazione con il computer e la piccola e media industria", Milano.
Fisher W., Requicha A., Samuel N., Voelcker H. (June 1978)
 'Part and assembly description languages II: definitional facilities in the PADL-1.0/2.n processor'
 Technical memorandum No. 20b, Production Automation Project, University of Rochester.
Hunt A. (August 1978)
 'Representations in the PADL-1.0/n processor: the drawing file'
 System Doc. No. 14, Production Automation Project, University of Rochester.
Hunt A. (August 1978)
 'Processes in the PADL-1.0/n processor: the drawing file post processor'
 System Doc. No. 15, Production Automation Project, University of Rochester.
Lee Y. (February 1980)
 'Algorithms for computing the mass properties of solid objects'
 M.S. Thesis, Mechanical and Aerospace Sciences Dept., University of Rochester.
Okino N., Kakazu Y., Kubo H. (1973)
 'TIPS-1: technical information processing system for computer aided design, drawing and manufacturing'
 in 'Computer Languages for Numerical Control', Amsterdam, North Holland, pp. 141-150
Okino N. et al. (1978)
 ' TIPS-1 '
 Institute of Precision Engineering, Hokkaido University, Sapporo, Japan.
Requicha A., Voelcker H. (November 1977)
 'Constructive Solid Geometry'
 Technical Memorandum 25 Production Automation Project, University of Rochester N.Y.
Requicha A. (May 1977)
 'Part and assembly description languages I: dimensioning and tolerancing'
 Technical memorandum No. 19, Production Automation Project, University of Rochester.

Requicha A. (1980)
  'Representations for rigid solids: theory, methods and systems'
  Computing Surveys, vol 12, No 4, pp.437-464
Requicha A., Voelcker H. (march 1982)
  'Solid Modelling: a historical summary and contemporary assessment'
  IEEE C.G. and A., pp 9-24
Scardaccione A. (December 1984)
  'Il modellatore solido CADME di tipo C.S.G.'
  P.F.I. Obbiettivo CADME, Technical report.
Winograd T. (July 1979)
  'Beyond Programming Languages'
  Communications of the ACM, No 7, vol. 22

Chapter 7
Artificial Intelligence

Generative Design in Architecture
Using an Expert System

Eric Gullichsen[*] and Ernest Chang

Dept. of Computer Science, P.O. Box 1700, University of Victoria, Victoria, B.C. V8W 2Y2, Canada

ABSTRACT

The mathematician-architect Christopher Alexander has devised a theory of objective architectural design. He believes that all architectural forms can be described as interacting patterns, all possible relationships of which are governed by generative rules. These form a 'pattern language' capable of generating forms appropriate for a given environmental context.

The complexity of interaction among these rules leads to difficulties in their representation by conventional methods. This paper presents a Prolog-based expert system which implements Alexander's design methodology to produce perspective views of partially and fully differentiated 3-dimensional architectural forms.

1. THE PATTERN LANGUAGE OF CHRISTOPHER ALEXANDER

'From the sequence of these individual patterns, whole buildings with the character of nature will form themselves within your thoughts, as easily as sentences.' (Alexander 1979, p.xiv)

1.1. Patterns: Forms within a Context of Forces

What are the primitive 'atomic' elements which comprise an architectural form such as a room, a building, or a city? In answering this question, the environmental context of what may upon first consideration appear to be atomic elements must not be neglected.

According to Alexander, patterns, which consist of static physical elements (the form) in the environment, together with dynamic occurences related to the physical elements (the context) which in turn result from the interaction of certain relevant forces, constitute the entire physical substance of the world. To consider the world to be made of physical 'things' entails a misconception analogous to that held by classical physics in considering an 'atom' a thing. Western languages contribute to the perpetuation of the illusion that 'things' are fundamental, by their preponderance of nouns. In Alexander's view, a noun is simply a convenient label for a set of relationships amongst patterns.

What is it then that is repeated in an architectural form? Traditionally, physical entities are repeated hierarchically: an apartment building can be seen as a collection of suites, each of which is a collection of rooms. However, this classical view fails to explain how or why these elements tend to be associated with different sets of events. For instance, people who live in an apartment building do disparate things in their respective suites, and the modular viewpoint fails to account for this variation.

Alexander asserts that hierarchies of relationships, rather than of things, contain the architectural primitives we seek. Each pattern is a morphological law which defines a permissible set of spatial relationships within a given context. The taxonomy of these morphological laws is a hierarchy, as each pattern is itself a pattern of relationships among other patterns.

The relationships between patterns are the only entities repeated in the world. Patterns, consisting of a space and the events which occur there, are the atoms of the man-made universe.

---

[*]Now at: MCC-STP, Echelon #1 Suite 200, 9430 Research Blvd., Austin, Texas 78759 USA

According to Alexander (Alexander 1979, p.98) these patterns are only a few in number: a building is defined by several dozen patterns.

If this is accepted, the obvious question is then how these canonical patterns combine to produce the world we know. Before we attempt to answer this, a distinction must be made between 'good' and 'bad' patterns.

1.2. The Quality of Patterns

Alexander claims that patterns vary from 'good' to 'bad', and that the quality of a form to be created can be assured by objective scientific means. Good patterns possess a certain hard-to-characterize quality of holistic completeness or 'life' which Alexander terms the 'quality without a name'. Patterns which produce irreconcilable conflicts in humans and thereby increase their psychological stress are bad patterns. What then is a good pattern? As will become apparent, good patterns are those generated by a specific set of rules which take into consideration the forces acting on the pattern being designed.

Such a pattern has an ecological balance of internal and external forces acting upon it. Where this balance is stable, as in the forms found in nature, a pattern is good or 'alive'. These live patterns can interact to support each other.

Natural objects are always formed by the forces which arise within them. Objects created by man are also formed through the action of certain forces, but there may also exist additional latent forces which do not directly influence the form of the object. However, a design procedure which does not account for all forces acting on objects will inevitably lead to an unstable system.

Living patterns are easily recognized from their geometric character. Alexander stresses that a hierarchy of living patterns is never modular. Rather, the reconciliation of patterns with their internal forces make their details unique, like the leaves of a tree, or the waves of an ocean. To be whole and alive, buildings and other architectural structures must have this natural characteristic of responsiveness to internal and external environmental forces.

It is precisely this holistic characteristic of good architectural design requiring the interaction of large amounts of knowledge that makes the use of expert-system techniques suitable.

1.3. The Generation of Pattern Hierarchies by Pattern Languages

Good patterns cannot be brought into existence by a single monumental effort of intellect, but only through process. Just as life within a natural organism implies the maintenance of a balance of forces, so a building which is alive must be grown from a set of patterns in which the parts created are harmonious both internally and in their totality. Rules for combining patterns constitute

> 'a way of focusing attention on some particular holistic behavior in a thing, which can only be understood as a product of interaction among the parts.' (Alexander 1968)

Alexander claims to have discovered a simple set of generative rules which determine the structure of any environment. These rules are similar to a genetic code, and govern human acts of building. Architectural forms generated by this 'pattern language' are necessarily 'alive' since a balance of relevant internal forces follows inevitably from the manner of their creation. Details of the 253 patterns which comprise this pattern language have been published (Alexander 1977). Alexander asserts that the language represented by these patterns constitutes the archetypal core of all possible pattern languages.

He makes a clear distinction (Grabow 1983) between a generative design process, and design governed by constraints, which is the conventional method of formulating design rules in architecture. An appropriate analogy can be found in the field of linguistics. Chomsky (Chomsky 1956) was the first to develop generative grammars for languages, both natural and artificial. Until Chomsky, most grammatical rules were expressed in the form of constraints which sentences in the language obeyed. Chomsky's generative specification of grammatical rules was novel in that only correct sentences would ever be created. Therefore, complex and uncertain 'generate-and-test' methods were no longer required. A similar process occurs in nature, in which an organism grows from an embryo in accordance with the generative rules encoded in its chromosomes. The same efficient design methodology is possible, according to Alexander, in architecture.

2. FROM FORMS TO FORCES: DESIGN WITH A PATTERN LANGUAGE

We have postulated the need to achieve during its design process, a balance of forces acting on a designed object, for it to be 'alive' and have the 'quality without a name'. We now explore more thoroughly how this need can be satisfied through use of a pattern-based design process.

2.1. A Formalism for Patterns

In (Alexander 1979, p.247) Alexander gives a rigorous treatment of patterns, the basic entities of his design system. A pattern both corresponds to a certain class of thing which exists in the world, and is a rule describing the design (generation) of that thing.

The structure of a pattern language follows from the fact that individual patterns are not isolated. Each pattern occupies a position in a (possibly cyclic) network of related patterns, connected to the smaller patterns it contains, as well as the larger patterns in which it is contained. A pattern helps to complete the patterns above it in the network, and is itself completed by the smaller patterns below it.

A pattern has three components:

(1) Context. Where or when is the pattern applicable? The context of a pattern may be considered to be a set of preconditions which specify its applicability.

(2) The system of forces which define the problem solved by this pattern. Why is this pattern required? Recall that good patterns resolve or balance the internal and external forces acting on the thing designed. This component of the pattern provides the reason(s) for its application.

(3) The solution, or spatial configuration of entities implied by the pattern which permit the resolution of (2). What specifically is the invariant property common to all such solutions? As patterns are hierarchically arranged, this third component of a pattern may be highly complex, and usually involves other patterns.

Each pattern thus contains two logical statements, which must be empirically true. The first is that a given problem (2) exists within the stated context (1). Secondly, the pattern asserts that (3) solves (2). A pattern is objectively good if the problem (2) is real and configuration (3) solves (2).

To implement a design system based upon an interacting set of such patterns, the rigorous specification of (3) frequently proves to be difficult[1]. As seen in the next section, for patterns to be practically applied to a design problem, the solution may be a set of procedures which further differentiates the form being designed.

Alexander has published (Alexander 1977), 253 patterns which apply to architectural forms of varying scales are presented. The scales distinguished by Alexander are those of: towns, buildings, and construction. Our expert design system employs a subset of 84 of these 253 patterns, selected to consider the design of forms from the second of the three scales, those that pertain to individual buildings and the spaces between buildings.

2.2. Use of a Pattern Language: Differentiation

The use of a language of patterns to design an architectural form involves a process of differentiation: the creation of distinctions where no distinctions previously existed. A process of differentiation which results in the 'growth' of a design should not simply consist of the addition of modular components in a hierarchical manner; each part must be modified by its position in the whole design.

Alexander's patterns are arranged roughly in order of decreasing morphological importance to ensure that a whole, imprecisely-specified form is successively differentiated during the process of design. This successive differentiation ensures that subsequent design decisions do not conflict with earlier decisions, and eliminates the need for backtracking.

---

[1] The reader is challenged to provide a rigorous definition of a 'rough circle', an object which any child could sketch without hesitation.

Since patterns are ordered, no pattern can unexpectedly arise to act as a constraint on a partially-completed design. Patterns are applied successively in a generative manner. At each step, certain general configurations of the form are established, and details are then elaborated, conforming to the structure laid down.

More precisely, to design in a generative manner, the order of application of patterns should meet the following three heuristic criteria, listed in order of decreasing importance (Alexander 1979, p.380)

(1) If pattern A is above pattern B in the network of patterns, then A should be employed before B. For instance, if pattern A involves a living room, and B involves alcoves in a room, the living room design must be produced (roughly) before alcoves can be incorporated.

(2) Before employing pattern A, all the patterns immediately above A in the pattern network should be considered in the design, as contiguously as is possible.

(3) Similarly, after employing pattern A in a design, the patterns immediately below A in the network should be considered, as contiguously as is possible.

It is the burden of the designer of a pattern language to correctly structure the network of patterns so that features which are 'dominant' in a form which can be produced are characterized by patterns which occur higher in the network of patterns[2]. As Alexander has made explicit the structure of the network of patterns for his pattern language (Alexander 1977), we need not concern ourselves with the problem of discovering the pattern hierarchy.

2.3. Differentiation of the Structure of an Individual Building

In order to illustrate more clearly what is meant by the process of design by differentiation, let us consider in detail that subset of patterns (104-204) which deals with the design of individual buildings.

An examination of these patterns as presented (Alexander 1977), reveals that the use of this portion of the pattern language involves 8 identifiable steps of differentiation of detail of the form being designed.

(1) Initially, the position and rough shape of building(s) on the site is fixed. (patterns 104-109).
(2) Entrances, gardens, courtyards, terraces and roofs are laid out. (patterns 110-118).
(3) The gradients of space within the building are established. (patterns 127-135).
(4) Within building wings, the most important areas and rooms are defined. (patterns 136-145).
(5) The inside of the building is knit to the outside, by treating the building edge as a distinct place. (patterns 157-168).
(6) Minor rooms and alcoves are attached, to complete the main rooms. (patterns 179-189).
(7) The size and shape of rooms and alcoves are fine-tuned, to make them precise and constructable. (patterns 190-196).
(8) Finally, the walls are given depth as necessary for alcoves and windows. (patterns 197-204).

For the design of any form which is to be a complete building, patterns are usually selected from each of the 8 groups outlined above. Variation in the exact selection of patterns leads to variation between individual designs.

3. THE PROLOG-BASED EXPERT SYSTEM

The ideas and structure of Alexander's system of design as based on a generative pattern language have been presented. The entities of the system are the patterns, each of which has three principal constituents (section 2.1). A network of patterns is seen to form a language for design, where a useful language should be both morphologically and functionally complete. The structure of the

---

[2] It is reasonable to imagine that if patterns were represented by means of a sufficiently uniform and rich description language, an inference of the structure of the pattern network might proceed automatically.

network is governed by the morphological dependencies present between patterns. Heuristic design rules for traversing the network to apply patterns one-at-a-time in a top-down differentiating fashion have been discussed.

Computer-based experiments with generative architectural design were conducted using the very high-level logic programming language, Prolog (Clocksin 1982;Kowalski 1974). CProlog Version 1.4 was employed on a VAX 11/750, and a Raster Technology Model 20 colour raster graphics device was used to present graphical output interactively, employing a 3-d solids rendering package developed at the University of Victoria. Prolog was selected for a number of reasons, including: its suitability as a language for implementing expert systems (Clark 1982), and its overt descriptive clarity.

3.1. The Need for an Expert Design System

Expert systems are powerful tools in knowledge-intensive fields of human expertise. Heuristics are often used to search problem spaces too large or heterogeneous for formal techniques.

As Alexander has observed (Grabow 1983), the number of potential interactions between rules in a generative system increases so explosively with the number of rules that a conventional exhaustive mathematical treatment of all points in the design space is impossible for non-trivial systems. He has also recommended (Alexander 1979, p.538) that designers should be free from preconceived notions, apply the pattern language objectively, and be egoless. Computer expert systems seem to meet these requirements.

3.2. The Knowledge-Base of Patterns

A subset of the patterns of Alexander's pattern language constitutes the expert knowledge of our system. The morphological content of patterns is represented in part by Prolog axioms, and can be manipulated (displayed, changed, removed, summarized) within the expert system. The solution component of each pattern is represented through the procedural attachment of appropriate Prolog routines to the pattern. Knowledge possessed by the system is thus both declarative and procedural in nature. The declarative knowledge indicates when and for what purpose the pattern is to be used. The procedural knowledge determines how the form being designed is affected when the pattern is applied.

Declarative information is represented for each pattern. The pattern number and name are present, to identify the pattern. Alexander's judgement of the universal archetypal validity of the pattern (Alexander 1977, p.xv) is represented by an integer from 0-2. The context of the pattern is encoded by associating, with each pattern, lists of the patterns immediately above and below it in the network of patterns. The group to which the pattern belongs is represented by an integer between 1 and 8. The problem solved by the pattern is given in text form. Finally, the solution component is given both in text form for explanatory purposes, and as (a set of) Prolog procedures.

The Prolog procedures for a pattern embody knowledge of the processing required to apply the design rule(s) captured by the pattern. Since Alexander intended his language to be used by people who possess spatial and perceptual tools (not easy to implement in machines), the amount of computation required to apply a even single pattern is often large. In our system, the complexity of individual rules (patterns) is much larger than that typical of production-based expert systems.

For example, consider Alexander's pattern number 106, termed 'positive outdoor space' (Alexander 1977). This pattern solves the problem of unused spaces between buildings by making these spaces 'positive' in form, giving each some degree of enclosure. This intuitive notion corresponds closely to the mathematical idea of ensuring that the sum of areas enclosed by walls of buildings or segments which constitute the convex polygonal hull of the building's wings, weighted by the ratio of its enclosing perimeter (provided by the walls) to the entire perimeter of the hull, is sufficiently high.

Although the attachment of a plethora of procedures to a single pattern seems to violate the principle of modularization, it was necessary to create such complex rules in order to automate Alexander's system in its original form. The lower-level procedures typically employ geometric methods to solve technical problems which are simply taken for granted in human design.

3.3. Pattern Selection and Ordering

The first step in the design of a form is the selection of the patterns which are to be used in the design of the form. According to the instructions of Alexander (Alexander 1977, p.xxxviii), in order to design a form, one begins by selecting the single pattern which

> 'best describes the overall scope of the project [one] has in mind'.

The network of patterns is traversed forward from the position occupied by this initial pattern; all patterns below the initially-chosen pattern are presented to the user for selection or rejection. The user should select all patterns relevant to the form to be designed.

Alexander cautions the user against selecting irrelevant patterns:

> 'When in doubt about a pattern, don't include it. Your list can easily get too long; and it if it does, it will become confusing.' (Alexander 1977, p.xxxix)

One goal of the development of an expert system for design is to succeed in dealing with complexity without confusion. As the user traverses the network of pattern in the knowledge base, explanations can be given of the problems resolved by the patterns encountered, to help in deciding whether to include the pattern.

Following the selection of patterns, those chosen are sorted into the order in which they are to be applied, according to the heuristic rules of section 2.2.

3.4. Form Generation

At the beginning of the generation process, a number of global design parameters are requested of the user. For example, what is the square footage of the form to be designed? Although Alexander's patterns do not explicitly use such information, the creation of actual buildings requires it. Selected patterns are then used, one at a time, to differentiate the form.

The Prolog procedures attached to each of the selected patterns are then applied sequentially to differentiate the form. Prior to the application of each procedure, the user may chose to invoke one of several available options. If desired, an explanation of why the pattern is being applied is presented. At the end of the partial differentiation which results from application of a series of patterns from the same group, special postprocessing procedures are invoked, to 'clean-up' the form which results from the processing.

A graphical display of the form as it currently exists at a given stage in the design procedure is updated as the form is differentiated by the application of patterns. As design proceeds, the user may request explanations of a design step or request the retention of the design for subsequent reproduction.

At the earlier stages of differentiation, the building is represented as a 2-dimensional line drawing in plan view. After all patterns from the first group have been applied, the form is given elevation, and is rendered thereafter by perspective projection of the 3-dimensional model. Through the scene description language employed by the rendering software, the user is free to select viewpoint, lighting sources, surface colours and reflectance properties for the building and its background both during and subsequent to the design.

3.5. An Example of Design

The following example of form generation is intended to convey the level of design expertise currently present in our system. Nine patterns (Alexander 1977) were selected for use in the design:

104) Site Repair
105) South-facing Outdoors
106) Positive Outdoor Space
107) Wings of Light
108) Connected Buildings
117) Sheltering Roof
128) Indoor Sunlight
159) Light on Two Sides of Every Room
239) Small Panes

Pattern 104 prohibits the form from being generated in certain regions of the site, as buildings should be constructed on those parts of the land which are in the worst condition. Pattern 105 establishes the principal orientation of the building. Graphical output commences for this example with the application of pattern 107, which causes the building to be generated in the form of long narrow wings (Fig. 1).

Pattern 106, which occurs below 107 in the pattern hierarchy, is applied next, to ensure that sufficient space is enclosed by the proposed form (Fig. 2). Pattern 108 ensures that the building is connected, and pushes wings towards their center of gravity if any were disconnected. As by chance all wings were connected, the application of this pattern causes no change in the example design.

As the next pattern to be applied, 117, is in a different group than is 108, end-of-group processing for group 1 causes extension of the building into the second and third dimensions (Fig. 3,4). Pattern 117 causes the roof to be partially differentiated (Fig. 5), and the remaining patterns create and differentiate windows (Fig. 6). Figures 7 through 10 provide some views of the completed form.

4. CONCLUSIONS

Although our design system is still being developed, our results are promising, and convince us of the feasibility of a Prolog-based expert system which implements the pattern language of Christopher Alexander.

The usefulness of the system as a practical design tool is reduced by a number of factors. Alexander's design methodology, although formal and precise in many of its higher-level characteristics, requires the user to make many lower-level decisions based on intuition alone. That is, the language is morphologically complete in its specification of form only to a certain level of detail, beyond which it seems natural and simple for humans to continue on the basis of considerations which appeal to emotional feeling.

While the mechanisms for choosing patterns and applying the language are easily implementable, it is difficult to automate the entire process of form generation, because the intuitive feelings of human designers are difficult to characterize formally in expert systems. It is only due to the high degree of formal structure present in Alexander's system that the automation of design is conceivable at all.

We believe that introspection combined with experimental verification can in all cases reveal the formal substance of what is termed 'feeling' or 'intuition' about design. The production of a formal characterization of human feelings about design can in many cases be laborious; its difficulty was greatly underestimated at the commencement of our experiment.

Another problem encountered during the development of the system was the lack of a good programming environment for Prolog. In order to develop a convenient user interface for the system, a large amount of low-level Prolog code had to be written. Prolog routines for such tasks as list manipulation, I/O, screen management, menu presentation and raster graphics have all been created, and are now available for future projects and the continuing development of our system[3].

Our experiences with Alexander's design methods leave us optimistic about the future of complex knowledge-based expert systems in the field of architectural design.

---

[3]The Prolog source code for the system is available from the authors upon request.

REFERENCES

(1) Alexander C (1968) The Bead Game Conjecture. Lotus, an International Review of Contemporary Architecture 5, 151-154

(2) Alexander C (1977) A Pattern Language. Oxford University Press, New York

(3) Alexander C (1979) The Timeless Way of Building. Oxford University Press, New York

(4) Chomsky N (1956) Aspects of the Theory of Syntax.

(5) Clark KL, McCabe FG (1982) PROLOG: A Language for Implementing Expert Systems. In: Michie D (ed) Machine Intelligence 10. John Wiley & Sons, New York, pp 455-470

(6) Clocksin CS, Mellish WF (1982) Programming in PROLOG. Springer-Verlag, New York

(7) Grabow S (1983) The Science of Design: Christopher Alexander's Search for a Generative Structure. ReVisions 2: 36-45

(8) Kowalski RA (1974) Predicate Logic as a Programming Language. IFIP 74, North-Holland, 569-574

Knowledge Engineering Application in Image Processing

Kazuo Mikame, Naomichi Sueda, Akira Hoshi and Shinichi Honiden

Systems and Software Engineering Division, Toshiba Corporation, 1-1, Shibaura 1-chome, Minato-ku, Tokyo, 105 Japan

1. INTRODUCTION

To establish the logic and procedure for image processing, a specific software module must be selected from 350 software modules, named SPIDER in Japan, according to requirments and the original image. Highly specialized and experimental knowledge is required to select this software module.

By using the knowledge engineering method, the authors verified the selection and execution of these software modules. As a result, satisfactory processing has been made available to even nonexperts for use in image processing. In image processing execution, FORTRAN is used to perform a image processing and AI language Prolog is used to infer a suitable software module. By applying AI language, a greater number of image processings, covering a wider range, are expected.

Image processing technology application depends on image conditions (called the attribute in this paper) and the image processing specialist's know-how. It has not gained access to other fields easily.

From this standpoint, knowledge engineering has been applied to image processing in which specialist's know-how can be used. So, the authors called the established system "The image processing expert system."

Prior to the application of such knowledge engineering, the image processing engineer's knowledge was defined and, as a result, the image processing expert system, developed in the segmentation field, has been verified, making a reasonable part of it comprehensible to nonprofessional persons in image processing.

2. IMAGE PROCESSING KNOWLEDGE

Before presenting an analysis of image processing knowledge, the developmental background for the image processing expert system is described below.

2.1 Developmental Background

As far as pre-processing in two-dimensional image processes is concerned, basic approaches have been substantially established.

In Japan, The Electrotechnical Laboratory of the Agency of Industrial Science and Technology, under The Ministry of International Trade and Industry (MITI), has developed and edited SPIDER (Subroutine Package for Image Data Enhancement and Recognition). SPIDER contains approximately 350 subroutine packages for each process field (orthogonal transform, enhancement & smoothing etc.), which is programmed by FORTRAN. The image processing engineers select suitable subroutines from the package group.
To select a suitable subroutine, it is necessary that the engineer have special knowledge in regard to image processing.
Therefore, the authors have begun to study and develop an image processing expert system, in which these subroutine packages can be used, based on the image processing specialist's know-how.

2.2 Analysis of Knowledge Used in Image Processing

The knowledge base to image processing must be analyzed before the image processing expert system can be established.
The three most important steps for studying are mentioned below : -- using a typical example of image processing, namely, a segmentation process -- :

(1) Specialist's processing procedures
(2) Specialist's knowledge classification
(3) Knowledge representation

2.2.1 Specialist's Processing Procedures

(1) Process example

The image segmentation process must be studied prior to discussing the processing procedures.
The segmentation process can be widely used for material inspection etc.
The segmentation process procedure is shown in Fig. 1. The figure shows that the process contents considerably vary with different image attributes (brightness, noise, overlapping with the background, etc.). In other words, the processing procedures depend on the image condition.

(2) Approach procedure

The specialist's approach is expected to follow the procedures in Fig. 2, in consideration of (1). The specialist at this stage can be described as follows:

  i) He fully understands the attributes of the objective image.
 ii) He infers the conditions of the resulting image after processing.
iii) He understands the effects reaction of the target process.
 iv) He is familiar with the algorithm.

(3) Classification of Specialist's knowledge

The knowledge used at each stage according to the approach in (2), is classified into the following three categories:

(a) Knowledge about image attributes
(b) Knowledge about image processing procedures
(c) Knowledge about image processing algorithm

The relevant knowledge is shown in Fig. 2 marked with *.

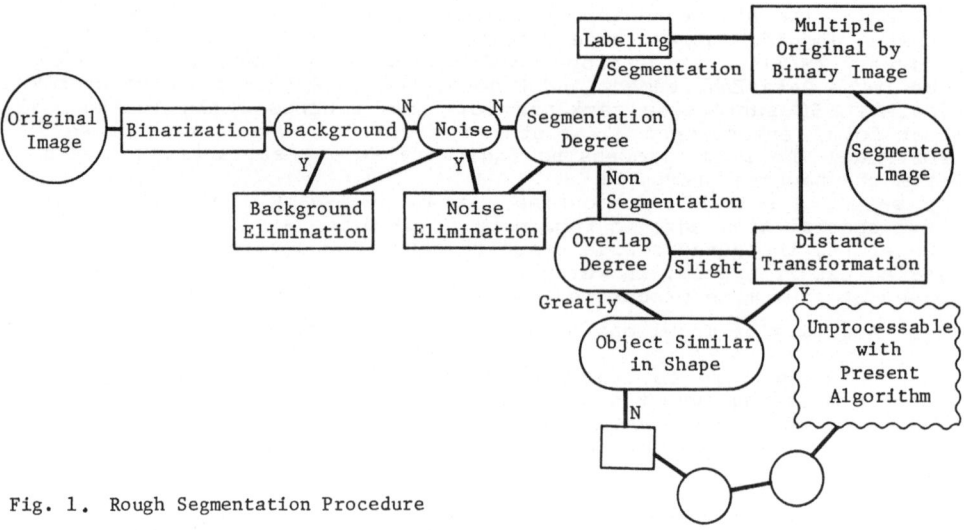

Fig. 1. Rough Segmentation Procedure

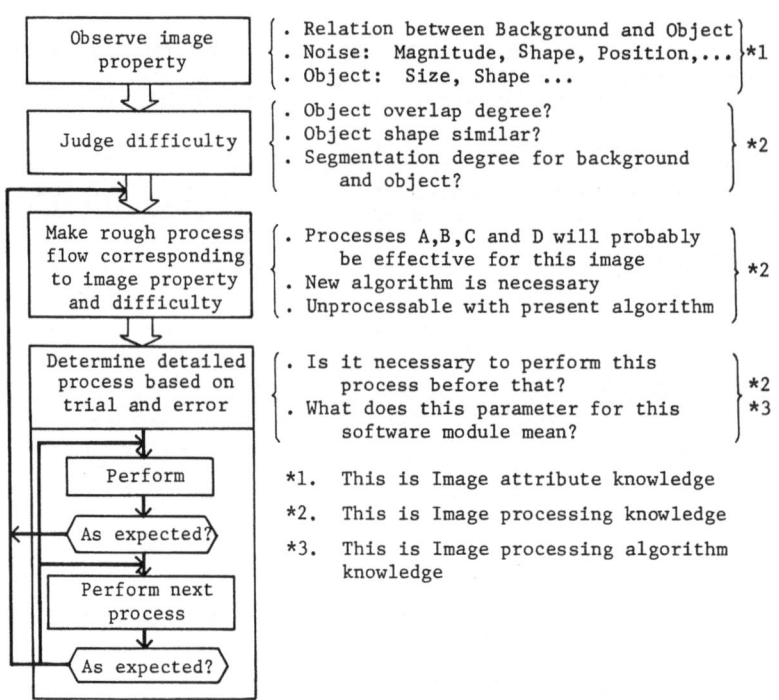

Fig. 2. Specialist's Approach and Classification of Knowledge

2.2.2 Knowledge about image attributes

The specialist, to whom the image to be processed is given, should understand:

i) Overall image
ii) Target conditions
iii) Relationship with the background
iv) Noise, Strain, Diffusion

Examples of such knowledge about image attribute are as follow.

(General) knowledge about background
    o Background is in an area other than the target area.
    o Background is often a larger area with the same features.
    o Background is often composed of two or more textures.

The knowledge is represented by three items image attribute, evaluation item, and evaluation value.
The Image attribute is "overall image" or "target condition" or "relationship with background" or something else.
For example, the evaluation items in the over all image of image attribute are average gray level, contrast, sharpness, and number of data bits.
The evaluation value means, for example, square, circle, and triangle for shape of the image attribute.

(1) Knowledge about image processing procedures

Knowledge about image processing procedures is broadly divided into the following two categories: knowledge about the basic process flow shown in Fig. 2 and knowledge -- so called specialist's know-how -- which regulates the processing in detail according to the correlation with the image attribute, or, simply put,

. Knowledge about basic processing procedures
. Knowledge about procedures which are defined as specialist's know-how.

Examples are given in Tables 1. and 2.

Table 1. Example of knowledge about basic processing procedures

(Binarization)
    o To an image over gray level 3, Set one or more threshold values.
    o Define sections outside of the two threshold values or the section between the theshold values as one (1), and define the others as zero (0).
    o Obtain an image comprising 0 and 1 only.

Table 2. Example of knowledge about procedures defined as specialists' know-how

(Additional information on segmentation)
    o If the objects overlap after binarization, binarize them again after calculating the overlap distance.
    o If the objective image has a low gray level, correct the gray level before binarization.
    o If the objective image contains any noise, eliminate the noise before binarization or grey level correction.

(2) Knowledge about image process algorithms

It is expected that, in image processing, the specialist's know-how attribute changes according to the process performed, which process routine should be used and how it should be applied. In other words, he has:

o Knowledge about effects/side-effects of image processing algorithms
o Knowledge about how to use software modules.

Examples are given in Table 3.

Table 3. Knowledge about effects/ side-effects of image processing algorithms

(Binarization algorithm)
 o When binarization is made, the grey level in other than the objective area equals 0.
 o When binarization is made, the grey level in the objective area equals 1.

3. APPLIED KNOWLEDGE ENGINEERING

The specialist continues to perform image processing according to the knowledge mentioned in the preceding, and tries to apply knowledge engineering to this process.

3.1 System Concept

To study the image processing knowledge application effectiveness, it is necessary to form the image process execution part characteristics (the knowledge effectiveness will be clarified only by execution of the image processing). The requirement is given by the user (for example, "Segmentation of the object from the original image"). The image processing expert system consists of the consultation section to infer the procedure, the execution parameter input section and the image processing execution section (Fig. 3).

3.2 Knowledge Representation

The structure suitable for inference is analyzed according to the knowledge analysis. Knowledge about the image processing procedure and knowledge about image attributes are described in detail below.

(1) Knowledge about image processing procedures

The knowledge structure is divided into the following categories:
(a) For process A, perform processes b, c, d, or e, f, g, --- .
     Meta-inference
(b) When the b_1 process is executed, the image attribute changes (greatly, moderately, or a little) and the attribute changes (greatly moderately, or a little).
     Effects on the processed image attribute (effects/side-effects)
(c) Process B should be performed prior to process C.
        Relationship between before and after processing

The knowledge structure can be described using the hierarchical structure shown in Fig. 4.

The relationship on level 3 in Fig. 4 is not strictly fixed, and an optimum processing combination is available depending on the image attribute. Knowledge about (b) and (c) affects this knowledge.

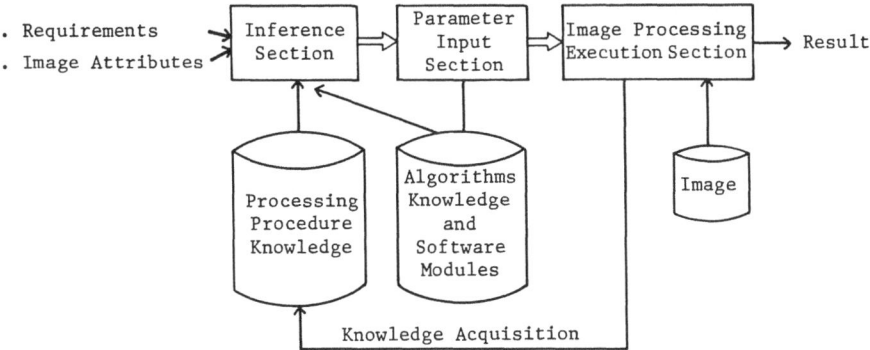

Fig. 3.   Image Processing Expert System Concept

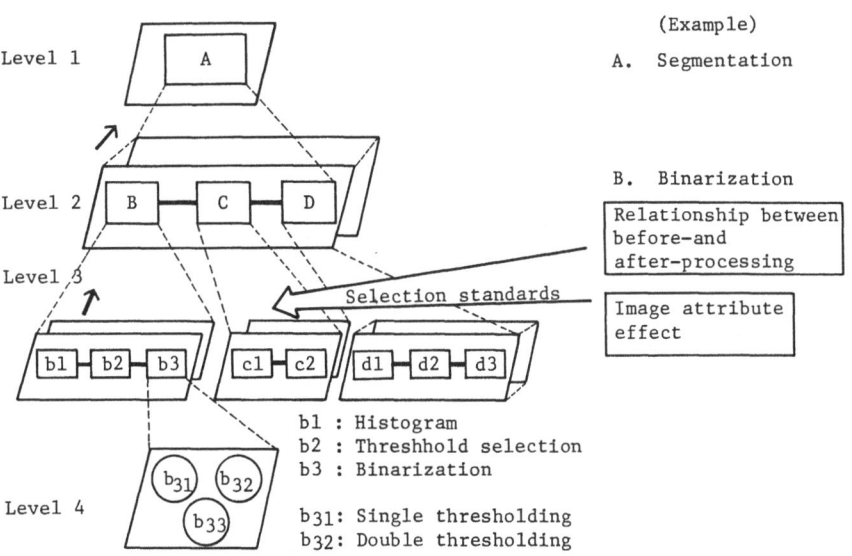

Fig. 4.   Knowledge Structure

It seems that this knowledge is not systematic, it is stored in fragments, and may correspond with, be inferred from, or be related to the image attribute when the knowledge is used.

This shows that the image processing needs rule base more than fact. Based on the above, image processing procedure knowledge is listed below, using the production rule (Fig. 5).

In this system, knowledge data parts and inference engine parts are individually separated. Thus, engine parts (programmed by PROLOG) interpret the rule below (Fig. 5).

```
Rule No.             : rule 21
Process request part: Binary image background elimination
Condition part       : IF
                         The gray level of the background and the object are
                         similar, and the background is larger than the object
Execution part       : THEN
                         Perform labeling operations and then area-cutting
                         operations
Effect part          : The background disappears
Process result image: Label image
```

Fig. 5. Image processing procedure knowledge example

The image attribute and its evaluation are formed according to the frame. Each frame is generated at each process level according to the process execution. Necessary information is inherited from the high-level concept to the low-level concept between attributes.

3.3 Inference Structure

The inference mechanism to select the software module makes undeterministic inferences, employing a so-called forward inference method, in which the inference is made under an assumption that "if the given image attribute is a, b, c, ---, perform processes A, B, and C".

This mechanism is shown in Fig. 6.

Levels 2, 3 and 4 in Fig. 6 correspond to the processing procedure knowledge levels 2, 3 and 4 given in 3.2 (1), respectively.

B and C in Fig. 6 are metaknowledge. The inference is made by the optimum inference procedure and the image processing is performed by selected procedure.
These mechanism is performed unification of the fact list with the condition rule, and after image processing executed, the fact list is updated by changed image attribute.
These mechanism is repeated until the user is satisfied the result of image. After performing the procedure of Large B, the next inference is perfomed for Large C.

4. EFFECTS

At present, the image processing expert system is considered a system whose application field is limited. To date, the system has been verified with approximately 300 rules and approximately 70 software modules. When processing is performed by a non-expert in image processing, about one hour is required to perform the steps from the introductory explanation to processing. On the other hand, achievement of a target image depends on the module functions and setting of

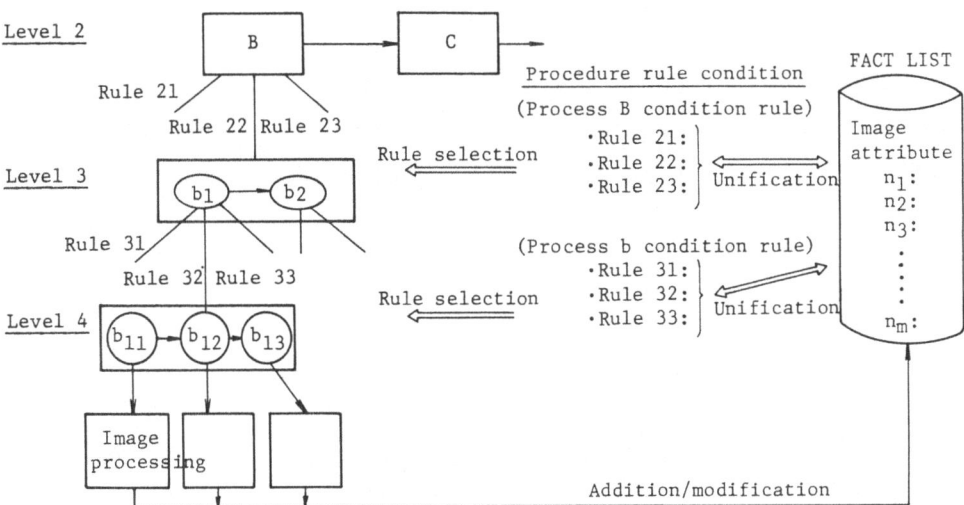

Fig. 6. Inference Process

optimal parameter values for module execution. Module functions are the subject of image processing technology, which should be further improved. For setting parameter values, since the application field is limited, the necessary values can be set at a very high probability.

As described previously, at present, the operator's load in the derivation of image processing procedures is markedly decreased.
The Image processing expert System is shown in Fig. 7.

Fig. 7. The Image processing expert System.

Inspection of flaws in IC chip "pins" is readily done by non-experts with the Image Processing expert system.

5. ISSUES TO BE SOLVED

The image processing expert system still has the following issues:

i) The system is not adapted for expression of an ambiguous image

ii) Action for objects, whose image processing technique has not been established, is difficult.

As described in 3.2 (2) concerning image attribute, definition problem (i) involves much ambiguity. As one image processing technique, an image quantitization technique, such as histogram analysis, profile analysis or label processing, can be used.

By quantitization using these techniques, it will become possible to reduce the portions left to the intuition of the user. Also to be studied is the Fuzzy theory in the expression method for information which is difficult to quantitize.
Though the system using the algorithm whose image processing technique has mostly been established is now being studied, it will be possible for expert researchers to develop a new algorithm on the basis of the existing algorithm.
When an unestablished algorithm is required, problem (ii) should be solved to assume and furnish conceptual processing for the user on the basis of the image attribute and procedure knowledge, thereby an assisting system for new algorithm development is required.

6. CONCLUSION

Up until now, when image processing technology has been applied to other fields, it has been necessary for the researcher in a particular field to start at the beginning, limiting technical application. However, through research and development on the image processing expert system, the authors found a clue to the image processing technology application to a wider range of fields by applying knowledge engineering. Thus, it is considered that image processing technology can be made easier to use by applying knowledge engineering.

ACKNOWLEDGEMENTS

The authors would like to thank Akira Ito and Masahiko Arai of the Systems and Software Engineering Division in Toshiba Corporation, who furnished the chance to write this paper.

REFERENCES

[1] Azriel Rosenfeld, Avinash C. Kak (1976), Digital Picture Processing, Academic Press, Inc.

[2] Avron Barr, Edward A. Feigenbaum (1981), The handbook of artificial intelligence, Willian Kaufmanm, Inc.

[3] Nils J. Nilsson (1980), Principles of Artificial Intelligence, Tioga Publishing Co.

[4] W. F. Clocksin, C. S. Mellish (1981), Programming in Prolog, Springer-Verlag.

[5] Hideyuki Tamura and five others (1982), SPIDER USER'S MANUAL, Joint System Development Co.

[6] Hideyuki Nakashima (1982), The Language Prolog and its Interpreters, Information Procesing Society of Japan VOL. 23, No. 11, P1049

[7] Takashi Matsuyama (1983), Knowledge Organization in Image Understanding, Information Processing Society of Japan VOL. 24, No. 12, P1437.

[8] Hideyuki Tamura, Katsuhiko Sakaue (1983), Three Kinds of knowledge for Building Digital-Image-Analysis Expert System, Paper of Technical group AL83-49, IECE Japan, P27.

[9] Shigeoki Hirai : Knowledge-Based System Tool, The Society of Instrument and Control Engineers VOL. 22, NO. 9.

[10] Motoi Suwa : The Current State and Future Trend of Knowledge Engineering, The Society of Instrument and Control Engineers VOL. 22, NO. 9.

[11] Shinichi Honiden,. etal (1985), "One Method of prototyping for real-time system", to appear in trans of IPSJ (in Japan).

[12] Naomichi Sueda, etal (1984), Prolog application in software reuse, Sumposium of the Role of Language in Problem Solving APL/Johns Hopkins University.

Heuristic Rules for Visualization

Laura R. Scholl
Laura Scholl and Associates, 135 Pleasant Street, Suite 208, Brookline, MA 02146, USA

ABSTRACT

In recent years there has been increased interest in heuristic methods in artificial intelligence. By and large heuristic research has been used with two modes of thought: mathematics and language (language being the vehicle for scientific research and search strategies). This paper focuses on another mode of thinking - visualization. The process is not to analyze visual perception as in the areas of pattern recognition and image understanding, but the complementary process to synthesize. Rather than dissect, the goal is to create. By using a visualization-system guided by heuristic rules, the artist can visualize the invisible. Discover new sets of heuristics for exploring new visual concepts. This paper describes the basis for a visualization-system. It is aimed at two groups of people. Computer scientists who are currently most influential in research in artificial intelligence and computer graphics, so that they may use visual thinking to better understand abstract concepts. Artists who are ever involved in developing and exploring new media (ie: computer technology) to realize their creative ideas.

KEYWORDS: Visualization, Heuristics, Computer Graphics, Artist, Creative Seeing

INTRODUCTION

> "Intuition enlightens and so links up with pure thought. They together become an intelligence which is not simply of the brain, which does not calculate, but which feels and thinks. Which is creative both in art and life..."
>
> Piet Mondrian

Important discoveries in science, mathematics, and art are rarely a result of pure scientific logic. They are brought to fruition through visual thinking: exploration of partially formulated ideas, fuzzy mental images and intuitive judgment. Visual thinking then, is a process of synthesis. It combines an understanding of structure, information, and manipulation. It is influenced by seeing and imaging; and is further stimulated through such picture making activities as drawing.

The artist, who copes with life by means of creating works of art is the ideal "expert" for an artificial intelligence based system for visualization. Historically, artists have always played an important role in the development of technologies and tools in order to realize their ideas through a visual medium. Euclid's Golden Section, a:b=b(a+b), was derived from the structural relationships in the Parthenon and the Temple of Athena. Perspective was discovered by the 15th century architect Filippo Brunelleschi. Le Corbusier devised the ordering system Modular, built around three main points of human anatomy: the top of the head, the solar plexus, and the tip of a hand (Giloth and Veeder 1985). So, an artistic viewing of reality reminds scientists that most natural phenomena are not described adequately if that description is attained only through accretion of isolated parts.

Computer graphics is an ideal "visual medium" to encourage creative thought through visualization. Aside from the obvious advantages of the computer: memory, precision, ability to perform routine tasks, fast manipulation of data, and network communication, new thinking strategies can be realized. Computer graphics can be used to correlate new visual data with previous stored data to overcome restrictions and develop new structural relationships. It may be used to articulate multiple perspectives through superimposed drawings, while maintaining an overview. It can be used to animate drawings to represent dynamic ideas [Hooper 1984]. It can be used to manipulate parts of drawings to gain a new perspective. Computer graphics allow the artist to simply make a rough sketch of an idea contained in the mind or to change the rules of physical reality.

HUMAN OBSERVATION / CREATIVE SEEING

Observation is the process of matching incoming visual sensations with visual memory. The eye is limited, however, by its ability to see even a small area equally focused at all points. So, it grasps portions that it then collects and stores. Creative seeing is the process of, as Cezanne said, "waiting for nature to free his eyes from their camera habits" [Rugg 1963]. It involves using the imagination to see new perspectives. It combines curiousity and a willingness to abandon old classifications for new possibilities.

How is creative seeing accomplished? Through a process of "unlearning". The natural tendency when faced with something new and different is to analyze, categorize and make familiar. This reductive method leads to stereotyping, black or white thinking, and superficial development of ideas. So, imagination must be harnessed to help us "unlearn". Imagination allows ideas to transcend space, time and physical reality by relaxing, looking at the world form different viewpoints, distorting and reclassifying imagery under new categories such as color, roundness, angularity etc. We must welcome the insecurity of newness and avoid premature judgment [McKim 1980].

Memory is an essential resource to creative visual thinking. Aside from matching incoming stimuli, it provides material for recombination. By the aid of the stored visual image the mind can take some part of an image out of its original setting and recombine it with a totally new event to solve a problem. Memory and seeing reinforce each other. Memory forces the ability to focus attention, to look and think about the perceived object rather than something else.

VISUALIZATION AND DRAWING

Although visualization can be illuminated through a number of vehicles (drawing, language, kinesthesia, etc.) Drawing works well within the context of computer graphics. There are two stages of drawing for visual thinking. The primary stage is explorational and the secondary, a more focused form of the first, is developmental [McKim 1980].

The first stage, exploration can be broken down further. It may be either deductive or inductive. That is, the incomplete, vague mental impressions that usually accompany creativity are recorded quickly through drawing. These drawings are general. They define structure, not a particular element. Sometimes an artist will work from the smallest manifestation of from and interrelationship [Klee 1968]. Either method is used as a point to departure for the developmental stage.

In the developmental stage. Drawings are chosen, refined and expanded for a more complete understanding of an idea that seems worth following through. (This is not a random activity.) These drawings are more detailed and thorough. Like the first stage these drawings are performed spontaneously and quickly. The approach is a flexible one. Ideas are expressed from as many viewpoints as possible. For example a computer may be represented by a drawing of its outer shell, by schematic drawings of its boards, or abstractly as a node on a communication network.

Drawing to stimulate visual ideas is not to be confused with drawing to explain and present fully formed ideas for communication with others. Visual idea drawing is for the artist's personal communication and is not for judgment. Obviously if these drawings are developed further, over time, they may result in a work of art.

THE PAINT SYSTEM PARADIGM

A "paint system" is one configuration of a computer. It comprises a computer, an image buffer, a variety of input devices such as a mouse, digitizing tablet and stylus, or digitizing camera, and a menu-driven user interface. These systems emulate, or attempt to emulate, traditional painting and illustrative operations and allow the artist to create electronic graphics with little or no understanding of computer graphics.

The artist chooses a method for "painting" from a fixed set of basic options. They include: point, line, rectangle, ellipse and so on. S/he can also create brushes made from the options or from areas of the existing image (rasters: rectangular arrays of pixels). A grid can be used to constrain the painting cursor to incremental locations on the screen for a minimal level of layout precision. Color can be easily altered in various ways, and areas of the screen can be filled with color. Text can be incorporated, although fonts vary from system to system.

Some systems provide more complex options like transformations (scaling, rotating, translating) or "Bit Blt" operations for "cut and paste" activities, where parts of the screen can be lifted and moved or rubber stamped. Other systems allow even more sophisticated processes like curve fitting, anti-aliased signal processing, or solid modeling (Giloth and Veeder 1985).

Still other systems have some form of animation capabilities. The artist can create each full screen "cel" as in traditional cel animation, create "sprites" or characters to be moved across the screen as in video games and some broadcast video graphic systems, simple color cycle animation, keyframe animation, and complex algorithmic animation.

Regardless of the level of complexity or number of features, the application for these systems is to create images to communicate well-formulated ideas (usually for commercial purposes). They tend to be idiosyncratic, imprecise, and often complicated to use. The interface is inflexible (only one configuration) and not usually designed by an artist. Paint systems are unlikely to provide the spontaneity necessary for stimulation of visual thinking.

THE VISUALIZATION - SYSTEM

This system is not a paint system. It is a new type of system for a different application. It combines some of the properties of a paint system with heuristic methods in artificial intelligence. The visualization-system is for the exploration and development of visual ideas. It allows the user to select from a variety of heuristic strategies for creative thinking. Unlike previous visual perception research such as pattern recognition, image understanding or image generating, this system does not analyze, but instead - synthesizes. It is used to discover new ways to be creative and so, discover new heuristics.

COMPUTER OBSERVER / CREATIVE SEEING

In the visualization-system the computer acts as an "unlearning" tool for creative seeing. It can generate variations on a theme input by the artist, by defining and revealing the structure and then applying associated heuristic operations such as: superimpose, circumscribe, complement, balance, fill-in, etc. It allows for manipulation of parts of the structure by allowing the artist to select and combine another set of heuristic operations to add dimension, rotate, transform (stretch, compress, scale). It provides image memory for recombination, to isolate a familiar, previously stored image in an unfamiliar relationship. The system can superimpose a grid to achieve or alter proportion.

The artist can stop the system at any point, save an instance, or continue working manually. The artist may retrace his/her steps because the computer saves an image, as well as, tracking a combination of movements and information (coordinate locations, colors, and function selection sequences).

The artist may also attach notes. The notes may be a part of the drawing or saved in a file related to the drawing. The system will also provide notes, so the artist may watch patterns emerge that s/he may not be aware of on his/her own.

The artist can create his/her own interface to the system by selecting and combining the basic drawing functions and heuristic operations with which s/he wants to experiment. The interface can be dynamically altered while working to increase flexibility in problem solving strategies. It is stored separately from the image so that it can be reused to develop other ideas/images.

COMPUTER AND DRAWING

The visualization-system includes a drawing tool for quick and intuitive drawing and somewhat more detailed drawing. The interface is flexible so that it may support many drawing styles. The operations available for the basic drawing tool are simplified and modular. The artist is allowed to: select and create brushes; generate: points, lines, rectangles, triangles, and ellipses; select and modify colors and pattern; move areas; copy areas; zoom-in (magnify); and fill enclosed areas. These operations can be combined to produce higher level operations that suit the individual artist. The drawing process is monitored by the system to provide structural information and develop concepts. This information then, defines the concepts to be processed by the heuristic functions.

VISUALIZATION - SYSTEM / HEURISTIC RULES

The visualization-system is still in the system-start up phase. The artist must work closely with it to help guide the selection of the heuristic rules. This allows the system to learn from the artist's selections. Once a rule is chosen, it examines the visual concepts tracked by the drawing tool, modifies them, and alters the original drawing and in turn, creates new concepts (Lenat 1983). It can continue to branch to other heuristic rules or the artist may intervene, draw, or redirect it to still other heuristic rules.

The syntax of heuristic rules are like the "if-then" construct in many computer languages. The left hand side: IF <CONCEPT>, returns true or false. The right hand side: THEN <ACTIONS>, modifies the concept (Lenat 1983). Below is a partial list of the heuristic rules used by this system:

> IF The drawing contains more than 10 shapes.
> THEN group elements together to form simpler shapes.
>
> IF The structure of the drawing repeats the same unit in the horizontal direction.
> THEN repeat the unit in the vertical direction.
>
> IF The structure of the drawing has two dimensional direction (moving in both horizontal and verticle directions).
> THEN rotate the drawing on its diagonal.
>
> IF The elements of the drawing vary in weight.
> THEN arrange the elements so that their value increases toward the center.
>
> IF The lines of the drawing are limited by fixed points.
> THEN add secondary lines that intersect the main line without intersecting the fixed points.
>
> IF The drawing is linear.
> THEN complete the lines to form planes.
>
> IF The drawing is planar.
> THEN fill each plane with color.

- **IF** The drawing contains two or more colors,
  - **THEN** create color harmony by balancing them in the red, green, blue, color space model.
- **IF** The combination of elements in the drawing are the same as another, previously stored drawing,
  - **THEN** superimpose the two drawings.
- **IF** The vertical axis of the drawing si to the left of the viewer,
  - **THEN** shift the axis to the right.
- **IF** The divisions of the structural units in the drawing are close to a:b=b:(a+b),
  - **THEN** correct the divisions to equal a:b=b:(a+b).
- **IF** The structure of the drawing is not repetitious,
  - **THEN** group the smallest recognizable entities.
- **IF** The drawing has two sources of energy: gravity and an obstructing object,
  - **THEN** determine which is dominant by projecting a diagonal line.
- **IF** The drawing has no apparent focus,
  - **THEN** define paths for the eye to travel along.
- **IF** The horizontality of the drawing is not proportionate to the height of the viewer,
  - **THEN** reposition the horizontal elements until they are proportionate.
- **IF** The drawing emphasizes symmetrical balance,
  - **THEN** redraw the drawing using a non-symmetrical balance.
- **IF** The rhythm in the drawing changes in a non-continuous fashion,
  - **THEN** try to impose a rhythm with defined steps.
- **IF** The direction of an element in the drawing ascends,
  - **THEN** redirect it to descend.
- **IF** The drawing is static because of excessive amounts of white,
  - **THEN** activate it with black.

CONCLUSIONS

This project is still in the conception stage. The design philosophy is to use the process of discovery, outlined for the system, to define the system itself. This is a process that will work back and forth from artist – computer – artist . . . ad infinitum. At this point, the artist must interject his/her "expert knowledge" while the visualization-system learns to mimic and eventually think visually on its own. The system acts like the creative imagination "unlearning" to stimulate creativity and subsequently new ideas. It allows the seemingly non-visual person to visualize and the artist to have a new medium with which to bring his ideas to fruition. Eventually, the system may be able to create art without the guidance of an artist.

ACKNOWLEDGEMENTS

I wish to acknowledge my colleagues who encouraged the development ot this research as well as being helpful critics. Specifically, Copper Giloth and Jane Veeder who helped refine the ideas for the drawing tool with their research. And Maxine Schur who edited the paper with me. I also wish to thank Robert Mallary at the University of Massachusetts who originally sparked my interest as an artist in this totally new art form called "computer graphics".

REFERENCES

Adams J (1979) Conceptual Blockbusting. San Francisco Book Co., San Francisco

Arnheim R (1954, 1974) Art and Visual Perception. University of California Press, Berkeley

Arnheim R (1969) Visual Thinking. University of California Press, Berkeley

Ghiselin B (1952) The Creative Process. University of California Press, Berkeley

Giloth C, Veeder J (1985) The Paint Problem. IEEE Graphics and Applications, July

Hooper K (1976) Imaging and Visual Thinking. The Open University Press, Santa Cruz

Hooper K (1984) People x Pictures x Computers: Some New Possibilities for Design. Proceedings of NicoGraph

Klee P (1968) Pedagogical Sketchbook. Whitstable Litho Limited, London

Krueger M (1983) Artificial Reality. Addison-Wesley, Reading, MA

Lenat D (1983) Nature of Heuristics II, Nature of Heuristics III. In: Pearl J (ed) Search and Heuristics. North-Holland Publishing Co., New York

Lenat D (1982) Knowledge-Based Systems in Artificial Intelligence. McGraw-Hill, New York

McKim R (1972, 1980) Experiences in Visual Thinking. Brooks/Cole, Monterey, CA

Perkins DN (1981) The Mind's Best Work. Harvard University Press, Cambridge

Rich E (1983) Artificial Intelligence. McGraw-Hill, New York

Rugg H (1963) Imagination. Harper & Row, New York

Winston P (1984) Artificial Intelligence. Addison-Wesley, Reading, MA

Chapter 8
Applications

Chapter 5
Applications

Computer Graphics for Multivariate Data

R. Cléroux[1], Y. Lepage[2] and N. Ranger[1]

Département d'informatique et de recherche opérationnelle[1], Département de mathématiques et de statistique[2], Université de Montréal, Montréal, H3C 3J7, Canada

ABSTRACT

The exploration of multidimensional data involves the use of a set of empirical techniques which aid in the discovery of interesting avenues to be pursued in later statistical analysis. Data exploration often directs this analysis. The availability and power of computers has changed the nature of statistical work and has made the exploration of multidimensional data more accessible. Graphical methods constitute one of the main tools for data exploration, and they are therefore of primary importance.

In this article, four graphical representation methods are presented and applied to atmospheric pollution data for the Montreal region. These representations enable the data from each monitoring station to be visualized and grouping may then be formed from observed similarities.

INTRODUCTION

Graphical representations have been in use for a long time in several disciplines. The usefulness of these methods lies in the capacity of the human eye to recognize shapes and to identify similarities and aberrations. For example, a two dimensional cloud of points reveals at a glance the essential relationship between the two variables. However, in several dimensions, even projections on different planes are insufficient to simplify the graphical representation, especially with a fairly large number of dimensions. Data in more than two or three dimensions is therefore difficult to grasp. However, the advent of the computer has facilitated the exploration of multivariate data in general and has, in particular, produced more accessible graphical representations for such data.

Data exploration is defined as the set of empirical techniques applied to data before the statistical analysis proper begins. The purpose of these techniques is basically to discover interesting avenues to be pursued in more detail. The techniques usually involve summarizing the information through elementary calculations, tables, diagrams, histograms and graphs. They provide a way of establishing intimate contact with the raw data and of learning about it. Data exploration often orients statistical analysis, and graphical methods are therefore of primary importance.

There are two main classes of graphical methods for multivariate data. Some methods are mainly used in the context of a geometric structure or statistical model following data analysis. All factor analysis methods belong to this class. Other methods are used mainly at the exploratory stage to represent raw data. This paper discusses only this latter class of methods.

Any graphical representation should have certain of the following qualities: it should communicate information easily and rapidly, help the reader to understand the information, produce a greater impact when the information is more important, have a mnemonic effect, in the sense that important information should be retained by the reader, be simple, compact and attractive, be clear, precise and without distorsion, be quickly and easily comprehensible, be constructed using standard forms, allow the representation of a large number of dimensions simultaneously, allow comparisons and groupings.

There are many graphical representation methods for raw data. A sampling is listed here: glyphs (Anderson, 1960), stars (Siegel et al, 1971A), faces (Chernoff, 1973; Chernoff and Rizvi, 1975), curves (Andrews, 1972), constellations (Wakimoto and Tagun, 1978), profiles (Bertin, 1967), triangles (Pickett and White, 1966), draftsman's display (Chambers et al., 1983), weathervanes (Cleveland and Kleiner, 1974), boxes (Hartigan, 1975), trees (Wakimoto, 1977), trees and castles (Kleiner and Hartigan, 1980). The interested reader will find other references on this subject in the bibliography. All are not, however, cited in the text.

In the next sections, we study four of these methods in more detail, applying them to atmospheric pollution data for the Montreal region.

THE DATA

The data to be considered consists of measures of the sulphur dioxide concentration in parts per hundred million (pphm), collected at various monitoring stations in the Montreal region during the year 1975. The data are collected by the "Services de Protection de l'Environnement du Québec" which also provides summary statistics. The results are published in the pamphlet "Qualité de l'air" by the "Editeur officiel du Québec" in the form of monthly tables of hourly or bi-hourly mean concentrations. The tables also provide 24 hour averages, monthly means for each hour and their respective maxima.

The monitoring stations chosen are sufficiently well geographically distributed to both adequately cover the territory of Montreal, and to allow the study of local pollutant effects. Since the purpose of this article is not to study the problem of sulphur dioxide pollution in Montreal but rather to present certain graphical representation methods, only monitoring stations 1, 12, 13 and 20 will be represented in the following discussion.

These stations are:

Station		Height above		Type of equipment	
No.	Address	Sea Level	Ground Level	Continuous	Sequential
1	Botanical Garden Montreal	55m	4m	Titrilog	
12	1125 Ontario East Montreal	23m	13m	Technicon	
13	1212 Drummond Montreal	35m	12m		Sequential
20	525, 9th Avenue Pointe-aux-Trembles	9m	6m	Beckman 906	

The presence of sulphur dioxide in the air is determined by several methods: some stations are equipped with automatic machines which register atmospheric gas concentration continuously, while others have sequential apparatus which takes samples every two hours which then have to be analyzed in a laboratory.

Each pollution monitoring station is represented by a vector of dimension 17. The first 12 components give the monthly averages of sulphur dioxide concentrations for the year 1975, and the other 5 components are determined by the relative frequencies of the daily maxima; component 13: % daily maxima of 15 pphm or over, component 14: % daily maxima between 10 and 15 pphm, component 15: % daily maxima between 5 and 9 pphm, component 16: % daily maxima of 3 or 4 pphm, component 17: % daily maxima of 2 pphm or less.

THE STARS METHOD

Let p variables be measured on n individuals to obtain n vectors of the form $X' = (X_1, \ldots, X_p)$. Using polar coordinates, the circle is divided into p equal angles. This division defines p planar vectors whose origins are located at the centre of the circle, and whose directions are determined by the angles. For i=1, ..., p, variable X_i is placed on the ith vector at a distance from the origin proportional to its size. The p variables are thus placed in the polar plane. The extremities of the vectors are then joined together to obtain a polygonal figure called a star (see Siegel et al, 1971A,B). We obtain n stars, one for each vector of observations. Similarities and differences between the stars may then be detected.

In certain practical situations, the initial variables must first be transformed to ensure a certain compatibility between them. Sometimes, a variant of this method may be useful. For example, a star corresponding to the vector of means might be constructed and then tranformed into a circle by multiplying each component of the observation vectors by an appropriate factor. Then, the standard deviations might be traced on each vector of the circle to indicate the dispersion of the variable with respect to the mean.

Fig. 1 indicates the arrangement of variables around a conceptual star, while Fig. 2 shows the stars corresponding to the 4 stations described above. For each representation, components 13 to 17 were multiplied by 5 to make them move compatible with the others.

It can be seen that pollution levels are relatively low at station 1 (botanical garden), high at station 20 (refineries to the East of Montreal) while the structures of pollution are somewhat similar for stations 12 (Ontario Street East) and 13 (Drummond Street) although the overall level is higher at station 13 than station 12.

THE CURVES METHOD

When n observations of the vector $X' = (X_1, \ldots, X_p)$ are measured, or in other words, p variables are measured for n individuals, each of the n observation vectors is represented by a function of the form

$$f_x(t) = \frac{X_1}{\sqrt{2}} + X_2 \sin t + X_3 \cos t + X_4 \sin 2t + X_5 \cos 2t + \ldots$$

and its graph is drawn over the interval $-\Pi < t < \Pi$. Thus, n different curyes will be traced. It would also be possible to draw the graph corresponding to the mean of a group, and then to repeat this for each group studied to compare these visually. This method has interesting statistical properties (Andrews, 1972).

Fig. 3 shows the curves $f_x(t)$ for the stations studied, as a function of the parameter t, $-\Pi < t < \Pi$. The values of the $f_x(t)$ are somewhat arbitrary but a large value of $f_x(t)$ implies a high level of pollution. The vertical axis can be taken as representing an axis of pollution.

It can be seen here, also, that the pollution level is low at station 1 (botanical garden) and high at station 20 (refineries to the East of Montreal). The pollution levels of stations 12 and 13 appear to be roughly similar.

THE FACES METHOD

Chernoff (1973) proposes the representation of a vector $X' = (X_1,\ldots, X_p)$ of observations using a human face whose characteristics are determined by the values of the components. Each component corresponds to a part of the face. More precisely, the parameters used to represent a vector of 20 components are as follows: parameter 1: width of the face, 2: level of ears, 3: height of face, 4: excentricity of upper face, 5: excentricity of lower face, 6: length of nose, 7: level of mouth, 8: curvature of mouth, 9: length of mouth, 10: level of eyes, 11: distance between eyes, 12: angle of eyes, 13: excentricity of eyes, 14: size of eyes, 15: position of pupils, 16: vertical position of eyebrows, 17: angle of eyebrows, 18: length of eyebrows, 19: diameter of ears, 20: width of nose.

The nose corresponds to a triangle, the ears and pupils are circles. Ellipses are used for the face outline and the eyes while the arc of a circle describes the mouth and straight lines are used for the eyebrows.

To use this method, each component must be brought to within a precise interval to control the dimensions of the face. In addition, when the dimension of a vector is less than 20, some pre-assigned values are used. Thus, n faces are obtained, one for each vector of observations.

Chernoff's faces suffer from the fact that extreme values of certain parameters diminish the effect of others (see Chernoff and Rivzi, 1975, and Bruckner, 1978). Conscious of these methodological limits, Flury and Riedwyl, 1981, presented a new "Chernoff face" which allows the appropriate representation of all observations and also increases the size of the vector considered.

The different parameters used are as follows: parameter 1: size of eye, 2: size of pupil, 3: position of pupil, 4: angle of eye, 5: horizontal position of eye, 6: vertical position of eye, 7: curvature of eyebrow, 8: density of eyebrow, 9: horizontal position of eyebrow, 10: vertical position of eyebrow, 11: upper outline of hair, 12: lower outline of hair, 13: outline of face, 14: density of hair, 15: angle of hair, 16: nose, 17: mouth size, 18: curvature of mouth.

The eyes and pupils are drawn as arcs of circles. The hair, nose and mouth, and outlines are drawn using parameterized curves (polynomials) (see Flury, 1980). This method allows the representation of pairs of vectors of dimension 18; asymmetry in the face obtained reflects changes in each component. Obviously, this also allows the representation of vectors of dimension up to 36. If the dimension is less than 18 or 36, as the case may be, some default values are used. Hence, n new faces are obtained, one for each observation vector.

Fig. 4 shows Chernoff's faces and Fig. 5 shows the new faces according to Flury and Riedwyl for stations 1, 12, 13 and 20. Again it is seen that the pollution level is low at station 1 (botanical garden) and high at station 20 (refineries to the East of Montreal). The levels at stations 12 and 13 are comparable although it is slightly higher at station 13.

THE TREES AND CASTLES METHOD

In the graphical representations illustrated so far, the order of variables in the vector plays an important role. In fact, each graphic would look quite different if the variables under study were permuted. Furthermore, these graphics contain a certain inherent correlation structure because of their design. For example, in Chernoff's faces, the length of the eyebrows is highly correlated with the length of the eyes. Both of the problems mentioned above are discussed by Chernoff and Rizvi, 1975. To eliminate these difficulties, Kleiner and Hartigan, 1981, developed a method which uses a hierarchical clustering algorithm on the variables to make them basically independent of permutation effects. This technique is known as the "trees and castles" method.

First, suppose the variables $X_1, \ldots, X_p$ are normalized with mean 0 and standard deviation 1. The most frequently used hierarchical clustering algorithm is the complete linkage method with Euclidean distances between the variables (see Hartigan, 1975). This algorithm is preferred because it tends to divide the variables into two clusters of the same size. The two variables which are closest to one another are joined to form the first cluster. The distance between this cluster and each of the other variables is defined as the maximum of the distances between each variable of the cluster and the other variable. The process is repeated by joining together the pair of clusters or of variables with the smallest distance between them, with distance then being defined as the maximum distance between pairs. At the final step, two clusters are joined together to form a single cluster containing all the variables.

For the 17 variables observed at the 14 monitoring stations, the results of the complete linkage hierarchical clustering algorithm are shown in the dendogram of Fig. 6. The first variables to be clustered together are June and September; February and March form the next group, followed by max 15+ (component 13) and July. The process continues until the cluster made up of max 0-2 (component 17) and max 3-4 (component 16) joins up with the cluster containing all the other variables.

The trees method represents each vector of observations by a tree. All the trees have the same typology as the dendogram of variables obtained from the complete linkage hierarchical clustering algorithm and each leaf of the tree corresponds to a variable.

Before drawing the graph, the width and length of the branches, and the angle between branches must be chosen. The width of a branch is proportional to the number of variables above that branch. A variable is said to be above a branch, if the path from the leaf representing this variable to the foot of the tree includes this branch. Thus, in our example, as each leaf has a width of 1, the base of each tree will have a width of 17, while the branch supporting the leaves for July and max 15+ is of width 2 increasing to width 3 when May is added (see Fig. 7). The angle between two branches at a division point is a linear function of the maximum of the logarithm of the distance between the variables above these two branches; the range of variation of these angles is a parameter which may be determined in advance. In our example, the minimum angle has been set at $5°$ while the maximum angle permitted is $95°$.

At each division point, the orientation of the branches must be chosen. Them stem of the tree is defined as the path which begins at the foot of the tree and at each division follows the widest branch until the division point with two branches of the same width. The stem alternates directions at each division point. At a division point not touching the stem, the widest branch will bear towards the right for division points to the right of the stem, or towards the left for division points to the left of the stem. In other words, the widest branches are furthest from the stem. When two branches have the same width, the choice is arbitrary.

The angle between a branch and the vertical is proportional to the width of the branch except on the stem where the angle is inversely proportional to the width of the branch. However, the sum of angles with respect to the vertical corresponds to the angle determined previously. Thus, the stem will tend to be roughly vertical. Finally, the length of a branch is proportional to the average value of the variables above this branch.

In Fig. 7, trees corresponding to the four pollution stations studied are presented. Those corresponding to stations 1, 12 and 13 have been doubled in size to facilitate the visual perception. Note that in general the level of pollution appears low for station 1 (botanical garden) and high for station 20 (refineries to the East of Montreal). Although not as high as station 20, the level of pollution at station 13 (Drummond Street) can be seen to be higher than that at station 12 (Ontario Street East).

The graphical representation using trees is very useful when the variables studied can be divided into clusters of highly correlated variables. It is also desirable that the measures of the variables be comparable. However, this method makes it difficult to compare variables of the same tree even if they are next to one another. Kleiner and Hartigan, 1981, suggest representing each point by a castle. This method is a mixture of the trees method and the profiles method (see Bertin, 1967) and it allows variables of the same tree to be compared. It also enables variables for the same observation to be compared more easily than in the profiles method.

Suppose that the variables take positive values which are comparable. Complete linkage hierarchical clustering using Euclidean distances on the variables is used to generate a tree. This tree forms the basis for the construction of castles. The width of each branch is set to be proportional to the number of branches above it, the angle between all branches is fixed at zero, and the order of the variables is that obtained by the complete linkage clustering algorithm.

In the following way, each vector is represented by a castle: the upper extremity of a branch is at a distance v from the base where v is the minimum value of all variables above the branch minus qd, where q is the number of branches joining the branch to the variable with the minimal value, and d is a value to be chosen.

The distance between the base and the extremity of the branch containing a single variable corresponds to the value of that variable, so this branch gives the same information as the profiles method. The position of the other branches reflects the information presented by the trees method. The value of d must be strictly positive to ensure that the tree structure is retained.

Castles for the 4 pollution stations studied are presented in Fig. 8. Note once more that station 20 (refineries to the East of Montreal) shows the highest pollution levels while the lowest levels appear at station 1 (botanical garden). The pollution level at station 13 (Drummond Street) is higher than at station 12 (Ontario Street East).

CONCLUSION

In this article, we have sketched several graphical representation methods for multivariate data. Great progress has been made since the work of Playfair, 1801, one of the fathers of graphical representation in statistics. However all the problems have not yet been completely solved. Development of and experimentation with new methods must continue, always keeping in mind that graphics should provide a simple way of communicating the information contained in a set of data.

BIBLIOGRAPHY

Anderson E (1960) A Semi-Graphical Method for the Analysis of Complex Problems. Technometrics 2: 287-292.

Andrews DF (1972) Plots of High-Dimensional Data. Biometrics 28: 125-136.

Banfield CF, Gower JC (1980) A Note on the Graphical Representation of Multivariate Binary Data. Applied Stat. 29: 238-245.

Beniger JR, Robyn DL (1978) Quantitative Graphics in Statistics: A Brief History Amer. Statistician 32: 1-11.

Bertin T (1967) Sémiologie graphique. Gauthier-Villars, Paris.

Bruckner LA (1978) On Chernoff Faces. In Graphical Representation of Multivariate Data. P.C.C. Wang (ed) Academic Press, New York.

Caporal PM, Hahn GH (1979) Computer Offerings for Statistical Graphics, An Overview. Proc. Comp. Sci. and Statist. 13th Symposium on the Interface.

Chambers JM, Cleveland WS, Kleiner B, Tuckey PA (1983) Graphical Methods for Data Analysis. Wadsworth Int. Group. California.

Chernoff H, Rizvi MH (1975) Effect on Classification Error of Random Permutations of Features in Representing Multivariate Data by Faces. JASA, 70: 548-554.

Chernoff H (1973) Using Faces to Represent Points in k-dimensional Space Graphically. JASA 68: 361-368.

Cléroux R (1982) L'impact présent et futur de l'informatique en statistique. CIPS Review 6: 18-21.

Cléroux R, Roy R, Fortin N (1980) Air Pollution in Montreal: A Statistical Analysis of Sulphur Dioxide Data. Water, Air and Soil Pollution 13: 143-156.

Cleveland WS, Kleiner B (1974) The Analysis of Air Data Pollution from New Jersey and New-York. Annual Meeting ASA. St-Louis, Miss.

Everitt BS (1978) Graphical Techniques for Multivariate Data. Heinemann Education Books, London.

Fienberg SE (1979) Graphical Methods in Statistics. Amer. Statistician 33: 165-178.

Flury B, Riedwyl H (1981) Graphical Representation of Multivariate Data by Means of Asymmetrical Faces. JASA 76: 757-765.

Flury B (1980) Construction of an Asymmetrical Face to Represent Multivariate Data Graphically, Technical Report No. 3, Université de Berne, Dép. de Statistique.

Friedman HP, Farrell EJ, Goldwyn RM, Miller M, Siegel, JH (1972) A Graphic Way of Describing Changing Patterns. Proc. Comp. Sci. and Statist. 6th. Annual Symposium on the Interface. Berkeley, Calif. 56-59.

Friedman JH, Rafsky LC (1981) Graphics for the Multivariate Two-Sample Problem. JASA 76: 277-295.

Gascon A (1978) Méthodes graphiques d'analyse de données multidimensionnelles, Masters' thesis. Dép. d'informatique et de recherche opérationnelle Université de Montréal.

Gnanadesikan R (1980) Graphic Data Analysis: Issues, Tools and Examples. Ann. Meeting Amer. Assoc. Adv. Sci., San Francisco.

Gnanadesikan R (1977) Methods for Statistical Data Analysis of Multivariate Observations. Wiley, New York.

Hartigan JA (1975) Printer Graphics for Clustering. Journal Statist. Comput. Simul. 4: 187-213.

Hartigan JA (1975) Clustering Algorithms. Wiley, New York.

Jacob RJK (1980) Correspondence on Fienberg (1979). Amer. Statistician 34: 252-253.

Kalence KW, Kiviat PJ (1973) Software Unit Profiles and Kiviat Figures. ACM Perf. Eval. Rev. (sept.).

Kent P (1982) An Efficient New Way to Represent Multidimensional Data. Doctoral Thesis. Ecole Polytechnique Fédérale de Lausanne.

Kleiner B, Hartigan JA (1981) Representing Points in Many Dimensions by Trees and Castles. JASA 76: 260-276.

Kruskal W (1977) Visions of Maps and Graphs. Proc. Int. Symp. on Comput. Assisted Cartography 25-36.

Kruskal JB (1964) Non-Metric Multidimensional Scaling: a Numerical Method. Psychometrika 29: 115-129.

Lee RCT, Slagle JR, Blum H (1977) Triangulation Method for the Sequential Mapping of Points from N-Space to Two-Space. IEEE Trans. Comput. 26: 288-292.

Lin CH, Chen HF (1977) Representation-Space Transformation for the Display of Multivariate Chemical Information. Anal. Chem. 49: 1357-1363.

Pickett R, White BW (1966) Constructing Data Pictures. Proc. 7th. Nat. Symp. on Information Display 75-81.

Playfair W (1801) The Statistical Breviary. London.

Siegel JH, Goldwyn RM, Friedman HP (1971A) Iteration and Interaction in Computer Data Bank Analysis: A Case Study in the Physiologic Classification and Assessment of the Critically Ill. Comput. and Biomed. Res. 4: 607-622.

Siegel JH, Goldwyn RM, Friedman HP (1971B) Pattern and Process in the Evolution of Human Septic Shock. Surgery 70: 232-245.

Wainer H (1974) The Suspended Rootogram and Other Visual Displays: an Empirical Validation, Amer. Statistician 28: 143-145.

Wainer H, Thissen D (1981) Graphical Data Analysis. Ann. Rev. Psychol. 32: 191-241.

Wakimoto K (1977) Tree Graph Method for Visual Representation of Multidimensional Data. Jour. Japan Statist. Soc. 7: 27-34.

Wakimoto K, Taguri M (1978) Constellation Graphical Method for Representing Multidimensional Data. Ann. Inst. Stat. Math. 30: 97-104.

Wang PCC (1978) Graphical Representation of Multivariate Data. Academic Press, New York.

Welsch RE (1973) Graphics for Data Analysis. Comput. & Graphics. 2: 31-37.

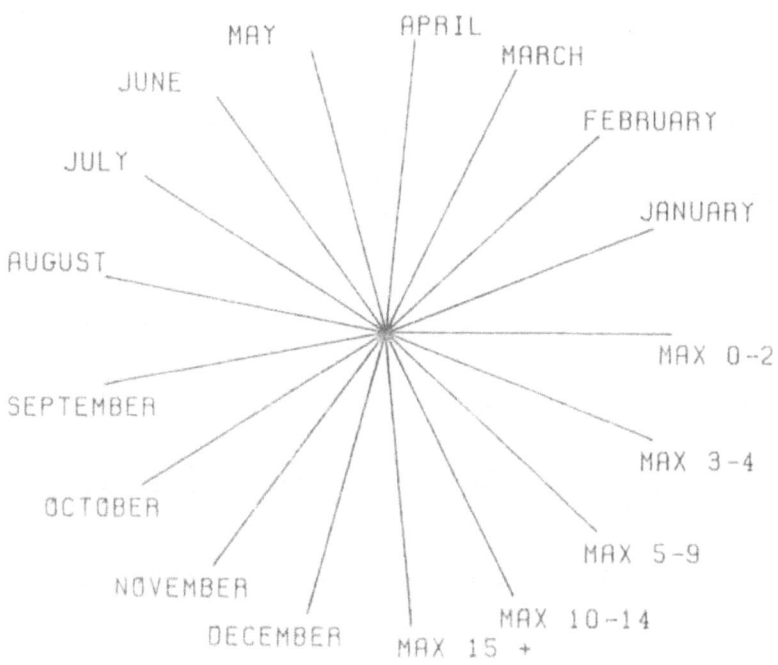

Fig. 1: Arrangements of variables around a conceptual star

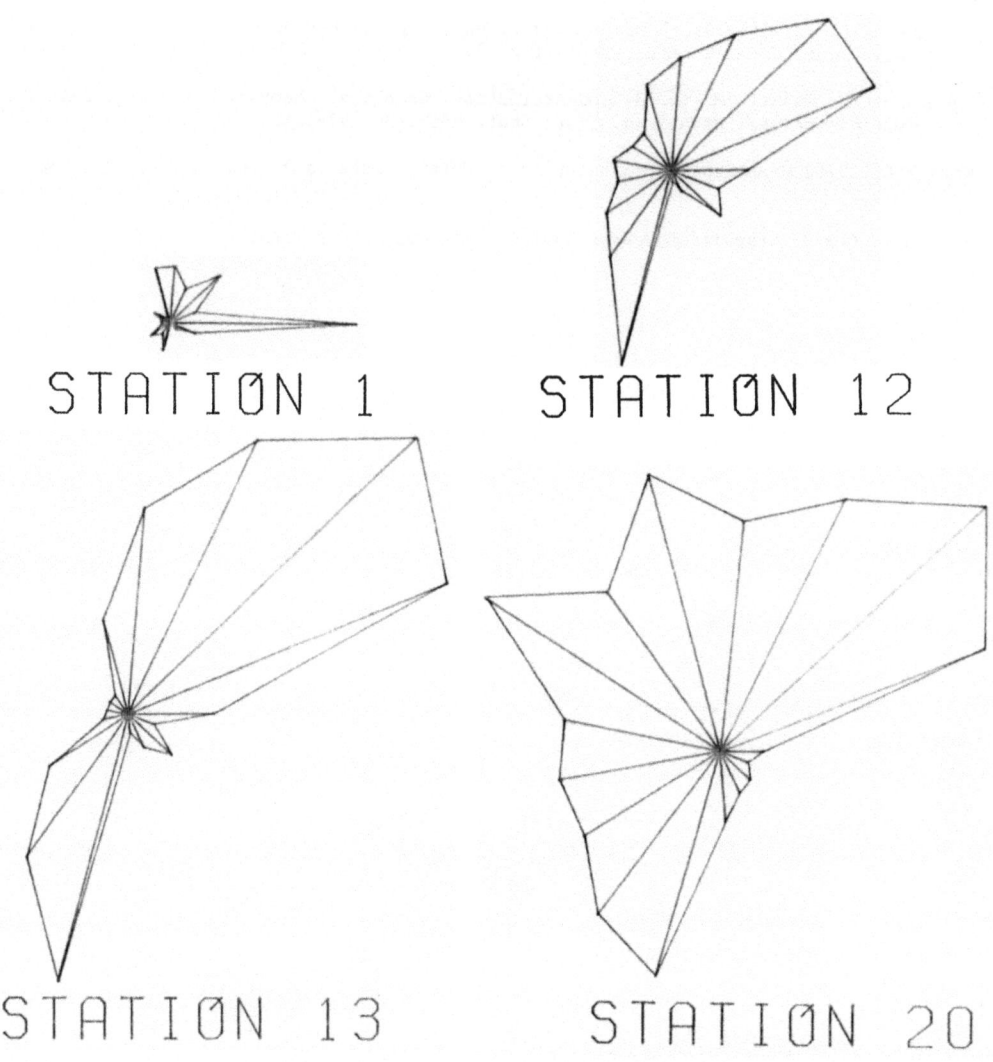

Fig. 2: Representation of certain pollution monitoring stations by stars

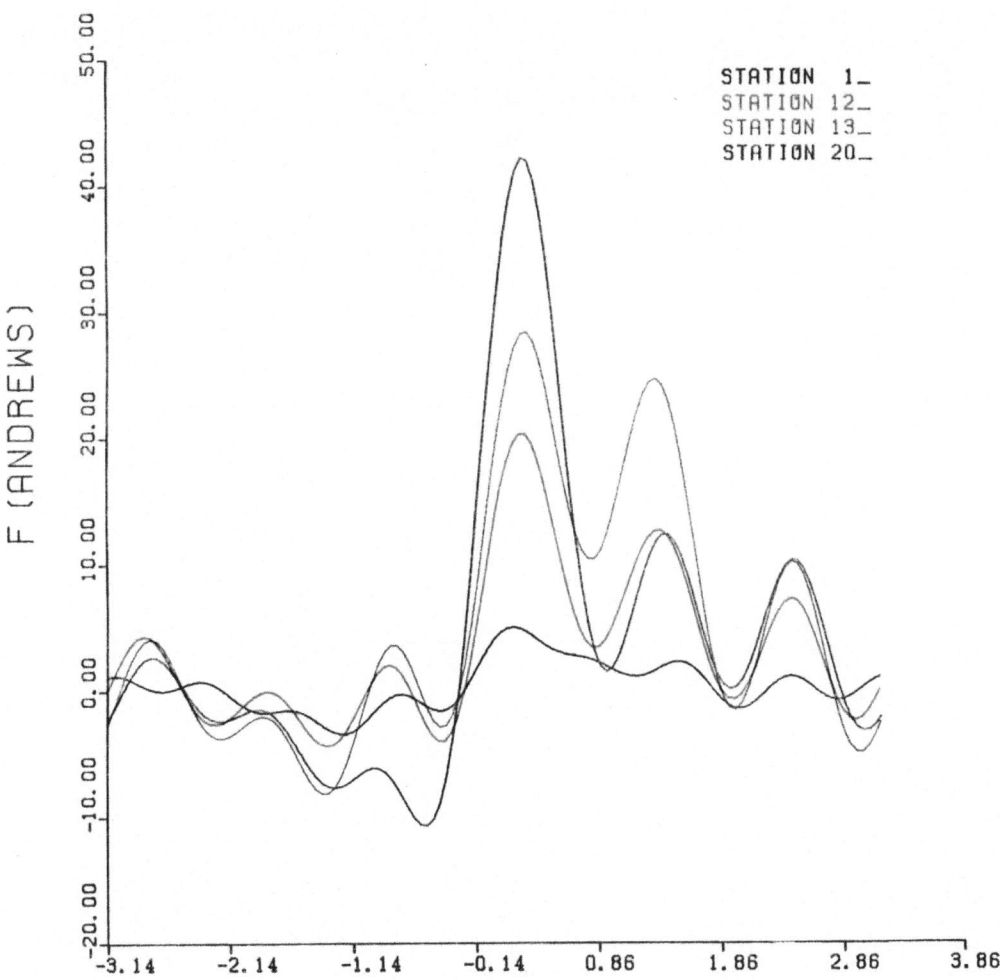

Fig. 3: Andrew's curves corresponding to stations 1, 12, 13 and 20

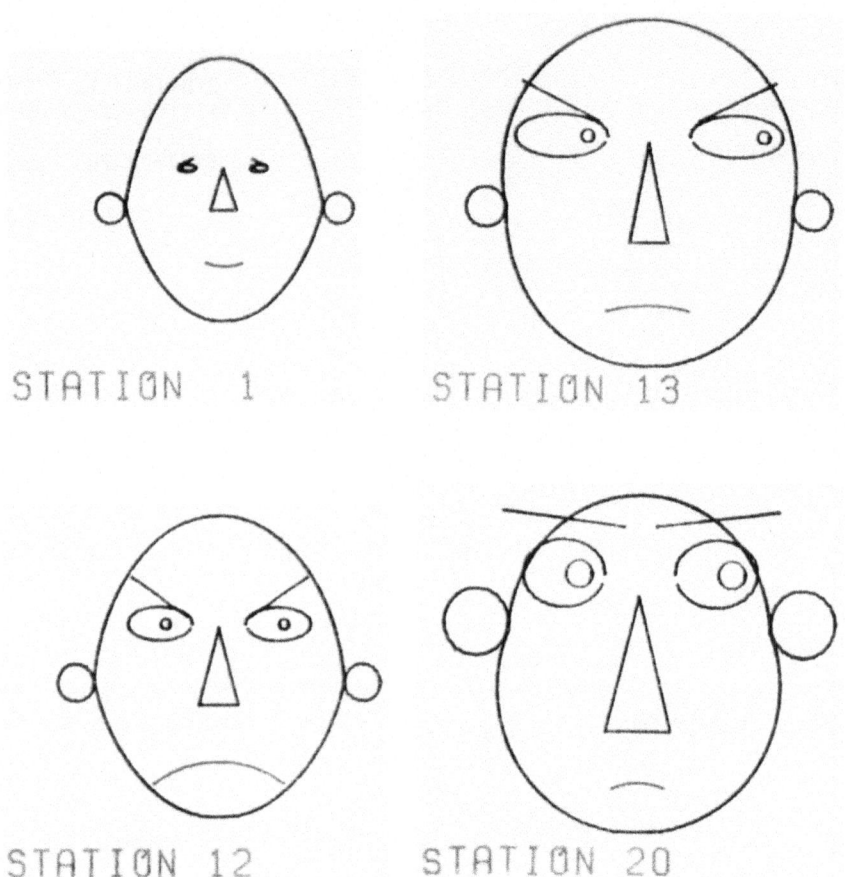

Fig. 4: Chernoff's faces for stations 1, 12, 13 and 20

Fig. 5: New Chernoff's faces as suggested by Flury and Riedwyl for stations 1, 12, 13 and 20

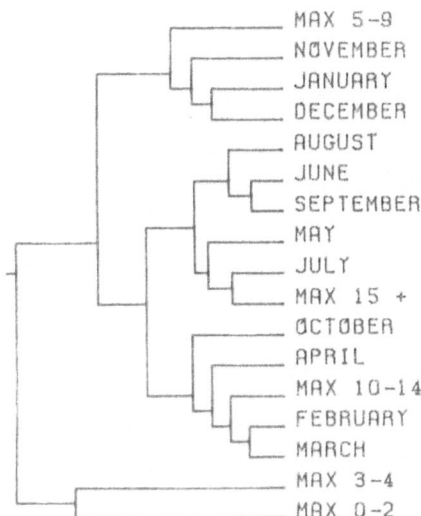

Fig. 6: Dendogram obtained by the complete linkage hierarchical clustering algorithm for the 17 variables observed at monitoring stations

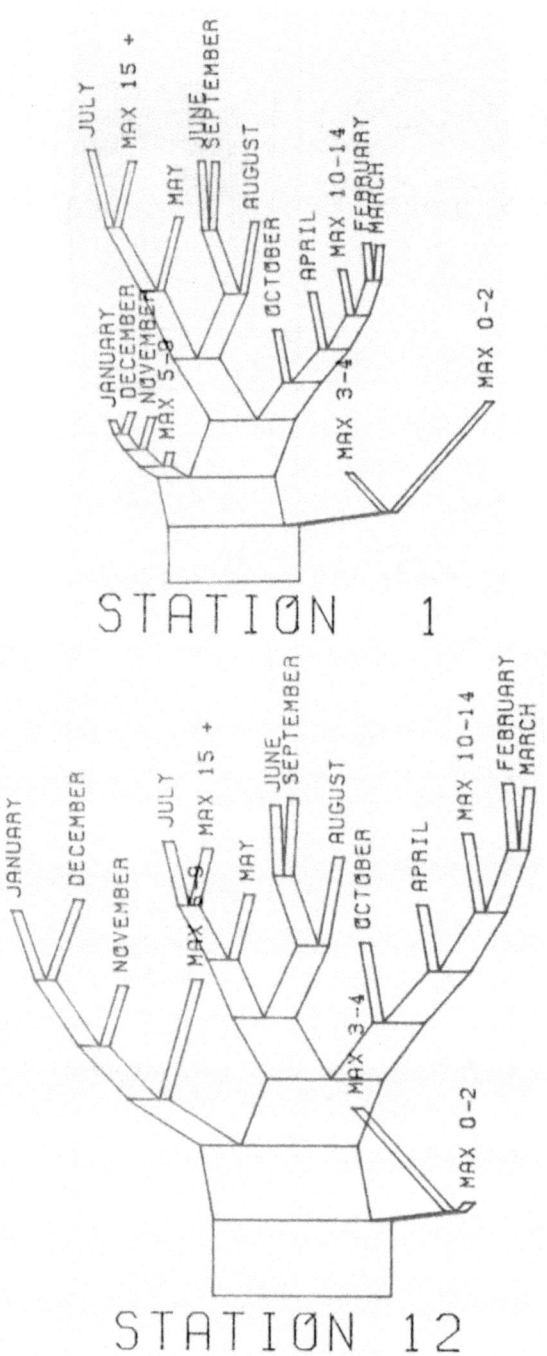

Fig. 7a: Representation of stations 1, 12 by trees

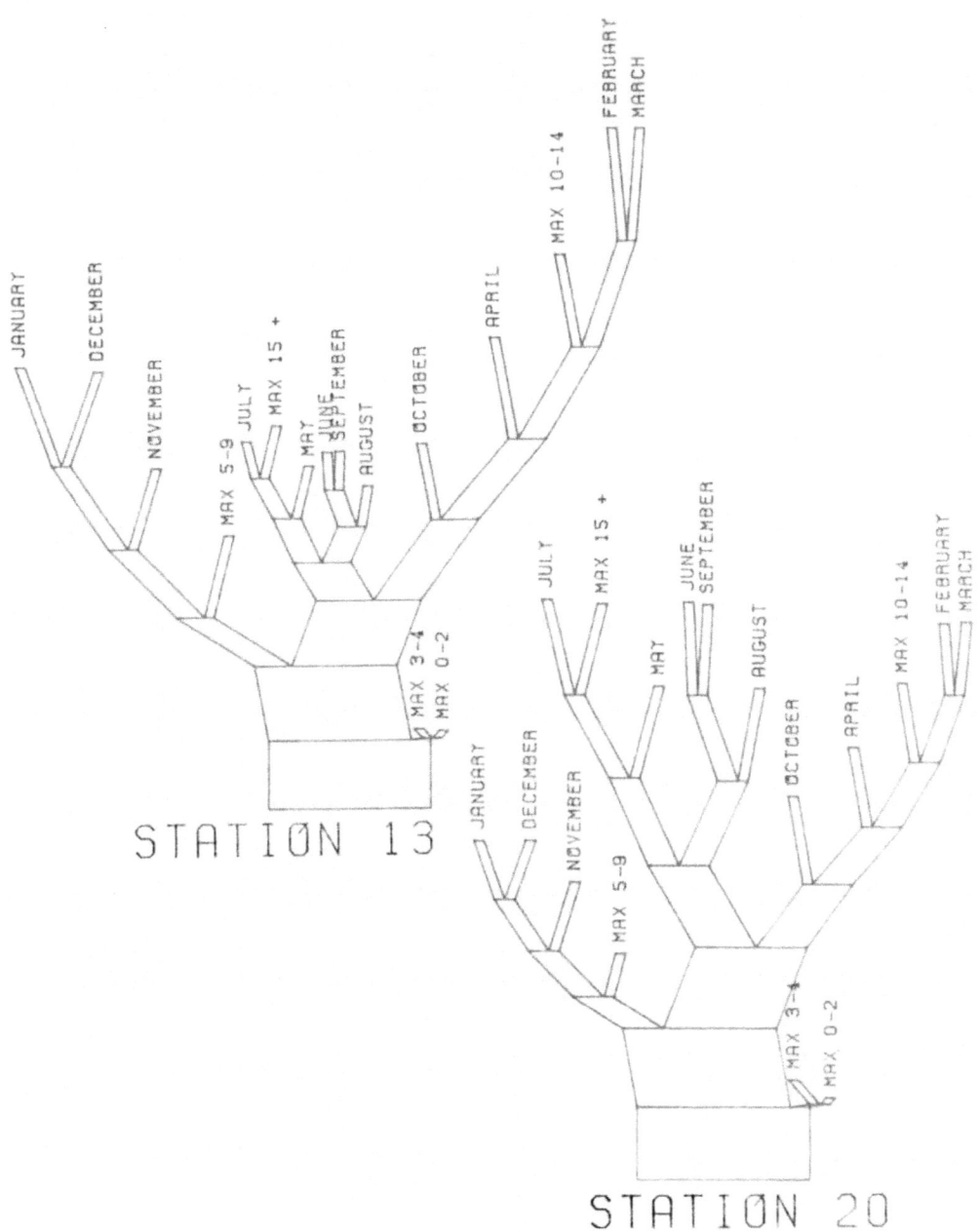

Fig. 7b: Representation of stations 13 and 20 by trees

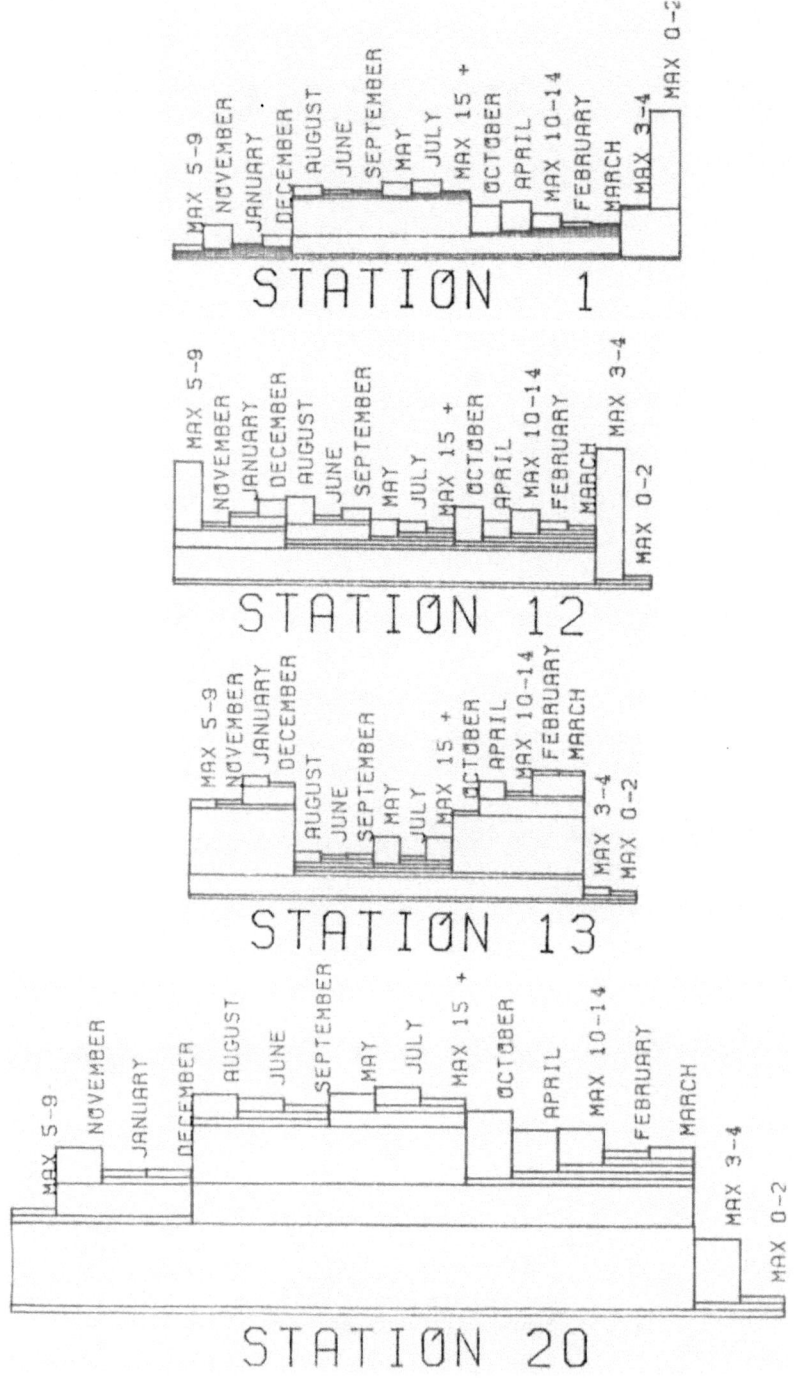

Fig. 8: Representation of stations 1, 12, 13 and 20 by castles

A Graphics Interface for Interactive Simulation of Packet-Switched Networks

J.L. Houle and L. Richardson
Ecole Polytechnique, Montréal, H3C 3J7, Canada

ABSTRACT

In the past the simulation of a communication network was usually performed using the batch processing mode. Presented in this paper is a more desirable way to design and evaluate a packet-switched network: the interactive simulation of the network using computer graphics to present the network states over a simulated time interval.

The concept of a software defined network is implemented allowing the use of an already existing network for a specific application related to distributed control systems. Moreover, the package presented could be used as a real-time network control system.

1. Problem definition.

In order to design the desired simulator, we had to focus on a particular aspect of computer communications: a distributed computer network for data acquisition and control, using the packet-switched technology. In many cases, computer control systems may be described as a hierarchy of computers distributed over thousands of kilometers.

These networks can be represented as two-layer systems. The first layer is the physical network, and the second layer the software defined network. The physical layer incorporates all the hardware and software requirements of an operational network such as links, node processors, buffers, communication based operating systems, etc. On the other hand, the functional layer is more relevant to the proposed application. The architecture of a control system is often based on a tree-like hierarchy, requiring that the flow of information be set accordingly. In our application the functional structure will be hierarchical, thus creating a hierarchical flow of information.

2. Methodology of design and performance evaluation.

With two layers to design and evaluate, it is understood that there are different performance criteria for each layer. Usually, the physical network used would be an already existing one, such as the Canadian DATAPAC network [1]. The main area of interest would be to design a software defined network in order to meet the requirements of a distributed computer control system.

The design and performance evaluation of computer communication systems usually focus on the sharing of resources and on the resulting queues. Normally there are two ways to evaluate these network queues: either to create an analytical model or otherwise to create a simulation model. In many cases it may be necessary to create both types of model.

2.1 Analytical modelling.

Analytical modelling is based on the abstraction of systems so that operational research and other tools of applied mathematics can be used to develop equations characterizing system performance [2]. Once the equations are developed, they can be solved by iterative numerical methods to produce the desired performance results under selected constraints. The analytical model can be more (or less) difficult to evaluate depending on both the complexity and the number of constraints involved.

The theoretical approach using queuing theory is a cost effective and practical technique to analyze the performance of a distributed computer control system. Networks of queues have been studied extensively in the technical literature in the past few years and a number of different models have been developed. The model we present here is a simplification of a model suggested by Samari and Schneider [3].

The model consists of one node and its output links, as shown in figure 1. The intervals between the arrival times of packets entering the node follow an exponential distribution, the processing time at the node is fixed and there is only one input queue. This node can be modelled as an M/D/1 system, and using the same notation, the links can also be modelled as M/D/1 systems. Such a model can be made much more complex by adding more nodal processors, or by including priorities on packets. But this is not our goal; we have chosen a simple case in order to describe the kind of analytical modelling required for a packet-switched network.

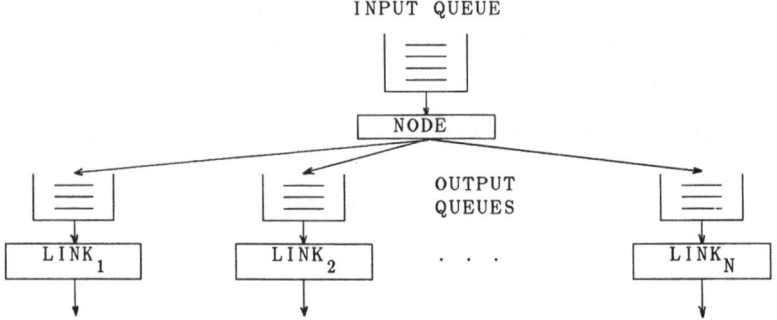

Fig. 1. Queuing model for a node processor and its output links.

Among the performance criteria we find the utilization factor of the node (ρN), and of each link (ρL), the average waiting time (including service) at the node input queue (tqN), and at each link input queue (tqL). Using the same notation as Martin [4], the following equations characterize these performance parameters:

$$\rho_N = \overline{S}\lambda_N \qquad (1)$$

$$\rho_L = \frac{\lambda_L}{\mu C_L} \qquad (2)$$

$$\overline{t}_{qN} = \overline{S}\left[1 + \frac{\rho_N}{2(1-\rho_N)}\right] \qquad (3)$$

$$\bar{t}_{qL} = \frac{1}{\mu C_L} \left[1 + \frac{\rho_L}{2(1-\rho_L)} \right] \quad (4)$$

where

$\bar{S}$ average service time at the node in seconds;

λ_N total input traffic at the node in packets/second;

λ_L total input traffic at a link in packets/second;

C_L the link capacity in bits/second;

$1/\mu$ the average packet length in bits.

Equations (1) through (4) are mainly used to evaluate the behavior of the physical resources. In order to evaluate the performance of the functional layer, characterized by the flow of information, we had to model the functional traffic. A packet sent from a functional node to another will take a route determined by the physical network, but the source and destination of the packet must be such that the hierarchy is respected.

The equations which follow are used to model the functional traffic. The concept of this model was presented by Samari and Schneider [3], with application to the physical network.

a) Traffic at the functional node i:

$$\lambda_i = \mu_i + \gamma_i \quad (5)$$

where

λ the total incoming traffic in packets/second;

μ_i the total internal traffic at node i;

γ_i the total external traffic at node i.

b) Total internal traffic at node i:

$$u_i = \sum_{j=1}^{N} \sum_{k=1}^{N} \gamma_j * DPT(j,k) \quad (6)$$
$$j \neq K, \; j \neq i, \; j \in \text{functional path } (j \to k, i)$$

where

N   the number of functional nodes;

DPT(j,k)   the destination probability table, giving the probability that a packet is sent from node j to node k;

j ∈ functional path(j -> k,i)
     the node j belongs to the functional path from j to k, passing through node i.

c) Traffic on a functional link:

$$\lambda_{SD} = \sum_{j=1}^{N} \sum_{k=1}^{N} \gamma_j * DPT(j,k) \quad (7)$$
$$j \neq D, [j \in \text{functional path}(j \to k, S)] \cap$$
$$[j \in \text{functional path}(j \to k, D)]$$

where

S   source;
D   destination.

Network mathematical modelling is generally the first step in network performance evaluation due to the direct relationship between the model parameters and performance measurements. In most cases this kind of modelling is too limited for the requirements of a real network therefore discrete event simulation becomes a good alternative.

2.2 Simulation.

The principal advantage of simulation is in its generality and flexibility. The complexity of the simulation model increases linearly with the network complexity, which is not the case for analytical modelling [2]. Criteria such as the implementation of a sophisticated protocol or a dynamic routing technique are extremely difficult to analyze, but simulation proves to be a useful tool in these cases.

Discrete event simulation can be described as a series of events associated with the network functions. [5,6,7,8] Some examples of typical events would be: the generation of a packet, the end of transmission of a packet , the statistical accumulation of events . A simplification of the model used is represented in figure 2.

```
          - packet generation at a node
    (1)   - enter the node
          - wait for service
          - wait for end of service
          - has packet arrived at
            destination ?
            yes:    remove it
            no:     perform routing,
                    get next node
          - wait for transmission
          - wait for end of transmission
          - go to (1)
```

Fig. 2. Simplified simulation model for a packet-switched network.

The simulator was written in Fortran 77 because of the need for short processing time. All computations are done with integer type variables, thus shortening the processing time.

Even if it is possible to evaluate the performance of a network using simulation only, the design of an analytical model should prove very useful for program verification and the validation of results.

2.3 Performance results.

The performance evaluation of a distributed computer network is done by a statistical analysis of resource and queue behavior. When the simulation model is appropriate and gives satisfactory primary results, the next step consists in carefully selecting the most sensitive parameters. These parameters should facilitate the accumulation of valuable information related to certain performance criteria, which include the total traffic at each node and link, the utilization factor of physical resources, the average queue length, etc. Some of this information may be relevant to the physical layer, but the need for information related to the functional structure is just as important.

Table 1 displays a comparison of the total flow at each node using simulation or analytical modelling for the physical and the functionnal structure. It can be seen that the analytical and simulation results differ by less than 1%. The physical and functional architectures can be found in figures 3 and 4.

Table 1. Comparison of the total flow at each node

Node	Total applied load at the physical nodes in packets per second.		Functionnal traffic in packets per second	
	Analytical	Simulation	Analytical	Simulation
HALIFAX	21.93	22.53	21.93	22.52
MONTREAL	54.23	55.24	59.16	60.13
OTTAWA	55.25	56.21	55.25	56.20
TORONTO	81.77	80.20	76.84	75.30
WINNIPEG	20.40	20.52	20.40	20.53
CALGARY	42.33	40.69	21.93	21.84
EDMONTON	20.40	18.85	20.40	18.85
VANCOUVER	20.40	20.49	20.40	20.50

The amount of data to be processed and analysed for the performance evaluation is quite large. Generally, the results are outputted in the form of printed tables or graphs. It is understood that the simulation program would have been run in a batch processing mode. A more desirable way of doing this would be to run the simulation interactively with a graphics interface for instantaneous display of network behavior.

3. A graphics interface for interactive simulation

The graphics software attached to the simulator has been developed on an IBM PC micro-computer, linked to a main-frame computer (IBM 4341), using the PC to emulate a Tektronix 4010 work station (storage tube graphics terminal). In order to create motion, the terminal software driver had to be modified so that parts of the screen could be erased and redrawn. Such procedures would not be possible on a real Tektronix 4010 graphics terminal justifying, in part, the use of a micro-computer.

At the beginning of the simulation the physical and functional architectures are read from a file which can be updated by the user during the simulation, and are processed in order to get a displayable format. The graphics interface is divided into three parts: the display of the physical structure according to the geographical position of each node, the display of the functional structure, and the display of simulation results as a set of histograms.

All three displays can be used either at the end of a simulation interval, or during the simulation interval where the values of selected parameters will be updated regularly. A menu is provided before each simulation to allow the user to select the parameter to be evaluated, and to select one of the three displays available. At the end of the simulation interval, the same menu is presented enabling the user to visualize the accumulated statistics. The simulation clock is displayed in the upper right corner of the screen on all displays.

3.1 Display of the physical layer.

The physical network display consists mainly of lines and squares. Each node is represented by a square, labelled with its geographical position (i.e. Montreal, Ottawa,...), and the lines joining the nodes represent the physical communication links. The resulting display is a geographical representation of the network. Occasionnally a group of physical nodes are located close together, for this reason a zoom option is available to decongest the overcrowded area. This option allows the user to either view the entire network or to select a zoom in on one or more nodes, thus concentrating on the behavior of the selected nodes only.

In the event that the designer wishes to use the physical network display during a simulation interval, he will see the numerical value of the selected parameter at each displayed node or link. As the simulation progresses, the values will be updated according to the network state. Figure 3 shows a physical network display with no selected parameters.

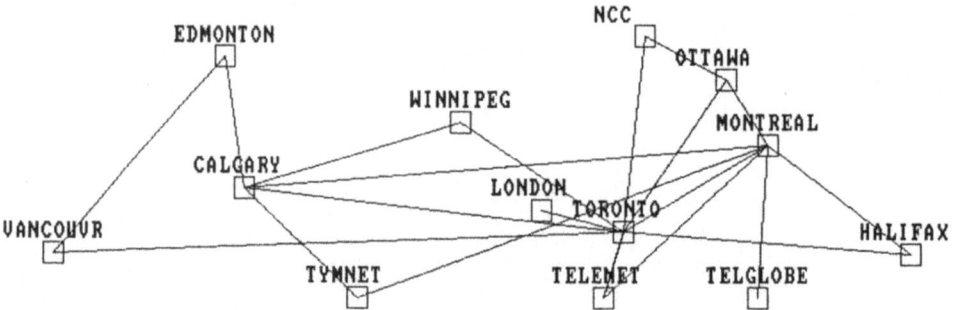

Fig. 3. Physical structure of the network.

3.2 Display of the functional layer.

The functional structure display uses a different format than the physical network display, except that nodes are not represented according to their geographical position, but according to their level in the control hierarchy. Because all physical nodes are not necessarily members of the hierarchy, there could be fewer functional nodes than physical nodes.

The simulation can handle a maximum of 30 nodes, but with 30 functional nodes, the screen could easily be congested and very difficult to read. Therefore, a zoom option has been implemented. The zoom option allows the user to select the display of the whole hierarchy, or of a sub-tree of the hierarchy. Figure 4 shows an example of a functional structure display, with a selected parameter related to functional links.

A choice of 8 colors is available for the foreground and the background allowing the possibility of 64 color combinations representing different hierarchical levels.

If the functional layer is selected for the display during a dynamic simulation, the values of the selected parameter will be displayed at the proper place, whether nodes or links have been chosen, and will be updated regularly during the simulation interval.

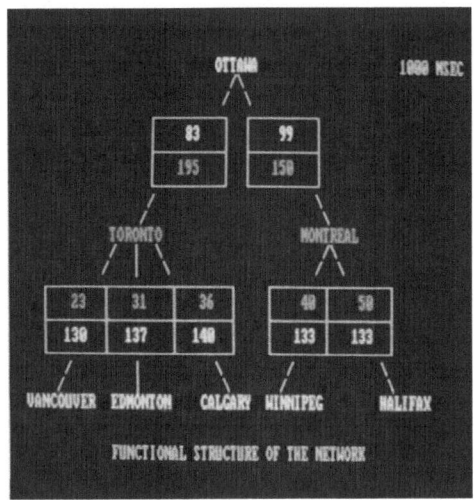

Fig. 4. Functionnal structure of the network.

3.3 Display of histograms.

The use of the histogram display enables the designer to view any layer of the network, physical or functional. The selection of this display at the end of a simulation interval will produce a standard graphic representation using histograms. The most attractive part of this display comes when it is selected for a dynamic simulation. The histograms will be displayed as a static graphic representation, but as the simulation progresses, the heights of the histograms will vary according to the value of the selected parameter, thus creating a motion effect. Using this display, the designer can easily detect the most congested area of the network, without knowing the exact value of the selected parameter, and make appropriate changes.

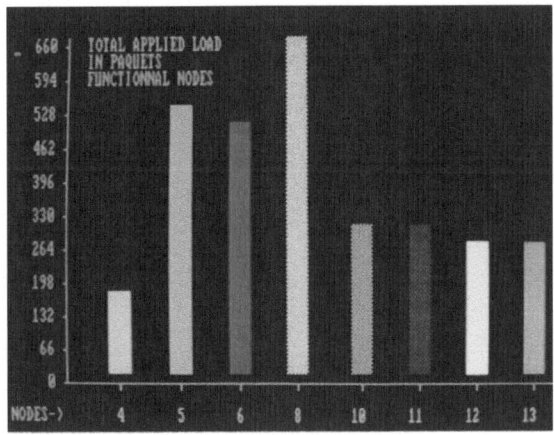

Fig. 5. Dynamic histogram of the network.

Conclusion.

The graphics interface for the present simulation package is a key element in that it allows excellent interaction between the network designer and its design tool, the simulation model. The large amount of intermediate results required to achieve the final results and desired network performance favors the use of an interactive color graphics display. Moreover, the results are strongly dependent on the geography; it is therefore natural to represent the designed network along with its actual topology.

References.

[1] Sproule, D.E., and Mellor, F. "Routing, Flow and Congestion Control in the Datapac Network", IEEE Transaction on communications, April 1981, pp. 386-391.

[2] Sauer, C.H., and MacNair, E.A. "Simulation of Computer Communication Systems", Prentice- Hall, 1983.

[3] Samari, N.K., and Schneider, G.M. "A Queuing Theory Based Analytic Model of a Distributed Computer Network", IEEE Transactions on computers, November 1980, pp. 994-1001.

[4] Martin, J. "Design of Real-Time Computer Systems", chap. 26, Prentice-Hall, 1967.

[5] Gomberg, G.R.A., Ken, I., Richards, J.S., Price, W.L., and Solomonides, C.M. "A Design Study of a Hierarchically Connected Packet- Switching Network Using Simulation Techniques", Computer Networks 3, North-Holland Publishing Company, 1979, pp. 114-135.

[6] Chlamtac, I., and Franta, W.R. "A Generalized Simulator for Computer Networks", Simulation, October 1982, pp. 123-132.

[7] Haenle, J.O., and Giessler, A. "Simulation of Data Transport Systems of Packet-Switched Networks", Computer Networks and Simulation, North-Holland publishing company, 1978, pp. 101-117.

[8] Boorstyn, R.R., and Livne, A. "A Technique for Adaptive Routing in Networks", IEEE Transactions on communications, April 1981, pp. 474-480.

[9] Gerla, M. "Controlling Routes, Traffic Rates, and Buffer Allocation in Packet Networks", IEEE Communication magazines, November, 1984, pp. 11-23.

Design and Implementation of an Interactive Route Editor

Guy Lapalme[1], and Michel Cormier[2]

Département d'informatique et de recherche opérationnelle[1], Centre de recherche sur les transports[2], Université de Montréal, C.P. 6128, Succ. A., Montréal, P.Q. H3C 3J7, Canada

INTRODUCTION

Operations Research techniques now provide us with many algorithms for real life routing problems (Bodin 1983; Chapleau 1984; Chapleau 1985). Unfortunately, being often heuristic in nature, their results must be evaluated by hand (by eye would be a more appropriate term). This evaluation must take into account not only the usual constraints (capacity, length, time duration, etc) but also other unwritten ones (overall shape of the route, going back on one self, certain types of vehicle might not be able to go over certain roads, etc). This process usually prompts some more modifications who then in turn must be evaluated.

The best way to appraise such routes is their drawing on a road map; usually many of them are on a single territory and we are interested in having a more global improvement than one route at a time; to differentiate them, we give a distinct color to each route. Hand drawing those results is very slow and tedious, so the generated routes are accepted as they are or worse they are rejected as a whole. So what we need is an automatic draughting tool to display both the road network and the routes in color. This implies a high resolution so that the drawing appears as it would on a real map. For that purpose, we can think of two kinds of hardware: color plotters and color graphic screens. The first tool gives a very good resolution and beautiful drawings but does not allow easy interactions to achieve the fast modifications that we plan to implement. This paper describes a tool to answer that need: a route editor which displays the routes and permits easy and fast changes in them.

We will show that this system has essentially the same structure as any text editor found in computer systems today [Meyrowitz 1982]. As those editors have been in use for many years now, we can expect that they are now on solid grounds and that their main commands correspond to the needs of a user changing a text already in machine-readable form. So if our commands parallel those of to the editor, we are confident that our foundamental needs will be fulfilled.

STRUCTURE OF A TEXT EDITOR

We first give a brief overview of the fundamental structure of a typical interactive text editor. Its commands can be classified in three major categories:

- file reading and writing commands to choose the file to be modified and to keep it for future use

- modification commands to change the contents of the file: we can insert new lines, delete lines, move lines, change only a few characters in a line. We need also a way to indicate which lines are affected by the changes

- display commands to list the contents of lines before or after the modifications

STRUCTURE OF THE ROUTE EDITOR

We think that a route editor should accomplish the same modification tasks on a file describing stops in routes a text editor does on a text file. If we consider the following analogies: a route corresponds to a line of text, a stop in a route corresponds to a character in a line. So we can create new routes and delete old ones; we want also to remove, add or reorder stops in a route. The main difference will be in the display commands where on one side, a text editor works on a linear basis (characters in a line) but on the other side, the stops in a route are given by coordinates in a 2-D space; this implies a more elaborate set of display commands not found in a typical text editor.

The overall scenario of an editing session is as follows: we first choose the routes to worked on; they are displayed over the road network, they are modified on line and are then written back to the file storage system. Table 1 lists the main commands.

EDITOR COMMANDS

```
    Modification
        add         route or stop
        delete      route or stop
        move        stop(s) to a route
        reorder     stops within a route

    Display
        visibility  on/off of a route
        colorswap   between two routes
        zoom        in/out of a region

    Others
        option settings
        undo
        help

            Table 1
```

DISPLAY COMMANDS

Those commands are very straightforward in text editors but are less so in our context because of the many variations that can occur: for example, we can display the whole network (see Fig. 1 were 2000 nodes and 3000 arcs are displayed) or just enough to display the chosen routes, the stops can be linked either with the shortest path on the network or as the crow flies (see Fig. 1 where stops are indicated by dots over the network). Each route has a district color different from the base network.

Once the routes are displayed, we may need to clear up the situation for a better evaluation: for example, by changing colors of the routes, by removing a few ones from the display or even zooming in on a particular area of interest (Fig. 2 was obtained by zooming on a region of Fig. 1). Once we have a satisfactory display, we can start the modifications themselves.

The implementation of these commands is quite straightforward once we have the basic informations about the network: for each arc representing a portion of a street between two corners, we keep the node numbers of its ends and its length; for each node representing the street intersections we have their x-y coordinates and pointers to the arcs coming in and out of this node; the routes are lists of stops each comprising a node number and other problem specific informations: stop number, number of persons to pick up, time of pickup, etc.

We see that we have all the information needed for drawing the network lines to be drawn (possibly clipped) between coordinates. The routes also follow the same pattern except when the exact path between each stop has to be drawn. Memory limitations do not allow keeping constantly in memory these paths which can involve hundreds of arcs, a typical route being 30km long. So before drawing that path, we first compute it using a classical Dijkstra shortest-path algorithm stopping as soon as the destination has been permanently labelled and keeping in each node the number of the preceding node in the path. We then follow the pointers to draw the whole path. This whole procedure is usually quite fast (1 to 10 seconds) between each stop and gives the user a very good feeling about the shape of the route; this is much better than the "crow fly" approach and so it is worth it.

Changing the colors of the routes or making them visible or invisible is done almost instantly because it only involves changing a few bytes in the color look-up table.

MODIFICATION COMMANDS

We have three levels of modification:

- route level: we can create or delete new routes

- stop level: we can add, remove stops from a route; reordering of stops within a route has proven itself very useful in our context. It is also possible to move stops from one route to another. When the modifications are made the result is immediately reflected on the screen.

- within a stop: a number of attributes characterize a stop; for example, the quantity of goods to pick up of deliver, the time window for servicing, the names of the people to pickup, etc. Updating that information does not involve 2-D spatial information and can be done with the usual text editing functions. But care must be taken to update the global attributes of the route accordingly: for example, total quantity, total time length, total number of people, etc.

It is very important that the modifications be done almost instantly, but some of them may require a certain amount of time and memory, for example to find the shortest path between each stop in a route. To be effective, we must have a very fast computer and a high transmission rate. We have chosen to implement this system on a dedicated work station composed of a high resolution bitmap color screen with a MC68000 based microcomputer running an UNIX like operating system. This is surely a very expensive piece of equipment but we must realize that the operations we want to optimize are very costly ones where a small part of the expected savings can pay off the investment.

The implementation of the commands involves processing the lists of stops: removing stops from one list and moving them to another, reordering of lists, deleting items from lists, etc. When lists are modified, the old version of the route is redrawn using the background color and the new modified route is redisplayed.

INTERACTION ASPECTS

The fact that we have a dedicated computer is very important to achieve a constant interaction rate. The user is not slowed down by the works of others like in a time-sharing mode. So simple commands are done almost immediately and more complicated ones take a longer time; the user expects this and can appreciate that it is his command which ties up the system.

We have also implemented a very simple interface consisting of menus and cursor positioning with a joystick, the keyboard is almost never needed. This allows direct manipulation of the objects (in our case the stops and the routes) which is recognized as one of the easiest way to interact with a system [Schneiderman 1983].

Another important aspect of the system is the possibility of undoing commands. If we realize that we made an error in specifying the nodes involved in a command or that a command did not give the expected improvements then, by touching one key, we can go back to the situation before that command. This feature is very important because in this way, one can freely experiment with the system without having to find the inverse of an erroneous command. In our system, we can currently go back over the last five commands; before that, the modifications are committed, but there is always the possibility of not saving those modifications in the case of an earlier error. The implementation of that feature is quite intricate because we have to execute the inverse of each command; in the case of reordering of stops, this inverse is almost impossible to find so the original order is kept in heap memory in case of backing up.

As it is very difficult to give a real feeling of such an interactive system by writing, we have produced an eight minute Super-8 film which shows how modifications can be made in a real context.

This system is closely related to the works of Cullen [1982], Fisher [1983] and Babin [1982] but these systems are not as much oriented towards the interactive route editing approach as ours. Cullen and Fisher use color graphic microcomputers mainly for the display, the main computations being made on a remote mainframe linked by a telephone line. Babin features a transit planning system running on a stand alone powerful microcomputer. It aims more at displaying analytical results in form of tables and graphs than at showing routes over a network; this system also includes an interactive network editing module but not a route editing one.

CONCLUSION

Our experience with this tool has proven that it is very user-friendly, easy to use and very cost effective. It has allowed users to evaluate and modify more than 150 routes in two days. We have focused here on the modification aspects of the editor but it can also be used to create new routes from scratch. We are currently involved in other works to improve the editor by integrating the notion of time and other basic algorithms for example: clustering, traveling salesman, insertion, etc..

ACKNOWLEDGMENTS

We would like to thank Serge Lafrance, Claude Mallette and Alain Choquette for bearing with us in the many program modifications which have been going on over the years. Special thanks also to Jacques Ferland and Jean-Marc Rousseau for believing in this project and putting much time and money into this interactive approach to routing and scheduling.

BIBLIOGRAPHY

Babin A., Florian M., James L., Spiess H., (1982) "EMME/2: Interactive Graphic Method for Road and Transit Planning", Transportation Research Record, 866: 1-9.

Bodin, L., Golden B., Assad A., Ball M., (1983) "Routing and Scheduling of Buses and Crews", Computers and Operations Research, 10: 69-211.

Chapleau L., Ferland J., Lapalme G., Rousseau J-M., (1984) "A Parallel Insert Method for the Capacitated Arc Routing Problem", Operations Research Letters, 3: 95-100.

Chapleau L., Ferland J., Rousseau J-M., (1985) "Clustering for Routing in Dense Area", European Journal of Operational Research, 20:

Cullen F.H., Jarvis J.J., Ratlif H.D., (1982) "Interactive Optimization in Distribution Analysis", ORSA/TIMS Joint National Meeting, San Diego.

Fisher M., Greefield A., Thomson K., (1983) "Real World Experience with an Interactive Color Graphic Interface for ORSA/TIMS Joint National Meeting, Orlando.

Meyrowitz N., Van Dam A., (1982) "Interactive Editing Systems", Computing Surveys, 14: 321-415.

Shneiderman B., (1983) "Direct manipulation: A Step beyond Programming Languages" Computer, 16: 57-69.

Figure 1

Figure 2

Business Graphics and the Stakeholder Approach
An Exploratory Field Experiment

Albert Lejeune, François Bolduc and Nadia Magnenat-Thalmann

MIRALAB, Ecole des Hautes Etudes Commerciales, Université de Montréal, Montréal, H3C 3J7, Canada

ABSTRACT

In this article, the concept of a stakeholder is borrowed from the strategic management literature. Our question is, "Which graphics format will influence a stakeholder network in the most efficient way?" To answer this question we define two categories of business graphics: (i) "circulation" graphics intended to circulate from node to node inside a network and (ii) "terminal" graphics in which the specific use is localized at only one node in a network. With the help of the GRAFEDIT, GRAFANA and CINEDATA software packages, we generate various graphic formats (line charts, pie charts, bar charts, pictographs, pictorial unit graphs and 3D charts). Finally an exploratory field experiment is set up to verify the following hypothesis: for a given problem and for a multiple stakeholder network, managers manipulate graphics formats to inform and influence different stakeholders in different ways. The results show the importance of the stakes (defined by a specific problem) and the stakeholders (internal or external to the organization) in the choice of a graph format. Some cultural aspects may also explain differences between functions and position in the hierarchy.

ACKNOWLEDGMENTS: We wish to thank Rhéal Boucher (chief communications division, Gulf Region), Moktar Outtas and Leontine Rousseau for their assistance in this study and Ann Laporte for the revision of the English version. This research was supported by the Natural Science and Engineering Council of Canada.

1. Introduction

Most researchers base their work on a rational or economic perception of the organization or enterprise, and focus on the use of graphics as rational input to the decision making process.

On the other hand, today's literature on "strategic management" encourages a multidimensional approach to understanding organizations. This approach draws attention to the cultural and socio-political dimensions of organizations (1) which complicate the pseudo-rational model. Even MIS researchers are not free from these concerns, and the notions of culture (2) and power (3) now appear in their literature.

In our view, the individual who chooses the graphic forms in which data will be distributed throughout the enterprise has considerable latitude to influence the impact of the information in desired ways. This latitude will be best used by those who best understand human information processing characteristics specific to the graphics display method (4).

The present study aims to establish, by means of exploratory research, the hypothesis that for a given problem, managers may use business graphics strategically by informing each stakeholder network, be it internal or external to the enterprise, using graphics formats (line charts, bar charts, circle charts, pictographs, pictorial unit graphs and 3D charts) which are most likely to influence this network's members.

The graphics used in this study were constructed using the following software packages: GRAFANA (5), GRAFEDIT (6) and CINEDATA integrated in a complete provider system designed for TELIDON.

We borrowed the notion of "stakeholder" from R. Edward Freeman (7).

2. The stakeholder approach and "compunications"

"The point of a stakeholder approach to organizations is to force organizational managers to be more responsive to the external environnement". Hence Freeman's definition of external stakeholder: "any group or individual who can affect or is affected by the achievement of the firm's objectives". The groups mentioned by Freeman are: employees, environmentalists, suppliers, governments, local community organizations, owners, consumer advocates, customers, competitors, media... "Each of these groups has a stake in the modern corporation", hence the terms "stakeholder", "stakeholder model or framework", or "stakeholder management". Freeman also considers the notion of "internal stakeholder": "Quite simply, the internal stakeholder must be seen as the conduit through which managers can reach other external stakeholders". Freedman finally develops "typical stakeholder maps" according to the managers' function: marketing, manufacturing, finance, public relations, and personnel.

In particular, this approach defines consistency networks, which are communication networks in which games of influence, inside a given network, or between different networks, are played
Currently, these networks, both internal and external, are being modified by technological changes and are moving closer and closer to the "compunications" phenomenon

defined by A. Oettinger (8). Office automation (word processing, decision support systems, data storage, retrieving and copying...) mixed with local networks and videotex will lead to "blurred boundaries between work and home telecommuting" (9) and between an organization and its external stakeholders.

It is reasonable to believe that stakeholder maps will become electronic maps, and that the format of business graphics circulating inside a given network, or between networks, will be of strategic importance for researchers and managers.

3. Presentation and decision aid graphics vs "circulation graphics"

As we are interested in dynamic communication networks, the distinction between presentation graphics and decision aid (and strategic planning (10)) graphics does not seem to generate mutually time-exclusive categories of graphics.

In other words, a presentation graphic created by A may well become a decision aid graphic for B; and a decision aid graphic for A may be later used to justify a decision to B. We live in a complex communication network, and, from node to node, the same graphic may take on a different nature depending on whether it is used as input for X's decision, or as output to justify X's decision another node of the network.

We suggest that business graphics design should not be restricted to a single specific application (node A in a decision process of nature X); graphics should rather be designed in such a way that they may circulate through the communications network(s) of the organization and/or its environment where they should be understandable by everyone. Depending on whether we are dealing with a decision's input or output, graphics will serve as presentation or decision aid graphics.

We therefore define two kind of graphics: (i) those which are designed to circulate throughout a network; these are mixed presentation/decision aid graphics and (ii) those which will never leave the network node at which they were developed; these lose all utility as soon as they have been used at point A in a given node (decision aid or presentation). These graphics will be called respectively (i) circulation graphics and (ii) terminal graphics.

4. Action graphics vs decision graphics

In a standardized organizational context, where the rules of the game are clearly defined and problems come to the manager in a structured way, the concept of action defines exactly what the manager must do: once warned about something wrong, he or she takes corrective action. In this case, when focusing on the context of the decision process, warning system graphics or "VIEWS" (Visual Early Warning Systems) graphs are most appropriate. These are mainly decision-aid graphs, which become presentation graph as they circulate through the network to warn managers or employees down the organizational hierarchy. However they are also "terminal" graphics in the sense that once read and understood by a manager, an action is initiated (direct action or verbal orders) and the "VIEW" graph loses its value as the process continues. New graphs are now awaited as feed-back to the corrective action.

Are these action graphics of the same type as those used in unstructured decision processes? The answer to this is, "No" because the decision process is quite different. Following Mintzberg et al. (1976) (11), who studied 25 unstructured strategic decision processes, the many iterations characterizing these processes can be classified into three main phases: identification, development and selection. Graphics formats used in unstructured decision processes must be tailored to the different steps of the process. These may be complex in the development phase (search and design routines), more formal and schematic in the selection phase (screening, judgment, analysis and bargaining routines) and easier to read (use of colors and icons) at the end on the decision process to better communicate the results of the process.

Note that one characteristic of unstructured decision processes is that they begin with problems, opportunities or crises from various different origins. Problem recognition is therefore complex, intuitive and synthetic rather than rational or analytic, and "VIEW" systems are of limited usefulness. Decision making is at the strategic level rather than the operational level. Bertin (1981) (12) suggests decision graphs for the identification stage and Chernoff (1971) (13) Moriarity (1979) (14) and Jarett (1983) (15) give examples of action graphs, designed to trigger an action.

5. Methodology

5.1 An exploratory field experiment

In order to understand the relationships between graphics format (as the dependant variable), a stakeholder network and a problem (as independent variables), we first chose an organization, a problem, and a series of business graphics to illustrate the problem for different managers (staff and line) in relation to active internal and external stakeholders.

5.2 Organization choice

We chose as the site for our study the Canadian Federal Ministry of Fisheries and Oceans, Office of the Gulf Region, Memremcook, N.B.

Several pressure groups (the main species management committees, producers and consumers associations, fishermen and plant workers' unions, ecologists, chambers of commerce, other municipal and provincial governments...) are stakeholders in this organization. We can even pinpoint corresponding internal stakeholders: the protection service (for the fisheries' officers), the communications service (for the media, and for the bulletin distributed to fishermen), the statistics service (which answers public requests and transmits data to the federal ministry of fisheries in Ottawa), the biology and economy services (which make people aware of pertinent issues, and maintain links with research centers and universities) all serve as contacts between stakeholders and the organization.

5.3 Problem choice

We simulated two problems which are very close to the usual kind of questions this organization has to deal with continuously. The first problem is a regulation problem following over-exploitation of lobster stock in a particular fishing ground. The second problem, at the other end of the scale, is an opportunity for higher quotas for salmon fishermen in another particular area. Both problems are presented as very current (and similar to real situations) and require information to be sent in graphical mode to several external or internal stakeholders.

5.4 Questionnaire

After studying the Gulf Region's organizational chart and the usual decision process followed to settle a regulation problem leading to higher or lower quotas, we designed a questionnaire. This consisted of a matrix of 10 situations and 5 graphics formats. For each situation, the manager was asked to arrange the 5 graphics formats labelled A to E, from 1 ($\simeq$ the best) to 5 ($\simeq$ the worst) for each situation. Note that graphic C, a pie chart, is included only as a means of control. It is not viewed as an adequate representation of time-series data.

5.5 Pictures

and once for the salmon problem. We standardized the forms and the colours after many trials and tests with people knowlegeable in the domain of commercial fisheries and others who knew nothing about the field. Finally a consensus was reached on 10 pictures (5 for the lobster problem and 5 for the salmon problem); several pictures are shown at the end of this article.

5.6 <u>The test</u>

During two full days we met 22 people from the 5 main services: economics and statistics, ressource allocation, protection and regulation, research, communication and the Director General. Twenty questionnaires were completed. The setting of the experiment was the same for all the members of each service as meetings took a place in a conference room, one service at a time. Practically, after a short introduction, a page presenting the first problem was distributed to the members of a service. Then, a questionnaire was given with the ranking instructions. Envelopes containing the 5 different pictures were then distributed. The test took 15 minutes to complete. As soon as this was finished, the second problem was presented and the same procedure was followed.

6. <u>Software description</u>

All plots shown in this paper were produced using two interactive systems: GRAFANA (5) and CINEDATA.

GRAFANA is a two-dimensional program which allows the user to produce cartesian plots, bar charts, network diagrams and pie charts. Two other kinds of charts may be generated as shown in our example:

- Pictographs: charts where each value is represented by a pictogram, whose size is proportional to the value;

- Pictorial unit graphs: charts where each value is represented by a small number of similar pictograms. This number is directly proportional to the value it represents.

CINEDATA is a three-dimentional program that is used to produce two main types of charts:

- Three-dimensional bar charts;

- Figurative charts where a symbol represents a certain number of elements as in pictographs of GRAFANA.

In our software, symbols are two-dimensional and constructed as a combination of filled polygons. The objective of this technique is to take into account the hidden surfaces of the drawing.

GRAFANA and CINEDATA are elements of very complete information provider system designed for TELIDON, the Canadian Videotex system. The complete system produces TELIDON pages using two graphical editors, GRAFEDIT (6) and HORIZON (16) the MIRA (17) graphical programming language and GRAFANA and CINEDATA. The software was implemented using MIRA, which is a graphical extension of PASCAL. It runs on a DEC VAX 11/780 with VMS. Images may be produced either on TELIDON terminals or on various graphical terminals. In this paper, pictures were produces using a Raster technologies.

7. Results

In order to determine whether graphics formats were associated with particular stakeholders for a specific problem, we conducted a correspondance analysis that allowed us to obtain the 3-D data (stakeholder - graph format - problem) on a 2 dimensional map (see fig.1)

The computer analysis calculated as the "X" axis the tri-D axis, opposing a first choice for the tri-D-graph and a fifth choice for the pictogram against a last choice for this graph format and a first choice for the pictogram. This axis shows the greatest dispersion between all the responses to the quetionnaire. The "Y" axis, calculated to obtain the greatest variances between all the variances non-correlated with the first axis, shows an opposition between a bar-graph as a second choice (and a pictogram as a fourth choice) an a bar-graph as a fourth choice (and a pictogram as a second choice). The external stakeholders are clearly associates with the right of the "X" axis, especially for the lobster problem.

The internal stakeholders are clearly associated with the left side of the "X" axis, but very disseminated along the "Y" axis, in opposition to the external stakeholders who are centered around the "X" axis.

A first conclusion is that there are greater differences between people's choices concerning internal stakeholders than external stakeholders.

A second conclusion is that the nature of the problem generates different stakes and this may influence the preferred graphics format. A female junior advisor said after the test: "I would never send pictograms with lobsters on thems to fishermen to tell them they can no longer trap lobsters!"

As well as these two conclusions concerning the stakes and stakeholders, a third conclusion emphasizes differences between organizational cultures in the 5 different services, and along hierarchical levels. In short, between services, two services, Economics and Statistics and Ressources Allocation, chose the most clearly the 3-D

FIGURE 1 RESULTS OF THE CORRESPONDANCE ANALYSIS

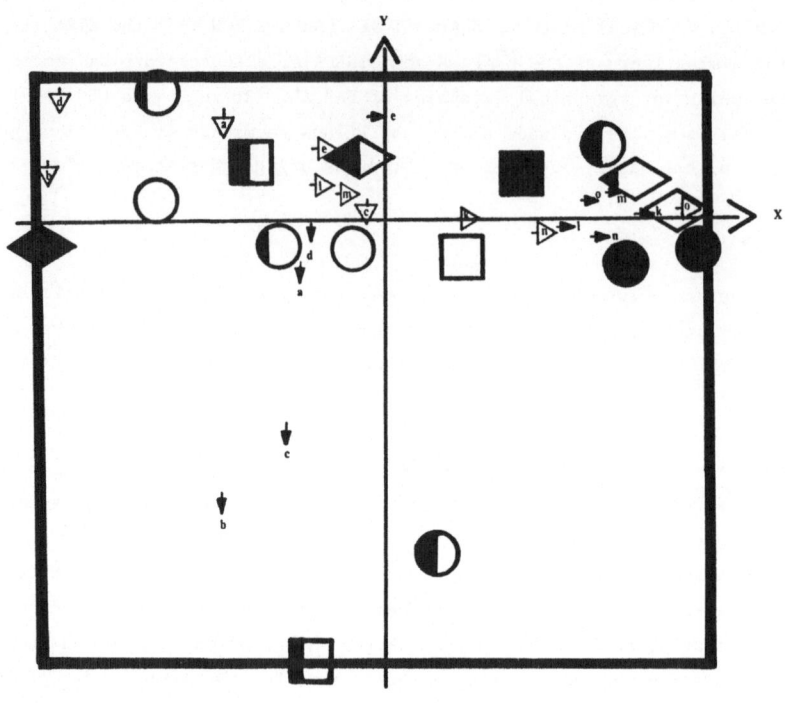

LOBSTERS:

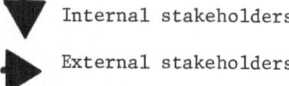 Internal stakeholders

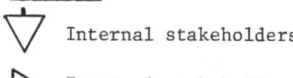 External stakeholders

◇ 3-D Graphs

○ Pictographs and Pictorial Units Graphs

□ Bar Charts

SALMONS:

▽ Internal stakeholders

▷ External stakeholders

RANKING:

1   2   4   5

a Regional Director
b Research Services
c Fisheries Officers
d Transformation Industry
e Council of Ministers

k National Television Networks
l Regional Newspapers
m Fishermen's Unions
n Gulf Region's Bulletin
o Mayors of the Municipalities or Chiefs of Indian Reserves

charts as their first choice and the pictograms for their last choice both for the internal and external stakeholders; and along the hierarchy, the senior advisers chose the 3-D format as their first choice in opposition to the secretaries and the Director General who preferred the pictograms. When we consider the variables sex and language French or English we obtain an opposition between French women and English men, the first (women) supporting histograms and 3-D charts and the last (men) choosing the pictograms.

8. Conclusion

Our simple field experiment shows that political, cultural and perceptual factors may be important in the selection of graphics formats.

Political influences can be observed as people try to inform different stakeholders with different graphics formats in order to present a situation in different ways to different persons or groups. In our experiment, we observed this kind of behaviour.

Cultural influences can be observed as people of the same language, sex, hierarchical level, service or organization tend to make similar choices, more or less independently of the problems and the stakeholders. This also emerges from our data.

And the influence of private perceptions can be observed as people prefer certain sizes of pictogram to others, the scratched lobster to the scratched salmon, and are more sensitive to the red colour instead of the pink or the New York skykine look of the 3-D chart instead of the salmon profile. And everyone has personal preferences.

However, we did observe certain regularities between graphics formats, types of problems and stakeholders. We suggest that the political aspect of format choice may be very important, and should be investigated further especially in the context of unstructured decision processes.

FIGURE 2:

Pictorial unit graph

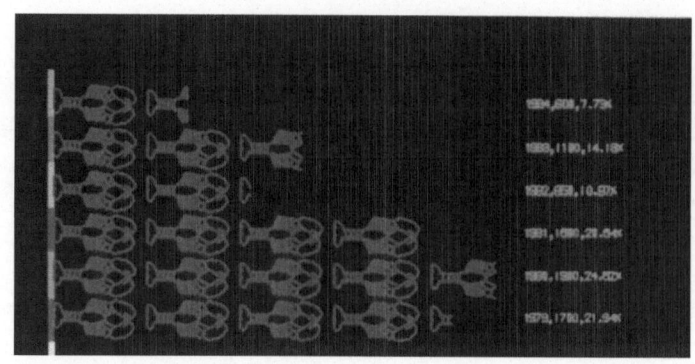

FIGURE 3:

Pictograph

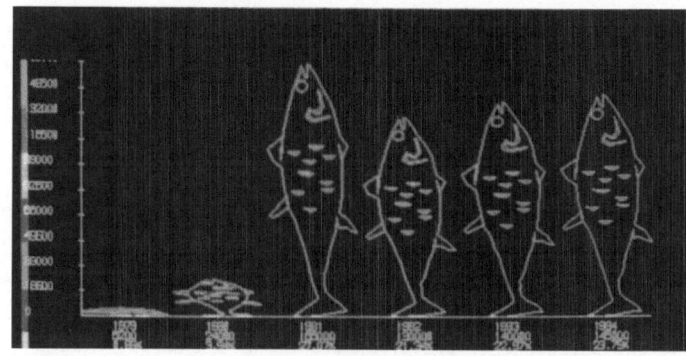

FIGURE 4:

Three-dimensional bar chart

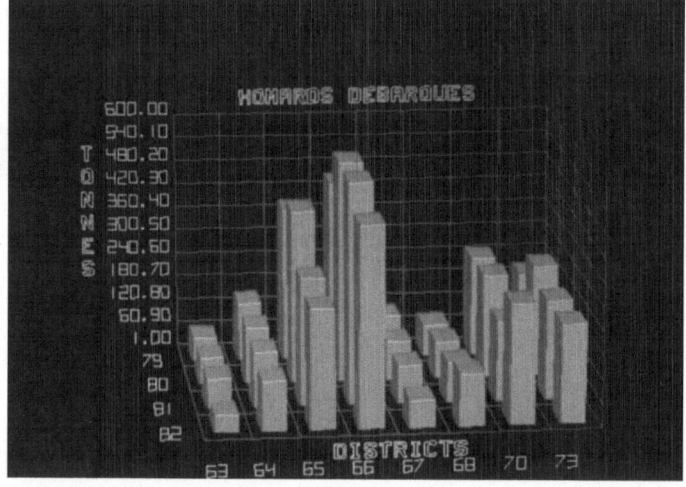

REFERENCES

(1) MINTZBERG, H., Power In and Around Organizations, Prentice-Hall, Englewood Cliffs (N.J.) 1983.

(2) OLSON, M.H., "New Information Technology and Organizational Culture", in MIS Quaterly, Special Issue 1982, pp. 71-92.

(3) MARKUS, M.L., "Power, Politics and MIS Implementation", in Communications of the ACM, June 1983, Vol.1

(4) DeSANCTIS, G., "Computer Graphics as Decision Aids: Directions for Research", in Decision Sciences, vol. 15, 1984, pp. 463-387.

(5) THALMANN, D., "An Interactive Data Visualization System", Software - Practice and Experience, Vol. 14, no.3, 1984, pp.277-290.

(6) MAGNENAT-THALMANN, N.; TAHLMANN, D.; LAROUCHE, A. and LORRAIN, L., "Grafedit: An Interactive General-Purpose Graphics Editor", Computers and Graphics, Pergamon Press, Vol.6, no.1, 1982, pp.41 à 46.

(7) FREEMAN, R.H., Strategic Management, A Stakeholder Approach, Pitman, Toronto, 1984, 276 p.

(8) Quoted by BELL, D., The social Framework of the Information Society, in Dertouzos, M.L. and Moses, J. (eds) The Computer Age: a Twenty-Year View, MIT Press, Cambridge (Mass.), fourth printing, 1983, 491 pp., p.176.

(9) TYDEMAN, J. et al., Teletex and Videotex in the United States, McGraw-Hill, New York, 1982, 314 p.

(10) PROBERT, D., "Business Graphics for Strategic Planning", in Computer Graphics, 1983, pp.57-62.

(11) MINTZBERG, H., RAISINGHANI, D., THEORET, A., The structure of "unstructured" decision processes, Administrative Science Quarterly, Vol. 21, (June 1976) pp 246-275.

(12) BERTIN, J., Graphics and Graphic Information Processing, Walter de Gruyher and Co., (1981) 273 p.

(13) CHERNOFF, H. "The Use of Faces to Represent Points in N-Dimensional Space Graphically". Technical report no.71 Department of Statistics, Stanford University, December 1971.

(14) MORIARITY, S., "Communicating Financial Information Through Multidimensional Graphics" Journal of Accounting Research, Vol. 17, no.1, (printemps 1979) pp. 205-224.

(15) JARETT, IL., Computer Graphics and Reporting Financial Data, John Wiley & Sons, New York, 1983, 359 p.

(16) MAGNENAT-THALMANN, N., THALMANN, D. and LAROUCHE, A., "An Interactive and User-Oriented Three-Dimensional Graphics Editor", Graphics Interface '83, Edmonton, 1983, pp. 39-46.

(17) MAGNENAT-THALMANN, N. and THALMANN, D., "The Use of High-Level Graphical Types in the MIRA Animation System", IEEE Computer Graphics and Applications, vol. 3, no 9, 1983, pp. 9-16.

An Integrated System for Printing and Publishing Applications

S. Cavaliere, M. Fantini and A. Turtur

IBM Italy, Rome Scientific Centre, Via Giorgione 129, 00147 Rome, Italy

ABSTRACT

This paper describes the architecture of a system, providing an integrated approach to the printing process, starting from the input of the basic components (images, texts, and graphics) up to the definition and modification of page layout and finally to driving high resolution output devices. The system allows an interactive management of the documents to be printed as well as of their elementary components, i.e. the pages, and at a lower level, the boxes, containing texts, images and graphics. The main peculiarities of the system architecture are interactivity, modularity and non-procedurality discussed in more details and some of its functions are illustrated by means of some system outputs.

INTRODUCTION

The publishing process, from page layout definition to printing plate production, is usually broken into a number of activities unevenly automated and very seldom completely integrated.
Composition of texts, for instance, is nowadays almost fully automated, while image manipulation is carried out independently and is often based on manual operations.
The definition and composition of a page is managed by the editor, who, on the basis on his own experience, gives the draftsman the page requirements needed to prepare the fool proof of the page to be printed.
Several trials are usually needed and as many proof-readings, before the press-proof is ready. The whole process is therefore long and expensive.

The present paper describes a system, a prototype of which is being developed by the authors at IBM Rome Scientific Centre, aiming at achieving an extensive automation and a complete integration of the above process as far as allowed by available hardware and software technology.
In the next section, a short overview of the system functions is presented in order to give the reader an idea of the provided features. The description of the system architecture follows with a presentation of the hardware and software tools on which the system is based. The image editor is there described in much more details by means of some examples illustrating the available functions. Than the logical data scheme is synthetically reported in order to show how a document and its elements are stored into the database; finally some examples reporting some pages obtained by using the available system functions conclude the paper.

THE SYSTEM FUNCTIONS: AN OVERVIEW

The system manages a set of documents, which are collections of numbered pages identified by name and characterised by date and comment.
A page is a rectangle of an arbitrary size, where one or more boxes are located. Boxes are characterised by a type specifying the nature of their content, i.e. images, graphics, or texts.

Documents, pages and boxes are defined and manipulated by means of a number of editors operating in independent functional states. These editors have been described in detail (Cavaliere et alt, 1984). The present paper will present a longer discussion of the image editor in a later section.

The user can interactively define an initial page layout, put in some contents and progressively modify them until he gets the desired result.

Besides operating on the page components, the system creates, manages and updates an integrated database by means of a Data Base Management System (DBMS) (Date, 1977).
The database contains not only image,text and graphics descriptions, but also information concerning the operations performed on them during the several phases of manipulation. This avoids storing intermediate products as digital images, thus allowing a considerable reduction of the required memory.

When a page has reached a satisfactory aspect, two more operations must be performed before plate preparation: first, changes applied to low-resolution page components are to be transferred to high resolution ones in order to fit output device characteristics; second, the image files, generally representing bands in additive chromatic decomposition (Red, Green, Blue), must be converted into the band files required for subtractive synthesis (Yellow, Cyan, Magenta) (Pearson, 1975).
These operations do not need the user's intervention but require a large memory and considerable CPU time. Therefore they are achieved off-line by the system which, moreover, issues messages indicating correct completion of the different steps.

SYSTEM ARCHITECTURE

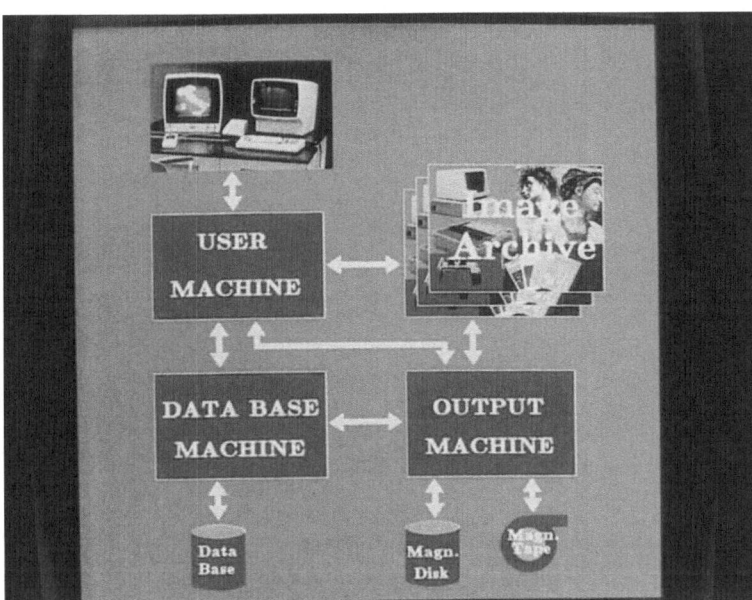

Fig. 1-System Architecture.

Before describing in details the system architecture, we review the concepts underlying the chosen data organisation.
Two kinds of data must be managed: image and text files, on one hand, and the formal description of documents, pages, boxes and descriptions of the operations on the other.
The former is characterised by large size and unstructured form, the latter has small size and structured form.

Therefore image and text files my be stored on several different devices, while the document components description is stored in a database, containing also information about the physical devices on which images and texts are stored.

When the user requires to load an image into a box, the system must retrieve from the database the information related both to the box and to the physical allocation of the image. This information is then supplied to a module able to load the image and put it into a box.

On the basis of the above concepts the system architecture (Fig. 1) is built on three functional environments, which, in our case, are three virtual machines (IBM VM/370, 1980):
the USER MACHINE, interacting with the user through the IBM 7350 Image Processing System, the DATA BASE MACHINE, and the OUTPUT MACHINE.

The user Machine

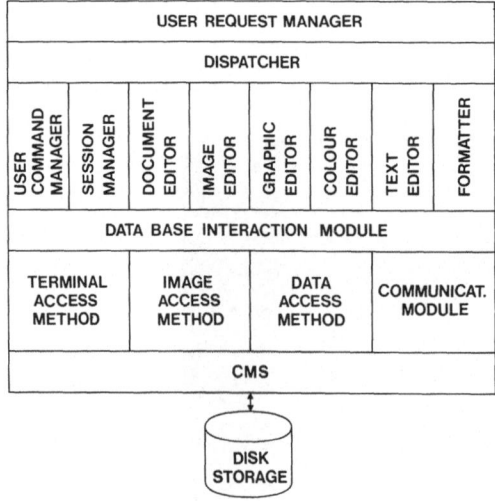

Fig. 2-User Machine.

The USER MACHINE (fig. 2) includes the following modules and subsystems.

MODULES:

User Request Manager
    This module provides the full screen management of the alphanumeric display of the work-station IBM 7350 and performs an initial analysis of user information correctness; if some errors are detected, a user intervention is required; when correctness has been checked this module gives the control to the dispatcher.

Dispatcher
    Gives the control to the proper subsystem, according to the user's request.

SUBSYSTEMS:

Document Editor
: Includes functions for document, page and box management. It simulates on the IBM 7350 color monitor the "cut and paste" operations.
By using its commands the user can, in fact, create or delete boxes, move them on the page, align them, cut and/or expand them, copy them in other positions, etc.

Image Editor
: Allows to load images into a box and provides also many important functions such as image windowing, rectangular and generalised cropping, retouching, filtering. Moreover it provides also a photomontage feature among several images. A more detailed description of the image editor functions is reported later on.

Text Editor
: Allows the user to edit the text and place it into a box. Moreover changes can be made on selected substrings, in terms of font, size, colour, angle of rotation etc.

Graphic Editor
: Provides a set of functions to draw simple shapes, give them a name for later usage and store them into the database.

Colour Editor
: Allows to give a name to a colour chosen out of a palette, so that the colour can be referred to simply by name, whenever a colour attribute is required, e.g. for text, box and page background.

User Commands Manager
: Invokes the module related to the command added by the user and manages also a simple interaction between the system and the user.

Formatter
: Sends commands with proper parameters to the OUTPUT MACHINE to enqueue an output request for a given page.

Database Interaction Module
: All the above listed subsystems interact with the DATA BASE INTERACTION MODULE which, on one hand, formulates data base transactions to satisfy the user's requests and, on the other one, processes the results of the previous transactions.

Finally at a lower level the access methods are located to drive the devices used by the system. The access methods include HBUS/VM (HBUS, 1983) for IBM 7350 image processing work-station, GDDM, for full screen management (GDDM, 1982) and a proper image access method to manage the digital images (Cavaliere et al., 1984).

The database machine

The DATA BASE MACHINE (see Fig. 3) contains at the top level the communication module, which can exchange data with the USER MACHINE. At the second level a monitor is placed able to receive the Database statements from the communication module, submit them to the DBMS module (Astrahan et al., 1976). and finally pass the responses back to the communication module The database transactions are formulated in the SQL language (Chamberlin et al., 1976).

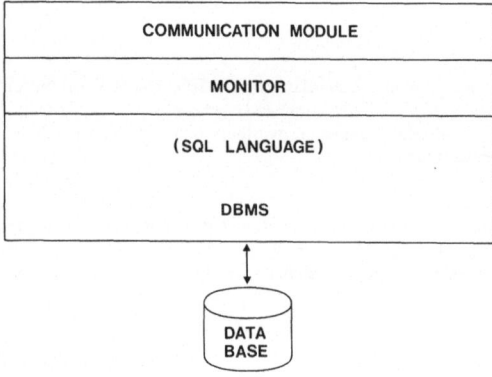

Fig. 3-Database Machine.

The output machine

The OUTPUT MACHINE architecture (see Fig. 4) contains, in addition to the communication module, the formatter, interacting with the DATA BASE MACHINE in order to retrieve the formal description of the components of the page to be printed (e.g. images, texts, boxes). On the basis of this information the formatter produces the output files for high resolution output devices, e.g. an output scanner.

A final aspect of the system architecture to be underlined is the possibility of including new storage devices to store large amounts of data (images for instance), by adding new ACCESS MODULES.

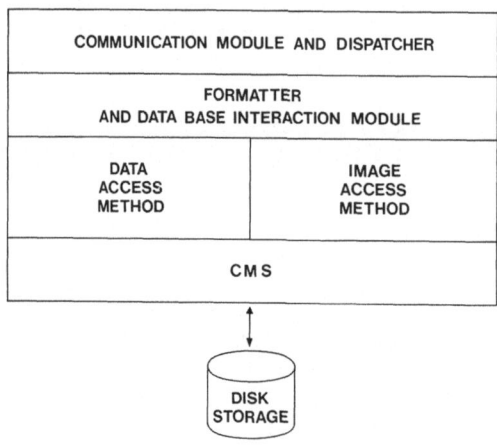

Fig. 4-Output Machine.

The Image Processing System

The IBM 7350 Image Processing System (P. Franchi, 1983; IBM 7350, 1983) is an intelligent work-station that can be attached via channel to a host system such as IBM 370/xxx, IBM 30xx or IBM 43xx.
It is structured in four subsystems:

The controller
    It is able to manage the communication protocol between IBM 7350 and the host computer, and supervises the operations performed by the other subsystems.

The display subsystem
    It consists of a colour monitor, a scroll-zoom logic, a cursor logic, a colour look-up table and a series of display controls. The monitor displays 1024x1024 pixels. The colour look-up table has 4096 15-bit words (5 bits for each primary colour component), so 32768 colours can be displayed, although only 4096 different ones can be active at the same time.

The Image Processing subsystem
    It is composed of up to 8 1-Mbytes band buffers, an image processing unit, an x/y processor, an interpolator and a histogrammer; it can perform locally several image processing operations at a very high speed.

The Graphics subsystem
    It provides the conversion from vector to raster representation, the polygon filling and the character generator features.

IMAGE EDITOR

A prerequisite to any digital image processing is image acquisition, that is achieved by using special devices, such as optical scanners. The acquisition process must be usually carried out at high resolution so that in the printing process a high quality reproduction of the image can be obtained by suitable output devices. This generates two problems: first a large file is produced and must be handled, second the digital image cannot usually be displayed on commercially available monitors since their resolution is considerably lower than that of the output equipment.
In order to solve the above problems, the system manages two copies of the same image: a coarse resolution copy is used for interactive manipulation and display, the fine resolution copy is used only when all the composition process has been completed. This implies that the system must store into the database information on the modifications performed on the images. This information is retrieved and modifications are actually performed on the fine resolution copy only when the final output is prepared.

A brief description of the main functions of the image editor is reported in the following paragraph.

Functions

The image editor functions can be divided in three major classes:

A) functions for loading and positioning;
B) functions for colour editing and image composing;
C) functions for image saving;

CLASS A.

This class includes a set of functions allowing the user to place an image into a box in the way he considers the most satisfactory. The user can select a window in the box where to put the image; moreover he can scroll the

window on the image, rotate the image, magnify/reduce it according to the scale factor he chooses.
Another interesting point is the possibility of loading several levels of images in the same box. The different levels can be interchanged or suppressed and new levels can be added. Finally, images can be moved or copied from one place to another.

Figure 5 shows some results obtained by using functions belonging to class A. In fact the image of a Madonna by Beato Angelico has been rectangularly cropped at different scale factors. The same operation has been done with the Primavera by Botticelli and San Girolamo by Leonardo da Vinci. Different loading points have been checked.

Fig. 5-Class A functions.

CLASS B.

The system provides several functions operating on the image colour components: they modify the contrast and brightness of images and balance the colour chromaticity of different images thus performing the some tasks of the usual photographic filtering.

Other functions allow the user to make image compositions by using a generalised cropping function. This can be obtained by using two types of contour following mechanism: the first one is semi-automatic, the second one is manual. On a chosen detail, the user can however apply all colour editing functions. Other functions, belonging to this class, give the user the possibility to perform an electronic make-up to modify some details by simulating a painting process. Special effects can be achieved by means of mirroring and shading functions.

Figure 6 shows results obtained by using the above functions; texts, images and graphics have been used. The images have been loaded and scaled, then corrected and balanced chromatically. After cropping, two of them, representing fishes, have been composed with graphics drawn by means of graphic features such as the one generating the background.

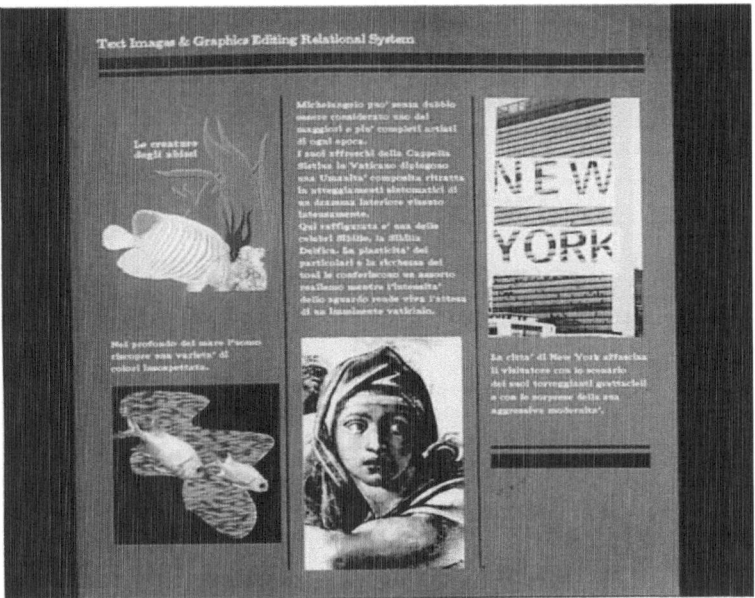

Fig. 6-Class B functions plus graphics and texts.

CLASS C.

The system is equipped with two different functions to save images onto disks. The first one is used to save intermediate versions during an interactive session. It operates on the coarse resolution image and saves a compressed form of it (16 levels per band). The second one operates on the high resolution copy and produces the final version (256 levels per band), that can be used to prepare the printing proofs of the page and, when no further modification is required, the printing plate.

DATABASE LOGICAL SCHEME

This paragraph reports a short description of the logical scheme adopted in the design of the database.
All the entities managed by the system and their functional dependencies are organised logically according to the extended relational model (Codd, 1970; Codd, 1979), representing the data scheme in terms of tables or relations.
Figure shows a simplified representation of the above logical scheme: the boxes represent the relations and the lines represent the links among relations.

The "document" is the entity at highest hierarchical level: it is described in the table DOCUMENT. This relation reports for every document its unique identifier, its name, and other information describing the document itself.

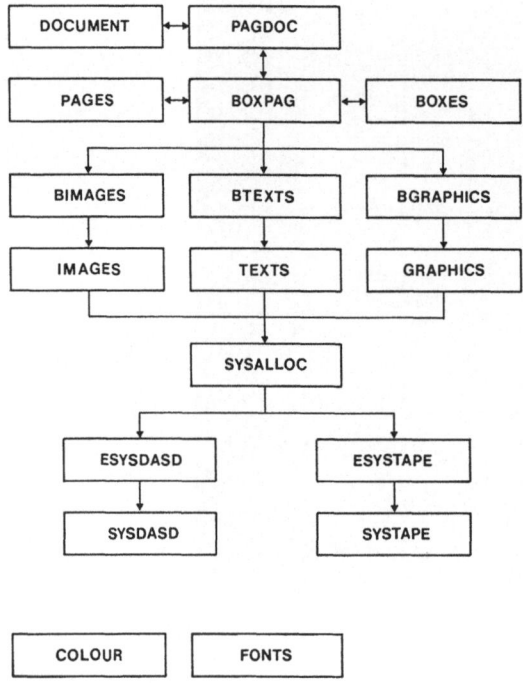

Fig. 7-Database logical scheme.

At an intermediate hierarchical level there are the "pages", listed in the table PAGES, where the page identifier, the page format and other page attributes are reported.
The relationship between pages and documents is represented in the table PAGDOC reporting for each page identifier the corresponding identifier of the document to which the page belongs. Similarly, since a page is defined as a set of boxes with different types, the table BOXES reports the identifier, the type, and all the information describing the box attributes, such as box background, colour identifier, frame thickness, frame colour identifier, etc. The table called BOXPAG specifies the relationship between boxes and pages by reporting for every box identifier the identifier of the page to which it belongs as well as its position in the page.
Moreover since the boxes, as before mentioned, are characterised by their contents (image, text or graphics), three more relations are needed to report the information about such contents. This is accomplished by the tables BIMAGES, BTEXTS and BGRAPHICS reporting respectively: the description of the properties of "image type" box (image identifier, description of image window, description of operations performed on that window, such as retouching, cropping, photo-montage, etc), of "text type" box (text identifier, font identifier, size, text, colour identifier, etc.), and of "graphic type" box (graphics identifier and other information).
The navigation among the BOXES table and the above three tables is managed by using an UGI (Unconditional General Inclusion) type table (Codd, 1979).
Whenever a transaction on a box is to be executed, the system retrieves from the BOXES table the box type, and from the UGI table the relation name, according to the box type, that will be accessed successively.

Finally the contents of the boxes (texts, images and graphics) are described in the proper tables called TEXTS, IMAGES and GRAPHICS respectively, reporting their identifier, name, creation date, comments etc.

UGI

SUB	SUP	PER
BTEXTS	BOXES	"TEXTS"
BIMAGES	BOXES	"IMAGES"
BGRAPHICS	BOXES	"GRAPHICS"
ESYSDASD	SYSALLOC	"DASD"
ESYSTAPE	SYSALLOC	"TAPE"

Information about the physical allocation of the entities is supplied by the relation "SYSALLOC", which reports the identifier of the physical device on which the entity has been stored for each entity identifier known by the system.

Storage devices has been divided into several classes according to the device type. Therefore, on the basis of the information retrieved from the table SYSALLOC, the system finds in the tables ESYSDASD (if the object to be retrieved is on disk) or ESYSTAPE (if it is on tape) the description of the related files, while information on the physical device is reported by the tables SYSDASD and SYSTAPE, respectively. Using another storage device would require the addition of two more tables, one describing the files and the other describing the physical device.

The tables COLOUR and FONTS are dedicated to the description of colour and font entities, respectively.

This kind of data scheme implies more simple formalisation of the functions performed by the system with respect to others types of schemes. In fact all functions can be expressed in terms of data base transactions. For instance the page creation implies the addition of a new tuples to PAGES and PAGDOC tables. The modification of the page background colour implies the update of the related tuple in the PAGES table.

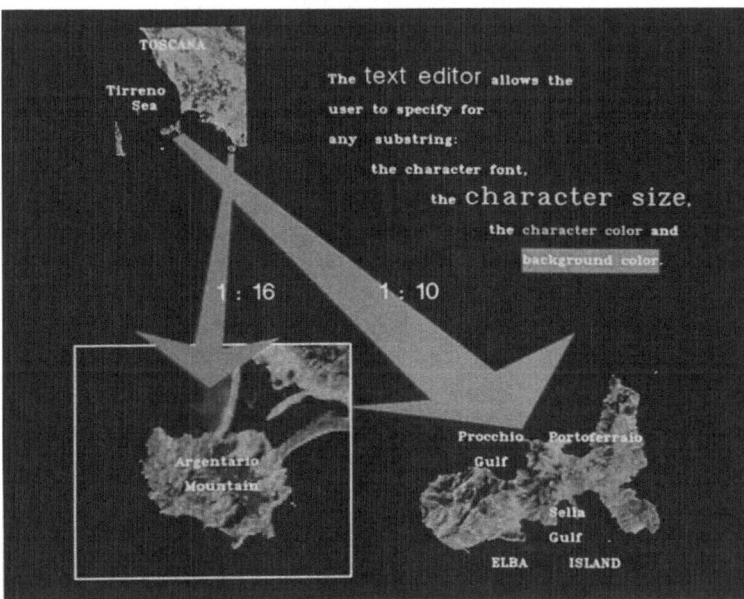

fig. 8-Example 1'.

EXAMPLES

Figure 8 reports in the left upper corner an image of Toscana taken by Landsat 3. The image is composed of some bands related to different frequency ranges. Three of them have been assumed as RGB bands and displayed. Two details have been enlarged. The scale factors are written on the arrows. Some lines of text have been placed and the attributes of selected strings have been modified.

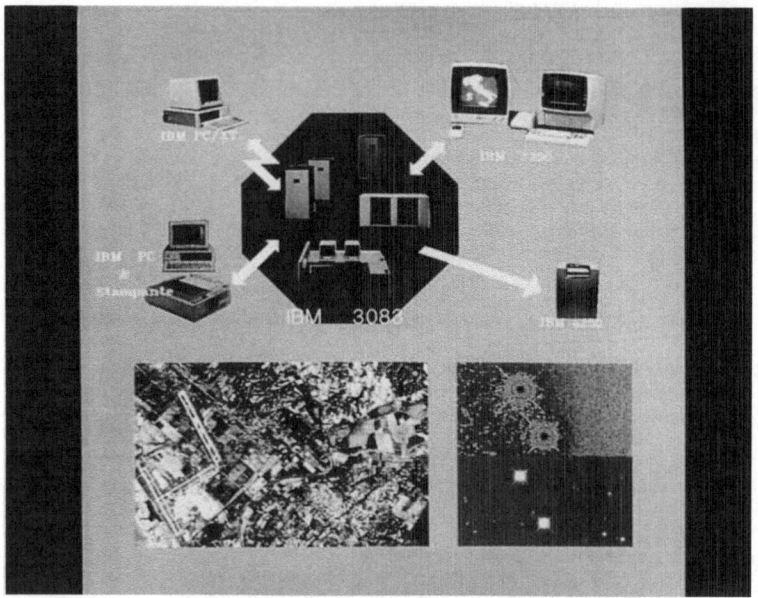

Fig. 9-Example 2'.

Figure 9 contains, on the upper side, a photomontage realized with details cropped out from images of IBM devices. The lower side shows, on the left, a Landast-4 image of the Leonardo da Vinci international airport; on the right, a detail taken from an astronomical plate and displayed in two different ways: direct and false colour.

All the figures of this paper have been prepared by using the system described.

CONCLUSIONS

An interactive system able to automate and integrate the editorial process has been considered. The architecture of the system, characterised by modularity and flexibility, has been described; moreover it has been underlined how the different modules are related to the different tasks of the editorial process.
The logical data scheme, followed to organise the information managed by the system has been reviewed.
The prototype is in the development phase; however the most important functions concerning the document editor, the text editor, and the image editor are available as shown by the reported examples.

REFERENCES

Astrahan M. M. et alter (1976) SYSTEM-R: a Relational Approach to Data Base Management. ACM Trans. on Database Systems, vol.1, n.2

Cavaliere S., Fantini M., Turtur A. (1984) Un sistema per la gestione integrata di testi ed immagini. Proceedings of Computer graphics, CAD, elaborazione di immagini: sistemi ed applicazioni (AICOGRAPHICS84), pp. 217-229, Milan Italy

Cavaliere S, Fantini M., Turtur A. (1984) Text, images and graphics management system for editorial environment. Proceedings of CAMP 84, pp. 493-496, Berlin Germany

Cavaliere S., Fantini M., Turtur A. (1984) An Image access method for IBM 7350. IBM Technical Report, Rome Scientific Centre G513-4053

Chamberlin D. D. (1976) SEQUEL 2: a Unified Approach to Data Definition, Manipulation and Control. IBM J. Res. Develop., vol.20, n.6

Codd E. F. (1970) A Relational Model of Data for Large Shared Data Banks. Comm. ACM, vol.13, n.6

Codd E. F. (1979) Extending the Database Relational Model to Capture More Meaning. ACM Transaction on Data Base System, Vol. 4, N. 4

Franchi P. et alter (1983) Design Issues and Architecture of Hacienda, an Experimental Image Processing System. IBM Journal of research and development, Vol. 27, N. 2

Date C. J. (1977) An Introduction to Database Systems. Addison-Wesley Publishing Company

Pearson D. E. (1975) Transmission and Display of Pictorial Information. Pentech press, London

IBM 7350 Image Processing System System Overview. IBM GA19-5343, available through IBM branch offices, 1983.

IBM Virtual Machine/System Product: Introduction. IBM GC19-6200, available through IBM branch offices, 1980.

Graphical Data Display Manager (GDDM): General Information. IBM SC33-0100, available through IBM branch offices, 1982.

IBM 7350 Host Basic User Subroutines Programming RPQs: Programmer's Guide. IBM SH19-6298, available through IBM branch offices, 1983.

Project Management Using Graphics

Fábio Pettinati
Tecninger Sistemas Ltda, Av. Rouxinol, 200 Cj. 71, 04516, São Paulo, Brasil

ABSTRACT

This paper addresses the problem of lack of visualization most managers face when using computer-based project control systems: although highly relevant information is generated, usually no graphical output is produced. This paper presents a system called UniPert that automatically produces high quality drawings showing all activities present in a project and the relationship among them. A detailed description of UniPert's major components and algorithms is presented as well as examples of its actual use. The main contribution of this paper is the integration of many different techniques and concepts that led to the development of the UniPert system.

INTRODUCTION

The last twenty years have seen a tremendous growth in the use of computer-based project control systems. The increased availability of such systems is mainly due to the following facts:

- The expanding familiarity of project management personnel with this tool;

- The pressure to complete work quickly before inflation takes a large share of the budget;

- Management hope that an investment in computerized project tracking will shorten project time and decrease costs.

A project control system consists of computer programs that analyze the activities present in a project, as well as the topological relationship among them. Inside the computer, a project is represented as a network composed of activities that have to be completed and a set of relationships that have to be observed.

The two most common types of network notations are:

- ACTIVITY ON NODE or PRECEDENCE NOTATION

    In this notation, each activity is considered to be a node in the network and relationships between two activities are called precedences and represented as edges connecting the nodes associated to the activities. Different types of precedences are allowed and, for each type, a minimum time span (referred to as a lag) must separate the beginning or the completion of both activities (referred to as predecessor and successor).

- ACTIVITY ON ARROW or ARROW DIAGRAM

    In this notation, each activity is designated in the network by an edge (arrow) that starts at a predecessor node and ends at a successor node; both nodes are called events and have time values associated with them.

Project control systems using any of the above notations will calculate start and finish dates for all activities, indicate how long each activity can be delayed (referred to as float) without delaying the whole project and highlight the set of activities with critical float values.

In spite of the power and extended usage of project control systems, even today project management is sometimes considered to be an art which involves skills for dealing with a great number of concurrent and resource sharing activities. This is due to the fact that those involved in this sort of activity often rely on their own previous experience and intuition rather than on objective conclusions.

Part of the problem is caused by the project control systems available in the market today. In spite of being widely used, these systems usually provide users with just lengthy user-specified printed reports. To overcome this lack of visualization and also to enhance comprehension, several companies started offering systems that provided users with graphical output more suited to their needs. Another solution that is also available in the market today acts as a post-processor to existent project control systems and generates the desired drawings.

Both approaches were not readily available in Brazil in 1982, a time when several companies started looking for this kind of graphical output. Due to the restrictions posed by the Brazilian government for companies to import software, it was felt that a locally developed system acting as a post-processor to available project control systems should be the solution. That was the start of the research that led to the development of the UniPert system.

THE UNIPERT SYSTEM

The UniPert system comprises a control program that accepts user input parameters, reads in project data and produces the desired drawings. UniPert can be interfaced to project control systems using the precedence notation for networks and will produce both precedence diagrams with activities sorted in topological or chronological order and Gannt barcharts.

UniPert was developed with the following objectives in mind:

- Drawings produced by the system should have the same quality as those produced by draftsmen;
- System portability and graphics device independence should be enforced;
- The system should expend as little computer resources as possible;
- The system should be user oriented, requiring neither extensive training nor excessive data input.

The UniPert system can be divided into five major subsystems, each one comprising several routines:

- CONTROL PROGRAM

    This subsystem coordinates the proper operation of UniPert's remaining subsystems while ensuring correct data flow.

- DATA ACQUISITION

    This subsystem is responsible for interfacing UniPert to various project control systems such as PROJACS, CIPREC or MAPPS. This interface consists of a file produced by the project control system containing all activities and precedence information present in the network used for project analysis.

- COMMAND INTERPRETER

    This subsystem is responsible for reading and parsing all free-form commands provided by users. These commands are keyword oriented, can be abbreviated or written in full and their syntax is extremely flexible. Parsing is accomplished by a non-recursive top-down command syntax analysis, error reporting and by calling action routines associated with the commands.

- GRAPHICAL OUTPUT

    This subsystem is responsible for drawing all charts produced by UniPert and it consists of a suite of routines patterned after the GKS standard (strict adherence to GKS is not enforced, but all important concepts and functions are present). Although the list of available device drivers includes both raster terminals and pen plotters, only the latter are used by UniPert; the reason is that users usually take copies of the drawings for distribution and further analysis.

- ALGORITHMS AND DATA STRUCTURES

    The algorithms and data structures employed play a vital role in UniPert: both are responsible for enhancing system overall performance. From holding project data to positioning activities and routing precedences accross the network, these are only a few examples of algorithm and data structure usage in UniPert.

Almost all UniPert's routines were coded in BLOKFOR, a structured language based upon FORTRAN-77; the only exceptions to this rule are some low level routines for address manipulation that in some machines (e.g. IBM) have to be coded in assembly language.

The BLOKFOR language can itself be translated into machine code by a two-pass procedure: the first pass generates an intermediate program by translating each BLOKFOR statement into equivalent FORTRAN-77 statement(s) and the second pass inputs this intermediate program to the FORTRAN-77 compiler.

UniPert can be run on computers providing virtual memory allocation that can be directly controlled by an application program. At present there are two UniPert releases running on IBM computers under OS/VS1, MVS and CMS and on VAX computers under VMS. Although there are some minor differences between both versions, source code management is easily handled by the BLOKFOR compiler itself.

The following sections will provide readers with aditional information about the preceding subsystems.

THE DATA ACQUISITION SUBSYSTEM

UniPert can be interfaced to various project control systems by means of a file containing selected activities and precedences comprising a network.

Although the format of this interface file may change according to the system in use, its structure must remain the same: activities have to be sorted in lexicographic order and after each activity there must be a list (possibly empty) of its precedences. Besides activity and precedence data, an interface file contains several header records that allow UniPert to identify the incoming network, its work breakdown structure or run date; this general information is used afterwards to properly place legends in the charts to be drawn.

The format of the interface file to be used by UniPert can be found in a master file which describes the attributes associated with activities and precedences. For activities, the minimum set of attributes includes identification code, float and a start date; for precedences, the minimum set includes preceding activity code, precedence type and lag. In addition to a flexible interface file format, users may specify which information will be displayed in the charts produced by UniPert; this option allows users to effectively taylor UniPert's output to suit their needs.

Since interface files may contain several networks, each one with an unknown number of activities and precedences, data acquisition is performed by a two-pass procedure repeated for each network present: the first pass writes the next network in the interface file into an intermediate file and allocates enough virtual memory to hold all activities and precedences; the second pass completes the process by reading the intermediate file and storing activities and precedences into the virtual memory data structures.

THE COMMAND INTERPRETER

The command interpreter used by UniPert can be classified as a 'one-symbol-lookahead without backtracking top-down parser' [WIRT76], [WIRT77]. The parser is similar to a recursive-descent parser except that recursion is removed by using an internal stack. Grammars accepted by the command interpreter are of class LL(1) [LEWI76] and they are represented inside the parser as a syntax graph. This syntax graph consists of nodes that correspond to the terminal and non-terminal symbols present in the grammar to be parsed.

Command parsing is performed by traversing the syntax graph in response to the tokens recognized by a scanner. The scanner recognizes identifiers, keywords, literals, numbers (both integer and real), symbols, indirect command files [DEDO80] and passes these tokens to the parser that will compare them to the syntax graph node contents. Graph traverse is aided by a stack which holds pointers to the nodes that have yet to be recognized. A pointer to the successor of a node is pushed-down into the stack whenever this node corresponds to a non-terminal symbol. Upon a non-terminal symbol identification, a pointer is popped-up from the stack and the analysis proceeds with the pointed node.

Every node in the syntax graph has attached to it the number of a 'semantic' routine that corresponds to the action one has to take upon node recognition; this scheme provides great flexibility since it allows for a complete separation of syntax and semantics [SETZ79].

GRAPHICAL OUTPUT PRODUCED BY UNIPERT

UniPert produces two types of graphical output: precedence diagrams with activities sorted in topological (Fig. 1) or chronological order. The main difference between both precedence diagrams is how the activities are placed: in the topological order, activities are sorted so that each activity is placed to the right of all its preceding activities; in the chronological order, activities are sorted so that all activities to the left have lower start date values than those to the right.

When drawing precedence diagrams, activity placement plays a trully important role: it determines how aesthetic the final chart will be and how long it will take to route precedences through the set of rows and columns activities had been placed into (activities are placed as boxes into the rows and columns of a matrix). The distance between rows is constant, allowing up to six horizontal precedence segments to be routed through. The distance between columns, on the contrary, is not fixed and varies according to the number of activities placed into them; this scheme garantees that no two vertical precedence segments will overlap each other.

Associated with every activity, there are two points called leading (to the left) and trailing (to the right) connectors. These points collect all precedences so that arrivals are always made at the left side and departures are always made from the right side. To make clear which type of precedence is connecting two activities, UniPert draws along the precedence's horizontal segment its type and lag value. UniPert always draws this information between activity columns in a position where no precedence will ever cross it. As it was stated before, users can specify which information will be posted inside activity boxes. Up to fifty user-specified formats can be accomodated and UniPert provides a default format that includes: activity code and description, early start and finish dates, duration, float and a milestone flag. Activities with critical float values are properly highlighted so as to reflect their importance. Highlighting is accomplished by drawing critical activities and precedences with a different linewidth.

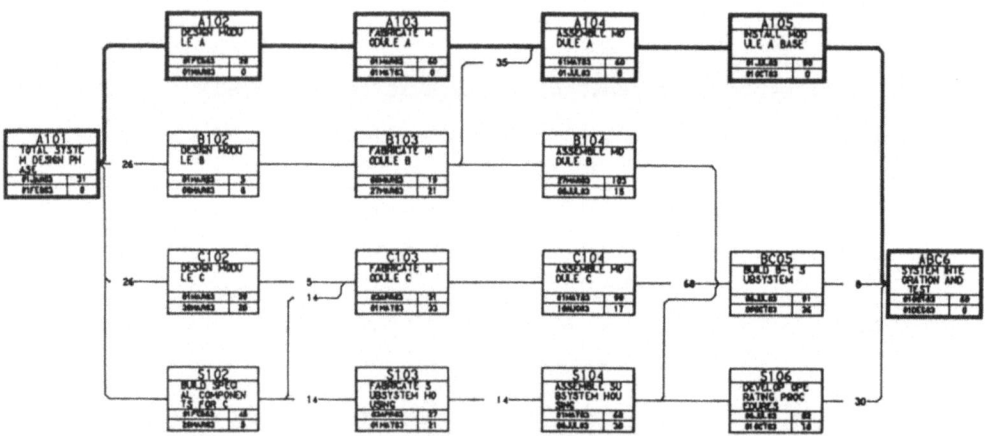

Fig. 1 - Precedence Diagram (topological order)

ALGORITHMS AND DATA STRUCTURES

The main data structures used by UniPert comprise a table for storing activities, a queue for sorting activities in topological order and several linked lists for storing precedences and precedence routing; all these data structures are considered to be dynamic since they only exist in virtual memory at run time. As it was seen before, activities are placed as boxes into the rows and columns of a matrix. Column placing is accomplished by first sorting activities in topological or chronological order and assigning activities to the columns in a left-to-right process. Row assignment is accomplished by distributing activities so that for each activity the sum of the vertical distances to all preceding activities is minimized.

Precedences are routed through channels placed like a grid over the drawing. To easy the routing process, activity boxes with leading and trailing connectors are transformed into channel obstacles so that the router's only task is to find pathes that avoid obstacles and join activity connectors. Path finding is accomplished by extending vertical lines through both connectors, by searching for an horizontal segment that goes from one line to the other without hitting any channel obstacles. The algorithm used for precedence routing is very efficient and overall performance is very high: a network consisting of 77 activities, 110 precedences took 23s of CPU time to be completed in an IBM 4341; running time is proportional to both the number of activities and precedences.

CONCLUDING REMARKS

UniPert has been used for the last two years by several companies as an aid to solve their project management problems. Among these companies, one can find a major civil construction company that used UniPert to manage the building of an international airport in Brazil, and an engineering company that used UniPert to manage the construction of a chemical processing plant. Looking at the software modules that comprise UniPert, one can see the fusion of several computer science techniques that led to the production of a system that is not only modular in nature but also easy to use, understand and modify.

BIBLIOGRAPHY

[DEDO80]   Dedourek JM, Gujar UG (1980) Scanner Design.
           Software-Practice and Experience, Vol. 10, pp 959-972

[LEWI76]   Lewis II PM et al (1976) Compiler Design Theory.
           Addison-Wesley Publishing Co.

[SETZ79]   Setzer VW (1979) Non-recursive Top-down Syntax Analysis.
           Software-Practice and Experience, Vol. 9, pp 237-245

[WIRT76]   Wirth N (1976) Algorithms + Data Structures = Programs
           Prentice-Hall

[WIRT77]   Wirth N (1977) Compilerbau (in german)
           B.G. Teubner (ed)

Chapter 9
Geographic Information and Databases

How Map Designers can Represent their Ideas in Thematic Maps
Effective User Interfaces for Thematic Map Design

T. Yamahira[1], Y. Kasahara[1] and T. Tsurutani[2]

[1] C&C Systems Research Laboratories, NEC Corporation, Kawasaki, 213 Japan
[2] Production Engineering Laboratory, NEC Corporation, Kawasaki, 210 Japan

ABSTRACT

Problem analysis in designing thematic maps and user interfaces which assist map designers in incorporating their ideas into maps are presented.

Problems in designing choropleth maps are analyzed from the map designers point of view. A graphical user interface, called "Histogram Interface" is implemented as a countermeasure for problems in designing choropleth maps. The user interface can assist the map designers in representing their ideas and achieving the desired resulting maps through the designing process. The user interface operations, which correspond to the map designer's ideas, are explained. The user interface effectiveness is confirmed by resulting map examples and the corresponding graphical patterns of the interface.

A concept is proposed concerning the importance in any computer graphics field, which the designers should consider in designing how to incorporate their ideas into pictures.

KEYWORDS: thematic map, user interface, computer mapping, human factor

INTRODUCTION

Computer mapping systems (e.g., Dutton, 1983; Tsurutani, et al., 1980) are effectively used, especially in the regional planning field. Planners who are concerned in regional planning in local governments often use thematic maps in order to explain some ideas. For example, population density maps, housing maps and geological features maps are often used for explaining the regional planning. Planners may also use the thematic maps when they intend to emphasize their ideas to map viewers, such as mayors, members of a regional planning committee and citizens. The important effect of using thematic maps is that the maps can effectively convey the planners' intentions to map viewers.

However, there are cases wherein the thematic maps do not always agree with actual circumstances or planner's intention. For example, based on experience in designing choropleth maps, which showed a relative comparison of earthquake danger, there was a case where two neighboring areas, which were considered as being identically in danger under normal circumstances, were classified into different groups. If planners design thematic maps without considering the representation of their ideas, the resulting maps will not always be appropriate to convey their intentions. An inappropriate map is not able to effectively convey designers' intentions to the map viewers. It can also easily cause misunderstanding.

With the advent of computer mapping, thematic maps are becoming to be used actively. As many people, such as planners in local governments, have been using thematic maps, undesirable problems are increasing. Therefore, problems in designing these kinds of maps must be carefully considered.

In this paper, as a case study on idea representation, the problems and developed Histogram Interface effectiveness for designing choropleth maps are described, including the results obtained from an actual experiment. The concept regarding how computer graphics designers can incorporate their ideas into resulting pictures is also discussed.

PROBLEMS AND ANALYSIS

Choropleth maps are used for regional situation investigation, information presentation activities and market surveys. Figure 1 shows a choropleth map example which shows Tokyo population distribution. It is easily understood that the population increases closer to the outlying areas.

In recent years, as these kinds of maps are designed actively in computer systems, it becomes important to pay attention to the problems in designing choropleth maps. For example, though a planner designed a choropleth map according to his intention, there were cases where the resulting map cannot reflect his ideas. By analyzing this sort of problems, in regard to representation of map designers' ideas and/or intentions, problems are categorized as follows:

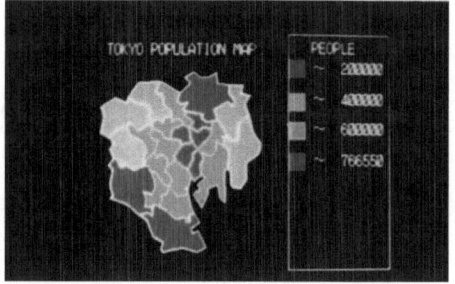

Fig. 1. Choropleth map example.

(1) Excessively detailed or too all-inclusive information.
(2) Disagreement relating to differences in statistical values for specific areas.
(3) Unsuitable color or pattern impression.

First problem and analysis

Excessively detailed or too all-inclusive information, compared with the planner's intention, is often expressed in a choropleth map. Figure 2A shows a choropleth map, which is an example of the excessively detailed information problem. A planner classified the statistical value range into six groups, in order to express the rough population distribution tendencies. However, the impression presented by the map has become too complicated for the viewers to readily understand the rough tendencies. On the contrary, if a designer represents the data too all-inclusively, the map viewers cannot understand much of the information presumed to be supplied by the designed choropleth map.

Classifying data into too many classes makes the information complicated. Also, classifying data into too few classes obscures the information. The number of classes influences the understanding of the regional tendencies portrayed in the entire map.

Second problem and analysis

The statistical distribution represented in painting patterns on the map does not often agree with the planner's intentions. Utilization of such maps is attended by the danger that the information which the planner intends to present therein could be misunderstood. Figure 2B shows a choropleth map which is an example of the second problem. The lowest class statistical value range is too wide for the viewers to readily understand the population differences between areas. If a planner intends to express population differences between areas, the impression presented by the map does not agree with the planner's intention.

Inappropriate classification causes cases wherein elements, which should be classified into the same group, are classified into different groups. It also causes the opposite cases concerning elements which should be classified into different groups. According to the statistical value classifications, which are determined by the lower and upper boundaries, the number of areas belonging to each class gives a map a unique impression. Therefore, the lower and upper boundaries are important factors.

Third problem and analysis

Figure 2C shows a choropleth map example of an unsuitable pattern impression problem. Though a planner intends to express the population distribution, the pattern assigned to each class

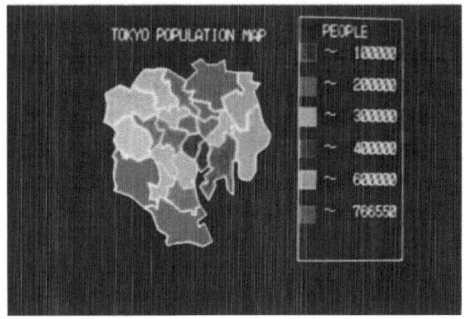

A. First problem choropleth map example. Map includes excessively detailed information.

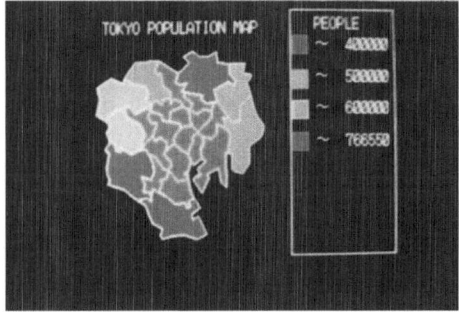

B. Second problem choropleth map example. The difference in statistical value for areas expressed in the map does not agree with planner's intention.

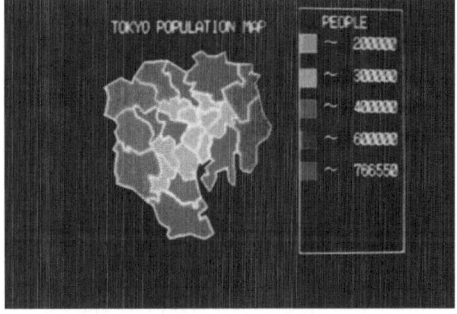

C. Third problem choropleth map example. Pattern assigned to each class causes difficulty in understanding the statistical distribution.

Fig. 2. Choropleth map examples which show the choropleth map designing problems.

causes difficulty in understanding where dense and sparse population areas are. In population maps, in general, an impressive pattern should be assigned to the classes whose statistical value representations are denser than other classes if the planner intends to express the quantitative relations.

Patterns can be ranked according to their own impressions. As severl patterns are assigned according to the statistical data represented in a choropleth map, the mutual relationship between individual patterns must be considered (e.g., Cleveland, et al., 1983; Vertin, 1982). If it is necessary to emphasize a specific feature in a set of statistical data, a stronger impressive pattern should be assigned to the classes to be high-lighted.

Unsuitable pattern assignment causes difficulty in understanding the information represented in the map, even if the other important designing factors were appropriately satisfied.

The following three important factors in designing a choropleth map are extracted from the problems and analysis described above.
   (1) Number of classes.
   (2) Lower and upper boundaries for classes.
   (3) Pattern impression order.

Planners must satisfactorily recognize the factors during the map designing process. If planners designed the maps in consideration of these factors during the designing process, maps could be designed sophisticatedly. However, if planners do not recognize the factors, they may fail to effectively represent their ideas.

HISTOGRAM INTERFACE

Taking these factors into consideration, the Histogram Interface allows the designers to classify the statistical data according to their intentions.

Histogram Interface functions are:
   (1) Indicating the statistical distribution tendencies to planners.
   (2) Allowing designers to control, according to the planners' intention, the statistical distribution in the form of a histogram.
   (3) Providing a tool for pattern assignment.

The first function enables the designers to change the number of classes. By this function, designers can easily recognize the statistical distribution. Map impression can be controlled according to the designers' intentions. For example, designers can operate the number of classes so that the resulting maps can make an impression (such as detailed differences or rough tendencies), which designers intend to represent, on map viewers. The function also provides the maximum, minimum and average value to the designers, so that they can set up the appropriate number of classes. This function reflects the factor for the number of classes.

The second function enables adding and deleting the boundaries and showing the number of elements in each class. The designer can clearly indicate a change in the number of elements in each class by moving the histogram boundaries. Designers can estimate the

Table 1. Intentions and corresponding Histogram Interface operations.

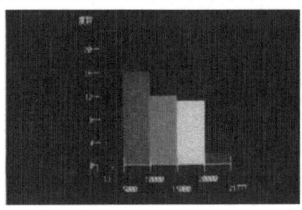 A. Initial histogram.	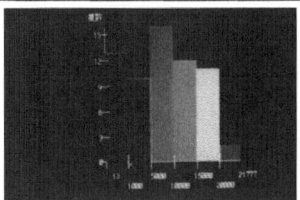 B. Histogram after adding operation. Statistical value 1000 is a new boundary.

Emphasizing statistical differences between areas and characteristics for specific areas.

<u>Adding</u>
Adding means to increase the number of classes. Designers set a boundary by moving a cursor which indicates the statistical value corresponding to a new boundary. B indicates a reworked A.

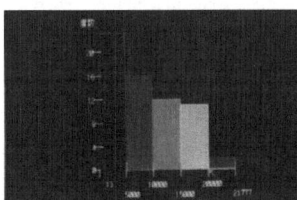 C. Initial histogram.	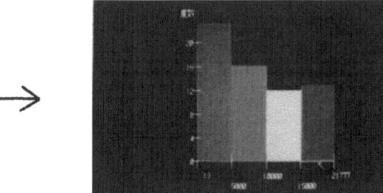 D. Histogram after deleting operation. Statistical value 20000 has been deleted.

Obscuring the statistical differences between areas and emphasizing the rough statistical distribution tendencies.

<u>Deleting</u>
Deleting means to decrease the number of classes. Designers delete a boundary by moving a cursor. D indicates a reworked C.

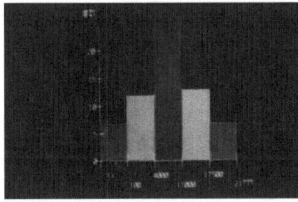 E. Pattern assignment example.	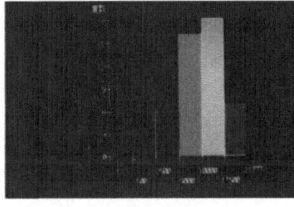 F. Pattern assignment example.

Considering the pattern impression and what is to be expressed.

<u>Pattern assignment</u>
A pattern selected from a palette is assigned to a corresponding class in a histogram, as shown in E and F. In E, patterns are assigned to show statistical value variation from average value. In F, impressive patterns are assigned to higher classes.

resulting maps, with reference to the statistical distribution shown in a histogram pattern. This function reflects the factor for the lower and upper boundaries.

The third function enables the designers to assign a pattern to each class and to confirm the pattern contrast. Designers can assign appropriate patterns, according to their intentions and the statistical contents which they are representing. This function reflects the factor for pattern impression order.

Some intentions and corresponding operations for the Histogram Interface are shown in Table 1. Typical designer intentions, emphasizing and obscuring, are indicated in this table.

EXPERIMENT

Experiment 1

In order to confirm the Histogram Interface effectiveness, the Histogram Interface is applied to Japanese population density map design. The following designers' intentions are assumed in this experiment.
(1) Emphasize dense population areas.
(2) Emphasize sparse population areas.
(3) Emphasize population density differences between areas.

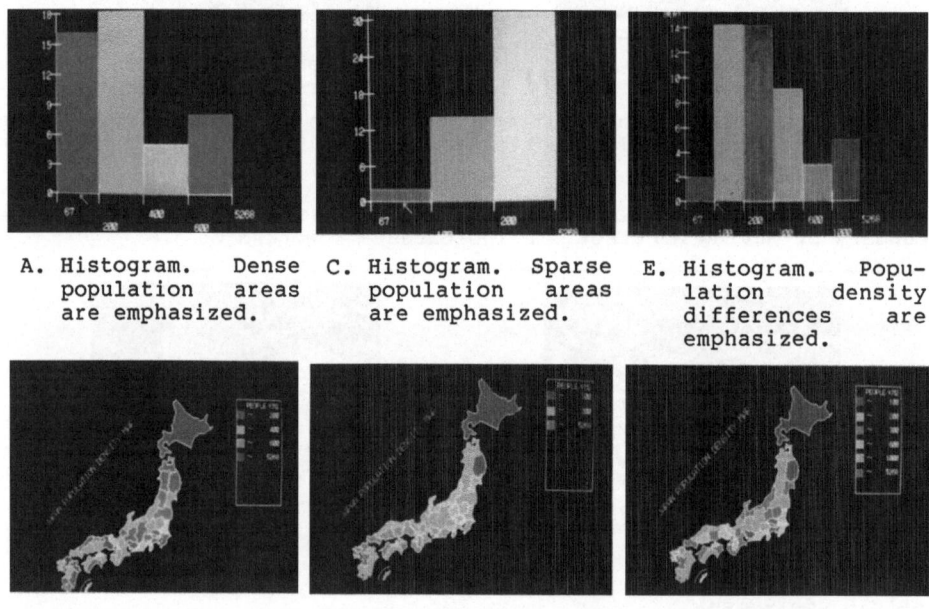

A. Histogram. Dense population areas are emphasized.

C. Histogram. Sparse population areas are emphasized.

E. Histogram. Population density differences are emphasized.

B. Resulting map corresponding to histogram A.

D. Resulting map corresponding to histogram C.

F. Resulting map corresponding to histogram E.

Fig. 3. Histogram patterns and resulting maps corresponding to ideas for experiment 1.

In this experiment, maps were designed in consideration of expressing the statistical distribution tendencies in addition to the designers' above purposes.

Histogram patterns and resulting maps are summarized in Fig. 3. The intention, which involves emphasizing dense population areas, is performed as shown in histogram 3A and resulting map 3B. The higher population areas, such as Tokyo and Osaka, are well recognized from the characteristics in resulting map 3B. In histogram 3C, there are a few areas in the lowest population density class. In corresponding choropleth map 3D, two blue colored areas are emphasized as extremely sparse population areas. In histogram 3E and resulting map 3F, the rough population distribution tendencies presented throughout the map are not easily recognized, but the population density differences between areas can be well recognized.

Experiment 2

In order to show another Histogram Interface use, the Histogram Interface is applied to a practical regional planning problem. It is assumed that Tokyo regional area planner designs a population density choropleth map for regional development to represent the suitable areas to develop. It is also assumed that the planner well recognizes the tendencies that the eastern areas in the Tokyo region have excessively dense populations and the population density becomes sparser closer to the western areas.

The histogram patterns and resulting maps are summarized in Fig. 4. Figures, from 4A to 4D, represent histograms and maps which are obtained by the following general classifying methods A and B.

Table 2. Designing process and histogram patterns for experiment 2.

Design process
Intention: Understand the rough statistical distribution tendencies.
Operation: Divide the statistical data into four groups.
Impression: It is difficult to understand the characteristics of the areas in the lowest class.
Intention: Classify the areas in the lowest class into several classes so that the characteristics in the western area can be expressed.
Operation: Select 100 and 1000 people per square kilometer as the boundaries.
Impression: The areas belong to the fourth class are considered as the object for development. The higher classes classification are too detailed, since the areas in the classes are not objects for development.
Intention: Emphasize that the most crowded areas are spreading over a wide area.
Operation: Delete two higher boundaries and select 10000 people per square kilometer as an appropriate bounday.
A. Initial histogram   B. Intermediate histogram   C. Final histogram

Intentions	Histograms	Resulting maps
Set up the boundaries so that the range for each class would be identical.	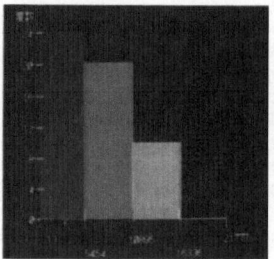 A. Histogram. Individual statistical value ranges are identical.	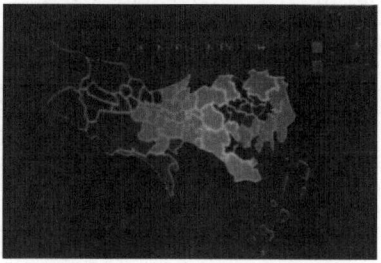 B. Resulting map corresponding to histogram A.
Set up the boundaries so that the number of elements in each class would be identical.	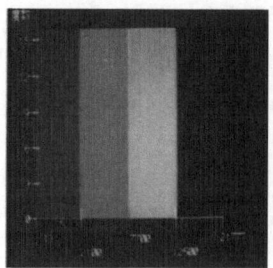 C. Histogram. Number of elements in each class is identical.	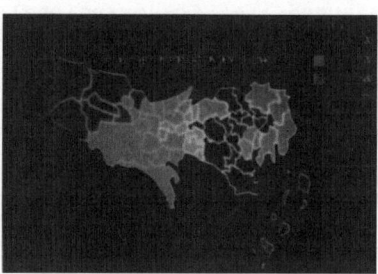 D. Resulting map corresponding to histogram C.
Show the suitable areas for regional development.	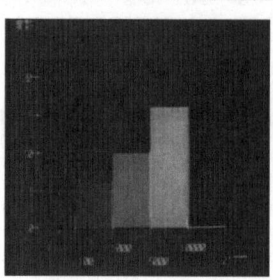 E. Histogram obtained according to planner's intention.	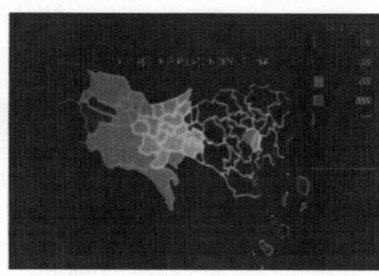 F. Resulting map corresponding to histogram E.

Fig. 4. Intentions, histogram and resulting maps for experiments 2.

A. Set up the statistical boundaries so that the range for each class would be identical.
B. Set up the statistical boundaries so that the number of elements in each class would be identical.

The Tokyo regional area population distribution can be understood from these maps. However, it is difficult to understand the details about the western areas from the maps, in which all of the western areas are painted in the same pattern.

Figures 4E and 4F are a histogram and a resulting map obtained according to the planner's idea. Table 2 shows the processes and corresponding histograms to obtain the relevant map. The intermediate class in final histogram C in Table 2 shows the object areas for development.

The designer can classify the statistical data by using the Histogram Interface in order to express his idea on a map, as shown in the examples. As the user interface function graphically indicates important factors, designers can easily recognize and handle the factors according to their ideas. The Histogram Interface is considered as an effective tool to incorporate the intentions into maps in designing thematic maps.

DISCUSSION

Histogram Interface limit

Idea representation on choropleth maps can be effectively carried out by using the Histogram Interface. However, more detailed consideration is needed for designing multiple kinds of maps, which have statistical relationships with each other.

For example, how can the population density change in time dimension be represented? Figures 5A, 5B and 5C represent 1960, 1970 and 1980 population density maps for the Tokyo regional area, respectively. No changes can be observed from patterns on these maps. It seems as if there were no changes in the past twenty years. The reason why the change cannot be expressed is that the designer has designed a choropleth map without paying attention to the statistical relationships between resulting maps.

From another point of view, the Histogram Interface limit is considered. In actuality, the Histogram Interface allows designers to effectively represent their ideas into maps for any kind of statistical and geographical data. However, in order to perform better classification using the Histogram Interface, it is desirable that designers should know the relations between statistical distribution and corresponding geographical circumstances. For example, experimental results described in this paper show that the designer's knowledge of the Tokyo population distribution was very useful in designing a better map. As the Histogram Interface alone does not possess a function which directly shows the relations between statistical data and geographical circumstances, designers might not create appropriate maps unless they know about the regional circumstances.

With reference to the example, the Histogram Interface has a using limit. Therefore, the designer needs to consider how to use the

Histogram Interface so that the resulting map can represent what he intends to express therein during the designing process.

Map drawing selection

In the choropleth map case study, a method to express designers' intentions on choropleth maps was presented. Another important issue, in regard to expressing designers' ideas on maps, is a pertinent selection of a relevant kind of thematic map. For example, pie-charts, shown in Fig. 6, are often used in representing statistical data on a map. The size of a pie-chart corresponds to the total amount of statistical values. In this case, map viewers cannot easily understand the differences between statistical values A and B. If the planner intends to indicate a statistical difference between the elements, using pie-charts is not appropriate. Choosing an appropriate map drawing method is also one of the important factors with reference to this example.

Extension to other computer graphics fields

At present, user interfaces design has been centering around a concept which is represented by a term, "user friendliness". However, a user interface, based on user friendliness alone, does not always sufficiently assist designers in expressing their ideas.

In computer graphics fields, designers have their own intentions, which must be emphasized according to the objective for designing a picture. They are emphasizing, extending, or obscuring and so on. For example, in displaying the result of simulation experiments, the precise movement derived from the experiment result is not always appropriate. The movement is often too fast or too slow for the viewers to

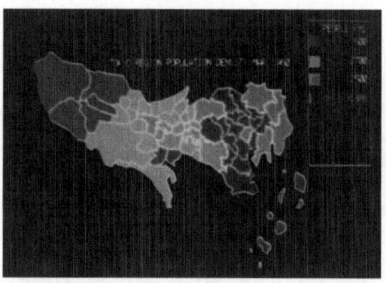

A. Tokyo region population density map in 1960.

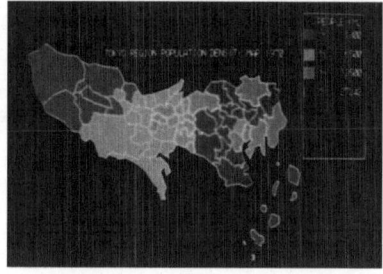

B. Tokyo region population density map in 1970.

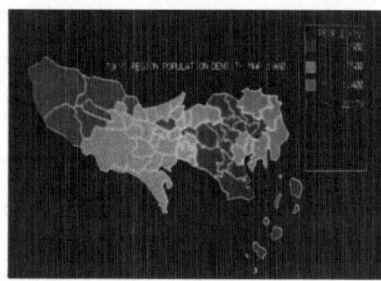

C. Tokyo region population density map in 1980.

Fig. 5. Inappropriate map examples to show the population change in the past twenty years.

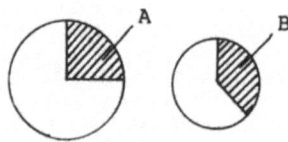

Fig. 6. Pie-charts used in thematic maps.

understand. This is a case where the speed for representing the movement of things is an important factor and it must be changed to be readily understood by viewers. The important factors to express designers' ideas must be considered during the designing process, in the same manner as when designing thematic maps.

The concept, which the designers should consider in determining how they can incorporate their ideas into pictures, is very important for any computer graphics field, as well as the case of thematic maps design.

Subjects for future study

Several subjects are considered for future study. An important one among them is the pattern impression problem to be projected such as color or hatched pattern. At present, the designers select arbitrary patterns according to their own sense. However, pattern meanings must be made known to the designers during the designing process. The impression projected by different patterns, such as heavy, light, strong and weak, must correspond to the statistical meanings.

CONCLUSION

As a case study for representation of designers' ideas into resulting pictures, a choropleth map designing process is described. The problems in designing choropleth maps are (1) excessively detailed or too all-inclusive information, (2) disagreement relating to differences in statistical values for specific areas, and (3) unsuitable color or pattern impression.

The Histogram Interface was developed to cope with the problems. It enables to control three important factors, (1) number of classes, (2) lower and upper boundaries for classes, and (3) pattern impression order.

By using the interface, designers' ideas are effectively expressed on the maps. However, some limits can be considered for using it. Detailed consideration in multiple maps designing and assistance of knowledge concerning relations between statistical distribution and regional circumstances are necessary. Map drawing selection is another important factor in designing thematic maps.

In any other field of computer graphics, the concept, which the designers should consider in determining how they can incorporate their ideas into pictures, is very important.

ACKNOWLEDGMENT

The authors would like to express appreciation for continuous encouragement from Dr. M. Naniwada. They are particularly grateful to Mr. Y. Koyama of NEC Scientific Information System Development, Ltd. and NEC Software, Ltd. members involved in this project, for their assistance and cooperation in this collaboration.

REFERENCES

Cleveland WS, Horris CS, & McGill R, (1983) Experiments on Quantitative Judgment of Graphs and Maps. The Bell System Technical Journal, July-August: 1659-1674.
Dutton G, (1983) The ODYSSEY GEOGRAPHIC PROCESSING SYSTEM. AN overview. NICOGRAPH '83: 359-376.
Foley JD, & Van Dam A, (1982) Fundamentals of Interactive Computer Graphics. Addison-Wesley Publishing Company.
Kasahara Y, Saigusa H, Miyashita T, & Tsurutani T, (1984) WING: A Geographic Information System for Regional Planning and Facility Management. NEC R&D: 66-75.
Marcus A, (1983) Designing Iconic Interface: A Review of Three Systems. NICOGRAPH '83: 103-123.
Miyashita T, Kasahara Y, & Tsurutani T, (1984) A Method of Regional Information Overlay for Regional Analysis. SCSC '84: 958-963.
Nakatani LH, & Rohrlich JA, (1983) Soft Machines: A Philosophy of User-Computer Interface Design. CHI'83: 19-23.
Newman WM, & Sproull R, (1979) PRINCIPLES OF INTERACTIVE COMPUTER GRAPHICS. McGRAW-HILL BOOK COMPANY.
Tsurutani T, Kasahara Y, & Naniwada M, (1980) ATLAS: A Geographic Database System. SIGGRAPH '80, July: 71-77.
Vertin J, (1982) LA GRAPHIQUE ET LE TRAITEMENT GRAPHIQUE DE L INFORMATION. Tokyo Inshokan Publishing. (translated into Japanese).
Yamahira T, Kasahara K, & Tsurutani T, (1984) Personal Mapping System WING-mini: Evaluation of the user interface. 28th National Convention of Information Processing Society of Japan: 1567-1568. (in Japanese).

Challenges in the Application of Graphics Technology to the Management of Geographic Information

I.K. Crain and C.L. MacDonald

Canada Land Data Systems, Lands Directorate, Environment Canada, Ottawa, K1A 0E7, Canada

INTRODUCTION

A Geographic Information System (GIS) is a system designed to capture, store, manipulate, retrieve and display data which are referenced to geographic locations (Poiker and Crain, 1985). Such systems are distinct from automated cartography where the primary goal is the production of printed graphic output. The goal of a GIS is to manage geographic data, and graphic output represents only one mode of data retrieval and only a subset of the system functions, which may include a wide range of spatial as well as non-geometric data manipulation. Graphic output capabilities have often been developed as an after-thought to a GIS which was primarily designed for tabular statistical reporting. In practice, however, the output of graphic images in the form of some sort of "map", almost always forms part of the retrieval repertoire of a modern GIS.

Many such systems began as aids to straight-forward resource inventories, but user demand has forced an evolution to their use as decision support tools. This in turn led to the requirement for distributed interactive graphics facilities. (Crain and MacDonald, 1984).

The Canada Geographic Information System (CGIS), the world's first GIS, was initially implemented (in the early 1960's) with no graphic output capability. Now, over 20 years later, it is incorporated into the comprehensive Canada Land Data System (CLDS) and provides an extensive variety of interactive and hardcopy graphics on a daily production basis. These are applied to problems in ecological land evaluation, land use monitoring, natural resource planning, wildlife habitat conservation, and so on (Thie et al., 1982, 1984). The implementation of computer graphics techniques into a high volume multi-user production environment has been a long and gradual process presenting a series of challenges to system designers.

GRAPHIC OUTPUT REQUIREMENTS OF A GIS

There are two principal types of graphic output required in a GIS - Statistical Graphics which include conventional displays such as bar-graphs, pie charts, scatter diagrams, linear plots etc, and Cartographic Graphics which include a range of map-like products. Statistical graphics are hardly unique to the GIS. These are addressed readily by the many packages available and will not be discussed here.

The cartographic output requirements are more challenging and range from simple diagramatic maps where no spatial accuracy is expected, to large size monochrome or colour maps with accuracy approaching that expected of high quality production printed cartography.

Any cartographic product presents challenges for computer production because of the need to combine vector elements such as line-work, space filling elements such as polygonal areas, textual annotation in several fonts and sizes, and other special features such as scale-bars, north-arrows, borders, legend boxes, etc. (Waugh and Taylor, 1976). In addition there are elements of esthetics and readability to be balanced with technical accuracy.

Cartographic outputs can be classified into three categories according to their intended use, as follows:

Interactive Analysis Graphics

These graphic outputs are required for interactive analysis of geographic data bases by users seeking to explore relationships between data elements, and to a lesser extent to make land resource decisions directly. The essential query is "show me where" qualified by various attribute and/or spatial criteria. The user wishes to select, display the mapped result, reselect, and redisplay repeatedly, often interspersed with non-graphic queries and reports (Foley and Van Dam, 1982). Another common need is the direct retrieval, qualified only by region - the "show me what exists in this region" query.

The desired graphics are ephemeral; no permanent record is kept. To be useful the images must be created and displayed quickly, usually in less than one minute. This in itself is a problem as the data bases to be queried are large and complex, and the algorithms needed to respond to the queries are commonly elaborate.

Working Diagrams

This second group of graphic outputs take the form of hard-copy maps and cartographic diagrams, often page-sized, for use as working documents - for desk reference, internal reports, group discussions, strategy and research decisions, administrative decisions, and as preliminary "proofs" for the design and selection of ultimate high quality publication graphics. Neither these nor the interactive outputs are accurate cartographic products, but rather, diagramatic representations in map form. It is not expected, for instance, that measurements of distance and area will be made from these diagrams. Fast output, preferably at or near the work location, is essential. Reproduction is desired usually in limited quantity if at all.

Publication Quality Maps

Publication quality graphics require the production of cartographically accurate maps, often heavily detailed and multi-coloured, with textual and symbolic annotation and legends. These are usually reproduced by conventional printing techniques in quantities of a thousand or more for distribution.

GRAPHICS IN THE PRODUCTION ENVIRONMENT

It is always a long and perilous step from successful research and pilot demonstration to production implementation. In a GIS, solutions found in a pilot project with controlled test data sets often do not stand up well to general implementation with massive sets of imperfect data. It is conventional wisdom that an operational system must have versatile, friendly, yet bullet-proof software. It must operate on reliable, continuously available hardware. This limits the use of experimental and unproven technology.

Data files in a GIS are often extremely large and have complex structures, involving data compaction techniques, multi-threaded chains, and topological index files. (Tomlinson et al, 1976). (Some files in CLDS have over 1,000,000 polygons comprised of about 6,000,000 line segments each of which may have hundreds or thousands of x-y pairs, along with large volumes of attribute data). Queries are complicated, difficult to predict and the output graphic requirements for maps vary widely from project to project, in map scale, projection, texture and density of information, nature and quality of annotation etc. No one output device or medium can meet all the categories of graphic output for all data sets.

An added dimension faced by CLDS and other systems is that many users wish to operate remotely from various nationally distributed centers. This presents challenges of data communication standardization and management.

Notwithstanding the long and successful history of the CLDS, success in meeting the challenges of the user's requirements for effective, reliable graphics at a reasonable cost has been a slow and gradual process, and has often had to await technological advances at each step.

SOME SUCCESSES

Although the original design of the early CGIS around 1963 included the concept of maps being displayed on a graphics screen based on queries, the actual production implementation of such a capability had to await the routine availability of the "low-cost" storage tube graphics terminals, such as the early Tektronix 4000 series. The earliest implementation of the system provided no graphic output whatsoever, only tabular reporting, and the addition shortly thereafter of a flat-bed pen plotter went only a short way towards meeting the needs for working diagrams, even less for publication quality maps and did nothing for interactive analysis graphics.

The introduction of the storage-tube screens in the early 70's provided for the first time simple rapid, on-the-spot graphics. Coupled with poor quality (but adequate) hard-copy attachments, these terminals also provided simple working diagrams for desk reference. This type of output, used mainly to display outlines of regions which met selection criteria, proved to be a workhorse for geographic data analysis for over a decade. Increases in software sophistication have greatly expanded the query capabilities and interactivity, but this basic graphic product, such as in Fig. 1, is still in production use.

The limitations of monochrome graphics are obvious, even for interactive analysis and working diagrams. The information content of this essentially binary medium is highly constrained to depict "selected" or "not selected", "in" or "out", etc. The use of shading patterns to depict multiple themes is of limited additional benefit, especially when small areas are to be identified. The solution is the colour graphics screen, and again, production implementation had to await the relatively recent commercial availability of these devices. Colour working diagrams have only been feasible in the last two years with the availability of ink-jet plotters for colour screen copying, and these devices still have questionable reliability for routine production use.

The colour screen enables the depiction of multiple themes on a map and improved discrimination of relatively small areas. Resolution restrictions of common low-cost terminals restrict the annotation capabilities and maps must, by necessity, be relatively simple and small in area. In spite of these restrictions the majority of the requirements for interactive analysis and working diagrams are achieved. Fig. 2 shows an example of such a map, reproduced from the graphics screen.

Very high resolution interactive colour graphics for data analysis purposes on a production basis remains unachievable (at reasonable cost) at the present time.

The requirements for working documents extend beyond hard-copy reproduction of graphics screens. There is a need as well for accurate large format maps as desk references, for interim display or use in the field during further studies. This requirement is best met through the use of a high quality flat-bed or drum plotters on various media. The plots are designed and commanded through the interactive user terminal, but produced off-line at a central facility, since the plotters required are too expensive to warrant user-site replication (CLDS uses a Gerber model 4200 drum plotter).

The two most commonly requested products are labelled polygon plots in black-and-white, and colour shaded maps. The former consists of an outline map with attribute labels placed centrally in each polygon. Automatic placement of these labels can be algorithmically complex, especially where polygon sizes are relatively small and the required attribute labels contain many characters (eg. ten characters). Consideration must be given to placing labels so that they do not overlap with others and yet remain clearly referenced to the correct area, and the minimum size of the label is constrained by readability (Ahn and Freeman, 1983).

The approach used in several systems is to tie the label to the polygon with a pointer if it will not correctly fit in the region, and to compress the large labels in extremely crowded areas to a one or two-digit code number, which is expanded in an accompanying automatically generated legend. Fig. 3 shows a portion of such a map.

To produce colour maps, colour fill is generated by horizontal shading on the plotter, with ball-point type pens. A much more limited number of themes can be identified this way compared to the labelled map, however the colour shaded map is commonly desired as a "proof" for designing a publication quality map, or as an inexpensive desk reference. (Fig. 4)

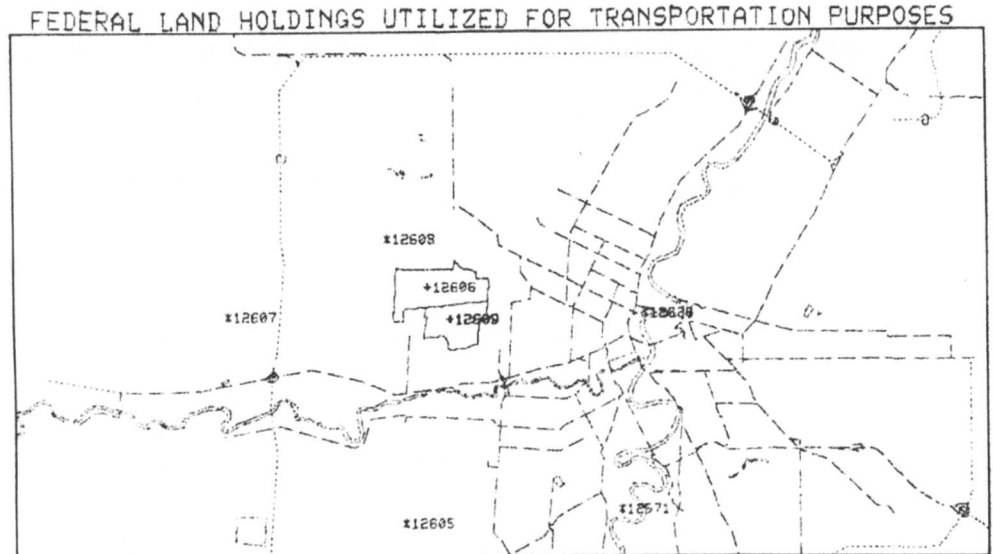

Fig. 1. Interactive monochrome output from storage tube terminal.

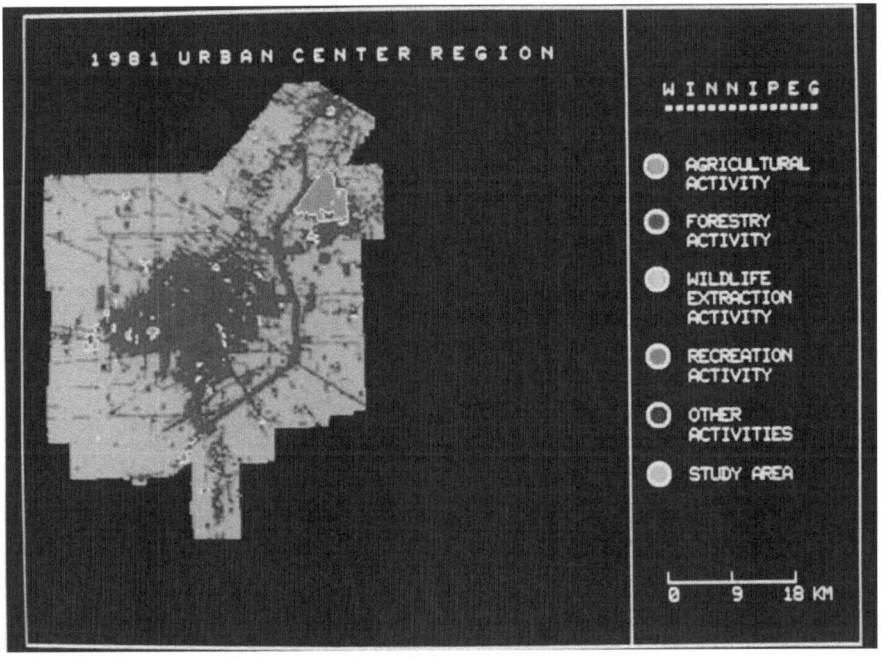

Fig. 2. Interactive colour map.

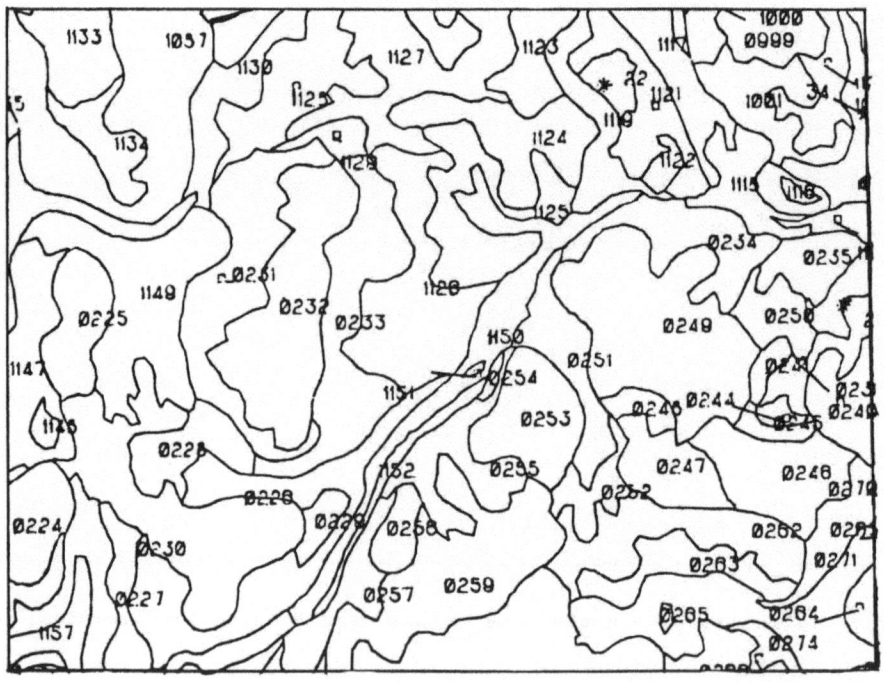

Fig. 3. Detail from labelled map.

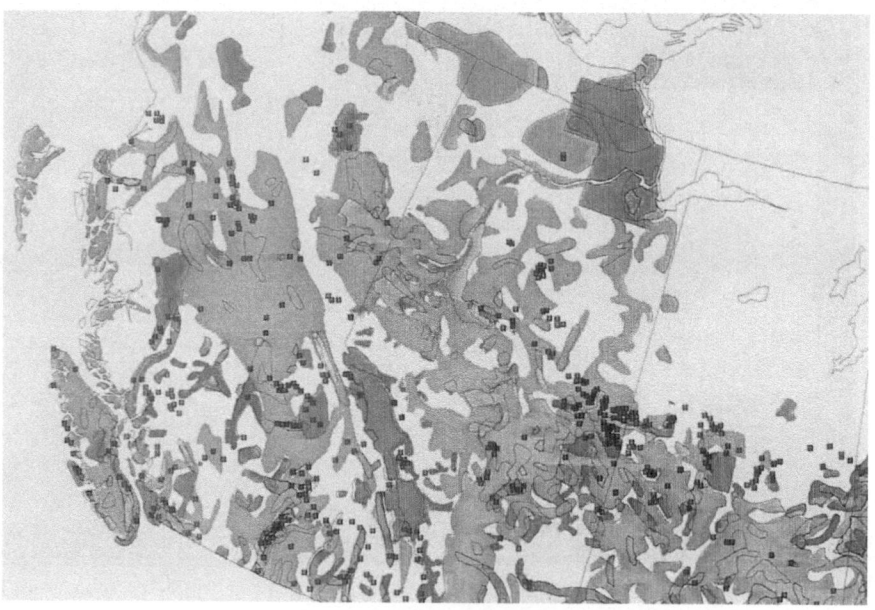

Fig. 4. Detail from colour-shaded map.

Meeting the need for publication quality maps has been a difficult task for most operational GIS. Common methods including those used until recently at CLDS, continue to be clumsy, slow, only partially automated, and relatively expensive. One approach uses the flat-bed or drum plotter to generate thematic separates where each polygon of a theme is completely filled with black ink. Such a map is produced for each theme - ie. each colour shade on the final map. These thematic separates are then photographed and colour dot screens added to eventually produce three-colour printing negatives. All annotation is drafted manually or by partially automated means, and integrated as a fourth black overlay. Registration of a large number of themes is a major problem, small areas are often poorly defined, colour choice by the user is awkward and so on. The various manual steps and photography add to the costs and delays.

The practical solution to this problem recently adopted comes close to completely automating this process while keeping costs and turn-around to a minimum. The output device used for the coloured polygon fill is a laser scanner/plotter. (In the case of CLDS an Optronics X4040). Although this device is primarily designed for input, ie. to scan documents for data capture, it also can output binary images in raster form with adjustable pixel resolution from 25 to 200 microns. The adopted process first uses software to rasterize the colour-fill areas of the output map directly from the GIS. This raster grid is then assigned the ultimate printing colour by the user as chosen from a master colour chart (of 4096 colours). These colour assignments are then used to reformat the grid by applying various dot patterns to three separate files representing the three primary colours (cyan, magneta, and yellow). Registered full size negatives are then exposed directly on film using the Optronics scanner (Crain, 1983, 1984). An intermediate step is usually used to produce an approximate colour-proof map on a large format ink-jet plotter for final approval or colour reselection by the user.

Annotation and any necessary black line-work on the map is produced through a commercial interactive map drawing package called GIMMS, (Waugh and Taylor, 1976), which provides a wide range of fonts, borders, north-arrows, scale bars, etc. This output is pre-viewed interactively, test plotted in ink on the drum plotter and finally plotted directly on film using a photo-head attachment on the plotter. The four negatives then can be applied directly to make the three colour and one black printing plate. Fig. 5 a,b,c, show the three colour separates and Fig. 6 shows the result (with the black plate) of such a process.

THE REMAINING CHALLENGES

The ultimate goal for graphic output in a GIS is for the user to be able to select and view any part of his data set interactively and to be able to design and pre-view planned hard copy outputs, including publication quality large format maps. These goals are not achievable with today's technology. Reasonable cost data communication and colour display terminals allow only a simplified approximation to be achieved in a production system. Additional break-throughs in high speed data communications, efficient data structures for cartographic representation, and high resolution display are needed to make these further steps. Current research activities indicate that there is reason to be optimistic of rapid progress.

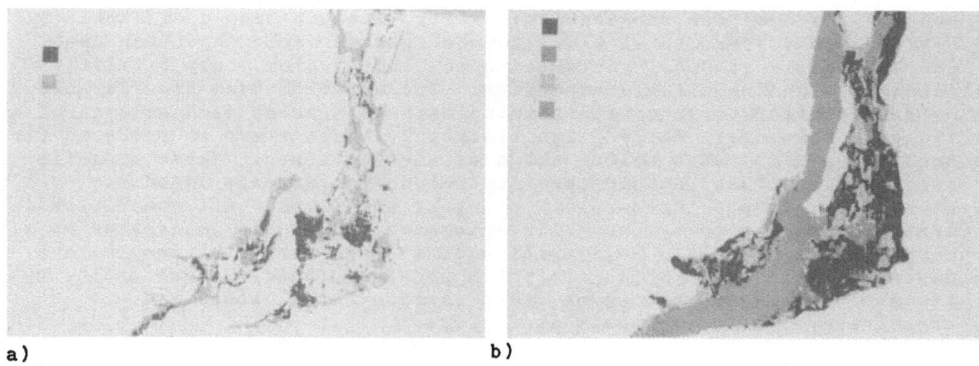

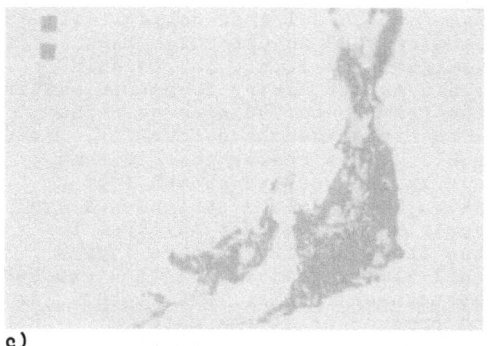

Fig. 5. Colour separates from laser plotter
a) magneta, b) cyan, c) yellow.

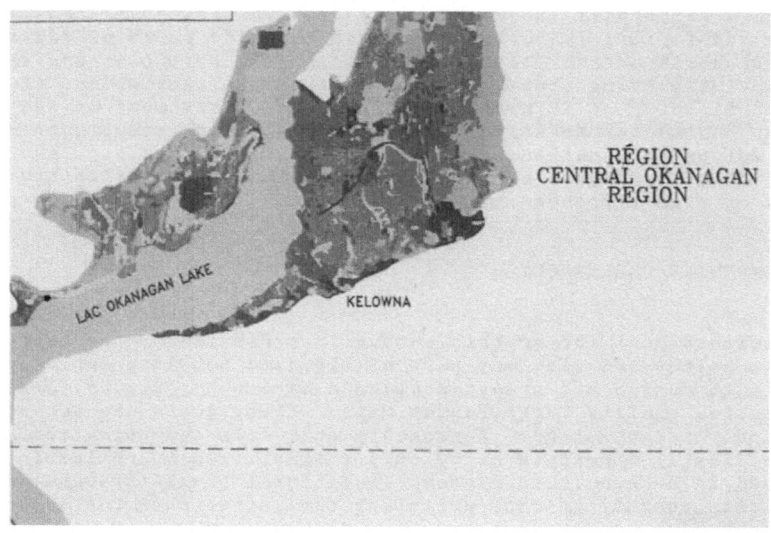

Fig. 6. Detail from printed colour map made from laser-plotter separates.

REFERENCES

Ahn J, Freeman H (1983) A Program for automatic name placement. In: Proceedings of Autocarto Six, Ottawa, p 444-453

Crain IK (1983) SIRE System Progress Report No.1. Canada Land Data System Internal Report R001160, Environment Canada, Ottawa

Crain IK (1984) SIRE System Progress Report No.2. Canada Land Data System Internal Report R001161, Environment Canada, Ottawa

Crain IK, MacDonald CL (1984) From land inventory to land management- The evolution of an operational GIS. Cartographica 21: 40-46

Foley JD, Van Dam A (1982) Fundamentals of Interactive Computer Graphics. Addison-Wesley, Reading

Poiker TK, Crain IK (1985) Geographical Information Systems. In: The Canadian Encyclopedia, Hurtig Publishers, Edmonton, p725

Thie J, Switzer WA, Chartrand NP (1982) Das "Canada Land Data System" und seine Anwendungsmoglichkeiten in Landschaftsplanung und Bewirtschaftung der Ressourcen. Natur und Landschaft 57: 433-440

Thie J, Switzer WA, Chartrand NP (1984) The Canada Land Data System and its application to landscape planning and resource management. (English translation of Thie et al, 1979). In: Selected Papers III, Canada Land Data System Internal Report R001071, Environment Canada, Ottawa

Tomlinson RF, Calkins HW, Marble DF (1976) The Canada Geographic Information System. In: Computer Handling of Geographical Data, The UNESCO Press, Paris, 1976, p27-73

Waugh T, Taylor DRF (1976) GIMMS - An example of an operational system for computer cartography. Canadian Cartographer 13: 158-166

An Image Management Kernel for the Design of Relational and Pictorial Data Bases

Ph. Chassignet

Lactamme, Centre de mathématiques Appliquées, E.R.A. - C.N.R.S. 747, Ecole Polytechnique, 91128 Palaiseau Cedex, France

INTRODUCTION

Picture allows to make use of the analytical wealth of the eye in the understanding of complex informations. Thus, one largest and largest part of the data, which are today generated or processed by computer, is expressed as digital images. So, it is of a great interest to be able to handle these in a similar way to other data whether those are elementary as numbers or more complex as sets of facts and rules.

Our project is intended to define a system that permits to finely connect the synthesis of images and the management of relations between these and other data. Thus, some of those are refered to in the images descriptions and, therefore, they may be used for synthesis. Naturally, for any specific application, the peculiar data, which are basically independent of the graphical representations, may be also linked alike to these.
This first applies to the realization of an "enlarged pictorial system" for arts, animations or scientific visualizations. The improvement mainly concerns the add of a high-level user-interface. For instance, previously defined images may be considered as a base of both good and bad experiences that may be browsed among to provide help by examples or to ensure an automatic but fitted choice for default-parameters. Such an interface so permits both an easy access by non-specialist user and a noticeable speed-up in image perfection.
A second kind of applications concerns the integration of graphical functionalities in a "general data base". Images may then be defined (and whence generated) as functions of various informations. They are, thus, much more powerfully managed than the recorded pictures of a "slides library". Reciprocally, images provide an useful interface to access and update other data. Typical areas are therefore illustrations for education, decision, etc...

To this end, *Relational Data Base Management Systems* are proving very suitable owing to their basic properties (Codd 1981; Date 1982). Main of these are the dynamism, the independence and the elementary presentation of the data, an easy and safe keeping of coherence and a certain access-flexibility, e.g. with Q.B.E. (Zloof 1975). With only respect to some elementary rules, most informations may be naturally expressed according to the relational frame, that is in the form of regular tables.
Hence, Relational Systems are being use for some graphical applications (Chang and Fu 1980; Yamaguchi and Kunii 1982) and particularly for geographic databases (Smedley and Aldred 1979; Vaidya, Shapiro, Haralick and Minden 1982).
But, compared with these applications, our project also implies to emphasize the image synthesis abilities.

GENERAL FUNCTIONING

So, in the present work, owing to performances, the D.B.M.S. does not directly handle images. This task is imparted to a system that is specialized in their synthesis and that must mainly perform three functions, which are storage, processing and display of low-level representations. These may be graphical (Newmann and Sproull 1979; Foley and Van Dam 1982) or iconic (P.A.R.C. 1978; Guibas and Stolfi 1982). Consequently, this system is named an *Iconographic Machine* and its three main components are respectively indicated as the *Physical Images Base*, the *Iconographic Processors* and the *Display Means*.

On account of their size, the most pictures this machine may display are not permanently stored in the form of their explicit representations. These must thereby be generated from a basic library and by using of the processors, which allow to modify and combine them. The programs that describe these computations are then stored by the D.B.M.S. and can be simultaneously managed as descriptive data that are subject to various requests and that may occasionally be updated. For this purpose, image-programs are composed of *iconographic entities*, each whose tallies with one operation. The relational schema that organizes these entities may, thus, be regarded as a skeleton that is defined independently of any application. The application-designer must then implement the aggregate schema around this *Iconographic Skeleton* by properly relating other data with the iconographic entities.
Note that the relative compactness of these representations thus allows to handle a very large base of images but, of course, at the cost of the computation time required before display.

Meanwhile, owing to its conceptual flatness, the relational frame is found too limited to handle the hierarchical structures of image-programs. Thus, some extension tools are required and we collect them in the concept of *Iconographic Kernel*. To ensure a good portability, this Image Management Kernel is intended to be easy implemented on any system build around both an Iconographic Machine, such as defined above, and a standard Relational Data Base Management System.
The first of two essential tools is the *Iconographic Editor* which allows to define, select or modify the iconographic entities. The second one is the *Piloting Interpretor* which is in charge of monitoring the Iconographic Machine to compute and display the requested images. All the tools have obligatory access to the Iconographic Skeleton through the *Extension Interface* that formats the requests for the Relational System.

Hence, the following sketch summarizes our functional decomposition.

Iconographic Machine
    Physical Images Base
    Iconographic Processors
    Display Means
    Control Interface

Iconographic Kernel
    Iconographic Skeleton
    Extension Interface
    Iconographic Editor
    Piloting Interpretor

Relational System
    Management System
    Relational Interface
    Data Base
    (application-dependent)

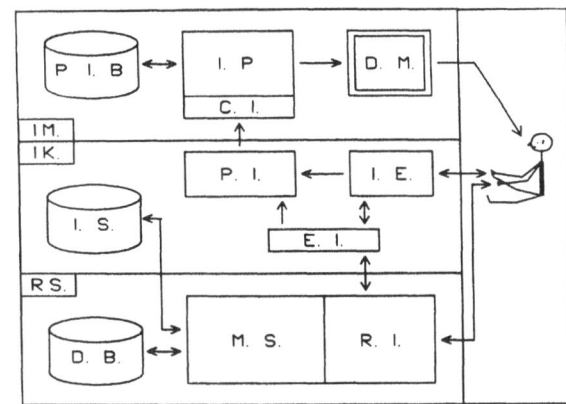

Fig. 1. Functional Decomposition. Arrows show the main data flows.

Then, the purpose of this paper is to describe some main points of the Iconographic Kernel. So, we present the principles of images descriptions and the formalism we use to bring these principles close by the relational frame. We shall finally introduce the *Interpretation Function* that occurs in the computations of pictures.

DESCRIPTION OF ICONOGRAPHIC ENTITIES

As a general rule, any iconographic entity is defined by references to other entities. The few exceptions to this are named *intrinsic* entities. All the others are, as a function of the context and of their own semantic, discerned between *images*, *processors*, *sequences* and *lists*.

Image-Entity

Images constitute the basic type of entity. Such one is defined as the result of a *virtual iconographic operation* of the form :

$$(\text{Proc}, \pi)(\text{Arg}_1, \ldots, \text{Arg}_k)$$

Proc denotes the processor that must be considered as a generic item and thus needs parameters to exactly specify the operator. For example, the zoom-processor requires the setting of the magnitude and the center-coordinates. So, given π a record of parameters values, (Proc, π) and $(\text{Arg}_1, \ldots, \text{Arg}_k)$ respectively denote the present operator and the list of its operands.

Proc and the Arg_i's are other entities that may be either intrinsic or recursively defined by virtual operations. On the other hand, parameter-values are always plainly stated in π. Then, both the Piloting Interpreter and the Control Interface are such that the most elementary instances of virtual operations may be directly submitted to the Iconographic Machine so as to materially perform them.

Actually, we take up the following representation :

$$(\text{Proc}, \text{Arg}_1, \ldots, \text{Arg}_k)(\pi) \qquad\qquad [1]$$

that regroups in a same list all the entities that are refered to by a given image and that will be expressed in two respective relational sets of tuples.

Processor-Entity

From a formal point of view, a processor is a function of entities and parameters whose result is an image-entity. A processor may also be described by an expression that is similar to Exp. [1], considering it as a variable image. Then, this variability is based on the three following applicative principles :

P1: For some i, the refered entity Arg_i is the result of such another processor that is function of the same (entity- and parameter-) arguments.

P2: Some parameters of π are expressed as functions of the parameter-arguments.

P3: $(\text{Proc}, \text{Arg}_1, \ldots, \text{Arg}_k)$ contains formal references to the entity-arguments.

The additional concept, which occurs in the description of a processor-entity, is that of *default-image*. Then one result can be assigned by default to each "incomplete operation", provided that a processor is refered to. According to Exp. [1], this notion may be expressed in terms of "hollow lists". Thus, the utmost expression (Proc)( ) defines the default-image of the processor Proc. Then, the more complete one operation is, the more its result differs from this generic image.

To this aim, each principle of variability is completed by one specific rule for the assignment of a given value when some of the required arguments are failing.

R1: Arg_i is the default-result of the refered processor.

R2: One default-value is bound to each parameter-function.

R3: One default-entity is added to each formal reference.
If the refered entity is a processor then rule R1 applies after this.

By the above rules, any processor also implicitly describes a set of sub-processors having the same but fewer arguments. Each default-element may then be fixed to yield automatically a "generally satisfying" result.

What is more, a processor generates a class of images whose any instance is determined by one peculiar choice of the arguments. Then, fixing some of these, we explicitly define a sub-processor that only generates a restricted class. Image is thus the limit case of constant processor whose class is considered as identical to its single result.

In practice, the use of implicit sub-processors is proving more spontaneous but certainly more limited than the one of explicit sub-processors.

Sequence-Entity

A sequence is one particular case of processor which generates a class of images that are solely functions of one parameter. A sequence may be defined by giving a processor and any path through its arguments "space". Thus, when the path-parameter is time, such an entity represents one given animation whose images are then generated depending on both the rhythm and the temporal resolution.

List-Entity

This term denotes expressions like $(Arg_1, \ldots, Arg_k)$ that degenerate from Exp. [1] by the absence of processor and that are considered as ordinary lists of entities. Such an entity may be used as a list of arguments in the description of images. It may also be useful for conversing with the D.B.M.S. In the latter case, it acts as a relation and thereby may be either the argument or the result of any request.

FORMALIZATIONS

Notations

Let d be an integer and Θ be a set of *constants*. Then, let Γ be the set of the *applications* defined from Θ^d to Θ. Now, for any $f \in \Gamma$, define the set $\Delta(f)$ as follows :

$\Delta(f)$ is the set of integers $i \in [1..d]$ such that there are :

$(c_1, \ldots, c_{i-1}, c_{i+1}, \ldots, c_d) \in \Theta^{d-1}$ and $c, c' \in \Theta$, all such that

$f(c_1, \ldots, c_{i-1}, c, c_{i+1}, \ldots, c_d) \neq f(c_1, \ldots, c_{i-1}, c', c_{i+1}, \ldots, c_d)$

Let $\dagger$ be one special function such that : $\Delta(\dagger) \cap [1..d] = \phi$.
Lastly, let E be a set of *iconographic entities*.

References

Let $R \subset (E \times N)^2$ be the set of the *references* that exist between entities of E. Whatever references r, r', assuming $r = (\alpha, i, \beta, j)$ and $r' = (\alpha', i', \beta', j')$, they must answer to the following property :

$$\text{if } \alpha = \alpha' \text{ and } i = i' \text{ then } r = r'. \qquad [2]$$

Under these conditions, we shall say that integer i is the *position* of reference r. In the case of $j = 0$, r is named a *constant reference* to entity β. In the other cases $(j > 0)$, r is a *formal reference* and the refered entity is the possible argument in position j or, by default, β. We shall note :

$Ref(\alpha) = \{ (\alpha, i, \beta, j) \in R \}$ and $Arg(\alpha) = \{ (\alpha, i, \beta, j) \in R \text{ such as } i > 0 \}$

Parameters

Let $P \subset E \times N \times \Theta \times \Gamma$ be the set of the *parameters* that are bounded to the entities of E. Whatever parameters p, p', assuming $p = (\alpha, i, c, f)$ and $p' = (\alpha', i', c', f')$, they must answer to the following property :

$$\text{if } \alpha = \alpha' \text{ and } i = i' \text{ then } p = p'. \qquad [3]$$

Further, it must be $i > 0$. Then, we shall also say that i is the *position* of parameter p, that constant c is its *default-value* and that f is the *parameter-function*. We shall also note :

$$Par(\alpha) = \{ (\alpha, i, c, f) \in P \}$$

Whatever $c \in \Theta$, the *constant parameter* of value c will be noted $(\alpha, i, c, \dagger)$.

Classification Rules

An entity α will be called an *intrinsic* one if $\text{Ref}(\alpha) = \emptyset$
and, respectively, a *list*-one if $\text{Ref}(\alpha) = \text{Arg}(\alpha) \neq \emptyset$.
In the other cases, there thus exist $\beta \in E$ and $j \in N$ such that $(\alpha, 0, \beta, j) \in \text{Ref}(\alpha)$.
Then, will shall say that entity α is a *processor* (that should be an image) and that entity β is its *operator*.

Iconographic Skeleton

Let the *directed graph* $K = [E, R, P]$ be defined by :

(1)   the set of its vertices is E,
(2)   any vertex α is labeled by the set $\text{Par}(\alpha)$,
(3)   its arcs are the couples $(\alpha, \beta) \in E^2$ such that $(\alpha, i, \beta, j) \in R$,
(4)   the arc (α, β) is then labeled by i, j.

Thus, any processor-vertex, the set of its outcoming arcs and their respective labeling are representative of one *virtual iconographic operation*. Hence, by transitive closure of the R-connexity, the sub-graph that is rooted at a given processor constitutes the *description* of the latter.
Then, we shall say that K constitutes an *Iconographic Skeleton* if :

(1)   it is a Directed Acyclic Graph,
(2)   its leaves are included in a given set of intrinsic entities.

These properties are of prime importance, since they will secure the computability of the Interpretation Function and of the various extended requests that are based on the R-connexity.

INTERPRETATION FUNCTION

Notations and Definition

Let $K = [E, R, P]$ be an Iconographic Skeleton and let Σ and Π be respective parts of R and P. We suppose hereafter that this two subsets are *consistent* with the Interpretation, that is saying they both satisfy to :

whatever the integer i, there is at most one reference $(\alpha, i, \beta, j) \in \Sigma$ [4]
and, respectively, at most one parameter $(\gamma, i, c, f) \in \Pi$.

Let α be an entity of E. Then define $\alpha' = I(\alpha, \Sigma, \Pi)$ as the entity that is equivallent to the *Interpretation* of α in the *context* given by Σ and Π. Then, I is plainly defined as a function of α, Σ and Π by giving the references and parameters that characterize α'. So, put :

$$\text{Ref}(\alpha') = \Sigma_1 \cup \Sigma_2 \cup \Sigma_3 \quad \text{and} \quad \text{Par}(\alpha') = \Pi_1 \cup \Pi_2 \cup \Pi_3$$

and then define these six subsets by the following rules :

Interpretation Rules

Let Σ_1 be the set of references $(\alpha', i, \delta, 0)$ such that there is one integer $j > 0$ such that :

(1)   there is $(\alpha, i, \beta, j) \in \text{Ref}(\alpha)$ (so, one but only j, due to Prop. [2]),
(2)   there is $(\gamma, j, \delta, k) \in \Sigma$ (so, one but only δ, due to Prop. [4]).

According to variability principle P3, this rule expresses the *substitution* of the formal references by those to the calling arguments. It affects the operator when $i = 0$.

Let Σ_2 be the set of references $(\alpha',i,\delta,0)$ such that :
(1) there is one integer j such that :
   (11) there is $(\alpha,i,\beta,j) \in \text{Ref}(\alpha)$ (so, one but only β, due to Prop. [2]),
   (12) either $j = 0$
        or whatever $(\gamma,j',\epsilon,k) \in \Sigma$ then $j \neq j'$.
(2) if both conditions are checked then put either $\delta = I(\beta,\Sigma,\Pi)$ if $i > 0$
                                              or $\delta = \beta$ if $i = 0$.

According to variablity principle P1 and default rule R1, there is no substitution, either because the reference is *constant* ($j = 0$), or by *default of argument*.
Thus, according to the general clause $i > 0$, arguments are propagated to entity β and, owing to the fact that Skeleton is a D.A.G., this recursive definition always ends. The special clause $i = 0$ acts according to default rule R3 and should also retain the operator of α.

Let Π_1 be the set of parameters (α',i,k,t) such that :
(1) there is one application f such that :
   (11) there is $(\alpha,i,c,f) \in \text{Par}(\alpha)$ (so, one but only f, due to Prop. [3]),
   (12) $\Delta(f) \neq \emptyset$,
   (13) for each $j \in \Delta(f)$ there is one but only $(\beta,j,c_j,g) \in \Pi$ (Prop. [4]),
(2) if these conditions are checked then put (unambiguously by the definition of Δ) :
   $k = f(c_1,...,c_d)$, after completing (in any way) the sequence of the c_j's.

In this case, the application f is "valuable" on Π and, according to variability principle P2, k is taken as the *resulting value*.

Let Π_2 be the set of parameters (α',i,k,t) such that there is one function f such that :
(1) there is $(\alpha,i,k,f) \in \text{Par}(\alpha)$ (so, one but only k, due to Prop. [3]),
(2) either $f = t$
    or there is $j \in \Delta(f)$ such that whatever $(\beta,j',c,g) \in \Pi$ then $j \neq j'$.

In that case, the function f is constant or, more generally, "unvaluable" and therefore, according to default rule R2, k remains as *default-value*.

Thus, abovedefined references $(\alpha',i,\delta,0)$ and, respectively parameters (α',i,k,t), are, in a one to one way, straight derived from all the members (α,i,β,j) of $\text{Ref}(\alpha)$ and, resp. (α,i,c,f) of $\text{Par}(\alpha)$.

Finally, the following rules just regroup, by *recopy*, the references of Σ and parameters of Π that are not defined again in the description of α and are consequently *visible* from α'. Then, the rules for visibility are almost the same that those existing for identifiers scope in most structured languages as PASCAL.
Hence :

Let Σ_3 be the set of references $(\alpha',i,\delta,0)$ such that :
(1) there is $(\gamma,i,\delta,j) \in \Sigma$ (so, one but only δ, due to Prop. [4]),
(2) whatever $(\alpha,i',\beta,k) \in \text{Ref}(\alpha)$ then $i \neq i'$.

Let Π_3 be the set of parameters (α',i,k,t) such that :
(1) there is $(\beta,i,k,f) \in \Pi$ (so, one but only k, due to Prop. [4]),
(2) whatever $(\alpha,i',c,g) \in \text{Par}(\alpha)$ then $i \neq i'$.

Use in the Pictures Computation

Pictures computation is based on the *Representation Function*, that is a function Rep defined from E into the set of computable (by the Iconographic Machine) Physical Images.

Thus, Rep associates to any processor-entity "its" representation. But, it is beyond our present purpose to deal with a full description of the functioning of the Piloting Interpretor.

To say briefly, special rules concern cases of intrinsic operators. So, a necessary but sufficient set of two intrinsic entities is aimed at the access to the Physical Images Base and at the using of the Iconographic Processors. Some additional are structuring entities which provide different kinds of iteration and a "case of" selection.

However, the more often as not used rule is the following one that applies "inside" the D.A.G. :

Let α be a processor and let β be its non-intrinsic operator then :

$$\text{Rep}(\alpha) = \text{Rep}(\ I(\beta, \text{Arg}(\alpha), \text{Par}(\alpha)\ ).$$

CONCLUSION

This paper was presenting some aspects of the Iconographic Kernel that acts as the middle component of a Pictorial and Relational System, also build around both an Iconographic Machine and a Relational Data Base Management System.

In spite of their formal sights, the depicted principles are staying very close to the relational frame. So, references and parameters may be directly translated into relational quadruples. Then, the Interpretation Function may be easy implemented onto these in terms of the basic relational algebra, that is by operations as, e.g., selection or join.

ACKNOWLEDGEMENTS

I would like to acknowledge Pr. Erol Gelenbe who suggested this project.
I express all my thanks to Dr. J.F. Colonna for his profitable comments on the pictorial aspects of this work.

REFERENCES

Chang NS, Fu KS (1980) Query By Pictorial Exemple. IEEE Trans on Soft Eng 6-11
Codd EF (1981) The capabilities of relational database management systems. RJ 3132. IBM Res Lab San Jose
Date CJ (1982) An introduction to database systems. 3rd edn. Addison Wesley
Foley JD, Van Dam A (1982) Fundamentals of Interactive Computer Graphics. Addison Wesley
Guibas LJ, Stolfi J (1982) A Language for Bitmap Manipulation. ACM Trans. on Graphics 1-3: 191-214
Newmann WM, Sproull RF (1979) Principles of Interactive Computer Graphics, 2nd edn. McGraw-Hill
Palo Alto Research Center (1978) Alto User's Handbook. Xerox, Palo Alto
Smedley B, Aldred B (1979) Problems with geo-data. In: Data Base Techniques for Pictorial Applications. Lecture Notes in Computer Science, vol 81
Vaidya PD, Shapiro LG, Haralick RM, Minden GJ (1982) Design and architectural implications of a Spatial Information System. IEEE Trans on Comp 31-10
Yamaguchi K, Kunii TL (1982) PICCOLO logic for a picture database computer and its implementation. IEEE Trans on Comp 31-10
Zloof MM (1975) Query By Example. In: Proc International Conference on Very Large Data Bases, ACM

The Scientific and Technical Issues in Integrating Remotely Sensed Imagery with Geocoded Data Bases

W. Murray Strome and Berne Grush

Perceptron Computing Inc., Downsview, Ontario, M3H 5S8, Canada

ABSTRACT

Since the launch of LANDSAT-1 in 1972, major advances have occurred in computer technology, which have in turn led to improvements in our ability to more effectively analyze digital remotely sensed data. The decreasing cost of computer equipment, especially on-line and off-line memory, has led to an explosion in the use of digital mapping technique.

For several years, many have recognized that the full potential benefits of satellite remote sensing would not be realized until digital analysis of satellite image data and automated cartography/geocoded information systems become more compatible and integrated.

Some of the difficulties associated with this integration will be explored, as well as some of the efforts being made to overcome them.

KEYWORDS: Geographic Information Systems, remote sensing, automated cartography, LANDSAT

INTRODUCTION

Workers in many disciplines associated with resource management, environmental monitoring and land use planning are required to collect, store, analyze and display spatial data collected from several sources. For decades, the main sources of such data have been maps, ground surveys and aerial photography. Until relatively recently, the spatial data processing was performed using paper maps, transparent overlays, human interpretation and manual drafting.

Over the past decade or so, new technological tools have become available. Computer systems have permitted a more automated approach to map making as well as to the storage and manipulation of geographic information. The launch of LANDSAT-1 in 1972 ushered in a new era for the collection of data concerning the earth's surface. For the first time, synoptic data in digital form became available regularly and repetitively for all land areas of the earth. The high quality of the data and its abundance, coupled with advances in computer technology have led to considerable progress in developing digital processing techniques for analyzing the remotely sensed data from satellites. These advances have increased our ability to determine more accurately and objectively the material present on or near the earth's surface and its condition.

For some time, it has been recognized that the key to realization of the full potential benefits of satellite remote sensing for land applications lies in the successful integration of the data from this new source with geographic data bases. Much success has been achieved using manual techniques such as overlaying satellite images and maps. However, the task of integrating satellite data into computer based Geographic Information Systems has proven difficult.

GEOGRAPHIC INFORMATION SYSTEMS

A large number of digital Geographic Information Systems have been developed over the years. The basis for computer processing of spatial data lies in the creation of consistent digital data files which can be manipulated in a manner to extract the particular information desired for any specific purpose. The files are usually generated initially by digitization of existing maps (hopefully, ones which are accurate). The systems are intended to permit the user to manipulate and integrate data files in order to bring together information from several spatial data sets into a composite for either visual display or analytic modelling. To bring these data sets into spatial correspondence is known as overlaying, which demands a reference to a common geographic coordinate system(s).

The typical products of a Geographic Information System (GIS) are documents in tabular or graphical form which are directly usable by a professional planner, resource manager or decision maker without further manipulation or modification (Calkins and Tomlinson, 1977). The utility of a GIS cannot be measured in terms of its complexity, but rather, its ability to provide the right data to decision makers in the proper manner and at the right time. A GIS may be manual, computer based or a combination of the two.

A typical series of questions which might be posed to a GIS are: in a given geographical region (e.g. country),

a) how much land was converted from agricultural to urban use in the past five years? Ten years?

b) how much land is suitable for future urban development, and where is it?

c) how much of this land is not prime agricultural land, and where is it?

d) how much xxx land is within y km of rail service?

e) Which land is best for which crops based on soil type, rainfall, slope and aspect?

The replies to these questions could take the form of printed information as well as maps showing the location of all land satisfying the query criteria.

A GIS generally deals with many data characteristics, three of which are: the actual phenomenon, classification or measurement; its geographical location; and the time at which the data were measured. It is important to note that an effective spatial data management system must permit location and nonlocation (attributes) data to vary independently, as the attributes may change character without changing spatial location or vice versa. For example, a field planted with wheat one year may be left fallow the next, or a river may change its course over a period of time.

In attempting to make the transition from a manually map-based GIS to an automated computer based system, two fundamentally different approaches have been taken. The first approach is based upon the manner by which the spatial location of objects is depicted on maps using points, lines and polygons. These are most commonly defined on maps using x, y coordinates such as latitude and longitude. In a computer based GIS, the location(s) of points are recorded. A single point will have one set of coordinates whereas both lines and polygons will be defined by a sequence of coordinates. Once the location of a geographic entity is defined, it must be identified or assigned attributes. There are several approaches which may be taken for the storage of the spatial information and the attributes (e.g. a line may represent a river, a specific highway etc.; a polygon, a city, county, wheat field etc.; and a point an aircraft beacon, lighthouse, etc.). The manner in which the data are stored has an important impact on the way analyses may be performed. An excellent description of the options available has been given by Dangermond (1983).

A second approach to the computer based GIS is to represent the geographic data by grid cell encoding. The area of interest is subdivided into a large number of grid cells and each cell is assigned the attributes corresponding to its location from a map. Usually the grid cells are square, although some interesting coding efficiencies can be achieved using hexagonal cells as is done with a system called AGIS/GRAM.

The conversion of map data to digital form using each of these approaches is illustrated in Figure 1. In the first instance, geographic entities are defined by a linked list of coordinate pairs with a reference to an attribute list. Attributes may be assigned to an object or in the case of a line representing a boundary, to the object on either side of the line. Grid cells usually form an array with a label assigned to each cell. To conserve space, the data are often run-length encoded.

POLYGON DATA BASES

There are several hundred different polygon or line segment based Geographic Information Systems in existence. In the U.S. Geological Survey alone, it has been reported that there are over fifty such systems in use. Since no standards have been developed, each system uses a different internal data structure, making it very difficult to combine the data from different systems.

Two factors resulted in bias toward polygon databases. Because the original data source was usually on printed or hand drawn maps, it was natural to digitize these by tracing the lines on the maps to define points or lines and polygons to define areas. Perhaps, more importantly, this approach leads to efficient use of computer memory. When the original systems were devised, computers were equipped with relatively small amounts of internal memory which was very expensive. Even external memory was at a premium. The key to a useful GIS is its ability to manipulate the data by overlaying the information from different data sets. This is a complex problem, especially when the data are stored in the form of a linked list of coordinate points defining lines and polygons. The complexity of the computing required to effectively manipulate the data was deemed worth the effort in order to minimize the cost of storage.

Today, the cost of memory has fallen drastically so that space efficiency is no longer a primary consideration. However, the line segment or polygon representation of data still has two major advantages. First is the fact that a tremendous amount of geographic data has been collected and stored in this format. Secondly, and perhaps more importantly, this representation most accurately corresponds to the hard-copy format of maps, which are the major tools of resource managers and land use planners.

The Canada Geographic Information System (CGIS) developed in the mid-1960's was one of the most ambitious projects for collecting, storing and manipulating spatial data. The highly innovative design work on this, one of the largest and most complex GIS in operation, created a system which has been able to migrate through several generations of computers and which is still one of the most cost-effective in existence (Calkins and Tomlinson, 1977) after two decades of operation. (The Canada Lands Data Systems (CLDS) Group which now operates CGIS has received the URISA award for Exemplary Systems in Government in 1985).

One of the most innovative aspects of the CGIS was the method chosen for data entry. Most such systems to that time (and even today) captured the line data from maps by manually tracing the lines using a point digitizer. Later systems have used automated line-following digitizers. The CGIS system uses a high resolution drum scanner to digitize maps into a raster format. Complex software then converts the raster data into the usual linked list of point coordinates to represent points, lines and polygons. The results are plotted using a graphical plotter or are displayed on a graphic terminal where they are edited with manual assistance.

GRID CELL DATA BASES

The principal attraction of grid cell geographic data bases is their conceptual simplicity. Overlaying data from different sources is a relatively simple task. Since the data are laid out in computer memory in the same way for each layer of data, it is easy to perform logical and arithmetic operations among data sets. Manual data entry from maps is easily performed by placing a gridded sheet of mylar or tracing paper over the map to be coded. Identification labels are then entered into each cell. The data may then be entered into a computer. Expensive peripheral equipment, such as high precision plotters are not required to display the results, as they may be printed using a standard line printer.

The original major objection to the simple grid cell approach was the vast amount of computer storage required. In the very simple example shown in Fig. 1, the polygon, line and point shown could be represented by about 30 sets of x,y coordinates. Including attributes, this could be represented by less than 70 data elements. The grid cell representation, however, requires 720 data points, an order of magnitude greater. For very large bases with complex maps requiring very small grid cell sizes, the difference can be several orders of magnitude.

Today, with the cost of storage much less important than it was in the past, the grid cell approach still has important limitations. Unless the grid cells are extremely small, the output products "look different" than the maps. Depending upon the particular users and applications, this may or may not be important.

One of the better known grid cell systems is the Maryland Automated Geographic Information (MAGI) System (Maryland, 1981). While the system itself is independent of scale or grid cell size, the State of Maryland uses a system based upon its 1:63,360 scale maps and the Maryland State Coordinate Grid Lines which are separated by 10,000 feet in each direction. Each 10,000 x 10,000 foot square is subdivided into 25 2,000 x 2,000 foot 91.8 acre grid cells, which may be further subdivided into twenty 400 x 500 foot 4.57 acre grid cells. The system is easy to use, is being constantly updated and is very comprehensive with respect to the wide variety and completeness of resource, environmental, demographic and cultural data contained.

The MAP Analysis Package (MAP) (Tomlin, 1983) is particularly useful as a teaching aid. It is a set of computer programs that provide for the input, output, and transformation of cartographic data stored in a grid cell format. Because of its low cost availability and ease of use, it is a popular tool for demonstrating the fundamental GIS concepts to students. The system has been used to implement at least one small scale practical geocoded data base (Tomlin, 1982).

REMOTELY SENSED IMAGE DATA

Image data acquired by remote sensing satellites are provided in two basic formats: photographs and digitally recorded computer tapes. The photographs may be used in a manner similar to that used for aerial photographs. They can be interpreted and the data transferred to base maps for later digitization and entry into a GIS.

The digital data may be handled in a similar manner: after analysis and classification, perhaps using digital techniques, the data may be converted to hard copy using a line printer, plotter or photographic output. The analysed data may then be transferred to base maps using standard manual or semiautomated methods and then entered into the GIS.

The vast majority of satellite remote sensing data now available has been acquired by the LANDSAT series launched by the National Aeronautics and Space Administration (NASA) and later the National Oceanographic and Atmospheric Administration (NOAA) in the United States. The early satellites carried Multi Spectral Scanners (MSS) which provide digital data for four spectral bands in a two dimensional array covering an area on the ground of about 185 x 185 km. The individual points or picture elements (pixels) represent an area of about 57 x 80 metres in the original data. The good radiometric fidelity of the data has helped to foster significant advances in computer assisted analysis and classification of the digital data. Data from the Thematic Mapper (TM) carried on satellites launched after 1982 are even better quality radiometrically and provide better spatial resolution (30 x 30 metres).

It has long been recognized that the acceptance of LANDSAT data by the resource management agencies was somewhat hampered by the difficulty of incorporating the data into existing geographic information systems. While the geometric fidelity of the

LANDSAT data is excellent in comparison to aerial photography or that from other satellites, the coordinate system is non standard and the errors in position are too great for direct input to a GIS. In most countries, even the geometrically corrected LANDSAT data are in a coordinate system which is based on orbital geometry rather than on standard mapping coordinates.

Canada is fortunate to have high quality base maps for the entire country based on a single standard projection system: Universal Transverse Mercator (UTM). Furthermore, through the Canadian Advisory Committee for Remote Sensing and the National Remote Sensing Program administered by the Canada Centre for Remote Sensing, and excellent dialogue is maintained between the user community and the technology developers. This resulted in what has proven to be a significant decision with regard to the format of digitally corrected satellite data distributed in Canada. It was decided that MSS data should be made available to Canadian users in a format which exactly corresponds to standard UTM map sheets. The resampled pixel size is 50 x 50 metres and the orientation is along the map coordinates (Northings and Eastings). Thus, after the data are digitally analyzed, no further coorections are required in order for the data to match digital data bases which were keyed to the national mapping system. This philosophy is being carried over to the Thematic Mapper data, where the resampled pixel size is 25 x 25 metres and to SPOT (to be launched by France in 1987) where the pixel sizes will be 12.5 x 12.5 metres for the 20 metre multispectral instrument and 6.25 x 6.25 metres for the panchromatic sensor.

INTEGRATION OF REMOTE SENSING AND GIS

The integration of remotely sensed data analysis automated cartography and digital GIS offers several benefits. If the data can yield the correct information, it provides the most economical method for repetitive data collection over large areas for updating geographic data bases. On the other side of the coin, the best analysis of satellite data requires the input of all available ancilliary information. Much of this could be obtained from existing geographic information systems.

The data from LANDSAT have been used to update and even to create georeferenced data bases, and information from such data bases has been used to assist in the analysis of satellite data. However, most work to date has used the two systems more or less independently. Part of the reason for this lies in the differences in the training and background of the scientists and engineers responsible for the technological developments in the two areas. The developers of Geographic Information Systems had strong cartographic and photogrammetric influences. The remote sensing equipment developers were influenced by the environmental sciences, physics, (in particular, spectroscopy) and signal processing. The differing backgrounds and influences resulted in systems whose data did not mesh naturally.

In the United States, where there are a fairly large number of grid cell based geographic data bases, the geometry of corrected LANDSAT digital products is incompatible (for MSS, 57 x 57 metre pixels aligned along the axes of the Space Oblique Mercator projection, which was devised to minimize the corrections required for data acquired by satellite). In Canada, the bulk of geocoded data is stored in polygon format.

With the advent of LANDSAT, there was considerable pressure (much of it from the remote sensing community) to move from ploygon based systems to grid cells. The arguments used were that it is much easier to manipulate data stored by grid cells (which is true) and that the cost of computer memory was no longer an impediment to this approach. This format also happens to correspond, in concept at least, to the raster format of satellite data. Thus, it was felt that it would be easier to encourage resource managers and planners to adopt remote sensing data and analysis technology if the data bases they used had a similar internal format. Many have predicated the demise of the polygon data base. This is unlikely for the forseeable future, simply because the format is inherently too useful! Moreover, while it is difficult to manipulate the data (e.g. to create overlays) in the sense that this requires complex, sophisticated software, the problems have been solved, more than once!

Some of the impediments to the successful integration of automated cartography or digital GIS technology and remote sensing are simply symptomatic of the difficulty experienced in integrating data from one data base into another. In particular, there are difficult problems in moving data between polygon and grid cell data bases and vice versa. Indeed, the difficulties occur in attempting to merge the data from two different data bases of the same type. The fundamental source of the problem is that each data set is a (mis)-representation of the real world, and is subject to errors in measurement. Fig. 2 illustrates the difference between the map (which was probably different than the world it represented) and each of the two representations, line segment and grid cell. The important point to be made here is that these errors are different. If two different people had digitized the lines or encoded the grid cells, the results would have been different again.

It is possible to design a GIS system which is based upon a vector approach for digitization of maps for data entry. The data may be converted to grid cell format for ease of internal manipulation. The resulting output products cannot exactly match the original maps, unless the grid cells are extremely small. If maps are an unimportant byproduct, or if the user can be educated to accept the differences, this approach is quite acceptable.

Remotely sensed data is provided in what is inherently a grid cell format. In Canada, where the cells are oriented along the standard mapping coordinates, the data could be quite easily integrated into a grid cell based GIS. Since most of these systems in Canada are vector or polygon oriented, successful integration required conversion between grid cell and polygon representations. In addition to the differences in the representation of the earth's surface using these two approaches, there are other difficulties to be overcome, especially in any attempt to automatically convert between the formats.

When a map is converted to a grid cell format, it is possible to assign an attribute to a cell to indicate whether it corresponds to a part of an area, a part of a line or an isolated point. Hoever, when the data are obtained from satellite, ambiguities arise. Does a single isolated pixel represent a small area, a point or part of a line which is not connected because of errors in classification? Do two or three adjacent pixels represent part of a line, or a small elongated area? These are problems which cannot be solved on the basis of the satellite imagery alone. Moreover, with today's state of the art, it is not practical to define the location of a boundary to subpixel accuracy.

B.C. MINISTRY OF FORESTS SOLUTION

Provincial legislation passed in 1978 placed a requirement on the B.C. Ministry of Forests to report annually on the current status of the forest resources in that province, which covers 52 million hectares. The task would be virtually impossible without automatic cartography and remote sensing technology. Because the current state of the art, integration of these technologies has not advanced very far. Instead, a pragmatic and highly practical approach has been taken (Hegyi and Quenet, 1983). Complete LANDSAT coverage of the province was used to update the entire forest inventory in 1981-82. New LANDSAT data are geometrically registered to the forestry base maps (which may be in error). Changes due to selective logging and other disturbances are detected automatically and displayed as a (grid) overlay to the existing (vector) digital map base. A human operator verifies that changes indicated by the satellite data analysis are valid. On the basis of general knowledge of the area as well as field data and aerial photography, the polygon boundaries may be modified in the data base. At this stage, no attempt is made to automatically convert between the grid and polygon format, nor to automatically update the data base using the satellite data. The changes in the forest are flagged for human operators who make the final decision.

The computer is used to analyze vast amounts of satellite data in order to identify those area where changes seem to have occurred. Again, the computer is used to store and manipulate similar amounts of geographic data for the province. However, the human operator is much more efficient at using contextual information (some of which may not even be in the data base) to determine if a change really has occurred, and if so, exactly where with respect to the original map.

THE FUTURE

One attempt to automate the process of integrating remote sensing digital image and automated cartography technologies is the development of an Expert System (Goldberg, et al., 1985). In this system, expert knowledge is encoded in symbolic form to attempt to emulate the human activities involved in selecting appropriate image processing and analysis techniques, recognizing valid changes in the forest conditions and making intelligent decisions regarding map boundary changes. The system is based upon the forest inventory update procedures now performed by the B.C. Ministry of Forests in a less automated manner.

The system design includes the incorporation of a large number of existing image analysis programs developed for the LANDSAT Data Image Analysis System (LDIAS) at the Canada Centre for Remote Sensing and is based upon a hierarchical organization for the forestry map updating problem. The overall design is now complete, and a number of the "experts" have been coded. To acquire new knowledge to incorporate into the system, a number of maps of different regions in British Columbia will be used, together with multidate LANDSAT MSS and TM images to detect logging. As the system becomes capable of handling change detection in forests in British Columbia, it will be applied to other regions and expanded to include sensor inputs from the SPOT satellite, airborne synthetic aperture radar and eventually, RADARSAT.

REFERENCES

Calkins H, Tomlinson RF (1977) Geographic Information Systems, Methods and Equipment for Land Use Planning,(1977). U.S. Geological Survey, Reston, VA

Dangermond J (1983) A Classification of Software Components Commonly Used in Geographic Information Systems. A Chapter in "Design and Implementation of Computer-Based Geographic Information Systems". IGU Commission on Geographical Data Sensing and Processing, Amherst,NY

Goldberg M, Goodenough DG, Alvo M, Karam G (1985) A Hierarchical Expert System for Updating Forestry Maps with LANDSAT Data. To be published

Hegyi F, Quenet RV (1983) Integration of Remote Sensing and Computer Assisted Mapping Technology in Forestry, No 2, Vol 1, Canadian Journal of Remote Sensing, December (1983)

Maryland (1981) Maryland Department of State Planning Publication #81-13, Revised April (1981)

Tomlin DC (1983) An Introduction to the MAP Analysis Package. (1983) National Conference on Resource Management Applications: Energy and Environment, CERMA International Conference Series, Aug. 22-26, (1983), San Francisco, CA

Tomlin SM (1982) Market Analysis for the Mount Tom Ski Area of Holyoke, Mass. Staff paper 82-3, Department of Agricultural Economics and Rural Sociology. University of Connecticut College of Agriculture and Natural Resources.

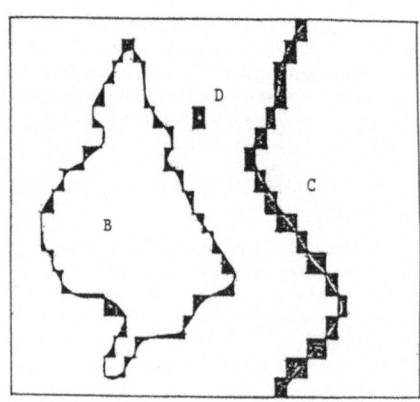
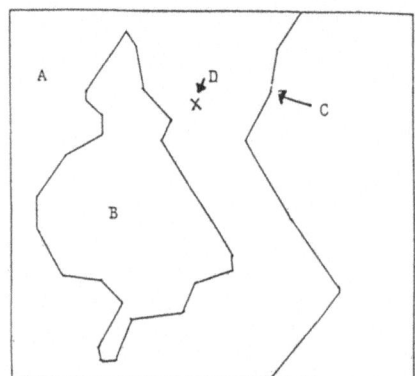
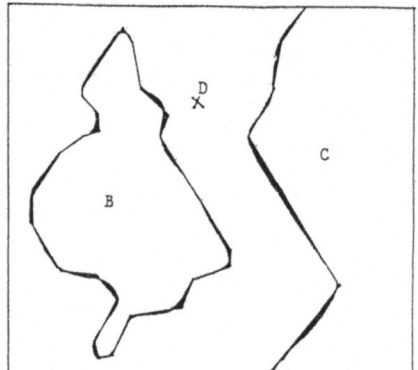
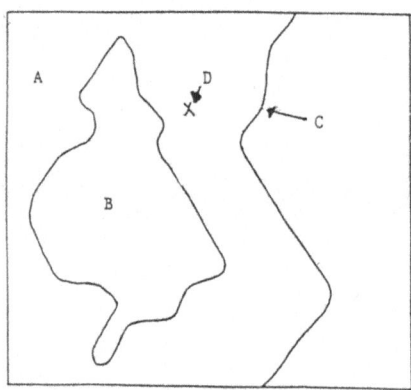
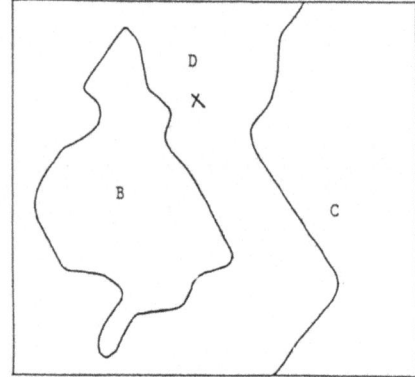

Figure 1. Representation of a map (bottom) in polygon (centre) and grid cell (top) formats.

Figure 2. Difference between original map and GIS grid cell (top) and polygon (centre) representations.

Author Index

Akmann, V. 176
Appel, R. 118
Armstrong, W.W. 203
Barsky, B.A. 11, 56, 153, 159, 209
Beaulieu, J.-M. 87
Bizzozero, C. 356
Bolduc, F. 425
Bournique, R. 269

Camarero, R. 330
Candrea, R. 269
Cavaliere, S. 436
Chan, Y.K. 342
Chang, E. 302, 367
Chassignet, Ph. 478
Christopher, M. 125
Cléroux, R. 395
Cormier, M. 419
Crain, I.K. 469
Cugini, U. 356

DeRose, T.D. 11, 159
Dill, A.R. 79

Eaton, R. 321
Erradi, M. 291

Fantini, M. 436
Fishkin, K.P. 56
Flavell, R.B. 307
Fortin, M. 45
Fournier, A. 35, 153
Franklin, W.R. 176
Frasson, C. 291

Funk, M. 118
Goldberg, M. 87
Green, M.W. 203
Greenberg, J.M. 260
Grush, B. 485
Gullichsen, E. 367

Hartman, D. 269
Heath, A.M. 307
Hochstrasser, D. 118
Honiden, S. 376
Hoshi, A. 376
Houle, J.L. 411
Hudson, S.E. 278

Kasahara, Y. 457
King, R. 278
Kunii, T.L. 137, 189

Lapalme, G. 419
Lejeune, A. 425
Lepage, Y. 395
Levine, M.D. 79, 106
Léonard, N. 45
Lichten, L. 321

MacDonald, C.L. 469
Magnenat-Thalmann, N. 45, 249, 425
Malowany, A.S. 106
McPheeters, C. 26
Michaud, C. 106
Mikame, K. 376
Milligan, T. 35
Mills, M.I. 3

Müller, A.R. 118
Ngai, W.B. 342
Noma, T. 189
Novacek, M. 26
Ozell, B. 330
Pellegrini, C. 118
Pettinati, F. 448
Prusinkiewicz, P. 125

Ranger, N. 395
Ratib, O. 98
Richardson, L. 411
Righetti, A. 98

Scholl, L.R. 386
Speer, L.R. 11
Strome, W.M. 485
Sueda, N. 376

Thalmann, D. 45, 249
Tsurutani, T. 457
Turtur, A. 436

Wilhelms, J.P. 209
Wyvill, B. 26
Wyvill, G. 137

Yamahira, T. 457
Zeltzer, D. 230

Author index

Subject Index

Active semantics data model 279
Actor 255
- -based sublanguage 250
Adaptive motion 233
Ambient light 46
Analytical modelling 411
ANIMAT 262
Animation block 255
Animator level 232
ANIMEDIT 46, 250
ANIMENGINE 189
ASAS 240

Backfacing polygon 48
BBOP 239
Bias 154
Blade-to-blade channel 331
BLOKFOR 450
Bounding volumes 14
Box 280
Branch-nodes 83
building blocks 344

CADME 356
Camera 4
Canada Geographic Information System 469, 487
Canada Land Data System 469
CAVITY 261
CGIS 469, 487

CINEDATA 430
CINEMIRA-2 250
Circulation graphic 427
CLDS 469
Colour map 305
Constructive solid geometry 137
Control polygon 154
Control vertices 154
CSG 137
CUPID 293
CURVES METHOD 397

DATA BASE MACHINE 439
Decision aid graphic 427
Decreasing light intensity 47
Deva 220
DI/DD 274
Dijkstra shortest-path algorithm 421
Directional sources light 46
Display Manager 192
Display Means 478
Document 444
Dynamic analysis 210

8-connected 57
ELSIE 119
End-branches 83
Energy of acceleration 212

Engineering animation system 189
Expert systems 371
External coherence 36

FACES METHOD 398
Fill algorithms 56
Focus 111
4-connected 57
Fractal 26
Frame buffer 32
FRANCIS turbine 337
Frontfacing polygons 48
Functional abstraction 235
Fuzzy laws 250

Geographic Information System 469, 486
Gibbs-Appell dynamics 212
GIS 469, 486
Global Controller 192
GRADIAL 273
GRAFANA 430
GRAFEDIT 431
GRAMPS 240
Graphicsland 27
Guiding mode 232

Hierarchical Step-Wise Optimization (HSWO) 87
Higgens 279
Histogram Interface 460

Hologram-like 128
HORIZON 431
Hue 308
Human camera 4
Iconic interface 296
Iconographic Machine 478
Iconographic Processors 478
Image-Entity 480
Image plane 14
Incremental curvature 82
Inference mechanism 382
Intensity based scheme 79
Interactive Planning Work Station 269
Internal coherence 36
Interpretation Function 479
IPWS 269
Ishihara colour blindness test 312
KAPLAN turbine 337
Key pose 239
- systems 239
Key-transformation 239
- systems 239
Lagrangian mechanics 204
Lightness 308
List-Entity 481
Manipulator dynamics 204
MELANIE 118
MELANIX 120
Message passing 107
MicroDesign 321
MIRA 240, 431
MIRANIM 45, 250
Motion recording 238

Multiple-inheritance 236
Multiply 30
- recursive objects 30
Naplps 302
Navier-Stokes equations 330
Nominal coding 307
Notation-based systems 239
Obel 177
Octree 141, 176
Ordinal coding 307
Originating object 14
Page Creation System 303
Painter's algorithm 196
Paint system 388
Parametric continuity 159
Particles 26
Patterns 367
PCS-UVIC 304
Physical Image Base 478
Polyhedron-clipping algorithm 47
Positional source light 46
Pressentation graphic 427
Procedural abstraction 234
Procedural actor transformation 253
Procedural Image Generator 28
Procedural law 252
Procedural objects 251
Processor-Entity 480
Profile 331
Project control system 448

Propagation algorithm 56
Query-by-Example 293
Query by Pictorial-Example 294
Radionuclide angiogram 100
Ray coherence 12
Recording Manager 192
Region 57
REMOTELY SENSED IMAGE DATA 488
ROUTE EDITOR 419
Saturation 308
Segment tree 88
Sensor 115
Sequence-Entity 481
Shannon-Wiener information theory 315
Shape 116
- -interpolation 238
- parameters 154, 159
Silhouette 49
Simultaneous contrast 6
SPIDER 376
Split-and-merge 88
Stakeholder approach 426
STARS METHOD 397
Start 256
Stereoscopic cameras 51
Stochastic 35
Stochastic modelling 35
Stop 256
Structural abstraction 234
S-turns 64
Subactor 255
Surface patch 168

Task level   232
TELIDON   431
Template model   199
TEMPUS   240
Tension   154
Terminal graphics   427
Token matching schemes   79
Traversal algorithm   126
TREES AND CASTLES METHOD   399

THE CAVITY CONVERTOR BOX   263
TYCHO   119

Undo systems   278
UniPert   449
User friendliness   466
USER MACHINE   438
User reversal and recovery systems   278
U-turn   65

Virtual buttons   304
Vision   6
VISUALIZATION-SYSTEM   388

W-turns   64

X ray cineangiograms   102

Zoom   111

848.3.6–27.11.85

Computer Science Workbench

Editor: **T. L. Kunii**

N. Magnenat-Thalmann, D. Thalmann

Computer Animation

Theory and Practice

1985. 156 figures, 54 of them in color.
XIII, 240 pages. ISBN 3-540-70005-6

Contents: Introduction. – Conventional Animation. – Computer Animation. – The Development of Computer Animation in Various Organizations. – Key Frame and Painting Systems. – Modeled Animation. – Hidden Surfaces, Reflectance and Shading. – Transparency, Texture, Shadows and Anti-aliasing. – Human Modeling and Animation. – Object-oriented and Actor Languages and Systems. – Case Studies. – A Case Study: **Dream Flight**. – References. – Appendix A–C. – Subject Index.

Computer Animation: Theory and Practice is the first presentation of all aspects of computer animation in a single volume. It is conceived as an introduction for designers and animators, a reference book for professionals in computer graphics, as well as a manual for university teachers in computer graphics and computer animation.
Both theoretical and practical aspects are presented in detail. Computer animation is treated using concepts familiar to those working in traditional animation. Readers will find techniques involved in computer-assisted animation such as key-frame interpolation and coloring and painting techniques, as well as a great deal of information on the state-of-the-art in computer animation and a history of animation systems and languages. The book also includes a complete list of computer-generated films produced between 1961 to 1984.

Springer-Verlag
Berlin Heidelberg
New York Tokyo

Computer Graphics

Visual Technology and Art
Proceedings of Computer Grahpics Tokyo '85
Editor: **T. L. Kunii**

1985. 179 figures, 50 of them in color. XI, 382 pages.
ISBN 3-540-70009-9

Contents: Computational Geometry. – Graphics Standardization and Packaging. – CAD/CAM. – Graphics Networks. – Visual Communication and Interfaces. – Computer Animation. – Computer Art. – Medical Graphics. – Author Index. – Subject Index.

Frontiers in Computer Graphics

Proceedings of Computer Graphics Tokyo '84
Editor: **T. L. Kunii**

1985. 266 figures, 82 of them in color. XI, 443 pages.
ISBN 3-540-70004-8

Contents: Geometry Modelling. – Graphic Languages. – Visualization Techniques. – Human Factors. – Interactive Graphics Design. – CAD/CAM. – Graphic Displays and Peripherals. – Graphics Standardization. – Author Index. – Subject Index.

Computer Graphics

Theory and Applications
Proceedings of InterGraphics '83
Editor: **T. L. Kunii**

1983. 292 figures, some in color. X, 530 pages.
ISBN 3-540-70001-3

Contents: Graphics Techniques. – Graphics Standards and 3D Models. – CAD/CAM. – Office Automation. – Computer Animation. – Graphic Applications. – Image Processing. – Author Index.

Springer-Verlag
Berlin Heidelberg
New York Tokyo